THOMAS MANN 1875-1955

Reflections of a Nonpolitical Man

Translated, with an introduction, by
Walter D. Morris

FREDERICK UNGAR PUBLISHING CO. NEW YORK

Library of Congress Cataloging in Publication Data

Mann, Thomas, 1875–1955.
  Reflections of a nonpolitical man.

  Translation of: Betrachtungen eines Unpolitischen.
  Includes index.
  1. Mann, Thomas, 1875–1955—Political and social
views. 2. Germany—Politics and government—1918–
1933. 3. European War, 1914–1918—Influence and
results. I. Title.
PT2625.A44B513 1982   833′.912   82-40249
ISBN 0-8044-2585-X

Original title
Betrachtungen eines Unpolitischen
by Thomas Mann
© S. Fischer Verlag, Berlin, 1918
by arrangement with the original publishers

Contents

Translator's Introduction

Before the first World War, Thomas Mann had shown little interest in politics. His novels and stories had dealt more with personal and artistic themes; he was, or at least seemed to be, a nonpolitical man. Indeed, if any political trend at all can be found in his prewar works it is the liberal one in his light novel, *Royal Highness*, which moved toward a democratic outcome even though it also contained some antidemocratic, aristocratic thoughts and characters.

Moreover, Mann was surprised by the outbreak of the war. "I still feel as if I were in a dream," he wrote to his brother Heinrich on August 7, 1914, "but one should probably be ashamed of oneself now not to have considered it possible, not to have seen that the catastrophe had to come." Soon, however, he recovered from the shock and to almost everyone's surprise promptly allied himself intellectually with the patriotic national conservatives, speaking out strongly in favor of the war and of German tradition. In the essay "Thoughts in War" in *Die neue Rundschau*, September 1914, he praised Germany's musical, metaphysical, pedagogical and subjective culture, contrasting it with the more analytical, skeptical, political and social civilization of the West. Mann felt that Germany, the moral country, had been attacked, and he welcomed the war as a glorious opportunity for his country to prove itself in meeting the challenge. Writers, he said, should join with soldiers as they joyfully faced the dangerous, exciting life ahead.

Mann expressed similar thoughts in an article for the Swedish newspaper, *Svenska Dagbladet,* and he soon followed these initial expressions of patriotic enthusiasm for his country's cause with the superbly written essay, "Frederick and the Great Coalition," which he finished by December 1914. Although the Frederick essay had been planned and researched to a great extent before the outbreak of the war, its theme and content were admirably suited to express Mann's enthusiasm for the war. Frederick's struggle for survival in 1756–63 could be thought of as Germany's struggle in 1914; the Prussian king became a symbol of the German character. Thus, in a period of four months, Mann had produced some rousingly patriotic works that revealed a body of ideas on politics, history, art, and Germany.

Apparently it was not just an initial outburst of patriotism that caused Mann to react so strongly at the beginning of the war, for after these writings were completed he began to plan the more extensive development of his ideas in *Reflections of a Nonpolitical Man.* He wanted to show that Germany was a great and special nation that had an important role to play in the European community and in the world. Germany's defeat and democratization, he feared, might lead to the loss of this important special culture. Not long after he had begun writing *Reflections*, however, his brother Heinrich, who was liberal, democratic, and pro-French, shocked him with an essay on Emile Zola and the Dreyfus affair. The essay was a thinly veiled criticism of Germany in which Heinrich might easily be substituted for Zola, and the Wilhelmian Empire for the France of Louis Bonaparte. In addition to its pro-French message, the essay argues that politics and literature are inseparably bound to one another, that the intellectual must act to further liberal causes. Beyond this, Thomas felt that several sentences in the work were meant as attacks on him. Heinrich had referred to those "false intellectuals" who "turned injustice into justice," and who stood "in elegant array against truth and justice." He urged that these "entertaining parasites," who were aspiring to become national poets, be knocked from their pedestals and cast into the abyss.

Thomas was deeply offended, and he immediately began to plan a new *Reflections*, which would now, in addition to being a description of German national character and of a romantic, nonpolitical world view, also be an answer to his brother. Now the European struggle was reflected in miniature in the struggle between the two brothers, and the whole book was set in a tragic framework, reminiscent of *Hamlet.* On the international level, Germany became the nation that had to bear courageously and tragically a fate to which she was called but not born, while on the personal level Thomas, like Hamlet, was the unlikely one who had the terrible task of setting things right. At the same time, Heinrich became "civilization's literary man," a Claudius-like traitor who scorned his nation's values and accepted those of its enemies.

Germany then also became the intellectual battleground on which European antitheses were fought out.

Mann now felt a challenge to himself, to his country, and to all the values he had cherished. His efforts to defend and to justify himself turned into a painful search for identity that often became an unreserved self-confession. He searched for the origins of his strong convictions in his own works, in Goethe, Schopenhauer, Nietzsche, Wagner, and in many other writers, foreign and native. He wanted to make everything clear, to omit nothing, to define the essential words, to show what it meant to be a German and a German creative writer.

For the next two years he worked on the essays, trying to bring all the themes together into an artistic whole; in the spring of 1918 he wrote the introduction, trying once again to bring the threads together, to obviate error and misunderstanding. It was his war book, the effort of a writer who was well established within Wilhelmian Germany, conscious of being a part of a great German cultural tradition and eager to preserve what he could of it. As he became more pessimistic of success and more certain of the coming of democracy to Germany, he began to call *Reflections* a delaying action. In the end, a spirit of irony pervades the book, for Mann felt that he himself, as a literary man—even against his will—was also contributing to civilization's triumph over German culture, for literature, by Mann's own definition, belonged to civilization.

Even before *Reflections* was complete, Thomas Mann began to think of it more as a work of fiction than as a series of essays. For the book is by no means straightforward, one-sided, simple and to the point. On the contrary, it is much more like an intricate drama, full of irony, plot and counterplot and suspense, with the many players—people, nations, ideas—enjoying their moments on stage, arguing, struggling and revealing their characters. It is like a Wagnerian opera with its leitmotifs, its romantic-modern style, its complicated passages and delayed resolutions. Finally, the book is like Germany herself, the stubborn, protesting nation so full of contradictions that courageously pursues its struggle and its destiny, determined to stick things out to the end. Both humorously and seriously the book not only describes the qualities of the German character, it also embodies them.

When the book was published, Thomas Mann awaited the public's reaction with a great deal of curiosity. The war was just over, the Social Democrats were in power, and Germany had become a republic. He did not regret what he had written, but he was not at all sure how people would react, whether the book would have any effect at all, whether it would be understood and by whom, and whether he might personally be harmed by it. On September 11, 1918, he wrote in his diary, "Curiosity about the adventure of the appearance of *Reflections*. Secret and utmost humor in the expectation of everything possible." But probably even he did not suspect that the book would dog his path throughout the rest of his life.

At any rate, the "nonpolitical" man found that he could not avoid politics. The book sold well, and he soon found himself popular with the conservatives, although they did not completely accept him because, after all, he had not been a conservative before the war, and his book was difficult, sometimes confusing, and not something with which a conservative could be completely comfortable. As for Thomas Mann, he soon found his association with the conservatives a little more than uncomfortable; many of them actually frightened him, and when he found they were placing national considerations above humane ones, he could no longer count himself one of them.

In the years following the war, Mann gradually shifted his support from the conservative cause to the new German republic. Many critics have called this shift a basic change in Mann's thinking, but he always resisted this interpretation and probably rightly so. The change was not so much in his basic convictions as in the cause he was defending. During the war he had thought of Germany as maligned, mistreated and attacked both from without and within, and he had stepped in to help. But in 1920 the Wilhelmian empire no longer existed and one had to live in the new times. Now the Republic was being unfairly, sometimes viciously attacked, and ironically perhaps but also consistently Mann began to lean toward the democratic government. He was no doubt influenced by liberal critics of *Reflections* such as Julius Bab, who, while agreeing with much of Mann's analysis of the German character, still pointed out faults in the former empire and the necessity for the people's participation in politics and democracy. Mann received this criticism well, as he began to regard many attempts to resist the new government as both wrong and cruel.

Mann even began to think of *Reflections* as not so much the end of an epoch as a continual ironical tension pointing in a Hegelian sense toward the future. He was helped in these thoughts by a manuscript he received in the mail on February 29, 1920, "Metaphysics and History: An Open Letter to Thomas Mann," by a young scholar named Alfred

Baeumler. Baeumler's manuscript gave Thomas Mann a way out of the dead end in which *Reflections* seemed to have left him. Baeumler said that for many years Germany had strayed from the reality of history and the power of logical historical thought as represented by Hegel. Spengler, for instance, was far from Leibnitz and Hegel, but Thomas Mann in his *Reflections* was a historical thinker. Spengler was a metaphysician, an eastern mystic, a translator of Schopenhauerian will into history; his work represented an end, while Thomas Mann's was a beginning.

Baeumler praised Mann's ironic method as eternal tension without resolution. The ironist is patient; he deals with reality, history and politics dialectically. Baeumler contrasted Mann's ironical attitude toward life with that of the radical who is impatient, hates life, and remains nihilistic and selfish. The radical wants to mold life through institutions, but history, like art, recognizes the tension between intellect and life, and both politics and art seek the middle path. Neither history nor art believes so much in institutions as in moods, ways of thinking, dispositions. Even though the total mood of *Reflections* might be pessimistic, the total meaning was not so. The book pointed toward the future.

Mann was excited and pleased when he read the manuscript, and he immediately used his influence to have it published. When it appeared he wrote in his diary on October 18, 1920, that his wife, Katia, "read Baeumler's open letter to me in the *Rundschau* . . . and it provides her, as it does me, with great pleasure."

In the first years after the war, Thomas Mann still could not forgive Heinrich's remarks in the Zola essay. In January 1922, however, there was a tentative reconciliation between the two brothers, and for the new edition of *Reflections*, Thomas took the opportunity to eliminate several lines, which altogether added up to about thirty pages, in which he had spoken harshly against Heinrich and against Romain Rolland, the French Nobel Prize laureate. Not only did the changes soften the personal excesses, they also allowed for a slightly more favorable attitude toward the Weimar Republic. This change in the direction of Mann's sympathies was greatly accelerated on June 24, 1922, when the Republic's foreign minister, Walter Rathenau, whom Mann admired, was assassinated by radical reactionaries. Mann decided to speak out. In October 1922, in Berlin he delivered a speech "On the German Republic," arguing for freedom and finishing with the words, "Long live the Republic!"

The speech caused quite a stir. Thomas Mann immediately lost the favor of the conservatives and found himself together with the Social Democrats. People spoke of a basic change in Mann's convictions, but the speech itself as well as Thomas Mann's later comments on it show clearly that no such basic change took place. For Mann, freedom remained a Germanic idea involving morality rather than the political freedom of the West. For the speech, he had derived his concept of freedom partly from Friedrich von Gentz and from Immanuel Kant, but mainly from the romanticist, Novalis. He had remained a monarchist at heart but had become a republican through reason; he still retained his romantic view of the German character, but he no longer believed, if he ever did, that silence was better than political expression. From then on he was to speak out courageously and frequently against cruelty and injustice.

The conservatives would never forgive Thomas Mann his speech on the German Republic. They thought he had gone against *Reflections,* and in 1927 a young critic named Arthur Hübscher attacked Mann in an article, "The Reworked Reflections of a Nonpolitical Man," accusing him of having falsified the contents of the book in the 1922 edition. Mann immediately replied that he had made only a few changes and that the meaning of the book had not been changed at all. Hübscher countered with a line-by-line comparison of the two editions, emphasizing that Thomas Mann had not mentioned the changes in a preface to the new edition, and continuing to insist that the changes substantially altered the tenor of the book. No doubt Mann was right when he said that thirty pages made up only a tiny part of the whole, that the book had remained essentially the same. The argument had only proved that the conservatives would continue to hold a grudge against Thomas Mann, and that they would seize every opportunity to attack him.

However, just as the conservative Germans looked back in anger at Mann's seeming repudiation of his views, the rest of the world would not let him forget the book, either. Even after he had been forced from Germany by the Nazis and had become an American citizen, he still felt the sting. In the *Atlantic* in May 1944, in an article entitled "What is German?" Thomas Mann emphasized the dangers of a cultured society remaining nonpolitical. The article was in no way pro-German. Nevertheless, such a noted scholar as Henri Peyre felt it necessary to remind Thomas Mann of his essay on Frederick the Great and of *Reflections.* He suggested that Mann explain what had happened to cause his conversion "from his former Pan-Germanist and pro-Nazi views." The attack was unnecessary, but typical of the lasting effects that *Reflections* called forth in the West. Since Thomas Mann had never been a Pan-Germanist or a pro-Nazi, and since his record of political decency and courage was open to all, he could and did—gently and correctly—fulfill Peyre's request for clarification, and to Peyre's satisfaction, but to many Americans Thomas Mann still remained suspect.

Thomas Mann never disavowed *Reflections.* The book was a sincere, painful self-analysis, a stage in his intellectual development that made future work, particularly *The Magic Mountain,* possible, and it also showed his deep affection for and defense of the German culture that he knew and loved, and of which he was a part. As far as the Nazis were concerned, it is clear that Thomas Mann would never have accepted them, even in his most conservative period. What he wrote to Reinhold Niebuhr on February 19, 1943, is undoubtedly true: "If I had remained at the level of *Reflections of a Nonpolitical Man,* which was, after all, not an antihumane book, I would still have taken a position with the same rage *and with the same justification* against this horror as I do today— *sit venia verbo*—as a 'democrat.'"

In speaking of *Reflections,* Thomas Mann was fond of quoting Goethe's words on Wieland: "The clever man liked to play with his opinions, but I can call upon all contemporaries as witness that he never played with his basic nature." Thomas Mann was a man of irony, of dialectics; his nature was often ambivalent, and he was courageous enough to admit this and to try to do justice to all his thoughts. This courage sometimes caused irritation and misunderstanding, but those who thought of him as a sophist with no convictions at all certainly misunderstood his honesty in the search for truth.

In America he became a democrat and dutifully travelled around making speeches in favor of democracy, but he was honest enough to admit that he often felt a little strange in doing so. The straightforward, sometimes platitudinous speeches he was making seemed much less interesting than *Reflections,* which had been so rich in ambivalence. He did not completely separate the good Germany from the bad one; he knew that the German past formed a unity and that he, as well as his countrymen, was part of it. As late as November 25, 1949, he could write to Willy Sternfeld: *Reflections* is a correct book with a false omen." The book was part of him and he would never deny it.

Except for some concessions to American format and punctuation, I have followed the original German edition as far as possible in style and atmosphere as well as in sentence and paragraph structure. For the most part, this will present no problems to the reader, but at times he may come across a rather long and complicated sentence with several qualifiers and differentiations, which may strike him as strange. There are reasons for this somewhat involved style.

First, Mann took great pains to write with precision. He was by nature complex and often ambivalent and spared no effort to say exactly what he had in mind, even if the reader might not easily follow him. But he was also aware of this tendency in himself, and sometimes in a kind of self-irony, he enjoyed making fun of his own style. Thus what may at first seem a bit pompous and stuffy is often really just Mann exaggerating and laughing at himself, and also inviting the reader to join in the fun.

Beyond this, *Reflections* is a very German book in its fullness and variety, in its tendency to include everything relevant. This follows a long tradition in German culture that goes back as far as Wolfram von Eschenbach, who, in *Parzival*, eschewed the simple style and purposefully wrote in a sometimes tortuous language that befitted the difficult nature of his subject. For writers in this tradition, to simplify things is to falsify them.

Finally, since the book is, to a great extent, a conservative treatise that combats the coming of democracy, the style also resists simple, easy-to-read, platitudinous writing. In particular, Mann wants to emphasize the difference between his style and that of the rhetorically passionate, and sometimes gawdy approach of "civilization's literary man," the herald of the new era. Therefore in his aristocratic aloofness and deep sympathy with German culture, Mann seems to state: "What I have to say is worthwhile; if you want to benefit from it, you must make the effort to come into my world."

There are no footnotes at all in the original work. For the most part, Mann made at least general references within the text to his sources, but he did not try to be thorough. Throughout the book some two hundred and fifty names are mentioned and many historical events, literary themes, and philosophical problems are referred to. There are also personal references. To footnote all of this would make the book far too pedantic, and it would also deviate too much from the original. The reader will no doubt be familiar with many of the references; in any event, he will not find it necessary to know all of them in order to understand and to enjoy the book, which is, as Mann suggests, much more a story and an inner-personal conflict than a scholarly treatise. Nevertheless, footnotes have seemed necessary here and there, although they have been kept to an absolute minimum.

Throughout the book, Mann uses many, many quotations—from his own works, from those of other Germans, and from foreign writers as well. He also quotes extensively from poetry, mainly German. In several cases, he skillfully weaves the material into the main narrative, often skipping around in his sources, selecting those items that suit his purpose, eliminating words and sentences that are not pertinent, and even adding his own emphasis when he feels it necessary. Accordingly, in order to have an accurate translation of Mann's book, it was necessary to translate the quotations directly from it rather than using published English translations. Therefore all of the translations from the original German excerpts are my own, and I have even followed the German translations of the Russian and French. My translations agree in essence, if not in exact wording, with published English translations of these passages. Excerpts from English sources are, of course, another matter. Here I have used the original English text in every case. As a supplement to the translations of German verse, the originals have been included as footnotes.

I am grateful to Iowa State University for granting me leave during the academic year 1979–80 so that I might have time to do this translation. My thanks go also to the many people, who, over the years, have helped me with this translation. Particularly deserving of my thanks are Johannes Bechert, W. F. Michael, and Barbara von Wittich, who solved many a problem in the interpretation of German words and phrases, while Eugene V. Smith and Jeannette Bohnenkamp read the entire manuscript and made excellent suggestions on style and readability. Will Jumper was helpful with the translation of an Eichendorff poem, and Jeannette Bohnenkamp and Thora Runyan gave generously of their time in reading proof. Many thanks go also to Hans Wysling and Therese Schweizer of the *Thomas Mann Archiv* in Zurich for their generous assistance in my research on the background of *Reflections*. I am also indebted to Golo Mann for discussing family details with me, particularly with regard to the relationship between Mann and his brother Heinrich.

By far the greatest help, however, came from Frederick Ungar, who read and compared original and translation, line by line, and made innumerable suggestions that greatly improved the translation in style and accuracy. It has been a pleasure and a privilege for me to work together with a man so experienced in editing and publishing literary translations, who also has a thorough knowledge of the German language and literature.

I must add that in all matters the final decision was mine, and that I am responsible for any faults and errors that may remain in the translation.

Ames, Iowa

WALTER D. MORRIS

Summer, 1982

Que diable allait-il faire dans cette galère?

Molière, *Les Fourberies de Scapin*

Compare yourself with others! Know what you are!

Goethe, *Tasso*

REFLECTIONS
OF A
NONPOLITICAL
MAN

Prologue

When, in 1915, I had presented to the public the little book *Frederick and the Great Coalition*, I thought I had discharged my duty to the day and the hour and that I would be able, even in the turmoil of the times, to rededicate myself to the artistic endeavors I had begun before the outbreak of the war. This proved to be an error. I was, like hundreds of thousands of others who were taken from their paths by the war, "drafted," estranged, and held for long years from my true calling and occupation. It was not the state and the army that "drafted" me, but the times themselves: to more than two years of military service of the mind—for which I was, by birth and by skill, finally just as little suited spiritually as was many a companion in misfortune physically for real duty on the front or at home, and from which I, not exactly in the most even frame of mind, a war casualty, as I should probably say, return today to my deserted worktable.

The harvest of these years—but I will not speak of a "harvest." I will do better to speak of a residue, a remainder, and a sediment, or also of a trail, and indeed, to tell the truth, of a trail of suffering—the *remnant* of these years, then, in order to correctly twist the proud concept of remaining into a noun that does not have an excessively proud character, makes up this volume, which I shall, for good reason, beware of calling a book or a work. For twenty years of not completely thoughtless artistic practice have after all taught me too much respect for the concept of a work or composition to claim these terms for an effusion or a notebook, an inventory, a diary, or a chronicle. Here, however, we are dealing with just such a piece of writing, something that has been piled up—although the volume does, at times, and with some justification, by the way, take on the appearance of a composition and work. With some justification: a basic thought that is organic and omnipresent could be pointed to—if it were not just the wavering sense of such a thought, with which, to be sure, the whole work is permeated. One could speak of "variations on a theme," if this theme had only attained more precise form. A book? No, we cannot say that. This searching, struggling, and probing toward the essence, toward the causes of an anguish, this dialectical fencing all the way into the fog *against* such causes—the result was naturally no book. For among these causes there was undoubtedly an antiartistic and unaccustomed lack of mastery of the subject, a lack to which my clear and shaming awareness was always alert, and that instinctively had to be concealed by means of a light and sovereign manner of speaking. Nevertheless, just as a work of art can have the form and appearance of a chronicle (something I know from experience), a chronicle can also, in the end, have the form and appearance of a work of art; and thus this bundle of papers shows, at times at least, the ambition and *habitus* of a work: it is something intermediate between work and effusion, composition and hackwork— even if its point of existence lies so far from the exact middle, in truth, so much more on the side of the nonartistic, that one would do better to take it, in spite of its composed chapters, as a form of diary, the early parts of which can be dated from the beginning of the war and the later sections approximately at the turn of the years 1917–18.

If, however, these notes do not form a work of art, the reason is finally because, *as* notes and reflections, they are just too much the work of an artist, of an artistic nature—for they are that, in fact, in more ways than one. They are that, for example, as the product of a certain indescribable irritability with intellectual tendencies of the times, of a touchiness, sensitivity and nervousness of perception that I have always recognized in myself. At times I believe I have derived advantage from this as an artist. Nevertheless, it has always produced the dubious side inclination to react in an immediate literary, critical, *polemic* way to these stimuli. This is particularly true when, yes, precisely when, it is not just a question of a superficial tingling of the skin, but when I am to a certain extent inwardly involved in what I perceive. It is simply a literary pugnacity or quarrelsomeness, based on the need for balance, and therefore, for its part, committed again all too strongly to angry one-sidedness. All this happens before my critical understanding is intellectually ripe enough in awareness, language, and analysis for me to be able to hope seriously for essayistic resolution. In my opinion, this is how artistic works come into being.

These essays are also the work of an artist in their dependence, in their need for help and reference, in their endless quotations and appeals to strong affidavits of support and to "authorities"—in their expression of reveling gratefulness for favors received, and in the childish urge to force literally upon the reader everything I have selected in my reading for consolation, instead of letting it form the silent and calming background of my own diction. By the way, it seems to me that, in all the unbridledness of this desire, there was a certain poetic sensitivity and taste at work in its satisfaction: quoting was perceived as an art, similar to the art of tightening a story by inserting dialogue, and the attempt was made to practice it with similar rhythmic effect.

An artist's work, an artist's writing: a person speaks here who, as it says in the text, is not accustomed to speak but rather to have others, people and things, speak, and who therefore "has" others speak even when he seems to be, *and thinks* he is, speaking directly himself. A trace of the actor, the lawyer, of play, artistry, detachment, of lack of conviction and of that poetic sophistry that allows the one speaking at the moment to be correct, and who in this case was I, myself—this trace is undoubtedly to be found everywhere; it scarcely stopped being half-conscious—and still, what I said was at every moment truly my intellectual conviction, my heartfelt emotion. It is not for me to solve the paradox of this mixture of dialectics and genuine, honestly striving will to truth. In the end, the very existence of this book vouches for my seriousness.

For I certainly hope that its feuilletonistic tone will deceive no one of the fact that the years in which I piled it up were the most difficult of my life. Yes, it is the work of an artist, and not a work of art; for it stems from an artistic nature that is shaken in its foundations, endangered in its vital dignity, and called in question, from an artist who is disconcerted to the point of crisis, who absolutely could not express himself in any other way. The insight from which it grew, and which made its production seem to be unavoidable, was above all that every work would otherwise have been intellectually overladen—a correct consideration, which, however, still did not do justice to the true state of affairs; for in truth, a continuation of the work on these other things would have shown itself to be completely impossible, and did show itself, upon repeated attempts, to be completely impossible: thanks, that is, to the intellectual conditions of the times, to the agitation of everything calm, to the shaking of all cultural foundations, to an artistically hopeless turmoil of thought, to the naked impossibility of *creating* something on the basis of an *existence*, to the breaking-up and impugning of this existence itself by the times and their crisis, to the necessity of understanding, clarifying and *defending* this existence that had been called in question and brought into distress, and that could no longer be understood as a firm, self-evident and instinctive basis for culture; thanks to a pressing need, therefore, for a revision of all the foundations of this artistic nature itself, for its self-study and self-assertion, without which its activity, impact, and cheerful fulfillment, its every action and creation, seemed from now on to be quite impossible.

But why did things have to seem this way to me, of all people? Why the galley for me while others went free? Of course I know very well that there were artists of all types who met this crisis and turning point at about the same age as I did, who, if they were physically spared by the war, were only temporarily inhibited, if at all, in their work. Works of belles lettres, music, and visual arts have been created in these four years and made public, and they have brought their creators appreciation, fame, and happiness. Youth arrived and was greeted. But also artists of an older generation, older even than mine, have progressed, completed what they began, produced their work as before in accordance with their cultural background and their talent, and it almost seemed as if their creations were the more welcome the less they touched upon and reminded people of what was happening. For the demand of the public for art had ever risen, its appreciation of creative work was livelier than usual, the prospect of every type of reward, including the material, particularly favorable. What I am saying here is a *captatio benevolentiae*, and I make no secret of it. Really, I am attempting to conciliate by pointing out how much renunciation the book has involved. I put off my dearest plans, which many awaited not without desire or impatience—whether to their credit or discredit—so that I might finish a piece of writing, the extensiveness of which I was admittedly, this time as well, not even vaguely aware; otherwise I would, in spite of everything, hardly have allowed myself to embark on it. I remember well that my enthusiasm in the beginning was great; that I was driven by the belief that I had many good and important things to say to myself and to others. But then: what growing unrest, what longing for "freedom in limitation," what pain from the enormously compromising and disorganizing nature of all speech; what gnawing worry about the loss of months, of years! But when the point where it is still possible to turn back, to abandon the material and to walk away from it, has passed, then "carrying on to the end" becomes more of an economic than a moral imperative—even if the will to bring it to completion definitely takes on heroic proportions when its growing to completion is unthinkable. There is only *one* motto for action and writing such as this that explains its foolishness and pain without condemning it completely. It is found in Thomas Carlyle's *French Revolution*:

> Thou shalt know that this Universe is, what it professes to be, an *infinite* one. Attempt not to swallow *it*, for thy logical digestion; be thankful, if skillfully planting down this and the other fixed pillar in the chaos, thou prevent its swallowing *thee*.

Again, why did "my body have to labor in place of Christendom," to speak with Claudel's Violaine? After all, was my psychological condition so particularly grave—that it seemed so much in need of discussion, explanation, and defense? Forty is probably a critical age; one is no longer young, one notices that one's own future is no longer the general future, but only—one's own. You have to live your life to the end—a life that has already been overtaken by the course of the world. New things have come over the horizon that negate you without being able to deny that things would not be as they are if it had not been for you. Forty is a turning point in life; and it is no small matter—I pointed this out in the text, I believe—when the turning point in an individual life coincides with the thundering of a turning point in the world; the awareness of this becomes terrifying. But others, too, were forty, and got along better. Was I weaker, more vulnerable to consternation, to destruction? Did I lack pride and inner strength so that I lost myself polemically in new ideas at the risk of bringing about my self-destruction? Or must I attribute to myself a particularly sensitive feeling of solidarity with my epoch, a particular intensification, sensitivity, and vulnerability because I belong to a particular time?

Be that as it may, I reduce the origin of these pages to its common denominator when I call it *conscientiousness*—a quality that makes up such an essential part of my artistic gift that one could say briefly that it consists of it: conscientiousness, a moral-artistic quality to which I owe everything it has been my lot to accomplish, and that now has played this trick on me. For I know well how close it comes to pedantry, and whoever would like to label and explain away this whole book as monstrous, childishly hypochondriacal pedantry would hardly miss the mark; many times it has not seemed otherwise to me. More than once, more than a hundred times, throughout all my explorations, explications, and expectorations, the question of the motto has forced itself upon me with the laughter that accompanies incomprehensibility. In retrospect, when I consider my clumsy efforts on the political question, I notice some of the same feeling that will certainly come over my readers. "What the devil did it matter to him?" But it *did* matter to me, it was truly and passionately close to my heart, and it seemed absolutely necessary somehow to clear up these questions according to my best understanding, belief, and ability. For the times were such that one could no longer tell the difference between what concerned the individual and what did not. Everything was excited, stirred up, the problems stormed into one another and could no longer be separated. One could see the interrelationship, the unity of all intellectual matters; the question of the human being himself was there, and the responsibility to this question also included the necessity for a political point of view and resolution. It was the magnitude, the weight and the limitlessness of the times that left the conscientious person and somehow—I do not know to what or to whom—the responsible person, the person who took himself seriously, nothing that he did not have to take seriously. All pain for the sake of things is self-torment, and the only person who torments himself is the one who takes himself seriously. One will pardon all my pedantry and childishness in these pages when one has pardoned me for taking myself seriously—a fact that becomes clear when I speak directly about myself, and certainly a quality that one can recognize and smile at as the very origin of all pedantry. "Lord, how he takes himself seriously!"—My book certainly provides continual opportunity for this exclamation. I have nothing to say against this except for the fact that I have never lived nor could live without taking myself seriously, except for the knowledge that everything that seems good and noble to me— intellect, art, morality—comes from human beings taking themselves seriously; for the clear insight that everything I have accomplished and produced, indeed the charm and value of every single bit of it, every line and expression of my life's work up to now—as much and as little as this may say—can exclusively be traced back to my taking myself seriously.

But closely related to conscientiousness is *loneliness*—it is perhaps only another name for it: that loneliness, you see, that is so difficult for the artist to differentiate from *public life*. All in all, he is not even disposed to distinguish between the two. His life element is a public loneliness, a lonely public life that is of an intellectual nature, and whose feeling and concept of dignity differ completely from civic, material-social public life, although in practice both can, as it were, coincide. Their unity consists in the literary public life that is both intellectual and social at the same time (as in the theater) and in which the emotion of loneliness becomes socially acceptable, civically possible, and even civically meritorious. The recklessness, the extremity of the artist's communicative dedication, may lead him to the prostitution and revelation of his personal life, to the most complete Jean-Jacques shamelessness—nevertheless, the dignity of the artist as a private person remains completely inviolate. It is possible, it is even natural, for an artist who has just sacrificed, surrendered, yes, even abandoned himself personally in his work to step out at the next moment among people without the slightest feeling that he has compromised his civic existence in the least—and a cooperative, cultured public, that is to say, one that equates itself as much as possible with the intellectual public, will support him; the merits he has earned as a lonely public person may even stand his civic honor in good stead.

But all this is only conditionally valid; a personal confession to the social public through literary publication is only valid when it is worthy of the intellectual public—otherwise, publication makes it into a joke or a scandal. One must hold to this law, this criterion. But I must now ask myself whether the publication of these pages, the product of a loneliness that is accustomed to being public, is justified; that is, whether they may show themselves worthy of the social public *because* they are worthy of the intellectual public—and I will be helped little here if I can only defend their publishability, their *right* to publication, or the public's right to them, with reasons that are only human and personal. Nevertheless, such reasons must be included. My production suddenly stopped; announced works did not appear; I seemed struck dumb, lamed, seemed to have left the field. Did I not owe it to my friends to tell how I had spent the years? And if it was not a question of a debt—was it perhaps a question of a right? For after all, I had struggled and renounced, had taken great pains, had honestly tried to achieve understanding, even if with insufficient and dilettante powers, and it was human to wish that all this should not be borne, tolerated, done completely "in vain" in private, nonpublic loneliness. I say that such reasons should be included—they are not the decisive ones. The publishability of these pages must be proven and their publication justified from the point of view of the intellect: it is a question of their intellectual right to publication—and truly, I think such a right exists.

This writing, which has the uninhibited nature of a private letter, offers, in fact, to the best of my knowledge and belief, the intellectual foundations of what I have had to give as an artist, and what belongs to the public. If this has been worthy of the intellectual public, then the following statement of accounts must also be so. And since it was the times that irresistibly demanded it of me, it seems that the times have a right to it: a document, it seems to me, has been presented that is not unworthy of being known by contemporaries and even by future generations, if only for its transiently symptomatic value, for its boundless intellectual excitement, its eagerness to talk about everything at once. But even the misgiving that I may not only have shown myself to be a poor thinker, but that I may also have compromised my artistic gift itself by revealing its intellectual foundations, cannot justify my locking up the manuscript. Let what is true see the light of day. I have never pretended to be better than I am, and I want to do so neither by talk nor by clever silence. I have never been afraid of revealing myself. The will that Rousseau expresses in the first sentence of his *Confessions* and that seemed new and unheard of at the time: "to show a man in the whole truth of his nature, and this man is I," this will that Rousseau called "unprecedented until today," and that he believed would find no imitators—has become an inveterate matter of course, the intellectual, artistic ethos of the century to which I essentially belong, the nineteenth; and the verses of Platen stand over my life as well as over the lives of so many sons of this age of confession:

> I am not yet so pale that I need make-up;
> Let the world know me that it may pardon me!*

I repeat: a fixation of a problematical nature, whether it be image or speech, is suitable for the general public if it is worthy of the intellectual one. If it is, one's private dignity remains completely untouched. Here I have a human-tragic element of the book particularly in mind, that intimate conflict to which a series of pages is particularly dedicated and which also colors and determines my thought in many other places. It is true of it, too—especially of it—that its exposure, as far as this was at all times possible, is intellectually justified and therefore not offensive. For this intimate conflict takes place in the intellect and has, beyond all doubt, enough symbolic dignity to have a right to publication and, once presented, not to have a rude effect. A cultured general public, that is, one that equates itself as much as possible with the intellectual public, is not scandalized by the revelation of personal matters that are worthy

---

* Noch bin ich nicht so bleich, daß ich der Schminke brauchte;
Es kenne mich die Welt, auf daß sie mir verzeihe!

of the intellectual public and to which the latter has a right. The *trust* implied in such a revelation may prove to be much too "lonely" and optimistically gullible: if it is mistaken, the one who cherished it will not be dishonored.

I said I had *served the times* by writing this book, by trying conscientiously or pedantically to "put down" in connected sentences the excited, stirred-up foundations of my being. But many a person, after he has taken note of the following chapters, will judge that I have served the times in a very questionable manner, without a healthy love for them, without discipline; that I have "served" obstinately, with a hundred manifestations of hostile disobedience and ill will, and that I have done little to further their fulfillment, completion, and realization. They will say I had not only, or not just, shown myself to be a bad thinker, but also, and much more, to be one who thinks bad thoughts, has a mean disposition and a bad character: by attempting, you see, to support and defend what is dying out and falling away, and to oppose what is new and necessary, to do harm to the times themselves. To this I must reply that one can serve the times in more ways than one, and that mine does not definitely have to be the wrong, bad, and fruitless one. A contemporary thinker has said: "It is not so difficult to discover the direction a culture is taking, and it is not so wonderful as the half-wits all around the country think to join it with great fanfare. To recognize the true path of life, the reversals, the contradictions, the tensions of life, the counterweights it needs, the opposing forces that tense it anew where it has become weak through expenditure of effort, the antagonists, without whom the drama of life does not progress—not only to see all these things, *but to feel them alive in oneself, struggling against one another*— this makes the person who is the complete human being in his times." A beautiful statement that strikes a chord in my soul. I do not think that it is the essence and duty of the writer to join "with great fanfare" the main direction the culture is taking at the moment. I do not think and cannot from my very nature think that it is natural and necessary for the writer to support a development in a completely positive way by direct, credulous-enthusiastic advocacy—as a solid knight of the times, without scruple and doubt, with straightforward intentions and an unbroken determination and spirit for it, his god. On the contrary, authorship itself has always seemed to me to be a witness to and an expression of ambivalence, of here and there, of yes and no, of two souls in one breast, of an annoying richness in inner conflicts, antitheses and contradictions. What is, after all, the origin and purpose of writing if it is not an intellectual-moral effort in behalf of a problematic ego?

No, granted, I am not a knight of the times, nor am I a "leader," and I do not want to be. I do not love "leaders," and I do not love "teachers," either, for example, "teachers of democracy." But least of all do I love and respect those small, empty people who have good noses and who live from knowing what is going on and from following the right scent, those servile and conforming vermin of the times who, with incessant announcements of their contempt for all those who are less quick and mobile, trot alongside the new; or also the fops and up-to-date people, those intellectual swells and elegant ones who wear the most recent ideas and catchwords just as they wear their monocles: for example, "spirit," "love," "democracy,"—so that one can hardly hear this jargon today without being disgusted. All of these people, the conformers as well as the snobs, enjoy the freedom of their nothingness. They are nothing, as I said in the text, and therefore they are completely free to express opinions and to judge, and always, of course, according to the latest fashion and *à la mode*. I honestly despise them. Or is my contempt only hidden envy, since I do not share their frivolous freedom?

But to what extent do I not share it? To what extent am I bound and determined? If I am not nothing, as they are, what am I, then? It was this question that forced me into the "galley," and by "comparison" I sought to find the answer. The understanding that repeatedly tended to appear was wavering, misty, insufficient, dialetically one-sided and distorted by effort. Shall I, at the last minute, try again to nail it down to tolerable satisfaction?

I am, in what is intellectually essential, a genuine child of the century into which the first twenty-five years of my life fall: the nineteenth. To be sure, I find in myself both artistic-formal and intellectual-moral elements, needs and instincts that no longer belong to that epoch, but to a more recent one. But since as a writer I feel myself strictly speaking to be a descendant (naturally not a member) of the German burgherly art of storytelling of the nineteenth century that reaches from Adalbert Stifter to the last works of Fontane; since, as I say, my traditions and artistic tendencies reach back to this native world of German masterfulness that charms and strengthens me by an idealistic confirmation of myself as soon as I come into contact with it, my intellectual center also lies on the other side of the turn of the century. Romanticism, nationalism, burgherly nature, music, pessimism, humor—these elements from the atmosphere of the past age form in the main the impersonal parts of my being as well. But it is especially in a basic disposition and spiritual tendency, in a character trait, that the nineteenth century, taken as a whole, differs from the previous one, and, as is becoming increasingly clear, from the new, present one as well. It was Nietzsche who first grasped this difference of character and put it best into critical language.

"Honest but gloomy," Nietzsche called the nineteenth century in contrast to the eighteenth, which he found, as Carlyle had, feminine and deceitful. But the eighteenth did have in its humane sociability a *spirit in the service of desirability* that the nineteenth century did not know. More bestial and ugly, yes, more vulgar, and precisely for this reason, "better," "more honest," than the former, the nineteenth century was *truer, more subservient to reality of every kind.* To be sure it was, in the process, weak in will, sad and darkly covetous, fatalistic. Neither for "reason" nor for the "heart" did it show awe and respect, and through Schopenhauer it even reduced morality to an instinct, namely pity. As the scientific century that was unpretentious in its wishes, it freed itself from the *domination of ideals* and instinctively sought everywhere for theories to justify a fatalistic *submission to the factual.* The eighteenth century sought to forget *what one knew of the nature of the human being* in order to adapt him to its utopia. Superficial, soft, humane, enthusiastic for the "human being," it advocated, with the use of art, *reforms of a social and political nature.* On the other hand, Hegel, with his fatalistic way of thinking, his belief in the greater reason of the victorious, signified quite essentially a victory over sentimentality. And Nietzsche speaks of Goethe's opposition to revolution, of his "will to deify the universe and life in order to find peace and happiness in his *visualizing and fathoming.*" Nietzsche's critique, never unsympathetic, becomes highly positive; in truth, it rewrites the *religiosity* of a whole age by rewriting Goethe's nature as an "almost" happy and trusting fatalism "that does not revolt, that does not weary, that tries to form a totality out of itself in the belief that only in totality is everything solved, does everything appear as good and justified."

Nietzsche's critique of the last century, of this powerful but not very "high-minded" epoch, one that was intellectually not very gallant, has never seemed to hit the mark more splendidly than when it is seen from the point of view of the here and now. Recently I found in print that Schopenhauer had been "social-altruistic" because his morality had peaked in pity—I marked the passage with a large question mark. Schopenhauer's philosophy of the will (and Schopenhauer never tended to forget what is known of the nature of the human being) was *without* all social and political *interessement.* His pity was a means of salvation, not a means of improvement in any sort of intellectual-political sense that went against reality. In this, Schopenhauer was a Christian. One should have talked to him about the role of art in social reform!—to him for whom the esthetic condition was a blessed predominance of pure contemplation, a stopping of the wheel of Ixion, a *breaking away* from the will, freedom in the sense of redemption and in *no other* sense. Here we have Flaubert's hard estheticism, his boundless doubt with the *nihil* as a result, with the scornful resignation of *"Hein, le progrès, quelle blague!"* Here Ibsen's burgherly evil head stands out, similar in expression to Schopenhauer's. The lie as a condition of life, the bearer of the "moral demand" as a comical figure, Hjalmar Ekdal as the human being as he is, his coarsely realistic wife as the upright one, the cynic as a querulous person: here we have the asceticism of honesty—the harsh nineteenth century. And how much of its brutal and honest pessimism, of its particularly stern, masculine and "unpretentious" ethos, still holds sway in Bismarck's *Realpolitik* and anti-ideology!

I see that this often varying tendency and basic disposition of the nineteenth century, its truthful, blunt, and unfeeling submission to the real and factual, which is averse to the cult of beautiful feelings, is the decisive inheritance that I have received from it; I see that it is this that limits and sets my being against certain aspirations that are now appearing and that negate my world as being without ethos. The novel of the twenty-five-year-old, which appeared at the threshold of the century, was a work completely without that "spirit in the service of desirability," completely without social "will," completely without solemnity, eloquence, sentimentality. On the contrary, it was pessimistic, humorous, and fatalistic, truthful in its melancholy submission as a study of decadence. One single unpretentious quotation will be enough to—forgive the expression—indicate the significance of the book in intellectual history. Toward the end, bitter and farcical school stories are told. "Whoever," it says,

> among these twenty-five solid young people, was strong and capable of living life as it is, took things at this moment completely as they were, did not feel offended by them and found that everything was obvious and as it should be. But there were also eyes that were focused in dark reflection toward one point . . .

And these eyes belonged to the latecomer of the burgher family, little Johan, who had been sublimated by decay, and whose only remaining talent was in music.

Little Johan stared at the broad shoulders of the boy in front of him, and his golden brown eyes with their bluish shadows were full of disgust, resistance and fear . . .

Well, the resistance, the highly sensitive-moral revolt against "life as it is," against what is given, reality, "power"—this resistance is a sign of *decay*, of biological insufficiency: intellect itself (and art!) is understood and presented as a symbol of this, as the product of degeneration: this is the nineteenth century; this is the relationship of intellect to life that this century sees—but admittedly again in a special and extreme nuance that was only possible after the culmination of that melancholic-honest tendency in Nietzsche.

Nietzsche, you see, who has depicted the character of this epoch in the most sharply critical manner, signified in a certain sense such a culmination: the self-denial of intellect in favor of life, of "strong" and especially "beautiful" life. This is undoubtedly a most extreme and final escape from the "domination of ideals," a submission to "power" that was by now no longer fatalistic but enthusiastic, erotically intoxicated, a submission that was no longer quite masculine but—how shall I say— of a sentimental-esthetic nature—and moreover a find for artists of quite a different degree from Schopenhauer's philosophy! From an intellectual-poetic viewpoint, there are two brotherly possibilities pro- duced from experiencing Nietzsche. The one is that ruthless Renaissance estheticism, that hysterical cult of power, beauty, and life that found favor for a while in a certain literary school. The other is called *irony*— and here I am speaking of myself. With me, the experience of the self- denial of intellect in favor of life became irony—a moral attitude for which I know no other description and designation than precisely this one: that it is the self-denial, the self-betrayal of the intellect in favor of life—and here I define "life" just as the Renaissance estheticism did, but with a different, lighter, and more reserved nuance of feeling that signifies lovableness, happiness, power, grace, the pleasant normality of lack of intellect, and of nonintellectuality. Now to be sure, irony is an ethos that is not completely of a passive nature. The self-denial of the intellect can never be completely serious, completely accomplished. Irony *woos*, even if secretly; it seeks to win for the intellect, even if in vain. It is not animal but intellectual, not gloomy but witty. But it is still weak in will and fatalistic, and it is at any rate very far from placing itself seriously and actively in the service of desirability and of ideals. Above all, however, it is a completely *personal* ethos, not a social one, just as Schopenhauer's "pity" was not social; not a means of improvement in the intellectual-political sense, not exalted, because it does not believe in the possibility of winning life for the intellect—and precisely for this reason it is a form of play (I say form of *play*), of nineteenth-century mentality.

But even the person who has not already been aware of it for ten or fifteen years now can no longer fail to see that this young century, the twentieth, is clearly showing signs of taking after the eighteenth much more strongly than its direct predecessor. The twentieth century declares the character, the tendencies, the basic mood of the nineteenth to be discredited, it defames its form of truthfulness, its weakness of will and submissiveness, its melancholy lack of belief. It *believes*—or at least it teaches that one must believe. It tries to forget "what one knows of the nature of the human being"—in order to adapt him to its utopia. It adores "the human being" completely in *dix-huitième* fashion; it is not pessimistic, not skeptical, not cynical and—most of all—not ironical. The "spirit in the service of desirability" is obviously the spirit it favors; it is its own—a spirit of social humanitarianism. *Reason* and *heart* are again foremost in the vocabulary of the times—the former as a means of bringing "happiness," and the latter as "love," as "democracy." Where is there still a trace of "submission to reality?" Instead, one finds activism, voluntarism, reform, politics, *expressionism*; in short: the domination of ideals. And art must propagate reforms of a social and political nature. If it refuses, judgment is passed upon it: critically it is called estheticism; polemically, parasitism. The new sentimentality is not a product of the war, but there is no doubt that the war has strongly intensified it. No more of Hegel's "state": "Mankind" is again the order of the day: no more of Schopenhauer's denial of the will; let intellect be will and let it create paradise. No more of Goethe's ethos of personal culture: society rather! Politics! Politics! And as far as "progress" is concerned, by which Flaubert's heroic Faustian couple reached such an ironical end—progress is *dogma*—and not a *blague* for the person who wants "to be considered." This, in sum, is the "New Passion."* It combines sentimentality with toughness; it is not "human" in any kind of pessimistic-humorous sense; it heralds "resolute love of humanity." Intolerant, exclusive, with French rhetorical maliciousness, it insults by

---

* One of the expressionist magazines of the time was entitled *Das neue Pathos*, and the name became one of the symbols of the expressionist movement. I have used the words, "New Passion," because the German "Pathos" implies "passion" and not "pity" as the English "pathos" does. "Passion" has been used fairly consistently for "Pathos," but sometimes related words such as "fervor," "enthusiasm," "feeling," and "emotion" were selected.

claiming all morality for itself—although in the end other people, too, claim with some justification not to have lived exactly as debauchees, purely for pleasure, even before the rule of virtue was proclaimed, and they might be tempted to answer as Goethe answered a reproachful patriotism:

> Everyone does his best, each according to his God-given ability. I can say I have allowed myself no rest day and night in the things nature has determined to be my daily work, and I have granted myself no time for recuperation, but have always struggled and searched and done as well and as much as I could. When everyone can say the same of himself, things will be fine for us all.

As far as I am concerned, I have tried at various places in the following essays to make clear to what extent I have to do with the new times, how much there is also in me something of that "resolution," of that denial of the "indecent psychologism" of the past era, of its lax and informal *tout comprendre*—of a will, then, that one might call antinaturalistic, anti-impressionistic, and antirelativistic, but which, in the artistic as in the moral sense, was, after all, a will and not simply "submissiveness." I have made this quite clear in my work—not because I had a need to join, but simply because I only had to listen to my own inner voice to hear the voice of the times as well. Why did I nevertheless have to come into conflict with the new, to feel myself pushed aside by it, negated, offended and *actually* abused and insulted by it, the more unbearable and poisonous because it was done by the highest literary skill, with the most rapacious writing, the most practiced passion it was capable of? Because it confronted me, me personally, in a form that had to call forth from me in opposition the deepest and most basic element, the most personal-impersonal one, the most involuntary, inalienable and instinctive one, the basic *national* element of my nature and culture: because it confronted me in *political* form.

The word "politics" can in no way be avoided in any analysis of the New Passion. It is completely a part of its optimistic-ameliorative nature that it is always but two steps from politics: approximately—and not just approximately—in the sense in which Freemasons and *illuminati* of a Latin tint are always but two steps from it, and never even maintain these two steps. But whoever asks what kind of politics the New Passion follows shows himself to be caught in an error, as if there were two types or even many types of "politics," and as if the political attitude were not always one and the same: the democratic one. When, in the following discussions, the identity of the concepts "politics" and "democracy" is defended or treated as obvious, it is done with an extraordinarily clearly perceived right. One is not a "democratic," or, say, a "conservative" politician. One *is* a politician or one is not. And if one is, then one is democratic. The political-intellectual attitude is the democratic one; belief in politics is belief in democracy, in the *contrat social*. For more than a century and a half, everything that has been understood in a more intellectual sense by politics goes back to *Jean-Jacques Rousseau*; and he is the father of democracy *because* he is the father of the political spirit itself, of political humanity.

I met the New Passion, then, as democracy, as political enlightenment and the humanitarianism of happiness. I understood its efforts to be toward the politicization of every ethos; its aggressiveness and doctrinary intolerance consisted—I experienced them personally—in its denial and slander of every nonpolitical ethos. "Mankind" as humanitarian internationalism; "reason" and "virtue" as the radical republic; intellect as a thing between a Jacobin club and Freemasonry; art as social literature and maliciously seductive rhetoric in the service of social "desirability"; here we have the New Passion in its purest political form as I saw it close up. I admit that this is a special, extremely romanticized form of it. But my destiny was to experience it in this way; and then, as I have already said, it is always at any moment on the verge of assuming this form: "active intellect," that is: an intellect that is "resolved" to be active in favor of enlightened world liberation, world improvement, world happiness, does not long remain "politics" in the more abstract, figurative sense; it is immediately so in the strict, real sense as well. And—to ask the question again foolishly—what kind of politics is this? It is a politics that is *hostile to Germany*. This is obvious. The political spirit that is anti-German as intellect is with logical necessity anti-German as politics.

When, in the following pages, I have held that democracy, that politics itself, is foreign and poisonous to the German character; when I have doubted or argued against Germany's calling to politics, I have not done so—personally or impersonally—with the laughable purpose of spoiling my nation's will to reality, of shaking its belief in the justice of its international claims. I myself confess that I am deeply convinced that the German people will never be able to love political democracy simply because they cannot love politics itself, and that the much decried "authoritarian state" is and remains the one that is proper and becoming to the German people, and the one they basically want. A certain amount of courage is required today to express this conviction. Nevertheless, in doing so, I not only intend no derogation of the German nation in the intellectual or in the moral sense—I mean just the opposite—I also believe that its will to power and worldly greatness (which is less a will than a fate and a world necessity) remains completely uncontested in its legitimacy and its prospects. There are highly "political" nations—nations that are never free of political stimulation and excitement, that still, because of a complete lack of ability in authority and governance, have never accomplished anything on earth and never will. The Poles and the Irish, for example. On the other hand, history has nothing but praise for the organizing and administrative powers of the completely nonpolitical German Nation. When one sees where France has been brought by her politicians, it seems to me one has the proof in hand that at times things do not work at all *with* "politics"; and this in turn is a sort of proof that things can also work in the end *without* "politics." Therefore no misunderstanding should arise when people like me declare the political spirit to be an alien and impossible spirit in Germany. What provoked the deepest element in me, my national instinct, was the cry for "politics" in *that* meaning of the word that belongs to the intellectual sphere: it is the "politicization of the intellect," the distortion of the concept of intellect into that of reforming enlightenment, of revolutionary humanitarianism, that works like poison and orpiment on me; and I know that my disgust and protest is not something insignificantly personal and temporary, but that here the national character itself is speaking through me. Intellect is *not* politics. As a German, one does not have to be bad nineteenth century to fight to the death for this "not." The difference between intellect and politics includes that of culture and civilization, of soul and society, of freedom and voting rights, of art and literature; and German tradition is culture, soul, freedom, art and *not* civilization, society, voting rights, and literature. The difference between intellect and politics, as a further example, is the difference between cosmopolitan and international. The former concept comes from the cultural sphere and is German; the latter comes from the sphere of civilization and democracy and is—something quite different. The democratic bourgeois is international, even though he may drape himself everywhere ever so nationally; the *burgher*, also a motif of this book—is cosmopolitan *because* he is German, more German than princes and "nation": this man of the geographical, social, and spiritual "middle" has always been and remains the bearer of German intellectuality, humanity, and antipolitics.

In Nietzsche's literary remains an interpretation of the *Meistersinger* was found that is unbelievably full of intuition. It says: "Meistersinger— *antithesis of civilization, German tradition against the French.*" The statement is invaluable. Here in a blinding lightning flash of ingenious criticism there appears for a second the antithesis that this whole book struggles with—the antithesis that for cowardly reasons has been much denied and disputed, but that is nevertheless still immortally true, of music and politics, of German tradition and civilization. As far as German tradition is concerned, this antithesis remains a matter of the heart that can only be acknowledged with hesitation; it is something emotional that cannot be grasped rationally and is therefore nonaggressive. For civilization, however, it is political hatred. How could it be otherwise? Civilization is politics through and through, politics itself, and its hatred, too, can only be, and must immediately be, political. The political spirit as democratic enlightenment and "humanitarian civilization" is not only psychologically anti-German; it is also by necessity politically anti-German wherever it holds sway. And this has determined the attitude of its internal German adherent and prophet who haunts the pages of this book as civilization's literary man. Historical research will reveal what role the international *illuminati*, the world lodge of Freemasons, excluding, of course, the unsuspecting Germans, has played in the intellectual preparation and actual unleashing of the World War, the war of "civilization" *against Germany*. As for me, even before there was any evidence, I had my own exact and irrefutable convictions about this. Today, it is no longer necessary to allege, let alone prove, that, for example, the French lodge is political to the point of identity with the radical party—the radical party that in France literally forms the hotbed and fertile soil for intellectual hatred of Germany and of the German character. It is not the *nouveau esprit* of young France that really nourishes hatred of Germans; this spirit, too, is at war with us today, but to it we are an honorable enemy. Germany's enemy, in the most intellectual, instinctive, venomous and deadly sense, is the "pacifistic," "virtuous," "republican" bourgeois rhetorician and *fils de la révolution*; this born three-point man—and he was the one with whose word and will the German representative of the political spirit, the one who deals with the New Passion in the sense of "humanitarian civilization," could immediately, in 1914, unify his own word and his own will, and whose disgusting argot he spoke as he had always done. I repeat: the German representative was not in agreement with the upstanding, nobly respectful foreign enemy, not with the *nouveau esprit*, which in the intellectual-moral sphere basically sympathizes with Germany, but with the political, the venomous enemy who is the founder and shareholder *"d'un journal qui répand les lumières."* This enemy was his hero, the German representative wished for the enemy's victory, he longed for his invasion of Germany; and this was logical. The triumph of *one* "military way of thinking" (to use the words of Max Scheler) over the other would have made little sense; what was urgently desired was the victory of the pacifistic-bourgeois "militarism with a cause" (with negro armies) over the "military way of thinking": And it is here, at the latest here, that our opinions, those of the political neoenthusiast and mine, separated; in the pressure of the times, the contrast between us became acute; for there were constraints of my being and essence that caused me to long for Germany's victory.

In Germany, one must take the greatest pains to explain and to excuse this wish. In the country of Kantian esthetics, it is above all advisable to emphasize that one desires a German victory in a *disinterested* way. I am neither a power-proud Junker nor a shareholder in heavy industry, nor even a social imperialist with capitalist connections. I have no life-and-death interest in Germany's trade dominance, and I even entertain oppositional doubts about Germany's calling to grand politics and to an imperial existence. Finally, for me it is also a matter of intellect, of "domestic policy." With my heart, I stand with Germany, not as far as she is competing with England in power politics, but as far as she opposes her intellectually; and for the German defender of "humanitarian civilization," it was soon not so much his political hostility to Germany as his spiritual hostility to German tradition that bothered me and awakened my fear, hatred and resistance—especially since for his part, as well, "domestic" policy soon supplanted "foreign" affairs, and hostility to Germany retreated behind opposition to German tradition, or more correctly: fell away from it and left it as its center. His hostility to Germany soon had little more to hope for: the military invasion of Germany by civilization's troops had failed. What he has continued to put his hopes in, not without a strong semblance of correctness, is the intellectual invasion that is possibly by far the strongest and most overpowering *political* invasion by the West that has ever become German destiny. Germany's spiritual conversion (which would mean a real transformation and structural change) to politics, to democracy: this is what he is hoping for. No! This is what has become for him, not without a strong semblance of correctness, as I said, a triumphant certainty, indeed, so much so that he deems it possible today, and does not think it a blemish on his honor, to unite himself with Germany in the first person plural; now he forms words on his lips that he has not used all the days of his life; the words, "We Germans." "*We Germans*," civilization's literary man says in a manifesto that appeared at the turn of the years 1917–18, "now that we have grown up to democracy, have the greatest experience of all before us. A nation does not reach self-government without learning much about human nature and without managing life with more mature organs. The play of social forces lies in nations that govern themselves in full public view with the individuals educating one another and learning about each other. But if we act now at home, the barriers abroad will also soon fall; European distances will become shorter, and we will see our fellow nations as family members travelling the same paths. As long as we persisted in the national status quo, they seemed to us to be enemies—doomed because they did not also persist. Has not every revolution come just before the end? Was it not ruin to try to realize ideas in battles and crises? This destiny shall now be ours as well . . ."

What unspeakably painful resistance rises up in my inner being before this hostile gentleness, before all this beautifully stylized unpleasantness? Should one not laugh? After all, is not every sentence, every word in it, false, translated, basically mistaken, grotesque self-deception—the confusion of the wishes, instincts, and needs of a novelist who has been spiritually naturalized in France with German reality? "This destiny shall now be ours as well!" A sublime and brilliant but basically Latinized literary man who long ago renounced every feeling for the particular ethos of his people, yes, who even ridicules the recognition of such a special national ethos as bestial nationalism, and who opposes it with his humanitarian-democratic civilization and "social" internationalism. This literary man is dreaming! He thinks that just because Germany is in the process of broadening her basis for selecting her political leadership, calling this "democratization," that things will now be as magnificently pleasant for "us" as they are in France! Caught up in mania and confusion, he is flinging at his country and people a destiny that never, never can or may belong to it—is this not so? I will let his reference to Germany's "growing up to democracy" stand—a form of government and society that Paraguay and Portugal have long ago "grown up to." I will pay even less attention to the chamber tirade about "self-governing nations." The important thing is that *never*, no matter how much democracy he assumes, will the German human being ever "manage" his life with the "more mature organs" of a boulevard moralist. The German will never mean society when he says "life," never elevate social problems above moral ones, above inner experience. We are not a social nation and not a bonanza for wandering psychologists. We think and write about the ego and the world, not the role that an ego sees itself playing in society, and not the mathematically rationalized social world that forms the subject of the French novel and theater—or did until the day before yesterday. To be able to think that "activity"—especially "subjective" activity—only means social, critical, and political activity, and to believe that it is proper for the German "to continue this frightful activity and also to waver this way and that"— precisely this is what I call *alienation*. In the cosmopolitan world of art, such alienation would be completely suitable for the production of goods of bizarre value, but it becomes unbearable from the moment when, as political prophecy, it attempts to set the direction of the nation's moral life, and presumes to lead it by the hand. Here confusion and distortion reach the point where he claims that we were completely wrong in looking upon our well-meaning fellow nations (the dear and good ones!) as *enemies*. Does he want to ridicule us, then? We saw them as enemies? We have done only too little of that! Our good-natured, nonpolitical humanity has always led us to think that "understanding," friendship, peace, and good relations were possible, and we would never have allowed ourselves to dream, we had to learn for the first time in the war with shock and horror, how much *they* hated *us* (and not we them!) all this time—hated us, indeed, not so much because of economic competition, but rather—something much more venomous— hated us *politically*. We had not imagined how, under the guise of peaceful international intercourse, in God's wide world, the hatred, the unquenchably deadly hatred of political democracy, of the Freemason-republican, rhetorical-bourgeois of 1789, was doing its cursed work against us, against our form of government, our psychological militarism, our spirit of order, authority and duty.

"Their destiny shall now be ours as well"—that is, "to work for the realization of ideas in battles and crises." What foolishness! It can never be and never will be Germany's mission and task, her "destiny," to realize ideas politically. The politicization of the intellect, as civilization's literary man sees it, strikes here against the deepest, most instinctive, most steadfast opposition, because here it is an elementary, essential, and basic part of our national ethos to believe that in this politicization both politics and intellect will go to the dogs, that both are equally jeopardized when a philosophy is made into the way of thinking and the basis of society and of the state. Ask all those who know, all those who understand national souls: they will tell you about the reserved character of German democracy. They will convince you that this reserve does not come from a lack of respect for the intellect, but from *reverence* for it; because reverence for the intellect makes one skeptical of programs of action for its political "realization." German democracy is not genuine democracy, for it is not political, not revolutionary. Its politicization in such a way that the antithesis of Germany and the West in this point would be leveled out and made to disappear is an illusion. Even its proponents do not deny that such a revolution could not be brought about by institutions, suffrage reforms and the like: only a spiritual change in Germany's structure, the complete transformation of her national character, would be able to bring it about—and this is, of course, what the German *zapadnik** *wishes* and what he therefore *believes* in. He is daydreaming and he is wrong. German "democracy" will never be anything more than economic equalization for the liberation of individual creative powers; at the most an administrative-pedagogical way of freeing natural political talents—as long as it is strictly German democracy, more "German," that is, than "democracy"; and its essence will *not* be "politicized intellect," that is to say, it will not consist of realizing "ideas" politically and staging intellectually sparkling affairs between saber and aspergillum on the one hand and "justice" on the other. Is not all this true?

And still—what triumphant certainty, no longer warlike, but transformed into a happily beaming mildness, speaks from the phrases cited from that manifesto! Is it possible to pass over so much subjective assurance of victory with a shrug of one's shoulders? And did I not say myself that his hopes, his belief, his triumph, had a strong semblance of correctness? Has the Western intellectual-political invasion been as completely frustrated as the military one? From the beginning this was clearly improbable, for Germany's national ethos cannot resist nearly as well as her armies can—let us admit what we know! The intellectual invasion has *not* been frustrated and could not be, for it has encountered not only ethical weakness, but also positive cooperation: the path had been prepared for it, and not just from today and yesterday. Germany's national ethos does not match those of other nations in clarity and

* A *zapadnik* is a Russian who favors the West.

distinctness. It lacks both self-awareness and self-assurance. It is not well defined, it has such "bad boundaries" as Germany herself. But its greatest weakness is its lack of readiness with the word. It does not speak well; and if one *defines* it in words, they sound paltry and negative, like the statement that it is not Germany's business "to realize ideas." Civilization's political ethos, on the other hand, with its high-minded, rhetorical-literary ability, has the scarcely resistible dash and verve of attacking revolutionary troops. It has admirers, friends, and allies within the walls, betrayers because of high-mindedness, who open the gates for it. Soon it will be fifty years since Dostoyevsky, who had the eyes to see, asked almost incredulously: "Can it be true that cosompolitan radicalism has already taken roots in Germany, too?" This is a way of asking that is equivalent to astonished confirmation, and the idea of cosmopolitan, or more correctly, international radicalism, itself contradicts the protestation that it is a "mirage" of our present enemies that the national democracies could ever unite into an intellectually unified European or world democracy. By "cosmopolitan radicalism," Dostoyevsky meant that intellectual tendency that has the democratic civilization-society of "mankind" as its goal; *la république sociale, démocratique et universelle*; the empire of human civilization. A mirage of our enemies? But mirage or not: those who see this mirage hovering before them must definitely be enemies of Germany, for it is certainly true that a union of the national democracies into a European, a world democracy, would leave nothing of the German character: the world democracy, the imperium of civilization, the "society of mankind," could have a character that would be more Latin or more Anglo-Saxon—the German spirit would dissolve and disappear in it, it would be obliterated, it would no longer exist. Richard Wagner once declared that *civilization* disappears before *music* like mist before the sun. He never dreamed that one day, for its part, music would disappear before civilization, before democracy, like mist before the sun.

This book dreams of these things—in a confused, difficult, and unclear way—but this and nothing else is the content of its fears: "*finis musicae*"—the phrase appears somewhere in it, and it is only a dream symbol for democracy. The progress from music to democracy—this is what it means throughout when it speaks of "progress." But when it claims and tries to show that Germany is really moving rapidly and unavoidably in the direction of this progress, then admittedly this is *first of all* a rhetorical method of defense. For it is obviously resisting this progress; it opposes it conservatively. Indeed, all of its conservatism is only opposition in this connection; all of its melancholy and half-hypocritical resignation, all of its sinking into the breast of romanticism and its "sympathy with death," is nothing else, either. It denies progress altogether in order at least to deny this progress; it argues quite indiscriminately and even enters into doubtful alliances; it runs up against "virtue," covers up "belief" with quotes, expresses itself provocatively about "humanity"—all this to oppose this progress, Germany's progress from music to politics.

But why the effort? Why the harmful and compromising galley service of this book that no one demanded or expected of me, and from which I will have no trace of thanks and honor? One does not worry to this degree about something one does not *need* to worry about, that is none of one's business because one knows nothing about it and has nothing of it in oneself, *in one's own blood.* I said that Germany had enemies within her own walls, allies and advocates of world democracy, that is. Is this possibly repeated in miniature? Do I contain elements in my own conservative inner nature that aid and abet Germany's "progress"? Could it be true that my being and—as far as one can talk about such a thing—my impact, too, do not correspond exactly at all to my thoughts and opinions, and that I myself with a part of my nature was and am fated to further Germany's progress to what in these pages is given the quite figurative name (and which has only superficially to do with universal suffrage) of "democracy"? And what part would this be, then? The *literary* part, perhaps? For literature—let us once more say what we know!—literature is democratic and civilizing from the ground up; even more correctly: it is *the same* as democracy and civilization. And could it be my authorship, then, that, for my part, has caused me to further Germany's "progress"—*while* I was fighting it conservatively?

With what I have said and asked here, I have summarized the motifs of the following reflections as in a musical prelude. At the same time, I have said what they are. They are the detailed product of an ambivalence, the presentation of an inner-personal discord and conflict. It is this that makes this book, which is no book and no work of art, almost into something else: almost into a story.

CHAPTER 1

The Protest

In his pathologically light, uncannily ingenious manner that is always somewhat reminiscent of the degenerate prattle of certain religious characters in his novels, Dostoyevsky speaks—1877—about the problem of Germany in the world, about "Germany, the protesting kingdom." As long as there has ever been a Germany, he says, her task has been protestantism:

> not merely that form of protestantism that developed at the time of Luther, but her *eternal* protestantism, her *eternal* protest as it began with Arminius against the Roman world, against everything that was Rome and Rome's mission, and later against everything that was transmitted from the old Rome to the new, and to all nations that received the Roman idea, formula, and element, *protest* against the heirs of Rome and against everything that constitutes this heritage.

In great sweeps, he then outlines the history of the Roman idea: beginning in ancient Rome with her concept of a universal unification of mankind and her belief in the practical realization of this concept in the form of a world monarchy. This formula died, he said, but not the idea; for the idea was that of the European people; their civilization has developed from it, and they exist solely for its sake. The concept of the Roman universal monarchy was replaced by that of unification in Christ; whereupon there followed that split of the new ideal into an *eastern* part, which Dostoyevsky says is characterized by the ideal of the wholly spiritual unification of mankind, and a *western European* part, which was Roman Catholic, papal. In its western form, the idea certainly did not surrender its Christian, spiritual character, but it also preserved the old Roman political-imperial tradition. After this, Dostoyevsky goes on, the idea of universal unity continued without interruption to progress and to change, but the development of the endeavor led to the loss of the essential body of Christian principles. The heirs of the ancient Roman world, who had succeeded in discarding Christianity intellectually, also discarded the papacy with it: this happened in the French Revolution, which was nothing more (basically, nothing more) than the last reshaping or reimbodiment of this same ancient Roman formula of universal unification. The realization of the idea—we are still following Dostoyevsky's thought—the realization was quite inadequate. To be sure, there was the most complete satisfaction in that section of human society that had won political supremacy for itself in 1789, namely in the bourgeoisie: it had triumphed, and now held that it was no longer necessary to go farther. But those intellects, who, according to the immutable laws of nature, are destined to create eternal disturbance in the world, to search for new formulations of the ideal and of the new word—both so indispensable to the development of the human organism—joined those downtrodden and neglected ones who had benefited little or not at all from the revolutionary formula of the unification of all people: socialism proclaimed its new word.

And Germany? And the Germans? Dostoyevsky says,

> The most characteristic, most essential trait of this great, proud, and special people has always been, since the first moment of its appearance in the historical world, that it has never, neither in its destiny nor in its principles, wanted to be united with the far Western World, that is, with all the heirs of the ancient Roman destiny. Throughout all these two thousand years, Germany has protested against this world, and even if she did not express her own word—and has still never expressed it at all, her own sharply formulated ideal as a positive replacement for the ancient Roman idea she destroyed—still, I believe—

(this is a powerful passage; one realizes suddenly where one is: with the foremost psychologist of world literature!) "still," he says,

> I believe that in her heart she has always been convinced that one day she will once again be in a position to proclaim this new word and to lead mankind with it. She began her struggle against the Roman world as early as the time of Arminius. During the era of Roman Christianity, more than any other nation, she fought with Rome for supremacy. Finally, she protested in the most powerful way by taking the new formula of protest from the most spiritual, most elementary foundations of the Germanic world. The voice of God resounded from her, proclaiming freedom of the spirit. The split was terrible and universal—the formula of protest had been found and was fulfilled—even though it still remained a negative one, and the positive word still had not been expressed . . .

After this deed, Dostoyevsky continues approximately, the Germanic spirit fades for a long time. The Western world, however, influenced by the discovery of America, by the new science, new principles, "seeks to recreate itself in a new truth" and to enter a new phase, and the first attempt at this transformation is the Revolution. What a confusing event for the German spirit! For basically, Dostoyevsky suggests, it understands as little about the Revolution as the Latin spirit does of the Reformation. Indeed, it is close to surrendering its individuality and to losing its belief in itself.

> It could say nothing against the new ideas of the far Western world. The era of Luther's protestantism was long past, but the idea of the free spirit, of free research, had already been accepted for some time by the world scientific community. More than ever, the gigantic German organism felt that it had no body, no form to express itself. And at that time there arose in it the urgent need to form itself, outwardly at least, into a single, solid organism: in consideration of the new, approaching phases of its eternal struggle with the far Western world . . .

Whoever devotes himself to the intellectual contemplation of great upheavals and crushing catastrophes, always runs the risk of falling under the suspicion that vanity is goading him on to test his cleverness against an earthquake. In great and terrible situations, intellect can very easily seem frivolous. But without intellect, nothing, not even the smallest thing, let alone great historical events, can be understood. They all have two aspects. If one removes "the philosophy" from the French Revolution, there remain the hunger revolt and the upheaval in property relationships. But who would deny that this would do a great injustice to the French Revolution? It is no different with our present-day experiences, and it is impossible to agree with the embittered purists who insist, admittedly out of understandable fear of the feuilleton, that the only reality of this war is its manifestation, namely unspeakable misery, and who argue that it is shameless to try to make sense of it, to distort and to embellish this loathsome reality by seeking to explain and to interpret it. The demand for such restraint is inhuman, even though it has its origin in humanitarian grief at the fall of brotherhood. Humanitarian is not always the same as humane.

Dostoyevsky's view of European history, or rather of the special role of resistance that Germany plays in it, is not less valid for its brilliance. I believe I see that his interpretation takes liberties, is sometimes one-sided, and even contains errors. When he states, for example, that the development of the Roman idea of unity led, in the Revolution, to the loss of the *essential* body of Christian principles, he seems to me to confuse what the Revolution itself confused, namely Christianity with the church; for all the cult of reason, all hatred of the clergy, all scorn unleashed against the dogmas and legends of positive religions in general and against the "bastard of an unfaithful wife" in particular, did not prevent the Revolution, as far as it bore Rousseauean intellectual traits, from being based upon a good bit of Christianity, of Christian universality, of Christian sensitivity. It was not in vain that Madame Roland, in her letter to the Pope, spoke of "those evangelical principles that the purest democracy, the tenderest love of humanity, and the most perfect equality breathe." It is also easy to establish that all Rousseaueans, all radical democrats, all revolutionary epigones, even up to the present day, are ready at any moment to moralize in a Christian way; yes, even consciously to call upon Christianity as an ally. And finally, there is probably something to the charge that Germany's enemies in this war have been able to hurl against her from "civilization's" camp that Germans are *heathens* who secretly pray to Odin— there is probably something to this, I feel, because the joke originated in our midst that the only Christians in Germany are the Jews. But as to the relationship of the German spirit to the Roman world, I think that Dostoyevsky sees only one of the two great symbolic German events and experiences, while probably intentionally overlooking the other: he sees the German event, "Luther in Rome"; but he does not see the other one, "Goethe in Rome," which to many a German is more dear and important—but we must be content here with these formulalike hints.

Dostoyevsky's *aperçu* is grandiose and one-sided, but it is profound and true—even though one must remember that true thoughts are not at all times equally true. Dostoyevsky wrote his reflection under the influence of Bismarck's personality, a few years after the Franco-Prussian War, and at that time it was to a high degree true. In the intervening time it lost some of the intensity of its truth; we could read it without being particularly moved by it, yes, without properly feeling and understanding it. Today we do not need to read it to be fully aware of its message and to contemplate its truth. For it is a warlike concept, of warlike truth, and in times of war this concept of the "protesting kingdom" shines out clearly to everyone in the greatest force of its truth—yes, from the first moment there was basically complete and general unanimity on it: Germany agreed with her enemies on this thought, and not only with her foreign enemies, but also with her so-called domestic ones, with those intellects among us who protest against the German protest—intellects, about whom we will have more to say later, who turn in trusting love to the European West. Everyone, I say, friend and foe, was and is of one opinion, even if not of one disposition— for that is, to be sure, something else. When, for example, Romain Rolland says in his war book that I was, in a certain article that some of my readers may possibly remember ("Thoughts in War," November 1914), like a raging bull with head lowered, charging into the sword of the matador; that I had claimed all the enemy's accusations as so many terms of praise for Germany and had provided ammunition for Germany's enemies—that I had, in short, in the most imprudent way, *agreed* with them, then he only clarifies that distinction between opinion and disposition that is actually the basis of all intellectual enmity. For where there is not the slightest community of thought, there can be no enmity. There is only indifferent remoteness. Only where people think alike but feel differently is there enmity; this is where hatred grows. Finally, dear and good M. Rolland, the issue is one of European *fraternal strife*.

In my opinion, then, there has been the most complete unanimity from the first moment that the intellectual roots of this war, "the German war," as it is called with every possible justification, lie in Germany's inborn and historical "protestantism," that this war is essentially a new outbreak, perhaps the grandest, the final one, as some believe, of Germany's ancient struggle against the spirit of the West, as well as the struggle of the Roman world against stubborn Germany. I will not be dissuaded from the belief that all German "patriotism" in this war—especially that which manifested itself so unexpectedly, or almost unexpectedly—was and is, in its essence, instinctive, innate partisanship for precisely this protestantism, partisanship that was often only reflected upon later; that Germany's face has remained pointed toward the west in this war—despite the great physical danger that has threatened from the east, and that has not ceased to threaten. The eastern danger was terrible, and it was necessary to shift those five army corps from the western front with the result that the French gained their *grande victoire sur la Marne*—each one of us would have agreed if he had been asked, for things could naturally not continue as they were in East Prussia. But this does not negate the fact that in the present war, dangerous, clumsy Russia is merely the tool of the West; she can only be considered from an intellectual point of view today to the extent she is liberalized in a Western manner—precisely as a member of the *entente* to which she is adapting spiritually as well as she can (the fascinating conversation that the Russian foreign minister, Sazonov, carried on with an English novelist about the Christian-human meekness of the sinner and the unbearable "strict morality" of Prussia shows that this adaptation is going rather well—a very good, witty conversation that our press tried to make fun of in the most inappropriate manner): as a member of the *entente*, I say, which, America included, is the unification of the Western world, of the heirs of Rome, of "civilization" against Germany, against the Germany that is now protesting with more primeval power than ever before.

CHAPTER 2

The Unliterary Country

There is considerable self-restraint in Dostoyevsky's description of the Germans as a "great, proud, and special people," for we know that he was far from loving Germany—not because of enormous sympathy for the countries farther west, but because to him, Germany, despite her protestantism, was still part of that "frivolous" Europe that he hated to the depths of his soul. Considerable self-restraint and appropriate moderation, then, the result of great, free, historical intuition, underlie his way of speaking about Germany. For instead of "proud, and special," he could just as easily have said "stubborn, callous, malicious"—terms that would, of course, have been mild in comparison to those that the Roman West, with its excellent manners, has used against us during the war. Indeed, Dostoyevsky's formulation of the German character, of German primeval individuality, of what is eternally German, contains the whole basis and explanation of the lonely German position between East and West, of Germany's offensiveness to the world, of the antipathy, the hatred she must endure and defend herself against—in bewilderment and pain at this universal hatred that she does not understand because she knows little about herself and has not developed very far at all in matters of psychological understanding—the basis and explanation also of her enormous *courage* that she has unflinchingly displayed to the surrounding world, the world of the Roman West that today is almost everywhere, in the East, the South, even in the North and across the ocean where the new Capitol stands—of that blind-heroic courage with which Germany is striking out everywhere with a gigantic reach. And it also explains the good sense of the charge of "barbarism," a charge that one cannot logically reject with indignation, because the heirs of Rome, articulate as they are, could indeed find no better, simpler, more effective, more persuasive word than precisely this one to characterize those who have instinctively, from time immemorial, protested against their world. For the worst thing was not that Germany never wanted to combine her word and will with that of Roman civilization: she only opposed it with her will, her disturbing, stubborn, obstinate, "special" will—but not with her word, because she had no word. She was speechless, she did not love words, and she did not believe in them as did civilization; she engaged in a silent, inarticulate resistance, and there is no doubt that it was not so much Germany's resistance itself as her wordlessness and inarticulateness that were perceived by civilization to be "barbaric" and hate-inspiring. The word, the formulation of the will, as with everything that has to do with form, has a conciliatory, winning effect, it can reconcile itself eventually with every type of will, especially when it is beautiful, generous, convincing, and clearly programmatic. The word is absolutely necessary to win sympathy. What good is great courage without the generous word? What good the stubborn conviction that "one will once again be in a position to speak one's word and to lead mankind with it" if one cannot or will not utter it at the crucial moment? (For it comes to the same thing: ability comes from desire; fluency comes from love of words, and vice versa.) One cannot lead mankind without the word. Gigantic courage is barbaric without a well-articulated ideal to guide it. Only the word makes life worthy of a human being. To be without words is not worthy of a human being, is inhumane. In the innate and eternal conviction of Roman civilization, not only humanism—humanitarianism in general, human dignity, respect for human beings, and human self-respect, are inextricably bound to literature. Not to music—or at least in no way necessarily to it. On the contrary, the relationship of music to humanitarianism is so much looser than that of literature that the musical attitude seems to the literary moral sense at the very least to be undependable, at the very least, suspicious. Nor to poetry, where the relationship is too much like that of music; in it words and intellect play a much too indirect, cunning, irresponsible, and therefore also undependable role. Rather expressly to literature, to linguistically articulated intellect—civilization and literature are one and the same.

The Roman West is literary: this separates it from the Germanic—or more exactly—from the German world, which, whatever else it is, is definitely not literary. Literary humanitarianism, the legacy of Rome, the classical spirit, classical reason, the generous word to which the generous gesture belongs, the beautiful, heart-stirring phrase that is worthy of a human being and that celebrates his beauty and dignity, the academic rhetoric in honor of the human race—this is what makes life worth living in the Roman West, what makes the human being human. It is the spirit that was at its height during the Revolution; it was its spirit, its "classic form," that spirit that in the Jacobin hardened into a scholastic-literary formula, into a murderous doctrine, a tyrannical, schoolmasterly pedantry. Its champions are the lawyer and the literary man, the spokesmen of the "Third Estate," and of its emancipation, the spokesmen of the Enlightenment, of reason, of progress, of "the philosophy," against the *seigneurs*, against authority, tradition, history, "power," kingdom and church—the spokesmen of the *spirit* that they consider to be the unconditional, sole, and dazzlingly true one, spirit itself, spirit in itself, while it is really just the political spirit of the middle-class revolution that they mean and understand. It is an historical fact that cannot be denied that "spirit" in this political-civilizing sense is a middle-class *concern*, even if it is not a middle-class invention (for spirit and culture in France are not originally of the middle class, but of noble-seigneurial descent; the middle class only usurped them). Its representative is actually the eloquent citizen, the literary lawyer of the Third Estate, as I have said, the representative of its spiritual as well as, not to forget, of its material interests. The victorious advance of this spirit, its expansive process, which is the result of colossal, turbulent, explosive forces within it, can be defined as a process involving the simultaneous conquest of the world by the middle class and by literature. What we call "civilization," and what calls itself civilization, is nothing more than precisely this victorious advance, this propagation of the politicized and literarized middle-class spirit, its colonization of the inhabited areas of the globe. The *imperialism of civilization* is the last form of the Roman idea of unification against which Germany is "protesting," and she has never done so more passionately against any of its other manifestations; she has never had a more terrible battle to wage than against this one. The agreement and unity of all those communities that belong to the imperium of the middle-class spirit today is the "*entente*"—a French name, how proper—and it is truly an *entente cordiale*, a unity full of the most heartfelt, spiritual, essential agreement despite many differences in temperament and despite divergencies in power politics: directed against Germany, which is protesting the final completion and conclusive establishment of this imperium. The Battle of the Teutoburg Forest, the struggles against the

Roman pope, Wittenberg, 1813, 1870—all this was mere child's play compared to the terrible, perilous, and, in the most magnificent sense, irrational struggle against the world *entente* of civilization, a struggle that Germany has accepted with a truly Germanic obedience to her fate—or, to put it somewhat more actively, to her mission, her eternal and innate mission.

CHAPTER 3

Civilization's Literary Man

> It was thought that the ideal of the Slavophiles was: "To eat radishes and to write denunciations." Yes, denunciations! They astonished everyone so much by their appearance and their views that the liberals had second thoughts and began to be afraid: What, did these strange people intend finally to denounce them, too?
>
> Dostoyevsky, *Works*

The great communities, however, do *not* possess—and it would be almost boring if they did—that spiritual unity that they seem to have, and then only temporarily, in time of war. The task of investigating the extent to which this applies to other countries cannot tempt us here. We must concern ourselves with Germany—and here the word "concern" must be taken somewhat etymologically, for it can be stated without any chauvinism that all intellectual concern for Germany has constantly proven to be particularly rewarding. We will now tell how, in our humble opinion, things stand with Germany.

The antitheses that loosen and call in question the inner intellectual unity and homogeneity of the large European communities are generally the same everywhere: they are basically European, but they are still strongly differentiated nationally among the various peoples, and they are unified under the national synthesis, so that, for example, a radical-republican Frenchman is just as much a genuine, correct, complete and unquestionable Frenchman as is a clerical royalist. A liberal Englishman is as English as his conservative countryman; finally, the Frenchman comes to an understanding with the Frenchman, the Englishman with the Englishman best of all and for the best. There is, however, a country and people in which the situation is different: a people that is not and probably never can be a nation in that definite sense that France and England are nations, because her cultural history and her idea of humanity are against it; a country whose internal unity and homogeneity are not only complicated, but almost abolished by intellectual antitheses; a country where these antitheses are more violent, fundamental, more malicious and less open to compromise than anywhere else; because there they are scarcely, or only loosely, enclosed in a national bond, scarcely combined on a grand scale as the contradictory wills of every other country always are. This country is Germany. Germany's internal, intellectual antitheses are scarcely national; they are almost purely European, opposing one another almost completely without national coloration, without national synthesis. In Germany's soul, *Europe's* intellectual antitheses are carried to the end—"carried to the end" in a maternal and in a warlike sense. This truly is her real national destiny. No longer physically—she has recently learned how to prevent this—but intellectually, Germany is still the battlefield of Europe. And when I say, "the German soul," I do not just mean the collective national soul, but quite specifically the soul, the mind, and the heart of the individual German. I even mean myself as well. To be the spiritual battleground for European antitheses: this is German; but it is not German to make matters easy for oneself and to manifest the national weakness, the—as Nietzsche says—"secret infinity" of one's people, by simply acting like a Frenchman. Whoever would aspire to transform Germany into a middle-class democracy in the Western-Roman sense and spirit would wish to take away from her all that is best and complex, to take away the problematic character that really makes up her nationality; he would make her dull, shallow, stupid, and un-German, and he would therefore be an antinationalist who insisted that Germany become a nation in a foreign sense and spirit.

A strange endeavor! Nevertheless, there are such Germans; and it would be quite wrong to believe that things were as simple in Germany as the great formula of the "protesting kingdom" would make it appear. Those who do not yet know, must certainly learn—for it is very important and interesting—that there are German intellects who not only do not join in the "protest" of their own community against the Roman West, but who even see their true mission and destiny to be part of a passionate protest *against* this protest, and who promote with all the power of their talents the intimate union of Germany with the imperium of civilization. But while the domestic opponents of the officials, of the spokesmen—oh, yes, of the spokesmen of France during the war, are still completely and decisively for their country, our antiprotestors give their struggling country no support and sympathy but enthusiastically confess themselves, as far as such a confession is permissible today, to be for the enemy, for the world of the West, of the *entente*, and especially of France, and why especially France will soon be explained. I will be careful not to call these people un-German. The concept "German" is an abyss, bottomless, and one should be extremely careful with its negative, the judgment of "un-German," so that one is not tripped up and hurt. Therefore, even though it may seem pussyfooting, I will certainly not call these people unpatriotic. I only say that their patriotism is manifested in such a way that they see the prerequisite of the greatness, or, if not of greatness, at least of the happiness and of the beauty of their country, not in its disturbing hate-provoking, "special nature," but, to repeat, in its unconditional union with the world of civilization, of literature, of elevating, rhetorical democracy that is worthy of a human being—with the world that indeed would become fulfilled by the overthrow of Germany: its empire would be complete and all-encompassing; there would be no more opposition to it.

The German proponent of this literary civilization is obviously our *radical literary man*, the one I have become accustomed to call "civilization's literary man"—and I do so because the radical literary man, the representative of the literarized, politicized, in short, of the democratized spirit, is a child of the Revolution, spiritually at home in its sphere, in its country. Actually, the phrase, "civilization's literary man," is no doubt a pleonasm. For I have, of course, already noted that civilization and literature are one and the same thing. One is not a literary man without instinctively despising Germany's "special nature" and feeling oneself bound to the imperium of civilization. To put it more precisely, being a literary man is almost the same as being a Frenchman, indeed, a classical Frenchman, a revolutionary Frenchman; for the literary man receives his greatest traditions from the France of the Revolution. His paradise lies there, his golden age. France is his country; the Revolution is his grand period. He was quite well off then, when he was still called a *philosophe*, and when he actually mediated, spread, and politically prepared the new philosophy of humanitarianism, freedom, and reason.

When I speak of the German radical literary man, for whom the national adjective seems so strange, I am not speaking of that ragtag, bobtail group that one honors far too much by any study one makes of them; not, then, of that scribbling, agitating pack of rascals that is propagating international civilization and whose radicalism is mischievousness, whose literary world is without roots and significance—these literary scum, as leaven and national ferment, may be of some value to progress, but their *lack* of any personal rank or humaneness makes them only worthy of being handled with fire tongs. I am speaking of the *noble* representatives of this type—for there are some. Generally speaking, there is no doubt a degree of innate merit, of intellect and art, that cannot be subjected to criticism on the basis of the national idea. On the contrary, people of this rank define, and perhaps redefine and correct this idea—I will not forget this. I will not fail to consider that with such high rank one is a factor and an element of the nation's fate—an unfortunate factor, perhaps—so much the worse for the nation! So much the worse for it, I say—for it is the nation's misfortune, it is its own fault, it lies in the nation, in its character, if it is left in the lurch in its most difficult hour by some of its best intellects. And not just left in the lurch. By fighting against such intellects, against their opinions in spite of their rank, one ceases to be an artist, for as an artist one was accustomed to respect rank and not to pay much attention to its opinions. One temporarily becomes a politician—and one must therefore guard oneself all the more carefully against political vices such as, for instance, attributing anti-intellectual, that is, base motives, to one's opponent, even if the reverse has already happened. The conviction of having "progress" on one's side obviously produces a moral certainty and self-assurance that borders on callousness, until one finally believes that one is ennobling vulgarity simply by making use of it. This is an excuse. We who feel ourselves less morally secure are necessarily more apprehensive. But let us get to the point!

Germany's radical literary man belongs, then, body and soul, to the *entente*, to the imperium of civilization. Not that he has had to struggle with himself, that the times have torn him in painful spiritual conflict; not that his heart is bound here *and* there, that he is trying by admonishing, punishing, appeasing, and preaching to pacify both sides, placing himself, like gentle Romain Rolland, above the fray. With full passion he thrusts himself *into* the fray—but on the side of the enemy. From the first moment he automatically took the *entente's* side—naturally, for it had always been his own. With unerring accuracy he felt, thought and said exactly what *entente* journalists or ministers said simultaneously or later. He was courageous, he was original, but only in German terms, only relatively. I believe he has shown signs of making his own isolation appear tragic—not quite justifiably so, for it only existed within Germany. He did not exactly think lonely thoughts; what he thought was not particularly sublime, superior, or lovingly all-embracing: it could have appeared in every *entente* newspaper, and it did appear there. In short, he thought as did every Tom, Dick, and Harry among our enemies abroad, and I do not call this tragic isolation. One can say he was well off during those first weeks and months of the war, times his compatriots who are not radical literary men will remember all their lives—the time when the world, the democratic public opinion of the world, was let loose upon Germany, when filth rained upon her: he was really quite well off, I say, for everything that this "great, proud, and special" people had to suffer then and later, both in word and deed—did not matter to him, did not make him hot or cold, did not touch or affect him—he excepted himself, of course; he said the others were right; what they said he had already said for a long time, word for word. Un-German? With all my strength I will resist calling him un-German, and I will not cease resisting it as long as my powers do not fail me. One can be extremely German and, at the same time, extremely anti-German. What is German is an abyss; let us stick to that. No, then! He is not un-German. He is merely an amazing, remarkable example of how alienated and disgusted with himself, how devoted to cosmopolitan ideas, how beside himself, a German may become even today, in post-Bismarckian Germany. It may be permissible to say that the structure of his intellect is *unnational*, but only insofar—or rather to the degree—that it is not German-national but nationally French: so completely so, in fact, that in more peaceful times it would be a real pleasure to study in him all the aspects of magnanimity, sentimentality, childishness, and maliciousness of the classically unbroken French national character that has as yet reached no critical self-reflection, no resignation. He is one of the best French patriots. Belief carries him and at times lends his style a magnificent tremolo, an admirable drive: the belief in the idea of the glory and the mission of his—of the French—people, that they have been called once and for all to be the teachers of mankind, to bring it "justice" after they have brought it "freedom" (which, however, comes from England). He does not merely think in French syntax and grammar: he thinks in French concepts, French antitheses, French conflicts, French affairs and scandals. He sees the war in which we are engaged entirely as the *entente* does, as a struggle between "power and spirit"—this is his principal antithesis!—between the "saber" and the idea, the lie and the truth, barbarism and justice. (I do not have to add on which side, in his opinion, saber, barbarism, and lie, and on which side the antithetically corresponding ideals are to be found.) In a word: this war seems to him to be a repetition of the Dreyfus affair on a colossally magnified scale—for those who do not believe this, I will provide completely convincing documentation. According to the analogy of this case, whoever is engaged in a spiritual struggle on the side of the civilization *entente* against the forces of the "saber," against Germany, is an intellectual. Whoever feels differently, whoever, following some kind of dark instincts in this tremendous struggle, remains loyal to Germany, is lost, a traitor to the intellect who stands against justice and truth—and whether he does so in elegant or sloppy style is justifiably immaterial to the moralist—he stands against them, and every suspicion of his motives is henceforth not only permissible but also imperative: eagerness for applause, acquisitiveness, the neat gift of profiting from the situation, probably also the only too human desire to seize the opportunity to outshine and to silence an opponent who is condemned to silence or to intrigue, to ambiguity—there is no guilelessness that civilization's literary man will not seize upon with a grimace to present siding with "the saber" in the correct psychological light. But since, however (certainly a point against Germany), it is a much more ticklish and complicated matter to speak for Germany than for "civilization," where only a good bit of dash and tremolo are necessary and the job is done—since to speak for Germany one must try, for better or worse, to dig a bit deeper, civilization's literary man refers in such a case, with marked disdain, to his opponent's "deep chatter."

This is the way civilization's literary man looks at things. His sympathy with the enemies of the protesting kingdom is intellectual solidarity. His love and passion are with the troops of the Western allies, of France and England, and probably also of Italy; he sees in them the armies of the spirit with which civilization marches. His heart goes out to them—to Germany his heart goes out quite indirectly: that is, in the sense that he yearns from the bottom of his heart for Germany's defeat. That his motives are of a more spiritual and therefore of a more noble sort is a matter of course. He wishes a German defeat because of its spiritual significance, because of the spiritual consequences it would entail for Germany and for Europe. He wants it for "domestic" reasons—as a substitute, as it were, for the revolution that Germany has of course lacked until today: for 1848 was a failure, and the unification of Germany did not result from the democratic revolution but from the worst and most unpardonable circumstance possible: from France's humiliation. To be sure, France's defeat blossomed into her greatest fortune, for it brought her the republic, that is: truth and justice. But if the only explanation of Germany's victory at that time is that providence smiled upon France (for from an intellectual viewpoint, according to civilization's literary man, Germany could never triumph under Bismarck, such a totally unintellectual man, such an anti-intellectual man of power), this is still no excuse for Germany. I do not know, it is hard to guess, what our radical literary man would have wished for at that time; today he wishes for Germany to be beaten *and converted* by the *entente*—its victory would be the victory of literature for Germany and for Europe, it would be *his* victory, just as its defeat would be his: so much has he made the cause of rhetorical democracy his own. He wishes, therefore, the physical humiliation of Germany because it would include her spiritual defeat; he wishes the collapse—but one says it more correctly in French: the *débâcle* of the *Kaiserreich* because such a physical and moral *débâcle* would—the moral one, by the way, may come before the physical one—finally, finally bring the warmly wished for, palpable, and catastrophic proof that Germany has lived in lies and brutality rather than in truth and spirit. Yes, if it could still be hoped for today, with all his heart he would certainly wish for the democratic invasion of Germany; he would not wish to let matters rest at any Marne-Valmy (it was, however, more like a Marne-Kolín), but to have civilization's troops march into Berlin with a full band—how his heart would welcome them! How he would find ways and means to give ambiguous expression to the triumph of his soul! Alas, this will not happen. It is a thankless business to play the blaspheming prophet in a country where consequences do not follow, in the country of half-measures, which is at best only overtaken by half-catastrophes and which is not capable of a tidy, novelistic fate! Civilization's literary man will not have the *débâcle* of the German *second empire* to write. Not at all. He will have to be content if Germany does not win far too impressively.

I ask you to believe me that if anything like scorn or bitterness may have forced itself into my lines, it has happened against my will. I have no desire at all to speak bitterly or scornfully; on the contrary, my efforts in this study are—let us say: to maintain a popular-scholarly style and to characterize a literary-political type. With this is mind, I hasten to make the following observation. The logical, psychological equation of the concepts, "beaten," and "converted," the equation of the physical and spiritual humiliation of a nation, proves that civilization's literary man is not really an opponent of war, not absolutely a pacifist, that he acknowledges incontestable intellectual validity in the decision to wage war, and that he sees in war an *ultima ratio*, yes, something like God's judgment. Striking, but true. Here we see a type of irrationalism that in truth is a spiritualized rationalism in which one proclaims war to be God's judgment as long as there is the slightest chance that Germany may in any way be beaten, even if only by economic suffocation. But on no account longer! For as soon as this prospect disappears, war becomes injustice and raw power, its outcome without spiritual significance. But this must not stop us from insisting that "spirit" is not necessarily pacifistic—as Italy's example teaches, where "spirit" actually made war: for is it not true, the republicans, Freemasons, radicals and literati of Italy who have waged the war represent "spirit" in that country—and certainly not the Social Democrats, who have resisted the war and who are really pacifists. The truth is that civilization's literary man does not denigrate war when it is waged in the service of civilization. Here he follows Voltaire's example, who, though disgusted by Frederick the Great's wars, could flatly demand a war (against the Turks, with whom Frederick had instead almost allied himself) for the sake of civilization. How, then, could the disciple of the Revolution—not to say; its epigone—condemn on principle the spilling of blood for the good cause, for truth, for spirit? "Resolute love of humanity"—the phrase belongs to civilization's literary man—resolute love of humanity is not fearful of shedding blood. The guillotine, just as much as the literary word, is one of its tools, just as the stake was earlier, which, to be sure, was not bloody. We do not need Gabriele d'Annunzio's lewd estheticism at all to point out where civilization's literary man is on principle *not* an opponent of war. He finds fault with *this* war because he sees it as a German war, an historical enterprise of Germany, as an outburst of the German "protest," because this war carries a German stamp, its activity, its great deeds, are German. He does *not* find fault with it to the extent that he sees it as a war of civilization against the barbaric stubborness of Germany. In this sense, for the other side, he sees it as good. In short, he does not so much find fault with the war as with Germany, and only herein lies the solution to all the contradictions of which civilization's literary man seems guilty, and which would truly seem amazing without this key. His attitude toward the war vacillates between humanitarian disgust and the greatest admiration for the military accomplishments of the enemies. On the one hand, he sees in the *entente* something tender, fragile, precious, nobly-weak, which is naturally in great danger of being brutalized by barbaric Germany. On the other hand, however, he has only the utmost contempt for those of his countrymen who underestimated the *entente's* military virtues and powers, or who even still underestimate them. He is delighted by the accomplishments of the powers of civilization; he admires their war materiel, their armor plate, concrete fortifications, aircraft formations, and poison and choking gas bombs, without asking how this fits the image of noble weakness, while he finds the same things on the German side disgusting. A French cannon seems venerable to him, a German one, criminal, repulsive, and idiotic. Here, too, he agrees with all the *entente* ministers and journalists that every German victory is only the result and proof of long-standing, sneaky preparation, while every *entente* success is a triumph of spirit over matter. On the other hand, however, his love cannot even abide the idea that an *entente* power, particularly France, could be poorly prepared or insufficiently armed. Armed? They are *splendidly* armed! Again, the logic of all this is not obvious. But who would be such a pedant as to demand logic of love!

As I have said, I want to remain scholarly and informative. But my sketch of civilization's literary man reveals that I do not quite agree with him. My position on the events—a position that I certainly did not "choose," a position that was at first quite unreflected and naively obvious—everything I said about it from the very beginning has embittered him. If I had not done so before, I have now ruined my relationship with him forever. With "pain and anger," he says, he has turned from me, but his pain did not prevent his anger from making ambiguous, half-public statements to me that may be excellent in a political sense, but that are, from a human point of view, simply outright meanness—clearly a nod that the "politics of humanitarianism" is still politics and not exactly conducive to humaneness. But this external estrangement is all the more regrettable because we are basically of one opinion—not of one feeling, but of one opinion on this war. He also agrees with Dostoyevsky's concept. He, too, recognizes in the war the ancient rebellion of Germany against the Western spirit, against his own spirit, that of the radical literary man—and the intervention of Rome (Western Rome, allied with Eastern Rome) against this rebellion; a war of intervention, then, of European civilization against stubborn Germany: for when the London *Times* announced one day that this war was being waged by the allies "in the interest of Germany's domestic affairs," this is assuredly almost exactly what one means by the words, "shameless audacity," but it was spoken completely in accord with the feeling of civilization's literary man who is also waging it for the sake of European interest in the domestic "conditions" of his country, and, like every Frenchman, after he suffered a period of demoralization in the first few weeks of the war, he has been convinced, since the miracle of the Marne, of the final victory. "Germany will have to conform," he said then, and his eyes glowed. Germany will finally have to be well behaved, he said, and she will then be happy, like a child that cries to be spanked, and, afterward is grateful that its stubbornness has been broken, that it has been helped over its inhibitions, saved, liberated. By beating Germany, by throwing her over our knee, by breaking her evil stubbornness for her own good, and by forcing her to accept reason and to become an honorable member of the democratic society of states, we are saving and freeing her.

I have already admitted that I cannot quite follow this train of thought. I will go further and admit that I find it quite unpleasant, that it somehow *personally* insults and angers me, touches my innermost honor, yes, when I first heard it, worked on me quite like poison and orpiment. But whence comes all this? Whence comes the rebellion of my final and deepest personal-suprapersonal will against the feelings of a good European, who, because he is a good European, wishes for and believes in the defeat of his fatherland, in the taming of his people by the powers of Western Civilization? I was never one of those who felt that an easy and triumphant German military victory over her enemies, with drums beating and trumpets sounding, would be good for Germany or for Europe. I said this very early. But whence comes the feeling that, from the beginning of the war, has ruled my whole being to the very core that I did not want to live—although I am in no way a hero and resolute in the face of death—that I literally did not want to live anymore if Germany were beaten by the West, humbled, her belief in herself broken so that she would have to "conform" and accept the argument, the rationale of her enemies? Supposing this had happened, that the *entente*, for its part, had won a splendid and speedy victory, that the world had been liberated from the German "nightmare," the German "protest," that the empire of civilization had been fulfilled, and that it had become arrogant from lack of opposition: the result would have been a Europe that was—well, a somewhat amusing, somewhat insipidly humane, trivially depraved, femininely elegant Europe that was already all too "human," somewhat implausibly adventurous and loud-mouthed democratic, a Europe of tango and two-step manners, a Europe of business and pleasure *à la* Edward the Seventh, a Monte-Carlo Europe, literary as a Parisian cocotte—but perhaps not a Europe in which it would have been much more advantageous for the likes of me to live than in a "military" one? Perhaps not an amusing, yes, a thoroughly amusing Europe, *lack* of desire for which, in a writer, would at least not testify to selfishness? For beyond doubt it would have been extremely arty, this *entente*-Europe for human freedom and peace, and the artiste, as far as he was precisely an "artiste," would have been able to feel as happy as a lark in it. He should consider this and one should give him credit for it.

Seriously, my rejection is quite remarkable! Remarkable for me—and I have the bad habit of forcing upon others as remarkable what seems so to me. Remarkable—for the fact remains that my own being and essence are much less foreign to those of civilization's literary man than would appear from the cold, objective critique I have subjected him to. What does he want, and if I do not want it—why not? It is, of course, not at all as if he were a bad citizen and patriot who did not care about Germany. On the contrary! He cares about her with all his might. He feels himself to the highest degree responsible for her fate. He wants and supports a development—that I consider necessary, that is to say, unavoidable, and that I also have a certain involuntary part in because of my nature, but that I still cannot see any reason to cheer. With whip and spurs he is hastening a progress—that to me, not seldom at least, seems irresistible and fated, and that I for my modest part am destined to further; but to which I nevertheless, for unclear reasons, am putting up a certain conservative resistance. I want to be completely understood. What I mean is, then: one can very well regard a progress as unavoidable and destined, without in the least feeling like egging it on with cheers and shouts—in my opinion, progress does not really need this at all. Progress has everything for it, above all, the good writers. If it appears that the good writers own the future, the truth in reality is much more that the future owns the good writers. A metaphysical proof of the goodness and imminence of a cause is the good writing in its behalf. However, one can also say that as long as a cause is supported by good writing, it, too, has value and justification, even if it is not progress. I repeat; progress has everything for it. It only seems to be the opposition. It is the conservative counterwill that in truth always and everywhere forms the opposition, that finds itself on the defensive, indeed, hopelessly on the defensive, as it well knows.

What is, then, this development, this progress I have been speaking of? Well, to indicate what it is about, I need a handful of shamelessly ugly, artificial words. It is about the politicization, literarization, intellectualization, and radicalization of Germany. It aims at her "humanization" in the Latin-political sense, and her dehumanization in the German one. It aims, to use the favorite word, the battlecry and hosanna of civilization's literary man, at the *democratization* of Germany, or, to summarize everything and to bring it over a common denominator: it aims at her de-Germanization. And I should have a part in all this mischief?

CHAPTER 4

Soul-Searching

> Could it really be true that cosmopolitan radicalism has
> already taken roots in Germany, too?
>
> Dostoyevsky, *Works*

And yet, I too have a part in it. And now, for simplicity, let us pass over all those apologies that are obviously most appropriate nowadays whenever anyone seems to be ready to talk about himself. "A turning point in world history!" I hear people saying. "The right moment, indeed, for an average writer to call our attention to his esteemed literary personality!" I call that healthy irony. On the other hand, however, I wonder if a turning point in world history, upon careful consideration, is not really the moment for everyone to look inward, to consult his conscience and to begin a general revision of his own foundations—at least such a need seems understandable and excusable to me when, even in great periods of foreign affairs and "power," domestic affairs and moral matters remain the dominant interest. To be sure, as long as the accusation of self-love and vain arrogance is at all possible, only the sympathetic person and not the indifferent or averse one can be convinced that one is speaking from one's conscience. As I prepare to indulge in bad taste, I must let myself imagine a small audience of friends, known and unknown to me; friends in the sense that their serious and cheerful interest in my previous activities and writings has produced a certain conscious co-responsibility for them. Friends, then, in the sense of that solidarity of conscience that binds an artist to his true public, and that I hope will be strong enough to help them and me through the discussions in the following chapters, which are so risky at this time.

To begin with, my right to "patriotism" may with good reason be doubted, for I am not a very genuine German. Partly of Latin, South American blood, I was from my youth on more oriented to European-intellectual traditions than to German-poetic ones—a difference, no, an antithesis, about which I hope there will be agreement from the start, so that I will not have to insist further on the matter. I have never tried to convince myself that I was a German writer like Gerhart Hauptmann or Herbert Eulenberg, for instance—whereby I hasten to add that I am not speaking for a moment of rank here, but exclusively of essence. The talent that is composed of synthetic-plastic and analytical-critical qualities, and that takes the form of the novel as its own, is actually not German at all, the novel itself is not really a German genre; here, in this country—in the "unliterary country"—it is at present beyond imagination to assume that a prose writer and novelist could rise up in our national consciousness to a representative position in the same way a poet, a pure synthesizer, a lyricist, or a dramatist can do. I say "at present," for civilization's literary man wishes things to be different, and he knows why. He is certain that a coming to the fore of the novel, or, more precisely, of the social novel in the public interest, would be an exact measure of the progress of that literarization, democraticization, and "humanization" of Germany that I spoke of, and that it is the radical literary man's real business and mission to spur on.

Let us return to personal matters! I said I was not a very good and genuine German—indeed, thereby dropping for myself that last caution which I was careful enough to grant civilization's literary man. I can treat myself with less care. But even here, I am not completely forgetting that it is almost part of higher German culture to present oneself as un-German and even anti-German; that a tendency toward a cosmopolitanism that undermines the sense of nationalism is, according to authoritative judgment, inseparable from the essence of German nationality; that one must possibly lose one's German character to find it; that perhaps, without some foreign admixture, no higher German character is possible; that precisely the exemplary Germans were Europeans who would have regarded every limitation to the nothing-but-German as barbaric. Fontane called the great Schiller a half-foreigner, and if Schiller's rhetorical drama is really at home in the *grand siècle*, then it is only a short step for Nietzsche to relegate the work of the other great German dramatist to the field of French romanticism. As for Goethe, at least *The Elective Affinities*, taken formally, is not a very German work, just as in general Goethe's prose is sometimes scandalously French (a phenomenon that cannot be more striking in the "Pole," Nietzsche), while Schopenhauer seems to have begun by translating his paragraphs into Latin in order to translate them back into German later with the gain of an immortal, metallic precision. We have thus become accustomed to accepting such national untrustworthiness in our great ones, putting a good face on it and deciding simply to incorporate it into the concept of the higher German character. By the way, I am not so foolish as to relate the Europeanization of my taste to my rank (but of course, rank should not be the subject of discussion at all). It is not a merit, even if it is not a fault, that what is intimately and exclusively German was never enough for me, that I could not do much with it. My blood needed European stimulation. In an artistic and literary way, my love for German tradition begins exactly where Europeans find it credible and valid, where it can influence Europeans, where it is accessible to every European. The three names I must acknowledge when I search for the basis of my intellectual-artistic development—Schopenhauer, Nietzsche and Wagner—are like a triple star of eternally united spirits that shines powerfully in the German sky—symbolizing events that are not intimately German, but European.

I can see before my eyes the small, upper-story suburban room in which, sixteen years ago, stretched out for days on end on a strangely formed *chaise longue* or couch, I read *The World as Will and Idea*. Lonely, erratic youth, passionately craving the world and death—how it drank in the magic potion of this metaphysical world whose deepest essence is eroticism, and in which I recognized the spiritual source of the music of *Tristan*! One only reads this way once. Never again. And what luck for me that I did not have to lock such an experience inside myself, that a beautiful opportunity to bear witness to it and to show thanks for it was immediately there, that a literary shelter was directly prepared for it! For two steps from my couch the manuscript lay open that was swelling in an impossible and impractical way—a burden, dignity, home and blessing for that strange age of youth, highly problematical in its public qualities and prospects—that had just grown to the point where it was time to have Thomas Buddenbrook die. To him, who for me represented the mystical-threefold image of father, offspring, and double, I gave the precious experience, the high adventure, wove it into his life narratively just before the end, for it seemed to me that it became him well—the sufferer who courageously stood firm, the moralist and "militarist" after my heart, the late, complicated burgher whose nerves were no longer suited to his milieu; the co-governor of an aristocratic city democracy, who, after having become modern and questionable, with nontraditional taste and with developed European-ized needs, had long begun to feel alienated from and to smile at surroundings that had remained healthier, more limited, and more genuine. In fact, the discovery Thomas Buddenbrook made before his death, in a dusty corner of his bookcase—was only seemingly a chance one. Not many years before, Europe, intellectual Europe, with which the middle-city dignitary nervously sympathized, had made the same discovery. Schopenhauer's pessimism held sway; it was the great intel-lectual fashion in Europe, for this German philosopher was no longer a "German philosopher" in the traditional, inaccessibly-abstruse sense. I dare say he was, indeed, very German (can one be a philosopher without being German?)—very German, for example, in that he was not at all a revolutionary, not an emotional orator, a flatterer of mankind, but a metaphysician, a moralist, and he was, to put it mildly, politically indifferent. But beyond this, he was also something surprising and gratifying, namely a very great writer, a *bel esprit*, a master of language, of the most encompassing possibilities for literary effects. He was a European prose writer of the type that has perhaps appeared among Germans two or three times before, and never among German philosophers. Yes, this was new, and the effect was great: on intellectual Europe that experienced the mode and "overcame" it, on Thomas Buddenbrook who died—and on me, who did not die, and for whom a supra-German intellectual experience became one of the sources of my "patriotism" that is in a literary sense so objectionable.

It was at the same time that my passion for the artistic work of Richard Wagner reached its height, or at least neared its height: I say "passion" because simpler words such as "love" and "enthusiasm" would not truly convey the idea. Often the years in which we are most capable of such devotion are also those of the greatest psychological sensitivity, which was, in my case, sharpened even more powerfully by a certain critical reading matter; and devotion together with understanding—precisely this is passion. The most intimately difficult and fruitful experience of my youth was learning that passion is *clairvoyant*—or it is not worthy of its name. Blind love, love that is only a panegyric, an apotheosis—is outright foolishness! I could never bring myself even to read a certain type of generally accepted Wagner literature. But the sharply critical reading matter I mentioned was from Friedrich Nietzsche's works, particularly so far as they are a critique of artistic genius, or what in Nietzsche says the same thing, *Wagner* criticism. For everywhere in those pages where he discusses the artist and artistic talent—and the subject is not treated gently—Nietzsche clearly had Wagner in mind, even if Wagner's name does not appear in the text: Nietzsche had completely experienced and studied the phenomenon of the "artist," if not of art itself—although this, too, could be argued—in Wagner, just as the much less worthy descendant passionately experienced the Wagnerian work of art, and in it almost art itself, through the medium of this criticism—and this in crucial years so that all my concepts of art and genius were forever determined by them, or, if not determined, at least colored and influenced—and indeed, in a way that was not at all sincerely trustful, but much too skeptically sly.

Understanding devotion, clairvoyant love—this is passion. I can assure the reader that the urgency of my passion for Wagner did not suffer in the least from being broken up into psychology and criticism—into a psychology and criticism that, as we know, match in refinement the elegance of their magical subject. On the contrary, only through this process did it receive its sharpest and most subtle spurs. Only in this way did it become real passion—with all the demands that real passion can place upon the elasticity of one's nerves. Wagner's art, no matter how poetic and how "German" it may seem, is in itself, of course, an extremely modern art that is not quite innocent: it is clever and deliberate, yearning and cunning; it can combine stupefying and intellectually stimulating techniques and qualities in a way that is in any case demanding on the listener. But involvement with it almost becomes a vice, it becomes *moral*, it becomes a reckless ethical dedication to what is harmful and consuming when it is not naively enthusiastic but fused with an analysis whose most malicious insights are finally a form of glorification and again only the expression of passion. As late as in *Ecce Homo*, there is a page on *Tristan*, and this would be proof enough that Nietzsche's relationship to Wagner, even into his paralysis, remained one of the strongest love.

The intellectual name for "love" is "*interest*," and he is no psychologist who does not know that interest is anything but a weak emotion—it is rather one that is, for example, much more intense than "admiration." It is the real writer's emotion, and not only does analysis not destroy it, but, in a very anti-Spinozan way, the emotion draws continual nourishment from the analysis. Thus it is not panegyric; it is criticism, and indeed, malicious, even hateful criticism, yes, even lampoon, provided it is ingenious and the product of passion—in which passionate interest finds satisfaction. Simple praise leaves interest with a flat taste; it finds nothing to learn from this praise. Yes, if interest itself should perhaps reach the point of productively celebrating the object, the personality, the problem for which it burns, the result is something strange that almost seeks its honor in being misunderstood, a product of insidious, slyly deceiving enthusiasm that may, at first glance, be confused with a pasquinade. I recently gave a little example of this when I contributed a historical writing, a sketch of the life of Frederick of Prussia, to the discussion of the war—a little work that was inspired, yes, provoked, by current events. At first, worried friends strongly advised me not to publish it—the war had not lasted long—not because of its "patriotism," which offended literature, but for diametrically opposite reasons.

I know very well where I am headed when I speak of these things. Nietzsche and Wagner—they are both great *critics of the German character*; Wagner in an indirect-artistic way, Nietzsche in a direct-literary one— whereby the artistic method, since it is modern, is not inferior in intellectual awareness and noninnocence to the literary one. As I have said, with the exception of Nietzsche, there has never been a school of Wagner criticism in Germany—for the "unliterary" nation is also the nonpsychological and antipsychological one. Baudelaire and Barrès have said better things about Wagner than can be found in any German Wagner biographies and apologies, and at this moment it is a Swede, W. Peterson-Berger, who, in his book, *Richard Wagner as a Cultural Phenomenon*, is giving us Germans a few hints about the best attitude with which to approach such a phenomenon that is in the most mon- strous sense interesting: namely, in a democratically upright attitude, that allows us to see anything of it at all. Here the Swede speaks of Wagner's nationalism, of his art as a nationally German one, and he notes that German folk music is the only element *not* included in his synthesis. To be sure, for purposes of characterization, Wagner could from time to time, as in *Die Meistersinger* and *Siegfried*, strike up the German folk tone, but this tone was neither the basis nor the starting point for his musical composition, never the origin from which it spontaneously gushed forth, as in Schumann, Schubert, and Brahms. Peterson-Berger pointed out that it is necessary to distinguish between folk art and national art; the first is directed inward, the second outward. Wagner's music was more national than folk, he said. It admittedly had many characteristics that *foreigners especially* would find German, but at the same time it had an unmistakably cosmopolitan cachet. Well, it is easy to hit the mark when one makes fine distinctions. Indeed, as an intellectual manifestation, Wagner is so powerfully

German that to me it has always seemed one absolutely had to passionately experience his work if one were to understand, or at least to divine, something of the deep magnificence and painful ambivalence of the German character. But *besides the fact* that this work is an explosive revelation of German character, it is also a theatrical presentation of it, indeed, a presentation whose intellectualism and billboardlike effectiveness reach the point where they become grotesque, *where they become parody*—a presentation that, to put it very crudely, is at moments not completely above suspicion of having connections with the tourist industry, and it seems to be made to bring a curious and awestruck *entente*-audience to exclaim: "*Ah, ça c'est bien allemand par exemple!*"

Thus no matter how powerful and true Wagner's German character may be, it is refracted and broken up in a modern way, decorative, analytical, and intellectual, and its power of fascination, its inborn ability for cosmopolitan, planetary effect, comes from this. His art is the most sensational self-portrait and self-criticism of the German character one can imagine. It is calculated to make the German character seem *interesting* even to an ignorant foreigner, and to be passionately occupied with this art is always at the same time to be passionately involved with this German character itself, which Wagner's art glorifies in a critical-decorative way. In itself alone, Wagner's art would be this portrait of the German character, but it becomes even more intensely so when it is actuated by a critique that, while it seems to be concerned with Wagner's art, is in truth concerned with the German character in general, even if not always quite as explicitly as in that magnificent analysis of the prelude to *Die Meistersinger* at the beginning of the eighth section of *Beyond Good and Evil*. In truth, if Nietzsche has rivals abroad as a Wagner critic, he has none, abroad or at home, who rivals him as a critic of the German character. He is by far the one who has said the most malicious and the best things about it, and the ingeniousness of the eloquence that grips him, that carries him when he begins to speak of German matters, of the problem of German character, is testimony to his fully passionate involvement with this subject. It is just as gross to speak of Nietzsche's hostility to Germany, which one does now and then in Germany—those abroad, thanks to their greater distance, see things more clearly—as it would be to call him an anti-Wagnerian. He loved France for artistic-formal reasons, although certainly not for political ones; but show me where he speaks of Germany with the same contempt that English utilitarianism and English lack of musical talent awakened in him! Truly, those political judges of morality cannot count on him; those who presume to chastise their people in a literary way, to censure them in the rattling terminology of Western democracy, but who never, never in their lives, could find a single word of understanding passion that would have sanctioned their right even to join in the conversation about German matters at all. What I wanted to say was: the young person, obliged by the times and by his own taste to make Wagner's art and Nietzsche's criticism the basis of his culture, to educate himself principally upon them, had, at the same time, to become aware of his own national sphere, of the German character as a completely remarkable European element that provokes passionate criticism; a type of psychologically oriented patriotism had to develop early in him, a patriotism that naturally had nothing to do with patriotic nationalism, but that nevertheless created a certain sensitivity in national self-consciousness, a certain impatience with *clumsy* insults resulting from ignorance; in about the same way, for example, as an art lover who has deeply experienced Wagner, but who has, for higher intellectual reasons, become an opponent of his art, nonetheless feels an impatience welling up within him when he hears the insults of backward Philistine ignorance. "Interest," to repeat in a reverse way, is the intellectual name of an emotion whose sentimental name is "love."

Schopenhauer, Nietzsche, and Wagner—a triple constellation of eternally united spirits. Until yesterday, until today, Germany, the world, stood under its sign—even if tomorrow no more. Their creative and ruling fates are deeply and inextricably linked. Nietzsche called Schopenhauer his "great teacher"; the world knows what a tremendous stroke of luck it was for Wagner to experience Schopenhauer; the friendship of Tribschen may have died—but it is as immortal as the tragedy that followed and that was never at any time a separation, but rather an intellectual-historical redefinition and re-emphasis of this "friendship of stars." The three are one. The reverent disciple, for whom their powerful lives became culture, would wish that he could speak of all three at once, so difficult it seems to him to separate the debt he owes to each one. If I have Schopenhauer's morality—a popular word for the same thing is "pessimism"—as my basic psychological mood, that mood of "cross, death and grave" that appeared as early as in my first efforts, then this "ethical atmosphere," to speak with Nietzsche, is also to be found in Wagner. His gigantic work stands completely within this atmosphere, and I could just as well cite his influence. If, however, this same basic mood made me into a psychologist of *decadence*, then it was Nietzsche to whom I looked as a master, for from the start he was not so much for me the prophet of some kind of vague "superman," as he was for most people when he was in fashion, as rather the incomparably greatest and most experienced psychologist of decadence.

Seldom, I think, has Wagner's influence been as strong and decisive upon one who is not a musician—and definitely not a dramatist—as I must admit it has been on me. Not as a musician, not as a dramatist, nor as a "musical dramatist," did Wagner influence me, but as an artist in general, as the modern artist par excellence, as Nietzsche's criticism had taught me to see him, and in particular as the great musical-epic prose writer and symbolist that he is. What I know of economy of means, of effect in general—in contrast to sensationalism, that "effect without cause"—of the epic spirit, of beginning and end, of style as a mysterious adjustment of the personal to the objective, of the creation of symbols, of the organic compactness of the single, vital unity of the total work—what I know of all this and have attempted to practice and to develop within my limits, I owe to my dedication to this art. Even today, when unexpectedly my ear hears a suggestive phrase, some solitary chord from Wagner's musical universe, I am startled with joy. But for the youth who found no place at home and who lived in a sort of voluntary exile in foreign circumstances he did not like, this world of art was literally the homeland of his soul. A sightseeing drive with a concert on the Pincio—and midst the internationally elegant crowd that was banally enjoying itself stood the wretched, half-neglected youth at the foot of the podium, under a deep blue sky that never ceased to irritate him, under palm trees that he despised, taking in, weak-kneed with enthusiasm, the romantic messages of the prelude to *Lohengrin.* Did he recall such moments twenty years later when war broke out between the spirit of the *Lohengrin* prelude and international elegance? Are such memories perhaps implicated in his impulsive-unliterary position on this war? A Wagner demonstration on the Piazza Colonna! Maestro Vessella, then director of the municipal orchestra (with kettledrums: when kettledrums were brought to the Piazza it meant that the city orchestra, and not the stupid military band, would play, and that Wagner would be on the program)—Vessella, then, the herald of German music in Rome, is playing the death lament for Siegfried. Everyone knows there will be an uproar. The place is packed; all the balconies are filled. One listens until the piece ends. Then everywhere a contest between ostentatious applause and nationalistic protest begins. Some scream, *"Bis!"* and clap their hands. Some cry, *"Basta!"* and boo.

It looks as if the opposition will win the day, but Vessella "*bisses*." This time there is a relentless demonstration while the piece is being played. From time to time, boos and calls for native music drown out the *piano* passages, while during the *forte*, enthusiastic cries of approval gain the upper hand. But I will never forget how under *evvivas* and *abbassos* the *Nothung* motif appeared for the second time; how it developed its powerful rhythms above the struggle of opinions in the street, and how, at its climax, at that penetrating, shattering dissonance before the double C-major chords, shouts of triumph broke out that irresistibly enveloped the shaken opposition, forced its retreat, and for a long time reduced it to confused silence. The twenty-year-old foreigner—foreign here like this music, *with* this music—stood wedged in among the crowd on the pavement. He did not scream with them, for there was a lump in his throat. His eyes kept watch on the podium, which furious *Italianissimi* wanted to storm, and which the musicians defended with their instruments—his face, which was turned upward, smiled with the sensation of its paleness, and his heart pounded with fierce pride, with youthfully morbid emotion. Pride in what? Love of what? Only of a controversial artistic taste? It is quite possible that twenty years later, in August 1914, he recalled the Piazza Colonna and the nervous tears that once, during the triumph of the *Nothung* motif, suddenly filled his eyes and ran down his cold face, tears that he could not dry because a foreign crowd kept him from raising his arms. Nevertheless, I will not deceive myself. Even if the intense experience of this art became a source of patriotic feelings for the youth—it was a supra-German intellectual experience, it was an experience I shared with intellectual Europe, just as Thomas Buddenbrook shared his. Of course, this German musician was no longer a "German musician" in the old, intimate, and genuine sense. I dare say he was, indeed, very German. (Can one be a musician without being German?) But it was not the German-national, German-poetic, German-romantic element in Wagner's art that enchanted me—or at least only insofar as all of this appeared intellectualized and in decorative self-display in it—it was much more those all-powerful European charms that emanate from it, and that are proof of Wagner's modern, almost extra-German position. No, I was not German enough to overlook the deep, psychological-artistic relationship between Wagner's methods and those of Zola and Ibsen, both of whom, like Wagner, were, above all, lords and masters of the symbol, of the tyrannical formula, and of whom particularly the Western novelist, naturalist, and romanticist seemed to be like him, to be Wagner's genuine brother in the desire and ability to overpower and mesmerize the masses. *Les Rougon-Macquart* and *Der Ring des Nibelungen*—the "Wagnerian" does not associate them. Nevertheless, they *belong* together, in one's intuition, if not also in one's love. For, to be sure, there are cases where one's intellect forces comparisons that one's emotion ever seeks to avoid. *Les Rougon-Macquart* and *Der Ring des Nibelungen*! I hope I will not have to choose. I am afraid I would decide "patriotically."

Schopenhauer and Wagner. Shall I also make a confession about the third "most sublime star"? How well I recall the smile, even the laughter, I had to suppress when one day some Parisian literati, whom I was sounding out about Nietzsche, claimed that he had been nothing else than a careful reader of the French moralists and aphorists. They might at least have mentioned Pascal. But they got no farther than Chamfort. This was some years before the war, and the war was not necessary to teach me about Nietzsche's Germanness. In any event, it is hardly this that must be insisted upon today. The colossal manliness of his soul, his antifeminism, his opposition to democracy—what could be more German? What could be more German than his contempt for "modern ideas," for "eighteenth-century ideas," for "French ideas," which, he insisted, had English origins? The French, he said, had merely been their apers, actors, soldiers—and their victims; "for the *âme française* had finally become so thin, so wasted away by the damnable Anglomania of 'modern ideas,' that one recalls today almost with disbelief its sixteenth and seventeenth centuries, its profound, passionate power, its creative nobility" (*Beyond Good and Evil*). One paragraph later he speaks of the "raving stupidity and noisy yapping of the democratic bourgeois"—not without that "deep disgust" with which the German spirit itself had risen up against the Anglo-French world of ideas. "With deep disgust." One sees how well Nietzsche, along with Dostoyevsky, understood the *refractory* role of the German character in European intellectual history. In other things, too, of course, Nietzsche also agreed with Dostoyevsky in the best possible way. "With deep disgust." There it is, the origin of this war, of the German war against Western "civilization"! Above all, however: if Nietzsche's "great teacher," Schopenhauer, was only an antirevolutionary—because of his pessimistic ethic, because of his hatred of the dishonest optimism of modern times and of the demagogues of progress—Nietzsche was himself *antiradical* in a sense and to a degree that was up to then unheard of, in a truly *radical* sense and degree, and in this quality and will, his German character came to an unparalleled primeval eruption. For antiradicalism—stated without praise or blame—is the specific, distinguishing, and decisive quality or peculiarity of the German spirit: this nation is unliterary simply because it is antiradical, or, to put it in a way that turns the purely negative thought, but again without praise or blame, into a positive one, positive in the *highest* degree—it is the nation of life. The *life concept*, this most German, most Goethean, and, in the highest, religious sense, conservative concept, is the one that Nietzsche imbued with new feeling, reinvested with new beauty, strength, and holy innocence, elevated to the highest rank, to intellectual dominance. Is not Georg Simmel correct when he claims that after Nietzsche, "life" became the key concept of all modern world views? In any case, Nietzsche's entire moral criticism stands under the sign of this idea, and if until then the boldness to free oneself from moral constraints had only had an esthetic dimension, if it had been completely encompassed in Platen's verse: "Let goodness itself bow before the high altar of beauty," it was Nietzsche, who with incomparably deeper and more passionate cynicism, first questioned the highest moral ideals, even truth itself, in their usefulness to life, as he placed the most radical psychology in the service of an antiradical and antinihilistic will. He did not bring goodness before the tribunal of beauty—he brought it before that of life itself. Or would that be one and the same? Had he perhaps only given beauty a new, divinely intoxicating name—the name of life? And also, was his rebellion against morality therefore more the rebellion of an artist and lover than that of a truly philosophical nature? I have often felt that Nietzsche's philosophy could have become a stroke of luck and a happy discovery for a great poet, as Schopenhauer's had become for the creator of *Tristan*; the source, that is, of a most highly erotic-crafty *irony* that moves playfully between life and intellect. Nietzsche has not found, or not yet found, his artist, as Schopenhauer has. But if I were to reduce what I owe him spiritually to a formula, to a key word—I would find no other than precisely this: the idea of life—which one may, as I have said, receive from Goethe, if one does not receive it from Nietzsche, in whom it appears, to be sure, in a new, more modern, more colorful light—an antiradical, antinihilistic, antiliterary, most highly conservative German idea, with which one is, indeed, for all the Frenchifying prose, for all the Polish noble blood, for all the superficial, philosopher's hatred of the "*Reich*" and its founder's landed-gentry, student-corps spirit—still hopelessly a German.

And still—the more quietly certain the speaker is of "the one side," of the matter, the more enthusiastically he may fence for "the other side"—still, the Nietzschean education does not provide an essentially and unobjectionally German education any more than does one from Schopenhauer or Wagner. Allow me to connect this to a word, a verse, from Stefan George, the lament with which he concludes the magnificent Nietzsche poem in *The Seventh Ring*. "It should have *sung*, not spoken, this new soul!" he cries out—*citing*, as one may or may not know, a sentence from his hero himself, from the late prologue to *The Birth of Tragedy*, where the cry is followed by the comment: "What a shame I did not dare to say as a poet what I had to say then: perhaps I might have been able to do it. . . ." Perhaps. It sounds almost coquettishly mysterious. His very Hölderlin-like sketch for an Empedocles drama was never developed. It comes from the years 1870–71, the time of the Dionysian work. But may one now say that the beautiful lament in George's mouth expresses more of George than of the one it was intended for? That the poet who began as a Parnassian and whose art and personality are today a completely German affair—that George, by generalizing a moment of regret inspired by an undertaking that was mistaken-inappropriate and that therefore failed and never materialized, relates and applies this undertaking to the total image of Nietzsche, and thus to a certain extent misunderstands and detracts from Nietzsche *as* a total image? For without doubt it signifies a misunderstanding and belittling of Nietzsche's cultural mission, it signifies a refusal to look at his final, involuntary, purely fateful impact, even to wish that the "stern and tortured voice"—it cannot be said more beautifully—that this voice might have sung instead of "simply" speaking, that Nietzsche should have fulfilled himself as a new Hölderlin and German poet instead of being what he was: a writer, that is, of the highest world class, a prose writer of still much greater worldly potentiality than Schopenhauer, his great teacher; a man of letters and essayist of the highest order; something very *entente*-like—let us be tasteless but descriptive!—in a word, a European intellectual whose influence upon the development, upon the "*progress*," yes, even the *political progress* of Germany, cannot be characterized by any Empedocles fragment or by any songs of Prince Vogelfrei, or even by Dionysian dithyrambs, but rather by works that in their attitude and taste, in their facility and maliciousness, their subtlety and radicalism, are as un-German and anti-German as the eternally admirable essay, "What is the Meaning of Ascetic Ideals?"

There can be no doubt. Without detriment to the deep Germanness of his spirit, Nietzsche, with his Europeanism, has contributed more than anyone else to Germany's education in criticism, to her intellectualization, psychologization, literarization, radicalization, or, not to shun the political word, to her democratization. I say that all of our civilization writers have learned how to write from him—and herein lies a contradiction that in the end is not one at all. Nietzsche, my dear voluntarists, is the most striking example of the fact that, as far as development, inevitable "progress," is concerned, the crucial question is what one is (or what one becomes and makes of oneself), not the question of one's volition and opinions. As a man of German destiny, he was the good brother of his great counterpart, Bismarck, whose final, involuntary, real impact also took this democratic direction. We shall return to this point later. For the moment, let us be content to maintain that volition, opinion, and tendency signify and decide very little for the effect and influence of precisely the greatest, the really fateful human beings, on developments on a grand scale. And if this is true with the powerful ones—how much more so it is with us little people! I could provide some pretty examples of the conflict between will and result, tendency and nature—a conflict that became acute in the crisis of these times, in clearly hard, inner struggles that became subjective and conscious so that overnight, as it were, an antidemocratic-conservative-militaristic Saul turned into an *entente*-Christian Paul who tore the thorn from his flesh that had been goading him for twenty months, and finally found himself. "Conversion"—is only another word for self-discovery.

Nietzsche's *teachings*, then, were less new and revolutionary for Germany, less important for German development—"important" in the good or bad sense, as one will—than *the way he taught*. His impact on the German way of thinking was at least, at the very least, as strong through his extremely Western method, his Europeanizing prose, as through his "militarism" and power philosophy; and his "progressive," civilizing impact consists in a colossal strengthening, encouraging and sharpening of the writing profession, of literary criticism and of radicalism in Germany. In his school, one became accustomed to allow the artist's concept to merge with the critic's, so that the distinction between art and criticism became blurred. He reminded people that the bow, as well as the lyre, was an Apollonian tool. He taught how to hit the mark, indeed, to strike fatally. He lent German prose a sensitivity, an artistic ease, beauty, sharpness, melodiousness, accentuation, and passion—

completely unheard of up to then, and of inescapable influence upon everyone who, after him, has dared to write German. Not his personality, oh no! but his impact, extraordinarily resembles that of Heinrich Heine, the Jew who adapted himself to Paris, whom Nietzsche praised and beside whom he placed himself as a writer—resembles it just as strongly in its bad as in its good aspects. It cannot be my task to analyze this here. It is a matter of judgment that one may quietly test. But I hope I have made clear what I mean when I say that the powerful strengthening of the literary-critical element in Germany that Nietzsche brought about signifies *progress* in the most dubious, most political sense, in the sense of "humanization,"—progress toward Western democracy, and that to be educated by him is not exactly what one could call an education in the spirit of preserving German tradition.

My own literary attitude corresponded only too closely to such influences, needs, and susceptibilities: so much so that people who were at their wits' end, like Adolf Bartels, wanted to make a Jew of me—against which, for the sake of truth, I thought I had to protest. If I, in my limited way, have contributed to the Europeanization of the German prose story, if I have been able to be helpful in raising the genre of the novel in Germany in rank and respectability, this was a consequence of my blood, not of my rank: for rank today is scarcely anything individual. It is a question of the national standard. It hardly justifies an aristocratic self-assurance, only a democratic one—"I am part of the German standard," the individual may say, "that is my rank"—a self-assurance, as one sees, that runs the great risk in times of national isolation and peril of degenerating into offensive patriotism.

Buddenbrooks, the story with which I, after a few light, psychological preludes, won the attention of a broader public, is certainly a very German book. It is German not only because of its milieu, my Hanseatic homeland, which is of the oldest German colonial soil, and not only in a cultural-historical sense, either, insofar as it reflects the spiritual development and differentiation, the—well, yes, the "humanization" of the German burgher class from my great-grandfather's generation to mine. Above all, the novel is German in the formal sense—by formal I mean something other than the purely literary influences and sources. I recall a review of the book from around 1908, in the *Mercure de France*, that said in a friendly appraisal that it was untranslatable because of its *structure*. Romain Rolland, as I know him, would perhaps think differently; but one can certainly imagine that in French this work would be monstrous and absurd. It became, it was not made; it grew, it was not formed, and precisely for this reason it is untranslatably German. Precisely this lends it an organic fullness that the typical French book does not have. It is not a well-proportioned work of art, but life. It is, to use the admittedly pretentious formula from art and cultural history, *Gothic*, not Renaissance. All of which, however, certainly does not prevent a completely European-literary air from circulating within it— it is perhaps Germany's first and only naturalistic novel, and also as such, certainly as such, it is of artistically international composition, of European attitude, despite the German character of its humanity. It has nothing of Raabe or Jean Paul; it has nothing at all to do with Spielhagen and other German novelists. The German influence is of a strange composition: of the humorous-low-German and the epic-musical element—it came from Fritz Reuter and Richard Wagner. The other influences came from everywhere—from Russia, England, France— the *entente* countries, as one sees, the countries of the psychological novel—from the Denmark of Bang and Jacobsen, the Norway of Kielland and Lie.

To cite, for their beauty, words from *Poetry and Truth*, I had "written down in the rich times of youth the events of the immediate past, and, boldly enough, at the opportune time, displayed them publicly." At the same time, I had created for myself in the extensive work a human-artistic foundation upon which I could base further works—I had built myself a violin, as it were, upon which I could now freely perform, one whose fine wood would always vibrate pleasantly with the notes, whose acoustical cavity would lend full resonance to my playing. There are people who claim that this playing has not been as good as the violin has deserved, that I could have spared myself the concert, that it will soon be forgotten, and that the well-built violin will be the only thing of value to remain. Well, at least once, at any rate, youth, the intellectual youth of Germany, born around 1880, decided differently: this was in the case of *Tonio Kröger*, the prose ballad that admittedly would scarcely have come into being without *Buddenbrooks*, and that was so much a song played on the instrument I had built for the large novel.

"Lively, intellectually unencumbered clarity of form," a later work of somewhat parodistic master-style says, "will delight the burgherly masses, but only what is problematical can capture passionately uncompromising youth." Here I was thinking of *Buddenbrooks* and *Tonio Kröger*. The former, completely plastic, art—and scarcely also intellect, continually occupied the educated middle class; but intellectual and radical youth, who were to be sure not yet politically radical, took to *Tonio*

Kröger as their own—the playing was more important to them than the violin. Where is he now, the Göttinger student of that time, with the thin-nervous face, who said to me with his bright, excited voice, while we were all drinking in Mütze's tavern after the lecture, "I hope you know, don't you—that your true work is not *Buddenbrooks*, your true work is *Tonio Kröger*!?" I said I knew it.

The point was that while in *Buddenbrooks* only the influence of Schopenhauer and Wagner, the ethical-pessimistic and the epic-musical elements, were dominant, in *Tonio Kröger*, Nietzsche's cultural principle broke through, the principle that would continue to be dominant in the future. The lyrical philosopher's dithyrambic-conservative concept of life, and his defense against the moralistic-nihilistic spirit, against "literature," had, in the experience and emotion that the story formed, become *erotic irony*, an enraptured affirmation of all that was not intellect and art, that was innocent, healthy, decent-unproblematic, and pure of spirit. And the name of life, yes, of beauty, was found here, sentimentally enough, transferred to the world of the *burgher*, to the world where the ordinary, the opposite of intellect and art, was perceived as blessed. No wonder this pleased youth. For if "life" came off well in the process, "intellect" came off even better, for it was the lover, and "the god" is in the lover, not in the beloved, something that "intellect" in this case knew very well. What it did not know yet, or put aside for the time being, was that not only does intellect demand life, but also that life demands intellect, and that life's need for salvation, its longing, its feeling of beauty—for beauty is nothing but longing—is perhaps more serious, perhaps more "divine," perhaps less proud and high-spirited than is "intellect's." But irony is always irony toward both sides, something of a mediator, a neither-nor and a this-as-well-as-that—just as Tonio Kröger, of course, also perceived himself to be somewhat of an ironic mediator between burgherly nature and genius, just as his name had to be symbolic of all kinds of hybrid ambiguity, not only of the Latin-German blood mixture, but also of the central position between health and decadence, decency and adventurousness, heart and artistry; a situational emotional appeal that again was clearly influenced by that of Nietzsche who derived the cognitive value of his philosophy precisely from the fact that he was at home in *both* worlds, in decadence and in health—he stood, he said, between decline and ascent. The entire product was a mixture of seemingly heterogeneous elements: of melancholy and criticism, ardor and skepticism, *Storm and Nietzsche*, mood and intellectualism. No wonder, as I said, youth was fascinated, that it preferred these ninety pages to the two thick volumes of *Buddenbrooks*! Youth aspires much more to intellect than to plastic form, and beyond doubt, what was exciting for it here was the way the concept of "intellect" was handled in the little story, how, under the name of "literature," intellect *together* with the concept of "art" was contrasted with unconscious and silent life. What captured them, without doubt, was the radical-literary, the intellectual-undermining element in the little work—and if the other element, the German, temperamental-conservative one, did not impair the pleasure, but even increased it, it was because it appeared as irony, and because irony itself is intellectualism to the highest degree. More than this, however, irony is an accessory of romanticism, and is thus in its proper place. For did one not see that Tonio Kröger was a latecomer of romanticism, and indeed, of a very German romanticism—that he was the good brother of Schlemiel, Undine, and Heiling, the Dutchman? No, and I myself did not see it at the time. Today I see it well, and when I am asked to what extent I am German, the story is my answer.

The problem appeared in a different form in *Fiorenza*. For while *Tonio Kröger* cultivated the antithesis of life and "art," in which "art" was understood in a very literary way, and thought of as united with "intellect," the dramatic story completely tore apart this hypothetical unity—and this was "progress"! The antithesis was now "intellect versus art," or also "intellect versus life," for here art was conceived of completely as life; life and art were fused into one idea, just as art and intellect had been before. Intellect, pure intellect, appeared separated as literature, as criticism, as "holiness and knowledge," and the hero of these discourses was the completely intellectual and religious man, the critic, the literary man, or, in his language, the prophet: for when he defines the prophet as the artist who is at the same time a saint, he also defines the literary man in the process. He, then, Brother Girolamo, was the hero of these scenes; and although dialectical justice gave him the artistically powerful Medici as a worthy opponent, still the secret intellectual sympathy of the Isar-Florentine author was nevertheless quite definitely on the side of the critical intellectual—somewhat as was Pico della Mirandola when he replied with his most supercilious smile to Polizian's remark that it was truly better just to make a chair, any kind of beautiful thing, than only to be born to judge things, "Well, I don't know! As a collector and fancier, I value things according to their rarity. In Florence there is a legion of worthy people who can make beautiful chairs; but there is only one Brother Girolamo." Pico is in error. The value of rarity is not found in intellect. There is much more intellect than art. But that secret sympathy and partisanship betrayed itself at least in the thickly served-up irony with which the praiseworthy tribe of artists was described, this cheerful group of parasites, rowdies, braggarts, and buffoons, talented, sensual and dumb as they could be, who stumbled so happily and morally irresponsibly through Careggi's house and garden. It would have been fair to contrast this group with something of corresponding human insignificance on the side of "literature": then it would have been clear that not second-rate artistic talent, but rather second-rate "intellectuality" is the shabbiest and most contemptible thing on earth.

At any rate, it is not these harmless creators who in any way came into consideration in the play as candidates for the control, the favor and love of "Fiorenza." The title was not less symbolic than that of the story about the writer; and it signifies what is personal and original in this attempt at a song in a higher tone: youthful lyrics about fame whirl around in it, the desire for and fear of fame in one who has been ensnared at a tender age by success, embraced by the world. "Oh world! Oh deepest desire! Oh amorous dream of power, sweet, devouring! One should not possess. Longing is gigantic power; but possession emasculates!" The rest is Nietzsche. For those two Caesars and "hostile brothers" who compete with each other for the erotic possession of the symbolic city, Lorenzo and the prior—they are only much too much the dithyrambist and the ascetic priest as both appear in the book: so much so that all attempts to present anything further, more individual, less theoretical, to bring their psychological types into connection with more intimate, more pressing problems, was understandably over-looked. The problem of *literary intellect* has occupied me my life long, and it occupied me above all here: this problem, which I have not liked even though I have borne it within me as a half-Westerner, but which intellectual duty nevertheless has continually forced upon me because I saw that it, although originally as un-German as possible, was, thanks to the efforts of civilization's literary man, daily coming nearer and growing to greater importance and timeliness for Germany. Nietzsche's ascetic priest, the one who would rather desire *nothingness* than *not* desire, this nihilistic Caesar, became for me—not at all unexpectedly—the radical literary man of the most modern type, and I did not spare the allusions to make it clear that he had become this for me. I made him into the representative of the *sacrae litterae*, into one who "conquered the city *with words*," who cursed "Florence," and whom this lustful

"Florence" loved for his having done so. "What do you call evil?" his dying lifelong friend asks him. He answers: "Everything that is opposed to intellect—inside us and outside of us." And the more penetrating question of the other, who does not consider himself to be without intellect, "Would you please tell me what you call intellect?" finds him prepared: "The power, Lorenzo Magnifico, that desires purity and peace." "Purity and peace!" Is this not, in the flat language of "civilization," "human freedom and peace?" In all seriousness: one must be allowed to translate the moral-philosophical formula into political language, for if "not to desire" is only philosophy, then "to desire nothingness" is politics, and the radical literary man is a politician: he has said so himself for years—loudly enough! proudly enough!—a politician and a voluntarist to the extent that he wants to help intellect to *power* and that he works "resolutely" for human progress toward purity and peace—toward human freedom and peace. Resolutely. Truly, it seems as if this motif, too, the motif of political literary-resolution, which is so tirelessly varied today by the writers of civilization, was not foreign to me at that time, not foreign to my intellect at least! For when my politicized monk broke out with the words: "I hate this vile justice, this lewd understanding, this vicious tolerance of the opposite! It will not touch me! Let it be silent!"—when he added that he was chosen, that he could know and still desire, that he had to be strong, and that there, as he stood, he embodied the "miracle of reborn impartiality";—when long before, at the very beginning of the play, His Excellency, Cardinal Giovanni, whispered the spicy novelty into the ear of his personal humanist *that morality was again possible*—then all this was to the greatest extent neopolitical and in the spirit of civilization's literary man, and I knew it well. I knew well that the Christian politician, Girolamo, represented the new, the latest word, against the esthete, Lorenzo, who was sinfully headed for his death—things that ten years later in Germany would be in such great intellectual fashion that youthfully brittle voices would make such a clamor that our ears would ring. And even if I had the perishing esthete cry to the political victor of the moment: "It is death that you are heralding as intellect, and art is the life of all life!"—yes, even if I share this opinion—my real interest, and I want to say this again, my secret intellectual partisanship and curiosity, was still for the representative of literary intellect and his trick of qualifying himself, by means of "reborn impartiality," as a theocratic demagogue.

May I be allowed, in this connection, to speak also of that attempt at a comedy in novel form that is called *Royal Highness*—and that, in spite of its highly individualistic title, represents at the same time an attempt at a reconciliation—even if not exactly without reservation—of "happiness" with "humanity"? Of my second novel, which was, from an artistic point of view, so strikingly different from its predecessor—and not at all advantageously so from a German way of thinking—that one would scarcely suspect the identity of the author with that of *Buddenbrooks*? Suddenly here is a book—not at all the result of "becoming" and "growth," far removed from all luxuriance and exuberance, a thoroughly formed book, attuned to measure and proportion, rational, lucid, dominated by an idea, an intellectual formula that is reflected everywhere, repeatedly called to mind, made as alive as possible, that seeks by a hundred details to create the illusion of life and that still never reaches life's original, warm fullness. It is sleight of hand, not life. Taken formally, it is Renaissance, not Gothic. French, not German. But to be sure very German internally, in its type (even if not in its form) of intellectuality and ethics, its perception of loneliness and duty. At any rate, it did not surprise me that French critics, so far as they are curious about things German, had much more liking for *Royal Highness*, for the purposes, for the prose of the novel than did the German ones—who found it absolutely and relatively too facile: too facile for the demands that one places in Germany on the seriousness and the emphasis of a book, too facile even for the author. Without considering the new element that was heralded in the tendency, they found the pact with "human happiness" that was concluded here, even if somewhat loosely, to be without character, and they examined the "plot" with a scrutiny that was too serious and objective for them not to find it like a story in a family newspaper. Now I am far from taking up arms in defense of the poetic value of the story about the little prince, who, in the most dignified newspaper style, is made into a husband and the bringer of happiness to his people—although I could still imagine today that old Anatole France would read this "family newspaper novel" not completely without pleasure. Although one did not consider its artistic value from a German point of view—one certainly did not underestimate its poetic value in the German sense, even if one did not exactly evaluate it very highly. But its *intellectual* value, if it has one, rests completely on its quality as a symptom of the times, as a sign of German development— and clever people, who found it worth their effort to apply their

cleverness to such a quaint phenomenon, saw this quite clearly. "Will,"
so runs the critical essay of an Austrian (it was Hermann Bahr himself),
"Will the Germans of our times realize that this novel is a sign?" And
he ends by calling my novel something like a beacon light of the new
democracy. Unjustly so? Was not in *Royal Highness* a small, lonely esthete
educated to be a political economist and an "active humanitarian," as
one would say today? And by what means? By love! But this is to the
highest degree in the spirit of civilization's literary man. And I would
be even more proud of such a high degree of progressiveness than I
seriously am, if, in the meantime, "love" had not become an intellectual
fashion, a literary-political program of opposition—and if I did not
find this to be quite shameless. Neither can it be denied that the book,
in spite of its democratic didacticism, presents a true orgy of individualism whose noblesse is tirelessly modified in a great variety of manifestations; that for all the book's advancement, it does not lack "conservative opposition"; that a deep hesitation accompanies that turn to
democracy, to community, and to humanity, yes, that this turn is actually
completed only humorously, only *ironice*, and that the heartfelt seriousness of the novelist—*and* of the reader: that is the result—never
ceases to belong to the aristocratic monsters, the impossible Collie dog
and the no less impossible Dr. Überbein. To be sure, Klaus Heinrich
becomes "happy," and Raoul Überbein, the romantic individualist, is
destroyed miserably in the most tendentious way. But one cannot think
that I am so common, so *political*, that I see an argument in "happiness"
and a refutation in destruction. This would be something different
from moral—it would be virtuous—and I have yet to say in these pages
what I think of virtuousness. On the contrary, those who make up
stories enjoy expressing their personal sympathy for certain figures and
their cheerful disregard for others by allowing the former to be
destroyed and the latter to become happy. However this may be, the
political-anti-individualistic tendency—a very un-German tendency, or
at least a tendency that is just now beginning to become German—was
present; even if it manifested itself in such a two-faced and nonbinding
manner that civilization's literary man became somewhat suspicious of
its final seriousness—the tendency was, to repeat, present. It was
included, it was not ignored, even if it was difficult to grasp, even if it
was strongly sicklied o'er with the pale cast of irony. There is a way of
writing, there is a *Western* attitude of intellect and style, that speaks
more clearly than all the didacticism of a fable; irony and *esprit*, they
themselves are radical literary powers; even Europe's wisest old man,

Anatole France in Paris, likes now and then to treat civilization with irony, and he is still the idol and grand monarch of all the civilization writers. In short, civilization's literary man had a right—whether he made use of this right or not—to *hope* for me and my modest abilities; and times came when nothing would have hindered him any longer from unreservedly *counting* on me.

In a magazine (it was *März*—a name full of the premonitions of political spring) an article appeared, a study dedicated to the "literary man," an explanation for Germans of the character and origin of this intellectual type that is to the highest degree *current*—and nothing more flattering has ever been said of him all the days of his life than what was said in this *März* article. I began by calling him a "brahmin," and I assured him loosely in the manner of the *Veda* that he had been born with more good sense and with a greater love of virtue than all the rest of the world. His good sense, I explained, was his knowledge of everything human, combined with high lust for adventure and a mastery in the field of words. His love of virtue was, however, the purity of the observer, the will to the absolute, disgust for concession and corruption, a scornful or ceremoniously accusing and judging insistence upon the ideal, upon freedom, justice, reason, goodness and human dignity. Nothing, I said, was more indicative of the literary disposition than the twofold and basically only uniform activity of those humanitarian journalists of the time of the Enlightenment, who, in criminological-political writings, summoned society to the forum of humanity, who educated their contemporaries to despise the barbarisms in the administration of justice, to be against torture and capital punishment, and who paved the way for milder laws—and who characteristically made names for themselves at the same time by pedagogical writings on language and style and by treatises on the art of writing. Love of mankind and the art of writing as the dominant passions of *one* soul: this meant something; not by chance were these two passions found together. To write beautifully meant almost to think beautifully, and from there it was not far to beautiful deeds. All the moral improvement of the human race—this could be demonstrated—came from the spirit of literature, and even the popular teachers of antiquity considered the beautiful word to be the father of good deeds. What a sermon! One believes one is listening to Woodrow Wilson, this highly placed patron of the human race, who, according to reliable sources, is said to be not a little proud of the style of his diplomatic notes. Was all of this only psychology, or was it sympathy, solidarity? I went on. I separated the literary man from art in a naive and candid sense, separated him from it in the name of intellect, of morality and of criticism. His drives for knowledge and judgment, I said, alienated him from the typical artist— from this cheerful and harmless creature who faced his severe brother with a mixture of antipathy and pious awe, or who would much prefer not to face him just yet. I described "the artist" faithfully according to the image of my Aldobrandino in *Fiorenza*: I portrayed him as the *maître des plaisirs* at the courts of the great, as the untroubled dinner companion at the table of the rich rascal, and I surmised that if any praiseworthy character trait were lacking in this worthy fellow, it might possibly be *decency*, which was positively not a matter of nature and "temperament," but rather of knowledge and criticism. The literary man, for his part, was the essentially decent person; he was decent to the point of saintliness, decent to the point of absurdity—for the absurd was what was intellectually honorable. And so it continued. To be sure, my papers teach me that I could, at the same time, think in exactly the opposite way. "The error of the literary man," I read from such a paper, "is his belief that only intellect makes one decent. But the truth is more the reverse: only where there is *no* intellect is there decency." Just the same, what I published is what counts. And it is certain, to speak in a Hamlet-like way, that it sat smiling to the heart of civilization's literary man. To be sure, I had remained in the intellectual-moral sphere, had not progressed to politics. But the political consequences of what I turned out there were quite clear: the political consequence of "love of mankind and the art of writing" is the radical republic, the republic of lawyers and literary men, as civilization's literary man cherishes them in his mind and in his heart. I repeat, I had hit the mark. Activists and men of "purpose" expressed their appreciation to me. In their way, not less advanced thinkers included the ideas of my article on the literary man with those things that "the new spirit of a most recent literature had to say to the spirit of the older one, one that had been modern since about Hebbel's time." There was no doubt, I found myself in the right boat; Lord knows I had made the connection! From *Buddenbrooks* on, the progress had been clear, the progress in a progressive direction. Finally, what could be more "intellectual" than *parody*? One has a part in the intellectual disintegration of the German character if, before the war, one was at the point of parodying the German educational and developmental novel, the great German autobiography, as the memoirs of a confidence man.

CHAPTER 5

Burgherly Nature

When the whole world was hostile,
Everyone found refuge within the walls:
The knight ducked inside,
The farmer in trouble found it quite nice.
Whence came the finest culture,
If not from the burgher?*

Goethe

Meistersinger: Opposite of civilization,
German tradition against the French

Nietzsche

And still, when the war started, did I have to betray literature? Did I have to disappoint civilization's literary man so bitterly with public expressions of nationalism and patriotism that were sometimes ironically sneaky, but also sometimes tastelessly excessive? Did I have to compromise my literary career more disastrously than I could have done with the worst possible story? How did this happen? The previous pages would have made it very difficult for me to answer this question if I had not almost answered it in them. For as I tried to say to what extent I was a European and a Western literary man, I always said, if I am not mistaken, at the same time something about the origin of my "patriotism." But to do a little more to complete the answer to that question of conscience of how this happened, I now intend to talk about the *nature of the burgher*, about burgherly nature and art, about burgherly

* Wie alles war in der Welt entzweit
  Fand jeder in Mauern gute Zeit:
  Der Ritter duckte sich hinein,
  Bauer in Not fand's auch gar fein.
  Wo kam die schönste Bildung her,
  Und wenn sie nicht vom Bürger wär'?

artistic nature—with the vague feeling that my objectionable attitude in this war may, in some way, have to do with it, and almost with the certainty that such an investigation will provide as a by-product some stimulation of an objective general interest in the subject.

There is a beautiful, profound book by the young Hungarian essayist, Georg von Lukács, entitled *The Soul and the Forms*. In it there is a study on Theodor Storm that is, at the same time, an investigation of the relationship of "burgherly nature and *l'art pour l'art*"—an investigation that to me, when I read it years ago, immediately seemed to be the best that had ever been said on this paradoxical subject, and that I feel I have a special right to cite, since the author was perhaps thinking of me—and at one place expressly mentioned me. Doubtless we have special claim to the knowledge to which we ourselves have contributed by our existence, and when we accept it as our own, we are somewhat in the position of a father who smilingly lets himself be taught by his learned son. Lukács, then, distinguishes above all between the foreign, violent and dissimulating, ascetic-orgiastic bourgeois spirit, whose most famous example is Flaubert, and whose essence is the mortifying denial of life in favor of the work—and the genuine, burgherly, artistic genius of a Storm, Keller, Mörike, which actually only realizes the paradox of its adjective by connecting a burgherly conduct of life, based on a burgherly profession, with the hard struggles of the most severe artistic work, and whose essence is the "artisan's excellence." "Burgherly calling as a life form," Lukács writes, "means first of all the primacy of ethics in life; that life is dominated by what is systematically and regularly repeated, by what returns in line with one's duty, by what must be done without regard to desire or lack of it. In other words: the dominance of order over mood, of the lasting over the momentary, of quiet work over genius that is fed by sensations." And as he continues, we see that he claims that this ethical-artisan mastery, in contrast to the monkish estheticism of Flaubert, whose burgherly conduct of life was a nihilistic mask, is the Germanic figure of the burgherly artist: estheticism and burgherly nature, he explains, represent here a complete and legitimate form of life, indeed, a *German* form of life; yes, this mixture of artistry and burgherly nature forms the actual German variation of European estheticism, the German *l'art pour l'art*.

This is brilliant—exceedingly beautiful and true! But may I be allowed not only to praise it, but also to recognize myself in it? For even with the repeated reminder that we are not speaking of rank here at all, but only of essence—I still lack precisely what the essayist seems to regard as the criterion of the German burgherly *l'art pour l'art*: the burgherly vocation, you see, the real form and order of life. But Conrad Ferdinand Meyer, whom one certainly can and must consider part of the German guild (and who, in 1870, recognized himself to be German, took Germany's side!)—lacked it, too, simply for reasons of health. But is this critical prerequisite really indispensable? Clearly, intellect loves to replace reality with symbols. One can live in a soldierly manner without in the least being fit for military service. The intellectual lives in symbols. That primacy of ethics in life of which the critic speaks—does it not signify the predominance of ethics over *esthetics*? And is this predominance not present even without a burgherly vocation, when life itself has primacy over the *work*? An artist is burgherly when he transfers the ethical characteristics of the burgherly way of life: order, sequence, rest, "diligence"—not in the sense of industriousness, but of faithful workmanship—to the exercise of art. Years ago in Vienna a clever Jew said to me: "What lends your works dignity and lovableness is that when you present them you seem to be saying, 'This is absolutely the best I can do.'" That was a doubtful but very penetrating compliment, and therefore I have remembered it. It was a youthful romantic illusion and youthful fancy if I ever imagined that I was sacrificing my life to "art" and that my burgherly nature was a nihilistic mask; if I, to be sure with candid irony toward both sides, gave art, the "work," precedence over life and declared that "to be completely creative" one could not live, one had to die. In truth, "art" is only a means of fulfilling my life ethically. My "work"—*sit venia verbo*—is not the product, meaning, and purpose of an ascetic-orgiastic denial of life, but of an ethical form of expression of my life itself: my tendency toward autobiography already testifies to this, a tendency that has ethical origins, but that, to be sure, does not exclude the most lively esthetic will to impartiality, distance, and objectification, a will, then, that is again only the will to faithful workmanship and that, among other things, produces that stylistic dilettantism that allows the subject to speak and that led, in *Death in Venice*, for example, to the astounding public misunderstanding that the "hieratic atmosphere," the "master style," of the story, was personal ambition, something I wanted to surround and express *myself* with and that I now had ridiculous ambitions to attain—when it was a matter of accommodation, yes, of parody. The important thing for me, then, is not the "work," but my life. Life is not the means for the achievement of an esthetic ideal of perfection; on the contrary, the work is an ethical symbol of life. The goal is not some kind of objective perfection; it is the subjective consciousness that "this is absolutely the best I could do." If this inner essence of my work can have an objectively esthetic effect on responsive people such as my Viennese patron, its subjective meaning is still completely ethical—so little is the likes of me a beauty fan, so little an esthete in the Bohemian sense, and so very much so one in the burgherly sense.

"How did this happen?" Perhaps in part from this essential reason. Perhaps I feel myself to be German because of my belonging to a burgherly-ethical artistic community that is German. Because people like me have nothing to do with the Anchoritism of Flaubert, nor with d'Annunzio's insufferable pontification about beauty. Because I, coming personally from an old, burgherly German sphere, in spite of all my questionable modern nature and Europeanizing needs, am in my way connected with those representatives of German workmanlike mastery of art, of whom Meyer and Storm are closest to me. Social and human sympathy pull me to Meyer. But my connection with Storm is one of kindred origin, and more than that. If *Tonio Kröger* is *Immensee* transformed into a modern problematic work, a synthesis of intellectualism and mood, of Nietzsche and Storm, as I said, then Lukács says very well in his study that in *Buddenbrooks*, late awareness (which has nothing to do with rank) made possible the monumentalization of that mood of decay that permeates Storm's burgherly world.

Ethics, burgherly nature, decay: they belong together; they are one. Does not music belong here, too? I remember well the words with which, as I am told, Stefan George rejected my *Buddenbrooks*: "No," he said, "this is nothing for me. This is still music and decay." Still! Late, yes, belated burgherly nature made me into an analyst of decay; and that "ethical air," that moralistic pessimism (with music) that I said I received from Schopenhauer and Wagner, was much more my own quality and nature that I found in these European Germans and that attracted and led me to them from the start. Not "beauty." I was never concerned with "beauty." For me, "beauty" was always something for Italians and tricksters of the intellect—it had basically nothing German in it, and it was especially not the subject and the taste of an artistic German burgherly nature. In this sphere, ethics is predominant over esthetics, or more correctly: a mixture and equation of these concepts appears that honors, loves, and cares for *the ugly*. For ugliness, sickness, and decadence *are ethics*, and never have I thought of myself in the literal sense as an "esthete," but always as a moralist.

Thus it was German, thus it was burgherly; estheticism in the literal sense, *the ecstasy of beauty*, that is, is the most un-German thing in the world and the most unburgherly at the same time; in the school of Schopenhauer and Wagner, one is not educated to be an esthete, one breathes ethical-pessimistic air, German-burgherly air: for the German and the burgherly character are one and the same; if "spirit" is at all of burgherly origin, then the *German* spirit is burgherly in a special way, German *culture* is burgherly, the German burgherly nature is *human*—from which it follows that it is not, like the Western one, *political*, or at least it was not up to yesterday, and will only *become* so on the way to its dehumanization.

To say that in Schopenhauer and Wagner one finds oneself in the burgherly sphere, that one receives a burgherly education from them, seems to be contrary to good sense; for it is difficult to connect the concept of the burgherly nature to that of genius. What could be more unburgherly than these highly tensed, tragic, intensely painful lives that led to the splendor of world fame! Nevertheless, they are true children of their burgherly age, and everywhere in their humanity and spirit there is evidence of their burgherly nature. Just look at Schopenhauer's life: his Hanseatic-merchant origins; his sedentary life in Frankfurt; the Kantian-pedantic stability and punctuality of his daily life; his wise hygiene based on sound physiological knowledge ("The reasonable person does not pursue pleasure but absence of pain"); his exactness as a capitalist (he wrote down every penny and by clever management doubled his small fortune in the course of his life); the tranquility, tenacity, economy, and steadiness of his working method (he wrote for publication exclusively during the first two morning hours, and he wrote to Goethe that *fidelity and honesty*, the characteristics he had carried over from practical into theoretical and intellectual life, formed the essence of his accomplishment and success): all this testifies strongly to the burgherly nature of his human side, and his burgherly *way of thinking* is expressed just as strongly in his decided hatred for the romantic Middle Ages, for the deceitful clergy, for knighthood, in his belief that one should insist upon classical humanity. By the way, this is part of his opposition to himself, and in it one can recognize the preliminary stage and preparatory school of Nietzsche's "self-destructive drive"—it is the strongest contradiction of inclination and nature, the intellectual denial of self; for who was less classical, who was more romantic than he! But as for Wagner, there is, of course, in his human and artistic personality, a trait that is not only burgherly but even bourgeois and parvenu—the taste for ostentatiousness, for "satin," for luxury, riches and burgherly pomp—above all a characteristic of his private life, that, however, also reaches deeply into his intellectual-artistic life. I wonder if the remark is mine, that Wagner's art and the *Makart bouquet* (with peacock feathers) are of the same temporal and esthetic origin? But if Wagner was somewhat bourgeois, he was also a *burgher* in a high, German sense, and his self-staging and costuming as a German "master" had its good intrinsic and natural justification: it would be unjust to overlook the old German element of artistic mastery midst the molten-volcanic, the demonic, and the ingenious nature of his work—the faithful patience, the handworker piousness and the thoughtful industriousness. "By their fruits ye shall know them." Wagner's European intellectualism is found again in Richard Strauß, but his German burgherly side is found in the skullcapped mastery and faithful diligence of the lovable Engelbert Humperdinck.

Burgherly artistic genius, a paradox come true, but a paradox just the same, a duality and inner conflict at any rate, in spite of the legitimacy that this intellectual way of life has, precisely in Germany. When I spoke of the determining influence that Wagner's genius had on me, I omitted something most questionable, saved it until now. It has less to do with Wagner's own burgherly character than with his relationship to burgherly nature, with his *effect* on the burgher. But this is precisely the point where Wagner's influence can become a type of undoing, and perhaps has become so for me: I mean what Nietzsche called the "double optic," seeing artistic *and* burgherly elements side by side, simultaneously, the instinct—for it is of course instinctive, not contrived, something completely objective, not at all subjective—to satisfy sophisticated and less demanding needs at the same time, to win the few, and the many to boot—an instinct that, in my opinion, is connected with Wagner's desire to conquer, his thirst for the world, his "sinfulness" in the ascetic sense, with what Buddha calls "attachment," with his longing, his sensual-suprasensual demand for love. There is, of course, a type of artistic genius in whom there can be no possibility of all or part of this, a chaste, strict, cold, proud, even stiff genius who has nothing but disgust and scorn for the "world" in his heart and spirit, and who is also untouched by demagogy, by the slightest unconscious consideration and condescendence, by worldly demand for effect, unity, and love. Wagner was very far from this. There is a place in his work that sums him up in both respects: it is the quote of the

motif of longing at the word "world" in the second act of *Tristan*—
("Even then I am the world!"). One will probably not object if I find in
Wagner's lust, in his world-eroticism, the basis and origin of what
Nietzsche called his double optic, an ability that arose from the need
not only to capture and fascinate the most sophisticated people—this
is obvious—but also the wide mass of simple ones: I say it arose from
a need, because I am convinced that every artist without exception
creates just what he *is*, what corresponds to his own esthetic judgment
and need. There is no such thing as a dishonest artistic genius who
would plan and achieve effects that would be ridiculous to him, that he
himself would be superior to, and that would above all be effects on
him. And therefore it follows that the objective effects of an artist,
including Wagner's broad burgherly impact, are always evidence of his
own being and essence. He was a yearning, or, to substitute the colder
word, an ambitious artist. But what one wants in youth, really wants,
and is justified by one's nature in wanting, not just what one falsely and
unnaturally convinces oneself that one wants—one has in abundance
in old age; and the result of that aristocratic-democratic, artistic-burgh-
erly optic, is *success*, which, as such, is always a double success: with the
artists *and* the burghers, for neither the purely bohemian and monastic
success nor the purely public one is deserving of its name. Let no one
believe that it is with the slightest self-satisfaction that I add I could sing
a song about "success," my little song! I see in it an experience in life
like any other, and I know that it characterizes its bearer in a rather
ambiguous way. Simply defined, it means: this fellow wanted the stupid
ones too. But what I also know is that the "success" that is the result of
that double optic, that one learns in a wicked, sinful way from Wagner,
is a precarious and uncanny abode; that it conceals mortal danger and
the vengeance of the furies; that in the long run a man must be
prepared for this success to be his undoing in *both* camps, with the
burghers as well as with the radicals; for me, the matter began with my
being a thorn in the flesh of the literati, or scarcely even that. One of
them, an Eternist* by trade, recently called me a "happy nature." Well,
that is the limit! No, it is still not the absolute limit. Every once in a
while it still happens that a pure and free expression of my being, such
as, for example, the essay on Frederick, obliges the literary sticklers, for
better or worse, to agree with the favorable judgment of the "burghers."
Was it not possible for a European magazine, *Die weißen Blätter*, to find

* Designation of a group of literary collaborators of the review, *Die Aktion*.

the essay masterful—even if its message naturally could not be approved of? It is Tonio Kröger's old song: "I stand between two worlds, am at home in neither and therefore find things a little difficult." But is one perhaps precisely for this reason *German*? Is not the German character the middle, the medium and the mediating one, and the German the central human being in the grand style? If it is already German to be a burgher, then it is perhaps even more German to be something between a burgher and an artist, and also something between a patriot and a European, between a protestor and a Westerner, a conservative and a nihilist—and to write exceedingly German essays, whose antiliterary tendency must fill every French-oriented heart with repugnance, but which nevertheless must unfortunately appeal precisely to the Westerners, the Europeans, and the literary men, as "masterful"?

This was musing! Let us get back to the point in the narrower—or broader—sense, and talk about burgherly nature *and politics*: I mean about the German burgher, the educated burgher, the human and artistic burgher and his relationship to politics—which, as we have already indicated, is basically a real nonrelationship, and which, after being worked on by Bismarck with doubtful half-success, is being worked on today by civilization's literary man in a "more intellectual" way. He has taken on quite a job for himself. For German higher culture thoroughly resists being politicized. Indeed, the political element is lacking in the German concept of culture. Even today, after a half-century of the *Reich*, the words of young Nietzsche in the third aphorism of *Thoughts out of Season* are valid for the higher Germans:

> For whoever has the *furor philosophicus* in him will have no time at all for the *furor politicus*, and he will wisely avoid reading newspapers every day or even serving a party; although he will not hesitate one instant to be *at his post when the fatherland is really in need*. All states are badly organized when people other than statesmen must be preoccupied with politics, and they deserve to be ruined by all these politicians.

But is what is said here of the typical German of a higher intellectual order, as he saw himself up to yesterday, at least—not also basically valid for Germans in general, for the German national character, yes, for the real German people? How these people behave when it is necessary "to be at one's post when the fatherland is really in need," we saw in the beginning of August 1914. They behave exceedingly well, we would like to think: no others behave as well. Therefore they look all the worse in times of shallow excitement that are, in the more narrow, more domestic sense, political—worse, probably, than any others; the process distorts them most unpleasantly, and they are basically aware of this themselves. I have my little memories of scenes in streets and streetcars on parliamentary election days. I see myself again on a forward platform, behind the driver, a man still young, with a marriage ring on the hand that is controlling the current switch. He is standing there surrounded by the public, in his solid service coat, and he rings the bell and peers through the rain-splashed windshield in front of his face. A man jumps on, his hat pushed back on his head, with wild eyes and flushed cheeks, starting to talk while he is still on the steps. He is going full steam, in a political rage. He has come from the polls, an agent probably, a recruiter, a vote chaser, at any rate a fiery party man. He cannot be quiet; one sees it; his heart is full of politics and half-education, and half-educated, excited street talk pours endlessly from him. He is speaking to no one and to all of us; he even sticks his chin over the driver's shoulder, this solid shoulder in the service coat, and prattles into his face from the side. He prattles about the "blue-black block" or similar inhumanly stupid drivel, he sticks his thumbs in his vest and with vulgar humor imitates a Jew. He was the very distortion of the nation, and I remember well the look with which the driver finally turned toward the embarrassing man and eyed him from head to toe, this sober, steady, quiet-unfriendly, depreciating, slightly disgusted look of the man in the service coat at the one who was drunk with politics and half-education, a look that seemed to me to be unforgettably characteristic of the relationship of the German people to politics. Was he an egoist, my driver? But when real trouble began, he was "at his post"; that I guarantee. His face was still sober, but it was devout then, and he has kept his post until the present day, whether on the earth or covered by it.

The meaning of the most steady of all nations seemed to me to lie in the look of this, its decent son. If I turn from him to the German artist, to the typically German variety of the creative human being, then I must try to grasp his image and essence "with my mind's eye," as Hamlet said. What do I see? I see a face turned slightly to the side and forward, of unforgettable and unmistakable national stamp, somehow like an old-fashioned woodcut, Nuremberg-burgherly, human in an unprecedented and original sense, moral-intellectual, hard and mild at the same time—an eye that looks inside and beyond, not a "fiery" one, but rather somewhat languid, a taciturn mouth, and signs of effort and fatigue on a forehead that is wrinkled with care but not with sullenness.

Ghibelline or Guelph? Oh, no: "Only a quiet artist who did his best, thoughtfully waiting for heaven's help." What would this faithful, worthy and humble man, this metaphysical handworker, have to do with politics in any vulgar, Western-democratic sense? He is national, of course he is, even though he is also much too human and urbane, cosmopolitan, and burgherly-cultured to make mischief by playing the trump card of nationalism in times of peace; he is national and becomes fervently aware of this when he sees the nation in physical, and particularly in spiritual danger. But a politician? A demonstrator and a rabble-rouser? A human rights' advocate and a freedom gesticulator? No, no!

It is not by chance that a medieval-Nuremberg face appears before me as I search for the image of burgherly intellectuality, of the burgherly-cultural type. One searches in books, one searches, in the distress of the times, for the farthest origins, the legitimate bases, the oldest spiritual traditions of one's hard-pressed ego; one searches for justification. Was it not so: the burgherly age of our history that followed the clerical and the knightly ones, the age of the Hanseatic League, the age of the cities, was a purely cultural age, not a political one; the burgher did not take up the political heritage of the knight. Nevertheless, the age was national to the highest degree, consciously national in dress and carriage; the burgherly culture has been called the first purely national culture. Which epoch was it that seemed to the Mosers and the Fichtes to be the truly brilliant period of German history? It is this one, the blossoming of the German Hanseatic League. The history of the German cities, Treitschke said in a defensive tone, was "thoroughly patriotic," and historians who regret, yes, who call it a German misfortune, that the political union between the monarchy and burgherdom delayed the foundations of the national state in Germany as it was formed in other countries at that time, loudly praise the significance of this history for the spread as well as for the deepening of the German character. Yes, the deepening of the German character—I am looking it up, and I remember that it is true—is the work of this nonpolitical burgher culture, of this time of an everyday structure, comfortably exact and satirically clear-eyed, of the time of sermons and mysticism, of Shrovetide plays, lawbooks, and *chronicles*—of a time of the rise of German individuality, according to one historian, and of the democratization of the idea of personality, according to the other; of the time of the most intimately dignified and nationally masterful engravers' art and painting—of a time, in a word, that has caused, in the German sphere, burgherly nature and intellectuality, burgherly nature and mastery of art, to remain intimately related in meaning.

And the "cosmopolitan burgher," is he not also—a burgher? What else does he represent than the combination of German burgherly nature and humanistic culture? Yes, just as the German word for "cosmopolitanism" includes the word and the idea of the "burgher," this word and idea itself also has immanent in it the cosmopolitan sense of a world without boundaries.

Who am I, where do I come from, that I am as I am, and can neither make nor wish myself different? In times of spiritual difficulty, one searches for the answer to this question. I am a city man, a burgher, a child and great-grandchild of the German-burgherly culture. My maternal-exotic blood may as a ferment have a disturbing, alienating and modifying effect, but it does not change the essence and the foundations, does not abrogate the main spiritual traditions. Were not my ancestors Nuremberger craftsmen of the type that Germany sent out to the whole world, even into the Far East, as a sign that she was the country of the cities? They sat as councillors in the Mecklenburg area, they came to Lübeck, they were "merchants of the Roman Empire"—and as I wrote the history of their house, a *city chronicle* that developed into a naturalistic novel, a German book that one may well place alongside the writings of the burgherly past, I found that I had mutated much less from this species than I had allowed myself to imagine. Yes, I am a burgher, and in Germany this is a word that is just as little foreign to intellect and to art as it is to dignity, solidity and comfort. My sense of elegance is of urbane origin; it is culture, and not international civilization, as it is with the elegant bourgeois. My sense of solidity is of the same origin. Even my instinctive demand for dignity and for comfortable abundance in life has older justification and differs in intent from the voluptuousness of the international bourgeois. If I am liberal, it is in the sense of liberality, and not of liberalism. For I am nonpolitical, national, but nonpolitically disposed, like the German of the burgherly culture and the one of romanticism, which knew no other political demand than the highly national one for emperor and empire, and which was so basically undemocratic that *its* spiritual influence alone caused the politicians, the members of the German student fraternities, and the revolutionaries of the *Paulskirche*, to want a hereditary empire, and made them, as Vogt wrote to Herwegh, "into complete aristocrats."

But I know very well that I am also a burgher in my attitude toward this war. The burgher is national in his essence; if he has been the bearer of the idea of German unity, it is because he has always been the bearer of German culture and way of thinking. Often, however, the teleological function of war in general has been seen to be the confirmation, preservation, and strengthening of the national character: it is the great defense against the rationalistic breakdown of national culture, and my participation in this war has nothing at all to do with world and economic dominance; it is rather nothing more than participation in that passionate process of self-knowledge, self-limitation, and self-reinforcement to which the German culture has been forced by terrible spiritual pressure and attack from without.

"Good: What you wish to call the 'burgherly nature' was a vital part of those quiet, impressive characters between 1820 and 1860, in the great time of German science and narration. But if one thinks of the highest and purest examples of this epoch, of Jakob Grimm, Uhland, Keller, Theodor Storm, it is impossible to overlook the fact that the steely core of their idealism clearly manifested itself at one time or another in a radical decision in matters of political freedom, Grimm as one of the Göttinger Seven, Storm as a citizen of Holstein, Uhland as a representative at Württemberg and at the *Paulskirche*, go to the limit of what a burgher could sacrifice in these times, relinquishing their lifetime positions for the sake of political causes. And these causes are the direct ancestors of contemporary democracy." Really? What does Storm's feeling for his homeland, his absolutely defiantly active resistance to Danish occupation, his sacrifice of his career as a lawyer in Husum, his bitter path into exile in Potsdam—what did the political passion of this sincere, deeply loyal man, whose feeling of freedom is expressed in the lines:

> Listen to me!—For all the rest's a lie—
> No man can thrive without a fatherland!*

—what did Storm's "politics," which was nothing more than a heartfelt cherishing of metaphysical life values, have to do with the democratic ideas of our radical literary men? With internationalism, human rights, radical enlightenment, the ideology of prosperity, the apotheosis of the social element, and the rhetorically sentimental spectacle of revolution? And was it essentially different with the political attitude of the other great burghers of that time? They were democrats, they were politicians,

---

* Hör mich:—denn alles andere ist Lüge—
  Kein Mann gedeihet ohne Vaterland!

because in their time, the national idea, love of the fatherland, was inseparably mixed up with that of democracy and of politics. They were national before they were democrats; they were so *by* being democrats— but the present war, the struggle of Germany against Western democracy, makes it extremely difficult for national feeling to be democratic; and "democracy" in Germany is another word for "cosmopolitan radicalism." No, these men were not actually radical literary men, these German burghers of 1820–60. Nevertheless, we must still remember Goethe's words to Eckermann about Uhland: "Watch closely. The politician in Uhland will devour the poet. Living in daily irritation and excitement is not for the tender nature of the poet. His song will end." And perhaps we may also remember Adalbert Stifter, who atoned in liberal literary histories for having declared in 1848 that he was a man of moderation and freedom, saying that both were now imperiled, unfortunately.

After all this, no one will want to hold up the young Richard Wagner of 1848–49 to me and point to what he later, not quite appropriately, called his "stupid pranks" of the time. Wagner was national, this above all, yes, uniquely so; coming home from Paris, the poor, nameless young artist fell on his knees at the bank of the Rhine, in solemn emotional transport, "swearing eternal loyalty to his German fatherland." His participation in the stormy movement of the times originated in his Germanness, his desire for a unified, majestic empire, not from any cosmopolitan-radical sympathies, and ten times over he confirmed that only police court officials could have prosecuted him as a political revolutionary, that the politics of the times had never really touched him in spite of the tumultuous nature of the situation, and that he had also left it completely untouched. One must not deny or forget that this wave of enthusiasm that passed over Germany in '48, carrying everything with it, was, in spite of its admixture of cosmopolitan ideology—no, precisely because of this German-universal admixture—a *national* flood, and that every intellectual attitude that devoted itself to it would also have been stirred by Germany in August 1914. One should rather emphasize the relationship and the belonging together, the common national stamp of the movements of 1848 and 1914; 1914 is only the return of 1848 at another level of historical development. What else is the idea of "Central Europe" than the rebirth of the pre-Bismarckian idea of Greater Germany? And even the appearance of that Christian professor, disciple of Frantz, and serious dreamer of the return home to the Holy Roman Empire of the German Nation—even *his* vision and teaching show the intellectual bridges that bind the present with that time in the past. To be sure, Dr. Foerster negates not only Bismarck, but also the Reformation, and it was right and proper to duel learnedly with the scholar and to refute him, but to curse him was boorish and wrong. How could it not happen, in spiritually uprooted and agitated times like ours, that his universal ideal of the Middle Ages would not also come to the fore—an ideal that one might call reactionary but that has very much to do with the most modern European longing for looking back beyond the proscribed border of the 16th century! Supranational, it seems to me, is something quite different and very much better than international; supra-German means being *exceedingly* German; and I like a hundred and a thousand times better the resolution of this Catholic German, as he has revealed it, than the unspeakably anti-German declamations of our Italo-French Freemasons, revolutionary epigones and opera singers of progress. No, at least Foerster is not one of civilization's literary men.

As for Wagner, it is certain that as an artist and an intellectual he was a revolutionary all his life. But it is just as certain that this national culture-revolutionary was not in favor of political revolution, and that he did not find the atmosphere of 1848–49 to be at all his element. In his memoirs he speaks of the "terrible shallowness of the spokesmen of that time," of their "rhetoric at meetings and in personal intercourse in general that was made up of the tritest of phrases." He said that it amazed him to hear and to read "with what unbelievable triviality it all happened, and how everything simply ended with the declaration that the republic was, to be sure, best, but, one could, if need be, put up with a well-behaved monarchy." And it certainly must repulse and offend civilization's literary man, the one who makes antitheses of power and intellect, not a little when Wagner, speaking of the Frankfurt Parliament, says that one did not quite see where all this powerful talk of the *most powerless* of men was going to lead. The most powerless! This brutal dreamer had a weakness, it would seem, for "power." He did not hesitate to come to terms with "power" in 1870—no, even to cheer it, to cheer it drunkenly, and to be more enthusiastic for it than he ever had been in the days of the *Paulskirche* spirit. According to civilization's literary man, then, he would have been "no fighter"—oh my God! He praised the "enormous courage" of Bismarck, celebrated the German army before Paris, the victory over France, the re-establishment of the empire, the crowning of a German emperor; all this overwhelmed his artistic heart; it broke out in a type of song that went something like:

"The rays of humanity's morning are beaming; now come forth, you day of the gods." In short, he was more enthusiastic than anyone who approved the war in 1914; for not one of us was so grand and violent of nature as to match his anti-intellectual excess. If one wants to clarify, to the point of amusement, Wagner's attitude toward politics in general and to the year 1848 in particular, one has only to remember that at the time he had only recently finished *Lohengrin*, and had crowned this most romantically graceful of all existing pieces of music with the prelude. *Lohengrin* and the year '48—these are two worlds joined at the most by one thing: national fervor. And civilization's literary man is guided by a correct instinct when he makes fun of *Lohengrin* in satirical social novels by treating it politically. Probably Wagner was thinking of the beautiful bass voice of his King Henry, when, in the Dresden "Fatherland's Club," he made that radically strange speech in which he declared himself to be a glowing adherent of the kingdom, a despiser of all constitutionalism, and implored Germany to send the "foreign, un-German concepts." namely Western democracy, to the devil, and to restore the only salutary, old-Germanic relationship between the absolute king and the free people. For in the absolute king, he said, the concept of freedom is elevated to the highest, God-fulfilled consciousness, and the people are only free when *one man* rules, not when *many* rule. Even Friedrich Wilhelm Foerster does not advocate stranger politics. This impossible forty-eighter certainly says strange things! For example, that art, at the time of its blossoming, was *conservative*, and that it would *become so again*. Furthermore, the pithy, indestructible sentence: *"The German is conservative."* Furthermore, the sentence that can only be opposed by Frenchmen and radical world reformers: "The future cannot be conceived in any way other than as determined by the past." Furthermore, the absolutely indisputable, the immortal and delivering sentence, "In Germany, democracy is a completely alien creature. *It only exists in the press.*" Certainly Wagner loved the idea of the brotherhood of nations, but he was very far removed from internationalist tendencies: otherwise the words "foreign," "translated," "un-German," would not have signified a judgment, a condemnation, yes, hatred in his mouth—and they did signify this. But why did he hate "democracy"? Because he *hated politics itself*, and because he recognized *the identity of politics and democracy*. Why do the nations that pursue politics with eagerness and talent believe in, want, and have democracy? Precisely because they are political nations! Nothing is clearer. The taste of a people for democracy stands in reverse order to its disgust for politics. If Wagner was in any way an expression of his people, if he was in any way German, German-humane, German-burgherly in the highest and purest sense, he was so in his hatred of politics. One may ascribe this to the intellectual disappointment he experienced from his participation in the Dresden May revolt, when he immediately afterward swore never to have anything more to do with such things and declared the field of politics to be "completely unproductive." But sentences such as *"A political man is repulsive"* (from a letter to Liszt) come from deeper, impersonal reasons; when would an Englishman, Frenchman, Italian, yes, even a Russian, ever have made such a statement? It came here from vague and heartfelt artistic broodings and hypotheses of a decay, of an anarchistic-doctrinaire politicization of the human race that dates from the breakup of the Greek state and the destruction of tragedy; of a "very definitely social movement" that had nothing at all to do with political revolution, but that, on the contrary, would create a human condition that would signify "the end of politics"; in which there would be no more politics at all, and in which, *therefore*, "art in its truth" would be possible; of a depoliticized, human, and artistic form of life and intellect, then, that would be so very much a German form, a form of life and intellect favorable to everything German, for "We Germans, it seems, will never be great politicians, but perhaps something much greater, if we judge our talents properly . . ." This spirit, which was mixed with German tradition and artistic genius, was dreaming of a de-politicization and humanization of the earth, of its becoming German in the word's most human and antipolitical sense, when he spoke of that passion that longed for "the only true thing—the human being": very much in contrast to civilization's literary man who "dreams" on the contrary of the "humanization" of Germany on the way to her democratic politicization. But of course I have already said that civilization's literary man knows well why he satirizes Wagner: he knows it instinctively, for he has not read him, and he does not understand a note of his music. But the new element for him, grist for his mill, is that Wagner was an imperialist—that, too, can be proved! As early as 1848, in that same radically strange speech that he made in the democratic "Fatherland's Club" in Dresden, he demanded the establishment of German colonies. "We want to do it better," he said, "than the Spanish, for whom the New World became a priest-ridden slaughterhouse, different from the English, for whom it became a haberdasher's stall! We want to make it German and magnificent!" The idea of colonies never ceased to occupy him; perhaps reminiscences of Frederick and Faust played a part here. But how could civilization's literary man fail to react satirically in the face of an intellect that behaved antipolitically—but nationalistically, antipolitically—but imperialistically: he who argued with practiced passion that one should definitely be political but in no way perceive things nationally, and who only spoke of "imperialism" as the most atrocious work of the devil and a crime against the human race?

The present war teaches us again that in stormy, turbulent times each finds his own. There is no world view, no ideology, no religious doctrine, no fad or fancy that does not find itself confirmed and justified by the war and that would not be joyfully convinced that precisely its time and future had come. Wagner found something of himself in the so-called German revolution; he was young and ardent enough to believe that it held the realization of his cultural dreams of the "end of politics" and of the dawn of humanity. It disappointed him most deeply; he disavowed his participation in it as "stupid pranks" and praised its mortal enemy, the sly-brutal founder of the empire, although Bismarck's solution to the German question did not at all signify the "end of politics," but its real beginning for Germany. And although those "stupid pranks" had very serious and burdensome consequences for Wagner's outer circumstances, it would still be completely absurd to claim that the political turmoil of '48 was a basic inner experience for him, his great spiritual experience. He had this quite a bit later, and it was as unpolitical as possible. It was a very German experience of a moralistic-metaphysical nature—it came to him during the loneliness of his Swiss exile, and it was only a book: it was the philosophy of Arthur Schopenhauer, in which he recognized the spiritual salvation of his real essence, the true homeland of his soul.

Schopenhauer, too, wrote about politics—to be sure, however, politics is a chapter of his *Ethics*. Its aspects are odd: they differ from those of civilization's literary man in essential elements. Apparently his general philosophy places freedom beyond appearance, not to mention beyond human institutions. But this is a bad beginning; it strikes a basic tone that is resigned, antirhetorical, actually already antipolitical, and it opens the gates wide to every form of skepticism and quietism. What is one to make of the statement that the difference between serfdom and landed property, in general between serf and tenant, owner, mortgager and the like, is more in form than in substance—for whether the farmer or the land belongs to me, the bird or its feed, the fruit or the tree, is of essentially little difference? Is he approving of slavery? Rousseau did, too, but for political reasons. He recommends it because people are needed to work, craftsmen to produce the necessities. These people, he says, must be slaves so that the citizen of the state will have the leisure to devote himself exclusively to politics. Schopenhauer, as I understand him, also would have been capable of such suggestions— but in no way out of head-over-heels love for democracy. His concept of the state is cynical-pessimistic—it cannot be characterized in a milder way. The state, he says, is not at all opposed to egotism in general and as such; on the contrary, it is founded on the clearly understood, methodically proceeding egotism that goes from the individual to the general, and it therefore arises from the summation of the common egotism of everyone and exists merely to serve this egotism—established on the correct assumption that pure morality, that is, right action based upon morals, cannot be expected; otherwise the state itself would, of course, be superfluous. This has a certain biting cheerfulness. But it is certainly true that in this way and no other, always and everywhere, the state, the state contract, and the law, must have arisen; and for Schopenhauer it makes no difference whether the prior condition was anarchy or arbitrary despotism. In both cases no state was there before, and the state is perfect or imperfect according to whether it is more or less unmingled with anarchy or despotism. "The republics," Schopenhauer says with cynical calm, "tend toward anarchy, the monarchies to despotism, and the middle path that has been conceived for this reason, the constitutional monarchy, tends toward domination by factions." Thought out in an ugly manner, and without dash! But it is true, nevertheless. And therefore if there is little hope for a perfect state— which governmental form does our philosopher declare to be comparatively the best? The monarchy. Obviously! That had to come. We suspected him from the first word. And why does he advocate the monarchy? Because his attitude toward reason—while not exactly antagonistic, is still quite casual. "The arbitrarily and artificially selected plant system of Linnaeus," he says,

> cannot be replaced by a *natural* one, no matter how much the natural one conforms to *reason* and how often the attempt is made, because, you see, such a system never provides the certainty and the solidity of definitions that the artificial and arbitrary one has. In the same way, the artificial and arbitrary basis of a governmental constitution . . . cannot be replaced by one that has a purely natural basis, one that, throwing out the above conditions, seeks to replace the rights of birth with those of personal merit, to replace the national religion with the results of ratiocination,

and so forth; because no matter how all this conforms to reason, it lacks that certainty and solidity of definitions that alone ensure the stability of the common system. A governmental constitution that only embodies abstract justice would be an excellent thing for creatures other than human beings: for, you see, the great majority of human beings are highly egotistical, unjust, inconsiderate, mendacious, even wicked now and then, and equipped with very scanty intelligence to boot; from this, therefore, there arises the necessity for a completely independent power concentrated in one human being who is even above law and justice, to whom everyone bows, and who is considered to be a superior being, a ruler by divine grace. In the long run, this is the only way the human race can be bridled and governed.

If ever one has written with grim humor about politics, it is here. This man's voice is completely lacking in tremolo, his style in every generous dash; it serves him to speak the exact and melancholy truth. With Rousseau, he shares the equation of nature and reason, but he does not maintain it pedantically; for at any moment he is also ready to use these concepts antithetically. The monarchical form of government, he says, is the one that is *natural* for human beings, almost as it is for bees and ants, migrating cranes, wandering elephants, wolf packs gathered for raids, and some other animals, as well, all of which place *one* leader at the top to guide their actions. In addition, every dangerous human undertaking, every military campaign, every ship, must obey *one* supreme commander. Even the animal organism is constructed monarchically: the brain, you see, is the leader and the governor. Even the planetary system is monarchical. Republics, however, are unnatural, artificially made, and the result of *reflection*—which is enough for this anti-intellectual intellect, this antirationalistic reason, to condemn them straight out. But when Schopenhauer talks about and advocates "monarchy," he obviously does *not* mean constitutional monarchy, just as little as Wagner meant it: he makes fun of it when he says that the constitutional kings have an undeniable similarity to the gods of Epicurus, who, "without mixing into human affairs, sit up there in heaven in undisturbed blessedness and peace of mind." But now they have become the fashion, he says, and in every tiny German principality a parody of the English constitution is presented, quite complete, with upper and lower houses, right down to the laws of habeas corpus and the jury. These forms are natural and proper to the English people because they arise from and presuppose the English character and English circumstances. But it is just as natural for the German people to be divided into many tribes that stand under just as many princes who *really* rule, with an emperor above everyone preserving domestic peace and representing the unity of the empire externally, because this arises from the German character and from German circumstances. He salutes the great understanding of the English as evidenced in their steadfast and true retention of their old institutions, morals and customs, even at the risk of carrying this tenacity too far, to the point of ridiculousness; because precisely these things were not hatched out of an idle head but grew slowly from the force of circumstances and the wisdom of life itself, and are therefore appropriate to them as a nation. "On the other hand," Schopenhauer writes, "the German Michel has been persuaded by his schoolmaster that he must strut around in an English dress coat; that there is nothing else to do. So he has insolently wrung it from Papa and now looks quite laughable in it with his gauche manners and clumsy shape." Here it should be noted that the English dress coat would still be comparatively a much more suitable piece of clothing for Michel than the French Phrygian cap that people *partout* want to put on his pensive head today. Wagner, Lagarde, Nietzsche, and other great Germans have had opinions similar to, yes, exactly the same, as those of Schopenhauer on the falsification of the German character by the importation of political institutions that are completely foreign and unnatural to it. Yes, Lagarde said that there never was a German history at all unless *the regularly continuing loss of German character* is considered to be German history. This regular progress is progress itself. Admittedly, Fontane thought that those of our democrats who saw England with their own eyes ridiculed and opposed the whole English "mess." Well, if parliamentarianism is a mess, and if nevertheless there is nothing else for a nation that has to politicize itself to do than to take over this mess because there is nothing better and because nothing politically new and original can be invented, then politics itself is a mess, and with this kind of devout confidence and enthusiasm, the German people are entering into their period of democratic world politics.

I said Schopenhauer's attitude toward reason was a rather casual one. His attitude toward *justice* is no better, no more "passionate." First of all, justice is simply a negative thing for him, merely the negation of injustice: whereby, beyond doubt, it already loses in fervor. Second, he states that justice in itself is powerless: it is force that rules by nature. To bring force over to the side of justice so that justice can rule by means of force is the problem of statecraft—which has always accomplished much when as little injustice as possible remains in the community; for complete justice, with no injustice remaining, is simply an ideal goal that can only be approximated. If, for example, injustice is thrown out from one side, it slips in again from the other, for injustice is deeply embedded in the human character. Also, all experiments here are dangerous, because one is dealing with the most unmanageable material, the human race, which is almost as dangerous to deal with as high explosives. "In general, however," Schopenhauer continues, and now the cloven hoof really appears,

> In general, however, the hypothesis could be made that justice is analogous in form to certain chemical substances that cannot be produced in a pure, isolated state, but only with a small admixture that serves as their bearer, or that provides the necessary consistency . . . so that justice, accordingly, if it is to take hold in the real world, and even prevail, needs a small admixture of arbitrariness and force so that in spite of its purely ideal and therefore ethereal nature, it may work and endure in this real, material world without evaporating and flying off to heaven. . . Things that may well be considered necessary for such a chemical basis or alloy might be all birthrights, all hereditary privileges, every state religion and many other things, for only in a really fixed basis of this kind can justice make itself felt and be carried out consistently.

Whereupon Schopenhauer spends quite a while mocking the country that has attempted to operate completely without such an arbitrary basis, that is, to let unalloyed, pure and abstract justice rule: the United States—whose example is not attractive; for, besides base utilitarianism, ignorance, bigotry, conceit, vulgarity, and simple-minded veneration of women, there is also enslavement and mistreatment of negroes, lynch law, unpunished assassination, the most brutal of duels, open disdain for justice and laws, repudiation of public debts, shocking political swindle of neighboring provinces, continually increasing mob rule, and more to boot in everyday occurrence. This testing ground, then, for a purely legal constitution hardly speaks well for republics, and it speaks even less well for the imitations of republics in Mexico, Guatemala, Colombia, and Peru.

It is difficult to make excerpts. But if with the above citations I have succeeded in angering our radicals, republicans, dialecticians of justice and power, and schoolmasters of revolution, I will not regret the effort. For they do not read Schopenhauer, but they do read me, and therefore I had to seize the opportunity to bring them a few confusing items from his statements on politics, by way of forced feeding, as it were. I have only presented a little bit, and only the most drastic part, by no means the most serious and profound one; but it is certainly enough to severely disconcert them. For where is the sovereignty of the people in such ideas? The sovereignty of the people, Schopenhauer says, is a fact, for no one can have the natural right to rule a people against its will. But he hastens to add: "Nevertheless, the people are like an eternally underage sovereign who therefore must, because of his youth, remain under constant guardianship and can never administer his rights himself without bringing about limitless dangers, because he, like all minors, easily becomes the plaything of treacherous scoundrels who therefore are called demagogues." Our theoretician also had the opportunity to realize in a practical way his feelings on people's sovereignty, and to express them in a practical way: this was in September 1848, when, on the Sachsenhäuser bridge, diagonally across from his house, a barricade was set up—and Schopenhauer in '48, that is a sight for the gods, full of immortal cheerfulness! *"The rascals,"* he writes to Frauenstädt, "standing right up by my house, aiming and firing at the soldiers in the street, while the soldiers' countering shots shake the house: suddenly I hear voices and pounding at my locked door: thinking it is the sovereign rabble, I bar the door with the rod . . ." But they are Austrian soldiers, and quickly he opens up for "these worthy friends" so they can "shoot at the sovereign ones" from his window, and he immediately sends his "large binoculars" to the officer who is reconnoitering "the mob behind the barricade" from the second floor of the neighboring house; the binoculars were not enough! Who does he designate—four years later before a notary public and witnesses—as the sole heir to his estate?

> The fund established in Berlin for the support of those Prussian soldiers who were crippled in 1848 and 1849 in the battles of insurrection and mutiny while attempting to establish and maintain legal order, and for the dependents of those soldiers who lost their lives in these battles.

A philistine? Tolstoy called him "the most ingenious of all human beings!" From this philosopher's testament, this demonstrative, grimly scornful deeding of his burgherly possessions, of the staff on which his life was supported, the basis of his spiritual existence, to the fighters for order—from this there speaks, I say, a defiance, a challenge to liberalism that runs no risk of being confused with philistinism, because it is so completely without fear and cowardice in appearing to be philistine; a challenge, scorn, negation, not only of liberalism and revolution, but also of politics itself; an antipolitical, or at least suprapolitical attitude that is German, German-burgherly, German-intellectual: and it has only been with the intention of throwing a little light on this attitude and spirit that I have spent such a long time with Wagner's and Schopenhauer's relationship to politics.

There are no personalities more national than those of these two great Germans of the late burgherly epoch. But the sense of this word, "national," is so vague and uncertain because it can refer both to what one is and to what one advocates, and because the two do not by any means always go together. One does not at all have to advocate what one is; one can, however, strongly advocate, want, and express it, and if one is national, one sometimes also plays the role of the nationalist. Wagner, the national cultural revolutionary, had nationalistic opinions even though he was antipolitical. Schopenhauer, completely unrevolutionary and so unpolitical that he expressly selected the old German verse, "I thank God every morning that I don't have to worry about the Roman Empire,"* for his motto and declared that he did not want to argue matters of state with those "who have the difficult job of governing *human beings*, that is, of maintaining law and order, peace and quiet, among millions of members of a species who are, in the great majority, boundlessly egotistical, unjust, unfair, dishonest, envious, evil, and very narrow-minded and contrary as well." Schopenhauer, then, *was* he not only national? Did he not also perceive, desire, think, and express himself nationally, too? We know that he condescended now and then to make his powerful universal intellect useful to German politics as well. But his literary participation in Germany's fate is limited to the defense against political Anglicizing and to that casual remark very much from on high that the dignity of the emperor, which had been shrewdly removed by Germany's archenemy, the first Bonaparte, had to be restored in the most effective manner; for German unity depended upon it and would always be only nominal or precarious without it. He added that the emperor's crown should alternate between Austria and Prussia for a lifetime. That was not much. Did Schopenhauer perceive nationally?

Caution is in order. Let us say: he did not perceive democratically— and what was democratic must have seemed to him to be the same as national. In this sense, he was antinational. In his human and most

* Ich danke Gott an jedem Morgen, daß ich nicht brauch' fürs Röm'sche Reich zu sorgen.

deeply intellectual character, Schopenhauer was an aristocrat, and his aristocratic attitude expressed itself mainly as radical individualism. For individualism is for Germans not so much a liberal as an aristocratic world view—as was evidenced later by Nietzsche. Schopenhauer's aristocratic attitude comes to the fore a hundred times and at every opportunity; he traces all enmity for anything at all distinguished back to envy, and if the envy of the mob, he says, should finally triumph everywhere, one will still have to allow the nobility of the intellect, of the great thinker, to stand. But his sympathy with all noblesse is so unconditional that he, the burgher who furiously ridicules knightly honor and aristocratic customs, does not hesitate to declare that intellectual nobility will always understand and be compatible with that of birth, with princes and great gentlemen: he says this out of spite against the mob and its envy. But I realized how far his aristocratic attitude reaches into the metaphysical realm in that happy-serious hour when I grasped his Kantian-based teaching on free will: the truth about freedom, he said, is precisely the opposite of what one has long believed; it does not lie in the *operari*, but in the *esse*—thus absolute necessity and determination rule in action, but being is originally and metaphysically free: the human being who commits a crime has of necessity, as an empirical character under the influence of certain motives, *acted in this way*, but he could have *been* different—and the pangs of conscience, too, aim at being, not at action. This is the deepest thought I could ever ponder, or rather: it belongs to those I had reflected upon before they were expressly thought out for me, before I had read them. For if one loves a writer very much, one has—not a logical—but a sympathetic anticipation for the thoughts on the pages one has not yet read, so that all that remains is a fortunate confirmation. I had a similar experience with Schopenhauer's equation of courage and patience.

As one sees, with his metaphysical definition of free will, Schopenhauer rescues, in spite of all determinism, the concept of *guilt*. One understands that this is an aristocratic concept, however, when one thinks of its complement, the concept of *merit*—with which Schopenhauer, as I understand him, was much more concerned than with guilt. Let me remind you that Goethe also likes to speak of "inborn merit"— a coupling of words that is actually absurd from a moral point of view, but incomparably aristocratic. Guilt and merit: an aristocratic double concept; and immediately it produces an aristocratic concept of *justice* that does not say, "To all the same," but rather "To each his own." But just as Schopenhauer's aristocratic attitude is one with his individualism, so also is his antinationalism one with his antidemocratic thought: he was antinational, or rather supranational, because he was an individualist and an aristocrat. He did not love peoples and nations, not even his own. He scarcely saw them, for the masses seemed pitiful to him, or generally to be negated. "Each nation," he says, "laughs at the others, and *all are right.*" He praised his Germans for their lack of national pride, a lack which proved their honesty, while he takes the French to task as only he can do for their tasteless ambition, laughable national pride, and shameless bragging. He is no less insulting to patriotism at home, to the demagoguery of the "German Brothers." Nevertheless, there is *one* point where Schopenhauer's antinationalism becomes weak, where a patriotic, yes, chauvinistic, feeling unexpectedly comes forth— I am referring to the *language.* Schopenhauer was an enthusiastic, fanatic, jealous champion and protector of the German language. This passion is expressed directly in many a proud word in its honor, and indirectly but more strongly through the rage with which he attacks those who spoil this magnificent language, which, in his opinion, was equal to Greek, those who corrupt and bungle it carelessly without love and respect. And his passion is also expressed with almost amusing partiality in the disdainful invectives that he, the European writer, applies to other European languages—particularly to French: "This paltry language, this disgusting jargon, this Italian that has been spoiled in the worst way with the horrible final syllables and the nasals." It is hardly an exaggeration to call Schopenhauer a language chauvinist, and this manifestation of nationalism is certainly the most intellectual one. But the question is whether this nationalistic prejudice does not also reach its ultimate profundity and passion in its highest spiritualization. The question is also whether an intellect that basically perceived aristocratically and that did not believe in the equality of languages could have believed in the equality of nations and could have regarded the "European balance" in a democratic league of nations as the ideal of international policy. The question is whether Schopenhauer's anti-nationalism was of such fully equally genuine origin as was his antidemocratic attitude—whether he did not simply confuse the one with the other under the influence of the times—whether the cosmopolitanism of the German burgher is not something different from democratic internationalism, and whether such burgherly cosmopolitanism does not get along quite well with deeper national ties.

I have indicated how far Schopenhauer was a "European" in the sense of civilization's literary man: he was European as a writer, as an essayist, and as a worldly literary man. But precisely in him, supra-Germanness is an intensification, not a blurring and abrogation, of German nationality, least of all an adoration of the political West. As a philosopher he was, of course, not only supranational, but also supra-European, an Asian, the first great admirer of Asia in Europe, and I would like to know, or rather, I know, what he would have said if he had read in a "European newspaper" that the English had "awakened the soul" of the Indians "to revolt." No, if the definition of the European that we have recently been presented: to wit, that he is nothing else than the humanitarian man of business and progress—if this brilliantly presented definition is correct, then Arthur Schopenhauer was not a European. But then, who has been, really, up to now, with the exception of the highly honorable members of the East India Company?

I said I wanted to explore here the meaning and spirit of German burgherly nature. What is important to me is the reinstatement of the very concept of the "burgher" in its purity and dignity, after it has been spoiled in the most abusive way by a literary group that lives and works in a world of foreign concepts. In truth, the word "burgher" as a favorite term of abuse of our literati is, to use Wagner's language, "in Germany a completely alien creature." It is the mechanical-literary translation of the French "bourgeois," as the Parisian *bohème*, the romantic gypsy world of 1830, saw and interpreted him: of the great unartistic, narrow-minded utilitarian who merely served with the sight of his miserable smugness to make the velvet-coated magnificence of the artistic libertine even more pleased with himself. German roman-ticism had no generally accepted word that would have corresponded to the French *bohémien*. And as far as the word "bourgeois" is concerned, it has, of course, been internationalized by the capitalistic era, but to translate it with "burgher" is mischief of the literati. German romanti-cism spoke of the "philistine"; but burgher and philistine are not only different, they are opposites. For the philistine is the essentially unro-mantic human being; while the German burgher definitely has a romantic element. The burgher is a romantic individualist, for he is the spiritual product of a suprapolitical or at least prepolitical epoch, of an epoch of humanism in which, as Turgenev says in his *Faust* critique, "society fell apart into atoms and went as far as its own negation, in which every burgher was transformed into a *human being*." Let us call the burgher—and of course one does so today—in his pure spiritual form, an atomist: it will always be difficult to equate this concept of atomistic cultural individualism with that of philistinism. The philistine is a narrow-minded townsman, a citizen of the *state*, and nothing more, nothing beyond this; thus Schopenhauer, who declared the state to be simply a protective institution against the inborn injustice of the human race, reviled the "philosophizers" (namely Hegel) "who in pompous rhetoric present the state as the highest purpose and blossoming of human existence and *thereby deliver an apotheosis of philistinism.*" The German burgher is today a citizen of the state and of the empire, and the war is working powerfully toward the completion of his political education. But he will never be a state philistine, a *Reich* philistine. He will never come to believe that the state is the purpose and meaning of human existence, that the destiny of the human being is found in the state and *that politics makes people more human.* The fact that was our starting point: that the mixture of artistry and burgherly nature in Germany is a legitimate intellectual way of life, teaches clearly and distinctly that there can simply be no question here of some kind of necessary-essential antithesis; and that the snobbishness of the artist and the intellectual toward the "burgher" is simply bad manners and in Germany something completely foreign. May the artist, the gypsy and libertine not forget, or may he finally realize, that there is a good bit of him in the German burgher: for artistry, the gypsy spirit, and libertinism make up the suprapolitical part of human nature, the part not consumed by the state and society—the atomistic-individualistic part that for the German burgher is almost human nature itself. What one calls "liberalism" may only be the political form and stagnation of this his human libertinism; and if liberalism is nothing of value, in secret has become another name for lack of character, this only proves that politics simply spoils everything. In any case, the arrogance with which the cosmopolitan literary man has been speaking of the "burgher" for ten years did not just begin yesterday to make me impatient: all the more impatient because I may previously even have given him the weapons. In the end, being a German burgher is not the worst thing one can be. German burgherly nature was always German humanity, freedom, and culture. The German burgher was really the German human being; and everything that strove for freedom and intellectuality, both from above and below, strove toward his center.

"But what kind of dreams are you speaking from! What vintage are you, when and where have you been living! Casually you mention that the word bourgeois has been internationalized by the capitalistic era; but you know very well, of course, that the thing itself, that the bourgeois himself, has been internationalized, that he is as much at home in

Germany as anywhere! Have you been sleeping? Have you slept through the development, no, the direct transformation, as if by Circe's wand, of the German burgher, his dehumanization and loss of soul, his *hardening* into the capitalistic-imperialistic bourgeois? The *hard* burgher: this is the bourgeois. The spiritual burgher does not exist anymore. You talk of times gone by, of 1850, perhaps, but not of 1900. In between was Bismarck, in between was the triumph of '*Realpolitik*', the tempering and hardening of Germany into a '*Reich*'; the entry of science into industry and of industry into science; the regulation, cooling and turning to hostility of the patriarchal-human relationships of employer and worker that had become impossible because of social legislation; emancipation and exploitation; power, power, power! What is science today? Narrow and hard specialization for profit, exploitation, and control. What is culture? Humanity perhaps? Breadth and goodness? No, nothing more than a means for earning money and for dominance. What is philosophy? Perhaps still not a way of earning money, but also very narrow specialization in the style and spirit of the times. Just look at him, your 'German burgher' of today, this imperialistic mine owner who would not hesitate to sacrifice five hundred thousand human beings and twice as many more to annex Briey and to be lord of the world! Again, you have been sleeping, you are still asleep, you are speaking in a dream."

Must I reply? This book is self-explanation and self-enlightenment— not polemics; although my self-explanation of necessity assumes polemic forms now and then. It would like to have *form*—and what may seem to be polemics is just a chiseling away, formation and contour. Thus here, too, I only want to explain and define myself, not to polemicize— there is not much to say against the above protest and alarm. For it is true, I have slept a little through the metamorphosis of the German burgher into the bourgeois. Still, I know about it, but scarcely otherwise than from rumor. Although I was born five years after 1870, I did not really experience it. How did this come about?

First of all, I spent my childhood and early youth in a politically independent, oligarchical city democracy of the northwest, in an old burgherly-ceremonious community of strongly conservative stamp that had not derived much material advantage from the creation of the empire (I wrote, you know, of the fall of a business establishment there midst the prosperity of victorious Germany—and of the adventurous excursion of its last proprietor into the field of burgherly-pessimistic philosophy) and whose social conditions, even though a social democratic parliamentary candidate not only ran for office but was even elected, retained a patriarchal character long into my life. When I recall the tone, the relationship, between my father and his warehouse workers, I am hardly ready to believe that emancipation and social legislation have furthered humanity and human dignity very much. I am careful not to revolt against the necessary changes of the times, and I do not shed tears over things that are passé, but I will not be persuaded that progress is always a progress toward something happier and better. Burgherly nature, then, indeed, partriarchal-aristocratic burgherly nature as the mood and feeling of life, is my personal inheritance. The burgherly nature that surrounded my youth and that had very little to do with the nature of the neo-German bourgeoisie, was, to be sure, on the average, anything but an intellectual burgherly nature; literature may well have seemed to it to be an oddity and an eccentricity that aroused suspicion. It was magnificently businessman-materialistic, and one could only call it artistic in a very objective sense, as a manifestation of its age, its tradition and culture, its style, in short, of its being and not of its feeling. But my real experience, which enabled me to give to literature a work characteristic of the history of German burgherdom, was the "decay" of such an old and genuine burgherly nature into something subjective-artistic: an experience and problem of overrefinement and loss of fitness, not of hardening; a life process that somehow I did not just experience critically at first hand as a contemporary, but that I was born to contemplate directly and deeply. In a word: what I experienced and formed—but I experienced it undoubtedly only *by* forming it—was *also* a development and modernization of the burgher, not his development into a bourgeois, but his development into an *artist*. And if I contrasted the rising burgher, the newcomer, the speculative buyer and successor, with the declining burgher, it was only in passing, without my in any way being particularly interested in this opposing type. The burning problem for me that stimulated me to write was not a political one, but a biological, psychological one; and it was again certainly very German for me, as an artist, to give all my attention to it: the psychological-human element was my main interest; I included the socio-political one only half subconsciously; it did not preoccupy me much.

Furthermore, it was in *Munich*, to where I was transplanted at an early age, that I wrote the book in which I gave form to that psychological experience—and this chance, or nonchance, again signifies an excuse for, and an explanation of, my political sleepiness. Obviously the

Bavarian capital took part to some extent in the transformation of things German. The penetration of a new German spirit, the Americanization of the German life style, expressed itself there in a certain clumsy corruption, in profiteering and enterprising ventures of a characteristically naive tone, and my indifference did not prevent me from getting to see this and that. The city, following its own law in modernization, maintained its historical character as a cultural center of the arts by eagerly developing it into a tourist industry; today, in times of peace, it is a metropolitan spa with a flourishing hotel business and with a sort of society for the preservation of local amenities at the top, which, with the heaviest of advertising, is intent on offering a lavish amount of elegant native, culturally enjoyable entertainment to a tourist audience streaming in from all parts of the world. Its deep-rooted, artistic culture is less spiritual than material; Munich is the city of applied, indeed, of festively applied art, and the typical Munich artist is always a born festival organizer and carnival man. That I, as long as I have been living here, have lived in a certain protest against this material, entertainment culture, perhaps lent a personal touch to that spiritually fanatic monastic criticism in *Fiorenza* that was delivered at the court of Lorenzo the Magnificent. That I *remained*, and did not move, say, to Berlin, was, however, not simple laziness. It would be idle to ask myself what would have become of me if I had spent these twenty-two years, the first half of which were decisive years of development, not here, but in the sharp air of the Prussian-American metropolis. At any rate, there is a stimulus and profit in living in protest and irony against one's surroundings; it elevates the feeling of life, one lives truer to oneself and with greater self-confidence under these circumstances. But when I reflect, I find that for this reason the atmosphere of Munich had and retained something congenial and suitable for me, that the old German mixture of art and burgherly nature is still very much alive and current here. This city is completely unliterary; literature has no footing here. But just as little as the Munich burgher knows what a literary man is—he actually has not the faintest idea; the writer lives here completely incognito—all the more does he know what an artist is; and not just because his kings have taught him. Frank Wedekind said once that the Munich burgher was himself an artist, because he wanted his peace and quiet, and because he wanted to amuse himself. This remains, of course, a highly Munich-like definition of artistic genius that will scarcely be understood in other places: it is precisely against it that I have lived for twenty years in quiet protest. But the most important thing is that here in an old, genuine way, artistic genius really arises from burgherdom and remains intertwined with it, that old, established Munich burgherdom and craftmanship are artistically combined: the intellectual-cultural, even the social, distance between the handworker (*artista*) of impersonal, nonscholarly culture and the academic artist is very small, and it is typical of Munich that of two brothers, bearers of an old burgherly name, the one is perhaps a baker or brewer (and a member of the "Art Union!"), and the other a famous architect or brass founder. These cultural relationships are very old German-townish—nowhere does one hear *Die Meistersinger* better than in Munich: better than in bourgeois Nuremberg—and certainly they contributed to the fact that I did not experience the development of the German burgher into a bourgeois: they kept a burgherly nature present for me that, to be sure, was even more unintellectual in the literary sense than the one of my home, and that did not possess the materialistic-aristocratic cultural life of my home, either, but that instead presented itself directly as a material-artistic culture; and what I saw growing out of the burgherly character was again not the hard bourgeois, but the artist, and this time without the slightest hint of degeneration.

In short, I must admit that I have been lucky; I have not experienced the development in a bad way. My origin and my experience have almost prevented me from seeing the transformation of the German burgher into a bourgeois. My "education" did it for me, too—if I, as an artist belonging to a generation of "naturalists" that was not exactly bent on positive erudition, can lay any claim at all to intellectual education. I have named the two geniuses who were my intellectual educators and who were not only close to the world of art, but who also, with a large part of their being, were active in it. I do not know the specialized bourgeois philosopher, I have not read him. I have not got beyond Schopenhauer and Nietzsche—and by my honor, they were not bourgeois. Schopenhauer was still completely a part of the burgherly-romantic age; and no matter how far Nietzsche reaches beyond the romantic and the burgherly epochs, no matter how much he inaugurates the new movement that is still nameless, or at least not to be named in a word: his intimate connection with German romanticism has been presented most beautifully in a learned-literary manner (Joel), and the finest roots of his being lie in a sphere of German-idealistic humanity that permeates even such late statements as these sentences from a letter to Overbeck (from 1880!): "I am so indebted to you, dear friend, for being allowed to observe the drama of your life so closely: indeed, Basel certainly gave me *your* picture and Jacob Burckhardt's . . . The *dignity* and *grace* of a special and essentially secluded path in life and knowledge: this drama was simply 'given' to me by the kindness of my fate, a generosity that cannot be appreciated too greatly." Is not this precisely the spirit from which the antithesis of the *furor philosophicus* and the *furor politicus* arises? Truly a German antithesis! "Philosophy" here means something highly un-French and also not exclusively erudite. The word is used here in the burgherly-cultural, in the German sense, and when Nietzsche, who called himself "the last nonpolitical German," placed the philosophical, intellectual disposition above the political one as better, higher, nobler, this, too, is most German, most burgherly in the sense I give to this word—and to me, no chronological objection seems to be valid against this idea of German nature as burgherly nature: as I live and breathe, I cannot help seeing it as something immortal that cannot seriously be attacked by any development or progress.

At the head of the *Reich* today stands a man who is known in the vernacular and in the satirical press as a "philosopher." This is a joke because it means that he is a bad politician. But if one admits that Herr von Bethmann Hollweg, politician or not, is in the right place, precisely during this time of war, as an honest exponent of the German character; if one finds it *good*, as I find it right and proper, that the smooth, stylish, and much more *entente*-like Prince Bülow does not occupy this position today; if one also recognizes that the statesman who represents the Germany of this war spiritual-politically is neither a Junker nor a bourgeois, but a representative of burgherly nature, of culture, of humanity, of "philosophy," of morality in the most spiritual, dignified sense: then one has admitted that German character still typically reveals itself under the sign of what I call the burgherly nature. I will never deny my sympathy for the person of this chancellor of the *Reich*, or at least for the type he represents, in spite of all my understanding of the concern, yes, the hatred, of the patriots who attack him. It is not by chance that he is governing today, nor is it by chance that he still stands so firmly in spite of all attacks. There are spiritual, yes, no matter how far-fetched it sounds, there are artistic, reasons why one would scarcely decide to remove him during this crisis of the German way of life.

Am I finished? Not quite. For after I have said why I, to a certain extent, slept through the transformation of the German burgher into a bourgeois—the reason was that I experienced the process of the loss of burgherly nature in an all too intimately psychological, completely unpolitical way—I do not wish to remain silent about how far the burgher in his *modernness* has nevertheless neither remained completely beyond my perception nor even beyond my emotional interest—yes, how far such perception and interest have taken form in my literary work. From the beginning, my insignificant prose has been so little able to do without a critical admixture that for me the concepts "prose" and "criticism" have seemed almost identical. But my critical attitude has always been directed at *life*, not at any political misfortunes, and even though to me writing, yes, fiction, has meant hardly anything else than intellectual criticism of reality, I have still perhaps been too positively attuned to be creatively disposed toward a purely negative characterization, toward lampoons, toward satire that is without pity. I do not believe that form can develop at all without sympathy—pure negation produces flat caricature. If I have understood anything at all of my times sympathetically, it is its type of heroism, the modern-heroic life form and attitude of the overburdened, overdisciplined *moralist of accomplishment* "working at the edge of exhaustion," and here is my psychological contact with the character of the new burgher, my only contact, but one that is important and moving to me. I have never created him in real, political-economic form; I had neither enough sympathy nor understanding to do this. But fiction has always seemed to me to be symbolic, and I may say that I have hardly written anything that has not been symbolic of the heroism of this modern, neoburgherly character. Yes, seen in this way, Thomas Buddenbrook is not only a German burgher, but also a modern bourgeois; he is the first figure in whose formation this decisive experience participated; and this experience worked formatively, creating symbols in my work from the main characters of the Renaissance play, through all the figures in the novel about the prince, all the way to Gustav Aschenbach.

I place some value on the fact that I sensed and discovered the idea that the modern capitalistic businessman, the bourgeois, with his *ascetic* idea of duty to his career, was a creation of the Protestant ethic, of Puritanism and Calvinism, that I came to this idea completely on my own, without reading, by direct insight, and that I only discovered afterward, recently, that it had been thought and expressed at the same time by learned thinkers. Max Weber in Heidelberg, and after him, Ernst Troeltsch, have treated *The Protestant Ethic and the Spirit of Capitalism*, and the thought is also found in greatly exaggerated form in

Werner Sombart's work of 1913, *The Bourgeois*—which interprets the capitalistic entrepreneur as a synthesis of hero, merchant, and burgher. That he is to a great degree correct is seen by the fact that as a novelist I had given form to his message twelve years before he presented it: assuming, that is, that the figure of Thomas Buddenbrook, the anticipatory embodiment of his hypothesis, has been without influence on Sombart's thought. But what I would like to add as something new is the conjecture, which is almost a certainty, that our agreement on the psychological series, "Calvinism, burgherly nature, heroism," comes from a higher, the highest intellectual source: from *Nietzsche*; for without this epoch-dominating experience that influences all experiencing of the era, even to the smallest detail, and that was, in an unprecedentedly new, modern way, a heroic experience, the social scientist would doubtlessly just as little have reached his Protestant-heroic message as the novelist would have conceived the figure of his "hero" as he did. Bernoulli, in his Overbeck-Nietzsche book, trying to give the reader an idea of Nietzsche's "heroism of weakness," comes upon the idea of quoting a passage from my *Fiorenza* dialogues; he would not have thought of this if the dialogue had not been saturated with Nietzsche's spirit. But this is also the same Swiss scholar who somewhere called Nietzsche a "godless Calvin," and at another place documented very well that Nietzsche, from a political point of view, was originally an advocate of the *middle class*.

My youth, I may say, did not prevent me from recognizing the moralist in Nietzsche at a time when his fashionable, vulgar effect had turned into a sort of hectic adoration of power and "beauty." But the psychological preconditions and origins of the ethical tragedy of his life, of this immortal European drama of self-conquest, self-discipline and self-crucifixion with the intellectual sacrificial death as a heart- and brain-rending conclusion—where else are they to be found than in the Protestantism of the Naumburg preacher's son, than in that Nordic-German, burgherly-moral sphere of Dürer where the engraving, "Knight, Death and Devil," stands, and that has always remained the native sphere of this stern, completely "un-southern" soul? "I like in Wagner," he writes in October 1868, to Rohde, "what I like in Schopenhauer: the ethical air, the Faustian smell, cross, death and grave." This was at the time in Basel when he heard the *St. Matthew Passion* three times in one week—Easter Week—cross, death and grave! He hurled his late, sulphurous lightning bolts against the "ascetic ideal," but he himself was the most unconditional and fanatic ascetic of intellectual history. He called Renan a clown *in psychologicis* because Renan brought the concepts "genius" and "hero" into the personality of Christ, but he, what was he, himself, anyway, if not hero, genius and "crucified one" in one person? For truthfully, one should not believe that the signature on that insane note to the Danish critic was an idiotic and meaningless signature.

Am I to be scolded because I speak or stutter of such high and terrible things when the subject at hand is much smaller, the bourgeois man of business and accomplishment and my psychological-symbolic sympathy with him that prevented me from perceiving him as a completely repulsive type? The world is deep—everywhere in every manifestation; and I see now that the tragic-ethical Nietzsche experience played a part in my experience of the burgherly moralist of accomplishment, even if this may not at all have been true for the learned psychologists of capitalism. I see further that precisely this insight of feeling into the connection between the capitalistic, neoburgherly character and the Protestant ethic comes from a certain modernity of my work that is critical of the times. And I see finally that my "patriotism" of 1914 was quite essentially a sudden and probably quite ephemeral politicization of this sympathy, of this symbolic participation.

Anno 1914, "civilization" declared it was taking the field "against militarism." Well, what "militarism" meant to me was almost nothing other than modernity and the dangerous and highly tensed existence with "bad borders." What I understood by civilization was the opposite, namely security and indolence. Germany's heroism, indefinable in its nature as attack *or* defense, seemed, to be sure, to be no heroism of weakness at all, but of robust power; nevertheless, it was still the same heroism that permeated the whole history of the development of this improbable and still so completely real *Reich*—of this empire in which, for foreign as well as domestic reasons, it is almost impossible to be political, and which nevertheless, by its power, efficiency, and modernity, is committed to great undertakings, great politics—of this nation, which, like Hamlet, was not actually born to action, but was unavoidably called to it. To be called, whether it be to knowledge or to action, to what one is not born to, has always seemed to me to be the meaning of tragedy—and where there is tragedy, there may also be love. Early on, admiration for the Schopenhauerian equation of courage and patience, the love of the "nevertheless," or—that I may once again release the miserably ridiculed phrase—of the ethos of "carrying on to the end," led me to the statue of that uncanny and popular king, whose deeds and suffering paved the way for all this. It was laughable how exactly I saw Frederick's history repeating itself in the history of the origin of our war. I wrote them down, one together with the other. I was enthusiastic, yes. But not as a *patriotard* or a zealous fellow traveler is enthusiastic, but enthusiastic because of history, of psychological recognition—and of endless sympathy. This sympathy for, this being deeply moved by, Germany's tragic-historical fate was "anti-intellectual" in the opinion of civilization's literary man, I know that. But I believe it was human and poetic, and I will never be ashamed of it.

CHAPTER 6

"Against Justice and Truth"

It is becoming clear: if I am to call my right to patriotism in question, if it needs defense before my conscience, the reason is not so much that I am not really a true German as that my relationship to *politics* is, in a good German fashion, a nonrelationship. For politics is participation in the state, zeal and passion for the state—and people like me have anything but a Hegelian attitude. I do not find that the state is "to be admired as something earthly divine." I see no "self-purpose" in it—I see something technical more than something spiritual, a machine to be supervised and taken care of by the experts. Not only do I disagree that human destiny should be absorbed in state and society, I even find this opinion repulsively inhuman; I think that the most important aspects of the human spirit—religion, philosophy, art, poetry, science—exist beside, above, and beyond the state, and often enough even against it; every application and applicability of these areas of the human intellect as agents of the state—every official, uniformed, and regimented spirit, that is—seems to me to provoke irony. I feel the same way about a "Department of Fine Arts"; personally, I have never liked to deal with the state. My feelings for it have always been as dissolutely lukewarm and individualistically unsubmissive as possible; I have been a nonpolitical human being, what civilization's literary man calls an "esthete." But is not patriotism politics? Does it not remain, *as* politics, an eccentricity for the artist? For politics is inhuman; but the artist's concern is, after all, if not "humanity," then at least what is human. I understand completely those who declare: "I cannot love or hate a whole nation; I know only human beings." Good. Now and then I also think that only this attitude becomes an artist—*although*. . . Although at first the sudden grotesque personification of the nations, the appearance of their humanity on a grand scale because of the war, had, especially for the artist, something highly vivid and exciting. Events like these suddenly powerfully emphasize the individuality of nations, their eternal physiognomies. Their original purpose, their "intelligible character," seemed to stand out like a rocky cliff: England, France, Germany and Italy have all conducted themselves so typically, so very much according to the book, to the fairy tale book, that in my opinion the artist was even more to be excused than the historian if the strongest desire to observe and reflect shook and inspired him. Politics? But it was *not* politics when one found the Chancellor's speech on the "injustice" Germany was supposed to be committing by the march into Belgium "*beautiful*," even if one also found it anything but political and not even accurate. For the deeply affected man's attitude and manner of speaking had no *intention* of being political. It was nonpolitical and antipolitical in the most German way; it was so genuine, so grand because of its genuineness, so suited to the suprapolitical, powerfully ethical moment, that political objections to it will always seem pitiful. A fresco-psychology, then, national-psychological understanding and self-knowledge, flourishes in times like these: one gets to know *oneself*, one is reminded most deeply of many things, and one becomes aware of one's nationality; and since, in times of trouble, self-denial would be a pitiful weakness; since in such times, self-knowledge and self-assertion are one, must be one, it is therefore hardly a step from knowledge of oneself to self-assurance, to warlike pleasure in oneself, to impersonal pride, to "patriotism." It is true: war favors, it almost forces, primitive views, primitive emotions; but should this definitely be an objection to it for the artist? It is true: to regard nations as mythical individuals is a primitive-popular way of regarding things, and patriotism itself may signify an emotion of more mythical-primitive than political-intellectual nature. But it seems to me that an artist to whom the primitive element had become completely foreign, who had become absolutely incapable of ever "relapsing" into the primitive, would be in a bad way. An artist is perhaps only an artist and poet as far as he is *not* alienated from the primitive; and even if he is a "burgher," he is still perhaps only an artist and poet as far as he is national and has not completely forgotten how to observe and feel in a nationally primitive way. "The people," Paul de Lagarde says in his polemic against universal suffrage,

> The people do not speak at all when the single individuals speak who make up the people. The people only speak when national character . . . becomes vocal in the individuals: that is, when the conscious-

ness of a common basic tribal nature of all the individuals awakens and clearly sees its relationship to great historical events. . . The people remain completely silent on individual laws and individual administrative measures, even if one seeks and receives their opinions, man by man.

It seems to me that in this sense, the political attitude of the artist and the creative writer is national. His political hour has come when "the national character becomes vocal in the individuals," not where technical governmental questions are concerned; it has come, to differentiate with Lagarde, when what counts is enthusiasm and not business. His concern is not for the state, but it is very much for the fatherland, and the experience of the war has shown him that he has, perhaps for the first time, come to see the fatherland clearly after such a long distortion of his view of it by politics and the state—to realize with deep emotion the relationship of the national character, which has also become vocal in him, to the great events of history.

But let us now, moreover, put ourselves in the position of someone for whom this defensive attitude and perforce nationally-intellectual self-assertion did not just arise in August 1914, as it did for most people, but who had rather lived for a long time in brotherly closeness to a significant way of thinking, that, for its part, was aggressive in a naive-French way, and that at the outbreak of the war had immediately been able to ally itself to the world that was foaming with rage against Germany; for no outpouring of foreign hatred exceeded or even matched its own uninhibited, pitiless and overwhelming rage against the being and essence, the historical experience, the real character of this country; a way of thinking that had long insisted with the most cuttingly intolerant sharpness that one either admit that Germany— Germany of all countries!—was the moral shame of humanity, or that one give up all claim to being a thinking man; a way of thinking that had regarded the German Empire as a complete facade of pomp and propaganda behind which lay only putrefaction and decay, brutality and slavish misery; a way of thinking that made a travesty of the deep honesty of German self-loathing, seeking to falsify in a satirically talented manner the Germany of the past forty years as a *second empire à la* Offenbach that was rushing toward a humiliating *débâcle*: and all this for the simple reason that Germany had not been a democracy in the elevating-Western spirit of "humanity"! How could I, who out of simple fairness had refused to share such doggedly mistaken doctrines— how could I not feel the deepest satisfaction when they were proven to be so ridiculously wrong; when Germany showed she could handle herself a little better in a storm than some kind of worm-eaten, prestige-empire of 1870! God save me from pigheadedness and wanting to be right in the end! I despise a person as crude both in a human and an intellectual sense who is not embarrassed at having won an argument, who does not immediately try to hush up the fact that he was right. But here, for this one great time, being right is sweet, and I do not have to be ashamed of it, since it is not a vain triumph of argument, but a moving self-revelation of truth—since it does not concern me, but a great and special nation beyond me.

Beyond me. Show me where I ever, in a moment of swaggering rashness, included myself, said "we," when I spoke of Germany: in the manner of certain insatiable stomachs from which the demand for abundant annexations resounds because "we" "must not have bled in vain"; show me such a "we," and I will be a chauvinistic braggart as long as I live. Never was the individual distancing of the *I* from the whole so much a commandment of propriety, a commandment of pride and modesty, as today when personal importance swells up behind the national symbol, and many a rascal may imagine he is less of a rascal because he can call himself a German rascal. Oh, that I were a Swede or a Luxemburger so I could provide documentation to counteract the suspicion that my patriotism is an attempt to decorate myself with borrowed plumes and to cover my nakedness with the national cloak of honor. No! Here I am, and there is Germany. My honor gains nothing from her virtue. I am detached. I observe. I prefer to be wretched on my own than to borrow fame from the nation by being "absorbed" in it. To be absorbed in the nation with a war cry—this is not a bad way of forgetting one's own weakness and causing others to forget it. I declare that I completely reject it, this way.

Beyond me. Truly, here is a further doubt about my *right* to patriotism! What do I basically have in common with this vigorous nation whose colossal ability today forms the horror and admiration of those who have joined together to destroy it? Chronicler and interpreter of decadence, fancier of the pathological and of death, an esthete with a tendency toward the abyss: how could *I* come to identify myself with Germany, How do *I* come to positive participation in the war, to patriotic enthusiasm? Does this suit me? Is it proper for me? Can it be genuine? Let me answer this with reference to a great man who was deeply ill from youth on, thoroughly pathological in every selection of artistic themes, hysterical, extreme, romantic, "hypochondriacal," a nuisance to Goethe. And who still, when Germany was in need, found the thunderous phrases of the "community" that could only be destroyed in a bloodbath *that would darken the sun*. Was this proper for him? Did it suit the suffering, complicated man to be simple? To love here, to hate there? Would it not have been more proper for this man of the spirit to honor Napoleon, to wish for the completion of the revolutionary imperium, the unified French Europe? This would undoubtably have been more literary. But quite clearly he was not literary. Quite clearly he was lacking in that "spiritualization" that, according to our radical literary man, who knows from experience, leads one "so far above one's compatriots that certain national events seem to make one appear as isolated as an enemy." No, he did not believe that he owed his genius such a separation. His disposition did not demand that he bear "banishment and silence" as civilization's literary man—with rhetorical blarney—insists he must do today. He spoke. And it was not a feeling of being misunderstood and arrogant alienation that spoke from him. The pathologically tortured artist, whose greatness was unrecognized by his contemporaries and who could not feel any obligation of personal gratitude, spoke for Germany in the most heartfelt, thrilling accents: yes, this hysterical Junker—logician, propagandist, daredevil and hot-head of irrationality and of regression to subhuman weakness, taking part in the struggle, irresponsibly spurring people on, beside himself with feelings of grandeur, became for Germany's sake an impetuous journalist. He wrote that article, those two pages of powerful and in the most serious sense oratorical prose with the title, "What Is at Stake in This War?" It could have been written word for word two years ago instead of a hundred, and it would surely have been branded by certain intellectual gentlemen as a rabble-rousing article. No doubt his spiritualization had not progressed very far. How, otherwise, could he have become guilty of the criminal thoughtlessness—if not something worse—of confusing the people, his people, the eternal people, with the chance living generation whose vices and errors he certainly knew; of confusing the humanly-faulty community of the living with that elevated one whose existence, as he said, had been sanctified by a third of a terrestrial era, the one that, unacquainted with the spirit of dominance and conquest, was as worthy of existence and of tolerance as any; that, far from having even a ripple of pride in its bosom, has not believed in its own greatness up to the present day, but has fluttered about tirelessly like a bee, absorbing everything it has found to be excellent, just as if it contained nothing in itself of original beauty, even though in its bosom the gods have preserved humanity's archetype more purely than in any other; with that community that has produced Leibniz, Gutenberg and Keppler, Hutten and Sickingen, Luther and Melanchthon, Joseph and Frederick, Dürer, Cranach and Klopstock, the community that even the savages of the south seas would rush to protect if they were acquainted with it, the community whose existence no German breast should outlive? How, I ask, could Kleist have become guilty of this thoughtlessness and confusion if he had not been a false intellectual, falsely enthusiastic, a flatterer and careerist who wanted to become a "national poet": just like us miserable ones of today who have not carried spiritualization to the desired height over our compatriots and whom civilization's literary man accuses of the same crime as well as of the same motives? One could object that the chance, humanly-faulty, living generation was just the contemporary manifestation of that high and idealistically transfigured community; that it is difficult in times like these to separate the contemporary people from the eternal people so completely; that the former are in danger with the latter; that the living generation must fight out in the flesh the cause of the eternal people, and that if they are not morally worthy of this task, then earlier living generations were probably not worthier of it. One could point out that, as Lagarde says, "a people, to be sure, has a natural basis and consists of individuals, but this natural basis in nationality is translated from the physical into the historical and therefore no longer exists as something purely physical." Finally, one could add: if it becomes all too unpleasant for civilization's literary man to think of such things, then he should rather spare the political moralizing. But such objections and reminders would be unnecessary, for the demagogic confusion that so embitters civilization's literary man does not exist—neither in Kleist's case nor with us false intellectuals of today, who, as civilization's literary man says, "are giving logical support to irrationality"—does not exist, I say, and I will prove it.

"Perhaps you think," the question is asked in the *Catechism of the Germans*, "that as matters stood the Germans were already at the height of all virtue, prosperity and fame?" The answer is, "Not at all, my father." And again: "Or that they were at least well on the way toward reaching it?" The answer: "No, my father, not that either." "What kind of bad habit have I talked to you about from time to time?" "Bad habit?" "Yes, that clings to the *present generation*." The answer is that this bad habit was an overexcited state of mind. The Germans reflected when they should have felt or acted. They thought they could accomplish everything by their wits, and they no longer paid heed to the old, mysterious power of the heart. But then: "What did they cling to," the questioning continues, "with immoderate and ignoble love?" "To money and property. They eagerly pursued business so that the sweat rolled quite pitifully down their foreheads, and they thought that a peaceful, comfortable and carefree life was all that could be achieved in this world." And then comes the question: "Why did the misery, which is part of the times, come over them?" And the answer: "To make these goods completely despicable to them and to stimulate them to aim for the higher, the highest things that God has given to mankind." "And what are the highest goods of mankind?" "God, fatherland, emperor, freedom, love and loyalty, beauty, science and art."

A crazy list! A crazy, highly antiliterary ranking of values. Religion first, fatherland and emperor second and third, freedom fourth, and literature at the very end! But is the present generation being confused here with the eternal people? Is it being treated with base flattery? Is it even being treated with indulgence? No, not at all; nor was it two years ago, either! No one told the German nation it had reached the height of virtue, or that it was well on the way to reaching it. Immediately, in the first frenzy of purification and of rising-up, reflection spoke, recalling the past. I do not envy the one, I envy no one, who could exclude himself at that time, who could remain unmoved by a shock that spread everywhere, whose waves immediately reached the man living out of the way and alone in the country, the man living beyond the seas, seizing them and awakening in every breast the most profound, the oldest, the simplest and the strongest feelings. I am repelled by a morality that points a pedantically raised finger at a challenged Germany and says that only when she has been morally purified by "internal politics," by some sort of Dreyfus affair, will she be justified in turning in any way toward the outside—as if the powerful and enthusiastic unification of the nation in preparation for its greatest test, in the high and joyfully serious preparation, which is free from frivolity and from arrogance, to face its moment of truth, its "day of fame," as Goethe called it in 1813 in that conversation with Luden—as if all this did not perhaps from a distance have everything to do with morality. I am suspicious of the stiffly rejecting coldness of a "spiritualization" that considers itself too noble to dream, if only for a day or an hour, a nation's dream of affliction and of deeds born of necessity, and that holds itself aloof in a malicious-stubborn way from this nation's accomplishments, which are unprecedented in all history and which are even looked upon with astonishment by its perceptive enemies as unprecedented—only because it would not otherwise "be right in the end"; because otherwise it would have to answer the question of whether a low-minded, servile people could be capable of such accomplishments—and that finally, in order to justify its obdurate position, feels it can call on Goethe, whom it otherwise taboos as an esthete, a quietist and a servant of princes, on the Goethe of 1813, for support: just as if Goethe, who saw on the opposing side not as we do Messrs. Asquith and Poincaré, but Napoleon Bonaparte, would have been a radical literary man and stupid enough to fall for the humanitarian lie proclaimed from democratic imperialism's raised bosom—he, who certainly was not less aware of Germany's "special nature" than was Dostoyevsky, who repeated his emperor's words that "the fate of the Germans had not yet been fulfilled," that they would have collapsed long ago if they had had no other task to fulfill than to crush the Roman Empire and to create and organize a new world. Finally, it is idle to the point of insipidness to cite the spirit of the master of a past national epoch in order to ascertain his opinion about the present world situation; for what one hears from such a childish experiment is not Goethe's word, but an empty and vacuous voice of a ghost that comes from ourselves, while we want to convince ourselves that it resounds from eternity. The immortalized spirit has entered into our world, not above or beyond it, and we cannot even seriously consider the spirit of the recently deceased one who in the flesh was called Friedrich Nietzsche to be judging us from above or beyond. Yes, it is senseless even to ask quite generally how a person of Goethe's rank living today would judge our situation; for there is no such person, and it is no accident that no such person is living; it is a result of the times, and the intellectual coupling of Goethean majesty with these democratic times that are not watched over by personal greatness is completely unprofitable and meaningless. In the meantime, there are literati who make the greatest effort to show the same attitude toward events as the sovereign of a cosmopolitan cultural epoch probably would have had, he who was only concerned at heart with the question: culture or barbarism, and who indeed would have preferred to see the French in Germany rather than our allies of that time, the Cossacks and the Bashkirs. I do not respect them at all. To repeat, I suspect that "spiritualization" that calls itself democratic when it is the opposite, namely the most arrogant alienation and aloofness; I not only suspect it, I saw and know what it is really about. I know and saw that this "spiritualization" is equivalent to a dogmatic anxiety for a pampered system of ideas that one suddenly to one's horror sees exposed to a stormy draft. "My ideas! What is going to become of my ideas?" This was their first question at the outbreak of the war and will always be their one and only question. But I was not aware that those who were not and are not a part of such a spiritualization had become guilty of confusing the present generation with the idealized people and of having flattered the former; on the contrary, I remember the complaints about pessimism and a tone of penitence that characterized descriptions of prewar conditions. At the time, it seems to me, many an extreme word was said about wolfish mercantilism, intellectual decay and anarchy, about the moral perplexity of the peaceful world that had collapsed and that nevertheless had been the world of the living generation—even if, to be sure, such criticism was not just meant nationally but referred to a world condition of which Germany was only a part; even if it did not pretend, in order to appear morally correct in domestic affairs, that things were only that bad in our country and very fine and noble everywhere else. Conscience spoke loudly, the hope for "renewal" spoke even more loudly and more polyphonically; and, let us be honest, we are a little ashamed today of all that dark and joyful impetuosity. Whoever had lived in the problematic sphere of literature might have been inclined to judge the conditions of life itself and of the nation by one's own suffering—of the nation that, beyond all literary imagination, had remained simple, calm and efficient. And on the other hand, the idealism of renewal has had to learn for better or worse that the human being is still "basely constructed" and is even today still eager "to bring himself humanly closer" to the heroic-historical element by food profiteering and similar humorous expedients.

But I have entitled this chapter "Against Justice and Truth," and that can only have *one* meaning: I wish to speak here for a moment about my contributions to the public discussion of the war, those two or three articles that were outfitted to do field service and that go together with the little book, *Frederick and the Great Coalition*—and in which, admittedly, there is little to detect of that Kleistian passion. For if I doubt whether a person like me is "suited" for patriotism, I have no doubt about whether certain things suit me or not. *Thunderous* words do *not* suit me. And I do not believe that they would be appropriate for anyone today. Probably they are best reserved for cannon. Literature today has a democratic character: no wonder the literati also demand democracy at other times, too. No, a different method, something other than thunderous words, was better suited for me to oppose the ingenious insults that literary civilization was heaping upon Germany, to oppose the boulevard psychology with which her saucily articulate enemies were befouling this nation that is not a nation of the word, that at this time, too, was not prepared to speak, and that therefore presented the look of literary helplessness. I remembered the European literary man in me, of whom I am, admittedly, not too proud, and it occurred to me that I *could also do* what the bourgeois rhetoricians over there could do, that I had, after all, learned how to write just as well as they—and that this case, my case, in which a Latin heritage of *esprit* was combined with passionate, indiscriminate partisanship for Germany, was a rarity, an exception, to a certain extent a stroke of luck that had to become manifest. I thought that one had to meet those over there with their own weapons, with the skill of a defense counsel, with intellect, antitheses, wit, verve, elegance and dialectical parrying. Brilliant? No, civilization's literary man is wrong when he says that I wanted to be brilliant. I wanted to serve, wanted to help. Or rather, far from believing that I really could serve and help, I wanted to make clear as quickly as possible my *desire* to help, to leave no doubt where my heart was: and thus there arose that early and rapid improvisation that was entitled "Thoughts in War," and in which much was anticipated with unusual presence of mind that was subsequently said better, more tenably, and with more validity: then came that essay that was dedicated to the "evil" king, an essay whose happy-light qualities I owe to my long preparation for it, and which was actually almost able to make "patriotism" acceptable in literary circles; and also the letter to the *Svenska Dagbladet*—this first and probably also last little political action of my life, truly something that one does not write to be brilliant, but to be useful. Am I wrong in assuming it is less the patriotic tendency of these articles than their Western-literary form that has caused bad blood with our literati? The clear contrast, which to many seemed deceitful, between their partisanship and the way partisanship was expressed in the articles? "In elegant array," civilization's literary man complained, I had "stood against truth and justice," and he made it clear with the word, "array," that the "elegance" in this case must be based on lies and deception; for he lives in the—not completely unjustified—conviction that "patriotism" and the style of a shoemaker are things that naturally and correctly belong together. But many a letter that I received at the time showed me that this contrast was also perceived and noticed by those who did not react with moral indignation, but who only observed and confirmed it. "A polemic against civilization," I heard there, "but in a form that would lead one to expect contents from the area of civilization. May I ask you to look at this passage? And to test the origin of all the words of emphasis in it? The thoughts and words are French. This other passage shows English language influences. Here again is a nerve system of completely French style." But it seemed to me that precisely this was the idea, the real point of the whole thing. And when a German scholar and soldier wrote to me later: "For you personally the problematic part of the matter is that your most characteristic means, the word, has been usurped by those others"—it seemed to me that on the contrary, I had usurped the most characteristic means of the others and used it against them.

Two writers of high rank have strongly attacked these war essays, of which, by the way, in my calm opinion, only the main piece, the Frederick essay, can be considered seriously from a literary point of view: the one directly and quite openly, the other indirectly, insinuatingly, and ambiguously-semipublicly—French the one, and a writer of European reputation, the other a—well, yes, of course! a German, then, whom spiritualization has raised so high above his compatriots that he has also become a Frenchman. The Frenchman by birth is Romain Rolland; and we see that he is a Frenchman, a Frenchman through and through, and thus basically completely without cosmopolitan talent, from his infinitely well-meaning little war book whose scandalous effect on Paris is not quite understandable, since its title, *Au dessus de la mêlée*, shows itself in the reading to be a complete deception. Is not this *"Au dessus"* also a naive presumption and impossibility in the Europe of today? Impartiality, suprapartiality, "neutrality," does such a thing exist today among the tolerably active intellects of the neutral or warring world? Was Norway's greatest prose writer, Knut Hamsun, neutral when he delivered his contribution to the German polemical work, *England in the Light of Cultured Humanity*? And can Romain Rolland, who supplied the King Albert's book with the highly sentimental article, *Au Peuple qui souffre pour la justice*, seriously believe that he is above the fray? He believes it. He believes that he feels just as directly and strongly for Germany, "the true Germany," *not* the Germany of this war that is combatting justice, as he feels for the true France that is obviously the same as the France of this war; and it is from this belief that he derives the right to scold me, a spokesman for the false Germany, so bitterly.

I must honor in the author of *Jean-Christophe* the master builder of a great work. Nothing must hinder me from perceiving the purity and goodness of his humanity, and from bowing before it. I also see very well that this writer is for his native land—but hardly for Germany—a very important and new intellectual phenomenon. His great prose work is not social criticism in the French manner, but an educational and developmental novel in the German style, and it even has a German musician as its hero. There are elements in Rolland's character that one may call antidemocratic, antirationalistic, and anti-intellectual, and that make him seem somewhat alien at home. This, however, is only true as far as he belongs to a France that is not identical to her officials and spokesmen—oh, yes, spokesmen!—not, therefore, to the centralistic-metropolitan France of chambers and newspapers, of doctrinary radicalism, of fanatic enmity to tradition, of the bourgeois rhetorician and of M. Poincaré. "You are still thinking," Rolland wrote one day to a mutual Austrian friend of his and mine,

> about France as she has appeared since the sixteenth century, but before this time she was infinitely broader and more profound. She continues to exist in this way in the hearts and minds of our provincial population. . . . Our literature gives a much too limited idea of our people; it was falsified by the old-new pseudo-renaissance of the sixteenth century and by the intolerance of the ruling generation that had conquered France— the King of the Isle de France and his ally, the Church. The other arts, less subordinated to reason, freed themselves earlier. Think of the bursting forth of impressionism. Never forget that we are the people who created Gothic architecture, the people of *chansons de geste* and of the Arthurian novels. *Our true books are our cathedrals.* Whoever deciphers the sculptures at the main portals of Amiens, Bourges, and Vezelay, reads in the soul of modern Picardy, Berry, or Burgundy. *This is our reserve strength.* . . .

"Our true books are our cathedrals!" A strange statement for the citizen of a country one is accustomed to think of as the literary country par excellence, and particularly for the citizen of the radical republic! I do not know how Rolland gets along in general with Maurice Barrès; at any rate, his feelings must have been on Barrès' side before the war when Barrès was fighting the desperate struggle for the defense of his country's Gothic monuments against the malicious destructive urge of the ruling apothecary-atheism—assuming, that is, that Rolland takes such French, all too French, conflicts at all seriously, that he is at all concerned with the unholy, life-threatening antithesis of the French intellectual and state constitution—an assumption that is probably, yes, obviously, *not* correct. No, he certainly does not find himself faced with the choice of being either a philistine of progress and a priest hater or a hysterical church commiserator. He knows that the antithesis that claims to be ardor itself while it is only witty signifies rigidity, bondage, sterility, hostility to life—and that it is *he*, a Frenchman, who knows this today best and most deeply perhaps in the whole world, is quite a remarkable fact. Perhaps one *must* be a Frenchman, at least to a certain extent, to have been able to suffer quite thoroughly through rationalism and intellectualism, and then finally to flee, like Rolland, to the creators, to Goethe and Tolstoy? In *Jean-Christoph* there is the truly decent and certainly immortal line: "Each one of our thoughts is only a moment of our life. What good is life to us if not to correct our errors, to conquer our prejudices, and daily to broaden us in heart and thought? . . . We use each day to obtain a little more truth. When we have reached the goal, then judge the value of our effort."

Sentences like this that are so congenial, so sublimely above doctrinairism and dogmatism, evidence of the deepest, most honest intent to live and to learn, are also found in no small amount in the little war book—this book in which the living Germany is so rigidly and sternly divided into a "true" and a "false" one; yes—what really should anger me—is that precisely the chapter that contains most of these sentences, precisely the one that contains, if I am not mistaken, the most remarkable and valuable part of the book, contains the main attack on the "*article monstrueux de* Thomas Mann (*dans la Neue Rundschau de novembre 1914*) . . . *proclamant que la pensée allemande n'avait pas d'autre idéal que le militarisme.*" The article is entitled "*Les idoles.*" It first appeared in the *Journal de Genève*, December 1914, and enjoyed, even at the time, significant public interest. I have before me a copy of the twenty-ninth edition of the book; the article forms the central core. It is advisable for me to say a few words in reply to Rolland's accusations.

He writes:

But I know well what the French intellectuals will think of the article, "Thoughts in War": Germany could not give them any more terrible weapon against herself. In an insane attack of pride and excited fanaticism, Mann tries at all costs to convert the worst criticisms against his country into embellishment and glory. While an Ostwald tries to bring the cause of culture together with that of civilization, Mann proposes the thesis that there is nothing in common between them. The present war is that of culture (that is, Germany's) against civilization, and carrying prideful boasting to the point of insanity, he defines civilization as reason, enlightenment, mitigation, morality, dissolution, and *intellect*, and culture as "an intellectual organization of the world" that does not exclude "bloody savagery." Culture is "the sublimation of the demonic." It is "beyond morality, reason and science." While, furthermore, an Ostwald, a Haeckel, only sees in militarism an instrument, a weapon, that culture uses to gain victory, Thomas Mann insists that culture and militarism are brothers, that their ideals are the same, that they contain the same principle, that their enemy is the same—and this enemy is peace, is intellect. Finally, he dares to give himself and his fatherland a standard from the verses (by Schiller):

The law is the friend of the weak,
But war allows power to appear.*

This is the way, then, the extraordinary Frenchman renders my thoughts of the time. In summing up, he says that I had demonstrated that culture was nothing more than "*la force*"; and he ends by calling the whole thing "a criminal excess of violence." "*Monstrueux*," "*Délire de fanatisme irrité*," "*Forfanterie d'orgueil*," "*Démence*," "*Surenchère criminelle de violence*": these are strong words in the mouth of a man of otherwise almost religious gentleness; wild, French words, directed against a statement whose dynamics knows nothing of such expressions; extremely hard words hurled against someone whom M. Rolland nevertheless seems earlier to have somehow valued and respected. I deduce this from various indications, for example, from the fact that he expresses almost admiring recognition for a German man of letters when he attacks me so completely "without regard" (*sans égards*). "Trick!" the German literary man in question would reply to this, I believe. As fate would have it, Rolland, too, held nothing back, and it would be fine for me and a little bit so for him, too, if the effort had not been quite so easy for him. I can imagine that his rage even arises from esteem. I must add: it comes from *over*estimation—I mean overestimation of my position and of the national, international weight to be attributed to my statements. How could he otherwise have come to denounce so bitterly precisely my article, from five hundred similar ones, to the French-reading public? In one breath he cites me together with Ostwald and Haeckel. But this is laughable. The foreigner's eye sees things here together that have extremely little in common. I am neither a monist nor an Esperantist, nor a friend of solutions to world

* Das Gesetz ist der Freund des Schwachen,
  Aber der Krieg läßt die Kraft erscheinen...

enigmas, nor an aping religious conformer, either. Above all, however, I am no very important person, no national dignitary, no bigwig, who, when he speaks, does so with the knowledge he is representing Germany abroad. My independence is that of a Bohemian. And the French intellectuals had already said so much about Germany that I could not care less what they said about my article. As I wrote it, I took part in my way in the quiet deliberations that outlawed and spat-upon Germany was conducting with her conscience under monstrous pressure from democratic public world opinion. That is all. And did I really, in the process, utter such horrible absurdities as your report would have a shocked international public believe?

Above all, *cher maître*, it seems to me that one should be more careful in the use of quotation marks than is obviously your wont. I never said that culture was "beyond morality, reason and science"—just as little as I said that it was "*force*," or that German thought had no other ideal than militarism. These are absurdities. But there is no strongly empha-sized statement that cannot be bent into absurdity and blunted if one wants to. You are a writer, Romain Rolland, and you have read my article and interpreted it as a dull-witted, intellectually clumsy philistine would have read and interpreted it. Even assuming that I really had stated that German thought was identical with "militarism," I would still have meant something different by "militarism" than what the *entente*-press means by it, that is, I would *not* have meant Junker rule and raw power; just as I, when I defined culture as "a certain intellectual organization of the world," that is, as the opposite of intellectual anarchy, meant something else by "organization" than its daily news-paper meaning. No doubt you consider my antithesis of "culture" and "civilization" to be an ad hoc improvisation that I would never have thought of earlier, an offspring, as it were, of war psychosis. This would be an error. Long before the war I had ordered my thoughts in this way for everyday uses; years ago I had publicly stated my definition of the two concepts in aphoristic form. I would, of course, hardly have been a German writer if I had never tried to vary this theme, to give my "definitive" description of these ambiguous and much misused words. This has been attempted hundreds of times in Germany before me, by thinkers and creative writers, without *one* interpretation ever being established for general use: unless it was the one that "culture" refers to spiritual matters, and "civilization" to material ones. I found this insufficient, yes, false; for it seemed to me that civilization was given far too little respect here. I said to myself that civilization was not only just as spiritual, but that it was even *spirit itself*—spirit in the sense of reason, of morality, of doubt, of enlightenment, and finally, of *dissolution*, while culture on the other hand meant the principle of artistic organization and formation, of the life-preserving, life-glorifying, principle. You call that "*pousser la forfanterie jusqu'à la démence*," but it is precisely you, just as you are, who would, if there were no war, probably discover neither *forfanterie* nor *démence* in it, and at any rate I can prove to you that such a concept is not at all foreign to French thought. Do you know the letters of Georges Bizet, the composer of *Carmen*? He writes to a friend about reason and art, about reason as the inexorable *enemy* of art. "I believe," he says,

> the whole *future* belongs to the perfection of our social contract. In the perfected society there will be no more injustice, and consequently no more dissatisfied people and no more attacks on the social harmony, no priests, no police, no criminals, no adultery, no prostitution, no spirited excitement, no passions and stop! no music, either, no poetry, no Legion of Honor, no press (ah, bravo!), particularly no theater, no illusion, that is, no more art! Miserable creatures that you are, your *inevitable and inexorable progress* is killing art! My poor art! I am sure of this. The societies that were the most superstitious were also great patrons of art. . . . Ah, just show me that we can have an art of reason, of truth, of exactness, and I will transfer with rifle and pack to your side. . . . As a musician, I declare to you that, when you eliminate adultery, fanaticism, crime, error, and the supernatural, not one more note can be written; I assure you I would write much better music if I believed in everything that is not true. To sum up briefly: art declines in proportion to the progress of reason. You do not believe it, but it is true just the same. Just make me a Homer, a Dante, today. With what, then? Fantasy lives on chimeras and visions. If you suppress the chimeras, then naturally imagination comes to an end. No more art! Everywhere science. If you ask me whether this would be an evil, I will release you right away and not argue anymore, because you are right. But it is definitely too bad, really too bad. . . .

"Because you are right": this is the ironical recognition of civilization's progress by a gifted French artist who sees in precisely this "inevitable" progress the dissolution and ruin of art. The antithesis of civilization and culture is not expressly stated in his words, but it comes out clearly as his conviction. When he says that the societies most steeped in superstition have been the great patrons of art, then it is culture that he ascribes to these superstitious societies, and he means the same as I do when I say that culture does not exclude "bloody savagery," while civilization softens savagery, clarifies superstition, discourages passions.

Culture binds together; civilization dissolves. This is obvious. Who will forbid me to see things in this way if I do see them this way? And again: do I not honor civilization? It has been called material. I deny that this is true. People have tried to define it simply as the human condition that has been regimented and tamed by the *state*: but this does not satisfy me either, for I see that it is much too intellectual a principle to stop at the state, that its will to dissolution is so strong that it will also seek the dissolution of the state. You are a Frenchman and you deny this? Civilization will not be satisfied with dissolving the state. It will put national passions to sleep and bury them in peace. It will create the pacified Esperanto-world in which war is impossible—I believe in it, you see; I believe in its future, and why not? It is the future and progress itself. Of course, pacifism is civilization's concern, at bottom its true and chief concern. It wants purity and peace, for it is literature, it is intellect. Must I still say what its strongest weapon, its most effective means of dissolution is? But it is *psychology*!—psychology, which has always seemed to me to be science itself, knowledge itself. Psychology discourages all folly and passion, it discourages life and art—through knowledge. For art becomes impossible, the artist becomes impossible, when they are seen through. Psychology has, therefore, anything but a culture-forming effect; it is rather to the greatest extent progressive-destructive, to the greatest extent civilizing. This is all quite clear. Obviously things can be formulated differently, but for the moment and in its way, this formulation is irrefutable.

I not only know, Romain Rolland, what displeases you in this matter, I can completely appreciate the essence of your displeasure. Still another foreign writer, the Swedish academician, *Per Hallström*, has, in an article that also appeared in German, given my war essays the honor of a critical analysis, but in a different sense and spirit than you have done: to wit, in the sense of political sympathy and in the spirit of essential agreement. Nevertheless, he says that no matter how exciting the idea of the antithesis between civilization and culture may be, this antithesis does not hold its sharpness for him. Is it not actually a question here, he says, of a *single* united, even if infinitely pieced together, being? And he suggests symbolizing this being as a tree, a tree with leaves and blossoms; culture is then the blossom, civilization the leaves. A *poetic* way of seeing things, is it not? Instead of an intellectual way. A Germanic way. But what, Hallström asks further, should one call the *life and unity* of the tree, the force that gropes about in the earth, that struggles up for light, that shines in the blossoms, that struggles in the storm—what should one call it? Not civilization and not culture. And then he speaks in strong, passionate words, in words, my dear Rolland, that could almost be yours, of the prime source, of the synthesis, of life itself in whose deep and dark realm the mystic powers, which I justifiably emphasized in defining my nation, dwell. "They are compelled into the light," he says, "in nations as in individuals, when the pressure becomes too strong and the limit of life's endurance is approached. They are immeasurable values, purchased only at the highest price. War is such a one, war, which threatens the fruits of a whole historical development and the most treasured possessions of a whole country, yes, its very existence. The simplest heart sees what is at stake here...." The simplest. Hallström says that I was too complicated, too romantic, ambivalent and sharp-witted in my basic conception of German heroism, for this heroism was sure of a quite direct and warm sympathy. "It was the clarity wrenched from bitter necessity and danger, the clarity that a rich and powerful nature gained over itself, over the innermost conditions of life, and over its own strength. From this, victory was born, and in this it will endure. Precisely because Germany, thanks to her enemies' hatred, has been so completely thrown on her own resources, *without the support of phrases and formulas that muddy reality*, but with that fire in her soul that burns to the foundations of life's values and there finds support, precisely for this reason she has been invincible." How beautiful that is! And how true! True in a more complete, stronger, purer way than my antithetical truth—I see it and admit it. I felt the need and the ability to lend intellectual, formulalike support to German heroism, support that this very unliterary heroism did not need at all, and that, had it been accepted, would only have troubled and confused it. Where life was concerned, I was witty and antithetical— where Germany was concerned, I was *French*. And precisely this French character of my formulation of things repelled you. For the remarkable thing about us, M. Rolland, is that you are Germanic enough to reject formulas and antitheses that are merely brilliant, while I am Frenchman and Latin sophist enough to be fascinated by them.

Do not believe that this fascination will be long lasting! That I am the man to stare all my life at an intellectual formula, as the Indian holy man stares at his navel! I am not this man. I am not a systematician, not a doctrinaire; I am not a slave to the shameful error of dogmatism, and I will never settle upon a truth that I consider to be *the* truth to feed upon it the rest of my life. Here I am prevented by a tendency to boredom and disgust and an all too lively need for new, fresh and refreshing truth. "Each of our thoughts is only a moment of our lives. What use is life to us if not to broaden us in heart and thought?" You are right! But are you unconditionally right? Or is not perhaps the idea that truth is only an experience of the moment, a very West European, anticonstructive, prodestructive thought that flirts with nothingness, an idea of Western individualism, of "civilization," and an idea that is to the highest degree anti-German?

"I asked Goethe," Eckermann relates, "which of the more recent philosophers he considered to be the best. 'Kant,' he said, 'is the best beyond all doubt. He is also the one whose teaching has shown itself to have lasting effect, that has penetrated most deeply into our German culture. He has also had an effect on you even though you have not read him. Now you do not need him anymore, because what he could give you, you already have.'" Well, Kant has also had an effect on me, simply because I am a German; I, too, possess what he could give me without my ever having studied him systematically. And now it seems to me as if the present war, which certainly, seen from one side, is a war for power and business, but which from the other side is a war of ideas, has already been waged in a purely intellectual sphere; as if the German spirit had already risen up once before "with deep disgust," as Nietzsche said, against "modern" ideas, Western ideas, the ideas of the eighteenth century, and as if it had been precisely Kant in whom the social, preserving, constructive, organizational German spirit rose up against Western nihilism after he had himself gone through all the depths of value-dissolving skepticism. As if he had answered the question of whether truth was more than an impression and an experience of the moment (he spoke in his fear-instilling, learned manner of the "possibility of synthetic judgments *a priori*") in a military, commanding tone with *yes*—for what is his "categorical imperative" other than the establishment of truth as duty, of *duty as truth*? It seems to me that Kant's warlike categorical intervention against the complete liberalization of the world is quite closely related to another powerfully *delaying* and restoring German act: that of Luther—which one may also regret in the interest of the progressive "liberalization" of the human race, without thereby in any way harming the missionary peculiarity and majesty of the German spirit that manifests itself in it. It seems to me, then, that the action of Bismarckian Germany of 1914, its intervention against the complete liberalization, civilization, literarization of the world, this intervention arising from the social instinct to preserve and delay, from the will to adhesion, to cult, and to culture—as if this war logically and characteristically aligned itself with previous German deeds. No, it does not just seem so to me, it is so, and again: at bottom there is unanimous agreement on this state of affairs. Why do all the conservative elements of the world, in Madrid, Rome, Athens, Bucharest, Stockholm, and St. Petersburg, secretly or openly sympathize with Germany, while all liberalism hates us like the plague? "The German is conservative," said Wagner. No, I am not staring idolatrously at an intellectual formula. I am not genuflecting before some "idol." I do not wish to obscure reality with phrases and antitheses. But how can you, Romain Rolland, keep me from seeing and perceiving most vividly what is most vividly true and realistically effective in the antithesis of "civilization" and "culture?" How can you want to prevent me from uniting the concept of culture with that of morality (I did it right away in that rashly improvised essay in the fall of 1914)—since, after all, as Schopenhauer already remarked in his writings on esthetics, the advantages of the German nation, like those of its art, are primarily moral in contrast to the intellectualism of Western civilization? How can you want to decry me as insane when I say that love of peace and warlike virtue are so compatible in the nature of the Germans because their military spirit does not come from passion for *gloire*, and is not the expression of a cocky, dashing and bravadolike desire to bully and to attack—like the early military spirit of the French, who are basically a much more warlike people than the Germans, and whose domestic policy is always dominated by the fear of some kind of saber Caesarism—but of a moral character, a heroism in the name of "need," precisely that "holy need," that has marked this war from the first moment on for the Germans, and that is quite wretchedly translated with "*nécessité*," M. Rolland, because the word "need" means something more than a dry, rational acknowledgement: the highest creative passion, you see— "need" was Richard Wagner's favorite word—all this, dear sir, is neither humbug nor bragging nor sophistry nor insanity, but spiritual fact, the basic fact of this war, which one can neither wash away with streams of philanthropic tears nor erase with unworthy, coarse insults. The nation became aware of this through extensive, searching, and hypercritical self-examination in days when a terrible compulsion made clarity, self-consciousness, and the understanding of its destiny an essential condition of its life—and I would like very much to know why in my own way I should not also have become aware of it, why I should not also have been permitted to put my thoughts and actions into the service of German self-understanding, of positive German self-criticism.

Do you remember, dear M. Rolland, a little study about two German writers—Emil Strauß and me—which one day—no one was thinking about war—appeared in a journal that was very close to you, the *Effort libre*? There was a sentence in it about me that I marked with my pencil at the time and have now looked up again. "*Car il est plus Allemand et moins Latin que vous ne pourriez le croire de premier abord,*" it said. "*C'est là son originalité.*" This originality, which at the time enjoyed such a peaceful-objective confirmation, had long been a latent originality, an originality of substance, but scarcely of knowledge. It had only found an automatic indirect-artistic expression. Suddenly, in midsummer 1914, it became acute, it became knowledge, entered into conscious feeling and began to struggle toward its origin and justification, toward clarity about itself. For the time being, simple existence, existence in art, was gone. The important thing was to know. The important thing was an existence based on thought. This became a conscientious duty for a whole nation; it became a conscientious duty for the individual, too, to create an existence based on thought during the most tumultuous, the most unfavorable conditions for contemplation. Did not Germany resemble a man who, forced to defend himself with all his might against a superior force of enemies who were trying to kill him, at the same time withdraws into himself with all his spiritual strength, and fights with an inwardly directed gaze? "The pressure," Hallström writes, "that the enemy's resourceful hatred and his agile mendacity concentrated on the greatest modern nation must have been hard for every German to bear." No word, no sound in your praised *Au dessus* book, Romain Rolland, gives an indication that the slightest idea of this thoughtful sympathy ever touched you. You belong to the best-loved, most indulged, and visible nation on earth, and your gentle heart beats strongly in the patriotic conviction that France is fighting "with pure hands and innocent heart," and that she is risking her life for divine justice. France! But not another word. It is not part of my task to explain to you that France's hands are not clean, and that "innocence" is not guiltlessness. Germany was never "innocent" enough to imagine herself guiltless. It seemed sneaky to her to be completely without guilt, not to want to become guilty. She has, without hypocritically balking, courageously accepted her measure of tragic guilt in this war; for her culture enabled her to see tragedy where you others saw, or convinced yourselves you saw, a sentimental-moral affair and melodrama. She laughed bitterly over the psychological Tartuffery that neatly differentiates between "defensive" and "offensive." She knew that there is a difference between frivolous "attacking" and fated "being on the attack"; she knew in the depths of her soul that she did not just find herself completely innocently on the defensive, but also in needful, creative attack—while France, the France of Poincaré and of Edward VII, the France of the Russian alliance, the France that in July 1914, in answer to Germany's last, decisive question on what she intended to do, answered that she would act "in her own interest": while this France rocked herself in vain innocence, and, in order to assure herself of the courage of her soldiers, lied to them that they had to free France's soil—as if this soil would not be evacuated the moment Germany was permitted to live. France innocent! France unwarlike! Her most peaceful, her most spiritual son is still more concerned with the military honor of the fatherland than are the members of the general staff in our country—yes, to you, Rolland, philanthropist and pacifist, I could prove that you privately defended and approved the reintroduction of the three-year period of military service, which in the opinion of knowing observers meant war and nothing else, because France's honor demanded it, because France had to be strong in order to be permitted to want peace. Enough! Enough!

In that passage where the Swede speaks of the pressure of the hatred that had gathered over Germany, he adds that people like me could not react so easily to this disgusting absurdity; my nature, he says, forced me to find a logical basis for the how and why, and from this there arose "a very interesting outline of the history of the German soul in its originality." This is not, in your opinion, what should have come of it. I should not have been moral—I should have been virtuous. I should have protested against the "Belgian crime," for only those nations are truly great, you say, who defend their immortal souls against the doctrine of the good of the state. As what nation has done? As France did in the Dreyfus case! One could reply to this that France's survival did not depend upon whether she finally acquitted the Jewish captain or condemned him I do not know how many times; that, however, Germany probably would not exist at all if Frederick had not marched into Saxony, and that she would perhaps not be able to rejoice in her immortal soul today if she had not acted in a similar way in 1914. But these objections are obviously feeble, and France, who acts "in her own interest," teaches the people of Schiller through your mouth that life is not the highest good. Standing high above the fray, you find the thinkers of Germany fighting honestly for the mortal part of their country but not worrying about its eternal life. In a word, we lack conscience. You have the impartiality to claim that Germany lacks conscience—the country that bled for thirty years for the sake of conscience and did not think of its earthly salvation, while in the process you others became what you are today. "It has been fifteen years," you write, "since that famous trial took place in which we saw one single innocent human being opposed to the power of the state. At that time we, we Frenchmen, opposed the idol of the good of the state and broke it because it threatened France's eternal salvation." Great France! Of course at the time she only symbolically broke the idol of the *salut public*—but just the same, she did so. It was not nearly so dangerous for France to rehabilitate the Jew as it would have been for Germany to maintain Belgium's holy neutrality (where would this neutrality be today?); but still, *"le geste était beau."* Would you believe, my dear Rolland, that the boasting about the noble fact that Captain Dreyfus was innocently convicted only for the second or third time and not also for the third or fourth time for the good of the state, seems to me like certain propaganda speeches of Theodore Roosevelt where he celebrated with gaping glibness the abolition of negro slavery in the nineteenth century as an incomparably moral and miraculous deed? Do you not think that actions such as the acquittal of an obviously wrongly convicted person and the elimination of a social backwardness that had become a scandal should take place quite gently, modestly, and in ashamed quietness instead of being announced with moral trumpet blasts to the world as great deeds for the "salvation of mankind?" Celto-Latin style! Humanitarian acts are not second nature to rhetorical virtue. They are heroic accomplishments that must constantly be held up for cultural propaganda purposes and for which one demands the world's admiration.

The Dreyfus affair was a spirited donnybrook such as Germany has admittedly never had up to now. Germany will catch up; civilization's literary man will do his part. But can we help it if there is no traitor among our officers and if the French political antithesis of saber and church on the one hand and "justice" on the other, of intellect and power, virtue-republic and the *salut public* of the *panache*, does not concern us at all? It does not concern us! Do you understand that? We can take part intellectually in the affairs that arise in your country from your dialectic, but they do not touch our own morality! The arrogant simplicity with which you other nations base your patterns of thought, judging us by your value systems—why don't you finally give it up! Morals! Domestic affairs! But if the justification of foreign adventures, of war, is to be decided according to the domestic conditions of a country, according to whether its social *conscience* is in good condition; then Germany would have the right to war *before* France, England, and Italy, not to speak of Russia. For the belief in the dignity of the state, in its moral calling, has been more alive here than anywhere else, the idea of the state as an institution for the protection of social justice. Germany has served "internal" affairs, that is, conscience and justice, more seriously, more practically, and more truly than you have with the bragging gesture of your affair—this is a reply, not an attack; a statement to ward off your continually aggressive boasting about virtue.

Dreyfus acquitted? But he was condemned! He was conclusively condemned I do not know how many times, indeed, at the moment when France gave the answer that she would act "in her own interest." What if she had answered: "We have entered into the Russian alliance to defend ourselves from attack and to preserve peace on the continent. But if Russia marches against Europe, then we stand with Europe?" The war would have been over. Instead of this, the French socialists entered the ministry and sank down, as Paul Lensch writes in his book, to the level of "receivers of stolen goods and accomplices of that international murder syndicate that has its spies in all capitals." Dreyfus was convicted in the hour when Jaurès fell, and he remains convicted so long as the French socialists serve their government as murderous fences. France innocent! But now really not another word.

If you and your *au dessus* opinions were correct, M. Rolland, France would not only be without political guilt in the war, she would also have found herself on the most noble defensive during the war. Of course you admit, "I am not prouder of the French intellectuals. The misuse they are making of the idols of race, civilization, and of Latin character gives me no satisfaction." But you do not name any names; you attack no one with "*monstrueux*" and "*délire de fanatisme*"; you control yourself admirably as far as your countrymen are concerned, and you speak bitterly only against the German view of the war, which by no means regarded the French as "stinking animals" and a race worthy of extermination—while this was almost without exception the way the French came to view us. Oh, how little you deserve the stigma of *enboché*, how little you deserve exile! How moderate your justice is! What an intolerant country it is to which you had to write the letter from Geneva, "*A ceux qui m'accusent!*" "I love no idol at all," you declare courageously, "not even that of humanity." But you add: "At least, however, the idols my people serve present fewer dangers; *they are not aggressive."* *"Elles ne sont pas agressives!"* This is what it says, and it still says so after one has rubbed one's eyes. The ideas and idols of France not aggressive! Why, then, the bigwig intellectuals in Paris have simply defended these ideas and idols against impudent challenges and insults from our side? Their behavior in this war would then be, after all, one of the most dignified superiority? The French intellectuals, dear sir, have acted like fools, that is the truth; and compared to the raving nonsense they spat out against Germany, all our "war literature," including my little musing on culture and civilization, was just harmless chatter. There has been no visible exception. I know well that it is disloyal to use the criticism nations exercise against themselves through their writers, but it was impossible not to remember Voltaire's definition of the Frenchman as a cross between an ape and a tiger. Europe's wisest sage, Anatole France, where was his knowledge, his doubt, his radical freedom? The melodrama took possession of his subtle brain and he foamed with rage. The French idols not aggressive! But history, M. Rolland, teaches that the French idols and principles have always existed only to hide French aggressiveness! Moltke said it in his article of 1841 on "The Western Border Question." "How many false excuses," he asks, *"how many completely contradictory principles,* have the French not already come to us with to rob us under the mask of assistance! They snatched Burgundy away from us in the name of the Pope, the Lorraine bishoprics and Alsace in the name of the Reformation as protectors of the Lutherans; Strasbourg and Holland they seized in the name of the absolute monarchy; Spain, Naples, and Lorraine they won in the name of legality, and finally Holland, the Netherlands, the complete left bank of the Rhine, they unified or at least allied in the closest way with France in the name of freedom and the republican principle. Four times they changed the principle, but each time they stole a country away from us." It is a lie that the revolutionary virtue-principle of freedom, justice and humanity that France cherished bore a less aggressive character than earlier ones. Do you value Max Scheler? You cite him at any rate. "The equality of nations and their equivalency in value," he says in a study "On the National Ideas of Great Nations," "is France's national democratic ideal and at the same time her ideological principle of stability— the same principle that runs through her whole philosophy and science. But since the Napoleonic wars, what she has considered to be precisely *her* special, foremost national mission, is to realize this specifically French concept of 'human rights' and of historical stability not only within *her* borders, but also to spread them over the world, to fill the world and *all* other nations with them. But this mission has been invested with the completely special Gallic value quality of the splendor of national glory. The glory (*gloire*), you see, of a "leader," "teacher," and "educator" of the human race—this is France's idea of a national mission. But *France has always overlooked in the most naive manner imaginable* that precisely this demand and principle makes its bearer *aggressive and warlike in the most extreme way*, aggressive against all nations that have another idea of their mission that France does not respect, or that, because of their own national spirit, will not submit to France's leadership." Is innocence guiltlessness? I mean that innocence, gentle master, that is expressed in your pleasant-sounding confession: "*Je n'ai jamais pu distinguer la cause de la France de celle de l'humanité.*"

Who did you think you were talking about, then, when you told the international public that I was war-mad? Perhaps I had not been a pacifist, no, not that. To me, pacifism had been a fancy like any other, a hobbyhorse for people who had nothing else to do than to ride large, cheap hobbyhorses. I found it superficial, maniacal and childish to want to cure the world with military peace; I did not believe that life could ever be peaceful, nor that the dear human race would look a great deal better in eternal peace than under the sword. I thought that as long as people did not wander around in white robes with palm leaves in their hands, exchanging literary kisses on their foreheads, there would be war now and then on earth; as long as they had blood in their veins, I thought, and not mild oil, they would want to shed it now and then. Therefore I could not have called myself a pacifist. But I had been peaceful, certainly not less peaceful than you, M. Rolland, and even though I had experienced the peaceful penetration of Morocco, about which you, to my knowledge, found nothing to remember; the Boer War, during which I was immoral enough to be very English, because I found England to be more important than the Boer Republic; the Abyssinian and the Libyan expedition, the Spanish-American, the Sino-Japanese, the Russo-Japanese wars and the Balkan wars: I would still have wagered my house and home that I and my world would not see the European war. I do not deny that a grain of contempt and self-contempt was contained in this unshakable conviction. No, I and my world would never see the war. The Archduke's murder, which was alarming for many, was not enough to change this conviction. The declaration of a state of war, even the mobilization order, was not enough to do so. Pressure and counterpressure, I said; you will see, it will come to nothing. How could I have thought otherwise? The international tendencies of the time seemed to me to counterbalance the national ones completely. The internationality of capital and of socialism, the economic intermeshing of Europe, the leading moderate ideals of "trade" and "security" seemed to me to make war unthinkable for the duration of the present era. As far as I was personally concerned, I had been a burgherly artist, national to a certain extent, to be sure, but much too urbane and cosmopolitan to make mischief by playing the trump card of nationalism in times of peace. My God, I even belonged to a German-French society for mutual understanding. *"Pour mieux se connaître"*! The din of the "Pan-Germans," as far as it reached me at all, had been a nonsensical and ridiculous matter for me, not less, I hope, than the roaring of the Patriotic League for you. When Herr Harden preached preventive war, I shrugged my shoulders in irritation. Then came the war. Not a political war, in my opinion. Not that preventive war for which Germany had passed up one favorable opportunity after another. Rather war at the final, most extreme moment, a moral war if the will of nations to self-preservation can be called moral at all. The physical danger was terrible, but if the war had been limited to the physical realm, it would only have frightened me, and my national participation would have remained only passive anxiety. What moved me to action was the rebellion of my sense of justice. It seemed as if nothing was left for my country to do than to disappear midst the hatred and scorn of the world: this was stupidity, hypocrisy, insanity. I knew from my Schopenhauer, and my own worldly experience had confirmed for me, that force ruled internationally and not justice. Would this ever change? Possibly. Certainly I could not object to that. But as long as it remained unchanged, it was still a shocking and stupid swindle to send Germany of all nations into the desert as a scapegoat, just because in her thoughts and speeches she had been more honestly pessimistic and less upliftingly rhetorical than the others. This shameless humbug-virtue did not shock me because I am something of a German, but because I have a very primitive, unaffected, undistorted feeling for justice and fairness. I did not see Germany as guiltier than the others; I did see the aggressive tendency in her rising up, but I found this in equal measure in the other nations. I saw the others just as ready and willing to make history as Germany. The disgusting political exploitation of the "Belgian crime" pushed me closer to Germany. I saw that everyone, Jaurès included, had always considered the march through Belgium to be the obvious and the only reasonable thing to do—just as obvious as a German-English war would result in a no less "unjust" blockade. I saw that neither England nor France had taken any steps in St. Petersburg for the preservation of peace that would have corresponded to the pressure exercised by Germany on Vienna. I saw that the government in Paris had hidden from its people the fact of Russian mobilization, because the republic wanted to reconquer Alsace-Lorraine for its eternal consolidation, and I saw the entry of the French socialists into this government. Never, not even when the "piazza" had not yet proved the opposite, had I been enough of a literary man to believe in the purity, innocence, and essential peacefulness of democracy. I had heard of *entente* plans for the partition of Austria, of Jean Jaurès' fearful struggle against the French war party, of Morel's accusations against the evil Morocco politics of the Foreign Office; I had understood this and that about the nature and purpose of the Parisian-Russian business, and I had to, or at least could, say to myself that there was no German counterpart to newspapers such as *Matin*, *Journal*, and the Northcliff press. I had known something about English history, known that democracy and imperialism formed anything but a contradiction there, and I had not doubted that England, even under a liberal government, would have to try to prepare the same fate for a new rival in the commercial and colonial field as she had prepared for those who came before. Admittedly, I also saw that the German radical literary man took the enemies' lying idealism deadly seriously, that no stupidity or infamy was so bad for him that he could not accept it, side with it, and use it against his country. But why, I asked myself, always only against his own country? Was that justice? Was it not very un-European, in this European moment, as well, to turn morality and conscientiousness so completely against his country alone and to utterly ignore all the others? I did not completely forget to consider my intellectual freedom. At a time when the waves of national enthusiasm were at their height, I devoted myself to quite independent thoughts about "defensive" and "offensive" that I recorded in my piece about Frederick the Great, and that convinced the neutral observers, the Swiss and the Swedes, of my desire for justice. Was I more German, Romain Rolland, than you were French? No. But the remarkable thing about our situation is that the modest amount of independence that you manifested in *Au dessus de la mêlée* caused great anger among your own people against you, while I, at home, brought anger and scorn upon myself by the extremely modest amount of chauvinism that I put into *Frederick and the Great Coalition*. *That is the difference between France and Germany.*

A little more than kin, and less than kind. It was not the foreigner, not the "enemy," who directed the most ferocious attacks against the position I was pressed into by the times, the emotional position that this book must serve to explain—not to justify, for emotion is free. Rolland scolded and complained with strong words, but he did not hiss. He thought he had to point out what seemed to him to be feverish aberration in order to deter it. His purpose was not to dishonor, to kill—and to insinuate himself into the place of the dishonored and slain one with the introductory cry: "Heed the one who loves!" It was left to a much closer person to have such a purpose, and such hatred. It was the German radical literary man who said the most poisonous and debasing things to me. Was it poison only for me? Debasing only for me? It is for him to think about this—for him through whose Latinly eloquent mouth civilization's literary man spoke to me.

I refuse to say whose mouth this was, for it is a melancholy and shameful matter. The war had not lasted long when a political writing of the highest literary quality appeared that had a certain family resemblance to my Frederick essay, for it also sought and found its magic and depth by mirroring the present and the past with each other. The role, for example, that the Seven Years' War had played in my article, the Dreyfus affair played here; as King Frederick's counterpart the French writer appeared who was the active hero of that forensic narrative. But the difference was that while I had run down my king so naturalistically that the character study could have had the effect of a pasquil on more naive readers, yes, that it provoked angry rejoinders— the other work raised its hero, Emile Zola, that is, the most impetuous man of power and violence in the history of art, an epic giant of animal sensuality, stinking extravagance, and filthy strength, to the "most encompassing intellect," saint of justice, and transfigured teacher of democracy ("His hair half-long in the nape of his neck"), to political civic glory. It was unfortunately also "fiction" precisely because it was so terribly far from the *truth*, from every desire and effort to keep its love under ironical discipline, from every deeper, stricter and more humane justice; its concept of truth and justice was forensically limited because in the case it celebrated, forensic truth and justice took on symbolic-political and civilizing significance; in short, it was "New Passion," political passion and one was reminded of Strindberg's admonition to Bjørnson: "Be truthful, Bjørnson! You are as untruthful as an after-dinner speaker!"

I will attempt neither a political nor an esthetic critique of this significant work. This is not the place, and of all people, it is not my job to appreciate the polish and the *geste*, the haughty conceit, the highly hysterical hatred, and the hard "love of humanity" in this ambiguous biography. I must defend myself against it from a purely personal, purely human point of view, must repulse the ingenious absurdities and raving baseness that it says behind my back or to my face: for, to give a relatively harmless example, when the author speaks of "those deep babblers who provide intellectual support for irrationality," he is clearly using the rhetorical plural, and all remaining doubt is removed when he goes on to say that "those deep babblers" flattered themselves that "they had understanding, and that beyond all understanding they could be the vainglorious advocates of ruthless force." This is quite unmistakable. For some place or another in my little war book I was guilty of writing the sentence, "The categorical imperative beyond the most unfathomable skepticism is German." Well, I do not deny that such thoughts and dicta, which are typical of the hasty trenchwork in our intellectual defense at the beginning of the war, seem a little tasteless to me today. But is there not still some truth to them? Yes, quite a bit. I thought *that way* at the time, and I can still quite easily think that way today.

Nietzsche's moral critique in the name of life, I thought, is essentially nothing other than Kant's "practical reason." Kant's practical philosophy, too, which followed his theoretical, radical, all-crushing one, is no longer concerned with "truth," but with practical ethical postulates—with "life." This desire for practical matters, for ethics, for the imperative, for life beyond the deepest understanding, is obviously typically national; it is German to relegate radicalism to the intellect and to act in a practical-ethical, antiradical manner toward life. This is the real *political* thought and instinct of the nonpolitical people. Without in the least being a "philosopher," I have also somehow come in for my share of this way of thinking and intellectual structure, of this *simultaneously ironical and categorical* concept of politics: at least I *know* just enough about it to have a right to talk about it in an alluding and intuitive way. But what does the *Dreyfusard* make of this? He understands from this that I "imagined I had understanding and that I could, beyond this understanding, be an advocate of lies and force." This is either not intelligent or not noble. In any case, it is only a harmless example.

What else is there? The most passionate of things! After only a few words, the elegant little sentence appears: "*Those who are destined to dry up early* step out deliberately when they have scarcely entered their twenties, a match for the world." I admit this is all one can expect from an advocate of love of mankind and a dyed-in-the-wool philanthropist. One can call this *radical* polemics. It is obviously a little squirt of sulphuric acid, *en passant*, into one's neighbor's face. It is true that I had hardly entered my twenties when I "stepped out," not so deliberately, but more or less a match for the world, it seemed. Not self-righteously, but right for the world—so early. How did this come about? There is, Goethe says, for every human being the hour when he is "driven out of the paradise of warm feelings to be a man and to find a new intellectual paradise in his work." This is true. But the hour Goethe is speaking of comes earlier for the one and later for the other. I remember I had planned during the work on *Buddenbrooks* to cite Platen's lines as a motto:

> Then I became quieter and finally cold,
> And truly I would now like
> To see the world from afar, as if outside it:
> My uneasy heart has suffered
> Longing and fear and dread.
> It has suffered its share of pain,
> And it places no trust in life;
> Let powerful nature for it
> Only become a means
> To build itself a world with its own strength.*

I do not know why I finally suppressed the motto. With heartfelt precision it expresses the condition, the destiny of early fitness for the world, *of fitness for work*, which has little to do with "ripeness," and nothing at all to do with cheap cleverness in living. I call it destiny, one of the forms human life takes, and in doing so, I claim some sympathy for it, no matter whether one thinks of it as a stroke of luck or as a misfortune. Is it necessarily a misfortune, does one pay so dearly for having been spurred on so early by the manliness of work, to have

---

* So ward ich ruhiger und kalt zuletzt
Und gerne möcht' ich jetzt
Die Welt, wie außer ihr, von ferne schau'n:
Erlitten hat das bange Herz
Begier und Furcht und Grau'n.
Erlitten hat es seinen Teil von Schmerz,
Und in das Leben setzt es kein Vertrau'n;
Ihm werde die gewaltige Natur
Zum Mittel nur,
Aus eigner Kraft sich eine Welt zu bau'n.

proved oneself right for the world so early with a work? If so, it must only be true of minor or middling talents, for clearly, very great talents, such as Goethe, for example, with the sensational novel of his youth, seem to prove the opposite. Is early withering the payment, the penitence that must unavoidably be paid for such a stern gift of destiny? Well, there are forms of artistic withering that find their enthusiastic admirers who perceive it as the exact opposite of withering: the form of political virtue, for example, in which Zola's withering occurred. Certainly this is not what fate had in store for me. If it were—I would perhaps, even probably, find sympathy where I now reap angry scorn. What is withering? Death is a part of life; life itself is dying and still growth at the same time. Particularly in artistic life, growth and withering are indivisibly enmeshed, and in contrast to early, fresh works, later ones may have, together with signs of withering, significant intellectual and artistic merits. From the beginning, an artist's life, like his work, is a unity, and finally, there is little that drives it from its course. The pleasure I feel in thinking of certain things I would still like to create offers me a guarantee that with them I will also awaken pleasure beyond myself, in others as well. Nevertheless, it is quite possible that I gave the best I was destined to give at an early age—a fate that one may call sad or even tragic as long as the one it befalls is still alive and struggling. When we rest in the ground, it will not matter much at which period in our lives we were at our best in what we were, and our most fortunate work praises our name, whether it stands at the beginning, in the middle, or at the end of our temporal life. The humanity of the arena cares little that an artistic life is also a human life. The same cruelty is evident whether it acclaims the gladiator's triumph or watches his defeat with curiosity and scorn. But should those who run the same risks, artists—should an artist who has selected "humanity" as his banner, adopt the vile harshness of this point of view? Could it be true that universal love, love directed far away, only flourishes at the cost of the ability to love "closer at hand," there, you see, where love has its only reality? And that it lulls its morally satiated possessor beyond his own growth or withering into an alienating sense of security?

No matter. The political acid-sprayer was aimed and it hit. Blind, and with a corroded and heavily bandaged countenance, one waits for the rest. And the rest, the real thing, does come—it bursts in at the moment when the humanitarian starts talking about the "reversion to subhuman states that is being brought about today in the country" (in the France of 1900), about the spokesmen and advocates caught in this reversion—and now the essay crashes and whips down without inhibition against the rhetorical plural. These spokesmen and advocates, it says—they may answer for themselves later if they can—"one thing is certain from the beginning: *It is easier for them.* Their opinions do not require them to suffer banishment and silence." (banishment? *silence?*) "On the contrary, *they take advantage of the fact* that we others are silent and banished; only they are heard, it is their most favorable moment. It would only be human *for them to profit from it and to proclaim their pretended patriotism even more loudly than they would perhaps do if it were not intended to drive us others into oblivion. One would have to take a look at them* to see whether they were not the ones who knew how to *profit* otherwise, as well. *Were they by chance fighters?* Or was it perhaps their nature to make the best of what power had brought—the power of human beings and of things—for their own good as well? What if one were to tell them that *they had with their own hands* brought about the enormity that is now reality" (the conviction of Dreyfus), "the ultimate in lies and disgrace" (here he is speaking of the conviction of the Jewish captain)—"by always reacting in a subtly skeptical way against such rough concepts as truth and justice. . . . In the extreme case, no, we certainly do not believe that in the extreme case they could *become traitors* to the intellect and to the human being. This is what they are now. Rather than reversing themselves, appearing before the people and urging them back, *they run together with them and their most disgusting corrupters, encouraging them in the injustice they are being enticed to commit.* They, the intellectual fellow-travelers, are more guilty even than those in power," (in the Dreyfus trial), "who lie and break the law. For those in power, the injustice they are committing remains an injustice; they are only arguing for their own interest, which they equate with that of the country. You false intellectuals are twisting injustice into justice, even into a mission, when it comes about by means of the very people whose conscience you are supposed to be. . . . The whole nationalistic catechism is filled with insanity and crime—and your *ambition* is preaching it, or, *what is even worse, your vanity . . . by pushing to become national poet laureates for half a lifetime, if your breath holds out that long*: but always running with the pack no matter what, always spurring forward, insane with pride, taking no responsibility for the coming catastrophe, *even as ignorant of it as you could be!*" . . . "Now it makes no difference if one stands in elegant array against truth, against justice; one stands against them and therefore belongs to those who are common and ephemeral. One has chosen between the moment and history, and one has admitted that with all one's talents one *has still only been an entertaining parasite."*

It was no pleasant business copying that; but now I am happy that it stands there: not merely in that European magazine, but also here in this book. For it belongs in this book, which is to be a document and to remain such when the waters recede. It belongs in this book, which is filled with the conviction that the present war is being fought not only for power and business, but also, and especially, for ideas, and which has already remarked in the early pages that Germany was the country where the intellectual antitheses of Europe oppose one another almost without common national coloring, without national synthesis—in whose soul the struggle between Europe's antitheses must be carried to the end. What! European wars will not be fought out anymore on German soil? They certainly will! European wars, as far as they are fought intellectually, and this they must always be, will be at the same time German *fraternal* wars; this remains the destiny of the European heartland, and in spite of all its physical strength, this is its inner, moral, political weakness—perhaps its misfortune. Germany has no brazen face like England; she does not have France's undivided, sentimental verve. Germany is not a nation.

On German soil, I say, even as German civil and fraternal wars, European wars are fought, and indeed, with weapons that are in no way inferior in refined cruelty to those that rage on the front. Here I stand in the dust cloud, the shell fragments, the yellow asphyxiation of a poison gas bomb, and do not know whether I am still alive. But yes, I am still alive all right. And therefore the thing to do would be to reply, to avenge with terrible countermeasures? There is no hurry. First there should be a general moral observation. It will be good to make it clear that as far as the struggle of intellects and pens, of criticism and polemics, is concerned, I do not at all consider cruelty and even infamy to be forbidden and dishonoring. "Infamy" is a very social reproach and a criticism that means little in a higher, more intellectual sphere. I am not talking about that shabby and negative infamy that one would do better to call ethical impotence: by the way, decency as a velleity, as something constantly on people's tongues, and as an impossibility, is a problem that forces itself on one and calls strongly for novelistic formulation. I mean rather that positive and passionate, bloodily insolent, proud and desperate infamy that does not at all perceive "decency" as its opposite, or that makes a childish error if it does, because it belongs to a completely different, a higher moral order, than decency. This infamy is like debauchery—of which Dmitri Karamasov says: "I loved debauchery, I also loved the disgrace of debauchery, I loved cruelty: for am I not a bug, an evil vermin?" This infamy is not egotistical; in every other sense than the civic one, it is anything but vulgar. It is a sacrifice, a casting away, a self-debasement, a relentless, fanatic, and humiliating devotion that not only is not without generosity, but is rather itself a dirty and bloody form of generosity. To the pure person—but I should rather say: to the clean one—the sight of infamy may awaken disgust, but not without at the same time inspiring him with a certain awe and teaching him presentiments of a mystical morality.

Above all, the passionately responsible critic must definitely have a right to infamy. Let us assume that a work appears that has an extraordinary effect on the public and on average critics because it is the product of extreme artistic effort, full of dazzling, awe-inspiring qualities and of the cleverest, most convincing subjective and objective defenses. Let us further assume that the book keeps the public on edge for months and sets a thousand pens to work in its praise—but one critic, made responsible by his gifts, his clearness of vision, sure of his instincts, sees that the work is essentially false, its effect fraudulent, harmful, destructive to culture: there would almost be—and I could even strike out this *almost*—no means he should not be allowed to use to discredit, denigrate, and destroy the admired work. For it is quite clear that the stronger the effective qualities of a bad work, the sharper and more unhesitating the means must be to bring its authority to a fall. Let no one demand that in such a case the critic should exercise "fairness"; that he praise, or even notice, the positive merits that might otherwise be credited to the work and its author: the merits must be more deserving of his hatred than the lies, for the merits are what give the lies effect, and his task here is not to acknowledge but to destroy. Let no one, least of all the author, complain about infamy when in such a case the critic exercises his legitimate malice on the author's person as well—one cannot be malicious without being personal; when he tries polemically to pursue the base work's origin into private-personal depths: work and life are in all serious cases much too intimately interwoven for passionate criticism not to be prepared at any moment to go over to a personal attack, and the demand for critical objectivity rests almost always on prudishness and lack of understanding.

Have I spoken gallantly, critic? I said this in order to prepare the categorical statement that there are infamies that I accept, because I have conscientious doubts about whether they might not be justified—

and infamies that I am completely resolved *not* to accept. The former are those primarily directed against my work, against my artistic gift, which like all artists I have before anyone else a grudge against; the latter, however, are those that touch my character, my intellectual honor. I think I see now and then that in spite of my best efforts errors may have gotten into my work. No one can be in a worse mood in such moments; no one can despise errors in his own works more bitterly, scornfully, and sadly, no one can recognize their problematic quality with more revulsion than I do—although it has long seemed to me that this quality is very much at home in the world of art; yes, that art is truly the most problematic area of human nature. I thought I had to deny the possibility of an artist's attaining real dignity, and from this denial I created a problematic work of art that still, above and beyond its problematic quality, has the intellectual honor of its doubt-plagued and pained honesty. Art is something quite different from literature, which is pure, rational, humanitarian and noble. It may be that the critic, who is a literary man and therefore a saint, and the artist, who is impure and of a problematic nature, may still finally find and understand one another in that ultimate honesty that is already extra-artistic, or precisely also still artistic. But there has perhaps never been an artistic nature without any trace of charlatanry, any tendency toward a feminine lie, and the artist in general, this "limitlessly sensual and vain ape," as Nietzsche called him, will always benefit greatly from the chastising rod of literature, of criticism, of malicious and even infamous unmasking, so that he will not decay intellectually and so that he will not receive with a stultified conscience the splendor and the honors with which the world appreciates his talent. I will never forget my shock when I first read Gogol's letter in which he speaks of the criticism his great novel was subjected to. "You are wrong," he says,

> to get so excited about the extravagant tone in which many of the attacks on *Dead Souls* are written; this also has its good side. Sometimes we need people who are furious at us. Whoever is completely taken with the beauty of a thing does not see its faults and forgives everything; but whoever, on the other hand, is enraged and embittered at us will *try to root up everything ugly, all the rubbish in us,* and to bring it so clearly to light that we must see it whether we want to or not. One so seldom gets to hear the truth that one should, for the sake of a small grain of truth, pardon the insult in the tone in which it is expressed. There is much truth in B.'s, S.'s and P.'s criticism, yes, even in the advice given to me that I should first learn Russian and then write books ... Yes, I even needed the epigrams and jokes directed against me, *even though I did not like them at all at first, and*

they were in no way pleasant to me. Oh, how much we need the constant blows and kicks, the insulting tone and the wicked jokes that wound us most deeply! At the bottom of our souls so much cheap, petty vanity is hidden, so much ugly, easily offended ambition, that we should be ceaselessly beaten and chastised by all sorts of rods, yes, we should be constantly grateful for the hand that punishes us.

I admit this is stated in a much too Slavic-slavish way for my taste. The artist may live more proudly, even if with more difficulty, if he carries his critic and punisher inside himself; he will react not only in a humble, but also in a basically friendly manner toward all criticism that comes from the outside, and he will accept the cutting truths and even the infamous half-truths about his work with a silence that may signify agreement, or that at least means: you are not telling me anything new.

But here we are not dealing with work and art. My human and intellectual honor is at stake here against the self-righteous intemperateness that poses as passion, that says it is love of humanity, and that hurls insults against me that are indeed something new and strange. It has to do with an intellectual and emotional position that I, in contrast to the German radical literary man, have adopted in this war, and with a "psychological commentary" on it that I not only will not bow to, but that, on the contrary, I can and must proudly and scornfully defy. For this position and partisanship of mine, even if it may have been abandoned by literature, was necessary, legitimate, consistent, genuine and true. It was the result, the quintessence, the direct expression of my character, my origin, education and esthetic training; it expressed my nature and my culture, which cannot be completely vulgar, not completely and utterly bad, because from it I have created two or three works that are good and that will last a while, and that have had as much effect on the times, the art of story telling, on language, hearts and minds, as any other work of the last quarter century—and whoever tries to debase this, my legitimate feeling, with psychological meanness; whoever says directly to my face with unbridled self-righteousness that through them I have become a traitor to intellect, that with them I have stood against justice and truth, that with them I have confessed myself to be a parasite, I will tell him *the name of his action* in a way he will not forget.

Recently a French journalist once again stated that his compatriots' national vice was always to impute bad motives to their opponents. Civilization's literary man is a Frenchman in this, too. Nothing could be more French than the confused mixture of venomous slander and fancy rhetorical pride that comprises his style. But from what basic tendency does this polemic vice come that that writer cannot help censuring in his Frenchmen? Why, it comes from the fact that they are psychologists! But psychology, of course, is the cheapest, most vulgar thing. There is nothing on earth in which dirt cannot be discovered and isolated by "psychological analysis," no action or opinion, no emotion, no passion. Just tell me what on earth psychology has ever been good for! Has it served art? Life? The "dignity of man"? Never. It can only serve the hatred that dearly loves "psychological commentaries," because through them everything can be utterly compromised. Anyone who is not a hater must find "psychology" the most superfluous achievement of recent times. What if I were to repay civilization's literary man in kind? If I were to meet him "psychologically"? If I urged him to turn against himself this type of knowledge he is using against me, and to ask himself if politics is not a pretext? If he had the slightest tendency toward moral hypochondria, he would have to turn pale and become silent. But he has no tendency toward moral hypochondria—alas, no. He is the most secure, the safest, the most virtuous person, he who dwells in justice and in truth. Here one should certainly make inquisitive youth aware that an arrogant carelessness such as his is never capable of doubt, of the flexibility of burgherly-artistic skepticism and of a wakeful conscience, but only of confirmed virtue.

Again, what have I done? In this war, I told the story of the king, through whose deeds, Goethe said, "the first true, higher, and characteristic essence of life came into German poetry." I told it in my way with a rather subdued and concealed enthusiasm, so that to well-wishers the writing seemed at first to be unpublishable. This did not prevent those who did not wish me well from thinking they could recognize in this selection of material a symptom of mercenary agility, of contemporary ability to conform to the times that does me little credit. I have indicated to them at the end of the last chapter how my relationship to the historical subject was not completely without legitimacy. But perhaps this legitimacy goes even deeper and broader. Intellectually, I belong to that race of writers throughout Europe who, coming from *décadence*, appointed to be chroniclers and analysts of *décadence*, at the same time have the emancipatory desire to reject it—let us say pessimistically: they bear the velleity of this rejection in their hearts and at least *experiment* with overcoming decadence and nihilism. Discerning people will find signs of this tendency, of this desire and attempt, everywhere in my works, and when a talented correspondent told me after my most recent work had been published that Maurice Barrès had written a story with almost exactly the same title—it is called *La mort de Venise*—he did not do so without allusion to a distant correlation. It is clear that Barrès' nationalism and Catholicism, his seizing and propagating of the idea of revenge as a means of *excitement*, meant nothing else than the attempt to overcome decadence; and it is just as clear what a strongly national origin this attempt had—and how a German version would have to be different. Of course the latter would not be *political* (and lead to the president's chair in a patriotic league) but *moral*; nor would it be *Catholic*, expecting everything to come from the outside, from the cult of tradition, but *Protestant*, appealing to the inner sense of duty, Kantian-Prussian. Am I making myself clear? Here is the intellectual legitimacy of my relationship to the Frederick material. I reveal it—not from joy in chilling self-revelation, but to counter the stupidity that insinuates I quickly began to swim with the stream anno 1914.

I called the timely manuscript a "Sketch for the Day and the Hour." That it was; and not only a sketch of history, but a hasty, and, as I still hope, a preliminary sketch of special, long-cherished dreams and plans of a creative nature whose intellectual nucleus I was in those days self-forgetful and heedless enough to publish as an essay. Thus the topical experience had its effect, but of course it would not have had such a strong influence on my thoughts had it not been for the historical-creative preparation. At least *one* sympathetic observer recognized and expressed what a strong and—I can say it—fruitful influence it really had on me: the Swedish writer whose study on the Frederick booklet I mentioned. There where Hallström speaks about the invasion of Saxony, where in agreement with my presentation he says that heroism in the face of danger, no matter how great, is "almost minor" in comparison to the heroism "of holding one's soul upright under the pressure of hatred, of bearing all the responsibility alone, of supporting alone all that is despairing and ill in a nation in mortal danger midst all the questions of why and what now"—there he adds: "I do not know whether Frederick's heroic courage, the basis of all his incomparable deeds, has ever been comprehended so strongly and intensely. It would not be surprising if this fateful period in Germany were the one destined to find the right measure—the historical past is repeating itself in the present in all essential elements. To have seen this with burning clarity and to have traced the parallels with sharpness and depth, this is what makes Mann's essay so significant." Why should I conceal the deep emotion with which I read and re-read this foreigner's words? And from this deep emotion, which is too proud and serious to have anything in common with everyday vanity, I now address the frivolous rhetorician who tells me that in that work I went along with the most disgusting corrupters of my people, encouraging them in the injustice they were being enticed to commit. If what the Swede says is true; if his "I do not know whether" actually means "I do not believe that," and if he is right with this "I do not believe"; if it is true—and I feel that it is true—that the mutual effect of historical-creative preparation and current experience enabled my soul to grasp so intensely and strongly the heroic courage of the man "through whose deeds the first higher essence of life came into German poetry," as it had never been grasped before (this would really not be surprising and would not signify an accomplishment at all, but only a fateful coincidence)—if this is true, how do you then stand before me, human being, artist, brother, with your wild chatter? An understanding and re-experiencing that never before was possible in such burning depth, and the fairly exact communication of this understanding and re-experiencing through the literary word: is this what an ambitious fellow-traveler does; can it be an example of pipe-puffing burgherly complacency? *Passion*, involuntary, not literarylike striven-for, hawked-out passion, but heartfelt passion, masked perhaps with irony and humor, is the only thing that makes something like this possible, the only thing that produces something new, something that has never before existed—suffering, then, pain, sacrificial devotion to something purifyingly suprapersonal. Have you no more regard for suffering, for experience? Do you insult them if they do not serve "intellect," that is to say: your radical teaching? Then you are lost! Then no matter how gaudy and dashing your prose, how ingeniously vivacious your gestures, how hot your breath, how melting your ballad—then you are no longer an artist and not a human being, either: then you are a doctrinaire and a schoolmaster, ossified in bigotry.

With this, everything has been said. For what should I repay in detail to the aria of hatred and suspicion from which I have cited a few particularly brilliant passages here? What should I perhaps respond to the accusation of ambitious patriotic striving? I recognize in myself the tendency to self-abuse, a readiness that is perhaps unmanly to adopt as my own hateful and obviously malicious stylizations of my being, and to affirm them. I can only look with a shake of my head at the criticism of ambitious striving; I do not know what to do with it. Cleverness in behavior toward the world and its powers has never been my strength; I was too much alone for this, too much "writer"; and this book also shows, it seems to me, that politics, in this sense as well, is alien to my being. When I see it in the artistic sphere, I observe it without anger but with smiling astonishment. I see a master publicly flattering the "younger generation," although he privately despises it; and this is clever. I hear another, or also the same, master declaring "the most insignificant reporter" to be his intellectual brother, provided only that his paper has democratic principles; and this is also clever, for in this way one becomes an idol and pet of the great, the leftist liberal press. I see a third, or again the same, master wooing the favor of the masses as he presents himself as a champion of democracy. I see him then making his work topical for domestic affairs, secretly mixing up love with mass distribution, joining virtue with profit. Is all this ambitious striving? Possibly. It seems foreign to me—humorous, but foreign. And ambitious *patriotic* striving? This obviously also exists. In all countries it is possible to do business with patriotism. But as for *me*, I know very well what it would have been like for me if, on the contrary, cleverness had dictated my attitude and style. I would have had to be quite outspoken, to throw the pacifist-humanitarian club between the legs of my fighting people, proclaiming over and over again that the war was a German crime against intellect—of course I would not have received a decoration for my Frederick essay, but my honor, my honor as a man of letters, that is, would have been saved. I could not do it. And since I could not, I am faced with the accusation that my ambition, oh no, my vanity, has preached the "nationalistic catechism."

No matter what the contents of the nationalistic catechism may be, I believe I am German precisely because I have never felt very secure in it, and in this respect the war has not changed much. It is true that the exaltation of 1914 carried me, too, to the belief and to the admission of this belief, that the nation to which I have the special honor of belonging had a great right to rule, a valid claim to participation in the government of the earth, in brief, to political power, and that it was justified in gaining the recognition of these natural rights through war, yes, that it had to do so. Today I have moments, at least, when this belief wavers and almost dies; for I say to myself that a ruling nation, limited, hard, egotistical and nationally firmly in the saddle, as a ruling nation must be, would hardly let itself be confused in its rights by its foremost intellects, as is the case in Germany. The rejoicing of the nation in itself and in its rights lasted five or six weeks, scarcely longer, even though it was only then that its accomplishments became tremendous, and—for the others—eternally remarkable. This national rejoicing was immediately perceived to be intellectually unnational, the counterpressure was immediately very strong, and the rejoicing was rapidly made despicable to the nation in a manner unimaginable in every other country. German nationalism—where is it? I wish I were capable of wishing something like that existed. Today, in the midst of this war, in the face of the enemy's unity and resolution that only a few of our people even try to imagine, a famous journalist turns, in a feeling of representing all of Europe, against Lessing, the national literary pedagogue, because he had called the French a vain people, attacked M. Voltaire critically, and put the figure of Riccaut into his Prussian soldier drama. Lessing had debased himself and caused incalculable damage, the journalist says. An enthusiastic cheer from the depths of the national soul: very true! Yes, this is truly a high point in German chauvinism. After two years of war, our national weakness is indulging in orgies; German self-abandonment and self-renunciation have long been almost complete again. If it were not for naked economic necessity—there would be no stopping of this rapid process of self-forgetfulness, of losing oneself again, there would be no "sticking it out to the end." Admiration of German deeds? Perhaps one can find this in Sweden, but not in our country, and this is the way it should be; one should not say that I would have it otherwise. Hatred of the mortal enemy? There is none. There is only admiration of the enemies—and the awareness of strength expressed in this is an awareness of physical strength, not at all of the strength of national character. It is the consciousness of border security, that ruin of all national fervor. For the deepest humiliation, the most extreme misery, is necessary to make national passion intellectually possible in Germany, and this war, which is unfortunate not because it is not going very well, but because it is not going very badly—this half-way situation that leaves the country secure, breeds indifference to events, public apathy and individual corruption— I admit that nothing worse could have happened from the national point of view. "No one," Goethe said, "looks pitiful when he feels he has some right to make claims." He also says: "Justice—a German quality and a German *illusion*." Who would deny that Germany is a cultured and a just nation? But a *commanding* nation? I doubt it. I doubt it to the point of *despair* every few days.

No, Germany does badly in the test of nationalistic catechism! And still: Is it not precisely this on which the best belief in Germany's mission is based? The nationalistic catechism lies in the hands and rules in the minds of the political, democratic nations; it is their spokesmen who preach it; the national principle belongs to the "immortal principles" of the Revolution, and today it must serve as ideological dynamite for Austria's destruction. Democracy and nationalism are of the same origin, they are one and the same thing. And *nationalistic democracy* is guilty—guilty (in order finally, for my part, to take up this word), guilty of the present situation in Europe, of its anarchy, of the struggle of all against all, and of this war. The national principle is the atomistic, the anarchic, the anti-European, the reactionary principle. Democracy is reactionary, for it is nationalistic and lacks all European conscience. Where is there a European conscience among Germany's enemies? In *England*, perhaps, not to speak of the brazen conduct of small national egoisms? European conscience, supranational responsibility, is solely alive in the nonpolitical and antidemocratic nation, in Germany—but the German radical literary man does not see this. He listens transfixed to the phrases such as "free society of states," "democratic league of nations," "democratic peace," that flow from the glib tongues of the Western rhetoricians—not really transfixed, for neither he nor any rational human being in the whole world seriously believes in this society, this league, and this peace. "Do you believe in the league of nations?!" M. Georges Clemenceau cried to his chamber . . . and the chamber was silent. No, it is not the nationalistic-international demo-cratic peace that Europe needs—for it is impossible, there would be no peace, only perpetuated anarchy. Europe's peace must not be interna-tional, but supranational; let it not be a democratic, but a German peace. The peace of Europe can only rest on the victory and the power of the supranational people, the people that calls the highest, most universal traditions, the richest cosmopolitan talent, the deepest feeling of European responsibility, its own. Let Europe's peace rest on the fact that the best educated, the most just, most sincerely freedom-loving nation is also the most powerful, the ruling one—on the power of the German *Reich*, which cannot be touched by any machination. If *this* means confessing the nationalistic catechism, well then, all right, I confess it, too; then I have always confessed it. And therefore, the humanitarian says, I have brought about the war "with my own hands."

No, not for this reason. I am mistaken. It was because I was a doubter. Because I "always reacted in a subtly skeptical way against such rough concepts as truth and justice." Rough concepts? These are not rough concepts. They are the highest and most pure. And whoever takes them in vain is a virtue-mouthing braggart. Doubting? I doubted truth and justice as eternal ideas, I never loved them, and on the two thousand printed pages I wrote in these twenty years, wrote slowly with the greatest deliberation, I was never concerned with truth—and therefore with justice? For are these not simply names—are not all the highest words, including "freedom" and "beauty," simply names for the one, the divine, the absolute? Justice! He who thinks justice is only a political slogan—a fanfare calling to bloody deeds, even if they are just literary deeds—does not know what it is. Only he for whom it is the highest form of conscience, yes, conscience itself, knows it as *intellectual* passion, as melancholy, and as truth. Admittedly, this justice may not be expressed in dashing fervor; it may be that it leads to quietism. But justice that is only aggressive, dogmatic, unscrupulous, and basically unjust—what is it if it never allows itself to be corrected by that other justice, what is it other than licentiousness and voluptuousness? Yes, I have doubted that it was proper to drag truth and justice day-in, day-out, through the political gutter; that it was right and proper to confuse them with the radical republic; yes, I have doubted this; and therefore I was a doubter and a quietist—the humanitarian may be right in the end.

But wait! Doubt and quietism brought about this war? Has an *action*, good or bad, ever come from quietism and "burgherly doubt"? This is new, this is paradoxical. But this war, you cry, is not an action, it is a catastrophe! Both. Every great upheaval has always been both the one and the other. You would be greatly offended if one wanted to remove the character of action from the French Revolution. This war, too, is just as much a common European *action* as it is a European catastrophe: and I admit I had always believed that it was an intellectual-spiritual constitution, custom, and *geste* completely different from doubt and quietism that produces, or at least prepares, or at least announces, the action—that is, a—even if artificial—*reinforcement*; a—even if spasmodic—new *will* and "New Passion," a—even if hysterical—call for *agitation* and *action* at any, definitely at any price.

One should not speak so frivolously about the relationship of intellect to events as the humanitarian is not ashamed to do in order to be able to accuse and to cast suspicion. Who cannot see that such a relationship exists, that this war is no accident, that it did not fall directly and unannounced from heaven or escape from hell? But it seems to me to be the most difficult of tasks to discover and to clarify this relationship, to establish, for example, the extent to which Dostoyevsky is a hero, the

Russian hero and prophet, of this war. Dostoyevsky was a great writer, an artist, a national *expression*—and one does not know if an artist is ever more than this, more than an expression and a spokesman, if he can also be a leader, dictator, shaper and teacher of his people. One does not know, that is, how much Dostoyevsky only received the Russian idea, Pan-Slavism, and the call to Constantinople, from the nation—only embodied it as a national writer—and how much the idea worked back on the nation through him. We know that this great Christian has praised and exalted war in general. And if the measure of political effect were to be determined by the measure of political will, then one would certainly have to see in him the hero of this war—more so than in Nietzsche, at any rate, whom I, at least, can never without bitterness hear called the author of political effects. "In an objective sense," Emil Hammacher says in his book, *Main Questions of Modern Culture*, "Nietzsche's greatest service *is the separation of metaphysical from social life*. . . . He rediscovered the insight that individualism is a mistake and that supraindividuality is still realized through personality itself and only through it; for him, social supraindividuality, *society*, is relatively unimportant and inferior in comparison to metaphysical supraindividuality." According to Hammacher, then, Nietzsche agreed with Christianity in the separation of the metaphysical from the social sphere; he was just as little a politician as was Jesus himself when he differentiated in that immortal sentence between duties to "Caesar" and to "God." If one wants to include among Nietzsche's political accomplishments the moving of a few mine owners or large market investors to think they were renaissance men, or the message that a few stupid young men and women got from him that they were to live amorally, "enjoying life to the fullest"—in God's name, this is not serious. But I know exactly *where* Nietzsche had very serious political effects, in a warlike sense indeed, and I will tell you.

Here I return to the recent apotheosis of Emile Zola, of the French novelist-activist, whose activity was admittedly directed against the movement in France that actually claimed for itself the name of activism, and that, in spite of the whole radical republic, remained very much alive after Zola's death: against the political activism of the *Action française* and the Patriotic League. Zola's activity was the individualistic indignation of justice against a *political enthusiasm for life* that declared itself ready to sacrifice a person who was probably "innocent" to the interest of the state—to sacrifice "truth" to "life." This was *politicized and therefore corrupted Nietzsche*. Never has anyone in Germany thought of politicizing the Nietzschean enthusiasm for life. This would have been completely un-German. It was left to the Latins to do that—as is proper. What in Germany is called "activism" is pacifistic, humanitarian, and antinational, in short: radical enlightenment; but the Latin activism is nationalistic and warlike, is radical reaction. The German "activist" learned how to write from Nietzsche, and this may have been a misuse, for Nietzsche was no enlightener. But the Latin learned *politicizing* from him and this is a much worse misuse. The politicization of Nietzsche is nothing else than the disfiguring of Nietzsche, and if the war has actively brought about anything intellectual at all, it is this: the inability of the Latins to keep philosophy and politics apart.

Of course it is precisely this inability that civilization's literary man values as the highest glory of the Western peoples. This is exactly what he wants to teach his people, and perhaps is really on the verge of teaching them. What is called activism, voluntarism, New Passion, is nothing other than the nonseparation of philosophy and politics: here, civilization's literary man sees the virtue that would have prevented the war if it had been dominant, while the opposite instinct, the separation of the metaphysical from the social, is in his opinion vice itself that did not prevent war, and this means: caused it. But things are not as simple as they seem to him who is intent on accusing, on blaming. The false Nietzscheanism of France teaches that the politicization of philosophy can just as well signify radical reaction as radical enlightenment, *war* as well as pacifism; and without accusation, without placing blame, I say that German "activism," even though its political doctrine is pacifistic, has had much more to do with the whole European action and catastrophe we find ourselves in, has heralded and prepared it psychologically, in gesture, much more than any "burgherly" quietism and "doubt," more than any apolitical artistry that seeks knowledge and form. Where would the psychological connections be, for example, between *my* German-burgherly-artistic production and the war—if I may here disregard certain purely symbolic-ethical connections that one admittedly tends today to perceive as "topical"? I know well that future events are somehow foreshadowed in me and through me, as they are through every somewhat sensitive instrument. The works I was engaged in when the war came and interrupted me were so much inspired by the rising events, which I did not consciously notice, that someone in the future, uncertain of the chronology, would without hesitation see the inspiration of the war in them. I also see very well, for example, how the story, *Death in Venice*, stands chronologically just before the war in its tension of will and its morbidity: in its fashion, it is something final, the late work of an epoch, on which uncertain lights of a new era are falling. But I do not mean such connections and purely sensitive-seismographical symptoms here. I am referring rather to sympathies of volition, temperament, gesture, and emotional needs—sympathies of which in me, a person well aware of an unusually epic *humanity* in himself, there is not a trace to be found and never will be, while a—not always according to age—younger, more "futuristic" type of production that is topical today shows a surprising amount of it. All honor to it! I repeat, I am not one intent on denunciation. In the meantime, it is, of course, quite obvious that what is called "activism" in Germany is nothing other than the transfer of a certain artistic taste and tempera-ment into politics. An artistic school ("Expressionism") of intensely activistic needs, disdainfully averse to peace and quiet, to observation, epic comfort, objectivity and cheerfulness, and based completely on speed, vehement agitation and the expression of the grotesque—de-mands one day that "the intellectual be active." This could be good. As far as I am concerned, I think with interest and gratitude of valuable and, in the Goethean sense, "significant" impressions of the exploding rage, cruelty, wild confusion, hardness, lack of cheerfulness, inexora-bleness, maliciousness, *inhumanity* with which certain of the most recent stories have been told, and I say to myself: it really matters little whether the political platform of these colleagues is pacifist or not—here is war! They sang it in every line before it was there, and there was never a better example of how little opinion proclaims being. And does not my clear insight agree with their own confession, their own pride? A leader of the expressionist movement, to be sure of the artistic rather than of the literary faculty, cried out in August 1914: "This is our moment!"

Of course the humanitarian thinks differently. He thinks that *my* most favorable moment is today, that the present favors the likes of me; for while he is condemned to "banishment" and to "silence," people listen only to us, only to me, and we are taking, I am taking, advantage of the favorable moment to insist much too loudly on my patriotism, thereby trying to drive "others" into oblivion, who, for their part, are also only a rhetorical plural. "*One would have to take a look at them,*" he says—the italics are mine, I value this turn of phrase, it *hisses* out so remarkably—"One would have to take a look at them to see whether they were not the ones who knew how to profit otherwise, as well." What this is supposed to mean, can mean, no one knows. It is suspicion in itself and in general, hissing suspicion without content and substance, softly tossed out from a twisted mouth. It is clear that in the humanitarian's opinion my "disposition" makes life quite easy for me—I am well off, according to him, and I have always been well off—"singing along through the world,"* as the song in the opera goes, thus it went for me, thus I lived all the time. Is hatred a better means of understanding than love? No, definitely not. At least not unscrupulous, rhetorical hatred. I do not want to speak of the past or of the warbling ease of my being and essence in it. "I stand between two worlds," Tonio Kröger said, "am at home in neither and therefore find things a little difficult." He also said that some people have to go astray because there is no correct path for them at all. Enough. For the moment, I only want to ask whether it might not be flashy progress-optimism and rhetorical humanitarianism that produce a comparatively "easy" way of life. I will be satisfied by stating that the one who accused me of having an easy life came to terms with events by first hurling a few Parisian chamber-tirades about saber and justice into the face of the German world, and then declaring the humanitarian businessman to be the European ideal—whereupon he, proud, cheerful, morally secure and surrounded by the clattering applause of politicizing youth, could turn again to the lasting joys of the art of letters. And I? I who am well off? Somehow I have been obliged to write this book. In other words, I run along with my people's corrupters, irresponsible and insane with pride, "as ignorant as I could be of the coming catastrophe."

"As ignorant as I could be"—this sentence has also made me think. Did I, and do I, know less about events than those who consider themselves to be completely free and noble because they spurn the "great times" out of petty literary concern about the cultural damage that war and patriotic confusion usually cause, in the year 1870, for example? Did I, in 1914, imagine this so-called "war," whose character and consequences only a childish fool would compare with those of 1870—did I even in the first moment imagine it to be a light, happy military romp to Paris and Petersburg? I did not compare it to 1870, but to 1756, as far as it was simply a "war"; I said it would probably last seven years—and since it is now in the third year, is this impossible? I had perhaps a clearer picture than most of my compatriots of the physical and superficially moral predominance we had to wage war against. I declared a "triumphant victory" to be unthinkable, and

---

* "mit Sing und Sang, die Welt entlang"

thought at most of a result similar to 1763. But if the seductive, national-historical parallels charmed me, I was still not completely captured and blinded. I saw well that what was happening was more, that it signified something greater and more terrible, than a bit of Prussian destiny. I may say that I was among the first who recognized in what rose up and overtook us, what only childish minds can consider a "war" like any other, an earth-shaking event comparable only to the most powerful revolutions, to breakthroughs and breakdowns in world history, the greatest history, then, and it had to seem stupid and wretched to me to "oppose" it in any pacifist-humanistic or literary-cultural way—a turning point in world history, at least the bloody-historical indication of the turn of the century. Only the German intellect seemed to be suited to such insight, and what disgusted it was precisely the cheap instinct of its enemies to falsify miserably and to transform a world event that, admittedly, as with everything elemental, hardly seemed to fit into our civilization, into a sentimental-moral, yes, even forensic affair with "guilt" and "innocence," "saber" and "justice." A good part of my patriotism came and comes from the comparison of the German-tragic concept of events to the forensic-moral concept of the enemies. But did I not also see in this turn of the century a turn of my own personal life and of all our lives? Did I not soon realize that "afterward" everything would be different, that nothing could become the same as before, that no one would be able to continue his life in the old style, and that whoever wanted to do so would outlive himself? What shook and shamed me was the incongruity between my personal rank and the roaring display of world history that marked the crisis of my forty years. No doubt it is fate to be placed so in time that a change in personal life comes together with a catastrophic change in the times. He is a happy man, I have often thought in these years, who can feel the same cultural and intellectual foundation under him his whole life long! I spent many an hour with the writings, notes and epigrams in which Goethe tried to come to terms with the French Revolution, and it was a consolation for me to see how this great man, who may also have thought he would have the same social and intellectual foundations under his feet until the end of his life, had so much trouble coming to terms with the new events, accepting them into his world, his work. Or was perhaps his heart, his spirit, wide and cheerfully open to new things? Was he not full of polemics, full of resistance? Was not his first and strongest instinct self-assertion, assertion of his world?

> In these confused times, French character is pushing back
> Quiet cultural development, just as Lutheranism once did.*

Or, to choose something else antidemocratic:

> What does the sacred freedom of the press
> Offer you in benefit, advantage, and fruit?
> You have a certain indication of this:
> Profound disdain of public opinion.**

Goethe, Schopenhauer, and Nietzsche taught the German pupil such things. And he should then have brought himself to take part against Germany in this war in favor of the democratic public world opinion that bore all the signs of superficiality, ignorance, sentimentality and meanness? Nevertheless, I repeat: Everyone who wanted to continue living as he had lived before would outlive himself. What more is this long monologue and writing than a glance back at what I was, what I was for a while with good reason and honor, and what I, without feeling *old*, will obviously no longer be able to be? No, I am scarcely as ignorant as I can be about the significance of the hour, for I even know that he who does not succeed in coming to tolerable terms with the new times will be old and will always be a man of yesterday.

As far as I am concerned, I must realize that I can probably accept, learn, seek understanding, correct myself—but that I cannot change my character and my education, cannot pull up my roots and plant them somewhere else. This period of change is "my hour"? Only as far as its thunder emphasizes in a direct-overpowering way the turn in my personal life—it signifies the *end* of my "hour," if I am not completely mistaken, not its beginning. My most favorable moment! Fool, do you not see that it is your most favorable moment, much more yours?! The politicization and democratization of Germany, the work of this war that you have negated in a humanitarian way, is it not creating the atmosphere in which your work and will, your political morality and political "humanity," can finally thrive gloriously? Is not your work blossoming? Are not your people coming together and proclaiming your name as a symbol to them of the new truth and honor? Are not

---

* Franztum drängt in diesen verworrenen Tagen, wie ehemals
  Luthertum es getan, ruhige Bildung zurück.
** Was euch die heilige Preßfreiheit
  Für Frommen, Vorteil und Früchte beut?
  Davon habt ihr gewisse Erscheinung:
  Tiefe Verachtung öffentlicher Meinung.

the critics bowing deeply before what has not existed before and what you are introducing: the artistic democracy? What I, who am, after all, much closer to German culture, German artistic burgherdom, than you, could never be convinced I was: a German writer—are not your people assuring you so eagerly that this is what you are, so that it would be "only human" if you believed it? Now comes turbulent success, modern-industrial success, almost in the style and taste of your Zola-like dreams; megaphone advertisements are coming, the yellow brochures of mass distribution, theater festivals—all in a political-democratic sense and spirit that was completely foreign to my "hour." Here's to you! Here's to me! The more you receive in full all you have wished, the more I can hope justice will be done to me, too; for every "hour" passes, and I do not believe that pure value judgments can be derived from the time it occurs in an individual's life. Meanwhile, however:

> Well, if I don't succeed, I *have* succeeded,
> And that's enough; succeeded in my youth,
> The only time when much success is needed:
> . . .
> Whate'er it was, 't was mine; I've paid, in truth,
> Of late, the penalty of such success,
> But have not learned to wish it any less.

Years have passed, more years than the war has lasted, since I marked the Don Juan verses in the book with my pencil. So early did I understand things, and even without complaining. I am capable of looking at my life and fate with calm, yes, with cheerfulness, with an independence for which *amor fati* is a much too emotional, moral phrase. Bitterness is my least danger. I *have* succeeded, and that's enough. Love, too, even the love of youth, still comes to me, and it can be sure that it does not come to an ungrateful one. But if I step back now; if I cannot and do not want to sing the song of the "spirit" that I hummed to myself early, experimentally, and with ironical softness, if I cannot and will not sing it in a politically organized chorus; if I, whose ethical symbolism at the moment has reached a certain national currency, will soon stand quite alone, without a following and "relations," an unorganized person, an outsider and "good for nothing": well, then it seems to me that a very new contentment could be bound to such unvirtuous loneliness and oblivion, a new freedom, lack of responsibility and bohemianism, something like a new gallows humor and high spirits, a condition that is quite similar to that dark, free, early one where one's name had not yet become the world's plaything, and where one, convinced of being an impossible fellow, did one's best work. Who says to you that it is not precisely this that I want and seek? That I do not perhaps consider the role of the impossible fellow to be more artistic and decent than that of a chorus leader of intellectual virtue? I am anticipating. I want to dedicate a special chapter to virtue. But is a moment that is so little mine, so obviously a part of you and your splendid rise—is, I ask you, this the right moment to hit me in the face as you are doing now? Was it worthwhile to remain fifteen years in noble freedom from envy in order to let yourself go with such abandon just at the moment when everything is changing? Is it not a misuse of your hour of glory to say to me to my face before assembled youth that all my life I have been nothing more than an entertaining parasite?

A parasite. For: "Were they perhaps fighters?" Oh, no, I was never a fighter, never anything close! I did not stand there, one hand on my heart and the other in the air, and recite the *contrat social.* I did not cry for the hanging of any "gentlemen" from the lamppost, and I did not plead for the abolition of great men because they oppressed the average man. I did not claim that the republic was the ideal of truth, neither did I scorn the human race, which is eternally burdened with sorrow, by insisting with a tremolo that it was headed toward "something beautiful and completely serene," nor did I call everyone who could not believe this an idiot or a rascal, and I did not cry: "Heed me, who loves!" I remember that I kept my distance from all that. And therefore I was not a fighter. Therefore I was a parasite. I want to be levelheaded. I do not want to say that slovenly, oratorical-carelessness is base, shocking insult; the extent of *my* case probably only merits calling it a small injustice. A great man walked back and forth in his little room with his hands behind his back and spoke to his listening famulus, his voice perhaps still shaking: "I know very well that in spite of the great pains I have always taken, all my writings are considered as nothing in the eyes of certain people, simply because I have disdained to take sides in political struggles. To justify myself to these people I would have had to become a member of a Jacobin club." May I *remember* these sentences, only remember them and nothing more, at the moment when I am told I have led the life of a parasite? The concept of *helping* has been delightful and dear to me ever since I became aware that it had a place in my life. I had not believed it before. I admit I had not begun with this social idea in mind. No, I had not allowed myself to dream I could help others, because my own questionable nature had occupied me so much. Today I know a hundred times over that by "having chosen the hard way" I have *helped* others *to live*. To help people to live. This is certainly something different from placing them with dash and tremolo into the one and only European condition, the one and only condition worthy of human dignity, the condition of political revolt, but it is not certain that it is something worse, something less moral, or even something more antisocial. My way of speaking, of letting life speak, was more bitter than sweet, even if, to be sure, humor and music were correlations of pessimism for me. A great burgherly artist, Adalbert Stifter, said in a letter: "My books are not just fiction; they are also valuable as moral revelations, as human dignity preserved in strict seriousness, and this will last longer than the fictional part." I have a right to repeat his words, and thousands whom I "have helped to live" *see* it, this right. The generation that decided around the turn of the century on the success or nonsuccess of a writer welcomed me—well, it also welcomed others who were often worse; this did not say much about the value of the effect I had. Perhaps it was based on ingratiating qualities, on pleasantries of accent. But at that time, when I began to write, people lay in their cradles who are today as old as the novel of decadence and the story of the burgher-writer. They grew up together with these creations, grew into life, into difficult life, and they let me know that these creations helped them to live. They taught me that no ephemeral, agreeable charm, that *human value* was at work in what I could give. But aggressive, always only self-righteously aggressive love of slander rises up and declares that instead of being a "fighter," I had parasitically taken advantage of what power had brought about.

"The name of his action"? What the humanitarian, civilization's literary man, the neoenthusiast and sly old fox has done here, what he has dared to do in his great, moral security, is the most thoughtless, unconscionable, humanly irresponsible slander. He claims nevertheless the moral superiority of this kind of "domestic policy" over the rage of patriotic zealots that is directed abroad: in no other contemporary have the qualities of reason, justice and humanity suffered greater shipwreck in the tempest of the times than in him.

CHAPTER 7

Politics

> What artist ever bothered much before about the
> political events of the day—He lived only in his art,
> and only in it did he walk through life; but ominous,
> difficult times have gripped the human being with an
> iron fist, and the pain is pressing sounds from him that
> were foreign to him before.
>
> E. T. A. Hoffmann, *Highly Absent-Minded Thoughts*

Objectivity is freedom, is cheerfulness. We breathe a sigh of relief,
we may be "scientific" again, as in the beginning of our reflections.
We ask: What is politics?

One will answer: "Politics is the science of the state." Or perhaps, as
a scholar formulates it with seemingly final exactness: "Politics is
practical behavior, including the rules derived from it, which, whether
it be on the part of government, particular groups of people, or even
individuals, sets as its goal the maintenance or the reformation of the
existing state." But today these are outdated definitions. The true
definition of the concept, "politics," is only possible with the help of its
opposite concept; it says: "Politics is the opposite of estheticism." Or:
"Politics is salvation from estheticism." Or, stated quite strictly: "To be
a politician is the only possible way of not being an esthete." We claim
and insist that only this offers a living definition of the concept of
politics that fits present conditions, although it does not escape us that
we are here defining an unknown with an unknown—that no definition
exists as long as we have not defined this second X, the concept of
estheticism, as well. We are ready to do this! What is estheticism? What
is an esthete?

In answering this question, it is customary to emphasize altogether
too much nonessential-secondary material, while neglecting the true-

essential characteristics, and above all, circumscribing the concept much too narrowly. Estheticism is not, for example, the beautiful spirit, the beautiful soul, the beautiful beard; it is absolutely not a criterion of estheticism for one to insist upon "dying in beauty," or always having figures of speech such as "wine leaves in the hair" on one's tongue. On the contrary, it is quite possible to perceive this wish to be unbearably affected and this manner of speaking rather trite, and still to be an esthete of the first water. Neither does that lack of warm-heartedness and humanity, that clever and intellectual mixture of triviality and sublety, or of brutality and refinement, which makes up the essence of many a modern, or no longer so modern, work of art, suffice to exhaust and to fulfill the concept of estheticism. Estheticism as the opposite of the political nature—for only within this antithesis does the concept become current and alive today! Estheticism is rather . . . But let us allow examples to speak!

Schiller, to single out the first good example that comes to mind, is an esthete when in *The Bride of Messina* he praises peace through the mouth of a chorus leader in the most ingratiating of words, compares it to a lovely boy resting by a quiet stream, surrounded by frisky lambs, luring sweet tones from his flute—but who uses—or misuses—his very next breath to speak of war with the same poetic dedication, declaring that it, too, has its honor, calling it "the mover of human fate," and then breaking out into that song praising human butchery—precisely those falsely moral verses that so angered Romain Rolland when I quoted them. Schiller, let us repeat, is an esthete here, because he is not a politician here—not one at all, neither a good one nor a bad one. He could have glorified war and called the pacifists cowards and snivelers: then he would have been a bad, a false politician, an enemy of humanity to be combatted. He could have been inclined to celebrate eternal freedom and to brand war as a return to subhuman conditions: then he would have acted as a good, enlightened and praiseworthy politician. But to immerse himself deeply into the essence of peace and war with the same dilettantish empathy, love, and free contemplation, precisely this was estheticism; it was the unprincipledness of the—I will say it: of the parasite.

Unlike Schiller, whose estheticism sometimes *seems* to be called in question by his morality, *Flaubert* is universally known to be a pronounced esthete; but it would be superficial to believe that he is so because of his chiseled artistic prose, which is weighed out with whimsical care. It is no more than a symptom, and scarcely that; for a good style is just as much the sign of the true, praiseworthy and humanitarian politician. No, something else stamps Flaubert as an esthete. It is, for example, the way he treats the two characters, the druggist and the priest, in *Madame Bovary*, as they sit together by Emma's corpse and as their philosophies clash—the famous world view of M. Homais and that of the country cleric. The poor sinner, Emma, has just died—these are austere, terrible, solemn pages. Well, as I said, philosophies clash against one another. "'Since God always knows what we need, what is prayer for?'—'Are you not a Christian, then?'—'I admire Christianity; it was the first to abolish slavery . . .'—'We are not talking about that. The Bible . . .'—'I do not care about your Bible! The Jesuits . . .'" At times they are interrupted by the entry of Charles Bovary, who is drawn to the corpse. He is the one whose wife has died, and it seems as if this somehow elevates him above the arguments of the two worthies. At any rate, he makes a very serious and respectable impression each time he enters. "As soon as Charles had left the room, the two began their discussions anew. 'Read Voltaire!' said the one. 'Read Holbach! The Encyclopedists!'—'Read *The Letters of Some Portuguese Jews*,' said the other, 'read the *Foundations of Christianity* by Nicolas!'—They got excited, their faces turned red, and they argued simultaneously with each other. Bournisien was irritated by the apothecary's presumption, Homais astonished by the priest's narrowness. They were both almost at the point of insulting one another . . ." Finally they go to sleep. "Thus they sat opposite one another, with their bellies sticking out, with their bloated faces full of wrinkles in their brows. After all their conflict, the same human weakness united them. They moved just as little as the corpse beside them, which seemed to be sleeping. Charles came. He did not waken the two. He came for the last time. To take leave of *her*." I will not add anything to this. It is estheticism; for here politics comes off badly in the most scandalous way.

Schopenhauer constantly betrays himself as an esthete; in the following two places he does not do so at all with particular impetuousity, but perhaps nevertheless with paradigmatic terseness. He speaks of fame, of accomplishments through which one attains fame: they fall, he says, into *actions* and *works*, and each of these two paths to fame has its advantages and disadvantages.

> The main difference is that actions are transitory while works remain. The most noble *action* still has only a temporary effect; the work of genius on the other hand lives and has beneficial and uplifting effect through all times. Only the memory of the actions remains, which becomes weaker

and weaker, more distorted and indifferent, and must even gradually disappear if history does not take it up and transmit it in a petrified state to posterity. Works, on the other hand, are themselves immortal and can, especially the written ones, live through all times.

In a footnote, Schopenhauer remarks that it is a poor compliment when, as is the fashion today, one thinks one is honoring works by calling them actions. For works are on an essentially higher level because they have arisen from intelligence, from *pure, innocent* intelligence, rising like a fragrance from this world of evil. This is the first reference. In another place, he says:

> Nature does not do as bad poets do, who, when they portray scoundrels or fools, do it so clumsily, so purposefully, that one sees, as it were, the poet standing behind each one, continually disavowing the character's attitude and speech, and calling out with a warning voice: "This is a rascal, this is a fool; do not pay any attention to what he says." Nature, on the other hand, does as Shakespeare and Goethe do, in whose works every character, even if he is the devil himself, while he is on stage and speaking, *is right*; we are drawn to his side and are forced to sympathize with him because he is *grasped so objectively*: for he is developed from an inner principle, just as the works of nature are, and his speech and actions therefore appear natural and necessary.

It seems to me that one can go no farther in politically hostile estheticism than to declare nature herself to be esthetic.

Even *Tolstoy* is an esthete and not a politician when at the end of his story, *Lucerne*, he breaks out with words:

> What an unhappy, miserable creature the human being is, who in his need for positive solutions is thrown into this eternally moving, shoreless ocean of good and evil, of facts, evaluations and contradictions! If the human being had only learned not to judge and to think so sharply and decisively, and not always to answer questions that are only asked him so that they will always remain questions! Would that he would realize that every thought is at the same time incorrect and correct! It is incorrect because the human being is one-dimensional, and it is impossible for him to grasp the whole truth in its totality; it is correct because through it a part of human striving is always expressed. Human beings have created compartments for themselves in this eternally moving, shoreless, infinitely mixed-up chaos of good and evil, they have drawn imaginary boundary lines in this sea, and they expect the sea to divide itself along these lines. As if there were not millions of other divisions of completely different points of view from and in other levels! . . . Civilization is good, barbarism is evil; freedom is good, restraint evil. This imaginary knowledge destroys

the instinctive, blessed, original striving for good in human nature. Who can define freedom, despotism, civilization and barbarism? What are the boundaries between these concepts? Who has in his soul such an infallible measuring stick for good and evil that he can measure all the fleeting and confused facts with it? Who has ever seen a condition where good and evil were not mixed up together? . . . Infinite is the goodness and wisdom of the one who permitted and ordered all these contradictions. They only seem to be contradictions to you, miserable worm, you who boldly and insolently try to penetrate his laws and counsel. He looks down mildly from his radiant, immeasurable height and rejoices in the endless harmony in which you all move in eternal contradiction.

What laxity! What doubt! Finally, what false transfiguration! And the starving peasants? Will they be sated by your "endless harmony"? It is not plaintive-conciliatory trains of thought that lead to the political action!

Strindberg relates:

The postmaster and the quarantine master did not, to be sure, see people and life from the same point of view, for the postmaster was a decided man of the Left, and the quarantine master was a doubter, but they could chat so well with one another . . . At times, the quarantine master's greater scope was expressed in disapproval, something like this: "You party men are like one-eyed cats. Some see only with the left eye, others only with the right one, and you can therefore never see stereoscopically, but always only in a flat and one-sided way."

Is this enough? At the end of *Black Flags* the same author says:

As a writer you have a right to *play with thoughts, to experiment with points of view*, but without binding yourself to anything, for freedom is the poet's vital air.

Is *that* enough? No, do not let yourself be confused. It is in no way enough to prove that Strindberg really belonged as a thinker and a personality to the European estheticism that Ibsen personified in Hedda Gabler—just as little as the above cited expressions would be sufficient to seriously stamp Schiller, Flaubert, Schopenhauer and Tolstoy as esthetes; for even Flaubert—as I believe we indicated—does not deserve this name in the narrow, pejorative, dandyish sense. But my examples, I believe, are quite sufficient to illustrate what estheticism as the opposite of the political nature is—and I repeat, this is its present, living, topical meaning.

In the Strindberg statement, the word "stereoscopic" stands out particularly strongly. It could mislead one to define the esthetic way of seeing as simply a physical way of seeing. This would be insufficient. There are spiritual, flat, one-sided intellectual products that nevertheless—even in their titles—bear the stamp of "estheticism." "Thoughts in War," for example—that would be such a title. It would be a limitation, the expression of a restriction of these thoughts, of a *reservatio mentalis*, to express myself in a Jesuit manner, the reservation of someone who knows that thoughts in war necessarily look different from thoughts in peace, who also knows that absolutely *everything* that is merely stated is limited and assailable, no matter how absolute and apodictic it may act and be perceived at the moment, and no matter how unassailably unique and alone the form; that the exquisite superiority of art over simple intellectuality lies in art's lively ambiguity, its deep lack of commitment, its intellectual *freedom*—the freedom that Turgenev always meant when he spoke of freedom. One must completely understand that someone who is not used to speaking directly on his own responsibility, but who is used to letting people and things speak—that someone who is used to creating *art, never takes* spiritual and intellectual things *completely seriously*, for his job has always been rather to treat them as material and as playthings, to represent points of view, to deal in dialectics, always letting the one who is speaking at the time be right. One does not understand the intellectual content in a work of art when one takes this context as an end in itself; it cannot be evaluated in a literary way—this is something that even sophisticated critics sometimes forget or do not know; it is useful for the composition; only in relationship to the composition does it have purpose and confirmation; taken absolutely, from a literary point of view, it can be banal, but within the composition it can be ingenious. Assuming that a mind of such structure and habit were to be brought to speak directly, to think outside of a composition, to write in the narrower sense: *on the one hand* he will find the conflicting inhibitions almost insuperable—first because in such a case he scarcely knows how he is to write, since he has nothing and no one to have speak and is without every artistic support; all in all, however, because as soon as he is not dealing with characters, he will not know what to do at all. "It always seems to me," Turgenev confesses, "as if one could always argue with equal correctness the opposite of everything I say. But if I talk about a red nose and blond hair, then the hair is blond and the nose is red—this cannot be argued away." *On the other hand*, however, it is precisely his strangely loose relationship to intellectual matters that easily lends him a touch of seeming unscrupulousness, frivolity, dialectic, and pettifoggery; unaccustomed to engaging personally in intellectual disputes, he will now hardly feel a sense of serious responsibility here, either. He will have himself speak in the same way he has things and people speak, and in addition, he will not identify himself any more profoundly with this role than with the earlier ones. The statement that no one has a conscience except the contemplator, that the man of action is always without conscience, applies here, too, even if in a nonclassical-complex way: The esthete is conscientious as a doer (maker, shaper), for his manner of action is so free and serene that it achieves the dignity and coolness of contemplation; but for him contemplation easily becomes action—perhaps he knows and wants it only as action—and it is precisely as he contemplates, therefore, that he tends toward unscrupulousness.

But I can hear the reply that all this is skepticism, relativism, frivolity and weakness! Weakness above all! For skepticism and relativism are the opposite of all genius, all primeval power and nature; they are also the opposite of all creativity and all religiosity. Is this certain? Is it not possible that in Tolstoy's doubt about the validity of the "compartments" that the human being creates for himself in "chaos" there is more religiosity than in any political position on what good and evil, civilization and barbarism, freedom and slavery are? Is not skepticism perhaps too light, too intellectual a word to characterize the Tolstoyan way of thinking—for his words definitely signify a devastating criticism of all intellectualism, of all drawing-lines-in-water? Skepticism is itself an intellectual attitude *vis-à-vis* intellect; it is not anti-intellectualism, for anti-intellectualism means reverence, and the concept of skepticism is never without a touch of frivolity. Reverence and doubt, absolute conscientiousness and absolute freedom—does this connection exist? Yes, it does, for *it* forms the essence of the esthetic world view.

Have we solved, at least to some extent, the task of defining the concept of estheticism by its present contrast to the political nature? If so, we have then indirectly also learned the essential thing about the politician—but in doing so we consider ourselves in no way exempted from a closer analysis of this incomparably more important and more topical character. It is clear, however, that we are not speaking of the politician in the ordinary sense of the word, of the professional, career politician. He is a low and corrupt being who is in no way fit to play a role in the intellectual sphere. No, the politician we mean is the man of intellect, indeed, of pure and beautiful, of radical and literary intellect;

he is therefore the man of the word, indeed, of the pure and beautiful, of the radical and literary word: we see before us the belles lettres-politician, the politician as a literary man and the literary man as a politician, the "intellectual," the "voluntarist," the "activist"—and whatever other noble names he bestows upon himself. But since he is a voluntarist—what does he want?

The highest! He is like Adalbert Stifter's beautiful youths at the beginning of the *Bachelor*: "Then comes the state. In it the most infinite freedom, the greatest justice and the most unlimited tolerance is offered. Whoever is against this, will be crushed and defeated . . ." What then does he want? He wants, for example: truth, freedom, justice, equality, reason, virtue, happiness—all in all, happiness! The absolute happiness of all, that condition toward which the human race is gloriously moving, that only now will become the condition of true humanity, and that the politician describes as "very beautiful and thoroughly serene." The guide to this goal is the intellect: the politician's intellect, of course, the political intellect, the politicized intellect, a heartfelt, inseparable, generous combination of politics and beautiful literature, of agitation and beautiful eloquence. But for spirit, this spirit, to dominate, it needs a certain social constitution that has not yet been perfectly established everywhere, least of all in Germany, and the politician's attention must therefore always be directed toward its establishment, for it signifies in the true sense of the word the preliminary step and foretaste of that final, desirable, "very beautiful and completely serene" condition of the human race. This state and social constitution is the radical republic, the republic of lawyers and literati with love of mankind and writing skill. But let us say it more correctly: love of mankind and writing skill, these *are* the republic, for the republic means nothing else than the dominance of politics, the unconditional and total politicization of minds and hearts—while, for its part, politics is nothing more than love of mankind and writing skill. We cannot make it more emphatic: love of mankind and writing skill, this is the definition of politics, it is the definition of the republic, it is also the definition of literature, of civilization, of progress, of humanitarianism. All these are one; yes, not only are literature and civilization one, as we recognized earlier on our own, literature and politics, literature and republic are also one. And this whole brilliant, philanthropically buoyant unity of ideas and purposeful efforts, with everything that goes with it, and what we will soon have to analyze more closely, the politician brings together in a name, a word, his special and favorite word, his war cry and hosanna, his magical formula for happiness that he tirelessly repeats like a fakir to the point of his own insensibility: he calls it *democracy*.

It will not have escaped the attentive reader that we are here renewing an old acquaintanceship, that the hero of the present lines, this man of will and savior from estheticism, is none other than our *entente* friend and partisan of justice, the German Westerner, the opponent of Germany's "special nature," the follower of the rhetorical democracy that is so heartlifting and humanly worthy, in a word: civilization's literary man! After such a long digression, this chapter is really nothing more than a continuation of that early one that was baptized in the name of civilization's literary man. But before we continue in the study of this significant type, we must, in order to avoid confusion, differentiate and hold apart, with our intellectual hearing, voices that are mingled in the noise of the times. It is the word "democracy" that forces such a differentiation and such polyphonic hearing, for many voices of the times are united by this word—united in noise and not in music, for they know nothing of one another.

We thought about Schopenhauer's disdainful rejection of every patriotic fervor (a rejection that only reverted to passionate partisanship where the German language was concerned), and we found that like everyone else at that time he equated patriotism and democracy, and that he could not and did not want to be a patriot and a "German brother" because he could not and did not want to be a political democrat, because his individualistic aristocratic feeling made him despise democracy. We remembered that Wagner never tired of declaring democracy in some sort of Western sense to be alien and un-German, that he hated it, indeed with the same hatred he had for politics itself, for everything political; because to him politics itself seemed un-German, anti-German, and nothing was more inimical to the wishes and dreams of this man of '48 than the democratic politicization of his people, whose talents were in his opinion called to higher things than politics. We saw, on the other hand, that the finest examples of Germany's burgherly-prebourgeois epoch, intellects such as Uhland and Storm, did not lack political passion, but that their politics, their commitment to democracy, that is, was obviously entirely at one with their national feeling, with their love for the fatherland; that they were politicians and democrats as far as they were patriots, and that these three words: politics, democracy, fatherland, signified for them, as for all political burgherdom, one and the same passion, one and the same longing and challenge. Nothing is more simple, and still it needs to be emphasized at this moment. Political freedom, in contrast to metaphysical freedom, means nothing other than the freedom of the patriot to take part in politics, his freedom to work on and in the state. If, as Wagner's case, as many others, as basically the whole burgherly age of our history proves, this was a cultural age and not a political one: if it is indeed altogether possible in Germany to be nationally but unpolitically, yes, even antipolitically disposed, then the opposite is logically not possible: it is not possible, or at least it should not be possible, to demand politics and democracy and at the same time to cherish antinational, antipatriotic opinions. Mazzini, the democrat and republican, in 1830 the pioneer of the present Italian war against Austria, demanded furiously that Austria be "struck in the heart by divesting her of the best of her territories"; as Italy's northern boundary he demanded "the upper range of the Alps"; he demanded Trieste. I call that a patriot and a democrat. Börne was liberal, radically so, in the spirit of political enlightenment; but he was a patriot, indeed so much so that Heine could say disdainfully of him: "The fatherland is his whole love." Herwegh was not only national, not only a patriot, he was an imperialist, he sang the "Song of the Fleet" to young Germany. If one wants to be like them today, if one wants to be a democratic politician, then one must declare oneself above all to be a patriot. But to call for democracy and to put on airs against all patriotism, all national feeling, this is not at all consistent. Democracy is nothing more than the right to be active as a patriot. Freedom and fatherland belong together. Or is this not so?

The great majority of those today who demand the politicization of the German people, that is, who demand that the German governmental system become democratic, really do this as eager patriots, yes, in the interest of German power: foreign policy completely determines their domestic political will—even if I admittedly think that they are not as clearly aware as would be desirable of the intimate connection, or rather of the identical significance, of "politicization" and "democratization." In the second year of the war, I could attend a meeting in Munich to organize a "Society for the Study of World Politics," one of those societies that set themselves the task of spreading political knowledge, understanding and enthusiasm in the German people. One of the first rules they decided to put into the bylaws was absolute nonpartisanship, absolute political tolerance and indifference: conservative, liberal, socialistic, one might be what one wanted, membership in this organization for the propagation of political thought was to be open to everyone. I had the correspondent of a leftist newspaper beside me at table. I said to him:

"If I may say so, I think that politicization and democratization are really one and the same thing."

"Why, that is what I always say!" he cried happily.

"Yes," I continued, "but the German conservatives know this as well as you, and that is why they say: Politics spoils character. This is a truly conservative way of speaking; recently some Junker or other used it to a great uproar in the parliament. Therefore if you want democracy by wanting politicization, you ought not to consider yourselves nonpartisan and invite conservatives to take part."

For the moment at least he did not know what to reply. And then also it seems to me that the logical objection I made then was well taken: I said that "political social studies" were essentially democratic arrangements whose political tolerance and all-inclusiveness was a conscious or unconscious deception. Strictly speaking, of course, the German desire for politicization, the insight into the necessity of politicization, is nothing new, not from yesterday; it would be wrong to date this will and insight even just from the formation of the *Reich*, and to make its founder, Bismarck, unilaterally responsible for this new will to politics and "reality," as Nietzsche always does: especially in that brilliant passage where he ironically hypothesizes a statesman who "would bring his nation to the point of having to continue dealing in grand politics even though it was by nature ill-disposed and ill-prepared to do so; so that it would have to sacrifice its old and reliable virtues to a new, doubtful mediocrity," and continues:

> Assuming that a statesman would condemn his nation to politics at all when up to then it had had better things to do and think, and when in its heart of hearts it could not rid itself of a cautious disgust [oh, magnificent!] for the unrest, emptiness, and noisy quarrelsomeness of the truly political nations:—assuming that such a statesman were to spur the sleeping passions and covetousness of his people, to make a fault of its former timidity and desire to stand apart, to call its affinity for things foreign and its secret infinity an error, to debase its most cherished inclinations, to confuse its conscience, to narrow its spirit, to make its taste "national,"—what! A stateman who did all this, a statesman for whom his

nation would have to atone throughout its entire future, if it had a future, would such a statesman be *great*?

Well, no matter how magnificent the sentence construction, the guilt, the act of violence hypothesized here is wrong; for it is wrong to act as if the German will had been violated in 1870 by Bismarck and forced into previously foreign and distasteful paths; as if to a great extent Bismarck had not been more its mandatary and executor. We know very well that the transformation of this will goes back a long way, at least ten years before 1870, that Bismarckian power politics and the "German idea" came together to the most remarkable degree around 1860. The Germany that at that time moved from her idealistic into her realistic period, and that would have done this even without Bismarck, was quite ready and willing "to sacrifice her old and reliable virtues to a new, doubtful mediocrity"; she scarcely needed to be "condemned" to politics, scarcely to be "goaded" into greediness. It was at this time that what one can call the realization, hardening, or also the politicization of Germany set in powerfully, that poetry and philosophy abdicated, natural sciences and history rose, all minds turned toward the foundation of the German state—and that the idea of freedom, which the liberal enlightenment had always been ready to place above that of unity, made its peace in the "national union" with the Prussian power principle. Of course it is true that Bismarck put Germany "into the saddle," but she already had one foot in the stirrup, and it looks as if Nietzsche, in his musical-Dionysian dreams of culture, had noticed nothing of this at all.

His polemic against Bismarck and the power empire has a somewhat mixed nature for us today, yes, confused, something both outmoded and anticipatory; it deals with conditions, I think, that, as he saw them, in part no longer exist and in part are *impending*—possibly. People have found that in his hatred for Bismarck, whom he is philosopher enough to accuse of lack of philosophical education, he became untrue to his own superman-ideal; and this is largely correct. In general, people censured his position on the national question as abstract and inconsistent: they said the military virtues he honored were bound to the national idea, and his internationalism was a regression into enlightenment. This is also true. But what Nietzsche really had in his heart against Bismarck and the "*Reich*" was not bitterness toward militarism, lordliness and power. What could he of all people have against power? He did not have anything against German power, either; for somewhere, for example, he expresses the wish for Germany to gain control of Mexico in order to set the fashion for the world with a new, exemplary forest culture in the *conservative* interest of the future of the human race. What he fought against was twofold: When he says, "The era of Bismarck (the era of German stultification), the exclusive interest devoted currently in Germany to questions of power, to trade in general, and—last but not least—to 'good living,'" then German culture itself is protesting through him, German cultural idealism, or, as strange as the words may seem here, German cultural liberalism, which actually determined his relationship to Bismarck's empire, and in which he did not nearly stand as alone as he wanted to convince himself he did, for people such as Mommsen and Virchow entered the opposition at that time—his German philosophical nature, the best and most fundamental part of his being, protested against the German conditions of the seventies and eighties, against the joint, interlocked nature of national self-righteousness and materialistic reaction, of the corrupt flowering of industry, of French farce and David Strauß-like contentment, which not only characterized the early years—in a word, this protest, which was the protest of a "burgher" in the most German meaning of the word, was directed against the perversion, hardening and falsification of a stateless culture into a cultureless state.

Was it philistine-satisfaction, ten years before the war, to find this aspect of Nietzsche's criticism of the "*Reich*" to be out of date? In a counterargument to myself I made every concession to the doctrine of Germany's hardening and loss of soul—a little academically, for personally, of course, my awakening to conscious intellectual life occurred in new, in different times—it occurred in the eighties, the time of the literary revolution and of the invasion of the naturalists; at eighteen I was a contributor to Conrad's *Gesellschaft*, when I was twenty, my stories appeared in the *Neue deutsche Rundschau*, which had just recently been formed from the provocative magazine, *Die freie Bühne*, and the literary—if not also the psychological—cosmopolitanism of *Buddenbrooks* marked me as a genuine child of this epoch, of an epoch of cultural revolution whose essence was opposition to precisely that Germany that the lonely Nietzsche had decried. The likes of me, it is true, never hated Bismarck or rejected him; I was always little inclined to play Goethe off against Bismarck, as disconcerted foreign countries and German radical literary men did. I found it foolish not to recognize the one in the other. I saw in Bismarck a powerful expression of the German character, a second Luther, a very great event in the history of the German self-experience, a gigantic German fact, set defiantly against European repugnance. But this affirmation was for his personality; I, too, opposed his work, or the spirit of his work, or at least the working of this man in areas where, in my opinion, it did not belong—as an example of this I may refer to my criticism of the Prussianization and dehumanization of the new German *Gymnasium* (*Buddenbrooks*, p. 722).

Did not a movement begin as early as with the "latest Germany," to which, after all, I belonged, that has not come to rest since? And was it not that of a new idealism? I hardly include the social legislation here. I consider it to be German to combine social tidiness with deep disgust for every overvaluation of social life. Just the same, it is not bad to read that at the beginning of this century a German-American could call social justice the ideal of present-day Germany, social work the basic demand of the new German education. But the sociopolitical, the welfare ideal is secondary. It had to do with something more spiritual. It had to do with the German spirit's rediscovery of itself, with something like reanimation, a redirection to an earlier path, a subsiding of natural sciences in all higher significance, no matter how gloriously the victorious advance of the monistic enlightenment might be perfected just at the time; a revitalization of philosophy, a seeking and finding of contact with the idealistic traditions of German thought, an urgent self-searching in religion, new possibilities in mysticism itself. Was this so, or not? Scheler's writings did not have much similarity to "beerhall evangelism" anymore. And just before the beginning of the war, almost *in* the war, there appeared in 1914 a book that to me seemed to sum up recent Germany, the Germany that had to enter the war, and not the Germany of 1875 anymore, seemed to present it intellectually in an astounding synthesis: *The Main Questions of Modern Culture* by Emil Hammacher, the young philosopher from Bonn who was killed in France, whom I would very much like to call my posthumous friend.

But Nietzsche continues: ". . .the rise of parliamentary stupidity, of newspaper reading, and of the participation of everyone in the literarylike discussion of everything . . . the growing rise of democratic man, and of the stultification of Europe and the diminution of European man brought about by this rise—" and with this continuation and turn of his criticism of the *Reich*, no matter how much here again it is German culture that is opposing, and indeed, opposing *in the conservative interest*: with this continuation of our quotation we are suddenly in quite another sphere; here Nietzsche not only does not seem to be surpassed, if he seemed to be so in the beginning, here his polemic *anticipates*,

anticipates a development he saw connected with almost complete inevitability to the life work of Bismarck, which at the time, however, was in its unpretentious beginnings, and which only after the expiration of the Bismarckian era, in a new epoch of German civilization and imperialism, could become clear in its meaning and goal: Germany's development to *democracy*.

Again it is important not to understand this word incorrectly, and not merely superficially, either: otherwise one could ask what there is to fear or to demand about the democratization of the world. In fact, small differences in forms of government do not prevent the world today from being democratized to the last corner; democracy is scarcely struggling anymore; it is triumphant; even in Tsarist Russia people speak correctly of "our democratic-burgherly society"—correctly, that is, as far as we live in a business epoch that is dependent upon the principle of utility, whose main motive is the drive for prosperity and whose rank-conferring ruler is money. Plutocracy and enthusiasm for prosperity: if this is the exact definition of democracy, then one may still maintain that refractory Germany is in this aspect, too, a bit behind the general development—but this Germany was still a true child of her time and shows herself to be loyal to it today as well. The speculator, the food profiteer during the war—what spirit does he belong to, anyway, other than to democracy, which has stamped money, profit and business as the highest values: the rulers, too, whose boundless awe of business makes them extremely hesitant to take action against speculative insolence. But as far as political freedom is concerned, seen even slightly from above, it of course rules more or less to the same extent everywhere today, and Gustaf Steffen, the Swedish sociologist, is probably right when he says that "in her way" Germany "practices just as great an amount of democracy through her army and through the widespread self-rule in her communities, cities and federal states," as the Western countries do.

But there is no talk of this when one teaches and demands that Germany be politicized and democratized—because, of course, it would not have to be so urgently demanded if it were already completed, or had at least progressed a long way. It is rather a matter of a real change in the structure of the German spirit, of the tendency to make Germany "free and equal," not so much at home as abroad, as in international relations, of a process of European leveling that is less economic and political than spiritual, a development that is leveling all national culture into a homogeneous civilization, yes, of nothing else than the total realization and final establishment of the world imperium of civilization that we spoke of at the beginning of our reflections: and Nietzsche, without detriment to his internationalism, which neither knows nor recognizes the national medium between the individual and the human race; without detriment, either, to the support that he himself, by the nature of his writing, as a writer who furthered a European style, gave to this development—Nietzsche was German enough, had a powerful enough *"conservative interest"* in Germany's special and refractory nature, to resist most vehemently the leveling process that he saw being connected to Bismarck's political foundation.

This is quite evident in all his statements on Germany's political and intellectual fate; the protest against the *nationalization* of Germany, in which he saw at the same time a *de*nationalization, internationalization and democratization, runs through his entire work from beginning to end, and it is a protest in the name of philosophy against politics—an extremely German protest, therefore, in which Nietzsche may possibly have had an "untimely," but in no way alien, impact, in which he was plainly a national spokesman, yes, in which he concurs precisely with all exemplary German thought and desire.

In 1870 a strange man died in Thorn in Prussia, Bogumil Goltz by name, humorist, philosopher and critic of the times, a writer who thought deeply and wrote much about Germany and the German character: *The Germans, On the Character and Natural History of the German Genius*, and more of the same. Somewhere he says:

> While in the Romance and Slavic nations only the masses bear a stamp, and only the "masses" think of themselves as a people, the German shows, as an individual, a particular intellectual physiognomy, a divine conscience and a disposition in which the history of the human race moves and is embodied. From a dozen Frenchmen, Russians, Poles and Italians, one can more easily draw a sketch of these four nations than one can understand the German people after having studied a thousand Germans. In every individual the German human being signifies a separate world; more than any other, he is a person; he is in the deepest sense of the word a human being with character, simply because compared with individuals of other nations, he is a person, a genius, an original, a person of feeling, because he is *not a figurant, not a social or a political animal* in the French sense, who, at the moment when one no longer regards him nationally but as an individual, reveals himself to be as lacking in character and feeling as possible. *The German nation can have no character the way other nations can*, because through literature and education in reason it has generalized and ennobled itself as a nation of the world that all humanity is beginning to recognize as its teacher and educator. Yes, we are, we

were, we remain the schoolmasters, the philosophers, the theosophists, the religious teachers of Europe and of the whole world. This is our genius, our ideal national unity, honor and mission, *which we must not trade for the thing or phantom that the French or the English call nation.* We are and remain a world-burgherly, world-historical people in a privileged sense, and for this very reason we cannot be a stupidly proud people that is brought together like animals and glued together, that, like wild geese, *flies together in a "V" formation,"* that, like the French and the Poles, *crystallizes itself in every meeting into a practice revolution or into a one-day republic.*

This was written in the 1860s, at the time, that is, when the German spirit was quite automatically preparing in national meetings to allow itself to be condemned to politics by Bismarck; and I have inserted the passage, which I really like, early to give resonance to what I will still have to say about politics. To come back to Nietzsche, it would undoubtedly have gone against his critical taste to call the individual German a genius, an original and a feeling person, and in contrast to call the individual Frenchman a person without character or feeling; but beyond doubt his own opinion about Germany agreed in all essential points with that of the good Bogumil Goltz. What Nietzsche, who called himself the "last nonpolitical German," hated in Bismarck was certainly not that Bismarck was a great man who denigrated the average man, a masterful man, a man of power. He hated him and doubted his greatness, if not also his strength, because he saw him working on the change of Germany's intellectual structure, on Germany's nationalization and politicization—and thereby on her democratization and simplification in the sense of homogeneous civilization. That is clear. But it is also clear that the great majority of those who for patriotic reasons call for politicization and civic education are not at all as aware of these connections as they should be—while the most important thing here is simply a clarity that distinguishes between what is necessary and what is desirable, and that does not automatically with fatalistic, uncritical enthusiasm acclaim what is necessary as what is desirable.

A giant put Germany into the saddle; now she must ride, for she must not fall off. This sentence seems to me to be the most calm, precise paraphrase, omitting all desirability or undesirability, of what I call the necessary part of the development. Those who today demand a democratic Germany that the *Reichskanzler* promises raise this demand not for doctrinaire, theoretical reasons, but for completely practical ones: first so that Germany can live, and second so that she can live powerfully and masterfully—to which, according to her heartfelt belief, she has the highest claim. These reasons, however, reasons that point toward an interest in life and power, are not those of domestic, but of foreign policy; for all strictly domestic policy is pedagogical, moral, not to say virtuous; it has no connections to the idea of power, and is only very loosely connected to that of life; it lives from a radical idea and is intent on nothing more than the high-minded realization of this idea. There is no talk of this at all in Germany. At most, the democratic thesis takes on a theoretical, domestic political character when it is expressed somewhat in the following manner: "The war has shown the German people to be a state people. The logical consequence of this is the demand for a *Volksstaat* appropriate to the high moral and political level and to the civic virtues of such a people." This is the serious and honest voice of the national democratic man, and it does not sound at all repugnant to my ear—for I must hasten to say that my ear in no way misses how much the good and honest word, *Volksstaat*, differs in sound and sense from the word, "democracy," with its humbuglike side noises. Here, then, the demand for a democratic *Reich* is morally justified because the democratization, the politicization, that is, of the *nation* is decreed as a domestically accomplished fact that honesty requires one to live up to through institutions. Here, then, the democratization of the state is regarded as the logical and moral consequence of the politicization of the people brought about by the war. Is the premise quite solid? One could doubt it. *One could seriously doubt* that in the course of thirty months the German people really have become a "genuinely political people" whose intellectual make-up demands institutions appropriate and peculiar to such peoples. By the way, however, the arguments of these patriotic democrats are also of a "foreign" nature, even when they seem related to domestic policy; they are those of practice, those of necessity. One says something like: "We must have people's politics, that is, politics whose subject—and not whose object—is the people; people's politics for the sake of the *Reich*, to keep the *Reich* and the state *strong* and vital!" Whereby characteristically, if not quite logically, strength is placed before vitality; where the idea of power not only does not follow that of life, but for the sake of clarity is placed above and before it as its sense and purpose. Then one continues with something like:

> The *Reich* has only been able to endure the enormous test of the war because in the storm of the times people and state have become one. But the tasks of peace will be no less enormous than those of war, and they will only be fulfilled when we succeed in salvaging and transferring the

accomplishments of war into times of peace, when the unity of people and state is preserved. Domestic strength is the precondition of a strong foreign policy, which will be necessary after the conclusion of peace. A state organization is necessary, therefore, that is established exclusively for the greatest national capacity for achievement; a state organization, that is, that the people can regard as their very own construction, and in which political rights assure them of participation and cooperation. We do not demand such a state organization for the sake of some sort of theory and doctrine, but for the sake of the life and of the global tasks that we earnestly believe the war's outcome will confirm for our people. Therefore let all education be education for citizenship: we say that it includes, without exception, all the purposes and goals of human education! The politicization, the democratization of all minds and hearts is necessary because—

Because, one may complete the sentence, Germany must ride and must not fall off.

This patriotic, opportunity-democracy, which equally combines "domestic" and "foreign" arguments according to the idea of life and at the same time of power, seems to me to be the predominant political opinion in Germany today. I will venture the attempt of a critique by sketching, in a few words, my relationship to the state as it existed instinctively before the war and as, with some reading and reflection, I have now become consciously aware of it.

As a boy I liked to personify the state to myself in my imagination; I thought of it as a stern, stiff figure in a dress coat, with a full black beard, with a star on its breast, and decked out with a mixture of military-academic titles that appropriately symbolized its power and legality: as *General Doktor von Staat*. The state (which here can be equated with its administrator, the government) probably appears in this image to young artists and sons of the muses, whose libertinism it threatens with punishment and strict discipline. And their sense of irony, which comes from a bad but still cheerful conscience, is not lacking in justice and dignity. The truth of their lives, the truth from which they live, is, of course, quite actually that there is a sphere that is undoubtedly superior to the state and to political life, that sphere to which art, religion, the humanities, and all deeper morality belong, a sphere of the most personally characteristic values and accomplishments. To be sure, of course, the one who is at home in this sphere will concede the state's qualification and authority to grant formal assistance, although he may find that His Excellency cuts a rather clumsy figure in the process. But, in accordance with his disposition, he will either passionately reject or disdainfully ignore every attempt at substantial regulation: in the one case because he sees that the state does not have the right to regulate in this way, and in the other because he knows that above all, and in the end, the power to do so is lacking.

This may be well and good. And yet, for all the estrangement, for all the stern distrust on the one side and all the irony on the other, they are related, have something in common. There is an extreme solidarity between the representative of the suprapolitical sphere, the sphere of the personality, and the state, as far as the state is the legal power of a national community—and the hour may come when both, the libertine and even the state as well, will become aware of this solidarity in the clearest way. It is true: what characterizes the human being as a social being is not what is actually admirable in him. The human being is not only a social but also a metaphysical being; in other words, he is not only an individual but also a personality. It is therefore wrong to confuse the supraindividual element with the social one, to place it completely in the social sphere: in the process one neglects the metaphysical supraindividual element; for the personality, not the mass, is the actual bearer of the general element. But is this not exactly the same with the nation—and therefore with the state as far as the latter is the crystallization of national life? The nation, too, is not only a social but also a metaphysical being; the nation, not "the human race" as the sum of the individuals, is the bearer of the general, of the human quality; and the value of the intellectual-artistic-religious product that one calls national culture, that cannot be grasped by scientific methods, that develops out of the organic depth of national life—the value, dignity and charm of all national culture, therefore, definitely lies in what distinguishes it from all others, for only this distinctive element is culture, in contrast to what all nations have in common, which is only civilization. Here we have the difference between individual and personality, civilization and culture, social and metaphysical life. The individualistic mass is democratic, the nation aristocratic. The former is international, the latter a mythical personality of the most charactistic stamp. It is wrong to place the supraindividual element in the sum of the individuals, to place the national *and* the human quality in the social mass. The metaphysical nation is the bearer of the general element. It is therefore intellectually wrong to pursue politics in the spirit and sense of the mass. It should be pursued in the spirit and sense of the nation so that there is at least the possibility of experiencing a unified political and national life, even if in the process it goes beyond the understanding of the mass as such. This demand, however, is today condemned to remain a theory. The advance of democracy is victorious and unstoppable. Only mass politics, democratic politics, that is, a politics that has little or nothing to do with the higher intellectual life of the nation, is possible today—this is the knowledge that the government of the German *Reich* has acquired in the course of the war.

The interest of the artist and the intellectual in the state, then, his relationship and solidarity with it, goes as far as the metaphysical character of the state goes. Admittedly, things are developing in such a way that the state is giving up more and more of its metaphysical character and appears about to take on a merely social one. In truth, the modern state is not particularly worthy of admiration. As egalitarian and as tolerant as it is, it no longer represents a definite world view, but rather presents itself as well as it can as an agency for the adjustment of class interests. A correspondence of political and—to use the most extensive word—religious life cannot be determined—and what would be the sense of the complete consummation of the personality in the state? A hundred forces are working on the disintegration of national culture and on the internationalization of life; and if one once said that the merit of militarism was to hinder the creation of a purely utilitarian culture, the sinking of the people into mere civilization, this merit finds little recognition today: the meaning, the teleological function of war, to serve the preservation of national character, seems invalid. Its connection with economic interests stands out obtrusively—a connection that admittedly has existed in all times and that has never prevented the honor of a nation from being more than the ideological glorification and embellishment of economic interests. But if this honor today really does not seem to be anything else; if earlier economic means seem to have become ends in themselves, so that war can generally be perceived as immoral and barbaric, and if here the last thing falls away that leads the masses, in a culture of expediency, to sacrifice themselves for supraindividual goals, for idealism—then it would be dishonest to conceal the fact that it is democracy that has caused this impression and that has taken away the dignity and spirit of war: internationalistic democracy is not waging war for spiritual reasons, for the protection and the honor of independent national culture, not for the sake of the German idea. It is waging it without ideas, really, only for export and therefore also with a bad conscience, midst pacifistic tears—whereby it swears that it only got into the war because it was "badly governed."

Whoever, out of sympathy for the mythical individual "German nation" and its heroic struggle, whoever has any sort of positive attitude toward this war, must properly cherish conservative, that is, national ideas, and participate in the war in their name. Democracy, which is basically of one mind with the civilization-*entente*, and which only "wants to do business where another is already doing business," as George says, is conducting a war without ideas, and therefore, as it itself feels, an immoral stock-exchange war. It is not even an idea *as* democracy, but only pure opportunism. "Under a democratic constitution one can do business better," is the way they argue. It can in no way be denied that the idea, and therefore the idealism, in this war is with the conservatives, and the criticism in democracy's mouth that the conservatives only want power is hardly correct—democracy obviously *also* wants power, indeed so urgently that it does not want to wait for the end of the war to secure it, because then the voice of the people or of the masses might be less favorable to the realization of democracy's will to power. The ruling concept is also implied in the word "democracy," and we know that it is not the people, but persons who "rule" in the democratic state. But as far as idealism is concerned, the conservative-national idea is still an idea, even if it has perhaps seen its day; but export is not one. When the conservatives assert that if universal suffrage is introduced into Prussia, Germany will have lost the war, they are beyond doubt serious. That they exaggerate in this is another matter to which we will return.

For the present, we repeat that the metaphysical character of the state is retreating more and more in favor of the social one, that the separation of the intellectual and the national elements from political life cannot be stopped. Naturally, this cannot be conducive to political participation by the intellectual and the artist. But there is still enough left to bind him not only logically but also emotionally to the state. Schopenhauer says in his "uncrowned prize essay" on the foundation of morality that the state is indispensable because thanks only to it the limitless egotism of almost everyone, the malice of many, and the cruelty of some cannot come to the fore: if one wants to learn what the human being actually is in a moral sense, he says, one must read crime stories and descriptions of anarchic conditions; and these thousands who mingle before us in peaceful intercourse must be viewed as just so many tigers and wolves whose jaws are well controlled by a strong muzzle, by the force of law, that is, and by the necessity of civic honor. This is a justification of the power of the state whose grim pessimism and skepticism admittedly hardly make it fit to be awarded a prize by academies. But it is valid, and individual love of mankind is no reason not to agree with it literally. Today, the monstrous, life-endangering, external threat to the state is bringing about domestic conditions that in part and in some ways approach anarchy, and immediately it is becoming clear what human beings in the great majority—for there are a few consoling exceptions who preserve one's faith—"actually are" from a moral point of view. Never has the difference between the people as a mystical character and the individualistic mass appeared more visibly; and no sense of awe for the former, no heartfelt participation in its heroic struggle, protects one from seeing the basically miserable nature of the latter, its cowardice, impudence, wickedness, lack of character, and meanness. On the contrary, there has never been a better opportunity to convince oneself what sort of pressure of force, fear and authority is necessary to hold the great majority of human beings in moral propriety. The democratic addition of the human race is not so much the addition of the good as of the bad in the human being, and the larger the sum, the more it approaches the bestial. Morally, the social sphere is a very questionable field; it has the air of the menagerie about it.

But there are of course more and still higher logical arguments for the affirmation of the state. It is the state that sets definite limits to human activity, to all human life and striving, and only within these limits can the human being prove his worth. It is the state that attempts to settle social conflicts, brings them *closer* to a reconciliation, and here it shows itself to be a necessary condition of culture. The artist, too, who needs a secure basis to develop his particular abilities, just as everyone else does, will not withhold reasonable recognition of this logical state role. Beyond this, however, he sees, at least when the times sharpen his perspective as forcefully as they do today, that the state, in spite of all its socialization, has not lost, and can never lose, a considerable remainder of metaphysical dignity and significance.

A nation's historical tradition, that treasure of experience from earlier periods of its intellectual development that is in itself a cultural value, cannot be completely appreciated and cared for by any other nation. The state, the supraindividual community, is beyond doubt the guardian of this treasure. But also, as far as the present is concerned, in spite of all internationalism, there is a radical difference between the experiences of philosophy, art and religion, and the progress of the homogeneous-international sciences. Even today these experiences are still dependent upon nationality in some kind of theoretical but admittedly indefinable

way, and it remains the metaphysical task of the state to defend them—
whereby it is completely immaterial whether its leaders approve of these
experiences, or whether they even know about them. To speak particularly of art, the likes of me knows very well how much it has been
subject to the general process of democratic internationalization. Palp-
ably national art, patriotic art, so-called native art, cannot very well be
considered to be higher art. But the *highest* art—does it not even today
still have a deep connection with national life, even though the connection is difficult to ascertain? Every artistic patriotism in times of war has
its origin and justification in this awareness that before had only been
a neglected emotion and that was only raised to consciousness by the
war. It is true, we saw very well that more and more one was forced to
separate national from political life; and still the mind of the individual
became aware at this time of a deep and unquestioned union between
state and intellectual life: as has been perceived and said a hundred
times, the German idea of the state and of freedom bears in it the mark
of its essential intellectual and cultural origin just as clearly as the
English idea contains its Puritan origin and the French idea its revolutionary one. When the war broke out, one could feel that the German
state, as it is, had taken in much of the German intellectual character,
and as far as intellect felt any national cohesion and solidity at all, as
far, that is, as it did not find itself irrevocably democratized and
internationalized, it could join itself emotionally to this fearfully threatened state—I say: It could do so. I do not say that it definitely had to
do so; for even in this case it is quite possible in Germany that not only
indifference to the state's destiny exists, but also that its humiliation
even belongs to the intellectual desirabilities.

This has its basis in the specifically German antithesis of power and
intellect; in the fact, namely, that seen historically these two, intellect
and power, seem to miss each other with apparent regularity, that
blossoming of the state and blossoming of culture seem to exclude one
another—and this is why the conviction could and did settle among
artists and believers in culture that a politically powerful Germany
would necessarily be opposed to intellect and culture, that German
intellectual blossoming would never be united with the flowering of the
state. When Goethe defined culture as "the intellectualization of the
political and military spheres," he was thinking in grand terms, holding
himself to a more general norm, and gazing sovereignly beyond German
conditions and realities. Nevertheless, the higher validity of his definition of the concept of culture justifies the conjecture or hope that

German disbelief in the possibility of a synthesis of power and intellect is a prejudiced disbelief. Perhaps nowhere is it written that things always have to be the way they usually have been; that Germany cannot desire power when she desires intellect. Bismarck's epoch was not a cultural epoch. But the real, general enthusiasm of the Germans at the outbreak of this war was of course that one was now stepping out of this epoch and into another—into what kind? Into one that would possibly give the lie to the old, antithetical prejudice that an unhappy history had firmly established. Was this not true? Today, to be sure, the belief seems rather to be widespread that after *this* war the whole idea of power in the world will come to an end, and that only the intellect, in the form of justice, will swing its scepter over a completely moralized earth— another German belief that, as far as I can see, is hardly shared anywhere else.

So much for the state in general. How do things stand now with our politics? With our opinion, that is, on how the state should be organized? I say "our" because in political matters it is of course presumptuous and wrong to speak in the first person singular. Here one never stands alone. There is no political originality. One takes sides, and one may only say, "We believe," or "I, too, believe." This stamps the political sphere, therefore, as inferior, because it is a nonpersonal sphere; in it opinions prevail, and opinions do not confer rank. Political opinions lie on the street: Pick one up and attach yourself to it, and to many, possibly to yourself, too, you will seem more respectable than before, but this is based on illusion. The fact that a person is conservative says nothing about his rank and worth; any idiot can be conservative. Neither does the fact that a person is a democrat signify anything about his worth and rank; every idiot *is* a democrat today. On the other hand, it would be erroneous to conclude from a man's high, nonpolitical achievements anything about his political insight, ability, and calling to join the discussion—just as erroneous as the reverse would be, to take proven political competency as a sign of a generally significant man. There is no extrapolitical criterion of political calling. Politics is the sphere of the (democratic) individual, not of the (aristocratic) personality. And as proof that an opinion *about* politics is already a political opinion, I offer the opinion that the only true and real justification of political democracy lies *here*, to wit, in the principle that can be summed up: "Where it is impossible to give each his own, everyone shall be given the same."

With this, we might actually already be finished. But to reach the goal too easily is not to reach the goal properly. We must begin again.

Every nonrhetorical person who loves truth and embraces a respectable pessimism will calmly recognize the irrevocable conflict between individual and society. He will recognize that social life is and remains the sphere of necessity, of compromise, of insoluble antinomies. He will declare it to be an unctuous betrayal of the people when positivistic enlightenment promises the realization of a harmony of individual and social interests by means of that impossible delineation of the "rights" of the individual in relation to the same "rights" of the others, that therefore promises "freedom," "individual prosperity," and "happiness." In practice, this is no reason to twiddle one's thumbs, but it is a reason to deny intellectual support to political enlightenment. Its unctuous high-mindedness, its self-satisfied confidence, will disgust such a person, not only because he sees that the "happiness" promised by this enlightenment is impossible to attain, but because it does not seem to him at all desirable; it seems unworthy of a human being, repulsive to intellect and culture, bovine-peaceful-cud-chewing, and without soul. He knows that politics, namely enlightenment, social contract, republic, progress toward the "greatest good for the greatest number," is no way at all to reconcile social life; that this reconciliation can be achieved only in the sphere of personality, never in that of the individual, only on a spiritual path, that is, never on a political one, and that it is insane to want to raise social life even the slightest bit toward religious consecration. It is precisely this tendency, however, that has existed in all positivism from time immemorial, and never has this tendency been clearer than today, when under the name of culture-religion, of religion of the "intellect," positivism is celebrating a triumphant *risorgimento*—while still remaining what it was, to wit, the morality of utility and nothing better.

Seen from without, the question of the human being presents itself in a two-fold way: as a metaphysical and a social question, a moral and a political, a personal and a social one. In truth, it is only one, and politics, that is, utilitarian enlightenment and the humanitarianism of happiness, is *not* the means to its solution. The opposite belief is that of the European West, of rhetorical democracy, and Germany, which has resisted this belief up to now because she knew that one cannot at all separate the political question from the question of the human being, that on the contrary the former, even as a political question, can still find its solution only in inwardness, only in the soul of the human being—Germany is about to go over to this belief, thinking that as she does so she is "politicizing" herself—as if a policy that in the long run is not compatible with any governmental form were worthy of its name. For no governmental form is compatible with the principles of utilitarian enlightenment. What they are creating is that vicious circle in which anarchy and dictatorship meet, and which a national, that is, an antidemocratic German statesman, who has admittedly become very old-fashioned today, namely Bismarck, did not wish for Germany. Neither anarchy nor despotism makes up a state at all, and in despotism it is immaterial whether "power" is based on the bayonet or, as in Kerensky's Russia, on "freedom," or rather whether freedom is held up "with blood and iron." To *differentiate* here is one of the most remarkable manifestations of human folly.

Since, as I have said, politics, social life, is the sphere of necessity and compromises, genuinely reasonable behavior in this sphere will always be moderate-middle, not to say: mediocre behavior, a middle-of-the-road policy. In many other spheres such as morality and art, radicalism may be permissible or necessary; in politics it is mischief. "Take sides! Take sides! Let us all take sides!" Herwegh sang—if one can call something like that song. At least once the apolitical Goethe took sides: when he said to Eckermann, that is, that every reasonable human being was a moderate liberal. And in his mouth this means about the same as "a moderate conservative." For as we understand him, by liberalism he did not mean enlightenment, egalitarian individualism, republic and "progress," not some kind of abstract ethics of human rights and duties and that ideal of "free competition," to which one owes the world-dominance of economic interests. No, Goethe did not believe in freedom "and" equality. He did not declare himself to be a democrat when he called himself a liberal. We hope, we fancy, we can define his "moderate liberalism" as we define our own in the following lines.

His cause is that of intellectual and social freedom. He is the enemy of democracy insofar as it behaves like a doctrinaire end in itself and not like a means. As a means, however, namely of aristocratic selection in the interest of the state, it is precisely what one calls social freedom, or more properly, social mobility: In an aphorism from *Human, All Too Human*, Nietzsche discusses the possibility of exchange between the two castes, the forced worker and the free worker castes: an exchange of the type "that the duller, less intellectual families and individuals from the upper caste are put down into the lower one, and on the other hand, the freer people from the lower caste attain access to the higher one." Nietzsche thought that culture should be vitally concerned with this possibility. But the state is also concerned with it. Beyond doubt, it is important for the state to have the greatest possible concurrence between personal and social rank. Therefore one must seek ways to thwart the educational privilege of property. The first, if not the best, method would be social tax legislation. But in this impairment of hereditary rights one must be particularly careful to spare the small *and middle* property owners, for culture has gained a hundred times from the fact that someone at twenty, by means of his inherited income, which might be a meager pittance, has been assured social freedom; and as far as real riches are concerned, there is justice in the reservation that certain values not only of a cultural but also of a political nature are bound to them. A happier solution, which is also, in a good psychological sense, more radical than the demand for social-democratic tax legislation, is the one that calls for the democratization of the means of education. This is the real way to assure that no one of special talent will be hindered any longer because of birth from following a higher career, and every public-spirited person will recommend this method, even if he does not forget that there are cultural values resulting from inheritance and breeding. The freest opportunity for education! This is very important. Democracy as a fact is nothing more than the continually growing public nature of modern life, and the spiritual-human dangers of this increasing democracy, the danger, that is, of a complete leveling, of a journalistic-rhetorical stultification and vulgarization, can only be met with an education whose dominating concept would have to be, as Goethe demanded in the Pedagogical Province, *reverence*: Goethe, this pedagogue by birth, this passionate educator who knew well that culture, education in the spirit of reverence, will be the only urgently needed corrective to the forthcoming democracy. And why is it this, finally? Because in the educational idea, the social-political question is put back where it belongs, namely into the inner sphere of the personality; because this idea puts the social-political question back into the sphere that it never should have left, into the spiritual-moral, the human sphere. The social-religiosity of the educational idea can bring reconciliation to social life. Only real, that is, metaphysical religion can do this by teaching that in the end the social element is subordinate. Or, if one does not want to speak of religion, then let one substitute education for it (whereby, naturally, we cannot mean scientific half-education), or goodness, or humanity, or freedom. Politics makes one rough, vulgar, and stupid. Envy, impudence, covetousness, is all it teaches. Only spiritual education liberates. Institutions are of little importance; character is all important. Become better yourself! And everything will be better.

So much for the concept of social freedom in our liberalism. As far as its concept of *intellectual* freedom is concerned, it is derived from the insight that the separation of intellectual life from the state cannot be rejected. For the state, as it is, cannot be the bearer of personal life. The absence of a state-directed cultural unity means that there is *no* complete human satisfaction in political life—from which, among other things, it follows that the doctrine of civic education as *the* education is rather bad romanticism. It is liberal to deny the agreement of intellectual and political life, or rather: to recognize their nonagreement. Human dangers lie here, too; but even if they are perhaps greatest of all in Germany, the German is also the most capable of resisting them, thanks especially to the Reformation, which taught him more generally to bear metaphysical freedom. Hegel said that France would never come to rest because she missed the Reformation. And Carlyle shows in his heroic-humorous way how the French Revolution was only a vengeful return of the Protestantism that had been rejected two hundred years earlier.

The democracy that our liberalism affirms is not a doctrine and not a rhetorical philosophy of virtue from the eighteenth century. It is twofold. In its public nature, which is still spreading, it is a fact of modern life that is not without psychological and intellectual danger; and in its social mobility and method for aristocratic selection it is a technical desirability for the state. It is therefore not something to be enthusiastic about but something to recognize calmly and reasonably. It has nothing at all to do with "intellect" or with virtue. But as a fact and as a desirability it is not only compatible with a *strong monarchical government*, such a government actually forms its necessary corrective. Political opinions are *volitional* opinions; this lies in their nature; and since, if the word combination can seriously be allowed, we are dealing here with a "political confession," I will therefore say what I want politically—and particularly what I do *not* want. I want the monarchy, I want a tolerably independent government, because it alone guarantees political freedom, both in the intellectual and in the economic spheres. I want it because it was the separation of the monarchical state government from the monied interests that gave the Germans leadership in social policy. I do not want the parliamentary and party economic system that causes the pollution of all national life with politics. I do not

want Dreyfus to be condemned and then acquitted for political reasons—for the acquittal of an innocent person for political reasons is no
less repulsive than his conviction on the same basis. I do not want the
lungs of the *petit sucrier* condemned to a chamber quarrel, the tubercular
man condemned to military service and to death because of reverse
class justice, because the public beast's foaming jaws "of justice" demand
a sacrificial lamb. I do not want politics. I want objectivity, order and
decency. If this is philistine, then I want to be a philistine. If it is
German, then in God's name I want to be called a German, although
this does not bring honor in Germany. And then, since we are talking
about German character and politics, I also want to say two or even
three words about the question of German or Prussian suffrage, which
has again become a burning question, from the point of view of the
German character and that of politics, two points of view that in my
opinion must be *well differentiated*.

The democrats maintain that the resistance of the conservatives to
the introduction of universal suffrage into the leading federal German
state, which takes up three-fifths of the total area of the *Reich*, comes
from interest in personal power. I argued against this that the conservatives are doubtless serious in their assertion that when Germany
condescends to Western democracy, she has lost the war spiritually.
They have this opinion because they are conservatives. Being conservative does not mean wanting to preserve everything that exists: the
conservatives assert their readiness for reforms. Being conservative
means: wanting to keep Germany German—and this is not exactly
democracy's will. The self-contradiction of the so-called "Fatherland's
Party" is that it ostensibly wants to "keep its distance" from domestic
policy, and, using the word "party" in a nonpartisan, nonpolitical sense,
only wants to bring Pan-Germany together in foreign policy. I call this
a self-contradiction: for when one combines "Pan-Germany," including,
that is, all those who are intellectually, and not just economically,
nationally minded and nationally inclined, one does not include democracy at all, but leaves it, as the hostile element, outside; this itself is
taking sides in a domestic and *conservative* way; for conservative and
national are one and the same—just as surely as democratic and
*inter*national are one and the same—no matter what democracy may
say against this.

In certain cases, democracy claims for itself the best German traditions. It finds its origins in German humanism, in the cosmopolitan
burgherly nature of our great literary epoch. But German humanism

is something different from democratic "human rights"; cosmopolitanism is something different from internationalism; the German cosmopolitan burgher is not a political burgher, he is not political—while democracy is not only political, *it is politics itself*. Politics, however, democracy, is in itself something un-German, anti-German; and the self-contradiction of democracy, or at least of a certain democracy, is that it wants to be both democratic and national at the same time, that it declares the name, "Fatherland's Party," to be an affront, and is mortally offended when anyone gives an indication of considering it less nationally reliable than the conservatives. In truth, it may be *patriotic* in its honest concern for the economic welfare of Germany, for her happiness and even for her power (for economics is of course a means and an expression of power) and in its opinion that Germany's industrial blossoming is only served by democratic "understanding"—it is not *national* and cannot be so: its abstract concept of humanity, its whole intellectual tradition, gives the lie to this claim. "Today," Rousseau has already said, "there are no more Frenchmen, Germans, Spaniards, or Englishmen to speak of; there are only Europeans who all have the same tastes, the same passions, the same customs, because none has received a national stamp from special institutions." Here is the tradition of all intellectual democracy that is not just opportunistic-political. The joining of the democratic with the national idea is today an inadmissible liberality, an intellectual impurity: I say "today," for seventy years ago that patriotic democracy, that politicism of the "German Brothers," which Schopenhauer despised, was obviously something intellectually possible. Not today. Intellectual possibilities also have their lifetimes; they are exposed to destruction. Have the times become stricter, more divisive, inexorable and radical in intellectual matters? They probably have; for in 1915 it is impossible to perceive the intellectual form of the national democratic man other than as an obsolete and faded form. It may be that those like me are from 1880. But national democracy is from 1848, and it only seems possible because every today finds the day before yesterday more elegant than yesterday.

I have mentioned the self-contradiction of the "Fatherland's Party" and that of the national democratic man. Let no one say that I am suppressing my own self-contradiction and that of those like me. It is a German self-contradiction: it grows out of the antithesis between German tradition and political character, out of this national antithesis that was represented in 1813 by Goethe, in 1848 by Schopenhauer, and after 1871 by Nietzsche against the passion of the politicizing masses, and that still remains in force today, no matter how much it may be denied by the advocates of the politicization, that is: of the democratization of Germany. The one and only possibility in Germany is for *national affirmation to imply negation of politics and democracy*—and vice versa. When one sees things in a conservative way, one sees them antipolitically. On the other hand, one is not a politician and a democrat without being antinational, without being a cosmopolitan radical. In the intellectual sphere, the call for Germany's politicization does not at all mean Germany's call to *power*—we learn this every day. It means rather the will to revolution and to the political dissolution of Germany. On the other hand, it is possible that that same national sympathy and attachment that makes one wish for Germany's victory, power, and historical greatness, also psychologically unquestioningly prescribes for one an antipolitical attitude, and makes one adopt completely the words that Overbeck wrote to Treitschke in 1873:

> If our German past is really so bad, if it really has repeatedly shown us in such a deplorable way our political inability, as you, not least of all, have demonstrated to us, then one may well doubt whether it is precisely in politics that our fortune awaits us, and whether we have not again fallen into a bad situation with our present political fever.

This yes-and-still-no is my case. I have myself to blame for this self-contradiction that is reconciled not in logic but in national feeling, just as my opponent's is reconciled in antinational feeling: it is the self-contradiction of this book, which at most presumes to present it, not to solve it.

So much for me. But as far as that democracy is concerned that gets hot-headed as soon as one accuses it of having less national interest than the conservatives, its sensitivity on this point is at best ignorance of its own deeper will—as far as it is not hypocrisy and tactics. At the right moment I notice a newspaper item that speaks quite remarkably to the point. It concerns a petition to both houses of the Prussian state parliament; it is from the German occupants of the Prussian eastern marches, and it has found more than sixty thousand signatures. The petition, it says, expresses the "deep concern" the eastern march Germans have about the imperial government's policy; that "the imminent change in Prussian suffrage and its logical consequence, the change in communal suffrage, will lead to a strengthening of the Polish influence in the Prussian state parliament *and to the complete Polonization of the hitherto German administration of the great majority of our cities.*" This appeared in a little south German paper that reprinted the report, perhaps innocently, from a conservative Berlin organ; it did not appear in *any* of the large leftist-liberal papers—the report would have been tactically inopportune, and even if it has to do with the realization of "justice," still the nationality of the eastern march city administration, the "deep concern" of the threatened Germans in these areas, is something of complete indifference to democracy.

I wanted to note and record this little known fact, and with it I am again at the more narrow theme of this section: the question of suffrage, on which a position must be taken for better or worse. I will admit, then, that the moral and intellectual arguments in favor of equal suffrage seem to me to be weak and not very sound. One says, for example, that democratic conviction, the will to participation in the state in the democratic spirit and in democratic forms, has been powerfully promoted by the war, on the basis of the sacrifices the people have made, that is. But *every* conviction and every opinion has been promoted and strengthened by this war: the conservative-national one not less than the democratic one; and to say "not less" is to say too little. I know people, I even know German women, who have sacrificed their loved ones in the war: lost them, that is, and who during these years, instead of moving toward the "left," have moved a good bit farther toward the "right." Whoever would claim that this is not an exception but even the rule—and indeed precisely in those classes that are in the end the intellectually important ones, the upper social classes, not to say: the educated ones—would scarcely claim too much; and the increase in membership that the "Fatherland's Party" is enjoying is only insufficiently explained by its campaign expenditures. Whoever travels and knows how to listen in Germany today will *not* return home with the conviction that the political opinion of the German people has been "democratized"—I am speaking from personal experience, and it has taught me rather the opposite. Let one visit the businessman, the academician, the artist (of course I do not mean the literary, intellectual one)—even the representative German artist of world fame, the musician; let one question the Pfitzners and the Straußes about their good wishes toward democracy and toward "equal suffrage," one will be very surprised and not at all in a liberal way. One will see that radicalism in artistic tradition and a politically quite conservative attitude get along admirably together. I heard a famous conductor exclaim: "It will reach the point where the orchestra will vote on whether to play a passage *piano* or *mezzoforte*!" Let him who does not think this is serious read what Nietzsche says in *Human, All Too Human*, about the *exemplary* nature of the relationship between people and government for the intercourse between teacher and pupil, master and servant, father and family, army commander and soldier, master and apprentice.

Now the large newspapers say, to be sure, that it is the politically naive, the laymen, dilettantes and idiots *in politicis* who are caught in the web of the "Fatherland's Party" and resist democracy. But is it not precisely democracy that teaches that politics is "no secret science" and that there is no such thing as political dilettantism and a political laity? Does political maturity exist only in the press? Or should we rather stick to Wagner's truth that it is democracy that in our country "only exists in the press"? By the way, the necessity of granting us democracy is based precisely on the fact that we have shown ourselves to be "ripe" for it. Ripe for democracy? Ripe for the republic? What stupidity! A people is either suited for this or that state and social form, or it is not. It is created for it, or it is not created for it. It never becomes "ripe" for it; and certain South American nations do not have a republic and "freedom" because they were "ripe" for it earlier.

The principle of general and equal suffrage is the principle of the plebiscite, and even dyed-in-the-wool democrats would prefer to reject this, assuming, for example, it involves debatable territorial questions. The plebiscite is then seen as a doctrinaire demand; one is of the hesitating opinion that there will be great difficulties in carrying it out, one doubts whether it would give the true picture of the people's will. Large groups, one says, would always be found that would call the result of the vote wrong and unjust, a strong minority perhaps, and who knows whether it would not include the truly decisive elements? In a word, one is not consistent, one forgets that the same doubts apply to general and equal suffrage, too, even if the territorial questions concern a population that is 75 percent illiterate and the question of suffrage concerns a well-educated mass. If a people is "more than the sum of its parts," then the people has not spoken when one has questioned the parts individually. It is not intellectual playfulness to say that the will of the people can be something else than that of the "sum" of the mass. A mechanical-democratic plebiscite in the Germany of the third year of the war would with lamentable probability produce an overwhelming majority in favor of an immediate and unconditional, that is, a ruinous peace. But here the principle of the plebiscite is carried *ad absurdum*, for that would by no means be the will of the people. The will of a historically rising people is one with its fate.

I repeat that all positive arguments in favor of equal suffrage, as far as they have intellectual and moral pretensions, seem untenable to me. What I for my part put in its place is the conclusion that in a sphere in which it is impossible to give each his own, nothing else remains but to give everyone the same. This is not just, but it has popular simplicity, and we live in a time that is not suited for the best thought-out justice but for the most easily comprehensible one. For me, there is no doubt that it is precisely in a differentiated people of great intellectual disparity such as the German that a multivote suffrage law tempered with wisdom and taking into account accomplishment, age, degree of education, and intellectual rank, as well as whether one had sons and therefore had not only an egotistical-personal interest in the formation of the state but also a farther-looking one—that such a suffrage law could be relatively more just than the universal one: for in all human efforts, there can of course only be a question of relative justice. But the more thought-through, aristocratic, ingeniously graduated and inventive in its approximation to justice such a voting law would be, the less it would be able to seem to be the right one to the masses, who, you see, only consider the most simple, the clumsiest, and the most primitive type of justice, the one that without much ado gives everyone the same, to be the right one. The fact that they even consider it to be *absolutely* just puts them in the moral position of resisting every aristocratic right with a fervor unattainable for those who realize the imperfection of every system of law, and with which they must carry off the victory. And politics can only be pursued today with the masses and their primitive, antiaristocratic enthusiasm for justice. All the political efforts of intellect, wisdom, and high acumen, such as we find in political thinkers, for example, like Adam Müller, whose reflections on political science are perhaps the most brilliant and true ones ever made on this matter— all this, I say, seems like a beautiful, luxurious and fruitless game in the face of the real, unchangeable and unstoppable course of political development that is leading directly into what is more and more suited to the mass-primitive element, into the radical democratic world. This can be established, and with that respect that one owes to fate, acknowledged. But precisely because of the fact that intellect, philosophy, and valuable thought quite clearly have nothing more to do and say in politics, there follows the necessity of *separating* intellectual from political life, of letting the latter take its fatal path and of raising the former above such fatality to serene independence. As things stand, no demand is more ridiculous and impudent than the one calling for the "politicization of intellect"—as if intellect had to be politicized because politics is not capable of intellect and is degenerating more and more into a type of rhetorical vulgarization. But intellectual life is *national* life, and it is this one must separate from political life—a decision that may and must admittedly seem difficult or impossible to the conservative politician. But let them consider that the national culture not only can reach out more extensively than the state, than public, legally organized life (it does so in the case of the German *Reich*, which, of course, does not at all encompass the German cultural area), but that it also—and this in any case—is more extensive, more personal than the legal system, and this is why one would do an injustice to ascribe to the latter an exaggerated importance for the higher and true life of the nation. It is just as much an intellectual impossibility for the personality to be completely absorbed in the state today (precisely because the state is giving up more and more of its metaphysical character and it is becoming less and less possible to maintain an agreement between political and religious life)—as it is for the legal system to absorb and transmit the personal element of a higher category, the national culture. The truth that the conservative politician finds so difficult to accept, and that he nevertheless will have to accept, is that the state, the legal system for the most part, or to a great extent, is a matter of international civilization and not of national culture. Are perhaps those people right who oppose the legalization of a specifically "German" freedom? "Freedom," says Büchner's Danton—and I cite the passage certainly not for the last time—"freedom and a whore are the most cosmopolitan things under the sun." It would therefore probably be too much to demand that freedom recognize nationality. On the other hand, there are expressions about freedom that prove that the insight into the unpoliticizability of the absolute is not a German privilege. "Liberty is the most treacherous, indeed, of all phantoms," Ruskin wrote in 1849 in his book, *The Seven Lamps of Architecture.* "There is no such thing in the universe. There can never be. The stars have it not; the earth has it not; the sea has it not; and we men have the mockery and semblance of it only for our heaviest punishment." This could have come from Goethe or Schopenhauer, or even Adalbert Stifter; and comes nevertheless from a person at home in the land where political freedom originated. One should perhaps not wish to treat politics all too nationally. It is not the material for it, it is not worth it.

To separate intellectual, national life from political life, and to differentiate between them is, however, a thoroughly German, a Kantian way of separating and differentiating. The difference between intellect and politics is that of pure and practical reason; and, far from even being able to be an object of intellectual enthusiasm, the granting of universal and equal suffrage to Prussia seems also to me, today, to be a postulate of practical reason. Faced with the decision, I will also vote for it. It could have been avoided if the government had in good time shown itself ready for reforms; as things stand today, it can scarcely be avoided without endangering the state itself, and its thwarting for intellectual reasons of principle would probably be, in quite a similar way, a sign of Germany's political nonviability and lack of a future, like an ideologically determined peace by resignation in foreign policy. That patriotic idea of expediency-democracy, no matter how illicit it may be from an intellectual point of view, has, in the end, its good, practical-political justification; and the intellectual and artist who, out of national sympathy or attachment, wishes Germany's political greatness, should not be prevented by this attachment, but moved by it, to advocate a democratic form of government in Germany today: realizing that one should not overestimate the significance of legal order for national life, with all intellectual reservations, by the way, and in the quiet confidence that the German *Volksstaat* will show important and quite national differences from the democracy of the rhetorical bourgeois.

I do not need more. This is the quantum of "politics" I need for everyday use. In it one notices some opposition to the principle that civic education is education itself. This principle is not German, no matter how honest the voices may sound that express it. Education is the formation of human beings, and never will the German spirit understand "the human being" to be exclusively or even predominantly the social human being. He will also never believe that culture is a means, that it amounts to something like the mastering of nature and to the greatest possible equal distribution of goods attained in this manner; he will rather hold fast to the opinion that culture is an "end in itself"; he will not cease to accord goals to it that have meaning in themselves, without regard, for example, to utility or to the state. Besides, nothing in these principles contradicts the demand, called forth by the war, for the *Volksstaat*. If it is truly a demand of the people, then it has ceased to be mere demand. The *Volksstaat* is nothing to be granted; it is here when the people are here who think and perceive of the state in this way. And my heart and my reason would be with the young people returning from the war who have to bring about the acknowledgement of a political *fact*, yes, have to force it. I want to leave no doubt about this here, either for myself or for anyone else.

The *Volksstaat*, the politicization of the people, to say it once more, is necessary because Germany has been put "into the saddle" and must not fall off; it is necessary for the sake of the governmental tasks she feels called to. But the thought is completely unbearable to me that it could even appear that democratic progress in the sense, say, of English ministerial speeches, had been forced upon us from outside, as if Germany had had to yield and to submit intellectually. And nevertheless, the national danger seems to me to lie in the fact that the *Volksstaat* in its domestic and foreign realization will be confused with democracy in the Western sense and understanding—even more that it could prove to be impossible to realize it in any other way than in the intellectual and political forms of the West; yes, that it would develop according to the minds of those who understand by the politicization of Germany not just a more popular formation of our public institutions, a more passionate, genuine and growing intimacy of the relationship between nation and state—who would not find this as desirable as necessary!— but rather the *complete politicization and republicanization of the nation*; and this would really mean that change in the structure of the German spirit that many would prefer to recognize as a necessity rather than a desirability; its leveling, narrowing, impoverishing, that is, the transformation of a world people into a political one, one "that flies in a 'V' formation," that "crystallizes in every meeting into a practice revolution or a one-day republic." In this case, democratization would be external conformance, conformance to the world level of civilization; nationalization in this sense would be denationalization, it would be the stultification of the German into a social and political animal, it would be de-Germanization—and what purpose in the whole world could German leadership tasks have after this?

Impossible? Such a process is *not* impossible! It is taking place, it is related to Bismarck's life work, who, to be sure, completed this work with aristocratic-conservative and not with democratic-liberal means. State and nation were not at all identical concepts for him, and he had no liking for the idea of Greater Germany, which was democratic. Admittedly, there is no Greater German state, and democracy is not at once the logically necessary appendage of the Small-German state. Nevertheless, Bismarck, too, in spite of his antiliberalism, considered democracy to be a part of his national state to the extent that he placed universal military duty alongside general suffrage; the development of his continental power-*Reich* followed a more centralist, imperialistic direction; and the phase of German politicization and democratization that has been achieved today, or that people are urgently being beseeched to achieve, is nothing other than just a new phase of that process that Bismarck started and that Nietzsche rejected "in the conservative interest" in order to preserve German tradition. But that this process will be accomplished in ways other than the prepatterned, traditional ones, even if they have in no way been proven successful, that it will be able to be anything different and more than a copying and hobbling after what is not just doubtful but notoriously unproven— is unlikely; for all demands that extend beyond the most general ones that are being expressed today have to do with continuous, mechanical democratization, the reform of suffrage, the formation of parliamentarianism.

"On the whole, however, I wish," Nietzsche writes, "that the idiocy of numbers and the superstitious belief in majorities would not yet become established in Germany as it has in the Latin races; and that one would finally *invent something in politicis*! There is little sense and much danger in allowing the habit of general suffrage, whose roots are still short-lived and easy to destroy, to become more deeply embedded, for its introduction was only an emergency and a momentary measure." The "habit" is no longer short and no longer "easy to destroy," I believe. But Paul de Lagarde, who observed things from a less precipitous height than Nietzsche, who did not pass judgment on them so casually and condescendingly, but who rather stood among his own people as a straightforward but also passionate patriot, expressed himself in a very similar way on suffrage and on the will of the people.

"One must understand quite completely," he says,

> that a nation does not consist of primordial voters. It does this just as little as a picture by Raphael is composed of canvas and bits of color. . . . The individuals stand as such, as egoisms, that is, even in contrast to the nation. . . . The nation does not speak at all when the single individuals who make up the nation speak. The nation only speaks when the nationhood (I am happy to use Goethe's very appropriate but forgotten expression) is expressed in the individuals: that is—

let this beautiful phrase be introduced for the second time; I love it very much because it seems to me to express perfectly how far politics is at all appropriate and permissible for the people *and* the artist, the intellectual —

> that is, when the consciousness of a common basic and tribal nature of all individuals awakens and clearly sees its relationship to great deeds of history. In wars such as those of 1866 and 1870, the nation speaks even when one only questions the sum of its individual members . . . in individual laws and individual administrative regulations, the nation remains quite silent, even if one goes from man to man for his opinion, and receives an answer man for man. As a totality, the nation thinks only about totalities . . . Where general suffrage is the last word of wisdom, one does not weigh the votes, one counts them. My pupils shall recognize this immoral way of reaching a conclusion to be immoral.

Thus Lagarde. And in all this, he begins unambiguously with the idea, which is democratic, if you will, that the nation itself has a voice in matters that affect it. Nevertheless, one can call him a conservative; for to be German-conservatively disposed does not mean: to preserve everything that exists, but it means: to want to keep Germany German, nothing more. And above all, it is German not to confuse the nation with the mass that is composed of individuals-atoms. "The principles of 1789," Lagarde says,

> have been transplanted to Germany, and one calls their representatives liberals. . . . Naturally, these principles can be even less successfully applied to Germany than to France. For if they arise altogether from theory, not from necessity and truth, if, as early as under Louis Philippe, they forfeited the most ruthless honesty of their raving, murdering, and dying fathers, then they have no more right anywhere on earth to be principles: their specific and very original Celtic flavor from the Paris of 1789 has made them neither more agreeable nor more justified to Germany, because Germany is basically aristocratic and could only become more un-German and therefore more unhappy from all that Celtic egalitarian nonsense.

To be sure, this does not sound democratic. But the aristocracy and conservatism of the *praeceptor Germaniae* are combined quite effortlessly with the most definite affection for his people, and nothing can be more national than this synthesis. When he demands "that one admit openly that in present-day Germany the possibility of freedom and self-government does not yet exist, that at present there is only government; that one, however, by seriously undertaking the genuine education of a few, selected *not according to birth but according to their ethical and intellectual capacity*, create a class that, appointed by and working for this people, and respected for this voluntary work, *supplementing itself freely from below*, can at some time in the future undertake self-government"; when he demands further "that one increase the wealth of the country so that such a class would also have the external means that makes it independent, without which self-government is a laughable farce or a martyrdom"; that one "put an end" to the parliament that has no power yet talks and votes and does not represent the people, then such demands do not seem to be from 1878 but from 1917: they are of the greatest timeliness today, and they have never ceased quietly to be timely; they are one with the demands for social freedom, unrestricted social mobility, and aristocratic selection that take precedence today over all merely political demands for freedom; they are national; but not democratic; and when Lagarde judges that paths other than those of the counting of votes must be taken to support the idea that the people themselves have the right to speak on matters concerning them, to help them to their rights, then this is only another formulation of Nietzsche's wish "that at long last one would invent something new *in politicis*."

The European philosopher does not say what this new element would consist of, and the national politician presents little to define those institutions that would unfold the true nature of the Germans. How could an artist who is taken away from his real, eccentric-personal tasks by the violent character of the times to reflect on his people's fate dare to contribute more than they! He can only repeat from deepest personal conviction what the great ones of his nation, say, the Nietzsches, Lagardes and Wagners, that democracy in the Western sense and taste is alien to us, an imported creature that "only exists in the press," and can never become German life and German truth.

"Germany must become politicized!" But would she become politicized by copying the political institutions of others, introducing a parliament, and then, without belief or hope, by hobbling after the Western nations into the area that is recognized as unproven? If the Germans do not possess enough political ability to create their own original, that is, national institutions, their own national type of freedom, or, as far as it exists, to maintain it; if, on the contrary, they find they must copy the "genuinely political nations," then they should not imagine that they are called to politics at all. What is freedom, anyway? Everyone answers me: it means to be allowed to live according to one's own laws of life. But no matter whether one calls it scholarly, burgherly, backward or tasteless—it is still true and will never cease being so that to politicize the German concept of freedom is already to falsify it. Our religious and philosophical history impresses itself so strongly on even the most unlearned person that he, forced to national consciousness by this war, cannot think and feel otherwise. There is a symbol for the German separation of intellect and politics, of radical theory and life, of "pure" and "practical" thinking: the two separate volumes of Kant's twofold critique that stand side by side. I know well that the fastidious person resists rethinking a thought, no matter how true it may be, that has been thought a hundred times. But here it is not a matter of the novelty and unusualness of the thought, but of the simple and lasting truth in it. And even if truths age and die; if it is disgraceful to fight new things with worn-out truths, there are still truths that do not become obsolete, do not become banal and despicable—or that can only become so for snobs and political esthetes: facts of the national spirit, bound to the structure of this spirit and incapable of aging. In my opinion, such a fact and unpretentious-unshakable truth is that the German concept of freedom will always be of a spiritual nature: an individualism that in order to reveal itself politically must create institutions other than those barren-abstract ones of the political West and of "human rights." Lagarde says that since it is important to achieve Germany's inner unity, one must reach back to the genuine German individualism of our fathers, for, enclosed within solid boundaries, this individualism will do no more harm. "All that matters," he says, "is granting the individual human being his rights, and for him to obtain these rights, there must, on the one hand, be institutions that will lift him above himself, while on the other hand all institutions that prevent him from developing his genuine individuality must be destroyed: the first thing to be done is to do away with the Prussian educational system." Here I pride myself a little that the only political criticism I have exercised within my literary production was directed against the Prussian secondary school!

Away, then, with the alien and repulsive slogan, "democratic!" Never will the mechanical-democratic state of the West be naturalized with us. Let one Germanize the word, let one say "national" instead of "democratic"—and one names and grasps the exact opposite: for German-national means "free"—inwardly and outwardly, but it does not mean "equal"—neither inwardly nor outwardly. Who would want to resist a more national organization of the *Reich*'s and of the public's affairs?

None of those, I guarantee, who in a certain sense resist with the most intense repugnance the democratization, the politicization of Germany. Germany as *res publica*—there is no objection. But Germany as a *republic*, as a virtue-state with a social contract, a democratic people's government and the "complete absorption of the individual in the totality"; Germany as a *state* and nothing more, and the German human being as a Jacobin and *citoyen vertueux* with the citizen's certificate in his pocket—this would be a fright! And especially: it would no longer be Germany. Evolution, development, originality, manifoldness, and richness of individuality have always been the basic law of German life. This life has always resisted centralization, has never received its customs from a principal, central point. The German has been free and unequal, that is, aristocratic. The Reformation was admittedly a democratic event: for the emancipation of the layman is democracy, and in the political area it is precisely what Nietzsche calls "a literarylike joining in the discussion of everyone about everything." But Luther's most original and profound impact, too, was of an aristocratic nature: he perfected the freedom and self-authority of the German human being by internalizing them and thus removing them forever from the sphere of the political argument. Protestantism took the intellectual sting from politics. It made politics into a matter of practice. From Kant we have the belief in the predominance of "practical reason," of ethics. From him we have the social imperative. But the coming of Goethe was a new confirmation of the legitimacy of the individual being, it was Germany's great artistic experience after the metaphysical-religious one that Luther had brought: an experience of culture and sensuality, completely human, foreign to all abstraction, hostile to all ideology, to patriotic ideology first, to all political ideology in general. A nation does not experience an intellect such as this, it does not even create one, without always having had and continuing to have a different attitude than the others toward those generous, magical-fraudulent words: mankind, freedom, equality, revolution, and progress.

Freedom, duty, and freedom again, that is Germany. One says to be sure that epochs of individualistic and of social thought alternate in history; but for the German intellectual constitution there is no conflict here and no necessity to shift and fluctuate between two hostile principles. It remains the peculiarity of German individualism that it gets along very well with ethical socialism, which one calls state socialism, and which is something different from the human-rights, Marxist type. For the social principle is only hostilely opposed by the individualism of the enlightenment, the liberal individualism of the West. There is an anti-individualism that includes the freedom of the individual, and to negate the individualistic enlightenment does *not* mean to favor the socialization of the individual and his absorption in the state—as one in all likelihood has believed in the West and as one will, we hope, never start believing here. "Organization"—a highly intellectual word! "Organism"—truly a word of life! For an organism is more than the sum of its parts, and precisely this "more" is spirit, is life. But if "organization," this other political slogan of today, is to mean enslavement of the individual by the state, state absolutism, that is, even if it is the absolutism of the *Volksstaat*, yes, even if it is precisely this—then down with it, too! For nothing would be more anti-German and antihuman than such an organizational absolutism: princely absolutism, under which the individual seldom came off badly, would be preferred with just as much calm as resoluteness to the unlimited rule of the state, even to that of the *Volksstaat*, if by such a state one means a Jacobin-virtue republic!

Truly, with the voices of those excessive adherents of state piousness in my ears, voices that categorically hold that human nature exists to be "organized," completely organized and socialized, and to be unconditionally absorbed in the state-social unit, I can hardly resist the temptation to select some of Lagarde's sharpest words about state and nation, state and freedom, state and human nature; and if I do not resist it, my possible readers should not reproach me for overloading this "book" with quotations. It has no claim to the form and appearance, or even to the name, "book": the likes of me naturally looks around for help at every step in order, in a work of anguish and pain such as this, to find authoritative support for his feeling; it is difficult enough for him even with it; he is full of gratitude for everything offered him, and he does not worry much about the readability of his composition. Lagarde, for his part, cites Madame de Staël, referring with bitterness to her statement that there are three qualities on which the superiority of the German character over the French rests: the independence of the spirit, the love of loneliness, and the special nature of the individual human being. Yes, this makes one feel good! This man abhorred politics and "politicization" as much as any great German before him; he wanted no politics in the state, but what he called the "selfless service of the ethos, that is, the full realization of the basic principle that the state stands in the same relationship to the nation as the housewife to the master of the house, that it has to take care of all external matters so that the nation can look closely at the really essential part of life and deal with it." He demanded "that one make religion, science and art independent because all these things only exist when they are independent." He demanded "a *Reich* that is only a state to the extent that the nation cannot do without the state," and "the recognition, education, and transfiguration *of our own nature*." He fumed against Hegel with a scorn and hatred such as before him only Schopenhauer had done; he protested against the idolatry of the state, against the teaching that the state is the highest form of human life—protested against this Roman and heathen viewpoint in the name of evangelical and Germanic freedom. He wanted to have the state looked upon "as an ancillary machine vis-à-vis which the issue was not at all conservative, liberal, freethinking, or Catholic, but only whether it worked to our content-ment, and, if possible, with modest costs." He wanted *no* career politicians in parliament. He wanted the government supervised only by those "who have already learned on a small scale to judge and to direct public life before they begin to judge and direct it on a grand scale." That is, he wanted no literarylike "joining in the discussion by everyone about everything." In his opinion,

> it is everywhere a matter of know-how, and to the extent that the people outside the civil service have this know-how, they may exercise a check on the government, but neither should those who do not have this know-how be so bold as to speak up, nor should those, who by the nature of things have learned all the ins and outs of their particular governmental specialties, be subject to the judgment of the uninformed.

There wouldn't be much of a *Volksstaat*, it would be rather an unnational, everyday dummy state, if all one meant by it were parlia-mentary democracy. It would be an abomination of politicization and organization if it meant the absorption of the nation in the state and the "absorption of the individual in the whole." The human being is not only a social, but also a metaphysical being; the German human being first of all.

The economic situation the war has produced will mean that for decades after the war everyone will have to work and earn almost exclusively for the state. Should the human being, therefore, not be allowed to belong to himself at least intellectually, spiritually? Will not the need for spiritual independence grow tremendously in the unprec-edented social constraint and compulsory serfdom that will come? The tenderest cultivation and care of the aristocratic-individual element, the highest curiosity and sympathy for the unique individual soul, the special spiritual value—are indispensable as a counterweight to the organized socialism in the state of the future: or life will not be worth a shilling anymore.

Voices of the times—they join together to make noise, not music, for they know nothing of one another. One must separate them, one must listen to them separately to understand them. When two people say "democracy," it is from the first probable that they mean something quite different; one must discuss things with them individually. If our hero and friend, civilization's literary man, demands "politicization," and "organization"—and he does so—he has something completely different in mind from the democratic patriot and the patriotic democrat whom we just heard using the same words. The difference, for example, between the southwest-German, Frenchifying liberalism of the thirties and forties of the last century, and the liberalism of the wars of liberation, that of Stein and Arndt, is small compared to the difference between the democratic theory of civilization's literary man and that of the patriotic national statesman. To be sure, we found that democracy is nothing more than the individual's right to be active as a patriot, and that it logically should not be possible to demand general politicization and democracy and at the same time to pay homage to antipatriotic, antinational attitudes. This logical postulate, however, is not fulfilled by reality. The democratic type, on whom we will now reflect again, namely civilization's literary man, has nothing to do with the patriotic democrat who is moved by reason and current events to demand the identity of people and state, the politicization of minds and hearts, so that Germany can live, so that she can live powerfully and masterfully. Civilization's literary man does not demand democracy because Germany "must ride and must not fall off," and because whoever wants the end must also want the means; he wants it for its own sake. For him, Germany's politicization is not so much necessity as desirability as such, as progress itself—progress, that is, on the way to European equalization, to that leveling development in the sense of the homogeneous civilization of which we spoke—this progress that Nietzsche himself, modern Germany's greatest prophetic spirit, certainly furthered, if not intentionally, although on the other hand he still opposed it in the "conservative" interest: a Janus-faced behavior in which he shows double loyalty, by which it is explained and made possible, that today, too, in one and the same individual, there can be just as much tendency to give this progress actual support as to argue against it.

No, our civilization politician is not concerned with any sort of German mission to live powerfully and masterfully! It is not enough to say that he does not warm up to the idea: he flatly rejects it, and would be quite agreeable to have the Rhine as a boundary: agreeable for no other reason but that the restitution of the Rhine border would also mean the restitution of the continent-wide, intellectual-political predominance of France, of the homeland of his soul. Truly, if he were not such an exemplary Frenchman, one would have to call him a German idealist, and indeed, one is not only tempted, but even forced to recognize in him a German idealist and nothing else when one hears the answer, the nobly evasive answer he gives without fail when one seriously presses him on the Rhine border question, when one urges him to say clearly whether he really could seriously desire its definite restitution. He will answer: "At that time Germany had a great literature."

That she had. But first of all, of course, it has not been lost. I even hear it said that this literature had something or other to do with the unification of Germany, with the establishment of the *Reich*, that is— for the Small-German *Reich* is, after all, the form in which the unification of Germany was completed. I hear it said that never in all the history of nations has a literature played such a role as German literature from 1750 on did for a whole century. Thus while other nations, out of patriotism, to further the progress of the country, have created for themselves a tendentious literature, while their art and poetry have served politics from the very beginning so that the artistic value of a work was probably of secondary importance to the purpose: while this is approximately what happened in other places, in Germany, science, literature and art have existed only for their own sake alone—*l'art pour l'art* it is called in French; I hear that all forces, all the sympathetic participation of the culturally educated people, have aimed for this goal; to be sure, they said it was always national, but never political, and that it pursued no other purpose than to serve truth and beauty. But the very strange thing was that German art, precisely *because* it "wanted" nothing else but honest accomplishment in its sphere, precisely for this reason, as the burgher, Freytag, says, its pure flame glowed through the tender heart of the Germans until it was hardened for a great political battle. What am I thinking of? Our classical literature politically without will, art for art's sake, egotistical, unburgherly in the public

sense and "burgherly" only in a completely different, parasitic sense—
was it nevertheless a political tool that served to prepare German unity?
Could one therefore be an "esthete" and still have a national-political
effect—could one even do this better if one did not stultify oneself by
becoming an activistic democrat, but simply worked *educationally* in
freedom, educationally in the sense of forming, of perfecting the
individual? This would be the overthrow of all moral order! In the
meantime, those I hear talking in this way could call to witness the
grand sovereign of that literary cultural epoch, Goethe, who, it is true,
at first declared in the conversation with the historian, Luden, that in
art and science, before which national boundaries disappear, he had
found the wings on which he could raise himself above Germany's
political misery, but who then added that the consolation they provided
was only a miserable consolation and did not replace the proud
consciousness of belonging to a great, strong, respected and feared (he
said brutally, "feared") nation; and, after he had expressed his belief in
the future political power of Germany, finished with the words:

> All that remains for us as individuals in the meantime is for each according
> to his talents, his inclination, and his position, to further, to strengthen
> the nation's culture, and to spread it throughout the people in all
> directions, as much, and preferably more, to the upper levels as to the
> lower ones, so that our nation will not stay behind the others, but will at
> least be ahead of them in this point, so that our spirit will not become
> stunted, but will remain fresh and cheerful, so that it will not despair and
> become faint-hearted, but will remain capable of every great deed when
> the day of glory dawns.

This last turn of phrase has an embarrassingly French quality. But does
not all this look as if Goethe thought of the great cultural epoch he
dominated as nothing more than a *preparatory* epoch—as if with his
esthetic, politically quietist artistic practice, he had almost consciously,
no, quite consciously prepared the "day of glory" the day of German
unity and rule?

"At that time Germany had a great literature." Oh, yes, that she had.
But after one has considered whether the restitution of the Rhine
border would provide a definite guarantee for the reappearance of a
classical literature, one can finally no longer keep from asking *who* is
really the "esthete" here, the one who wishes at the bottom of his
progressive heart that Germany, so that she can once again throw
herself into the arms of beautiful literature, be deprived of power,
broken up and set back a hundred years—or the one who not only

affirms Goethe but also Bismarck because he believes that in the end Bismarck understood and reimbodied Goethe better than the civilization democrat? We want to be honest! In the thought of leading Germany back to her previous nonpolitical, suprapolitical condition, there is a deep, emotional temptation for every intellectual German that we must neither misjudge nor underestimate. What advantages for the spirit the restitution of this old condition would entail! What superiority there is in standing apart, in observing, in not being involved, in not wanting, in the cynical philosophizing that only bids Alexander get out of the sun—what freedom, irony, cheerfulness, purity, humanity would be won in this way, even if the national reality would again be depressed, wretched, and without worldly dignity as before! But can one avoid admiring and defending this nation's universal will, its will to reality and influence, justified and demonstrated as it is by the most earnest application, by mighty deeds and stupendous accomplishments? No radical literary man is necessary to teach us that the "man of power," Bismarck, was a misfortune, or to express it in a somewhat more reverential, positive way, a destiny, not only for the peace and quiet of the dear old cultural empires of Europe, but also in a very definite sense for Germany, and that the reality of his *Reich* was not exactly the governmental form to further the national tendency to pure humanity, spiritualization, and intellectuality, as did the abstract condition of Germany a hundred years ago. But since civilization's literary man is definitely a shrewd politician and not a frivolous esthete—can he wish and demand that his people return to the nonpolitical humanity, to the egotistical atomism, to the egocentric culture of the Goethean epoch? Who, I repeat, is the esthete here, anyway? Civilization's literary man does not, on the whole, like Goethe very much, the antirevolutionary, the quietist, the servant of princes. A hundred times he has played Voltaire off against him, the man of the Calas affair against the one who dared to say that he would rather tolerate injustice than disorder. But he plays Goethe off against the *Reich* and agrees quite uncritically with everybody's democratic opinion that the power *Reich* is an affront to the spirit of Weimar. Should he not rather conclude from the equal aversion he cherishes against them both, against Goethe *and* Bismarck, that the two are related and belong together? Should he not conclude from this equal aversion that they both are powerfully characteristic examples—more like outbreaks—of that cursed, refractory German tradition that is inimical to literature, yes, that Goethe was this way, too, in spite of his refractoriness to the wars of liberation and his liking for

Napoleon—outbreaks of German tradition, I say, that disgust civilization's literary man, and into the midst of which he should neither bring himself nor presume to interpose himself as a political preceptor? Politics! The creation of the *Reich* was in an extremely German, that is, antiradical sense a "political" creation, a work of practical reason, a concession of thought to matter, so that reality, so that "life," could come into existence, and life is indeed not beautiful literature. The *Reich* is not less a German realization than, for example, the France of today is the realization of the French philosophy of the eighteenth century—a living *Reich*, with all the dross, errors and baseness of life, yes indeed. But if civilization's literary man absolutely must have the question answered of whether Goethe would have approved of the *"Reich,"* then one might counter with the question of whether Rousseau, for example, or that pedantic, murderous philistine who called himself his disciple, would have agreed with the reality of the *république française* as it presents itself today to the delighted gaze of civilization's literary man.

We have digressed. This book is a constant digressing, that lies in its nature—I wanted to say that the democratic type we are now considering would not allow Herweghian naval songs to cross his lips. Democracy and imperialism—this combination may be admissible somewhere else, may be intellectually possible in France and England—and indeed, in a way that the democracy sanctifies the imperialism—in Germany it is not permissible and downright impossible. For uppermost to Germany, uppermost to the German radical literary man, at least, is the antithesis that we, if I am not mistaken, characterized earlier as the supreme, the general antithesis of this sharp and passionately ingenious thinker: the antithesis of *power and intellect.*

In the end, one must see that the necessity and inviolability of this thesis for Germany can also be disputed. A passage in one of Adalbert Stifter's letters from 1859 comes to mind that does not recognize it, that obviously knows nothing about it. "And Germany," it says there,

> should she, standing at the top of the world in intellect and power, matching the divine image of Hellas, which she really does match in depth of thought, youthful warmth, high-mindedness and enthusiasm, shall she also, like the Greek image, be shattered by the disunity of her members?

Never, nowhere, have intellect and power formed an antithesis in the life of nations, for the basis of this life, what creates a state, has always been something spiritual, something like a religious idea, and the state has always been an institution to assure power to the national, intellectual treasury of ideas at home, and to assure it peace, expansion and triumph abroad. No matter. The "and" is no longer a copula; today it opposes, it separates the good from the definitely bad, it puts one before the choice, at the moral crossroads, when the democratic politician of civilization expresses it: For his antithesis of intellect and power—let us look at it more carefully! Is it not a political antithesis? And should one not also give it a political name? "Intellect and power," this is nothing other than "*domestic policy and foreign affairs*." But while in the honest opinion of the patriotic democrat, of the man of the *Volksstaat*, domestic policy and foreign affairs are inseparably connected, yes, while to him the democratization of the state, a national domestic policy, seems to be directed mainly toward the establishment of a strong foreign policy, civilization's literary man, when he says "politics," means purely domestic policy: for him, it is politics—not only "par excellence," but also politics itself, in toto. What one calls "foreign policy," in order not to call it plainly, "power politics," does not, in his opinion, at all deserve the name of politics, but only that of wrong, brutality, and crime; and it would be nothing else than this, nothing else than injustice, brutality, and crime, to permit the so-called foreign policy, the idea of power, to have the slightest influence on the true, domestic policy: On the contrary, domestic policy must be regulated exclusively by the radical intellect; it must—passages in *dix-huitième* taste are the only proper style here—"steadfastly take the principles of reason and justice as a guide."

The politician of civilization, as we have already said, is the man of intellect, of pure, beautiful, radical and literary intellect; he is the man of domestic policy, and indeed, to such an extent that the present demand for "politicization" means nothing other in *his* mouth than the most complete concentration of all minds and hearts on domestic policy—and on what a policy! "World-political study societies," and similar organizations for the political education of the German people, cannot please him at all; from the beginning they are bound to have for him the odor—not so much of democracy, but of imperialism. But politics, domestic policy, democratic policy, is not imperialism and the misuse of power, it is *morality*—and the politician of civilization is, above all, a moralist, nothing but a moralist—that is, a political one.

Now it must be admitted unquestioningly that in foreign policy, morality almost always gets the short straw. When Macaulay says: "The principles of politics are so constituted that the basest thief would be afraid even to hint at them to his closest accomplice"—he undoubtedly means, with this amusing rhetorical flourish, foreign policy; and one knows of founders of states who, after their work had been completed, said they did not know whether they could still be reckoned among men of honor. To be sure, any smart aleck could ask whether domestic policy is any more moral, whether it is not, on the contrary, even five times dirtier than foreign policy, and whether anyone has ever come out of *it* "with a pure soul." However, this would only be dialectical teasing and would have no relevance in this connection. More serious doubts could be raised about the unity of domestic policy and morality— about this unity represented and embodied by civilization's literary man—when one runs across differentiations in the literature such as, for example: "individual-moral—general-political." Things like this do occur. It happens in intellectual life that one finds the concepts "moral" and "political" being treated as opposites, as, for example, in that important passage where Taine compares the revolutionary Frenchman with his English counterpart, the Puritan, whose activity, he says, is above all directed inward, with self-denial as its first purpose; it is moral before it becomes political. The French type shows the opposite picture. He worries first of all about the political, not the moral side of things; he places much more emphasis upon his rights than on his duties; and instead of being a spur to his conscience, his doctrine flatters his pride. This is, as I have said, extremely important and interesting. It is a psychological antithesis that great writers have often treated independently of one another: Dostoyevsky did it in the deepest and most magnificent way in his immortal and unbelievably timely—timely for Russia *and* Germany—polemic against the liberal Professor Gradovsky—an enchantingly brilliant treatise on the social ideal and personal ethics, on politics and Christianity. One finds it, together with other vitally timely things, in the volume, *Literary Writings*, from the German complete edition of his works, and we will probably have to return to it.

But for now it is fortunate that we can stay in Russia for the preliminary maintenance of the antithesis, "moral" and "political," so that we may see things from the other side, from the opposing party's point of view. I promise that in the process we will come upon a short, lively, and accurate formula for our antithesis, a formula we will be able to use gratefully every time we need it.

Around the middle of the last century, at the time when Turgenev's *Fathers and Sons* appeared, a politicizing, radical group of young men appeared in Russia that "went to the people," young men to whom "everything not concerned with politics seemed ridiculous and even absurd." All of them were "literary activists," as the *esthete*, Turgenev, called them, all of them propagandists and demonstrators who would not pardon the aforementioned esthete because even though he did, to be sure, politicize in his masterwork, he only did so in a poetic, that is, in a human way; they would not pardon him for having been just to the conservatives, to the "reactionary mob," to the high tory, Paul Petrovich Kirzanov, as well as to the revolutionary and radical, Basarov—just and critical; for giving to both characters from his soul, his problematic soul that was both conservative, yes, reactionary and radical, both aristocratic and democratic, doubting and disciplined, melancholy and truth loving—yes, they even accused him of obscurantism and of abuse of progress, they found Basarov to be an attack, a lampoon, an insult, and what they said about Basarov's friend, the young Kirzanov, they meant also for the undependable esthete, Turgenev himself: "Kirzanov's son has, of course, neither impudence nor malice; people like him will not go beyond well-born humility or well-born indignation, both are hoaxes; we want to fight; *you want to criticize yourselves; we want to criticize others and to break them*; you just remain the soft, liberal, spoiled son of the ruling class." That is the formula! "You want to criticize yourselves; we want to criticize others and to break them," that is a good, clear, ever-valid differentiation and definition; it is the definition of the antithesis between personal ethics and social-humanitarianism, between puritanism and Jacobinism, between duty and right, between Christianity and socialism, between *domestic policy and foreign affairs*; and our hero, civilization's literary man, the political activist, the humanitarian who posits the antithesis of power and spirit, and the savior from estheticism, he who does not want to criticize himself at all, but who wants to criticize others and to break them—might he, then, in a moral sense, *not* be what he claims, the man of domestic policy, but rather much more of foreign affairs? Yes, so it is! The complicated and captivating difference between the belligerent politician and his opposite, whom we can only give the name of esthete, is this: the humanitarian is from a political point of view a decided follower of domestic policy (of the "intellect"); from a moral point of view, however, he is completely a man of foreign affairs ("wants to criticize and break *others*"). The esthete, on the other hand, becomes political at most for the sake of foreign affairs (of "power") that is, in moments "when the national character speaks in the individuals"; but from a moral point of view, his sympathy belongs completely to domestic policy—("wants to criticize and break himself")—and foreign affairs, that is, social life, the question of "institutions," is definitely of secondary importance for him: He thinks the latter has little weight, but that character, culture, goodness, humanity, and individual morality are all-important. And he disapproves of the pessimism, the *misanthropy* that believes it has to mechanize all human intercourse and to regulate and insure it with institutions in the spirit of abstract ideology.

I have created confusion. I am afraid that the gentle reader does not know anymore where his head is and what he is now really to understand by "domestic policy" and by "foreign affairs." The simple facts of the case are that one can understand the antithesis between domestic policy and foreign affairs morally or politically. The type we are speaking of understands it politically—well, after all, he is a politician! By "domestic policy," yes, by "politics" in general, yes, even by "morality," he understands exactly what the esthete understands by foreign affairs: the politician's morality is directed outward, aggressive, *agaçant*, revolutionary, a combination of agitation and excellent rhetoric, as we said. Revolt is for him the one and only condition worthy of a human being, as an outburst of the "dignity of the human spirit"; and we have here a significant clue for the understanding of what civilization's literary man actually means by the call for politicization: politicization is education to revolt. But revolt, he says, is above all something extremely European, and every time, for example, when it happens that the Indians revolt against their British masters, they should realize that it is not their own feelings but European feelings acting through them, that it was the Englishmen who "awakened their souls"—one can also say: politicized them. Whoever finds this objectionable will still have to find much literary wit in it—no wonder, because we are definitely dealing here with a man who is not only a master of literary sentimental rhetoric, of dash and corn, but also especially of literary wit. For what leads to the ideal goal, to political revolt, that is, what prepares the mind and heart of the nation, of the people, of the citizens for it, prepares both in a preliminary and in a final way, is of course humor, satire, the principle and element of decomposition, *criticism* and education to politics, above all—we know this from before—education in criticism.

What is criticism, anyway? Nothing other than morality. Nothing other than "domestic policy." But we must again remember that the politician understands precisely by "domestic" policy what the esthete means by "foreign affairs." The politician's critical activity, too, like his morality in general, is directed morally toward the outside, it is aggressive, for he himself *is right*, he himself is unassailable, the man of progress and of moral security: only the others need criticism, the community, the nation; the literary politician's criticism is the pedagogical mockery and satire of his own people.

Let one not be rash now and object that such an outwardly directed criticism is not the true one, that all criticism must begin with self-criticism, that only the latter is moral, that the purely self-righteous moral judge is not a very moral one, but a presumptuous figure, and that the question: "Where does he get the right?" remains unanswered. This would indeed have something on its side, but not everything. It would only apply to one side of the matter. For precisely because the literary politician's criticism and satire is *national* criticism and satire, precisely because it is directed politically inwardly, it is of course self-criticism—political satire is the *self-criticism of the nation by its writers.*

Here I will not forgo once again calling attention to the intertwining and crossing of intentions, to the insoluble entanglement and relativity of all intellectual-moral life. Civilization's literary man and democrat, as we know him, is of course generally not an advocate of nationalism. He does not want it, he denies it, he recognizes it in no way as a mediator between the individual and the human race, he is an enthusiastic, direct lover of the human race itself and of its homogeneous civilization; in a word, he is a politician of the human race—while his opposite type, whom we call a little figuratively but of necessity the "esthete," is significantly cooler toward civilization, and, let us be frank, even toward the abstraction, "the human race," and becomes political precisely "when the national character speaks in the individuals." But seen from the point of view of criticism and self-criticism, of criticism as morality, things are quite the opposite. As a critic and satirist, civilization's literary man absolutely needs the national instrument; his criticism does not really penetrate the general human level, or it only reaches it in its special political manifestation—precisely in the national manifestation, and his "self-criticism" consists in the literary chastisement of his own people: whom he finds in principle *wrong* and the others right in all matters, both in peace, and indeed especially in war—and here one must consider that in order to be permitted to call someone wrong, one must be right; and the politician *is right.* Especially in war, we say, does he behave in this way; for even if he is in no way unwarlike in attitude, his concept of politics is still too close to that of domestic policy, of morality, of national self-criticism, for him not to have to recognize in *civil war* the only moral form of war—and to consider its manifestation in *this* form to be highly desirable, highly worth supporting. The "esthete" is completely different. The esthete, *as a critic*—and why should criticism not be for him, too, a felt need of and almost the meaning of language?—has little inclination to consider the national, the political-social element, as a mediator between the ego and the human race. His criticism is also self-criticism, not in the political, but in the moral sense; it is directed inwardly but not toward the political inner part of the nation, but toward his own individual inner side, and when it meets the ego, it meets the human element itself quite directly. Therefore if the politician appears to be arrogant because he chastises and judges as a dogmatist and as one whose "intellectualization has raised him above his compatriots," and indeed, in the name of the human race whose cause he champions, then the arrogance of the esthete lies in his insinuating his own ego as a symbol of general human nature, in his both loving and censuring, affirming and denying human nature through his own ego. His criticism, when it makes use of the comic, does not actually become satire in doing so—assuming, that is, that satire means the ridiculing of political and social conditions. The esthete is much more a humorist, humanity's tragicomedian; and by passing over and excluding the national element in his criticism, he is *not* suggesting that only his own people are miserable and laughable, while the others are happy and noble—an idea that the political critic almost always at least seems to cherish, and always runs the greatest risk of awakening.

Finally, it is no wonder that there are at times reproaches against him because of such a misunderstanding—*if* it is a misunderstanding. One says that when he scorns and negates his own people he exposes them to the others; that he agrees with everything the others say, plays into their hands, gives them weapons and arguments against his people, reinforces them in their prejudices, in their delusion of being far superior to his people in happiness and virtue, in matters of truth, freedom, and justice, and it is said that he has thus contributed not a little to their moral courage in the war of annihilation against his own people. I do not like such accusations. I do not like accusations at all; and this is admittedly an aversion the politician hardly shares. I reject the above accusation because I understand that the politician as a critical moralist feels himself nationally bound, that political satire is a form of patriotism, a national function, nothing else, as I have said, than the self-criticism of the nation through its man of letters whom it itself has created for this very purpose—and that every misuse, every international exploitation of this self-criticism, signifies a disloyalty that one may despise.

This would be well and good, but Germany's case—and it is the one we are concerned with—is a special case, not constituted exactly as the others are, and German self-criticism is a special one that again and again seems to be essentially different from that of other nations. It may be because this nation's literary-moral organ is particularly sensitive, or because it really exceeds all others in inner coarseness, stupidity, ugliness, meanness and ridiculousness; there may be other reasons that we have perhaps already alluded to: the fact remains that German self-criticism is baser, more malicious, more radical and spiteful than that of any other nation, a cuttingly unjust kind of justice, an unbridled degrading without sympathy or love for one's own country, together with fervent, uncritical admiration of others, such as, for example, noble—no, this is not ironic defense!—doubtlessly very noble France: an expression of *loathing*—of self-loathing, remember!—which may signify generosity, freedom, boldness, depth, every imaginable moral virtue, but which one simply cannot designate as *smart*, as pedagogical in relation to the others, as *political*, therefore. Perhaps it would be better to call it—excessively esthetic. But this is a word too much here.

It seems to me that one shows one is not on such bad terms with criticism and satire when one confesses one's liking for Russian literature. Well, until 1917, when she rose up to become a democratic republic, Russia was considered generally to be a country particularly in need of political-social self-criticism; and tell me who can measure the depths of bitterness and sorrow from which the comedy of *Dead Souls* grew! Strange, however; in this book the great writer's national ties are not simply expressed as despairing comedy and satire; on at least two or three occasions they are expressed as something positive and heartfelt, as love—yes, religious love for grand little Mother Russia, resounds more than once like a hymn from the book, it is the original source of bitterness and sorrow, and we feel strongly in such moments that it is what justifies the bloodiest and cruelest satire, yes, what sanctifies it. Imagine such license of feeling in Germany! Imagine hymns rising up out of the satirical novels of a German writer—hymns to Germany! One cannot. Disgust chokes such fantasy. The simple word, "love," already has an embarrassing enough effect in this connection—it seems like the most impossible tastelessness under the sun.

A German satire in which any emotion other than alien spitefulness, alien gloating, were even alluded to would not be acceptable from a literary point of view, that much is certain.

But let us leave Russia as a state, society, or as politics. Let us take a critique of the Russian human being in Russian literature that is in a certain sense a devastating critique. Let us take Goncharov's *Oblomov*! Truly, what a painful, hopeless figure! What weariness, clumsiness, laziness, indolence, what incapacity for life, what slovenly melancholy! Unhappy Russia, this is your human being! And yet—is it possible not to love Ilya Oblomov, this bloated impossibility of a human being? He has a *national* opposite number, the German, Stolz, a model of intelligence, prudence, conscientiousness, dignity and efficiency. But what amount of pharisaical pedantry would be necessary to read this book and *not*—as the writer does, too, secretly, but absolutely beyond all doubt—to prefer fat Ilya to his energetic comrade, and finally not to feel and to admit the deeper beauty, purity and lovableness of his human nature? Unhappy Russia? Happy, happy Russia—who, in all her misery and hopelessness, must know that she is so beautiful and lovable in her innermost being that she, compelled by her literary conscience to satirical self-personification, puts an Oblomov into the world—or rather lays him on a bed of laziness! As for Germany, the satirical self-criticism she exercises on herself through her literary men leaves no doubt that she feels herself to be the truly ugly country, the country of ugly people: This is the manifestation of her "intellect"— which will then never be able to desire "power" with a clear conscience; this is her morality, her "domestic policy."

We realized earlier that a "coming to the fore of the social novel in the public interest would be the exact measure" of the progress of that process of Germany's literarization, democratization and humanization, the process that civilization's literary man finds his mission in spurring on. Here we add the opposite: Democracy, that is, the state that has been humanized and made capable of having a literature, that has become a society—and indeed, an amusing society—democracy, then, is the fertile soil in which political satire really begins to thrive; the social-critical novel is even an integrating unit, an important part of the inventory of democracy, of the amusing state, that is; even more than that: it is a power in it, a political power, stated quite practically, even a *path* to political power—so that in the amusing state the novelist can at any time become a minister, something he perhaps does not want to become, but still wishes to be able to become; and this is why the political moralist, the radical literary domestic politician, demands democracy, the republic of lawyers and literati in the Western style: it offers his kind that optimum of conditions of life that every earthly being instinctively strives for. Granted this is a skeptical interpretation of his will and essence, instead of a grandiloquent one that may seem uniquely appropriate to it, the reader will at least agree with me that here a beneficial interaction, a mutual assistance and promotion, is taking place: Civilization's literary man educates people to democracy by agitation and beautiful rhetoric, and democracy, for its part, the amusing state, the intellectually thoroughly politicized society, nourishes and stimulates the organ of social criticism, of social-psychological writing, to the point of hypertrophy, so that finally, through such reciprocity on the path of brilliant amusement, something extreme, a condition of scornful anarchy, world despair, and social-critical corrosion is reached that civilization's literary man is celebrating in advance as the goal, as the condition of true humanity, as a "very beautiful, completely serene" condition. But the progress toward this condition, which, no one will deny, is boundlessly serene, is *progress itself*, and there is no other.

In the course of these reflections, I have often expressed the conviction that Germany is on this progressive path. Yes, we will have it, democracy, the state for novelists, and we will be happy, or at least entertained! That evil, abstract, inhuman, and therefore very boring form of government that once tried to fool us by claiming to preserve the interest of the whole and to remove administration from the tumult of party campaigns will lie behind us in an unreal light; that form of government in which special knowledge, talent, and professional training were considered indispensable for the assumption of office. No more of that! Professional civil service has become a myth. Self-government! Rotation in office! To the victor belong the spoils! Whoever has the desire and two strong elbows can get to the state trough sooner or later—previous experience unnecessary. We have reached the stage where every office is open to every citizen, and only the obsolete dogma of the "expert," this bastard of humility and conceit, has prevented it from being reached long ago. Oh, what a cringingly faint-hearted stupidity of a dogma that was! Did it not cause political passivity in the best people—in the artist, for example? The person engaged in artistic activity is most deeply imbued with a regard for ability and mastery, with a disgust for bungling: sovereign mastery of the subject seems to him the prerequisite of all art, for to him, art is the absorption of the material by the form. Is it surprising that he was only too ready to succumb to the German dogma of the "expert" and to fall prey to political quietism? Nevertheless, he is precisely the one who is indispensable to democracy—indispensable in the struggle against that dogma that inhibits progress, because he does have certain qualities that counterbalance his disgust for bungling. Is he not almost always an *arrangeur* by instinct? Does he not understand how to hoodwink people? Does he not know how to make a lot out of a little—like his foster brother, the journalist, this experienced sauce maker who sets up a lead article of five columns from the scantiest bit of information? An actor's ability: is this finally not one of his basic instincts? As a novelist, for example—does he not, if it seems to him to strengthen the composition, write a whole chapter on national economy that looks as if he had never done anything else? Add a little pleasure in rhetorical intercostal breathing, a little talent for dash and sentimentality—what more is needed for the democratic politician, for the conqueror of the "expert"?

Democracy means the dominance of politics; politics means a minimum of objectivity. But the expert is objective, that is, nonpolitical, that is, undemocratic. Away with him! His successors are the lawyer as the owner of a weekly, the journalist, the rhetorically talented artist. They do things with a little spirit—and this is what democratic tradition wants. "Every Frenchman," we read in the memoirs of a contemporary of the Great Revolution,

> considers himself capable of overcoming all difficulties with a little spirit. Never did so many people imagine they were all lawmakers, that their task was to correct all the mistakes of the past, to remove all delusions of the human mind, to insure the happiness of coming generations. There was no room in their minds for doubt . . .

Is there any condition more horrible than the one in which there is no more room left in the mind for doubt? An obscurant's question! We will have it, the nondoubting and belletristic political system. We will have it, democracy—which as such is equality and therefore hatred, ineradicable and jealous republican hatred of every superiority, every expert authority. Who will make an industrialist Minister of Commerce? One puts a comedy writer or a cabaret entertainer in the position, and the principle is saved. It will be thought wrong to fill the ministries of agriculture and culture with other than lawyers and scribbling stockbrokers. And as far as military affairs are concerned, it would be a slap in democracy's face to make an exception for their sake. In military matters, ask the military! But that would be dominance of the saber! That would be corruption, the most extreme danger to the radical republic! For authority is not just hateful when it is of an unreasonable nature, based on tradition, birth, and privileges; no, it is hateful because the radical principle makes it so in general, in every case, even when it is derived from knowledge, efficiency, proven-practical superiority, and expert ability.

Once more: democracy means the dominance of politics. Nothing may, nothing will exist—no thought, work, or life—in which politics does not play a part, where political feelings and connections are not maintained. Politics *as atmosphere,* permeating all vital air so that with every breath drawn it forms the main element of all psychological structure; politics *as the displacer of music,* which up to then had usurped the highest position in the social-artistic interest of the nation—as its displacer, I say, in alliance with literature, which is to be understood as the twin sister of politics, *if not as identical with it,* and its natural ally in the fight against the predominance of music; politics, then, together with literature, to the extent that the latter is gregarious, that is, rhetorical, psychological and erotic—a mixture of both, politics perfumed with literature, literature spiced with politics as national atmosphere and life's breath: That is democracy, the amusing state, the state for novelists, and we will have it! Yes, civilization's literary man has recognized that Germany's literary morality, the literarization and psychologization of Germany that was powerfully furthered by geniuses such as Heine and Nietzsche, and whose promotion we all, I, too, whether consciously and intentionally or not, made it our business to further—that this literary morality has progressed to the point where it must change into politics, where the connection between psychological thinking and formal elegance steps out openly with political freedom. This is his hour, the hour of civilization's literary man; it is here; it is giving him those national rights that he has long enjoyed in other nations.

The first demand of this hour must be for the establishment of a German Academy—I have quietly promoted it for a long time. The German Academy, or at least something like a counterpart to the Roman "Dante Alighiere Language Club," whose chairman is Prime Minister Boselli; the establishment and yearly presentation of a "Grand Prize for Rhetoric"—such things are necessary components of the literary-political, *parliamentary* epoch we are entering. Let literature become official. Let the *literary man* become official—*that* is the demand of the political moment. We will have that humbug-dominance of the intellect that will perhaps manifest itself in saloon signs such as "*A l'Idée du Monde.*" The "Café Schopenhauer" as the center of the cattle trade in a little German market town will not be bad, and when French fishing boats are christened "*Pensée*" and "*Honneur et dévouement moderne,*" this must be translated into German, even though it may be difficult—intellect will no longer tolerate the shabbiness of our bearing names such as "Klaas," or "Schlutupp" on the bow; under its announced rule our armored cruisers will not be called "Blücher" and "Gneisenau," but "Goethe," "Lichtenberg," and perhaps also "E.T.A. Hoffmann," or "Wackenroder"—and if many find it more depressing when "Goethe" rather than some sort of Father Blücher is torpedoed to the bottom, this will only be a stirring of that lingering sensitivity that also takes offense when thieves are discovered in the "Philosophy" or the "Justice" hotel.

I beg pardon if instead of generously characterizing the splendid and cheerful condition that is awaiting us, I have lost myself in details. They are not unsuited for conveying a breath of the generous, political-literary atmosphere from which our national life will be reborn, by which it will then constantly be wafted. Two phases must be differentiated, wherever and whenever we are dealing with the realization of people's sovereignty and democracy. The first is the revolutionary phase: we will have to pass through it; I can add: we are about to cross its threshold. Who could today (I write in April 1917) misinterpret the revolutionary mood of the German mind? The *Volksstaat* that young and old are eager for—and strive for with undeniable temporal justification—what is it other than Rousseau's united will of the community represented in the state that is the actual state-forming element! Publicists speak of nothing else than Voltaire, Figaro, "mankind"; Marquis Posa is very much in fashion; and plays whose academic, revolutionary passion is only half-disguised by psychology, estheticism and hysterical eroticism, find the frenzied approval of the intelligensia. The first phase, we say, is the revolutionary one, where the belief that now the realm of justice and happiness has dawned and is flaming up dazzlingly, and the passion for politics is taking control of every single mind, even the most foolish and uneducated one. Taine describes the condition by citing a chronicle of 1790:

Every shop clerk who has read the *New Heloise,* every schoolmaster who has translated a few pages of Livius, every artist who has leafed through Rollin's works, every esthete who has become a journalist by memorizing the unclear language of Rousseau's social contract, is writing a constitution . . .

And Taine himself adds:

With the help of eight or ten phrases made palatable by the six-sous-catechisms distributed by the thousands in the country's suburbs, the village lawyer, the customs official, the ticket collector, and the guardhouse sergeant are becoming lawmakers and philosophers . . . The result is that they give lectures about all sorts of people and things that earlier seemed forever beyond them. They talk about them to the people, make petitions, are applauded and are proud of themselves for their ability to argue in such an excellent and high-sounding way . . . Every sensible conversation has been swept aside by preference for controversy, fault-finding and sophistry. Swindlers talk about morality, hetaerae about civic virtue, and the most depraved subjects about the dignity of the human race . . .

This, as I have said, is the first phase. It is not beautiful, not beneficial, not particularly humane. For the general political excitement of stupidity has an embarassing and humanly depressing effect—at least in our country, where in fact (and I am thinking here again of my friend, of the man in the service coat) there is the most instinctive dislike for this condition. At any rate, it will pass; and what follows will be a system rich in renunciation, an amusing-melancholy compromise, the "realization" of the principle, which obviously cannot be anything else than such a compromise, a condition that the great majority of the citizens, who are careful not to follow the general political line and who leave this to those who make a questionable and unseemly profession of it, will look upon with scorn and unconcealed skepticism—but precisely this frame of mind is a welcome one, for it contains the revolt within it, it turns the lifeless, anti-intellectual burgher into a lively and inflammable element, it makes him into a European, makes him into a human being. But the spectacle he observes in this progressive frame of mind is precisely the amusing state that has now been reached, the republic of the comrades and the *arrivistes,* the glitteringly rotating miracle of the annual fair and the merry-go-round of newspapers, women, legislatures, adventurers, the oligarchy of a "society" that is not exactly the "good" one, but that is certainly a literary bonanza, an extremely human-lively research area for the authors of satirical comedies and skeptical novels. The humanized state, literarized, erotically animated politics with a "psychological way of thinking" and with formal elegance, politics with ladies-in-waiting—we will have it! One hardly understands democracy if one does not understand its feminine touch. "Freedom and a whore are the most cosmopolitan things under the sun." What international *held on* even during the World War? The horizontal one. Up to now, the political-social ideals of our radical literary man have been realized more in Bucharest than in Paris. We will follow. We will also have the judicial acquittals of interesting murderesses—out of gallantry or out of party politics, or for both reasons. For what cause and question at all will not immediately degenerate into a trial of strength for the parties? Which ones will not immediately stand in the falsifying, distorting light of politics, of party politics, that is? Politics as a source of perception through which all things are seen; the administration—skilled in the spirit of the ruling parliamentary majority of the time; the officer corps—politically demoralized; the justice department—politically poisoned; creative writing—tendentious theater and psychology on the basis of social comparison, carried to the point of *tout-est-dit;* and affairs, scandals, political-symbolic conflicts of the times, magnificent ones that elevate and inflame the burgher in alternating dances, a new one every year—this is the way we will have it, this is the way we will live every day.

One tells me that this is impossible; that a general outbreak of disgust would prevent the realization of such images of the future in Germany. For here the belief cannot be uprooted that what has grown organically, what has developed from tradition and history, is with all its faults preferable to the product of reflection and of the dogma of reason. Humanity is at work both there and here; but the humanity of what has grown has something venerable, while that of the product of reason incites scorn and contempt. Good, good, I want to believe it, I know that this is the German emotional judgment. Nevertheless, it is impossible to hide from oneself that the development of German affairs as I have described it is taking place at this moment, and for the time being it is moving in the described direction under the sharp whiplashes of civilization's literary man. Second, however, I have already indicated that civilization's literary man strongly desires "scorn and contempt" as the generally pervasive attitude against the state and the government, that he desires this in a thoroughly planned way—and indeed, to such a degree that he tends to confuse this attitude with "intellect" itself, that for him poisonous hatred and scorn for everything that rules clearly signifies the criterion of intellectuality. He is a politician, yes; but he is a politician against the state, and he knows just as well as the young Nietzsche, yes, if he does not know it *from* him, that democracy is the decadent form of the state. "Disdain, decline and death of the state," Nietzsche said in *Human, All Too Human*, where he casts an eye at politics,

> the unleashing of the private person (I am careful not to say: of the individual) is the consequence of the democratic state concept; *here lies its mission* . . . to *work* on the propagation and realization of this idea is admittedly something else: one must be arrogantly proud of one's reasoning ability, and one must scarcely half-understand history to put one's hand to the plow right now—when no one can yet point to the seeds that will afterward be strewn on the prepared soil. Let us therefore trust to the intelligence and self-interest of the people that the state will *still* last a good while, and that *destructive attempts of overeager and rash, half-informed people will be rejected!*

This was the still-youthful Nietzsche whom civilization's literary man claims to admire, while in truth he has made the later, grotesque Nietzsche, who had become fanatic, much more his own, in spirit if not also in substance. As far as he, civilization's literary man, is concerned, he thinks highly enough of his reasoning ability and understands history well enough to put his hand to the plow with all the "resoluteness" appropriate to his love of humanity: to bring about the disdain, decline and death of the state as soon as possible seems to him to be *the* task of "intellect," and in this sense, we must admit, "democracy" is for him only a means and a transition—just as he longs for and demands the amusing, humanized state more in his capacity as an artist and novelist then in his second one, namely as a *prophet*. Let us finally appreciate him in this capacity! Let us briefly present his *teaching!* It is simple, axiomatically simple, and even if we are already partially aware of it, it will still be useful to reduce it here to its most pithy and compact formula.

Literature and politics, he teaches, both have the human being as their subject; they are, therefore, if not identical, then at least inseparably correlated: one cannot (must not) deal with the one without the other. And since there is—can be—may be—only *one* politics: the humanitarian–democratic one, the one of progress, there is and may be therefore only *one* literature: the one directed toward humanitarianism and democracy—the one that, in all its conceptions, incessantly pursues humanitarian-democratic progress, insinuates the concept of democracy into every work, into every beautiful creation, into all art, leaves this didactic-voluntaristic-political intention half-hidden and half-evident. There is no other literature, or no other may come into consideration. What is otherwise at times claimed for literature is immoral estheticism, decorative work at best, not *what is necessary*. What is necessary is at bottom not art at all but the manifesto, the absolute manifesto in favor of progress, the proclamation of the intellectuals through intellect. Art in and for itself and for its own sake, *l'art pour l'art*, once a cry against the philistines, has today become a burgherly concept. Art as life, art as the mastered, liberated and liberating knowledge of life through form—has been rejected, is to be rejected. What *good* is knowledge to us, and what good is form? The action is what matters—the intellectual action. The manifesto that calls to the action, that already is action, is more important than a hundred "forming" works. Art, as far as it wants to endure, as far as it wants to be considered, must be the tool of progress, of humanitarian-democratic politics. It has discovered its principal duty in moving consciously, purposefully and gravely with political responsibility toward world improvement. If it does not do this, if it serves at best only a decorative culture, but not civilization, then it is only a question of temperament whether one calls it a type of frivolous philistinism or villainy; and since the political prophet counts not only reason and humanity, but also passion among his prerogatives, he will usually choose the latter judgment. From his dogma, however, that there is, can be and may be, only one reason, one politics, one intellect, namely his, there results for him the conclusion and the demand for what he calls the "solidarity of all intellectuals," the "*organization* of all intellectuals," for the conquest of power, for the propagation of truth, of justice, of freedom, of happiness—in a word, of the democratic republic.

The conquest of power? And indeed, by the intellect? And the highest of all antitheses, that of power and intellect—what of it? But let us not get involved here in this contradiction! Let us free ourselves for now by saying that this antithesis is obviously extinguished and destroyed when it is precisely intellect that seizes power—political power. We have to go on. There are a few things to criticize in the teaching that we have presented in proxy; its rare combination of limitation and fanaticism even gives cause for amazement. It speaks of "what is necessary" and of the manifesto. But if what is necessary is supposed to be freedom, then the manifesto may be an extremely doubtful means of obtaining it. For a manifesto, if it is strong, may at most fanaticize, but only a work of art can *liberate*. The political prophet is beyond doubt a great free spirit, a *libre-penseur* and *esprit fort* of the first water, his contemptuous relationship to the national element proves it. But a *free* spirit of the type that prepared for the Europe of the end of the nineteenth century the most tragic and most heroic spectacle of world history, a spectacle of critical self-crucifixion—oh, no, that he is not. He has picked up a few grotesque accents and violent gestures from it, just as the feuilletonists picked up Heine's "facility" earlier, but he has not experienced the severe heroic epic of this life, and if he has ever experienced it, he has "overcome" it. How? By politics! No, it is not freedom he has in mind. What is the *good*, he asks, of freedom? It is just as worthless as knowledge and form! His cause is much more *resoluteness;* his cause is—now I present the most terrible combination of words ever invented, the overpowering tastelessness of which assures its inventor, civilization's literary man and political prophet, immortality—his cause is "*resolute love of humanity*." But it is resoluteness, and nothing more, purposeful self-stultification and logical shadow-boxing in the service of progress, that is, when he insists, for example, upon the identity or inseparable correlation of literature and politics, because, you see, "the human being" is the subject of both—a sophism that is so obvious and impudent that repugnance deadens our critical sensitivity. For we do not intend to bore ourselves and others by explaining polemically that the "human being" whom politics has as its subject is nothing more than the social human being in the sense and taste of Western *civilisation* and civilization—and that the type of "literature" and creative writing that has, to be sure, this subject in common with politics, is nothing more than the social novel according to the model of this same *civilisation* or civilization—the social novel that the German radical literary man proclaims to be *the* literature, whose spirit and essence he proclaims to be the spirit and essence of art, of creative writing in general, and this at the very moment when France, with the bitter taste of *tout-est-dit* in her mouth, wants to find something better, older, stronger—and indeed not at all solely in the person of Romain Rolland. "*Le roman m'a toujours semblé une sorte de confession*," Charles Louis Philippe wrote in 1905.

> "*Il faut d'ailleurs qu'une oeuvre soit l'espression de la vie de l'écrivain . . . Pour moi, je conçois le roman, non comme le développement d'une idée, mais comme quelque chose d'animé, de vivant, de réel, comme une main qui bouge, des yeux qui regardent, comme le développement de tout un corps. Aussi le roman à thèse me paraît extraordinaire. Je trouve vraiment extraordinaire qu'on ose faire du roman un prétexte d'études sociales ou psychologiques . . .*

Thus we Germans are to begin to see in the "human being" the social animal, and in the novel a pretext for social criticism, at the very moment when France is completely fed up with doing so!

Art and politics! Art and the manifesto! Is not exactly the same thing happening to us that happened in the Russia of the fifties and sixties to which "everything that did not belong to politics seemed incongruous and even absurd," and that, because *Fathers and Sons* was not a manifesto, burned Turgenev's photograph "with a cold smile"? The most sophisticated comment at the time came from a lady. "The true title of your story," she said, "should be '*Neither* Fathers *nor* Sons'—and you yourself are a nihilist." "I will be careful not to answer this," Turgenev muttered; "perhaps the lady was right." But she was not right, because a person who respects life as he does is not a nihilist. An esthete perhaps; he probably was an esthete—someone, that is, who tended more to "criticize himself" than to "criticize and break others"; and then he was a great lover of freedom! Does this sound loose and undisciplined? But the remarkable thing is that in the artistic sphere freedom and discipline mean one and the same thing. One knows that Turgenev, for his part, was a "zapadnik," a Westerner and anti-Slavophile, a believing follower of European culture; as an artiste he was a friend of the French; as an intellectual he came from Goethe and Schopenhauer. What did he do? He created for himself an ape, the Westerner Panshin, in *A Nest of Gentle Folk*, a changing parody of his own character, a fop of such tastelessness that he delivers himself of tirades of enlightenment such as: "All nations are basically the same; one need only introduce good institutions, and things will be fine!"—in short, a chatterer whom it is easy for the Slavophile, Lavretsky, "to refute in all points." This is almost incomprehensible. Turgenev's expressed principles, principles such as: "My personal inclinations mean nothing," "The strictest conscientiousness is to be required of the artist," "Love of truth, inexorable love of truth, is necessary in dealing with one's own feelings; freedom of observation and opinion are necessary; nowhere is freedom so necessary as in matters of art, of poetry: not for nothing do we hear of 'liberal' arts even in the official language of the government"—such phrases are not a sufficient explanation for this excess of self-discipline in which the love of truth does a somersault and becomes a persiflage of his own ideal. This is no longer simple "*impassibilité*," it is castigation, asceticism, it is art as the will "to criticize and to break oneself," it is an example on a small scale and with a humorous stamp—of that ethic of self-destruction that we Germans only saw toward the end of the century in a much greater, much more tragic-terrible example, in a philosophical one—and every kind of "resoluteness," every political voluntarism in a work of art, is by comparison with it nothing more than intellectual *voluptuousness*.

"No matter what youth may say," Turgenev wrote at the time to a friend, "art cannot die, and service to it according to one's ability will always bind people closely together." Was this a confession of estheticism? Politicization of art! As if art were not, no matter how much it is a matter of the lonely soul, of conscience, of protestantism, and of God's immediate presence—as if it were not in and for itself and in all ways a social power that "always binds people closely together"! Since historical examples teach that politically irresolute art that seemed to exist only for itself, and in any case only wanted to exist for itself, can nevertheless become a political tool in the grandest style and bring about the spiritual unity of a people; since personal examples teach that an art that never liked to assume a social attitude, a parasitic, nonpolitical art of personal ethics, can still *help* the human being *to live:* what have I to do with the call for the politicization of art and with the impudent and stupid differentiation of the "private writer" from the "*responsible* writer" that one likes to make today? Where is the insipid fool who believes that a productive drive could ever have an unsocial, antisocial character? The productive person's grudge against the receptive-idle one, his feeling of disdain for him, his inability even to understand how one likes to and can live in a receptive-idle way: does this not prove the social-moral sense of the productive drive? If our manifesto writers and "belletrists of action" knew how much they were distancing themselves from all German *culture* with their antithesis of "estheticism" and "activism," with their confusion of uselessness with wickedness—perhaps, but of course not at all certainly, their voices and courage would sink a bit. In an essay on Schiller, Wilhelm von Humboldt said:

> It is deeply ingrained in German character and feeling to allocate the high and solemn place I spoke of above to poetry among human endeavors and to defend it against the petty and trite opinions—the former mistake its dignity and the latter its individuality—that either make it into a trifling decoration and ornamentation of life *or* demand direct moral effect and enlightenment from it.

And Schiller himself said: "The human being is only completely human *when he is playing*."

German culture! German character! Goethe was delighted when he read Guizot's words: "The ancient Germans brought us the idea of personal freedom, which was above all characteristic of this people." "Is this not very pleasing," Goethe said, "and is he not completely right, and does this thought not still prevail for us today? The Reformation came from this source . . . and the manifold nature of our literature . . ." Oh, yes, this too. And precisely this protestant-individualistic, manifold nature is an abomination in the eyes of the political prophet— who in national affairs clearly greatly prefers "freedom" to "unity," but who cares little for freedom in intellectual matters, only thinking of the unity, militaristic organization, and political striking power of the intellect. But who could be surprised that by "politicization of art" he quite obviously, as if it had to be so, understands its politicization in the democratic spirit? The politicization of the German concept of art would itself of course mean its democratization, a most important feature of the democratic leveling and assimilation of Germany! It is no less pleasant to realize that all politicized artistic sense is opposed to nondemocratic greatness. The social-religious, aged Tolstoy (still gigantic, by the way, even then—but this did not give him any collegial feelings) called Shakespeare an immoral savage; Mr. Bernard Shaw agreed with this assessment; he said the author of *Coriolanus* was in no way timely, and had little to say to us moderns, because his hostility to the people and his undemocratic attitude were all too obvious. One cannot judge more honestly. In Germany, where reverence is still too much in vogue, it is important to work more with innuendos, and since Goethe often said things such as, for example, ". . . for a good work of art can and will have moral consequences, but to demand moral intentions from the artist is to ruin his work,"—it is doubtless with an innuendo toward him that civilization's literary man declares that the esthete is not even venerable in old age, that he has no maturity, authority, venerableness, that every great human impact is to be found in the moralist, that is, in the political moralist. Goethe—not venerable in old age, lacking authority as well, just a rather frivolous, senile esthete. Zola, on the other hand—Zola in his little garden, Zola with his hair half-long in the nape of his neck, a transfigured teacher of democracy. German artistic sense! Irritated, I once let the sentence slip out that art was a *form* of morality, but not a moral expedient. I was told that the words were obscure. Nevertheless, Fichte said that the German—and only he—practiced art *as a virtue* and a religion—which says the same thing and is an ever valid translation of the *l'art pour l'art* formula *into German.*

Politicization of art! Well, we have seen the like. Some seventy years ago we had the liberalism that became literature, the activistic Young Germany that overthrew romanticism, the estheticism of the time; the works that resulted from it were not exactly immortal. The experts do not credit it with extravagant conquests in the realms of the soul and of beauty. German romanticism, national but nonpolitical as it was, will always be celebrated as one of the most magical events of European intellectual and art history. As far as the young liberal writing of 1840 was concerned, it certainly powerfully furthered our political enlightenment. But what happens when the tenth muse, to wit, that of freedom, begins to *sing*, we see from those verses that Georg Herwegh wrote in the glow of the Alps:

> Mountain to mountain, fire to fire
> Flame up here together;
> What a glow! — ha! thus stood
> Ilium once in flames.
> A sinking royal house
> Smoking before my eyes
> And I cry out into the land:
> *Vive la république!**

The rhyme is unsatisfactory; and I would like to think that our activists of today tend to deny the burning passion of this strange impression of nature. But what a difference in taste and in artistic subtlety also separates them from their predecessors, no matter how much care they take to conceal politics, past recognition and understanding, under psychological skepticism and sexual pathology—the "warm ethic," on which their superiority over all esthetic inhumanity rests, can be summed up completely in the cry in which the arsonist's song of power finally breaks out, in the cry: "Long live the Republic!"— and indeed, in French.

Politicization of art! Finally: what should the person to whom *music*, for example, is the purest paradigm, the sacred and fundamental type of all art, have to do with this idea? And is it not really the truly moral

---

* Berg an Berg und Brand an Brand
  Lodern hier zusammen;
  Welch ein Glühen! — ha! so stand
  Ilion einst in Flammen.
  Ein versinkend Königshaus
  Raucht vor meinem Blicke,
  Und ich ruf' ins Land hinaus:
  Vive la république!

art that is art precisely because morality takes form in it, and that the German has preferred to practice all along "as a virtue and a religion"— the German *l'art pour l'art?* I want to have a musician intercede, Grillparzer's Poor Fiddler. "The eternal blessing," he says,

> and grace of tone and resonance, its miraculous harmony with the eager, languishing ear — that the third tone agrees with the first, and the fifth also, and the *nota sensibilis* rises like a fulfilled hope, the dissonance is bent down like a conscious malice or an impudent pride, and the miracle of ligature and conversion in which the musical second also reaches grace in the bosom of harmony . . . And the *fuga* and the *punctum contra punctum*, and the *canon a due, a tre*, and so forth, *a whole heavenly structure, one striking the other, joined without mortar, and held by the hand of God.*

And he speaks for absolute music, he wants no words and no "program": "Lord," he says, "speech is as necessary to the human being as food, but one should also keep the drink that comes from God pure." This is not literary, it is German. I have acquaintances among musicians, I know none who would not have felt nationally in this war and taken a national stand—yes, there were naive-political forms of expression for this declaration, such as the defiant and effusive act of Hans Pfitzner in dedicating his latest opus to Fleet Admiral von Tirpitz. This is nothing to be surprised about. The war forced the national feeling of the artist to politicize itself insofar as the political, patriotic element had remained in him from before. And the politicization of the artist—is it not true, master? We still prefer it to the politicization of art!

There is, I say, nothing strange in the fact that civilization's literary man is quite ill-disposed toward music—German music, that is—since it recently has even entertained a relationship with Fleet Admiral von Tirpitz; on the other hand, it is understandable that every mind in any way musically attuned and inclined is opposed "in the conservative interest" to the progressive plans of civilization's literary man, to his declared will to replace the national supremacy of music with the democratic dominance of politics and literature. I have been very exhaustive, I have covered pages to clarify for myself and for any imagined reader where I get the right to patriotism, to political national feeling, I could have expressed myself briefly and limited myself to the fact that I am, to be sure, a literary man but even more a musician, and that my life has stood for this very reason under the magical sign of that "three-star-constellation" and will always stand there because all three, Schopenhauer, Wagner and Nietzsche, were the same: literary men and musicians, but more the latter. Yes, I have a right to quotations such as those from Grillparzer's story: judge what I have done, my works of art, as you will and must, but *they were always good scores,* one like the other; musicians have also loved them; Gustav Mahler, for example, loved them, and I have often wanted to have musicians as public judges of them. Art as ethics in sound, as *fuga* and *punctum contra punctum,* as a serene and earnest piety. Like a building of nonprofane purpose where one thing intertwines with another, thoughtfully, sensibly, and bound without mortar and held "by God's hand,"—this *l'art pour l'art* is truly my ideal of art that I by no means represent, but that I will always try to approach. If this is German, then all the better—and worse; for it does not bestow a disposition toward progress, and it makes communication with civilization's literary man extremely difficult, because to him, music is the political cantilena, the tenor's aria accompanied by brass *unisono* in the Italian style—and for the rest, he hates music with his whole soul, thinking of it as a national stultifying drink and instrument of quietism. How could he feel otherwise, since he is interested in Germany's denationalization, in her integration in the world empire of civilization, and since this goal cannot be reached as long as music's national power is not broken? No small project! For it is clearly a power deeply rooted in four hundred years of history that has to be broken, a power as old as Protestantism and in eternal alliance with it: the education of the Germans to music began with Martin Luther, a pedagogue of defiantly national character, theosophist, religion teacher, and musician in one person, and so much in one that musicality and religiosity can scarcely be separated in him, that in his soul the one stands for the other—as the German character has remained ever since. "I have always loved music," he said, "it is a beautiful, affectionate gift of God *and close to theology.*" He also said that this art was "a semidiscipline and taskmaster that makes people softer and more gentle, more moral and more reasonable," and: "A schoolmaster must be able to sing, otherwise I will not consider him." Luther gave the artistic culture of his Germans the natural direction toward music, and it was in his spirit that Melanchton's school system in Saxony provided for *four hours a day* of musical training. The Saxon children must really have liked going to school at that time. Of course the church hymn also came from Luther, the German spiritual song that replaced the Gregorian singsong, so that it was a mockery and a scandal to the Catholics the way the Protestants praised God with such bad barrackroom singing, lewd favorites, and spinning-room warbling. Ever since

Luther's religious-musical influence, however, German music from Bach to Reger has been the *punctum contra punctum*, the great fugue, not only the resonant expression of the Protestant ethic, but with its powerfully polyphonic joining of self-will and subordination, the image and the artistic-spiritual reflection of German life itself. How should civilization's literary man, the man of Western "rights," not hate all this? And what, once again, would a musician do with his "teaching"?

No, one must not be musical if one is to qualify as an adept disciple of this teaching. The man whose ears are *not* offended by such dissonances as "resolute love of humanity" or "progress of the human heart" should cheer up; he can accomplish something in this school—providing his logic does not thwart him at the last moment and cause him to founder at the dogma—or the postulate, I do not really know what it is—of the "solidarity of all intellectuals," the "organization of all intellectuals." "Organization!" There it is again, the second key word and slogan of the moment, as a word common to all heroes of the times, even if not at all as sense and meaning. We know the literary infatuation with the word, "political"; we know that in the literary sphere it has become a constant refrain, the highest praise; the cry for "organization" is no different. In it, too, the rhetorically trained voice of civilization's literary man joins with the lesser trained one of a democratic patriotism—even if the literary man does not exactly mean it patriotically. "The organization of the intellect," he cries, "must be completed! And indeed on the basis of the solidarity of all intellectuals!"

On the basis of obvious absurdity then, to give our critical opinion, of absurdity that is transparent to the most burgherly human understanding. When one hears the politician of "intellect," no, of *the intellect*, speak, one is inevitably reminded of Schopenhauer's furious attack on the "crude insolence" of the Hegelians, who,

> in all their writings, without much ado and introduction, talk long and extensively about the so-called "intellect," confident that the listeners will be much too much nonplussed by their balderdash for one, as would be proper, to take on the professor and ask him: "Intellect? Who is that fellow, anyway? And where did you get to know him? Is he not perhaps just an arbitrary and convenient hypostasis that you are not even defining, not to speak of deducing or proving? Do you think you have an audience of old women before you?"

"That would be," Schopenhauer said, "the proper language against such a fake philosopher." We are far from making it our own. But we cannot possibly help being amazed and taking some offense when the heralds of the "solidarity of all intellectuals" act as if there were only one type of intellect, an intellect in itself, claiming it to be theirs, namely the intellect of the enlightenment and of progress. But this simply cannot be completely correct. Was Aristophanes not an intellectual? But he was conservative, an obscurant, if you like, a follower of the "old gods," the mortal enemy of the "corruptor of youth," enlightener and pre-existent radical literary man who was called Socrates. Was Dostoyevsky *not* an intellectual? But although he did not neglect the "human heart," neither was he exactly what one would call a man of progress. Are intellect and progress identical? Granted that democracy in relation to monarchy means political if not always historical progress: is democracy more intellectual than monarchy? Is our monism a more intellectual world view than that of the Christian church? One disputes it. Solidarity of all intellectuals! But it does not exist! To assert or to demand it would be to assert or demand the solidarity of intellects such as Dostoyevsky and Turgenev. They hated each other. Where is the solidarity of intellects such as France and Claudel? They would have to hate one another if they ever even took notice of one another. *Intellect is perhaps nothing more than hatred,* and in no way humanity, solidarity, fraternity.

Nevertheless, there *is* a "solidarity of all intellectuals," but it is not of an intellectual nature, let alone a democratic one. This solidarity is organic, it is constitutional. It rests on the homogeneity of the form of existence, on a higher, more tender form of existence that is more capable of suffering, more willing to suffer, more foreign to comfort than the ordinary one. It is comradeship in nobility, brotherliness in pain. *Here* is the source of all tolerance, conscientiousness, all courtesy of the heart and gallantry, in short, of all *morality* of the intellect. Here is also the source of what should be the deepest and most unconquerable disgust of every intellectual, *of the disgust for dogmatism.* The fact that the politician, precisely as a politician, does not feel this disgust, or has, for the sake of the "good cause," forcibly broken himself of it—should this not be an argument against his humanity, no matter how much he may insist on his claim to "humanity"? "*Ceux qui souffrent,*" a French writer has said, "*ont besoin d'avoir raison.*" This is beautiful and tender, it lays a soothing hand on all sickly obstinacy. But would it not be less sickly, would it not even be more proper, to suffer and still not to have to be right? An intellect in which the *will,* the political-dogmatic will, had the absolute upper hand over contemplation—esthetic, independent comtemplation—would such an intellect be an "intellect" at all? Is it intellectual to find every opposition, every doubt even, to be a sign of depravity, to exclude it coldly, haughtily and clearly from one's own sphere of virtue? Oh, the politician is stern, he is of firm character! He is very far from that lax morality of the intellect that still sees the comrade and brother in the opposing or skeptically resisting brother and comrade. Between himself and every intellectual who opposes the "teaching," he places the whole abyss that separates virtue from depravity. Over there are the esthetes, the selfish ones, the egocentrics, the bad citizens; here, however, are the activists, the ones who follow a manifesto, the democrats, the men of principle, the politicians. A clear separation is imperative for the sake of the "cause." Tolerance, courtesy of the heart, individual human friendliness, would be betrayal of it, would besmirch its existence. His respect for freedom of the intellect is politically conditional. His solidarity and brotherliness with all intellectuals is a very exclusive solidarity and brotherliness; it excludes, strictly excludes, what he is not, what doubts and opposes. The important things for him are not equality of rank and nobility, not humanity, but rather identity and reliability of opinion. Thus he surrounds himself with subalterns, with those who, even though they are not his equals, still hold the same opinion, and from whom he therefore does not have to worry about any opposition, any disturbance and insult. *Il a besoin d'avoir raison.* In this way, however, his conscience is completely lulled to sleep, his sense of truth and justice decays, and quickly that degree of demoralization and bigotry is reached where everyone who does not swear to the "teaching" is given the choice of being called villainous or idiotic. This is the intellectual freedom of the politician. This is the "solidarity of all intellectuals" that he means. This stiff and cold pharisaism preaches humanity.

But let us grant his premise. Let us follow the *credo quia absurdum* and recognize the dogma of the *intellectual* solidarity of all intellectuals: What about the final inference and final summons that the political prophet derives from it? The inference and summons, that is, of the organization of the intellect in order to seize power? Bad, bad! There is something to the antithesis of power and intellect: if for its sake we take the politician at his word, it is not to nail him in a seemingly logical contradiction, a sham contradiction. Does he not know that "intellect" declines as soon as it assumes power? That it does so faster and more thoroughly the *more* power it gets? It is not necessary to delve deeply into history! It is quite sufficient to observe the fate of *the* intellect that the politician quite obviously, quite doubtlessly, means when he speaks of "intellect": the fate of the *enlightenment.* What does all enlightenment want? The older, the new, and the newest of all? Well, happiness! The famous "greatest good for the greatest number." It is social eudaemonism, the morality of utility, the teaching of the "true benefit" of the human being. Definitely not anything else. But what is happiness? No one knows this, and no one can define happiness for everybody: Happiness is something completely relative and personal; it is "in you" or it is not in you, but it is doubtful that it can come from outside. Yes, it is doubtful that social conditions can promote happiness or hinder it, that social progress has increased the sum of happiness on earth. Was there no happiness in the ghetto? I am convinced that there was some. Is there no happiness in the Siberian deportation camps? I have always perceived the "death house" as *a life form,* in God's name, as a life form in the sense that European prisons or even barracks are not—Dostoyevsky himself doubtlessly perceived it so, for neither when he suffered this form of life nor later did ever a word of accusation or of revolt pass his lips: it made him impatient when one spoke to him later of the "sufferings" he had had to bear. "What suffering, then . . ." he said, gruffly breaking off and beginning to joke about inconsequential things—Strakhov tells the story. A life form, I say, and every life form that is at all humanly bearable is in the end something acceptable, life fills it out as it is in its mixture, its relativity of pain and comfort, desire and torment. It is undeniably true that even to think such a thought as this is a luxury made possible only by favorable social conditions, and that to have the desire and the strength to think it one must have a warm breakfast in one's stomach. But does one disparage the human race when one says that for the overwhelming majority of all human beings—and not just those who are starving—"happiness" is gorging and boozing—or, to say it more politely and scientifically: "the greatest enjoyment of economic goods"? This is the way things are beyond all doubt. But the result of this is that all enlightenment morality, every teaching of the "true benefit" of the human being, no matter how intellectual it is to begin with, even if in the beginning it defines the true benefit of the human being to be "life in God," definitely *comes down* to the same degree, that is, materializes, becomes economic and despiritualized, as it attains power and takes on the attitude of the mob; and that on the other hand the masses of human beings who believe in it definitely become more and more greedy, discontented, stupid, and irreligious. Yes, more irreligious. Liberalism errs when it believes it can separate religion from politics: Without religion, politics—domestic, social politics, that is—is in the long run impossible. For the human being is so formed that having lost metaphysical religion, he puts the religious element into the social sphere, elevates social life to religious consecration, and this leads either to an anticultural, social plaintiveness, or, since social antagonism is inevitable and the promised happiness does not appear, to eternal disputes about utility, and to despair. Religiosity is quite compatible with social conscience, with the need for social tidiness. But it *begins* only at the moment when the overestimation of social life *ends*, that is: with the insight that the reconciliation is to be sought elsewhere than in the social sphere; and it ends, it flees and leaves nothing more than despairing discord behind, where that over-estimation takes possession of the minds, where the unconditional apotheosis of social life begins.

This is the way it is with all antimetaphysical enlightenment: No matter how "intellectual" it may be in the beginning, it descends, descends to monism and even much deeper, when it attains "power," conquers the common man. For *"quand la populace se mêle de raisonner, tout est perdu." Voltaire,* my dear democrats! But as long as one does not show me the *essential* difference between the spirit of "resolute love of humanity" and that of the utilitarian enlightenment morality that actually does not have to scream for power anymore because it has already progressed much too far in its acquisition of power and in "democratization"—I will not find the connection, God help me; and it amazes me how one could dare recently to designate this intellect as "the" intellect, and precisely in its name to proclaim the solidarity of all intellectuals.

"Happiness" is a chimera. Never will the harmony of individual interests come down to that of the community, the unequal distribution of benefit will never end, and you cannot explain to the people why some remain masters and the others servants. But the principle of democratic enlightenment, once enthroned, will not suffer limits on its rule; it would have to admit defeat if it feared any logical conclusion. Let it achieve the realm of individual mass socialism— it will revolt against the hardship and constraint that even then—and precisely then—the individual person will have to suffer, and it will march forward to anarchy, to the "autonomous individual removed from all tradition." In the long run no governmental form is compatible with the principle of the enlightenment, and as it fulfills itself logically, it leads to the destruction of the conditions of all cultural life.

It is fortunate that the intellect is quicker than reality, that it does not have to actualize things in order to understand. A Frenchman, Sorel, realized early what others only saw at the outbreak of the war: to wit, that the parliamentary workers' movement can only strengthen the present-day state, that it has actually only strengthened it. He understood *the danger of reconciliation, of the corruption of the "intellect" by the political attainment of power.* At the same time he anticipated the knowledge of the tyrannical strain of socialism and founded, as he began to teach unpolitical-anarchic class struggle, the so-called "revolutionary syndicalism." Please pay attention! This final consequence of the principle of enlightenment, this step *beyond* radical socialism, signified at the same time the first step toward reaction. For what is the title of Sorel's programmatic work? It is: *Les illusions du progrès.* Well, this could be enough. But what does it say? It says that democracy leads to the destruction of greatness and to the dominance of mediocrity; that it also, by the establishment of an unavoidable central authority, makes itself illusory. It says more! It says that one must break every bond between the people and the *literature of the eighteenth century*, to avoid the danger of its becoming established in burgherly life. The man had insight. The day came, it had to come, when he realized the impossibility of his "syndicalism" as well (which could no more do without leaders than democracy could earlier), realized it with all the vehement honesty within him, and—*went over to the monarchist party.* To religion, too? To a more relaxed evaluation of social life and to the realization that politics without metaphysical religiosity is impossible? I do not know, but it is probable. But do you see the circle? From the most extreme radicalism to the most extreme conservatism is only one step. But the human spirit does not want to turn back. Whoever has been a syndicalistic anarchist cannot become a socialist anymore. He will make the step "forward," to where—in France—the Catholic church stands.

Admittedly, this danger is more significant in the realm of pure theory than in that of action. The *homme d'action* may not even perceive the corruption of the intellect by power, he may not even perceive *his own corruption.* Do you know the story of M. Briand? "It makes no difference, you could hear it again," Pedro says in the *Preciosa.* The lawyer was thirty-nine years old when he defended M. Hervé against the accusation of antimilitary agitation. At the time he said: "Like Hervé I am of the opinion that we cannot be satisfied with an idle critique of the standing armies, but that rather, in order to uproot the plague of militarism, we must seize the evil by the roots, I mean by what the bourgeois calls the fatherland." That was "the intellect"! But since M. Briand was a talented man, he became Minister of Education four years later, shortly thereafter Minister of Justice, and now that he has even become Minister President—but everyone who values the French parliamentary reports as entertaining reading knows well enough with what an iron fist he defended "what the bourgeois calls the fatherland" against the domestic enemy—against the domestic one for the time being! Did he even have an idea of his decline? No, probably not. For one does not betray the revolution when one behaves like a bourgeois, and decline is very difficult to differentiate from development. Concepts also develop: the concept of revolution, for example. For all times it stands written on the bronze tablet of history what *Le temps* once wrote about income tax. "Against *it*," it wrote, "our fathers made that revolution that has the immortal honor of having brought the spirit of freedom to the world." There we realized what "intellect" meant by freedom, after it had attained power.

Reflections of a Nonpolitical Man? One will only find the word accurate in the figurative sense. But no matter how much appearances speak against it—I don't side with any party; truly I am not fighting democracy. I was twenty years old when I first read the sentences:

> If the object of all politics is to make life bearable for as many as possible, then these many as possible should logically decide what they understand to be a bearable life; if they trust intellect to find the right means to this goal, what good would it do to doubt the efficacy of this path? The fact is, they *want* to be the makers of their own happiness or unhappiness; and if this feeling of self-determination, the pride in the five or six concepts their minds contain and bring forth, actually makes life so pleasant for them that they will gladly bear the fatal results of their limitation: then little can be said against it.

This comes from *Human, All Too Human,* and at that time they were just good, intelligent sentences, not very timely, that one consented to in a schoolboy way because of their graceful-noble resignation. No doubt they lived on in me while I was preoccupied with other things, and when the forty-year-old looks them up again under vexing circumstances, he find that they describe his relationship to politics today, too, in the briefest and most complete manner. Or perhaps not completely? Can we really only have a negative, purely resigned attitude toward what we feel comes from necessity? Is it not positive, does it not at least gain a bit of color and warmth from our disapproval of the absurdity of thinking of trying to prevent the inevitable? Admittedly, events such as those of today reinforce *every* tendency, and the war cannot fail, *must* not fail, to supply the conservative, delaying forces, and all irrationalism, all "reaction" as well, richly with new spirit, new blood. But I knew on the day of its outbreak that the war would above all signify a powerful step forward for Germany on the path to democracy, and I said so to the most bitter opposition from the political literary man who expected only the blackest things from it.

Just as Germany's political order has undergone many and great changes since the patriarchical police and vassal state of the seventeenth century, it is certain she must continue to go forward according to the exigencies of time and development. Just like anyone else I am convinced that much in our state order has gradually become *disorder*, is no longer to be tolerated, but must be set right, that unavoidable consequences must be drawn from so many social, economic and world-political changes, that rights result from the democratic educational institutions of general obligatory schooling and military service, rights of self-determination and co-determination of the people that need political, orderly expression, and that the state that refused to recognize reality would certainly fall. I repeat: it is not the coming democracy, which I hope will appear in a bearably German and not an altogether too humbuglike form, not the realization of some kind of German *Volksstaat*, which, of course, carefully considered, will neither have to be a mob state nor a state of literary men, that I reject. What infuriates me is the appearance of the intellectual *satisfait* who has systematized the world under the sign of democratic thought and now lives as a dogmatist, as one who is right. What galls me and what I struggle against is the secure virtue, the self-righteous and tyrannical thickheadedness of civilization's literary man who has found the bottom that eternally holds his anchor, and who announces that every talent must wither that does not quickly politicize itself democratically—his bold enterprise, that is, to commit intellect and art to a democratic doctrine of salvation. But what not only offends my intellectual need for freedom and decency but also particularly embitters my natural feeling for justice to its very foundations is the "objectivity," that is: the infatuated absurdity with which this all-too-German man morally supports the enemy civilizations against his country and people; it is his truly shameless doctrine of the "higher moral level of democracy," this doctrine from which he does not hesitate to draw the hidden or open conclusion that Germany, precisely because she has not been democratic, bears the guilt for the war, that the war and her defeat will break her mania for dominance, her crude advocacy of aristocracy, that she will be proved wrong, disciplined, broken, that she must and will be brought to the reason and virtue—of the others. If he called the war a chastisement, yes, a self-chastisement of *all* suffering nations; if he wanted to see in it an unconscious and religious attempt of all of them to purify themselves and to do penance for the sins and vices of the comfortable peace—I would be silent, I would even agree with him. Who has not had moments when he has been completely unable to regard the nations that are flaying one another as *enemies*? When he thinks he understands that all this has to do basically with a *common* European action—with a common attempt, even though perhaps with highly improper means, to renew our world and our soul? What Dostoyevsky said of his beloved nation:

> And just recently, when it seemed almost to be decaying from sin, drunkenness and immorality, it rose up in new spiritual elation and freshness and fought out the last war for the belief in Christ that the Moslems had trampled upon. It accepted the war, it *reached out for it, as it were*, as if for a possibility of purifying itself from its sins and vices by sacrifice; and it sent its sons there to fight and if need be to die for the holy cause, and it did not lament that the ruble was sinking and the price of food was rising . . .

does this not apply a little, does it not, compared with other things, apply very much to the warlike uprising of every nation, and also to this total uprising that is so thoroughly bewailed by humanitarians as a disgraceful "relapse"?

But what does the German radical literary man mean by "chastisement"?

> When the German workers have overthrown the military and Junker party, when they have hanged the Kaiser, the von Bernhardis, the von Tirpitzes and the others in this caste in a long row *Unter den Linden*, when they actually have begun to construct a democratic republic, then we will assume that they have delivered the proof of their wish and their intention to punish the criminal perpetrators of this war.

To be exact: it was not our radical literary man, it was the French social democrat, M. Hervé, who wrote that. But it comes to the same thing. Civilization's literary man also says exactly the same thing: not only in the same sense, but also in the same words, in the same wild and insipid *sansculotte* jargon. The arrogance with which the Celto-Romanic democracy, including the Anglo-Saxon one, "judges" German conditions, with which it insists upon "improving Germany internally," is infantile, hair-raising, foolish to the point of grotesqueness. This arrogance has never even received so much as a smile from civilization's literary man, let alone driven the blood to his temples. He encourages it, he gives his assent, in his own heart-stirring thieves' Latin he agrees with everything that comes from its impudent mouth. For democracy has "the higher moral level." And we, we have "*masters*."

Well, the others have masters, too, it seems. "You have no idea of the cowardice of your masters," Rolland has his Christophe say to the French. "You let yourselves be oppressed, insulted, stepped on by a handful of rogues." But these rogues and masters are democratic rogues and masters, and therefore they may still be rogues—they are not really such genuine "masters"; while on the other hand the Germans are possibly more masters than rogues. More exactly, however, there is still something else about them: to wit, that civilization's literary man is not only a prophet, but also an artist, and as such a decidedly wrong-headed thinker who has read too much in Michelet's *History of the Revolution*, just as Don Quijote did in his books of chivalry, and who is now fighting against flocks of sheep and windmills, which he has, for the sake of noble feeling, convinced himself are knights and giants—even though he probably does not really think they are. We have long known that he has been living and working intellectually in an epoch of one hundred and thirty years ago, in that of the French Revolution; the result is that he is quite playfully transferring the circumstances of that time into present-day Germany, dreaming them in. Since he hates the prerevolutionary *seigneurs* with his whole heart, hates them as a *sansculotte* of 1790 did, and since he does not simply wish to combat them historically but also rhetorically as if they were truly contemporary, he translates them into German as he is wont to do with all things, and calls them "the masters." We have masters; they are the military, the saber-Junkers who retain "power" in Germany, who represent "power" as such in contrast to "intellect," and one has absolutely no idea at all how depraved this master and warrior caste is until one has learned about it from civilization's literary man. To be sure, during forty years of peace they "attempted" nothing—started no war, that is—and accomplished nothing, but instead of this they have abetted the class struggle and the chronic civil war, and they have caused international crises, whether because of ineptness or cunning one seldom knew, and have derived benefit for themselves from the disunity of the nation and from its fears. The nation means nothing to them, it is the raw material of their rule, and only naked self-interest has kept them from destroying us, the raw material, completely. Yes, these are masters—seldom has one seen the like. But if the German people tolerated them, if they (literally) "suffered humiliation from them for generations," then the reason is that (and here the psychology of the literary man becomes "deep"—it is always "deep" when it has reached the point of sexuality and presents a mixture of Nietzsche and Krafft-Ebing)—that the misanthropy of the tyrants "appeals to all perverse instincts." One sees that it is quite simply and disgustingly an alternating game of sadism on the one side and masochism on the other. For perverse reasons the people have even done well under their "masters," and the "struggle" (*l'effort*) against the "masters" is really a "struggle" of the nation against itself, as it were. Nevertheless, the enormous affairs of Köpenick and Saverne have, in spite of all their masochism, raised a storm in the German people against their masters, that storm "that stirs up the deepest feelings"—and what does one call a government, civilization's literary man asks, that has the will of the whole nation against it? One calls it foreign domination, he answers quick-wittedly; and the nation would have given itself up and deserved to collapse if in the face of power it had become silent once and for all.

This dionysian galimatias—why I call it dionysian, I will certainly yet explain—was presented before the war, but it would be superfluous fairness to emphasize this: one would be wrong in assuming that the war had changed the literary man the least bit in his view of Germany. He would, he does, speak today as he spoke in May 1914. Foreign nations that seriously believed the German nation had been thrust into the war by the fists of its "masters," and that it longed to be liberated by the armies of civilization from these "masters," have been taught better by a few months of war. They have long known, every single one, that in this war they are dealing with Germany herself, with the people as an embodiment, with the nation, and not with any sort of ghostly "masters" of the country. A Frenchman of a refractory mood, who was opposed to the dominant spirit of his homeland, said to his bourgeois compatriots that they did not understand anything of "this heroic people." Another, the ex-Minister Hanotaux, spoke in the newspaper of "this terrible people" that had "dreamed of world mastery"—and if he was wrong in this, he was still wrong in a more correct way than the German radical literary man, who believes with all the fire of his talent in an alien dominance of masters in Germany, a rule under which the people voluptuously pant and moan; and since he knows how to express his literary scorn and hatred in such a passionate rhythm, we should therefore believe him when he says that a nation of masochistic slaves has performed the deeds of this war. A real politician, a politician, that is, who pays a little attention to reality and who does not look upon politics as a means of intoxication and a cheap opportunity for passion, the democratic representative, Konrad Haußmann, said in a democratic magazine: "*No trace*," he said, "no trace of a contradiction exists between army and people in the supposedly militaristic Germany. The field gray has replaced the 'bi-colored uniform' . . . The accomplishments of the reserve, the militia, and the home guard are worthy of those of the officers and men of the regulars." This is without doubt philistinism, but it is the truth; while the songs of civilization's literary man admittedly have talent and passion in their favor, they show little regard for truth, which in political matters, if not in expressionistic art, must finally have a little to do with *reality*. No matter how the nation may have behaved toward its masters, it does *not* really seem to have merited the "collapse" that civilization's literary man was not far from prophesying, for today it is putting up a resistance for which no mechanistic explanations are sufficient and at which the world has not yet learned to be properly amazed. One day it will become aware; and however the war may now end—it can certainly no longer bring a German defeat in any moral sense. What barker's spiel could have argued more powerfully for the right of this nation to take part in administering the earth than its present accomplishment? But if the laughter at the Köpenick farce, if our burgherly displeasure at the Saverne affair, had been "the deepest feelings" that could be "stirred up" in the German people, then they would have been less deep than one believed. In my opinion, the deepest feelings in the *human being* cannot be stirred up at all by politics. The deepest feelings of a *nation*, however, are stirred up by a decisive spiritual and physical struggle such as the one today—and not by any Saverne affair.

I am as little tempted to make an apology for the political leaders of Germany as it is my job to do so. Nevertheless, I believe that in this point, too, I am on better terms with justice than are those who have justice as their battle cry. I do not believe that our leaders and masters have shown themselves to be *humanly* inferior to those of hostile nations, and indeed, precisely for the reason that, as the terrible situation in Germany in the summer of 1914 proved, they have shown themselves to be so very much inferior to them *politically*. Moreover it is *a priori* probable to me that this inferiority actually existed: for in the end, a people has the leaders it "deserves," that it is ordinarily able to produce; and no matter how much these war years have "politicized" the German people—up to 1914 they were considered to be a politically untalented people, and they did not object to being considered so. Leaders, I think, are to be looked upon as exponents; basically one criticizes oneself when one criticizes them, and perhaps one would therefore do better to criticize oneself straight out. After one has done so, one may, by way of apology, make allowance for the vicious trickiness of foreign policy that one has faced so ineptly since one has been an empire—and one may precisely for this reason feel oneself driven to allow one's inborn sense of efficiency and accomplishment to hold sway, particularly in questions of leadership, and to think about finding surer methods of selection for all national offices. This would be well and good. But I detest the accusing, banishing into the desert, and the angry political squabbling with those "responsible"—the Roman gutter politics of "*Piove? Abbasso il governo!*" Germany's leaders may have conducted the empire's business very badly; they may have lacked all tact in the treatment of foreigners, used harmful words, made harmful gestures, and above all awakened the disastrous idea that Germany had become fat and cowardly and would, if she only saw herself opposed to a strong counteralliance, under no circumstances accept the war: one says all this, and it may well be true. In the essential thing, however, in the main thing that has to do with direction and goal, they have led Germany as she wanted to be led, namely on the *imperial* path—which, if a new and greater Bismarck did not show the way, and perhaps even then, had to lead to a collision with those who had "older rights." It would be silly to be deceived at the measure of aggressiveness that lay in the will of the nation to be led in this way. One should not deny this aggressiveness, not act as if the German people had not wished for anything better for themselves than to raise their cabbage in contented limitation, and not write—as I have read verbatim: that the predominant feeling of this German people at the outbreak of the war was "dread of the coming horror." We know different. What happened after the disaster of Echterdingen* was a strong portent. And the indescribable uprising in the summer of 1914 was an uprising of belief, of boundless readiness. Need? Oh, yes, it was the passion of the moment. But need

---

* In 1908 in Echterdingen one of Count Zeppelin's lighter-than-air ships crashed and burned.

is, as we have already explained to M. Rolland, neither mere "*nécessité*" nor desperado boldness; need is the solemn name for a *creative* emotion in which elements of defense are strongly mixed with those of attack. A nation does not rise up in this way, millions of its youth do not take up arms in this way, before they are called, if that nation wants nothing, nothing at all but peace, and if it is being seduced into lawbreaking and misdeeds by cunning "masters." The world nation of the spirit, strengthened to exuberant physical power, had taken a long drink at the fountain of ambition; it wanted to become a world nation as God had called it to be, *the* world nation of reality—if necessary (and obviously it was necessary) by means of a violent breakthrough. Had not Spain, France, and England had their moments of grandeur and honor? When the war broke out, Germany believed fervently that her own time had come, the moment of trial and of greatness. Whoever does not admit this today, whoever prattles about the "dread of the coming horror," is lying. The German people, *as* a people, completely heroically attuned, prepared to take guilt upon themselves and not inclined to moral pussyfooting, have not whined about what the radically merciless enemies have done to them in turn, but in an emergency they have not doubted their right to revolutionary measures, either; they have approved of such measures, and more than approved. They approved of the march into Belgium, and found nothing to criticize in it other than the words of the Chancellor about the wrong one was committing. They approved of the destruction of that impudent symbol of English mastery of the sea and of a still comfortable civilization, the sinking of the gigantic pleasure ship, the "Lusitania," and they defied the world-resounding hullabaloo that humanitarian hypocrisy raised. And they have not only approved of unlimited submarine warfare, they have cried for it and were bitter with their leaders almost to the point of rebellion when they hesitated to allow it to go on. It suits the democratic orthodoxy of the enemies, for whom "the people" naturally must be "good," just as it suits their political cleverness, to differentiate between the fine German people and their detestable "masters"; not us. And no matter how the war may now end: let us take the German share of the "guilt" upon us, each individual, with the exception, perhaps, of a handful of pacifists and literary saints—and not make some chance functionaries into scapegoats.

In spite of its esthetic attraction, the ghastly picture civilization's literary man draws of the psychology of the German "masters" reveals undeniable obscurities and contradictions. For forty years they attempted nothing, these crafty ones; that is, they did not go to war, but only, as they brewed international crises, threatened war and frightened the people in order to be able to hold them down more easily, the cunning ones. This is how we read it before the war. No sooner had it broken out than we heard that they had contrived it, and indeed, for the same purpose. For it is certain that masters of their type, executioners of democracy, that is, are never drawn into a war that they have not contrived first of all for the suppression of their own people. What, contrived? And at the most unfavorable moment, under the most difficult circumstances? After they had let pass one opportunity after another for decades to conduct it under much easier circumstances as a real "preventive war"? They threw themselves into the risky venture only after it had become gigantic—while they had shunned it when its success had seemed as good as certain? If it then failed, what would become of them and their tyranny? And what would become of it if Germany were victorious? Did they believe they would be better able to suppress the people more certainly with the help of a victorious war? Which social class would be the one to gain the main advantage from Germany's victory, anyway—which one other than the one that is called the "people" in the narrower sense, the German workers? Does one suppress the people by raising them up, enriching them, giving them an interest in the state? What even the likes of me with a politically untrained eye saw: that a people's war such as this one had to lead irrefutably, unconditionally, and even independently of its conclusion, to democracy—had not the "masters" seen this? But then, they were not only rascals, they were clearly so stupid, so stupid it cannot be expressed!

But stupid or sly or both—why should the masters not have contrived the war, since they, of course, and only they, were so disgustingly prepared for the murderous work? At least civilization's literary man has shown us the French enemy, who concerns him so much, in that bad condition "that all Germany's enemies were in at the beginning of the war and that German newspapers were aware of": the tattered peacetime uniform, the pack cord from which the sidearm hung, the cracked patent-leather shoes. And as he, the politician, suddenly shoves the individual-human element before the political one, he has the ghost of the peaceful Jean Bonhomme from the rustic Café Voltaire whisper melodramatically to his murderer: "I hated you and your countrymen much less than I did the fellow who wanted to take my girl friend away from me." He could just as well have had the ghost of a German farmer who was stretched out in the mud speak to the "enemy." He prefers the opposite, in honor of the Café Voltaire. Is it proper to misuse individual innocence with such tearful bliss, and the innocence of the "enemy," at that, when the lives of nations are at stake? "It has been firmly established," the Dutch Attorney General said in his argument against the editor of the *Telegraaf*, "that the *entente*'s expenditures for armaments before the war exceeded those of the Central Powers." If this is true, what happened to these expenditures that Jean Bonhomme must wear such pitifully cracked patent-leather shoes? What about the "*archiprêt*" that was megaphoned over the Rhine at every opportunity from the great Café Voltaire? What about the warlike rejoicing over France's headstart in air power "that the French newspapers were aware of," about the newly rekindled offensive spirit in general? Did Austria find herself at the beginning of the war facing a terrible Russian superior force or not? Did Germany have to suffer the invasion of East Prussia or not? If she prepared herself well—the tasks that would come to her in the war had given her good reason to do so. In the theaters of war at the end of 1916 her armies had a front of one thousand, eight hundred kilometers; the French six hundred, the English two hundred and fifty. Preparation! If it is French to say: "*On n'est pas prêt et on se bat tout de même*"—is it our fault? It was the same in 1870, too; but this time you were given time, lots of time to meet the height of the requirements—which everyone had very old-fashioned ideas about. Was perhaps the German preparation adequate for it? Did it reach as far as the colonies? Did it not fail more than once in Europe itself? Everyone was prepared for a war, indeed abundantly so. But no one was prepared for *this* war, that is the point, and the reason it could come is that everyone nevertheless believed that he was prepared for it.

In 1875, Theodor Mommsen, a highly liberal academician, a noble representative of German intellectuality, said the following words as Rector of the University of Berlin in a speech at the commemoration of its foundation:

> Of course we also know that the Kaiser above all, but every German statesman as well, shares this wish to be protected from further victories. Yes, beyond doubt the greater one's influence, the deeper one's insight, the more one shares this wish, the more seriously one strives for the suppression of every flareup of temper even if it is justified, of every even apparent misuse of the newly-won position of power, the more one is willing to risk everything, except the right and honor of the nation, on the creation of a lasting state of peace ... When a nation such as ours

exposes the highly-educated segment of its youth to the dangers of war to the same extent, yes, if one considers the ratio of officers to men, even to a greater extent than the less-educated segment, when it necessarily carries part of its best flowering to the grave, then there certainly lies in this enormous stake a warning against the game of war itself that no German statesman and above all no German ruler ever can and will ignore. Wars such as the ones the last French emperor mischievously began on distant shores and then against us, and often just as mischievously broke off, *are formally possible according to our political system, but in fact impossible* . . . Under the Hohenzollern dynasty it has happened that to the greatest detriment to the nation *necessary wars have not been waged*; no Hohenzollern has ever waged an unnecessary war, and he cannot wage one!

Ah, yes, the German masters; what bloodhounds. Does one have a sense of harmony? Would one like to hear a few bloodhounds howling right here and now? "Our people," the Quartermaster General and later Minister of War von Stein wrote on New Year's Day 1915,

> Our people would not have been well served by rapid and easy victories. The abuses that occurred after the successes of the campaigns of 1870–71 would have had an even greater impact. Since that time the violent upswing has caused a greater turn toward the material direction. The balance had not yet been reached between spiritual and material forces.

Oh, what a vile, doglike voice! How the desire resounds from it to bring us to generations of humiliation. Quiet now, the second one is howling. A letter appeared in the newspapers last year that the younger Moltke, a "master" beyond doubt, had sent to the editor of a magazine. "It was clear to me," he says,

> long before this war placed our nation on the gold balance of world development, that we are desperately in need of a renewal of spiritual life, and I have hoped with my whole heart that the nation might show itself worthy of the high task that world leadership has given it. It is spiritual weapons that are concerned here; only with them can the future be conquered. There is such an infinite amount of idealism, of upward striving in the soul of our people. It was long suppressed by the thick layer of material life; it broke through this when the war caused the externals of existence to disappear before the idealistic storm of love for the fatherland that swept through all hearts . . . Divided into classes, split up into parties, we scarcely knew each other before the war. We want to remove the barriers that the egotism of individual existence has erected between us and bring human being close to human being. *We must help*

nobility of soul conquer the business mentality . . . We will soon perish, but our nation shall live into the coming centuries. It shall live *upwardly* . . .

Gianettino Doria's rustic voice. A look into the atavistic mentality of one of those power louts and systematists of terror from whom the burgher "has suffered generations of humiliations." But is it not striking that he is speaking *his* language, this man of the saber—the language of German-burgherly culture and humanity? To "live upwardly . . . to help nobility of soul conquer the business mentality . . ." Have we heard such war aims from any other country? From England, perhaps, where master morality, master rights, master pride are truly at home *together* with democracy? His war aims are not exactly politically competitive; they might sound foreign to the ear of a bourgeois-imperialist. The knight is old-fashioned—well, that is why he is a knight. But when, in an old-fashioned way, he idealizes the meaning and goal of this war, which is, of course, to a great extent a war of bourgeois competition— there is no lack of reason to believe that the likes of him does not much approve of the outer stamp of modern warfare. A chemical industrialist makes a circle of high military men acquainted with a newly discovered lethal gas. He experiments a little, describes and recommends in a glib lecture the annihilating effects of his ozone. One of the officers has listened with a slightly displeased look on his face. Finally he turns on his heel and goes to a corner of the room, comes back and says: "Really quite atrocious. Really no longer beautiful . . . as a weapon . . . I cannot help it . . ." The chemist shrugs his shoulders. "Well, does His Excellency wish us to produce a *harmless* gas? We can do that, too." He had the laughter on his side.

It is true, then, they are sometimes old-fashioned, the masters. As far as modern trends are concerned, though, they are well-meaning to a fault. When Herr Delbrück with his hereditary nobility left civil service, the conservative press said he not only had no feeling for agriculture, but that he had also demonstrated more and more radical tendencies in social policy; they said that in his aversion to any special legislation protecting those willing to work he went so far as to reject the ban on picketing. A regime of masters and sabers! It seems that during the war the German people have wanted more of this than they have gotten. For it was not popular with the great majority when Dr. von Bethmann Hollweg defeated Tirpitz together with the whole iron party; and it is still remarkable that while in the France of Briand, the man of the right, a newspaper like *Action française* was pampered from on high, in our country there were complaints that the leftist-liberal, Western and internationally minded press was the one that the censor favored to the disadvantage of the conservative-national one. Others may check the justification of such complaints. At any rate, the main organ of burgherly culture in Germany, the *Frankfurter Zeitung*, defended itself in vain against the public opinion that it was *semiofficial*; and English loyalty saw to it that Bertrand Russell, a scholar who at the beginning of the war had resisted the wild atrocity propaganda against Germany, not only received no passport to America, but also lost his chair in Cambridge, while the pacifist and Christian Professor Foerster enjoyed complete freedom to travel and to teach.

This is approximately the way it was with the German iron fist regime, with the Junker and military despotism during the war. How was it before? I do not want to speak of social policy—of which I have heard that the education and the welfare of the people have been relatively decently advanced. But did the arts and sciences lie bound and gagged on the ground in Germany? Did the club swing at bold ventures of the mind? Terrible awakening! I, who thought of myself as quite thin-skinned, quite excitable and needing freedom, I have become forty years old in Germany without knowing, without noticing that I was a slave under the thumb of the "masters." Indeed, I lived in a country where a book could appear unsuppressed and uncontested that ends with the words: "I call Christianity mankind's one immortal disgrace." Such a country seemed *free* to me.

"Mankind's one immortal disgrace." Does one know the sound, the style, the gesture, the monstrous accent? Does one recognize it? Truly, it has by now become such daily nourishment for us, our ear has gradually become so deadened to it, that we are scarcely curious anymore about how it ever could have been dared in an unfree country that was hostile to the intellect. Admittedly, at the time the sulphuric curse was originally hurled with the most intense, most spiritual, most abstract passion in the titanic struggle against a moral value system that was to be delivered over to the contempt of intellect as belittling and slanderous to life. The terrible and ecstatic height of the polemic passion, the horrible intensity of the accent that was no longer critical but religious-execrating, corresponded to the sublimity of the sphere and of the subject. Moreover, it corresponded to a personal, psychological state of extreme and most terrible overtension and excitement, the final stage of an ineffably venerable life tragedy that truly "awoke fear and pity," in which the giggling of clinical megalomania already resounded perceptibly, and which was followed directly by psychic collapse, the onset of spiritual darkness. Since then we have seen the democratic exploitation of this late style for literary—what am I saying, for daily political use. Dionysian criticism—have we not already spoken of it? And have we not already noticed that our radical literary man has appropriated much more of the spirit, if not also of the substance, of the older Nietzsche, *who had become grotesque and fanatic*, than of the younger one who found "that everyone who violently represents opinions in word and deed should be perceived as an enemy of our present culture, or at least as one who has been left behind"?

It is a peculiarity of intellectual-technical development that imitative, exploitive talent holds mainly to the late and old-age works of the masters—as if the final results of personal development were really decisive for development in greatness, and as if it were not a childish masquerade when an artist at the beginning of his individual destiny speaks the language of a high age level, only because it seems to him to be the ultimate achievement. Thus twenty-year-olds have imitated Beethoven's last chamber music, thus Ibsen's and Wagner's late styles have had the greatest effect on the times, and thus it was not the Nietzsche of the early, ripening period who had the most influence, but the oldest one, whose methods and accents to be sure were not those of advanced age, but of a demonic phosphorescence of decay and of a psychological phase that preceded insanity.

Our political literary man has learned a medley of things from Nietzsche. Overbeck called his great friend, in comparison with Pascal and Schopenhauer, a *rhetorician* in the pejorative sense; and it is true: a powerful strengthening, yes, actually the first legitimization of the prose-rhetorical element in Germany, came from Nietzsche—we recognized a basic element of democracy in it, and we see well that Nietzsche's rhetoric is the point where the Western-politicizing literary man possibly touches German spiritual life. Nietzsche's brilliant tendency toward *satire* was also politically exploitable (is not the best in *Zarathustra* satire?)—above all, however, what goes with it, his caricaturelike late style *in psychologicis*: Nietzsche as a critic was finally completely a caricaturist and artist of the grotesque, his psychology of Christianity, of Wagner, and of the German character, for example, was a grotesquely distorted, a fanatic's psychology, and our literary-political criticism has its gestures, its monstrously ludicrous accent, from it. Christianity was finally "mankind's one immortal disgrace"—and how much is lacking, then, for civilization's literary man to hurl the same judgment against Germany, or at least against the regime of the German masters? He would scarcely have revealed to us that we had "taken" generations of "humiliation" under the masters if the New Testament critic had not previously called himself an "assailant of two thousand years of perversion and human defilement."

Is there anything more intolerable than titanic passion that is transplanted and democratically dissipated? The over-tensed, tortured language of a spirit reaching up to its full height to destroy and set anew the highest values—applied to political criticism, misused in practiced passion, but still in a completely secure state of mind for the purpose of democratic agitation! Truly, the fanaticism, the grotesque, caricaturelike nature of the political prophet's criticism need make no one worry about this critic's psychological health; it is not a sign of genuine, excruciating eccentricity and of excessive tension leading to a collapse. Insanity is not behind it—quite honestly, nothing is behind it except perhaps a completely irresponsible artistic pleasure in gesture. Sobriety goes very well with this heat, with a critically grotesque style that is not destructive passion but rather—literary school that one can live comfortably and successfully on. Tsarism and the Russian police state were at any rate something different from our "master" establishment, and Dostoyevsky had *suffered*. But never did a word against his government cross his lips or issue from his pen, nor did he lose faith in Russia. What in the world has the German literary man had to suffer politically, and how have German "conditions" hurt him? When he invited us to orgies of cerebral eroticism—the jailer kept a respectful distance. Unmolested, without risking anything, without even having to think about any kind of Siberia, the politician decreed his radical manifestos in favor of the republic, of the ideal of truth—and in doing so he speaks against the *Reich*, power, and the "masters," using Nietzsche's language against Christianity.

That is laughable. And it does not become less laughable by the fact that the great majority of Germans paid little attention to these manifestos. Is it unpardonable if one did not take them objectively seriously—if one took them as artistic diversions and escapades? If we had had forty-five years of arrest warrants, *lits de justice*, Bastille, Deer Park,* a parasitic court, a physically and spiritually pauperized people, in short, all the abuses of the Bourbon regime, then the despair of

* In the Deer Park French girls were brought to the king from the people.

civilization's literary man over what the nation "took" from its masters could not have raged more monstrously. *When*, however, he assured us at the time, the limit is reached; when even this apathetic people's patience comes to an end, and they proceed to a reckoning with the "masters"—then this judgment will be highly extraordinary and terrible! I do not believe this. History and its interpreters teach us that the fury and horror of a revolution always correspond exactly to the frightfulness of the misrule that finally caused it. All the terror and madness of the Grand Revolution, the childish helplessness of the "constituting" convention, the theoretical stupidities and practical crimes, of which the government of the literary men and humanitarians was full—they were the necessary consequence of the limitless political immaturity of the nation, they corresponded to the intellectual state of a people that had been made ignorant and cruel by oppression. Assuming that in the Germany of today or tomorrow a constitutional change of the extent and even of the outer form of a revolution would take place: I do not believe that the terrible threats of civilization's literary man would be fulfilled. I believe, rather, that to his gaze, which is lost in the vision of noyades, fusillades, guillotines, heads on spikes, and similar orgies of reason, there would present itself the image of a people that was well-prepared for new freedoms by those it already had, and that would run little risk of falling into the hands of theoreticians, petty peddlers of generalities, dogmatists, revolutionary schoolmasters, freedom priests, inquisition democrats and organizers of humanitarian masquerades.

Truthfully, then, one was not particularly moved by that rhetoric, one took it to be "an end in itself," an expression of temperament, political *l'art pour l'art*; one found no real connection between it and reality, for one found, for example, that there had been a "saber regime" at times in France, but never in Germany. One did not know that the German radical literary man, when he spoke of a saber regime, German slavery, miserable serfdom, and generations of humiliation, had expressed nothing more than the democratic world opinion of Germany that was and is his own: This became clear only at the outbreak of the war when the liberal press of all continents repeated practically word for word what he had always said—and then to be sure one felt oneself forced to defend onself. I say that every German self-contemplation, that the subjective consciousness of the nation, the domestic facts, strictly contradicted those declamations. I did not rely upon myself at the time—it could be that I was thick-skinned and not alert. But I have searched well, made many inquiries of people who were competent to judge, whom I had a right to trust, from whom it can hurt no one to learn—there were quite radical heads among them—and their verdict, their verdict that contradicted the raging of civilization's literary man—ensued with a unanimity that must mean something.

"We do not want to allow our pleasant, secure, clean, orderly homeland, *in which we are freer than almost all so-called democratic peoples*, to be abused . . ." That was Oppenheimer, an otherwise not very amiable scholar who wants to completely do away with large estates; and the italics are not originally mine, but his. But this is the way it resounded from all sides.

"Nowhere do personal freedom and human dignity suffer in our country."

"The freedom of the citizenry from governmental arbitrariness is protected just as well or better than anywhere else."

"All talk of a despotic German militarism hostile to culture is the talk of people who have or want to have no knowledge of our domestic circumstances."

"A free and proud people *that feels itself borne up by great future powers* . . ."

The most colossal self-deception? But no, this feeling of freedom, power and future was *objectified*, of course, in gigantic deeds, it was confirmed by the victory that can no longer, we repeat, result in a defeat in any higher sense; and wherever, among combatants and noncombatants, undeluded intelligence looks things in the eye, where historical instinct is active, there the pioneering, leading nature of the German character, which is completely unslavish and somehow pregnant with the future, is anticipated or recognized, whether with joy or with worry and bad conscience.

Since the outbreak of hostilities, of course, there has been no doubt that Germany has had world liberalism, which has thoughtlessly confused itself with world progress, against her, and that only conservative powers have given her moral support. But of course this was a highly confusing and misleading phenomenon that basically proves nothing more than the emptiness of political terminology. Georg Brandes, who certainly had always been a liberal, but especially a *free*, man, published in Germany during the war an essay entitled "Berlin Memories," in which he said:

When Bismarck's decisive break with the Manchester principles occurred, the way the free-thinkers conducted their campaign against him seemed so ridiculous to me that I published an article four years after my immigration to Germany, "The Opponents of State Socialism," in which, in spite of strong reservations, I had to agree with him against them. In it I wrote: "It would be rigid dogmatism if, in the political economic dispute, one wanted to call the government absolutely reactionary simply because of its position on religious reaction and because of its utilization of old prejudices of lineage and class, and to believe that progressiveness in this case means progress. On the contrary! This time it is Bismarck who represents the modern point of view, or, stated more correctly, the revolution, above all, the initiative, the brilliant risk, while the Progressive Party members represent the conservatism that is infertile and poor in thought."

It was not by chance that the clever old gentleman published this suggestive anecdote in a German magazine at that time. He wanted to say that progressivism does not mean progress in this war, either; he wanted to point out where in truth the "more modern position," the "revolution," the "initiative," the "brilliant risk"—and where the "infertile conservatism" were; and really, if world liberalism ("civilization") still represented progress, had the future on its side, then it would not have the whole world on its side and would not have pushed forward to the savages who are already enthusiastic for "freedom." Whatever the state of Germany's spiritual power of resistance may be today (May 1917), in 1914 she had recognized as superstition the belief that the Western ideas were still the leading, victorious and revolutionary ones; she was convinced that progress, modernity, youth, genius, and novelty were on the German side; she thought it patently clear that compared with the conservatism of the "immortal principles," her own psychological conservatism signified something truly revolutionary.

This belief, I say, was objectified in deed and in victory; it had the power, at least momentarily, to cause world liberalism to lose faith in itself. What was becoming clear to the authors of the *Manchester Guardian* when they, on the occasion of the voyage of the "Appam," compared the inventive daring of the German sailors with the accomplishments of the English sea powers and found that the latter "seldom distinguished themselves with that refreshing, restless, revolutionary attitude that alone causes great changes in the world"? What was becoming clear to that Roman journalist who wrote: "For wherever one's sympathies may lie, one still cannot ignore the fact that the Germans have shown a decisive initiative in all areas, and that the role of the other powers has been generally limited to copying the Germans"? What was becoming clear, finally, to Citizen Hervé when in his newspaper he called the

Germans an enemy that "disgusted" France but that *was renewing all the qualities of our fathers from the time of the Revolution*; organizational ability, power of decision, daring—"everything that we seem to be lacking today"? If qualities such as those he listed are not the firm possession of a nation, but if they go over from one nation to the other; what is it, who is it, that at the moment gives these qualities to the one nation, awakens them in it, and causes them to work in it and from it? Is it not the time, history, that shows such a remarkably talented people that its hand is over them at the moment?

This is how Germany thought in 1914, and rightly so. If she can no longer think in this way today; if she is about to capitulate intellectually-psychologically before she capitulates physically; then it is not completely because the pressure from outside was too strong, not only because she is unnerved by suffering. The unnerving comes to a good and worse part from within: I do not believe that I am paying too much respect to the effect of civilization's literary man when I assert that the process of decay that is spreading out is in good part his work, the effect of his teaching that we are in need of "reforming"—not, for example, as everyone else needs it, but reforming in the sense of the others, reforming *by* the others; of his teaching of democracy's "higher moral level." To repeat, I do not believe that with this claim I am exaggerating his influence; for when I am told that our psychological attrition is only the result of our national weakness, of the German tendency to self-betrayal, then I reply that one can recognize in civilization's literary man precisely the tool and the expression of this weakness and tendency. And the "higher moral level"? What about it? Shall we, in order to pass the difficult time, look it a bit critically in the eye?

The world was in a bad way before the war—who denies it? Whether it will ever be less badly off, whether it will not always be badly off, only in different ways, I do not know, yes, I confess that I do not have enough rhetorical high-mindedness to suggest this as definitely likely. It is certain that the forms of its sinfulness were gross and repulsive. It had sunk into senseless worship of affluence. The economy was its one and all, and the name, type and form of its economy was capitalism, or rather the imperialism that one could also call "capitalistic militarism"— the literary man, I believe, calls it this. Now admittedly I do not deny that the manner of this saint, when he speaks of capitalism and imperialism as if they were the most depraved works of the devil and a crime against the human race, has always seemed a bit laughable to me. As if, I said to myself, capitalistic expansion were not a necessary stage of development in economic life. As if, furthermore, there were any prospect that there would be, after this war, less "imperialism" than before: the future will, if everything is not deceptive, see a few gigantic world empires, which—whether Germany is one of them or not—will have divided the administration of the globe among themselves; and the phrase, "rights of small nations," will then generally be treated as the deceitful sentimental phrase it already is today. And especially: as if *democracy* were in any way a contradiction of imperialism or capital-ism—as if it were not rather almost in solidarity and identity with them. But wherever it is, or wherever it is in a rhetorically acceptable manner alleged to be, there it covers, in the eyes of civilization's literary man, all imperialistic sins with the veil of "beauty."

This is, in short, doctrinaire mendacity. It is not the free, just and true manliness that the liberal belief was quite capable of up to a short while ago. Just recently the newspapers published one of Theodor Mommsen's letters from 1898, the year of the Spanish-American War. "In my youth," he said,

> the belief was rather general that the world order was continually improving, and that this progress would be expressed by the more and more general introduction of the republic. One has gradually gotten rid of this youthful stupidity after one has had the opportunity to actually experience such transformations. But one was not prepared for the bitter disappointment that this war has brought to the friends of the republic. The hypocritical humanitarianism, the violation of the weaker ones, the waging of war for the sake of speculation and hoped-for stock manipu-lation, give this American enterprise a stamp that is even less worthy than that of the worst so-called cabinet wars, and are well-suited to disenchant the last republican.

Truly, it is good to hear the language of painful honesty after one has heard for six years or longer the language of a hysterical doctrinairism and beautiful-souled democracy ringing in one's ears! Where was the protest of the literary saint when Italy, with truly villainous frivolity, improvised the conquest of Libya "without anyone," as Guglielmo Ferrero wrote at the beginning of the World War, "giving a thought to the effects that such a severe affront to international law and such a sudden disturbance of the European equilibrium *could have had*"? Since it was a matter of the will of democracy—where was the anti-imperialistic anger of our radical literary man? He found words of tender psychological understanding for Italy's last-minute panic that for her the colonial gates would be closed, that was all. Where was his anti-imperialistic moralism when France, backed by England, with a mood no less impudent than that of before 1870, "penetrated" Morocco, unabashedly violating treaties? He admired France, he admired with one eye closed France's powerful colonial empire, he admired the imperialistic democracy. Disgusted with the brutal injustice of the Boer War, Germany's popular feeling was in agreement with France's; but at the time, our literary man probably still remained on the esthetic level and took no moral side. Did he ever take offense at the fact that England, without needing a defensive force, kept a mercenary army solely for wars of aggression and conquest? Never. This was quite all right. One cannot point out enough that the conscience, the moral sensitivity of this declared cosmopolite and friend of mankind has always shown itself to be intimately national. For the sins of others it has nothing but excuses; for what would not be excused, embellished and glorified by the name of democracy!

But as we toss out this rhetorical question, we find ourselves coming to the realization that "democracy" actually means the synthesis and reconciliation of power and intellect. We are at the point of realizing that civilization's literary man, this supposed preacher of the antithesis of power and intellect, as a political educator, really wants a synthesis of power and intellect under the banner of democracy. Let us take a good look: the oldest representatives of democracy are England and France, the classical country of political economy and the classical country of revolution. But political economy and revolution, these are *profit* and *virtue*, and precisely the name that brings these two together is "democracy." It is also "politics." It is also "civilization." Yes, all these are again just names for something even higher and more general, for Europeanism. "The European," according to a passage from the "teaching," "wants first of all to do business; but as he does his business, he wants secondly to bring about something moral as well, that is, something progressive-humanitarian." This is the definition of Europeanism; it is at the same time that of politics and civilization. What civilization's literary man wants to teach us Germans is the priceless psychological ability to see morality and business, humanity and exploitation, virtue and profit in one, to make them one—this is precisely what politicization consists of. During the war he celebrated the English spirit as the embodiment of this Europeanism. "The East India Company," he said, consisted of money men, but they were *humanitarian money men, prepared to profit by making people happy.* And if up to today they and their successors have been the harshest of exploiters—is there any doubt that they have been proven right and that a relative human happiness, even if only the greater security for their very lives, would never have come to the dark masses of India without England?

God forbid us to doubt it! In India the mortality rate has risen in the last thirty years from twenty-four to thirty-four percent—I have read it. And indeed, this happened thanks to plague and famine, in which the cold-blooded English masters see providence's remedy for overpopulation. "Just think!" the former American Secretary of State, W. J. Bryan, said one day,

> The English administration is justified because it prevents the Indians from killing one another, while the plague is praised because it carries away the ones the government has protected from being murdered.

So much for "relative human happiness" and "greater security for their very lives," this humanitarian accompaniment to the economic fact that roughly a hundred million dollars a year flows from India to England. But after all, we are dealing here with Asia, with "dark masses," with niggers. One is a "European" and an aristocrat toward other continents, even if a democrat at home. Meanwhile, Ireland lies in Europe, a beautiful, fertile country that has been conquered by a related, neighboring people, raped, annexed in our times, in the second half of the nineteenth century, whittled down to half its one-time population. How unimportant to mention it! Self-criticism! Self-criticism! Put your own house in order, patriot! But I find nothing! By my immortal soul I find nothing in German history that can be compared to England's treatment of Ireland; for valid reasons I can refuse to compare Schleswig-Holstein and Alsace-Lorraine to it, and I must leave it to antinational foreign nationalists who are also students of a rhetoric class to prove the moral plus and the relative human happiness in the Irish case, to prove it to be among the other high-minded endeavors of democracy's drive for enrichment: in the Boer War, in the Opium War, in the Spanish-American War, where Mommsen's Teutonic understanding could not discover it. Business and virtue! The nation of humanitarian moneymen has risen up in this war to slay a dragon that answers to the name of German militarism, to protect the small nations, to protect freedom and justice. But it has seized the opportunity not only to occupy with the greatest care and precision all important European and non-European points for the maintenance and expansion of its world mastery, beginning with Calais, but also to gain possession of worldwide business secrets through extensive postal espionage, to destroy German foreign trade, to eliminate the German overseas enterprises, to complete and to make permanent Germany's economic isolation by entangling all possible countries, including those of no military significance, in the war, and to organize a lasting economic blockade through the decisions of the Paris Conference of June 1916. This is how one profits while making people happy.

"While the Germans torture themselves with the solution of philosophical problems," Goethe said to Eckermann,

> the English with their great practical sense laugh at us and win the world. Everyone knows their declamations against the slave trade, and even though they would have us believe that humane maxims motivate this policy, we now see that their true motive is a real purpose, without which the English, as is well known, never do anything, and which we should have understood. They themselves use the negroes in their large possessions on the western coast of Africa, and it is against their interest to export them. In America they have founded large negro colonies, which are very productive and which deliver a great many blacks every year. With them they supply the North American demand, and since they are thus carrying on such a thriving trade, importation from the outside would be quite contrary to their mercantile interests, and they therefore preach, not without purpose, against the inhumane trade. At the Congress of Vienna, the English delegate still argued quite vigorously against it, but the Portuguese delegate was clever enough to answer quite calmly that he had not been aware that the purpose of the meeting was to deliver a general judgment on the world or to establish the foundations of morality. He knew the English purpose very well, and he also had his own, which he knew how to speak for and to attain.

This is the Goethe who, as I said, showed more Bismarckian traits than the Weimar-Potsdam dialecticians want to admit. However, it is highly unlikely that there will be a German delegate at the world peace conference who will answer the Englishmen as the Portuguese representative did.

If the English spirit, to wit, the happy instinct "not to act" before the "humane maxim" has been joined to the "real purpose"—if this spirit is the embodiment of Europeanism, then America is not far behind England in European spirit. Right now she is providing a splendid example of the democratic art of the good conscience, of the *political* synthesis of intellect and power, morality and business, by opportunely making herself, for the sake of "justice," and midst the praise of the democratic world, into a great world power through militarization and fleet construction. To learn how to become skilled in the laughable-miserable archswindle of the instinctive, naive reconciliation of virtue and profit that has long since ceased being hypocritical: again, that is democracy, that is what politicization consists of, and it is that to which civilization's literary man has been sent to educate his people.

The world, we say, was in a bad way before the war, and Germany with it. After she opted for reality and power, Germany took part in the general intellectual attitude that is most generally called "materialism." We were materialists. Were we more so than others? I ask this because we are talking about democracy's "higher moral level." If it is true, as it seemed to us, namely that in Germany the coming of the war was *mainly* perceived with a certain feeling of moral liberation as a disciplinary measure against materialism—(it may be, it is even probable, that some people in all countries thought of it in this way, but mainly, as I have said, it seemed to us in Germany to be true): if this is true, then— would this not be an indication that more resistance to materialism had remained alive in Germany than anywhere else? Was not *money* in France, in England, in America, in the *trois pays libres*, a greater, more decisive, more absolute power than it had ever been in our country? "Freedom" and the dominance of money have always been very closely connected. This was less true in our country because a few things, a few wavering forces, resisted the complete realization of democracy. Or is this not so? If materialism, and indeed materialism as morality as well as materialism as a philosophical attitude, marked the epoch—was this not precisely because it was a commercial epoch determined by the utility principle, in short, a democratic epoch whose predominant instinct was by far the drive for affluence? Seen from one side, the war is of course a result of this way of thinking, planned as democracy's competitive struggle for affluence. And still one can say that it probably would not have come, that it would nevertheless probably not have been psychologically possible, if *theoretical* materialism, materialism as a philosophy and as an epistemology, had not been on its last legs. How do things stand now? Do we not have good reason to doubt that this is what civilization's literary man really wanted and wants? No matter how "spiritual" the herald of a social message of happiness may act, must he not feel the strongest anxiety in the face of a growing, almost complete withdrawal from a materialistic explanation of the world? If his political activism sees in every metaphysical system an opiate of the people, then it is clear that every move toward *religious* rebirth must be met with his utmost invective, with the dismal word of terror, "reaction!" That monarchical wish of sovereign simplicity that religion be "preserved" for the people only seems anachronistic precisely because religion was taken away from the people long ago—midst endless rejoicing, while the unshakable truth remains that without metaphysical religiosity, this sphere of true humanity, social reconciliation is forever impossible. But let one ask the literary man—no, one would do better not to ask him— if he would approve of any efforts to give back to the people—if not religion, then at least something like religiosity! He is a monist, certainly not in a strict sense, but a monist just the same. For all antimetaphysical enlightenment, all democratic adoration of happiness, of utility, of science and of work, is different only in degree from the registered and documented monism, only insignificantly, only in gesture and in literary accent. Now, of course, there has been no lack of attempts in modern philosophy to reconsider a duality of body and soul, to see in the brain-organ only an instrument—but I can assure you that an accident almost took place when civilization's literary man heard of it. He saw red and used inelegant, unrefined language. "Just go ahead! Just go ahead!" he cried. "Just bring back the 'soul' again by underhanded means! That will do it! We will have the *whole mess* again!" One understands, I hope. But to return to materialism: can civilization's literary man logically oppose it? No, he cannot. Practical materialism, plutocracy, enthusiasm for affluence, form the basic character of democratic epochs; and without theoretical materialism, the "whole mess" comes back.

It will succeed, it has already succeeded, the effort to convince us Germans of the vital necessity of the psychological reconciliation of virtue and profit, of morality and business, in short of the necessity for democracy. We have seen that without democracy in the world no business can be done anymore, that one must Anglicize oneself in order to do business—the opportunistic desire for German democracy comes from this insight. But the further attempts of the democratic dogmatist and systematist to win intellect and art for this democratic teaching, this democratic doctrine of salvation, will scarcely succeed; if I may judge by myself, there is still some liberal defiance and resistance to this. At the bottom of this—one must say it: of this completely bigoted, impudent effort that is hostile to freedom, there is, as far as *art* is concerned, an excessive overestimation of politics altogether: as if artistic progress and bold invention were only possible together with political progress, as if the revolutionary principle in politics ever favored the revolutionary element in art in the least. Who was the first to have *Tannhäuser* performed in Paris? A despot. The same despot whose *coup d'etat* forced the immortal desperate sigh from the gentlemen, Bouvard and Pécuchet: "*Hein, le progrès, quelle blague! Et la politique, une belle saleté!*"—this expression of a psychological mood *that is the infallible means of producing general politicization.* On the other hand, French romanticism, which was the new, progressive element, developed under the protection of the monarchy, while the liberals and republicans stubbornly and conservatively defended classicism—it is clear why: because of virtue, you see. And Cézanne? A bold innovator beyond doubt! But he thoroughly despised Emile Zola, the worshipper of the masses, the prophet and servant of democracy, who called the public "our highest master"; he was far from all futurism and all "progressiveness"; he sneered at new principles, theories and movements in art, convinced like our Hans Pfitzner that there was only *one* art, precisely *the* one that lives in all master works of the past, and that a work of this one art cannot be "surpassed" by anything; he was a conservative, pious Catholic; to him, everything traditional, the monarchy, the army, the church, were inviolable. Was he therefore a wretch? Did his talent dry up in this attitude toward life and intellect? I know nothing about painting, but I think I can confidently leave the answer to the experts.

It is the monstrous and inflexible delusion of civilization's literary man to believe that conservatism and talent mutually exclude one another. But the connections between art and politics, if there are any, are completely different from what civilization's literary man would have us believe! In Gogol's magnificent story, *The Portrait*, there are the words:

> The monarchical governments are not at all the ones that suppress high and noble sentiments of the soul: works of intellect, of poetry and art are in no way despised and persecuted under such rule; monarchs are rather their natural protectors, only under *their* high-minded protection does a Shakespeare or a Molière arise — while on the other hand, a Dante could find no peace in his republican fatherland. True geniuses develop only in the splendid ages of powerful kings and kingdoms *and not under the influence of ugly political events and terroristic republics, which have up to now not given the world one single poet.*

It is an empress that Gogol has say this, and he has her add:

> One must richly reward and honor poets and artists, for they give the
> soul rest and peace and protect it from ugly passions and rebellion; the
> scholars, the poets, and all creative artists are the pearls and diamonds in
> the imperial crown: they are the highest decoration that crowns the age
> of a great ruler and grants him a magnificent splendor.

When the empress spoke these words, she was infinitely beautiful and
divine, Gogol concludes, and I believe it, for noble naiveté always has
a beautiful and divine effect, and the somewhat ladylike words of the
empress are at bottom completely true: even those about art giving the
soul rest and peace and protecting it from ugly passions. Schopenhauer
said this, too, although in a less imperial way; and no one will dare
defend the idea that political terrorism, the terrorism of politics, favors
art.

Does it favor the spirit? A "no" to this question is not enough. One
must add that all political terrorism has long been intellectually impossible. Politics has brought itself to ruin by mismanagement. No longer
will political life be able to rule intellectual life; never more will there
be a political power that gags intellect and brings it to the funeral pyre.
This is impossible, and least of all will the democratic doctrine of
salvation be able to do so. What stubbornness to believe anything else—
to want, for example, to make the democratic doctrine master over the
minds out of love of "freedom"! Before the war, the idea that democracy
provided more freedom was recognized as nonsense. One had realized
that the rule of the people made life completely public, that it only
could be represented by all sorts of laws and rules; that it therefore
meant limitation of freedom, increase of bureaucracy, continual control,
power of the majority over the minority, of those who are probably
stupid over those who are probably smart, that is. Today, in order to
justify political expediencies intellectually, or in order to brag about the
strength of one's belief, one seeks, in spite of the fact that one knows
better, to raise the democratic theory to a dogma. Truly, democracy as
dogma of the intellect! And here it is certain that equality not only does
not mean freedom, but that it is excellently suited, yes, it all by itself,
to be a pedestal of grandeur, of the master, of the tyrant—of whom
civilization's literary man speaks so badly!

The democratic republic, he says—will finally allow the trial to begin
that will decide the fate of *great men*—of these monsters, of the bane of
the little people whose share they gobble up, of these offenders and
oppressors of the human race. The great man must be eliminated,
rooted out, brought back to the common denominator, brother among

brothers: may the democratic republic help us with this! It is impossible not to admire the circumspection, the radical-logical consistency, with which this truly systematic intellect follows his principle, thinking it through to the end; how should our insight, our assuredly very clear insight into the *essential hostility to Germany* of his whole ideological system, change anything at all in this admiration? The literary man knows only too well that Germany is quite truly the land of great men—knows it as well as the poet who speaks to the Germans in "Star of the Covenant":

> . . . Mediocre growth blossoms and increases
> Over there more fully, more fragrantly than with you . . . :
> The most noble of the noble thrive only here.*

But the desire to get rid of the great man is as old as the wishful image of *civilization* itself, first conceived by the *Chinese*, among whom the saying goes: "The great man is a public misfortune." But it could just be that civilization's method of fulfilling this wish is unreliable— that the belief that leveling hinders the rise of the *master* is a mistake. "Yet I found no reason for discouragement," Nietzsche says in *Will to Power*.

> Whoever has instilled himself with a strong will and maintained it, together with an extensive mind, has more favorable chances than ever before. For people have become quite *trainable* in this democratic Europe; people who learn quickly, who conform easily, are the rule: the herd animal, highly intelligent even, has been prepared. Whoever can command finds those who *must* obey: I am thinking, for example, of Napoleon and Bismarck. The competition with strong and *un*intelligent wills, which thwarts things the most, is small . . .

The leveling of intelligent ones, not, for example, as a means against the "great man," but precisely as the native soil that leads directly to Caesarism—may one beg civilization's literary man to táke note of this point of view for the sake of his intellectual freedom? Does he prefer Caesarism to monarchy? That would speak for his taste, without being consistent. But German reality once knew—oh, it is like a dream!—a combination of both, of monarchy and Caesarism, it knew the genius as "a loyal German servant of his master"—and that was politically the most fortunate time for Germany, yes, it is easy to predict that Germany

---

* . . . Das mittlere Gewächs erblüht und schwillt
  Dort drüben voller, duftiger als bei euch . . . :
  Des Edlen Edelstes gedeiht nur hier.

will not be happy again until this blessed constellation has been re-established. But if in its absence and expectation one wanted to make Marshal Hindenburg, an Eckart-figure of monumental loyalty and objectivity, the Imperial Chancellor, let no one expect me to oppose such a rule of the saber out of devotion to "intellect." On the contrary: only under a leader who has the characteristics of a great man of German stamp will the *Volksstaat* offer a bearable appearance and be anything else than the humbug-democracy we do not "love."

Democracy, no matter how one may now slice and twist it, means *rule of the people*; and the belief in it, the belief, that is, that it is the most noble, most just type of rule that brings the greatest happiness, is as old as the state itself—and as old as the opposite belief. It would be impossible to think up new arguments for or against it. If the struggle could be decided, it would have been decided long ago; and it is amazing how political principles maintain their youthful freshness and energy in spite of all the wear and tear of history, of thought and practice, how they suddenly, by dint of a change in lighting, appear new and splendid to mankind, and are jubilantly seized as the "truth."

Rule of the people. The phrase has its terror. But let us observe all the same that it sounds least terrible by far in German. It is not just patriotic prejudice when one imagines and perceives in the strangely organic, unforced and poetic word combination, *deutsches Volk*, some-thing not only national, but also essentially different, better, higher, purer, yes, holier than in the expression, "English people," or "French people." *Volk* is a truly holy sound. But does it not in any event still have a living meaning just by its connection with the word, *deutsch*? The breakdown of our concept of *Volk* by the foreign spirit, by Marxism, this mixture of French revolutionism and English national economy, has gone far enough. And yet the German people have remained a people more than any other; they have degenerated least of all into class and mass; and on this emotional basis, therefore, those whose instinct is repelled by the cry for democracy may prick up their ears sympathetically to the word, *Volksstaat*.

Rights of the people. Truly, it would not be very fitting for a German today to dispute the right of the German people, the hero of this war, to take part in and to have a voice in the life of the nation. To be sure, it seems to me that this right and this beautiful possibility is not to be "expanded"—for it scarcely existed—but only to be created, and that nothing, or only what is harmful, is accomplished by the mechanical "expansion" of existing rights. At any rate, I have an open ear for warnings that come to me from the front and run something like: at every rejection of democratic uncleanliness, at every intervention against those who would use democracy to come to power, against impotent literary men and dirty mobs, I would unfailingly have the best ones on my side: but if I did not want to be completely alone, I should be careful not to impugn and denigrate the average man, "The German industrial worker who is winning the war and who is a magnificent fellow, devoid of hatred, full of humanity, with a deep feeling for justice and deprivation of justice, and with an inborn robustness and efficiency that is fully proven and is equal to any situation. . ." I am thankful for such words that bring life and reality closer to me and whose sentiment I proudly and happily share. But am I therefore obliged to forget everything human nobility ever felt in its heart and expressed with eternal sincerity against the people as a political monster, against the "animal with many heads," the "fickle, dirty mob"? Has Coriolanic perception become unnatural horror that a healthy mental attitude must shun?

> He loves your people;
> But tie him not to be their bedfellow. —

. . .

> — but your people,
> I love them as they weigh.

. . .

> Master of the people,
> Your multiplying spawn how can he flatter
> That's thousand to one good one —

. . . .

> Bid them wash their faces,
> And keep their teeth clean. — So, here comes a brace.

. . .

> Behold, these are the tribunes of the people,
> The tongues o' th' common mouth: I do despise them —

. . .

> It is a purpos'd thing, and grows by plot,
> To curb the will of the nobility:
> Suffer't, and live with such as cannot rule,
> Nor ever will be rul'd.

. . .

                    I say again,
  In soothing them, we nourish 'gainst our senate
  The cockle of rebellion, insolence, sedition,
  Which we ourselves have plough'd for, sow'd, and scatter'd,
  By mingling them with us, the honour'd number;
  Who lack not virtue, no, nor power, but that
  Which they have given to beggars —

Was this perhaps simply an "indirect character sketch"? Was it not stinging lyric and does it not stand there for eternity? Close to two hundred years later a man wrote with pen and paper: "The people are just, wise and good. Everything they do is virtuous and true, nothing exaggerated, mistaken or criminal." It was Robespierre. Have we reached this point again? Is our understanding, which has been so tyrannized by the times, again at the point of taking this miserable hypocrisy for the truth?

Still, it was progress. For social-political progress is only a result of the people discovering their strength. Disraeli answered it: "The people are never strong, the people can never be strong. The attempts of the people to assert their rights will only end in suffering and confusion. It is *good breeding* that has brought about that change and that continues to bring it about; *it is what teaches the educated person his social duties.*" I would have to be a liar and a hypocrite if I were to suppress and deny, for the literary man's sake, my convinced agreement with these words and the immediate applause they awaken in me.

My God, the people! Do they have honor, pride—not to speak of understanding? It is the people who sing and clamor in the streets when the war starts, but who begin to grumble and whimper and to call war a swindle when it lasts a long time and imposes sacrifices. Where they can, they revolt; but not on their own; for revolutions require intellect, and the people are completely without intellect. They have nothing but force, combined with ignorance, stupidity and injustice. They can revolt; but they would never bring about a revolution by themselves if intellect from above did not come to their aid, as in 1789 when they were encouraged in everything by an intellect that was not their own, and thanks to this intellect, which prevailed in the upper classes, they encountered no resistance at all.

Are the people perhaps more noble and better than the rulers? Are they more just because they demand justice? Justice is not demanded at all, it is *practiced* (for example by a ruling class that decides for the sake of propriety to grant the subject class equal rights)—otherwise it is called envy and greed, and not a virtue. Are the people more high-minded, do they believe more easily and better than the bourgeois in voluntary action, unselfishness, and higher humanity? Do they pander less to the cult of goods, of the economy, of utility, and has not the conviction that everything in the world is done only out of calculation and for the sake of money become remarkably quickly their axiom, a basic fact of life that they show little tendency to dispute?

You think the people have a progressive attitude? "The tendency of the herd," Nietzsche says, "is toward inactivity and preservation; there is nothing creative in it." This is a teaching that agrees with the often observed fact that nowhere is there more tendency toward inertia than in the lower classes, that the ideal of absolute inactivity is quite characteristically the ideal of the "working class," which certainly earns this title quite involuntarily. I remember I heard a man of the people say, when he saw a dog run by: "If I could run like that, I wouldn't do any more work either!" It was precisely the logical senselessness of the remark that impressed itself so amusingly on my mind. What pleasure the man must have had in the thought of doing nothing, how foremost and alive this thought must have been in his head for him to seize such a logically insufficient opportunity to talk about it! But inertia has nothing to do with progress, change, and revolutionary new events; work must be loved, one must stand in awe of inventive agility, if the world is to go "forward"; and precisely the "dignity of work" is not at all a popular concept, but a burgherly one: one needs *intellect* to be able to grasp it.

You also think the people love enlightenment and want it? That is an error. The people are as little inclined by nature toward enlightenment and progress as they actually perceive democratically—they have the most natural feeling for distance and rank: just as the greatest men of the people, on the other hand, were conservative, yes, from the point of view of the enlightenment, obscurantists. The aforementioned Aristophanes and Dostoyevsky were true men of the people (I pride myself a little on this combination), these defenders of religion, these arch enemies of progress, of "nihilism"; and "Seigneur de Ferney" was *no* man of the people. Are the people, after all, intellectually and morally prepared for the enlightenment? M. Barrès wrote one day: "There would be many a surprise if the old church were to disappear from the midst of the houses that it dominates. Just listen to what the Catholic and the Protestant clerics and the country doctor say to you. They unanimously state and assure that the ground lost by Christianity will not be conquered, for example, by rationalist culture but by paganism

in its basest forms: as magic, witchcraft, theosophic aberrations, spiri-
tualistic swindle." And if not by this, then by the lowest utilitarianism
and materialism, by the unconditional belief in profit and by insatiable
greed.

The rule of the people ensures peace and justice? The most certain
safeguard of peace is "democratic control"? That's what I'd like to
know! I would like to know whether in the hands of the masses the
decision on war and peace is more secure than in those of a minister
like Herr von Bethmann Hollweg. Do we not have the example of Italy
for those who consider the "people" to be a conscientious, enlightened,
controlled protector of peace? Who caused the Italian war if not the
"street," the "piazza," the democracy, the people, or those whom the
people did not prevent from claiming to be the people? Did you see,
August 1914, the London mob dancing around the Nelson column?
Even a convinced socialist like the Swede, Steffen, rejects with a shrug
of his shoulders the doctrine that the antagonisms, the discord of the
nations, and therefore the causes of war, would disappear by themselves
as soon as the proletariat exercised political power. Responsibility! And
since when has a divided responsibility gained in seriousness and
weight—placed upon many, upon all shoulders? Every experience
teaches that in this way responsibility dissappears altogether. *Now*, to be
sure, the people have long wanted peace, indeed unconditionally; they
probably want it everywhere, most recklessly-unconditionally, as one
must believe, in Germany: not only because there it is least supported
by the *word*, the phrase, but expecially because here the national element
is a force and accomplishment of unpolitical burgherdom, while the
politicized people remained nationally weak and took and take the
Socialist International more seriously than anywhere else. I have no
doubt at all that today the great majority of the army at the front would
immediately approve without debate the surrender of Alsace-Lorraine.
"For," so adds the observer who gave me this to think about, "if the
people and their elected representatives are to establish political goals,
then the needs of the moment and of the present generation will always
be decisive, and the people will always overlook the fact that the
'people' also have a temporal extension, because they know that their
kind like to resign themselves to the given situation." There is no doubt,
then: the realization of the *Volksstaat* as a government of the people
would, in the midst of the war, mean immediate peace and the triumph
of France and England—but just try to make the "common man"
understand that this would be an unpatriotic peace! And just try to

convince *us*, too, that such a peace would be a proof of the ability of the people to rule themselves! On the other hand, they do not want to be ruled anymore, that is clear; they are too suspicious to believe in a "government of the people" and in its good will: precisely because the deeper down the social scale the materialistic-economic conviction goes, the more solid it is. Scarcely have the "emancipated," the "enlightened," the "thinking" masses submitted to the leadership of their elected representatives than they intend to take them to task. But must the so-called ruling classes reproach themselves for having themselves plowed, sown, spread and raised the weeds of rebellion, impudence and mutiny, and for having raised impossible half-masters for themselves when they needed something quite different? The people as a creature that neither can rule nor allows itself to be ruled is not a modern creation. It has always existed and will always exist. This plight is timeless and inter-national. And international are the palliatives that one makes use of against it: they are called domestic policy, parliament, "democracy." But what the likes of me worry about in the idiotic, intellectual overvaluation of these miserable necessities that have become popular again today has—why do I trouble myself!—already been said in the best possible way; it has been summarized once and for all in Schopenhauer's essay, "On Jurisprudence and Politics," with which I shall close this chapter by quoting, and which runs briefly and forcefully:

> Everywhere and at all times there has been much dissatisfaction with governments, laws and public institutions; but this has largely been because people have always been ready to blame the governments for the misery that is inseparable from human existence itself; for the misery that is, to speak mythically, the curse that Adam received, and with him his whole race. But never has this false accusation been made in a more deceitful and impudent way than by the demagogues of the "present." As enemies of Christianity, namely, they are optimists: the world is for them an "end in itself," and therefore in itself—in its natural state, that is — quite excellently arranged, a real dwelling place of happiness. They ascribe the colossal evils of the world, which completely contradict this idea, to governments: if the latter would only do their duty, there would be heaven on earth, that is, everyone would, without effort or difficulty, be able to booze and gorge and breed to his heart's content, and then to croak: for this is the paraphrase of their "end in itself" and the goal of the "infinite progress of the human race" that they tirelessly proclaim in pompous phrases.

CHAPTER 8

On Virtue

The Jacobins have declared virtue to be the order of the day.

Büchner's *Danton*

Pécuchet, bilious and with a tendency to obstinacy, declared himself a sansculotte and even a follower of Robespierre.

Flaubert, *Bouvard and Pécuchet*

To speak of the opposite of a matter is also a way of speaking of the matter itself—even a way in which objective understanding is admirably served. Therefore I open this chapter with a look at an old, German book—the moment forces me to add: *still today* a German book, that to a truly immoral degree is devoid of virtue as I understand it and as it absolutely must be understood today, *political* virtue, that is: in such a way, namely, that the book not only wants to know nothing about virtue (this would still not be a lack of will), but actually knows absolutely nothing about it, and therefore finds itself to a simply startling extent for today in a state of political innocence and ruthlessness: I am referring to the *Good-for-Nothing*, Joseph von Eichendorff's story that is so marvelously sublime and free and lovingly imagined, which we have all read in our youth, and which has left forever in all our hearts the reverberation of a delicate string chord and the chime of bells.

From the Life of a Good-for-Nothing. Does one remember? And would one not like to refresh the charming memory right now, and defiantly to read the floating, resonant story again, which, when we read it before, was perhaps in the form of a dog-eared pulp edition, and in the meantime has taken on the most elegant book form: of imposing format, printed in clear and large Gothic letters on beautiful, strong paper, even decorated with drawings by an ingenious little gentleman who seems curiously anachronistic and who has the romantic-prepolitical name of Preetorius? This, you see, is the way it recently reappeared, in the midst of the war, and this, too, this bibliophilic honor that has come to the *Good-for-Nothing* just now is perhaps a sign of the times that a writing such as the one in hand has reason to take note of in some detail.

There is probably no reason for me to recapitulate the story? To call it unpretentious would already be saying too much. It is pure ironic playfulness, and the author himself makes fun of it when toward the end he has someone say: "Well, then, in conclusion, as is self-evident and fitting for a well-bred novel: disclosure, repentance, reconciliation, and we are all happily together again, and the wedding is the day after tomorrow!" But the novel is anything but well-bred; it lacks every solid center of gravity, all psychological ambition, all social-critical will, and all intellectual discipline; it is nothing but dream, music, letting go, the floating sound of a post horn, wanderlust, homesickness, luminous balls of fireworks falling in a park at night, foolish blissfulness, so that one's ears ring and one's head buzzes with poetic enchantment and confusion. But it is also a folk dance in Sunday best and travelling organ-grinders, an artist's Italy seen in a German-romantic way, a happy boat trip down a beautiful river while the evening sun gilds the woods and valleys and the shores re-echo with the sounds of a French horn, the singing of wandering students who "swing their hats in the morning glow," health, vigor, simplicity, courting, humor, drollery, ardent lust for life and a continual readiness for song, for the purest, most refreshing, wonderfully beautiful singing. Yes, the melodies that resound there, that are strewn in everywhere as if it were quite natural to do so—they are not ones that we merely take for granted, they are jewels of German lyric, highly praised, old and dear to our ears and hearts; but here they are in their proper places, still without any patina of fame, not yet in the song treasury of youth and of the people, fresh, original, and brand new: things like "Wherever I go and look," or "Whoever wants to wander to foreign lands," with the final cry, "I greet you, Germany, from the bottom of my heart!" or "The faithful mountains stand guard," and then the magical stanza that a woman disguised as a wandering painter sings to the zither on the balcony into the warm summer night, a stanza that like all of the songs is prepared musically in a way that is still prosaic—"From far away in the vineyards one still heard at times a vine-grower singing; in between there was often lightning in the distance, and the whole area trembled and rustled in the light of the moon"—and which, to be sure, is no longer in keeping with the national tradition, but a *non plus ultra*, a bewitching essence of romanticism—

> Loud revels of the people rest:
> Earth now rustles as in dreaming
> With all trees in wonder streaming,
> What the heart has scarcely guessed,
> Olden times, their gentle weeping,
> And soft feelings, awesome, sweeping
> Summer lightning through one's breast.*

The good-for-nothing, then, to come to him personally, is a miller's son who has his bad name because at home he is good for nothing else than to loll about in the sun and to play the violin, and whom his father therefore angrily sends wandering so he can earn his bread in the world. "Well," the boy says, "if I am a good-for-nothing, that's fine; then I shall go into the world and seek my fortune." And while right and left his friends and acquaintances go to work, dig and plow, "just as yesterday and the day before yesterday and always," he wanders with "eternal Sunday" in his heart, with his violin through the village and out into the open world, and when he sings his brand new song, "To whom God wants to show real favor," he understandably draws the attention of the two ladies to himself who overtake him on the highway in an "exquisite coach." They take him along on the running board to Vienna, which he has named out of the blue as the goal of his journey; and with this there begins the dreamy roundelay of his German-Italian adventure, the story of his love for the very beautiful, gracious lady, this irresolute story that gets lost in an operatic intrigue to be settled to everyone's satisfaction, and in which the character of the one who experiences and tells it reveals itself so candidly-irresponsibly.

Here is the good-for-nothing's character. His needs fluctuate between such complete idleness that his bones crack from laziness, and a vagabond longing full of vague expectation for distant places that makes him see highways as bridges—bridges that swing out over the

---

* Schweigt der Menschen laute Lust:
  Rauscht die Erde wie in Träumen
  Wunderbar mit allen Bäumen,
  Was dem Herzen kaum bewußt,
  Alte Zeiten, linde Trauer,
  Und es schweifen leise Schauer
  Wetterleuchtend durch die Brust.

shining country far over mountains and valleys. He is not only useless himself, he also wishes to see the world as useless, and when he has a garden to take care of, he throws out the potatoes and other vegetables that he finds in it and plants it all, to the astonishment of the people, with selected flowers that he wishes, admittedly, to give to his high lady, and that therefore do have a purpose, if only an impractical-sentimental one. He is from the family of youngest sons and simple Simons of fairy tales from whom no one expects anything and who then nevertheless solve the problem and marry the princess. In other words, he is a child of God who receives the Lord's gifts in sleep, and he knows it, too; for when he goes out into the world, he is not guided by his father's words about earning his bread, but exclaims lightly that he is going to seek his fortune. He also has such a pretty face that in Italy, where as a result of the plot he passes for a while, without being aware of it, as a disguised girl, an enraptured student falls quite hopelessly in love with him, and absolutely all hearts are friendly to him. And yet, even though from his grateful soul he loves and ardently listens to the beautiful world of his travels, the vigorous crowing of the roosters over the lightly waving wheat fields, the larks flying between the morning clouds high in the sky, the serious noonday and the whispering night, he is still not at home in the world, and usually does not take part in the happiness of those who feel at home in it. "Everything is so joyful," he thinks, as he sits, as he often does, over the world in a tree top; "no one is thinking about me. And this is the way it is with me everywhere and always. Everyone has staked out his little place on the earth, has his warm oven, his cup of coffee, his wife, his glass of wine in the evening, and is quite satisfied . . . to me, nothing is right anywhere. It is as if I had arrived everywhere too late, as if the whole world had not planned on me at all." He compares himself to a rolled-up hedgehog, to a night owl that squats in a dilapidated house, to a bittern in the reeds of a lonely pond. And then he takes his violin from the wall and says to it: "Come here, you loyal instrument! Our kingdom is not of this world!" He is an artist and a genius—something that is not his own claim nor the author's, but that is proven most beautifully by his songs. Nevertheless, his character does not have the slightest trait of eccentricity. Its nature is not problematic, demoniacal or morbid. Nothing is more characteristic of him than his "horror" at the wildly beautiful, overexcited speeches of the painter in the Roman garden, a bohemian of decorative manner who blusters with grotesque gaiety about genius and eternity, about "thrills, wine drinking and the pangs of hunger," and who in the process looks quite as pale as a corpse in the moonlight with his hair tangled from dancing and drinking. The good-for-nothing slips away. Although he is a vagabond, a musician, and in love, the bohemian life is not in his nature at all—for the bohemian life is an extremely literary form of romanticism that is alien to nature, and he is completely unliterary. He is of the people, his melancholy is that of the folksong, and his joy in life is of the same spirit. He is healthy, but in no way vulgar, and he cannot put up with crazy things. He "commends himself to God's guidance, takes out his violin, and plays through all his most beloved pieces so that the lonely forest resounds quite cheerfully." This romanticism, then, is neither hysterical nor phthisic nor lascivious nor Catholic nor fantastic nor intellectual. This romanticism is completely nondegenerate and on track; it is human, and its basic tone is melancholy-humoristic. Wherever this tone becomes droll, it is noticeably reminiscent of that of a very great contemporary Germanic humorist who is also of the people and a passionate vagabond: of Knut Hamsun. "*Parlez-vous français?*" I finally said fearfully to him. "He shook his head and I was very glad, for of course I could not speak French, either." The good-for-nothing also reveals himself to be a humorist in matters of love. His love is not "pale as a corpse." It, too, is human, that is, melancholy, passionate and humorous. He would never, as the Latin student who takes him for a girl does, fall at anyone's feet with *Iddio* and *cuore* and *amore* and *furore*. When "everything, everything, is fine," and he can have his grand lady, since she is, praise the Lord, only a doorman's niece, he is "so completely satisfied in his soul," and from his pocket he takes a handful of unshelled almonds that he still has with him from Italy. "She took some of them, too, and we cracked and stared contentedly into the quiet countryside." This is so spontaneously humorous that no unwanted comicality can arise, and one remembers that the simple Simons of fairy tales do not conduct themselves more exaltedly, either, when they win the princess. The good-for-nothing is innocent to the point of clumsiness in sexual matters, and gets, untouched and unaware, out of very tricky situations that he falls into because of the intrigue. It is a great poetic accomplishment that his purity does not have the effect of stupidity. It is the purity of the folksong and of the fairy tale, and therefore healthy and not eccentric. He has a naiveté and a free human nature in common with figures such as Wagner's forest youth, the hero of the *Jungle Books*, and Kaspar Hauser. But he has neither Siegfried's muscular hypertrophy nor Parzival's saintliness, nor Mowgli's half-animal nature, nor Hauser's psychological cellar color. These would all be eccentricities; the good-for-nothing, however, is in no way extreme. He is a human being, so much so that he cannot and does not want to be anything else at all: this is exactly why he is a good-for-nothing. For obviously one is a good-for-nothing when one claims to be nothing else than precisely a human being. Also, his human nature is hardly differentiated, it has something abstract, it is really only defined in the national sense—but this, to be sure, very strongly; it is convincingly and exemplarily German, and although its format is so modest, one would like to cry out: this is truly the German character!

Preetorius understood and rendered this figure wonderfully. It is only two inches high in his sketches, but full of poetic and symbolic life. The good-for-nothing before the magistrate, on the weather-beaten garden wall, in his dressing gown before the little customs house; the good-for-nothing strolling and playing his violin at dawn, or meditating in the tree over the wide countryside; the good-for-nothing swinging his instrument before the silhouette of Rome, or finally with his beloved on the balcony overlooking the deep valley; these are pictures of tender and impressive imagination. The illustrator does not make his hero "beautiful," although the book says of him: *"Come è bello!"* But the good-for-nothing's beauty is certainly nothing more than the shining through of his divinely childlike nature, and the illustrator acted correctly in following the drift of his humoristic talent and in not showing an ideal youth but rather a clumsy Simple Simon. His good-for-nothing—and now one will probably always have to see him this way—is a fellow in a brown swallow-tailed coat and awkward trousers, with stand-up collars, a comical, unruly growth of hair and a sharp-nosed, endlessly naive, simple and good face. The artist gave very much with very sparing, but exact and ingeniously appropriate means: with the writer's formula in mind, he produced a symbol of pure humanity that is touching and cheerful in its unpretentiousness, of affable humane-romantic humanity, once again, then: of the German human being.

"Understand me well! I am full of praise for those who spoke up for beauty when it was still the cause of the few, and as long as morality sat foolish and unquestioned in its chair. But since beauty has become a vulgar public cry, virtue is beginning to rise in price." These sentences are twelve years old. I had my little Medician cardinal anger the palace humanist with them, and I believe the more alert among my readers saw that they were not at all meant "historically." *Fiorenza* was, of course, not least of all a satire on the democratization of the artistic sphere, on the childlike eagerness with which the times, our times and world, had come to appropriate art and beauty, so that they actually saw the spiritual element only under the sign and meaning of the esthetic concept; and it was appropriate to this satire for me to allow a completely different type of intellect, intellect as *morality*, to come forward as a new and fascinating possibility in my fiction, because in liberal times such has long since not been considered possible, and to allow it to dominate the minds. Admit that the author of these conversations was not so naturally inept that he did not dream of some antiesthetic repercussions, of a necessary reaction against general art-infantilism—yes, of the rehabilitation of virtue. But I must admit the insufficiency of my intuition: what I did not dream of, would never have allowed myself to dream of—and indeed certainly not because my knowledge was bound to my personal self, to my own existence, and had not extended sensitive literary antennae outward—what I could *not* allow myself to dream of was the resurrection of virtue in political form, the renewed possibility of a moral priesthood of sentimental-terroristic-republican stamp, in a word: the renaissance of the Jacobin.

It is a fact—and is it not true, we are the last to close our eyes to such a remarkable if also loathsome fact! Even earlier, at that place in the previous chapter where we talked about the dogmatic intellect, about the *pharisaism* of the intellect, it dawned on us that it was a pharisaism that had long been known historically and long been studied psychologically; not by chance, even if involuntarily, were there reminiscences of Taine's Jacobin-psychology. Everywhere where literature and politics permeate one another, where intellect is politicized, where all the great abstractions: truth, freedom, justice and humanity, stop being moral-philosophical problems of the ultimate, highest type, and take on purely political significance, where they are totally related to state-social matters, and, depending upon their individual definitions in this connection, all in all signify quite simply the radical republic; where politics in turn is literarized and takes on the character of the high-minded phrase worthy of a human being, of rhetoric in honor of the "human race": in all these places (it seems unavoidable) an intellectual type must appear that completely reproduces all the characteristics of Jacobinism.

Our political intellectual, civilization's literary man, is such a type. He is not a Social Democrat, naturally not. How could not the objective activity of the labor unions, even before the war, but have bored and irritated his fiery spirit? What philistines these war financiers were, these Scheidemanns, Heines, Davids, Franks, and the others who stood by Germany at the moment of most pressing vital need—as Bebel and others had predicted, by the way. They had to—let that be said in their favor. If only for the sake of the party, of their flock of lambs, the working class, "who would have had to taste the cup of sorrow to the bitterest dregs," they could not, would not, allow the *Reich* to be overwhelmed, crushed, its political and economic future ruined—this is how they justified themselves. But there is the well-founded suspicion that they not only "*had to*" with their heads, but also a little with their hearts: and this was the philistinism, the mortal sin against the intellect, that will not be pardoned. It is unnecessary to say and to explain why the socialist "Policy of 4 August" in Germany was something incomparably more despicable than in the *free* countries! What, after the split in the German party had been completed, Comrade Renaudel pointed out in Jaurès's newspaper to the German minority: namely that they must not imagine that French socialism now also favored the shortening of the war and would support any peace other than one that the defeat of Germany implied; beyond any doubt, the situation of the German socialists was different from that of the French ones, and the latter would now remain all the more dedicated to national defense—to be sure, this proud message met in the bosom of civilization's literary man with an understanding that was equivalent to agreement. He has a heart, too, but as the song goes, it is "not here." From the rostrum Wilhelm Liebknecht has called the words, "defense of fatherland," a "phrase meant to confuse": this was meant for Germany, not for nobler peoples. Let one beware of raising the trivial objection: if the rise of a strong "left" is desirable for Germany, then first the positive participation of social democracy in the state is desirable, or, as far as it exists, to be saluted! It would be a misunderstanding to believe that our politician is concerned with *politics*—that is, with the reform, compromise, adaptation, and reconciliation of reality and intellect, or, to use old Adam Müller's words, of "justice" and "good sense" at all—and not rather with high-minded disorder, the foolish destruction of the state, the permanent rise of the mob, the revolution. Nor should one try to confuse him with a trick, by saying that the Russian revolution would not have been possible if one had enabled the Tsar to enter Berlin by denying appropriations for national defense! How could such a purely logical argument accomplish anything against the indescribable disgust that necessarily arises in him when he hears words such as those of a comrade named Alwin Saenger about the Western front, dated November 1915, long past the first excitement of the war:

> Today there can no longer be a Social Democrat who could ever be brought by mistakes of his own country to prefer to be an Englishman or a Frenchman. Today, there is no longer a Social Democrat who would not rise with the strongest words against every foreign criticism of us, of people, statesman, and prince. Today, there can be no Social Democrat who would not believe in an overwhelming influence of his great fatherland on the future history of mankind. Whoever does not feel his heart beating faster today when he hears the word, "German," is a poor, sick man!

By heaven, no, the politician of the intellect is not a Social Democrat. He would be one, possibly, if our anarchist-socialists and international revolutionaries of the most extreme type, to whom he is close intellectually, if not formally, were to be included in the left wing of the party—something that in my opinion would be a mistake, since these gentlemen are to be evaluated as pure geniuses, but hardly also as party politicians. But it is not really their language he speaks, either. His language, I hardly need mention, is not spoken at all in Germany; it is spoken in France. It is the jargon of a French party: of the *radical* one, of those *"fils de la Révolution,"* who inherited their political vocabulary, a chauvinistic-humanitarian phraseology, from the Jacobins; with them, the radicals of the Parisian parliament, civilization's literary man is the bearer and preserver of the immortal principles that official France, the France of the rhetorical bourgeois, proclaims. His is the vocabulary of the bourgeois revolution. Far from believing that political dilettantism, political bungling, can exist at all (this would be an assumption incompatible with democracy) he is replacing, as the Jacobin did, the study and serious understanding of living reality with "reason," *bel esprit*, and literary bravura. The human being, human rights, freedom, equality, reason, the people, the tyrants: he deals with these concepts with the same bewildering certainty that the Jacobin did, and like the Jacobin, he formulates a radical dogma from them whose radicalism certainly seems to a more conscientious mind to be frightful superficiality. Proudhon called J. J. Rousseau a person *"en qui la conscience n'était pas en dominante"*; and as is proper, the new Jacobin is a Rousseauean of the first water. Thus, for example, he does not pay the slightest respectful concern for the highly differentiated nature of our troubled continent. "Today there are no Frenchmen, Germans,

Spaniards, Englishmen anymore, no matter what one thinks about this; there are only Europeans who all have the same taste, the same passions, the same customs, because none has received a national stamp from particular institutions." This is what Rousseau said, and the neo-Jacobin believes it, too. He goes farther, as his predecessor also went farther; he finds that there are only human beings, human beings in general, that is, to say it in his language, the language of the eighteenth century: "feeling, reasonable beings, who, as such, avoid pain, seek pleasure and therefore happiness, who strive, that is, for a condition in which one perceives more pleasure than pain." Very simple. Too simple, in fact, to be flattering to "the human being." Nevertheless, our democrat means it to be flattering. He has the Jacobin's optimism; his preconceived idyllic ideas of reason and of the beautiful heart of the human being, his tendency toward demagoguery in the grandest style, toward flattery of mankind—the tendency to speak inanities to the human race. He has the Jacobin's bent to anarchy *and* to despotism, to sentimentality *and* to doctrinairism, terrorism, fanaticism, to radical dogma, to the guillotine. He has his terrible naiveté. Like the Jacobin, a stickler for the principles of humanity, he has a predilection for the scaffold. He also has the operatic gestures of the Jacobin, the eternally magnanimous pose—one hand on his heart and the other in the air. Above all, he has his instinct to pay exclusive attention to the political side of things, not their moral side, to be incomparably more interested in rights than in duties; to neglect conscience, but to give "pride in being a member of the human race" a wicked overnourishment. The outlawing and expulsion of those who disagree is completely consonant with his concept of freedom, just as it is with the Jacobin. He has the Jacobin's self-righteousness, his certainty and his sense of psychological security, which is intellectual callousness. Since he believes he possesses the truth, "the blind—ing—ly clear truth," his love of truth is in a bad way; for whoever is, so to speak, married to the truth, naturally has his role as lover and wooer far behind him. But his truth, this system of ideas that he has concocted for himself, that he is infinitely proud of, and that he never, not for a moment, abandons, so that he will not catch an intellectual cold—let one not believe that there is anything special about it; it is composed of radicalism, maudlinism, and humanitarian sentimentalism of a rather insipid kind, but put together in such a way that it is right, so that with it one can be *right* in the end: and dogmatism, egotistical self-preservation, is the basic instinct of this intellect. All by himself he has worked out an intellectual-political world view that has long been known and long been named: it is called the cosmopolitan-radical view, democratic internationalism. But since he worked his thinking through to this well-known cosmopolitan radicalism alone, independently, and almost without any reading, it seems to him so uniquely and overpoweringly true, so much the truth and the light, that he considers everyone to be an idiot or a scoundrel who refuses or even hesitates to profess it as well. He did not come upon and join this party and world view as something established, known, and in its way legitimate, he personally conceived of it and thought it out anew, it came over him as a gradual illumination and took hold of him to the point of delusion, of fanaticism. If he had come to know it as a world view among other world views, as one party among others, he would be more tolerant. Thus the childish man sees in the unconditional acceptance of this idea the criterion of all decency, all intellectual honesty, integrity, and virtue; he imagines himself justified, yes, morally bound, to relegate to the deepest pit every way of thinking that cannot and does not want to recognize what glitters so absolutely for him to be the light and the truth. There is only a "yes" or a "no," sheep and goats, one must "come forward". Tolerance and delay would be a crime. He believes he has to save his soul by not spending one more hour of even apparent companionship with obstinate fools who do not see what he sees. With pain and anger he separates himself from such a person in the steadfast belief that he owes it to truth and light to stride resolutely over human relationships. In all this there is much respectability, but also just as much comedy, yes, real foolishness, the French malignity of the doctrinaire, and all the ruin that is caused by the shameful delusion of dogmatism.

There is, I say, much respectability in all this: alas, only too much, too much respectability is in it, the righteousness of our type, of the political literary man and new Jacobin, has something scandalous in it, as did that of his ancestor, and for him the words seem to have been coined that Büchner's Danton directs to Robespierre: "Robespierre, you are shockingly righteous. I would be ashamed to run around between heaven and earth for thirty years with the same moral physiognomy just for the sake of the miserable pleasure of finding others worse than me. Is there really nothing in you that does not say to you quite softly, secretly: You are lying, you are lying!?" No, nothing. We are far too dignified to summon up such criticism and doubt in which *morality* would really just begin, or even to allow it to have any voice at all, because virtue beckons to us in a much too new and youthful light as the conqueror of estheticism and of *burgherly* doubt. The "rehabilitation of virtue" *against* doubt and criticism is of course our very own creation, at least it is a form, the true form, of this rehabilitation; we did *not* restore virtue as many would like to do, for example, by reclothing the attitude of humility and reverence that had become alien to a materialistic age with new justification and new beauty; on the contrary, our virtue is reason; the *dignity* of reason, free of doubt and completely without humility; we found it again by the means and on the path by which and on which it is always found and only can be found: it is the *idea*.

"General *ideas* and *great arrogance*," Goethe says, "always tend to cause terrible misfortune." Obviously a statement inspired by the Revolution. But what a juxtaposition, that of the "idea" with "great arrogance"— quite apart from the effects ascribed to this explosive combination! Is the idea necessarily bound to arrogance? Yes, this seems inevitable. All Jacobinism, old and new, proves it. And how could it be otherwise, how could the idea not lead to virtue, and that means: to arrogance, since it *is* of course virtue itself, since it contains precisely that highly idealistic, political righteousness from which the satisfaction arises of finding others worse than oneself?

In an essay with the significant title, "Zarathustra Glosses," a German scholar and liberal philosopher, Leopold Ziegler, spoke recently about the *idea* and—taking a phrase from Adalbert Stifter—about that "humanitarianism of the dignity of reason" that one owes to the idea and that definitely is the most noble accomplishment of the rising middle class—the dignity of reason—a beautiful phrase! a humane, a humanistic phrase. And still—if dignity, the firmly established dignity of intellectual virtue, is a high and noble burgherly condition, it is not really a very moral, religious, or artistic, in short, not a very human condition, and—one must say it—it contains the danger of callousness. Should the human being be "dignified"—or should he be free, soft, pliable, approachable, humble, and open to the dangerous-harmful element? Which is the better, the more humane, and—why shy away from the phrase!—the more God-pleasing humanitarianism? That is the question; and the esthete—I mean the type that the politician calls an esthete—wants to know nothing about the rhetorization and the political exaltation of the idea as the politician manipulates it with such imcomparable dignity of reason. "The most noble accomplishment of the rising middle class." Here we face the question again of *who* here actually is the "burgher," anyway—the esthete, or his conqueror and adversary? The cult of the magnanimous idea is the burgherly democracy of 1789 and 1848. The idea, the virtuous phrase, was the irresistible explosive material of the burgherly Revolution, the only and the terrible weapon of the third estate and of its leader, the literary man—it, the idea of virtue, was what poor Louis XVI meant when he said that the cause of the third estate "appealed to noble feelings, and *therefore would always have public opinion with it*"; and it is the virtuous phrase, the politicized high idea, that is, that now once again has the democratic public world opinion with it—against Germany, and which one has now been beating and smashing us on the head with so long that it really would not be surprising if a certain stupefaction and confusion had finally taken hold of us, if we, shaken, had begun to lose faith in our psychic "special nature," to waver in our intellectual resistance.

We want to state that this is the way it is. The German, as he entered this war, had a few religious and philosophical experiences behind him that gave him a feeling of disgust for the political-democratic virtuous phrase. For many months he was disgusted at what seemed to him to be shameless humbug: at how, you see, the high ideas of the human race, such as "truth," "justice," and "freedom," were dragged through the political gutter, misused, dirtied, disfigured, made hypocritical, and degraded; he was truly disgusted by the venom these words produced in the loud mouth of democratic public world opinion, and that thickly coated it. But public opinion is crushingly strong; in political matters there is no other court of appeal. And even if the pressure from outside had been less terrible: Germany bore within herself the intellectual forces that could help to subvert her power of resistance—not long ago, just a few weeks, civilization's literary man, he who is urging the democratic politicization of the intellect and is handling the idea of virtue with the highest rhetorical dignity of reason, took up his splendid agitation again with a passion fired by current events, and worked with ever-growing success for the intellectual capitulation of Germany, which must, as our allied opponents also know very well, precede the physical capitulation. If, however, his democratic zeal was directed mainly at the disavowal, yes, the abolition of the "great man," then he knew well why: at all costs he must neutralize the psychological aftereffects of the *great man of the German nation* if he ever wants to achieve his goal, the democratic leveling and conformance of Germany—whether this great man is called Luther, Goethe, Bismarck, or Nietzsche.

Nietzsche and Bismarck! Is it permissible, is it possible, to place the two together, to name them together? But if Bismarck's struggle against the "ideologists," against humanitarian liberalism, in short, against the *idea*—was not exactly the same thing in politics as Nietzsche's criticism of morality and of the "raised chest" was in the philosophical-ethical sphere: then I do not understand anything, then I will never again believe I understand anything at all about spiritual things! I see and declare that what is now happening in Germany, that this process directed by civilization's literary man, who is preparing the intellectual capitulation of Germany and her integration in world democracy, is *reaction*—pardon the word, but it hits the mark—reaction against Nietzsche *and* Bismarck at the same time: and from this it can be seen how much the two, in spite of all the surface enmity that the one had for the other, are sons of one and the same spirit. *Liberal reaction*: this apparent self-contradiction is the experience of our times, and it signifies essentially the "rehabilitation of virtue," the restoration and re-enthroning of the humanitarian-democratic ideology, of the idea—I come to this conclusion with a sort of enraptured amazement. Nietzsche, who argued that the good European basically conducted a war against the eighteenth century, called it the *progress* of the nineteenth that it always understood the "return to nature" more and more decisively in the opposite sense from the way Rousseau understood it. "*Away from the idyll and the opera!*" That it was always more decisively anti-idealistic, more objective, more fearless, more industrious, more moderate, more distrustful of sudden changes, *antirevolutionary*. We have everything again: the idyll, the opera, the "idealism," the rhetoric, the slander of "doubt," the belief in politics, that means: in revolution; we have him again, the Jacobin. Enraptured amazement! To the "esthete" "the dignity of reason," as far as it meant the renunciation of doubt and freedom, the tyranny of the idea, its elevation, no, its debasement to a political idol and fetish—to the "esthete," the politicization of the intellect had seemed to be the corruption of intellect and nothing else. The great abstractions in the Phrygian cap: to the esthete they seemed to be intellectual mischief, a humanitarian masquerade similar to the one that the late Anacharsis Klootz* arranged. The great abstractions, truth, justice, freedom, humanity, stripped of shame and conscience, raging through the streets with flapping breasts as revolutionary furies: we knew that this had to be experienced once, that it had once been

---

* In 1792 Klootz, as a member of the revolutionary convention, advocated the spread of the revolution throughout Europe.

possible in Europe's history, thanks, that is, to a catastrophic cooperation of the shallowest philosophy that ever ruled with evil social conditions that would certainly have come to an end with terror in one way or another. That the political madness of the idea, the radical political subservience of the intellect, would ever again be possible with good intellectual conscience—could that be dreamt of? "Morality is again possible"—I know, I know. But that it, a single human lifetime after the draft of Nietzsche's main work (1887!) would be possible again in *this* form, as revolutionary sentimentalism and Jacobin virtue—but what am I saying: be possible!—*would establish itself as "the intellect" itself*—no! I did not believe this, and who can be surprised that I have gazed in amazement at it for a few years before bending over any kind of work again?

Art politicized, intellect politicized, morality politicized, the *idea*, all thought, feeling, desire, politicized—who wants to live in such a world? In a world where freedom means general and equal suffrage and nothing more? "In many spiritual orders, too," Treitschke said, "the superiors are elected by general suffrage, and who ever sought freedom in a nunnery?" Thus speaks, one should believe, a completely politically attuned thinker; a German, however, whose very Germanness makes it impossible for him to allow the concept of freedom to become absorbed in the political sphere, even for a moment. That is something for the Italian Carbonaro, for Giuseppe Mazzini, for example. "The election law," he cries, "*the principle of every freedom*." That is clear. When I want to read something that makes my stomach turn, that turns everything in me into contradiction (and this can, at times, be useful), I open up the volume of Mazzini that one day, quite without any effort on my part or credit to me, came into my hands, as if sent by heaven, and to which I not only owe the beginning of my meager insight into the essence of political virtue, but which also taught me where the German radical literary man actually got the style, gesture, breath control, and passion of his political manifestos. Here I have the Latin Freemason, democrat, revolutionary literary man, and rhetorician of progress in his purest form and in his blossoming; here I learn to grasp "the intellect" as a thing between the Masonic Lodge and a Jacobin club as it should and must be understood again today after the rehabilitation of virtue. Here I can look with amazement at an activist who is sicklied o'er with no pale cast of thought, who sometimes stands declaiming before the people with the grandest of gestures, his eyes directed toward heaven, and sometimes struts around with his hands on his hips and with hissing breath, inciting, instigating, and agitating. Here the barricades are called "the people's throne," here I hear a person saying: "Morality and technology!" "*Christ and the press!*" Here the impossibility of reconciling freedom, *true* freedom, with the monarchial form of government is asserted with the highest passion, here the "*dogma*" of equality is "*raised to the religion of souls*," and the "revolutionary symbol" is summarized in the monstrous two words: "A principle—and its consequences." And its consequences! This formula, which Mazzini even needlessly designates expressly as the *revolutionary* symbol, is the formula of all intellectualism. Not for nothing does the political literary man call himself the true intellectual. And we know now, in a flash we grasp it quite clearly, that what he understands by intellectualism, and what we understand by it with him, is the dullest, most callous, inhuman doctrinairism, and nothing else.

But at the same time it is *virtue*, indeed, virtue in several senses, first of all, for example, as the Rousseauean return to nature, as *simplification*—even if only as a tendentious simplification, a selective simplification. The man who follows his principles to their logical conclusions finds it embarrassing when present-day thinkers again dare to approach the idea of God. He finds it hypocritical to speak of "God" a hundred and thirty years after the *Critique of Pure Reason*. But the reactionary, the *obscurantic* shamelessness with which today, in the land of moral criticism, the highest and intellectually most equivocal words: truth, freedom, and justice, are thrown around politically, signifies precisely that powerful simplification that is a manifestation of virtue.

From Russian books we know the watchword and the velleity of "self-simplification," where it has the same meaning as the personal "mixing with the people" of young idealists: of Nezhdanov, for example, the thin-skinned revolutionary in Turgenev's *Virgin Soil*, a politicized esthete who suffered so much from "simplification" because drinking bad brandy went with it. "If one has to drink brandy in order to 'simplify oneself,'—then I most humbly say no thanks!" he cried. Well, our activists of "intellect" and of a politically resolute love of humanity are far from trying any real "mixing with the people." Their relationship to the "people" is altogether of a platonic, principled and impractical nature—a human impossibility, since they are completely lacking in all humor, all gentleness, congeniality, direct human friendliness, in short, in the *love* that is necessary to really speak the language of the people; and their "love of humanity" is basically a rhetorical, ridiculously cheap, writing-table high-mindedness that requires no personal sacrifice at all.

The "simplification" is therefore limited in their case completely to the intellectual sphere; not even their artistic nature is involved in it, because it is very far from renouncing aristocratic refinement. Nevertheless, would they not fare the same as poor Nezhdanov, who quickly despaired of simplification because he could not stand brandy? If the "dignity of reason" means the politicization and rhetorization of the idea, its degeneration to the democratic phrase of virtue—then I most humbly say no thanks! Would they not learn one day to speak like this?

Alexei Nezhdanov was not only of aristocratic background, but also an artistic nature, and Turgenev makes it beautifully clear that this was why he had to fail. One should not lie to oneself for the sake of a system: art is not on good terms with virtue, it has seldom or never been so, as far, that is, as virtue means democratic progress—and this is what it is supposed to mean, is it not? Nevertheless, it is precisely this lie that one today, "for the sake of life," wants to make acceptable. To place art in the service of progress, to make it the chief witness for progress, to raise the degree to which it promotes progress to the criterion of its rank and value: this is seriously being attempted today; and the criticism, for example, that a German radical literary man recently made of Werner von Heidenstam's novel, *Charles XII and His Warriors*, in which he declared that we were no longer interested in military-heroic matters, but in oppressed humanity that was not treated justly in those (this is very pretty), in *those* confused times; the increasing self-awareness and revolt of the subjects were more important than the egotism of the kings, and *Charles XII* was definitely only a "backwards-oriented novel"—this criticism was such an attempt. But art will always be "backwards-oriented," reactionary. It is not for nothing that it is included, together with religion, among the anti-intellectual powers; and it is democratic humbug to equate the artist with the "intellectual." Art will never be moral in the political sense, never virtuous; progress will never be able to depend upon it. It has a basically undependable, treacherous tendency; its joy in scandalous antireason, its tendency to beauty-creating "barbarism," cannot be rooted out, yes, even if one calls this tendency hysterical, anti-intellectual, and immoral to the point of being a danger to the world: it is an immortal fact, and if one wanted to, or could, extirpate it from the world, one would certainly have freed the world from a grave danger, but at the same time one would almost certainly have freed it of art as well—and only a few want that. An irrational power, but a great power; and the attachment of people to it proves that people neither can nor want to make do with rationality, that is; with the famous three-part equation of democratic wisdom, "reason = virtue = happiness." Let one read, in this connection, the sinfully enthusiastic description that Baudelaire gives of the *Tannhäuser* march! "Who could," he cries, "in listening to these chords, which are so rich and proud, to this elegantly cadenced, magnificent rhythm, these royal fanfares, imagine anything else than a magical pomp, a parade of heroic men in shining costumes, all of great stature, all of strong will and naive belief, just as magnificent in their joys as terrible in their battles?" And who, let us add, could fail to recognize that it is, in the sense of political virtue, the most *questionable* ideas that art awakens here? Yesterday I heard Tchaikovsky's *Symphonie Pathétique*, this thoroughly dangerous work in its sweetness and savagery, which one neither hears nor understands without experiencing the irreconcilable antithesis of art and the spirit of literary virtue. I am thinking of the third movement with its *malicious* march music, which, if we had a censor in the service of democratic enlightenment, would absolutely have to be forbidden. So long as such things may not only be composed, but also performed; so long as this trumpet blare and cymbal clash is allowed among cultured people; so long, allow me to say, will there be wars on earth. Art is a *conservative* power, the strongest of all; it preserves spiritual possibilities that without it—perhaps—would die out. So long as poets are possible—and they will always be so—whose wish and lament is to lie down in the deepest woods to forget "these stupid times,"

> Of princely deeds and works
> Of ancient honor and pomp,
> And what may strengthen the soul,
> Dreaming away the long night — *

so long as their *forward*-directed longing will call forth the time when the Lord will put an end to things and tear from the deceitful ones their unjust power:

> Then Aurora will dawn
> *High* up over the forest,

---

* Von fürstlichen Taten und Werken,
  Von alter Ehre und Pracht,
  Und was die Seele mag stärken,
  Verträumend die lange Nacht —

Then there will be something to sing and defeat
Then, loyal ones, *awake* — *

(Joseph von Eichendorff wrote this poem, and Hans Pfitzner put it to magnificent music in 1915)

—so long, I say, will the rule of that three-part equation, will democracy
on earth, not be secure. Let every utopia of progress, let the sanctification
of the earth by reason—every dream of social eudaemonism be fulfilled,
the pacified, esperanto world become reality: air buses breeze over a
"human race" that is clothed in white, pious with reason, statelessly-
unified, monolingual, in the ultimate mastery of technology, with
electric television: art will still live, and it will form an element of
uncertainty and preserve the possibility, the conceivability, of relapse.
It will speak of passion and unreason; it will present, cultivate and
celebrate passion and unreason, hold primordial thoughts and instincts
in honor, keep them *awake* or reawaken them with great force, the
thought and instinct of war, for example. One will not be able to forbid
it, because that would go against freedom. Or will "the human race"
live under absolutism, under the *tyranny* of reason, of virtue and of
happiness? Then it is all the more probable that art will go completely
into the opposition—and that everything that finds itself opposed to
this ultimate tyranny will hold passionately to it. Art will seize the
leadership of that party that seeks to overthrow the rule of virtue—and
it is a ravishing leader. In short, then: war, heroism of a reactionary
type, all the mischief of unreason, will be thinkable and therefore
possible so long as art exists, and its life will last and end only with that
of the "human race."

But do let us speak more personally. Let us leave all conjectures about
the future role of art out of the picture and stay with its bearer, the
psychological species, "artist," and with *his* relationship to virtue—it will
immediately have revealed itself as a nonrelationship, or at least as a
quite loose and uncertain relationship. Not that we would be so foppish
as to recommend the life style of the artist to the curiosity of the
burgher as an immoral, "amoral" life style, as has sometimes been the
fashion: the measure of personal ethics and even of social love that is
inherent in a productive artistic life is, under all circumstances, a
respectable measure—we shall let this stand. But just as the artistic nature

---

* Da wird Aurora tagen
  Hoch über den Wald hinauf,
  Da gibt's was zu singen und schlagen,
  Da wacht, ihr Getreuen, *auf* —

is something quite different from cheap libertinism, so is morality something different, and indeed, something *completely* different from virtuousness, and circumstances force us to insist that this distinction not be neglected.

The moralist is different from the virtuous person in that he is open to the dangerous-harmful element; that he, as it says in the Bible, "does not resist evil"—something that the paragon of virtue always does with the most respectable success. What is the dangerous-harmful element? Shepherds of the soul call it *sin*. But this grave, frightful word, too, is still just a word and can be used in various ways. There is sin in the sense of the church and sin in the sense of humanism, of humanitarianism, of science, of the emancipation of the "human being." In any case, "sin" is *doubt*; the pull to the forbidden, the drive to adventure, to lose oneself, to abandon oneself, to experience, to explore, to understand; it is the seductive and the tempting element. Only philistines will rush to call this drive immoral; no one will deny that it is sinful. Let us even go back a little and digress to clarify the special case of sin in the humanistic sense.

In all nations there are individuals today, too, who need be neither stupid nor really bad because they cling less cheerfully and believingly to the bold and generous idea of "progress" than—well, than civilization's literary man. They recognize and admire progress in the technical area and in the sciences, from which, however, philosophy must already be excepted, and they find that in the field of the arts there is much less to be said of progress. Progress appears to them, therefore, to belong to civilization, not to culture; to be a matter of experience, cleverness, politics, practical world adjustment and progress in decency, in short, of civilization, but not of morality and the soul. They insist (together with old Karl Jentsch, who does so in his wise book, *Christianity and Church*) that

> all progress of science and technology and even of humanitarianism has never made the human being happier, never more content, but always only more discontented. Every improvement in external living conditions becomes, as soon as one has become used to it, something taken for granted that pleases no one anymore, and the demand is directed toward improvements that one cannot have right now. In the process, all cultural progress has not been able to rid the world of the terrible bodily suffering that at all times strikes thousands and threatens everyone. But as far as society can be made responsible for the existing evils, the hope of remedying them through a perfect social order proves to be utopian.

Cultural progress has eliminated certain abominable forms of torment. In general, however, the changes in the social situation occur in such a way that every technical, economic, *social, political* improvement brings us new evils to replace those it has eliminated. Every attempt to draft a plan for a technically or morally perfect social order becomes laughable and absurd; in the moral sphere simply because people have such different opinions about what is morally perfect and desirable that in more primitive times they smash each other's heads over the question, and in more polite times the parties hurl scorn and insults at one another, and not seldom *hate each other mortally because of such differences of opinion*. Moreover, a more perfect social state of the future could not help the billions of people who have suffered under the earlier, more imperfect conditions.

All this is true, is the simple, human truth, and whoever says otherwise is only being rhetorical. Lack of moderation in the evaluation of social life, dressing it up with unconditional and religious solemnity, seems to the type of people I have been talking about to be foolish and wrong, and for good reason they do not like to hear the belief in a "better and freer human race" proclaimed all too boastfully. They are willing to appreciate the intellectual means of progress, the enlightenment, that is; but their *love* belongs much more to what can never be explained, to the eternal secret, and they tend to find the human being more beautiful in an attitude of worship than in one of emancipation. This is a matter of taste, or, if the word sounds too frivolous, then one of mood. Conservatism in general, one may say, is a mood, while progressiveness is a principle; and here lies, it seems to me, the human superiority of the former over the latter. One may nevertheless call this mood *pathological* without running into much contradiction; for in a certain sense, for convenience let us call it the individualistic-cultural sense, disease is of course no counterargument. It has produced the most priceless works. And moreover, the idea of disease and depression is much too unclear for care not to be advised in dealing with it. It seems to depend completely upon one's point of view *which* periods in intellectual-political life one wants to designate and interpret as depressive: for we are reminded that Nietzsche blamed the "deep mediocrity" of the Englishmen for having caused a collective *depression* of the European spirit, and indeed at the time when they had introduced "modern ideas," the "ideas of the eighteenth century," into the world, and he called the Frenchmen their apers, actors, and first real victims. And whether one may or must devalue the French movement of the last decade before the war—a movement of doubtlessly reactionary nature, since it was mainly the protest of a young France against the radical break with her past, with her medieval period, with all prerevolutionary and preclassical cultural values: whether one may or must devalue this national movement as a manifestation of *depression*, is something that can be argued about, even if civilization's literary man declares the arguments to be inadmissible.

It is another matter when the humanist (and civilization's literary man is a humanist) stigmatizes that devious tendency and mood as *sin*—and indeed, as sin against the "human being": we feel with him that there *is* sin in the humanistic sense. But to this one can at least reply that doubt and sin are more productive and humanly liberating than virtue, the dignity of reason, the possessive pride of the truth-philistine, and the transfigured masculinity of a teacher of democracy. *Vérité, fécondité, travail, justice*—yes, the democratic humanist is a paragon of virtue, his uprighteousness is almost maddening, his claim that he finds others worse than he is so righteous it is a horror—and here again the cursed enigmatic question cannot be avoided—*who* is really the "burgher," after all: the esthete or his conqueror, the politician? An artist, I think, remains to his last breath an adventurer of feeling and of intellect, tending toward deviousness and the abyss, open to the dangerous-harmful element. His task itself requires psychological-intellectual freedom of movement; it demands from him that he be at home in many, and also in evil worlds; it tolerates no settling down on any truth, and no dignity of virtue. The artist is and remains a gypsy, even assuming that he is a German artist of burgherly culture. Since it is his job to speak through many characters, he is by necessity a dialectician. But dialectics, Goethe says, "is the cultivation of the *spirit of contradiction*, which is given to the human being so he can learn to recognize the difference between things." We know well that dialectics in the sense of belief and virtue is sin, is evil; it is precisely for this reason that the moral command, "Resist not evil!" is a command for artists and moralists—obviously not for politicians. For the politican *resists* evil—and how he resists it! Do we have to insist that he is not at all a gypsy and an adventurer, but much more the opposite of this, a pedant, a man of principle, a solid man, a virtuous man, a man of secure soul who has said adieu to every intellectual vagabondage, who looks neither to the right nor to the left, but steadfastly keeps his eye on *the* path, the narrow path of virtue and of progress that one can tread only by means of the doctrine? He obviously has a hellish fear of dialectics, and he quickly calls any objection to the "teaching" a sophistry—in spite of the fact that one could, with the same justification, call every one of his own principles of salvation sophistic. His "politicization of the intellect," his recovery of the "idea," his "rehabilitation of virtue," his marching forward to moralizingly pugnacious purposefulness, means—it is impossible to mistake it, it ought to be impossible for him, too—means the end of all bohemian life, of all irony and melancholy, all that is loosely bound together, that does not belong, all gallows humor, all innocence and childlikeness, in short, all that one had previously considered "decent," artistic; it means "masculine maturity," solid and transfigured masculinity, which no longer has much to do with artistic nature: now, with one's hair half-long in the nape of one's neck, one stands as a *praeceptor patriae* before the younger generation, harangues it in the classical style of virtue, instructs it in democracy, and is not ashamed.

One is not even ashamed anymore of being an *opportunist*—I mean: of rejecting and excluding with cold strictness everything as "not to be considered" when allowing its entry seems *not* to be opportune to the interest of the doctrine of progress, of purposefulness. Politics against the polis, the state, is allowed. To have intellect against "the intellect" is *not* allowed. That is forbidden. It is immoral because inopportune. The same is true to a great extent for beauty, which as the following example shows, can be found to be completely inadmissible.

Five years have gone by since I read and re-read with the greatest sympathy and joy *L'Annonce faite á Marie* by Claudel: I declared at the time that I had received the strongest poetic—altogether the strongest artistic impression from it that I had received for a very long time. Why not say that I enjoy admiring, that I like to lose myself, that I am basically bored when there is nothing to love, to conquer, and to master? Then I feel old, but enthusiasm for any creation teaches me that I am not yet old, and lets me live again as before, when the twenty-year-old passionately took in the work of Wagner. Well, at the time I was in love with the ingenious Christianity of that French drama, whose breath is so deep and sincere; with the precious mixture of clarity and mysticism that it offers, its divine humanity, its angelic voice, its high, tender and humble sensibility, the spirituality of its sickness, the devoted piety of its artistic nature—"*Va au ciel d'un seul trait! Quant à moi pour monter un peu il me faut tout l'ouvrage d'une cathédrale et ses profondes fondations*"—and I am completely assured that this tendency signifies something more and better than gourmand taste and literary dilettantism. Is it not above all a feeling of joy in becoming aware of a France that is much too lovable for one not to be allowed to call it the true France: the *douce*

France of our dreams, whose sight is salvation from the poisonous grandiloquence, the snub-nosed vulgarity of the France presided over by M. Poincaré? Claudel's France hates us, too, I know. But that is a better, nobler hatred than that of the rhetorician-bourgeois; this I will stick to. What does it matter that the poet of the *Annunciation*, who lived as a consul in Germany, disparaged Germany during the war from his ardent, patriotic heart? In the depths of his soul he must feel like that French landed aristocrat from the north, whose castle Wilhelm II visited, and who said to him: "Sire, you are our enemy; but still, you are an emperor and not a lawyer." France and Germany, they were once *one country* in the womb of time, before their life paths separated and deadly hatred came between them. They are bound by a common artistic-metaphysical possession, which cannot be solely attributed to either one of the two: From the German spirit France created the Gothic style. Has one noticed to what extent the *Annunciation* in Hegner's translation has the effect of an original work? How effortlessly Anne Vercors of the French text is transformed into Andreas Gradherz of the German one, Pierre de Craon into a Peter von Ulm, the *Maire* of Chevoche into the Mayor of Rothenstein? Yes, love for this work of art is above all joy in becoming aware of ancient brotherhood that was more than brotherhood, that was unity.

I was trustful enough to speak of this to the intellectual politician and radical literary man—tactlessly, as I immediately saw. He shrugged his shoulders, he did not want to know about it. No, that would not do. I urged it upon him in a completely tactless way. I pleaded for the work. I tried at least to awaken my companion's historical sense for it, to win him over at least to appreciating this unprecedentedly deep penetration into the soul of the Middle Ages, to make him appreciate objectively the most wonderful spiritually enriching discoveries about this soul. No. "But things like this must definitely be permitted," I cried, about to despair. He was silent. Perhaps he had a moment's horror at his magnificent virtue. A little more mildly he answered: "Perhaps. *But there are more important things.*" There are more important things! I do not know what more important things there are or can be than what is sublime and good, even if it does not prove directly useful to progress and to Prussian voting rights. Yes, if it not only did not do that, if it even indirectly worked against progress and the improvement of Prussian voting rights—could an artist for this reason shut himself off in a hard political way from the high and the good? Richard Dehmel, whom the young French lyricists have probably studied, had read

Claudel's drama at the time. He wrote to the translator: "Here all intellect's superior knowledge is silent, *here the soul looks on breathlessly.*" What does a radical literary man care about the soul? "There are more important things." Such as "intellect." Such as democratic progress and what promotes it. But what does *not* promote it—a poem, for instance, in which to be sure and by all means the scandalous phrase appears, "To each his due, therein lies justice"—is inopportune and therefore forbidden. Does one now understand what it means "to resist evil?" And did I say too much when I called the intellectual politician a Jacobin and a man of terror?

I am glad that the context offers a good opportunity to talk about an experience during this war that I want very much to relate; and I would be wrong to be surprised at this coincidence, because the work in question would not have become such an experience for me if it had been less deeply and intimately tied up with the intellectual connections I am investigating. A work of art, then, once again a foreign work, not of French-Catholic sentimentality, however, but German—*still* German (for it has a somewhat late, later-day German quality about it that looks toward the triumphant new era with intellectual melancholy, even though it is rich in artistic energies for its individual part). The *Annunciation* was an expedient, I see that now. Here is the same thing *in German*, and an incomparably more intimate, direct affirmation is possible here.

I have heard Hans Pfitzner's musical legend, *Palestrina*, three times now, and remarkably easily and quickly I made this difficult and audacious production into my own, my intimate possession. This work, something ultimate, consciously ultimate, from the sphere of Schopenhauer and Wagner, of romanticism, with its characteristics reminiscent of Dürer and Faust, its metaphysical mood, its ethos of "cross, death and grave," its mixture of music, pessimism and humor—it is completely "to the point," to the point of this book, its appearance at this moment brought me the consolation and blessing of complete sympathy, it agrees with my innermost idea of humanity, it makes me positive, releases me from polemics, and in it my feeling has been offered a great object it can gratefully join with until, healed and reassured, it is ready to create again itself; seen from this work, repulsiveness lies in an unreal light.

Did Pfitzner's musical poem have something new to say to me? Hardly. But I must have wanted to the point of languishing to hear what was deeply and intimately familiar, to make it my own again; yes, the extraordinary effect it immediately had on me at that first morning performance before an amphitheater of experts to whom I in no way belong, the rapidity with which I absorbed it, can only be explained by an unusual tension of preparedness and receptivity that the times, the hostility of the times, had brought forth in me. I shy away from an analysis, not only because I basically hate the effect of finality that the critical word produces, but especially because dissection means division, a sequence of observation, the separation of the intellectual and the artistic elements, for example, by which I am afraid of damaging the whole. Naturally there is nothing but unity here. But art is strong in and for itself, and it also overpowers those who would taboo the intellectual will it serves if they understood it. The product of a melancholically alienated way of thinking that is at odds with the times can be strong, happy, and victorious through the talent that helps it to triumph over the minds of thousands. In the process it happens then, of course, that something is taken—and probably even taken with the artist's consent—for talent, art, and pure stylization, which is really something quite different, something psychologically far more imme- diate. These archaic fifths and fourths, these organ sounds and liturgical finales—are they nothing but mimicry and historical atmosphere? Do they not demonstrate at the same time a psychological tendency and intellectual inclination in which one must, I fear, recognize the opposite of a politically virtuous tendency and mood? Let us put the question aside! Talent is what conquers. Let us admire it!

What great artistry, in combination with the most nervous agility, penetrating harmonic audacity with a pious ancestral style! One knows the master school where this was learned. The psychologically modern element, all the refinement of this insertion of harmonic retardations, how purely organically it joins itself to what is musical milieu, what, therefore, is humble-primitive, Middle Ages, frugality, the breath of the grave, crypt and skeleton, in this romantic musical score! The charming theme of Ighino, which is repeated most beautifully in the prelude to the third act, I immediately locked into my heart—this melodious symbol of the personality of a child full of wistfulness and loyalty who gladly leaves what is splendid and new and remains sympathetic to the old. The passage is wonderful; I believe the most subtle and the sweetest part of the work is connected with it. How much the work gains simultaneously in chasteness and in the power of deliverance when it is painfully born out of the music, when the music paints those agonies and inhibitions of the soul from which the final element, the difficult word, breaks free and strives upward: for example in the rhythmically incomparable measures that prepare Ighino's entry and outburst, "The old father's grief . . ." And what breast that was still breathing quietly would not suddenly—and inevitably, over and over—be shaken by sobs when the pure voice of the child sings of Palestrina's glory, his "genuine glory—

> that quietly and in time
> Enveloped him like a festive raiment?"*

A blessed-lyrical moment whose beauty gains self-confidence as the melodic passage is immediately repeated in lighter instrumentation. Very late, in the third act, it is touched on once more by way of allusion: there where Ighino assures his father that one will still speak of him in the most distant future; and with envy one perceives again here, as in other places, what possibilities of unification and of ingenious or intimately thoughtful deepening the Wagnerian-motif art work provides.

Again, I am leaving aside all ethical and intellectual considerations in order for the present to exclusively admire the esthetic powers and merits of the work. I survey the extensive but artistically compactly filled scenario of the first act, and find that it is joined together unusually beautifully and easily, in fortunate necessity. The conversation of the boys is followed by the emotional scene between Palestrina and the prelate; immediately there is the "predecessor" scene, faded and filled with ghostly sounds of the past, this heartfelt vision, the deep, struggling conversation in the night of a living person, piously and nobly filled with tradition, with the masters . . . they disappear, from distress and darkness the lonely one cries upward, then the angel's voice rises up heart-stirringly into the *Kyrie*, the tired one's hour of grace begins, he bends his ear to the shadowy mouth of his dead sweetheart, light bursts from the depths, the endless choruses break out in the *Gloria in excelsis*, to the accompaniment of all their harps they sing to him of perfection and peace. Then the high tension is resolved, everything becomes pale, Palestrina hangs exhausted in his armchair, and now? Could it be possible to close this act without exhaustion, an act that is a true celebration in honor of painful artistic genius and an apotheosis of music, after it has risen to such visions? To bring forth

* der still und mit der Zeit
  Sich um ihn legte wie ein Feierkleid?"

another effect that even exceeds such a climax? What joy to see how this is possible, how such a possibility has long been prepared with that exquisite, permissible, yes, imperative and enthusiastic cleverness, circumspection, and politics of art! Pay attention! Through the window of Palestrina's workroom one becomes aware of the cupolas of Rome. Very early, as early as the end of the first scene, when Silla, the promising pupil who sides with the Florentine futurists, looks out over Rome and takes leave of the conservative old nest with pleasantly ironical phrases, the orchestra, after the majestically sweeping motif of the city, begins a moderately strong, monotonous dinning in seconds that seems as if it will never end, and whose purpose, for the moment, is undiscoverable. The people exchanged amazed and smiling looks at this strange accompaniment, and there was no one who would have prophesied any dramatic future to this whimsically nonsensical idea. Pay attention, I say! Since then more than an hour has gone by in reality, but by illusion a whole night, and a world of things has happened. The disappearing angelic glory has left earthly dawn behind, the day is rising rapidly in a red glow over the cupolas outside, there is Rome, its powerful theme announced clearly and ostentatiously in the orchestra—and then, truly, the forgotten dinning of yesterday evening starts up again, it is like a ringing, yes, they are bells, the morning bells of Rome, not real bells, only imitated by the orchestra, but in such a way as massive swinging, resounding, droning and dinning church bells have never been imitated artistically before—a colossal swinging of daringly harmonized seconds in which, as in the roar of a waterfall that one's ears cannot master, every kind of pitch and vibration, the thundering, roaring and crashing, mix with the greatest string falsetto, exactly as it is when hundreds of resounding bells seem to have set the whole atmosphere into vibration and to want to blow up the firmament. It is an enormous effect! The master, who is slumbering at the side in his chair, the holy city in a purple glow that, as it shines through the window, glorifies the pitiful locale of nocturnal creative ecstasy, and in addition the powerful resounding of the bells that only retreats when the boys, who have had a good night's sleep, collect the sheets of music that are spread around the room and exchange a few lines; and that then resumes its powerful course again until the curtain falls.

I admire as a compositional beauty the way in which the powerful figure of Cardinal Borromeo, this boisterous patron, combines the clerical-intellectual world of Palestrina with the world of reality, the world of the second act. But this second act, standing as it does in its turbulent colorfulness between the first and the third, is itself a compositional beauty. Contrary to the esthetic judgment of most people, I enjoy this impossibility made possible, in a pure drama of ideas that is, if not "plot," then at least an intellectually illuminated, colorful event. Life in the light of thought—what better thing can art provide us, what more entertaining? I have actually heard the opinion: Meyerbeer, historical opera. This is completely erroneous. To tell everything—perhaps I was personally better prepared than others to avoid this misunderstanding; perhaps I had long been well-acquainted with the main intention here: to let the idea speak through historical detail, and only in this way to give this detail dramatic tension. At any rate, every reproof here attacks the whole work, the conception. One may believe that the idea of this composition: art, life, and art again, was the earliest fog, the first thing that the poet actually *saw*.

Pessimism and humor—I have never perceived their correlation more strongly and never more sympathetically than in the face of the second Palestrina act. The optimist, the reformer, in a word, the politician, is never a humorist; he is lofty-rhetorical. The pessimistic moral philosopher, however, whom one likes to call today quite figuratively the "esthete," will behave toward the world of will, reality, guilt and practical affairs with a natural preference for humor; as an artist he sees them as picturesque and amusing, in sharp contrast to the quiet dignity of intellectual life: and only in this contrast rests the dramatic nature of the Council scenes in which the product of that exuberant night that we experienced, Palestrina's mass, becomes an object of political negotiation. Truly, what type of life and reality would be more grotesque, tumultuous and funny in the sense of this contrast than politics? The second act is nothing other than a colorful and affectionately studied satire on politics, specifically on its immediately dramatic form, the parliament. That it is a parliament of clerical men increases the ridiculousness and lack of dignity to the extreme. Admittedly, music is original passion; and therefore the orchestral prelude, perhaps the most splendid musical piece of the evening, has a completely stirring effect: this crashing, storming, falling, breath-taking agitation, the most admirable moment of which is the fourfold, gasping onset of the main motif (piano score, page 174 at the top), tragically illustrates Palestrina's statement about the "movement that life constantly whips us into." It is a description, only too full of experience, of the dreadful Samsara. And still it is precisely this fundamental passion of the music that together with the human element creates the overpoweringly funny part. I am thinking of the figure of the patriarch Abdisu of Assyria and the sounds of unimagined and fantastic absurdity with which the orchestra accompanies his sacerdotal jubilation over "*the* day" and "*this* work," and his mildly unsuccessful parliamentary speech. Never at all has the moving comedy of doddering old age and venerable innocence been so thoroughly perceived and raised to such a special effect.

Say what you will, the act is entertaining. The richness of accents, the sharpness of the types, the transparency of ideas, lend it the sublime charm of victorious art. The spritely Bishop of Budoja, the unbridledly arrogant Spaniard, the conceited Cardinal Novagerio, in whose role the torture motif does its infamous work: life is in motion, art plays lights upon it, gathers it to its highest energy—and what a homecoming, then, to *art itself*, to the tidy cell of the creative artist, to the world of loneliness and of loyalty. The Pope sings hexameters—a singularly grand idea. The final note is of resignation and peace, "musical thought" on the harmonium, only lightly disturbed by distant, rapid *evvivas* to the chirping of the mandolins. And quietly the orchestra speaks the final word that was also the initial word, and is a secret.

I have not said anything yet about Pierluigi Palestrina, the musical hero of the work. I loved his figure from the moment he stepped with the prelate through the narrow door of his little room, the figure of the medieval master, of the artist, as popular romanticism does not at all dream of him, quiet, modest, simple, without claim to "passion," subdued and composed, wounded inside, dignified by suffering. I see him as, with his gentle, already graying head to one side, he lifts his hand slightly toward the young pupils and says, "Be pious and quiet." Infinite sympathy wells up. "Be pious and quiet!" How should a person obliged to create a work of art not be pious and quiet? Or should such a person perhaps run out into the street and make political gestures? But if this figure of an artist is not romantic in the cheap sense—it is still *romanticism*, simply by forming the lyrical center of the poem. Romantic art tends to be "backward pointing" in two senses: not only to the degree that it is, as Nietzsche says, "applied history," but also because it turns reflexively-reflectingly back toward the subject. Conversely, at least, all art that has art and the artist as its subject—no matter how skeptical-ironical the treatment of the subject may be—all *confessional* art, therefore, is *romantic* art; and especially here, even if also for some additional reasons, especially as an artistic confession, and indeed as one of the most ruthlessly radical type, *Palestrina* is a romantic work of art. But as far as politics is concerned, let one not hope that it has been dispensed with! Has it *never* been dispensed with, even though we were not aware of it?

At this moment, at the end of the third year of the war, Pfitzner publishes an essay entitled "The Danger of Futurism," written "on the occasion" of Busoni's *Plan for a New Esthetics of Musical Composition*—the prospectus of musical progress. Discussing esthetic questions, then, the German composer proves that he is well aware that the perspectives of his forty-five pages extend everywhere beyond the purely esthetic element. Truly, one would not go far wrong if one were to call his brochure a political pamphlet—although it even has antipolitical, that is, conservative tendencies. "Bach and Beethoven," he says, "are to be thought of as 'a beginning,' not 'as unsurpassable, final results.' Here we see in its most undisguised form this certain *goal-directed attitude* that I have always perceived to be hostile and opposed to all art." And after he has feuded with this "goal-directed attitude" for a page, he reaches one of those precise and truly profound statements that only genuine writers can find: "*Not art—the artist has a goal.*" Superb! But look closely at this: Is it esthetics or is it politics? Finally, it is probably something else, namely ethics—and therefore precisely what the intellectual politician calls "estheticism." But antipolitics is also politics, for politics is a terrible force: If one only *knows* about it, one has already succumbed to it. One has lost one's innocence.

Pfitzner says at another place—and I render here a quotation that fits this book as no other: "Well, we do not want to put a spoke in the wheel of the ruling world spirit; let what must come, come. Whether what comes is beautiful is another question; and whether it will be more beautiful than what we already have is a *crucial question for us*." And he continues:

> Busoni hopes that the *future* will bring everything for Western music, and he thinks of the present and the past as a stuttering beginning, as the preparation. But what if it is different? If we find ourselves at a high point or even if the high point has already gone by? If our past century or our past century and a half makes up the golden age of Western music, the height, the real period of splendor that will never return and that is followed by a decline, a decadence similar to the period after the blossoming of Greek tragedy? My feeling tends much more toward this opinion. Even Rubinstein has spoken seriously of a "*finis musicae.*" Should our present task not be, instead of seeking sixth tones, of wanting to rush forward in a raging tempo, of wanting to destroy everything that has been accomplished for the sake of something new—should our present task not rather be to encourage a loving contemplation of what has been

created and what is being created at present, and indeed, not just of what is floating at the surface? Error prevails in every age, but it is always of a different coloration. The stamp of the past epoch may have been philistinism; the stamp of the present one is much rather the opposite. The preceding era asked of all new things: Is this comfortable and understandable for me? The present one asks: Will I not look foolishly behind the times? That is the only difference.

It is the only one. One exaggerates only slightly when one claims that all the success of the past fifteen years has come from this new philistinism, which far exceeds the old honest one in ridiculousness and perniciousness; and what the German musician says here is exactly the same thing that a virile rationalist, the Dane, Johannes V. Jensen, says in his book, *Our Age*: "Futurism has also made its entry into New York salons. Never has a Moloch held slavish souls so much under his power as does the modern commanding shout of *progress*; even the Anglo-Saxons, from whom, after all, the concept of common sense comes, bend willingly to the whip; for one would rather run naked through the streets than be stupid, just like the dear old emperor in the fairy tale."

"The Danger of Futurism" is a child of the war, and it can therefore not be surprising that the essay shows a political coloring. *Palestrina*, on the other hand, was composed before the war—at least two-thirds of the score was finished before August 1914. Nevertheless, even at a quick glance, one can recognize the lines that unite the work with the polemic, and it is amazing to see how problems that the war "democratized," that it awakened to general, journalistic topicality, how every intensified emotion had urgently occupied us long before—and indeed not at all academically and in leisure hours, but most intimately, even in our works. We did not believe in the war—while we carried it within us.

The curtain has not been up ten minutes when young Silla bursts forth with the insidious verses:

> What a magnificently free impulse is going through our times!
> Do not thoughts go immediately
> To cheerful Florence,
> As if my own being might
> Free itself from the stupid yoke of the mob,
> And climb to the greatest height.
> As in my dear art the singing voices,

Always dependent, pitifully polyphonic,
Free themselves there to individual existence.
. . .
But I am pulled toward all the beautiful new things,
And as I see fame and life shining before me,
So strives certainly in constant liberation
The whole human race to unimagined heights!*

Again, is this esthetics, or is it politics? This time there is no third
possibility: it is politics—"by way of" esthetics. For liberation, individualistic emancipation in idealistic connection with the endless progress
of the human race, that is politics, *that is democracy*; and our poet
proclaims this through one who is "with it," one who "goes from one
end of the room to the other with elastically hopeful-joyful movements."

Palestrina, for his part, understands.

I know—but Silla thinks I still know nothing.
He is a youth, full of God's gift,
I feel no right to hinder him.**

And when Borromeo, the man of the strong church, asks zealously:
"Did you not even threaten him? Is your mood so mild?" Palestrina
answers: "Oh, I am the one who is threatened, not he!" Then he says:

The art of the masters of many hundred years,
Mysteriously united through the times
To build it continually into the wondrous cathedral,

---

* Welch herrlich freier Zug geht doch durch unsere Zeit!
Ist's nicht bei dem Gedanken schon
Ans heitere Florenz,
Als dürfte sich mein eignes Wesen
Vom dummen Joch der Allgemeinheit lösen,
Und die höchste Stufe erklimmen.
Wie in meiner lieben Kunst die Singestimmen,
Abhängig von jeher, erbärmlich polyphon,
Sich dort befrein zur Einzelexistenz.
. . .
Mich aber zieht es fort nach all dem Schönen, Neuen,
Und wie ich Ruhm und Leben leuchtend vor mir seh,
So steigt gewiß in stetigem Befreien
Die ganze Menschheit noch zu ungeahnter Höh!

** Ich weiß,—doch Silla glaubt, nichts wüßt' ich noch.
Es ist ein Junge, voll von Gottesgabe,
Zu wehren ihm fühl' ich in mir kein Recht.

To which they gave their lives, their trust,
And to which I, too, offered my poor existence:
He thinks it worn-out goods,
He believes it conquered, believes it dead.—

Now dilettantes in Florence have
From heathen, ancient writings
Artificially thought up theories
By which music will henceforth be made.

And Silla presses enthusiastically to them
And thinks and lives only in the new tones.
Perhaps he may be right! Who can know,
Whether the world now follows unimagined paths,
And what seemed *eternal* to us is not going with the wind?—
It's sad, of course—almost inconceivable . . .*

It would be impossible to express the psychology and mood of all conservatism more perfectly than with these words—I mean: a conservatism that is free, knowing, tender, intellectual, in a word: *ironical*, not a robust conservatism that believes in authority, like that of the cardinal, whom so much languid mood and doubt fill with healthy anger, and to whom the master "seems to be sick in his soul." For his part, Palestrina says to himself that the priest's soul is "quite secure," and speaks in thought to the deeply angered man:

Oh, if you only knew,
All that here is still murmuring, that would speak,

---

* Die Kunst der Meister vieler hundert Jahre,
   Geheimnisvoll verbündet durch die Zeiten
   Zum Wunderdom sie stetig aufzubau'n,
   Der sie ihr Leben schenkten, ihr Vertrau'n,
   Und der auch ich mein armes Dasein bot:
   Ihm dünkt sie abgegriff'ne alte Ware,
   Er glaubt sie überwunden, glaubt sie tot.—
      Nun haben Dilettanten in Florenz
      Aus heidnischen, antiken Schriften
      Sich Theorien künstlich ausgedacht,
      Nach denen wird fortan Musik gemacht.
   Und Silla drängt begeistert sich zu jenen,
   Und denkt und lebt nur in den neuen Tönen.
   Vielleicht wohl hat er recht! Wer kann es wissen,
   Ob jetzt die Welt nicht ungeahnte Wege geht,
   Und was uns *ewig* schien, nicht wie im Wind verweht?—
   Zwar trüb ist's zu denken—kaum zu fassen . . .

What darker thoughts, sinister—
You would deem the stake even too mild for me!*

An ambivalent master! Would one have thought that things could look like this in a conservative soul? Toward the cardinal he has an attitude of complete submissiveness, as is artistically good and the only proper attitude for the poor little conductor. But when things become serious, he refuses obedience in the most improper way. He does not want to write the saving mass, even if this should cause all the polyphonics to go to the devil. And when Borromeo, at the limit of his patience, asks: "And if the Pope orders it?" he answers: "He can order, but never my genius—only *me*." This is strong—and not very medieval. A pride and a freedom speak here that belong more to the "new times"—so that in the end the priest really finds that there is the smell of sulphur about him. If Palestrina is sick in his soul—and he surely is—his melancholy is nevertheless bound to a self-assurance that causes him to perceive the words from the mouths of his "predecessors."

The circle of exalted ones is full of longing
For him who will complete it: chosen one, You!**

Is it not true: we are inclined neither to perceive this predecessor scene nor the following one of angelic inspiration as a purely legendary miracle and as Catholic theater magic; for us these visions signify an illustration of the most ethical inner-being, and for us the call, "Chosen one, You!" comes from the same ego as the answer:

Not I—not I—I am weak, full of faults,
And my time of creation is past.
I am an old, dead tired man
At the end of a great time.
And before me I see nothing but sadness—
I can no longer force it from my soul.†

---

* O wüßtest du
Was hier noch alles flüstert, reden möchte,
Welch dunklere Gedanken, unheimliche—
Für mich der Holzstoß wär' dir noch zu mild!

** Der Kreis der Hochgestimmten ist voll Sehnen
Nach Jenem, der ihn schließt: Erwählter, Du!

† Nicht ich—nicht ich—; schwach bin ich, voller Fehle,
Und um ein Werden ist's in mir getan.
Ich bin ein alter, todesmüder Mann
Am Ende einer großen Zeit.
Und vor mir seh' ich nichts als Traurigkeit—
Ich kann es nicht mehr zwingen aus der Seele.

And whence this melancholy? Whence comes it that "in the middle
of life he finds himself lonely, deep in the forest, where there is no way
out of the darkness," and that he does not see how he could ever create,
rejoice, and love? But this, and no other, is the way it is when the height
and turning point of one's own life come together with the turning
point of the times, and when one is slow, attached, and already a little
tired. To have become mature in the atmosphere of *one* age and then
suddenly to see a new age approaching that one also belongs to with
part of one's being; to stand with one foot, say, in the Middle Ages, and
with the other in the Renaissance, is no small matter—always assuming
that one tends in attitude toward conservatism, which Palestrina definitely does. There is nothing more conservative than the words he
directs to the shades of the masters:

> You lived strongly in a strong time,
> That still lay darkly in unconsciousness
> Like a seed in the lap of Mother Earth.
> But the light of consciousness, deadly sharp,
> That rises disturbingly like the impudent day,
> Is hostile to the dream's sweet work, the artist's work;
> The strongest lays his weapons down before *such* power.*

And from here it is no longer far to the wish and resolution:

> With open eyes into the jaws of life
> I want to flee from the times—**

The anachronistic-Schopenhauerian paraphrase of a completely unseemly intention that is then also refused by the masters with categorical
sternness. "*Your earthly task*, Palestrina," they say, "your earthly task,
fulfill!"

---

* Ihr lebtet stark in einer starken Zeit,
   Die dunkel noch im Unbewußten lag
   Als wie ein Korn in Mutter-Erde-Schoß.
   Doch des Bewußtseins Licht, das tödlich grelle,
   Das störend aufsteigt wie der freche Tag,
   Ist feind dem süßen Traumgewirk, dem Künste-Schaffen;
   Der Stärkste streckt vor *solcher* Macht die Waffen.
** Mit off'nen Augen in des Lebens Rachen
   Will flieh'n ich aus der Zeit—,

The capstone to the building
Be ready to lay;
That is the meaning of the times.
When you show your whole picture,
When your form is completed,
Just as it has sprung from
The creative spirit from the beginning:
Then you will shine forth brightly, then you will resound purely,
Pierluigi, You,
On its beautiful chain
The last stone.*

What else do these verses intend than the prosaic words of the polemic: "Not art, the *artist* has a goal"? The contrary opinion would be optimistic enthusiasm. Palestrina is the man of pessimistic ethos. If the world "progresses" in a direction one does not at all believe in, even if one recognizes such progress to be necessary and unavoidable, and even if one by one's nature cannot avoid furthering it: then it is impossible to be lofty; the sense of the times takes on a personal-ethical character; "your earthly task" is essential; you must perfect your form; you must *bear* it—I do not say hold out to the end. Whatever he may be— Palestrina finds the strength to be it; and as he creates the necessary work, which only he is capable of because of his nature and his position in the times, the mass, which joins newly developed art with "ecclesiastical feeling," he also perceives the poetic joy of protecting the florid counterpoint from the flame—he becomes the "savior of music" by a preserving-creative act. He knows now what he is, where he belongs, and where not, or at least, how far he belongs here and there; he knows his fate, his honor and his place, and he "wants to be peaceful and content."

   This is of course a conciliatory fairy-tale ending, and still one has

---

* Den Schlußstein zum Gebäude
   Zu fügen sei bereit;
   Das ist der Sinn der Zeit.
   Wenn Du Dein ganzes Bild aufweist,
   Wenn Dein' Gestalt vollkommen,
   So, wie sie war entglommen
   Von Angebinn im Schöpfergeist:
   Dann strahlst Du hell, dann klingst Du rein,
   Pierluigi Du,
   An seiner schönen Ketten
   Der letzte Stein.

perceived Pfitzner's work as "hopelessly pessimistic," and this is quite
understandable and justified at a moment in which optimism has
reached the revolutionary stage. *Palestrina* is really a great work that,
although it stands higher ethically than artistically, completely lacks
progressive optimism, political *virtue*, that is. It is romanticism not only
as an artistic confession, but also much more deeply so, in its spiritual
tendency, its intellectual mood: its sympathy is not for the new, but for
the old, not for the future, but the past, not life, but—I do not know
what shyness keeps me from saying the word that is the formula and
basic definition of all romanticism. But has one noticed that the female
role in the work, Lucretia, does not belong to life, that she is only a
picture and a shade? She was Palestrina's wife, she died, and when she
died, Ighino sang that "he became dark and empty." But this is a special
type of gloom and emptiness, more productive apparently than much
brightness and abundance, for Palestrina's greatest work comes out of
this, and it is the departed one who whispers it to him. Would the living
woman have been able to do it? The music, when he stands before her
picture, finds chords of overpowering enthusiasm to express his love
for her spirit. Would it have the desire to create so much beauty because
of love for a living woman? To put the question frankly: would
Palestrina be the man, and was he the man, to love a living woman as
he loves a dead one? And in general: is life the inspirational genius of
this artist, after all, and not rather—

There is in the *Palestrina* score a theme—it is probably actually the
most important of all, and once we had almost started to talk about it—
the significance of which is not immediately clear and that cannot easily
be given a name, such as, for example, the Emperor Ferdinand and the
Council motifs, or the motifs of the cities of Rome, Bologna, and Trent.
It is a melodic figure of extraordinary beauty, consisting of two measures
that are presented, as it were, with sadly aware precision, to which a
nobly-perceived cadence is added that rises high up and returns to the
dominant, decoratively accompanied by a final flourish of sixteenths.
It appears as early as in the overture at the end of Palestrina's own
archaic theme, and its reappearance always accompanies or creates
moments of spiritual and poetic significance. It dominates the musical
scene when the cardinal encourages the tired master to create the
preserving and crowning work; it resounds also when the predecessors
announce to him "the sense of the times" and that of his own life; and
it forms, in an un-Wagnerian, untheatrical way, the quietly-resigned
conclusion of the whole work. What, then, does it mean? Undoubtedly

it belongs to Palestrina's personality. It is the symbol for a part of his character, or for his character in a certain connection: the symbol of his artistic fate and of his temporal situation, the metaphysical statement that he is not a beginning, but an end, the motif of the "capstone," the look of melancholy, the look backwards. But I have not yet said where this theme is *also* expressed: there, you see, where Lucretia's passing is mentioned—truly and unmistakably it forms the symphonic undercurrent to Ighino's sentence: "He became dark and empty"; therefore it is also at the same time the symbol of Palestrina's psychological condition after the death of his wife, the symbol of his love that is turned backward or rather downward to the shadow kingdom, the love that proves to be the inspiring force in that creative, miraculous night; it is, all in all, the magically melodious sounding formula for his special type of productivity, a productivity of pessimism, of resignation and of longing, a romantic productivity.

On a summer evening between the second and third *Palestrina* performances we were sitting on a garden terrace, discussing the work by making obvious comparisons with the *Meistersinger* both as a drama about an artist and as a work of art in general; we compared Ighino with David, Palestrina with Stolzing and Sachs, the mass with the prize song; we talked of Bach and of Italian church music as stylizing forces. Pfitzner said: "The difference is expressed most clearly in the concluding scenic pictures. At the end of the *Meistersinger* there is a stage full of light, rejoicing of the people, engagement, brilliance and glory; in my work there is, to be sure, Palestrina, who is also celebrated, but in the half-darkness of his room under the picture of the deceased one, dreaming at his organ. The *Meistersinger* is the apotheosis of the new, a praise of the future and of life; in *Palestrina* everything tends toward the past, it is dominated by *sympathy with death*." We were silent; and in his manner, the manner of a musician, he let his eyes move directly upward into vagueness.

It is not readily understandable why his last word shook and astounded me so much. Not that it was on material grounds a surprise for me; it was of course completely consistent. What startled me so was the formulation. "Sympathy with death." I did not believe my ears. It was my expression. Before the war I had begun to write a little novel, a type of pedagogical story, in which a young person, landed in a morally dangerous locale, found himself between two equally quaint educators, between an Italian literary man, humanist, rhetorician and man of progress, and a somewhat disreputable mystic, reactionary, and advocate of antireason—he had the choice, the good youngster, between the powers of virtue and of seduction, between duty and service to life and the fascination of decay, for which he was not unreceptive; and the turn of phrase, "sympathy with death," was a thematic constituent of the composition. Now I heard it word for word from the mouth of the *Palestrina* composer. And not pointedly at all, in a completely improvised way, it seemed, he had only spoken the words to give matters their correct name. Was this not quite remarkable! In order to characterize his elevated-musical work properly, this important contemporary had, with absolute necessity, hit upon an expression of my ironical literary work. How much brotherhood comes readily from contemporaneousness itself! And how much similarity in the direction of intellectual work is necessary for two intellectual workers, who, distant from one another, live in completely different artistic spheres, outwardly without connection, to agree upon the same literary symbol for whole spiritual complexes!

"Sympathy with death"—not a phrase of virtue and of progress. Is it not rather, as I said, the formula and basic definition of all romanticism? And that beautiful, nostalgic-fateful Palestrina motif, which we could not name at first, could it be the motif of creative sympathy with death, the motif of romanticism, the *final word* of romanticism? The artist who sang Palestrina was the same one who made such a strong impression on Romain Rolland in Basel as the evangelist in the St. Matthew Passion. At night at his table he looked grippingly like the author: with this, the confessional stamp of the whole performance became complete. It was not so much a matter of the culmination of Italian church music, as rather of the "capstone" of the structure of romantic opera, of the wistful end of a *national* artistic movement that finished gloriously with Hans Pfitzner, according to his own insight.

I want to say everything—that is the purpose of this book. The composer of *Poor Henry*, of *The Rose from the Garden of Love*, and of *Palestrina*, who, until midsummer 1914, must not have cared a damn about politics, who had been a romantic artist, that is: national but nonpolitical, realized through the war the unavoidable politicization of his national perception. Inwardly and outwardly he took a stand with a decisiveness that had to arouse quite a bit of antagonism, quite a bit of contempt, in all "literature," in all cosmopolitan radicalism. Truly this tender, ardent and spiritualized man took a stand against "intellect," revealed himself as a "power man," longed for the military triumph of

Germany, and, while the surge of submarine warfare was at its height, demonstratively dedicated a work of chamber music to Fleet Admiral von Tirpitz; in a word: the national artist had politicized himself into an antidemocratic nationalist. Who was surprised? In his music he had been German as no other; his instinct, his basic desire to preserve, had stood deeply hostile to all artistic "democracy," to all European intellectualism; and if, precisely for this reason, he came to see a foreign essence in politics—the day came when it turned out that a certain psychological-intellectual constitution quite definitely is inherent in, or at least corresponds to from a distance, a latent political attitude that no one can help assuming under present world circumstances. No Christian cosmopolitism, however, can stop me from seeing one and the same intellectual force in romanticism and in *nationalism*: the dominant force of the nineteenth, the "last" century. Before the war all analyses of the times heralded the end of romanticism; *Palestrina* is the grave song of romantic opera. And the national idea? Who would want, in a very firm and steady voice, to contradict the assertion that it is being consumed by *fire* in this war—a fire, to be sure, so gigantic that for decades the whole sky will stand aglow with it? The nineteenth century was national. Will the twentieth be so? Or is Pfitzner's nationalism, it, too—"sympathy with death?"

I hope that this theatrical excursion has contributed to the clarification of what I understand by "virtue," or, more correctly: by "virtuousness." It is the unconditional and optimistic advocacy of development, progress, the times, "life"; it is the renunciation of all sympathy with death, which is being disavowed and damned as the ultimate vice, as the most extreme corruption of the soul. "I have the gift of life," says the author of that lyrical-poetic prose-poem that has Emile Zola as its hero,

> for I have the deepest passion for life! What is the gift of life? It is the gift of truth . . . to love all powers of truth, science, work, democracy . . . to love one's times! . . . Whoever today is not on the side of science leaves himself crippled. One does not at all imagine what an irresistible force a man is given when he has the tools of the times in his hands and cooperates with the natural development of things. *Then he is carried along. He advances so quickly and so far*, because he has the passions of his times . . .

Here not only all the essence of intellectual virtue is incomparably expressed, here also its personal *reward*, its *dulce utile*, is shown—shown with how much proud gratefulness! Was there ever a more enthusiastic paraphrase of that three-part equation of classical democracy: reason equals virtue equals *happiness*? Because of reason, one is virtuous, swears allegiance to the flag of progress, furthers as a stalwart knight of the times "the natural development of things," rejects completely the sympathy with death that one is perhaps not alien to *personally*, and wins in this way, if one does not already have it, the gift of life, that is: one advances so quickly and so far.

Undoubtedly the subject here is the art of attaining health. But the problem of health is no simple one; the relationship of health and disease is not absorbed by that of optimism and pessimism, of progress-virtue and sympathy with death. Taken personally, Schopenhauer's pessimism was certainly something healthier than Nietzsche's dionysian optimism, for Schopenhauer reached a patriarchal age while denying life and playing the flute, and Nietzsche's affirmation of life is most disastrously compromised as paralytic euphoria. This, then, is the way things can be personally—even if in the process nothing has been said about the philosophical value of optimism and pessimism for health. But with all good will toward objectivity, I cannot completely avoid the personal element. Not everyone is suited by nature for the blessed pact with the times and with progress; democratic health is not exactly proper for everyone. If one has broad shoulders and strong teeth, if one is called Zola, Bjørnstjerne Bjørnson, or Roosevelt, then a harmonious effect may result. But if one entered the world a little noble and old, with a natural calling to skepticism, to irony, and to melancholy; if the blush of life that one displays for effect is hectic or cosmetic, if it is basically—estheticism, then the matter has its ethical offensiveness. I cannot overlook this. There is something I have always called in my heart the "betrayal of the cross." And virtue, too, "democracy," too, the voluptuousness of political enthusiasm, too, signifies at times only this: the betrayal of the cross.

CHAPTER 9

Some Comments on Humanity

Here I want to insert five or six thoughts and somehow string them together apropos of the greatest slogan and expression of virtue that democracy is always talking about, the watchword, "humanity."

Above all, it has never seemed possible to me that anyone could disagree that "humanity," a human way of thinking and observing, obviously signifies the opposite of all politics. To think and to reflect in a human way means to think and to reflect in a nonpolitical way, a thesis with which one of course immediately comes into the sharpest conflict with democracy. Democracy insists, you see, in the name of resolute love of humanity, that everything human be considered politically—but this does not stop it, in certain, in quite specific cases, where it seems useful and advisable, from considering political matters in a human way. In these cases the antithesis of politics and humanity appears as that of myth and enlightenment. This is what I mean:

Germany's popular fantasy created for itself a very repulsive image of the man who directed Great Britain's foreign affairs at the beginning of the war. The image was so satanic and dime-novel wicked that it could not even have been found in a rogues' gallery: the hollow-eyed demon of lies, deceit, and outrage has such features, it was a truly apocalyptical, vulturous and villainous physiognomy. This angered those who were informed, who knew better, and they soon spread the word that such a phantom as the average German imagined upon hearing the name of Sir Edward Grey did not exist. They said he was, rather, a sensitive, warm-hearted gentleman who tended toward solitude and the idyllic life, who was, to be sure, a man intensely English with no knowledge of continental languages, but in his way highly cultured and exceedingly humanely disposed.

They spoke the truth, and one must speak the truth, even when it has a confusing, sobering, paralyzing effect and calms passions, yes, precisely then. Admittedly it is questionable whether the better knowledge of the informed people really was better knowledge or only a more correct knowledge. I do not wish to go so far as to assert that Germany's popular fantasy had a good claim to *its* Grey image; but it certainly did not claim portrait-fidelity. This image was political myth, that of the informed ones was human enlightenment.

Prince Lichnowsky is to be counted among the enlighteners. In his statement he relates: One day when Sir Edward was with his family at table, he made the remark after listening to the chatter of the children for a while: "I can't help thinking how clever these children are to talk German so well!" Then he laughed quite heartily at his little joke. With this anecdote, the prince would like to refute the German belief in England's "guilt," and this is weak—enlightenmentlike and weak. For is it not true: no matter what England's "guilt" for the war may be—the human friendliness of those who thought they were governing in July 1914, is a very weak argument against it. "This," Lichnovsky exclaims, "this childlike, cheerful old gentleman, is the liar-Grey, the infernal creator of intrigues one has dreamed up in our country!" No, of course he is not. He is only a substitution, the substitution of the human element in place of the political one, as only a German can practice it, to confuse, discourage, and paralyze his own people. The moral identity and again nonidentity of the friendly old individual with the exponent of a political-historical power of the likes of England, which acts through an individual while the individual believes he is acting personally—to feel, to see, and to present this deeply complicated double psychology of a "governing" statesman would be a matter for a great writer; it obviously cannot be a matter for a society-diplomat who believes that he would have prevented the World War if one had only allowed him, who stood so well with the English gentlemen, to have his way.

Not only personally, but also on a grand scale, also as far as great England is concerned, for example, the political literary man, the enlightener, is intent on substituting the human in place of the political element and on destroying what we called the myth and which, in our unpolitical opinion, may and must in certain moments of history be considered from a definitely one-sided point of view. From a human point of view it sounds like a wild absurdity to call England a non-European and even an anti-European power that is completely lacking in European conscience and European feeling of solidarity. It sounds absurd, I say, for the English are, of course, a cultured European people in spite of what one says, it is impossible not to admire them as such. To be sure, their philosophy is not particularly elevated, and they were not creative in music. But their painting, for which I have had a weakness since my youth, has at least the advantage of insular originality, of independence from Paris; the novel has had a powerful European influence, the lyrics are exquisite, and *Hamlet* and *Manfred* came from there. And quite a few practically useful things that make life more agreeable also come from there, such as the bicycle, the water closet, the trimmed mustache, the safety razor, lawn tennis, and so on and so on. Moreover, if I may judge, there still lives on those islands the most beautiful and proudest human type of young people of all zones, Hermes and blonde Aphrodites, and then that dark, esthetic virginal type that one knows from Botticelli as well as from the angelic figures of the British pre-Raphaelites. Well, and? All this would not stop the day Field Marshal Hindenburg threw the English expeditionary forces into the sea—making England forever lose the desire to gain a foothold on the continent again—from being a day of celebration of the first order not only for Germany, but also for the whole world. For, taken in a political-historical way, that assertion that England is a non-European, yes, an anti-European power, is the pure, literal and inexorable truth. All great continental Europeans have recognized it as truth, above all, Napoleon Bonaparte, whose defeat by this power the English constantly rejoice in today to their invigoration; and finally, the European, Nietzsche, referred to the "understanding" with England, which he put in significantly undemocratic quotation marks, as an unavoidably approaching necessity. It is a tragic curiosity that each one of the great European nations comprises in its way a *potential disaster* for all of Europe— (Germany no less than others). But England does so in an especially egotistical, unconscious, cold, imperturbable and clever way. It has always been her affair to play the nations of the continent off against one another, to take advantage of their quarrels, to let them bleed for her cause. Her rulers may be the most friendly persons imaginable— they are only the executive organs of a political-historical power that must live and act according to the principle it began with, and whose vital interests are hostilely opposed to the welfare of Europe. She is not a European, but a world power, particularly an Asiatic power, and therefore, at the beginning of this century, she had to deflect the Russian drive for expansion from the East to the West—against Europe, of which she is psychologically, so to speak, a part. She did not do this out of malice, but under the fateful necessity of her political-historical life. For in politics, mechanical, extrahuman, extramoral laws rule that one can therefore call neither good nor evil, and that England, to be sure, always understood best how to dress up with humane interpretations and embellishments. But not only the Englishman, the human being in general needs morality; it is intertwined with his character, and he does not want to and cannot dispense with a moral way of looking at things, and precisely for this reason there arose in Germany the repulsive image of good old Grey, as well as of great England herself.

It was the myth. As I have said, the political literary man uses humanity to enlighten by substituting, in certain cases, the human-cultural element for the historical-political one. In so doing, he hopes to make the historical-political element repugnant to his people. He does this even though the two elements have nothing to do with one another, and even though in a war such as this our cosmopolitan cultural disposition and humanity need not in the least be impaired by our political partisanship. Thus he showed us the poor French infantryman with his cracked patent leather boots, whose ghost spoke to his military murderer: "I hated the fellow who wanted to entice my girl away from me much more than I did you!"—he shows us the young Englishman who saw Goethe in Karlsbad and stood flabbergasted because he had not considered it possible that the author of *Werther* could really walk around in the flesh. Noble, splendid young man! Is it permissible to wage war against your country and people—even assuming that this country and people declared war against us and not the other way around? Is it, let us ask on the other hand, permissible, is it not rather a base trick and meanness, to confuse the mind of one's own nation, which is locked in a fateful life-and-death struggle with a political-historical power such as England, with cultural sentimentalities?

Let us not ask. Let us stick to the facts—they show us the same marvelous intricacy of moral opinions that has often struck us in the course of our reflections. *When* namely, in which cases, or, more correctly: in which case does the democratic, or, said more personally, the political literary man, insist upon a human view of politics? In the case of *foreign* affairs. For in *domestic* matters, for opportunistic reasons, he completely forbids a human view of politics and insists rather on a political view of everything human. *Quite the contrary* is true for his opposite number, the nonpolitician, for whom we still have no better name than that of esthete. The esthete insists that in *foreign* affairs, at least now and then, the myth has an absolute prerogative to life—a prerogative over the individual human element, and that in such times the extrahuman, political-historical side of things is to be seriously considered, while the human-cultural one, although certainly not to be completely denied, must still retreat for the moment. In *domestic* policy, however, he thoroughly hates the myth, the politicization of everything human, and here, truly, he loves the human enlightenment as it is practiced, for example, by art or religion.

Is it human to present the landed aristocracy as a group of champagne-guzzling proboscidians? No, it is mythical, it is political, it is a demand and a demagogic tactic of the "politics of humanity." Whereby, to be sure, the question still remains whether it is actually political in any sort of higher sense, whether the democratic-socialist hatred of large land-owners, of the land east of the Elbe, has, besides "passion," anything of good common sense in its favor as well. It has often been explained—best of all by the clever and truly free old Karl Jentsch (whose death has, to my regret, just been reported)—that not every part of Germany is suitable for land distribution and small farming; that large farming is indispensable, precisely in the interest of progress, because it is what leads the way technologically; that large landownership is the necessary counterpart to the *metropolis*, which cannot be supplied without it, that the land east of the Elbe must not be more thickly populated than it is if it is to continue to deliver large amounts of wheat to the *Reich*, and so forth. However, to look at things in this way would be to look at them all too matter-of-factly, to observe them without *spirit*. The "feudal prin-ciple," every type of conservatism, religious, monarchical, national, moral, economic, every opposition to progressive degeneration and dis-integration, is rooted in landed property, and it is the natural opponent of that other principle, the democratic one, the principle of human rights, which has roots nowhere except in "reason." One would certainly think that reason above all, as far as it is in any way compatible with freedom and humanity, would have to deduce, from the sanctity and indispensa-bility of "landed property," a certain legitimacy of the principles em-bodied in it, and that it would also have to glean some skepticism about the absolute superiority of the opposite principles. But, as has been said, it is a matter of politics, of resoluteness, of the struggle of intellectual-material interest complexes—a struggle, by the way, in which there has long been no doubt which side is on the victorious offensive and which finds itself on the defensive. Also, the fact that the leftist-liberal press is better written and usually understands more about fine arts than the conservative press does not blind me to the fact that such refinement does not prevent this press from defending its interest against the agrarian block with the grossest perfidy, with demonstrably unfair means. Well, that is politics—in which spiteful partiality, injustice, lies, falsification, distortion, and incitement are the order of the day; which is also why no one can convince me that humanity and politics could ever stand in an attributive relationship to one another. And if it is, after all, true, that the most decent and humanly dignified of all ways of life, that of the landed gentry, is at the same time the politically most backward and despicable one, then this also speaks against the possibility of ever bringing politics and humanity into such a relationship.

That scene in Fontane, where the old gentleman, von Stechlin, who has been defeated by the Social Democrats in the parliamentary elections, and who, on the way home, finds the drunkard, Tuxen, who has voted for Torgelow from Berlin and who is now lying drunk in the night frost right in front of the wheels of the carriage, seems to me to be human, enlightening, and salutarily destructive of the myth, the way von Stechlin, shaking his head in Junker melancholy, speaks with Tuxen, puts him on the carriage, and takes him as far as Dietrichs-Ofen: "Now get off and take care you don't fall when the horses move forward again. And here is something for you. But no more for today. You have enough for today . . ." What makes the scene so charming? Hardly the bit of satire, hardly the contrast between the idea of general and equal suffrage, this concession to the "law of nature," the sovereignty of the people—and the humanity of old Tuxen who has exercised it and now lies drunk before the wheels. What has effect, what charms, is the nullification, disarmament, and destruction of politics by freedom, resignation, and goodness. "You know me, I don't rip anyone's head off. It doesn't make any difference," Dubslav says when he wants to know who "the old drunkard" has voted for. "It doesn't make any difference." Torgelow from Berlin has not progressed that far yet. But to think in this way, one probably must not be the victor.

Art, like religion, is the human sphere; politics disappears before it like mist before the sun. Art can assimilate politics, even use it as a subject, it can portray political events, but then art will humanize politics, illuminate it psychologically, and its objectivity will be serene and prodigious all the way into tragedy. By the way, no experience is better able to remove politics from consideration, to make it more completely insignificant, and to cause it to be forgotten, than the experience of the eternal-human element through art. At a moment when world political events of admittedly terrifying force affect the individual-human element everywhere most seriously, inundate it and carry it away—precisely at this moment it is fitting to defend against the megalomania of politics, the truth that politics will not even be able to touch the essential part of life, the human part. "In the meantime," Tolstoy says in *War and Peace*, after he has spoken of the political schemes of the years 1808 and 1809, and has mentioned the internal changes that at the time were taking place in all parts of the Russian administration and that had particularly occupied the interest of Russian society—"In the meantime, life, the real life of the people with its essential interests: health, sickness, work, and rest, its concern for thought, knowledge, poetry and music, love and friendship, hatred and passions—took its usual path, outside the political sphere, independent of the enmity against or friendship with Napoleon Bonaparte, and untouched by all reforms." What one calls human dignity also remained untouched by politics—it is foolishness to believe that life is "more worthy of a human being" under a republic than under a monarchy. Nevertheless, one is a politician only at the price of believing this.

The concept of what is human, the ideas about what is worthy of a human being in a social sense, are also quite varied within the civilized world. The Russian, accustomed to arbitrary conditions, coming from a country with a mixture of despotic and democratic corruption, complains in Germany about lack of personal freedom because he cannot, by handing over a banknote, succeed in being served at a counter ahead of those who have arrived before him. Order, justice opposed to corruption, therefore wound his human dignity, his type of freedom; and one can sympathize with him in this. Equality is a feigned and artificial condition that one maintains by denying as much as possible the real and natural distribution of power, and by superficially nullifying it. Equality and freedom—but this has probably been said all too often—obviously exclude one another; and as far as brotherhood is concerned, it is without moral value when it is based on equality.

It would mean attacking the Russian-French alliance with ineffective weapons if one declared it unnatural and shameful for a democracy to ally itself with an absolutist state. Only the politician, someone, that is, who overvalues and misunderstands the significance of political systems of government to the point of absurdity, can consider autocracy and democracy to be human antitheses, only he does not know that true, that is, human democracy is a matter of the heart and not of politics, that it is brotherhood and not freedom "and" equality. Is the Russian not the most human of human beings? Is his literature not the most human of all—saved by its humanity? In her innermost soul, Russia has always been democratic, yes, Christian-communistic—inclined to brotherhood, that is—and Dostoyevsky seemed to think that a patriarchal-theocratic autocracy represented a better political system for this democracy than did the social and atheistic republic.

That alliance seems to me a *mésalliance* not so much in the French as in the Russian sense, for democracy of the heart is humanly very much superior to democracy of principle and of humanitarian rhetoric, and to want to justify the power-political connection between Russia and France, to prove it humanly well-grounded, is not at all my concern, but completely that of civilization's literary man, who plays with words to this purpose: with the word, "democratic," for example, which he uses according to his need and convenience in a religious-human or a rational-political sense; or with the word, "psychological," as he craftily points out that the Russian and the French spirits have the "democratic" form of expression of the psychological novel in common—as if the elegant insight of French social criticism had anything at all to do with the Russian nature and soul. It is definitely one of the radical literary man's most irresponsibly dogmatic assertions that the human character of the Russian writers, that the great Russian literature has been understood and sympathized with best of all in France—an assertion set forth boldly, blindly, and irresponsibly, so that everything would fit together, and that it would seem quite plausible and completely justified for M. Poincaré to receive guarantees from the Tsarist government for Alsace-Lorraine and the Saar Basin. It was a Dane, Herman Bang, who first called Russian literature "the holy one"—something I did not know when I called it the same thing in *Tonio Kröger*. Just show me the Frenchman who could *boast* of such influence from Dostoyevsky as Hamsun and Hauptmann; and what the poet of *The Idiot* and of *The Brothers Karamazov* meant for Nietzsche cannot be measured by any compatriot of Anatole France—not even to speak of England, naturally. Russian literature had its strongest influence in Scandinavia and in Germany; to say that it had it in France is nothing more than a political, tendentious swindle.

For me there is no doubt that German and Russian humanity are closer to one another than the Russian and French, and incomparably closer than the German and the Latin; that here greater possibilities of understanding exist than between what we call humanity and the *vulgar humanity* of the Latins. For it is clear that a humanity of religious stamp, based on Christian gentleness and humility, on suffering and compassion, is closer to another one that has always stood under the sign of a humanly world-burgherly culture than to a third that is much more a political clamor. In Russian literature one finds much ridicule of German pedantry, much resentment of the intruder, the foreign teacher, much antipathy to his efficiency, which is perceived as humanly inferior and therefore objectionable. But just look at the French in Russian literature—their role is, if possible, even more unsympathetic than that of the Germans in French literature.

Polezhayev says:

> The Frenchman is a child,
> He quickly overthrows
> A throne overnight,
> Creates law and power,
> Is quick — as lightning
> And empty as a windbag.
> He provokes and acts,
> So that one is amazed and laughs.

And the great narrators? I do not think that my memory deceives me: Among the Russian narrators no Frenchman appears who is not a bag of wind, whether a malicious or only a laughable one. Tolstoy makes fun of them everywhere, particularly in *War and Peace*. The German and the French private tutors in *Boyhood*: these are types. Where does Turgenev, the friend of Flaubert, have a French figure equal in beautiful simplicity and grandeur to the German musician, Lemm, in *A Nest of Gentle Folk*? I also call to mind the disgust that was created when the visionary with the demon, Ellis, hovers over Paris (*Visions*). Leo Tolstoy was also in Paris once, 1857, twenty-nine years old, before he went to Switzerland. "The city," he says, "disgusted me until I almost lost my mind. What all didn't I see . . . First of all, in the *hôtel garni* where I stayed there were thirty-six couples, nineteen of which were common-law marriages! Then I just wanted to put myself to the test, and I went to an execution where a criminal was guillotined. Afterwards I couldn't sleep anymore and didn't know what to do . . ." I think an antipathy is poorly substantiated here, but the main point seems to me to be that it existed. Let one take Tolstoy's description of the visit that Déroulède paid to Yasnaya Poliana. Nothing is more laughable than the contrast between the rhetorically fastidious Parisian politician and the Russian human being. Even the Frenchwoman, I mean the Parisienne, or also the frenchified Russian woman—appears as a painted prostitute, the bearer of misfortune, scarcely anthing else, and worlds lie between her and the pure, earnest humanity of the Russian girl. Just think also of the effect of the French language in Russian books—of the way it is used. No one whom the author does not despise speaks it or mixes his honest Russian with it; it is the chatter of elegant superficiality; it is at any rate the idiom of maniacal-political radicalism, which has never been more deeply mocked than in *The Possessed*, there where the ideological suicide, Kirilov, signs the false confession in French as a *"citoyen du monde civilisé,"* and, in order "to correct himself with a curse," adds, *"Vive la république démocratique, social et universelle ou la mort!"*

"To become a genuine, complete Russian," Dostoyevsky says in an essay, "is perhaps only (this means "finally," do not forget that)—to become a brother of all human beings, a total human being, if you will." Have nationality and humanity, has the most human sense of nationality, ever been understood and expressed in a more German way than here as it is done by the greatest Russian moralist? The sentence is the positive complement to that mystifying mockery of the *république démocratique, sociale et universelle*, and it says that in order to be a human being, or to become one, one must above all have a nation, and that it is an erroneous and foolish way to begin as a *citoyen du monde civilisé*. A little farther on Dostoyevsky says: "But the main school of Christianity that the nation has gone through consists of the centuries of countless sufferings and misfortunes that its history relates, the centuries in which it was abandoned and trod upon by everyone, and at the same time worked for everyone and everything . . ." The history of the *origin* of German and Russian humanity—is it not the same, too—namely a history of suffering? What a kinship in the relationship of the two national souls to "Europe," to the "West," to "civilization," to politics, to democracy! Do we not also have our slavophiles and our zapadniks? It is no accident that it was a Russian, Dostoyevsky again, who, as early as a generation and a half ago, found the expression for the antithesis between Germany, this "great and special people," and Western Europe, the antithesis from which all our reflections began! "Dostoyevsky is *forgotten* in Russia," a Russian said to me before the war. Well, the revolution proves it—this desperate brawl between democratic-bourgeois French character and anarchial Tolstoyism. But we know that "forgetting" is a very superficial psychological process, and no one can convince us that the approaching Russian declaration in favor of the *république démocratique et sociale* seriously has anything to do with the Russian nation. No! If psychological and intellectual matters should and can serve at all as a basis and justification of power-political alliances, then Russia and Germany belong together: since the beginning of the war, my heartfelt wish and dream has been for their present agreement, their future alliance, and this agreement and alliance will be more than a desirability: it will be a world-political-spiritual necessity if the unification of the Anglo-Saxon world should prove to be lasting, as it probably will. Who could remain indifferent to a threat that before the war had already taken on the form of an impudently calm statement: "The world is rapidly becoming English!"

Humanity. As a revolutionary cry, it signified the collapse of a senile, aristocratic society culture, the emancipation of reason *and* nature from the chains of the civilization that Rousseau vilified—while on the other hand reason and nature, in the sense of the Voltairean-Promethean gesture, formed an antithesis. It signified, among other things, Beccaria's criminal love of mankind that persisted until the concept of guilt almost disappeared in the face of sheer humanitarianism, yes, so that at times, under the pressure of expert opinions, one scarcely dared lay a hand on the criminal and beheld in the death penalty the height of inhumanity—while in the eyes of every more serious person the concept of guilt bears, while not a humanitarian, to be sure, still a high-humane stamp, and is in no way destroyed by any kind of deterministic insight, but on the contrary only gains thereby in weight and horror.

To some extent, of course, the nineteenth century, in spite of characteristic contrasts to the eighteenth, was this eighteenth over again: romanticism in many ways goes back to Rousseau, and Tolstoy, for example, the social-religious prophet of recent times, was a genuine Rousseauean, and, as a humanitarian, completely eighteenth century. This is shown most clearly in his satirical rejection of the administration of justice in the novel of his old age, *Resurrection*, which is still of gigantic imaginative power—I am referring, of course, to the powerful series of chapters in which the trial of the prostitute, Maslova, a very tendentiously constructed case, is formed under the theme of the Christian "Judge not!" Judge not? No, God forbid us! What person, lawyer or layman, would want to make himself laughable and inevitably bring the curse of satire upon himself by presuming the ability to *judge* a fellow human being? But to *render justice*—if there is to be a social cultural life at all, if there is to be anything like a state, that is—we must certainly *render justice*; this social burden must after all be borne. I like very much to visit halls of justice, and I am enough of a writer to have an eye for the human fallibility of all administration of justice. But I confess that precisely in the face of the most serious of cases, the treatment of capital crimes before a jury, that is, I have scarcely ever felt in the mood to satirize the administration of justice—unless the jury *as such* gave rise to this mood. On the contrary: the scientific exactness and medically careful conscientiousness with which humanly disgusting cases of all kinds of incredibly bestial acts were treated in the courtroom have always filled me with respect, yes, admiration, and satisfaction at the amount of sagacity and the desire to be decent that the human being, as a social being, has cultivated in this area as well.

But to say nothing of state and culture, I do not at all think that that "Judge not!"—a prohibition that is nothing else but the statement of a final and higher inability—should be understood as calling for the criminal's acquittal. On the contrary, I believe it would be flabby egotism and in no serious sense humane to spare a guilty person the verdict of guilty, even if it means death, out of pity, or out of the consideration, "I am not any better." If one wants to understand the difference between the spirit of the eighteenth and that of the nineteenth century, between a humanitarian and a moralist, then let one read, after a few pages of Tolstoy, Dostoyevsky's essay, "The Environment," which is a part of his treatise on Russian nihilism. "By making the human being responsible," Dostoyevsky says, "Christianity recognizes his freedom. When one declares the human being subject to every failure of the social establishment, as the doctrine of the environment does, then one leads the human being to complete nonpersonality and releases him from every personal-moral duty, from all self-reliance, and thereby brings him into the greatest slavery one can possibly imagine." This, too, is humanity, but it is not humanitarian. By the way, it does not let the emotional appeal of "I am not any better" come off badly, either. "We must enter the hall of justice with the thought," he says in another place, "that we are also guilty, and precisely this pain of compassion that everyone fears so much now, and with which we leave the courtroom after a conviction, will be our punishment. If this pain is genuine and deep, it will make us better, and only when we ourselves become better *will we make the environment better. That is, of course, the point*, that this is the *only* way one can improve the environment." That is, of course, the point. For that is the difference between politics and personal ethics. It is well known that the liberal Professor Gradovsky declared that in Dostoyevsky's life work one feels a lack of any hint of social ideals.

But to say what is to be said: The politician, the humanitarian revolutionary and radical literary man, who is a demagogue in the grand style, namely a flatterer of mankind, when he speaks of humanity, has exclusively the nobility and dignity of the human being in mind, while his opposite number, the one he calls an esthete, tends rather to see in the word, "humanity," human weakness, helplessness, and pitifulness—the humanitarian politician, then, seemingly so much concerned with human dignity, is precisely the one (and not some kind of "esthete") who, with the help of the honorable concept, "humanity," is trying to remove all seriousness, all dignity and responsibility, from life, as his attitude toward the administration of justice, the question of guilt, and the death penalty already shows. All in all, this is a moral cheapening of the world and of life, which is not a matter everyone can take pleasure in, and above all, in my opinion, not a matter for the artist: who, you see, has the strongest interest in life's not completely losing its grave, deadly serious accents, and who would be at a loss in a morally castrated world. What has already entered into civilization as obvious, as the humanitarian idea of humanity of the eighteenth century, should no longer have to serve as a battle cry against everything that seriously, sternly, and vigorously reaches beyond the obvious—precisely as it happened and is happening with the idea and word echo, "humanity," this favorite word of rhetorical democracy, which has been anointed with all the oils of French rhetoric and Anglo-Saxon cant, with which it believes it can tyrannize, dishonor, and besmirch a nation that is engaged in its most serious, difficult, historical struggle. What was it other than mawkish lack of seriousness and pitiful lack of tragic sense when the *entente* world sentimentally deplored the execution by order of a court-martial of an Englishwoman who misused her nurse's uniform to help Belgian soldiers over the border? It was permissible to make a heroine out of her; but only under the assumption that Cavell was not a thoughtless ninny, but knew what she was doing, was acquainted with the possible consequences of her deed, which was not even purely patriotic (for she was not a Belgian), but political, and that she was prepared to take them in the given case. One did not dishonor her, one honored her by placing her before the firing squad, and—"Humanity is obvious," the officer who commanded the firing squad probably thought as he carried out the regulations by killing the woman, who had fainted, with a revolver shot, so that she paid for her serious and voluntary guilt, which was not dishonorable, with an unaware death. A political action that can lead to the firing squad should only be undertaken by someone who feels himself justified and called to the task, and who is to some extent certain that he will *not* faint before the firing squad. Turgenev relates with grotesque accents the military execution of a very unheroic Jewish "factor" who had been unmasked as a spy. He describes his tragicomic fear of death, yet does not bat an eye at the "inhumanity" of the process, but salutes the action as a man and an artist. It is not true, I deny it, that an intellectual or an artistic human being would be duty-bound to turn away with a humanitarianly covered head from everything that seriously transcends the everyday measure of obvious humanity.

This would then probably be the place to say and to admit a few more things about *war* and humanity. But I will do well, in case something like an objective confession *against* humanity should emerge in the process, to preface it with a personal avowal of faith *in* humanity. This is advisable; for I know well what I am risking, what misunderstanding I am exposing myself to, when I seem to plead the cause of antihumanity. But such an avowal will also be very easy for me, for truly, how could I be of an antihumane disposition in any way other than possibly that of the protest against a repugnant shallowness and castration of the concept of humanity! I am no monocle-Junker as he lives in the fantasy of the *entente* nations, no violent man and killer; I do not look like Zola's Bismarck, that is, like a gray-haired giant, laughing loudly in brutality. I feel myself a member of a nation whose national unification was prepared and made possible by an epoch of great literature, of the highest humane culture. I am conscious of being the descendant of a burgherdom that received its traditions from this same epoch, yes, that is more the product of humane culture than that of any other country. Without arrogance, I may say that humanity is obvious to me—and indeed, not only in intellectual life, but also in individual, everyday affairs. Morality is the air I breathe; I love, yes, I really respect only what is kind, vulgarity disturbs me, I fear personal hatred and suffer not less when I cause it than when I am the object of it, although I know well that in order to experience human life one must experience hatred, both actively and passively. If, in spite of all desire for artistic abandonment, one tends to shyness in direct speech, then one values the quotation as a calming medium. There is a passage in a letter by Adalbert Stifter that runs, "My life element is trust and friendliness; where this is lacking, I am paralyzed." I feel as he does. And in no way a reason-democrat, in no way an adherent of the principle of the "equality of human beings," I see in democracy of the heart a character trait, the absence of which astounds me. Equality is neither a fact nor a desirability, but let it be a human gesture; let it be that politeness of the heart that is not just related to love. Democracy as a standing institution would lack every individual merit, and social reconciliation is not a fruit of politics, but of sympathy and of individual improvement. As far as I am concerned, I find the challenge "to respect the human being in every beggar" to be beneath all self-evident truth, to be arrogant, obsolete-humanitarian, rhetorical and silly. I do not know the aristocracy of being human. I also "respect" my dog, and when the good fellow greets my by putting his front paws on my chest and laying his spotted head at the same place while I pat his thin shoulder blade, I feel closer to him than to many a member of the "human race." I do not "respect" the beggar out of the rational consideration that he is a human being ("Then he is something good," some Swift would remark); I am not particularly open to this argument from *The Magic Flute*; I respect him out of a warmer and more direct feeling that I will not name. Furthermore, I know that I am not at all capable of even changing my behavior toward people according to their class or social rank, and I remember many a situation where I embarrassed members of my own social class by forcing them by my behavior toward subordinates either to appear arrogant-undemocratic or to painfully overcome their reserve-lieutenant's reserve. But this nature of mine did not prevent me from seeing, on the contrary, it probably helped me to see, that the majority of human beings are little served, that it is not very appropriate and comfortable for them, but rather, if not embarassing, then at least quite bothersome, when one "respects" them all too much. In the story, *Royal Highness*, the remark is once made that in dealing with people, Klaus Heinrich took everyone for such a complete, serious, important, and *good* person, that the poor, overestimated, overstrained fellow just sweated. This is what I mean here.

Finally, however, I am an artist, a worker in the finest material, and even if refinement certainly does not have to mean goodness, it still remains true that "*artes molliunt mores*,"—a phrase, I would like to believe, that also works in reverse, also applies to the *artifex*, so that it would probably be difficult to be an artist and at the same time a brute. Impossible, however, to be something like a poet, a shaper of human beings, and at the same time to be indifferent to the human being, even assuming that hatred and scorn for human beings made up the formative principle. "The human race"—I admit that my relationship to this abstraction is doubtful; the *human being*, however, has long occupied my whole interest, the human being, and probably also the animal, but not, shall we say, art, or the landscape—on trips, for example. My books have almost no landscape, almost no scenery except for the rooms. But a lot of human beings live in them, and one says that they are "lovingly" observed and presented. Was this "love of mankind"? I do not know. Maybe it is a matter of egotism? Perhaps I am only so much interested in the human being because I am one myself? One of the last sentences of the artist story that I wrote as a youth (and that one still finds beautiful today) runs admittedly: "For if anything at all is capable of making a poet out of a literary man, it is this, my burgherly love for what is human, lively, and ordinary." Was that "love of mankind"? At least it did not take the form of doctrinaire bragging, of the habitual fanfare of civilization—forms in which, in my opinion, for the sake of good taste, it should never appear, least of all among creative writers.

I made a note of an anecdote that appeared in our newspapers at the beginning of the war. It had been taken from *Figaro*, and according to it, a French farmer had said of the German prisoners working in his fields: "These vermin! One would like to kill them, but still, one cannot because after all, they are also human beings." But the contributor to *Figaro* had also added: "Fourteen centuries of Latin culture reveal themselves in these words." There is no better example of what I mean and do not "mean." There we find ourselves in a sphere in which humanity is, in fact, *not* obvious, in the sphere of the bragging democrat, to whom it appears as intellectual and moral merit, as an occasion for tearful self-complacency. A social-ethical novelist, an adherent of humanity and a pioneer of democracy, discovered in his latest work that "the rich also cry." How wonderful, he exclaimed, they are human beings, notwithstanding, these rich people, they, too, I know it. They suffer at times, and then they cry. Had one considered such a degree of humanity, such an all-inclusive pity, possible? "The rich also cry!" This is what I call a poetic spirit! But to return to *Figaro* and to its enlightened farmer, one really has the impression that malicious ferocity and foolish crudeness are just about held in check here by the idea of humanity that is perceived as completely sublime, noble, and philosophically liberal.

One must take a lenient view of many things in the aristocracy of the old dominating nations: a certain noble narrow-mindedness and foolish inhumanity arises naturally in them, even though they champion political humanity. For the Englishman the idea of the "nigger" begins very early, even earlier the Frenchman's idea of the "barbarian." One must particularly take a lenient view of many things in the unfortunate France of this war, of her suffering, her "innocence," her half-conscious hopelessness, her natural character, which contains quite different, much more wicked, precipitous and poisonous possibilities of national hatred than the German one; of her childlikeness, too, which really consists of innocently-arrogant ideas about the childlike barbarism of the others, especially the Germans, and which revealed itself completely in the prudent eagerness with which, during the German advance against Paris, the villagers of northern France hung out their *pendules* before their house doors as offerings and indemnity, obviously in the belief that the Germanic invasion aimed, as had earlier ones, mainly at the acquisition of these mechanisms that so charmed the redbeards. One must, I say, take a lenient view of many things in the France of these years—but this does not have to prevent one from seeing that there, where humanity forms the favorite subject of rhetorical exercises in style, the danger of straying from it is obviously greatest. Whoever has read Maupassant's war stories understands why the leadership in the so-called atrocity campaigns against Germany fell to his compatriots. By the way, the taste for wicked imaginative pleasures is something that the Western nations, the bearers of "civilization" par excellence, have in common: in England, France and America there is an artistry of cruelty, a cold, nervous, and intellectual cult of the hideous, that has only recently been found in Germany, and probably not at all in Russia. If one thinks of the Grand Guignol's dramatic chamber of horrors, or of the blood curdling products of a certain type of novel writing with which the most widely-read Parisian daily papers fill their *feuilleton* columns, then it certainly seems that the French, simply because of a generally more lively talent, take the prize here as well. But this is an advantage that, together with hatred, suffering, "innocence," despair and childlike arrogance, helps explain why France's humanity in this war has suffered such a miserable shipwreck.

For it did not at all stop with excesses of fantasy, of course. Herr von Bethmann Hollweg's government has, true to its basically unwarlike system, made extremely moderate use of the available material to characterize the enemy's conduct in the war, particularly that of France. Anyway, one knows enough, and I will not dwell on what is known. The word torture is actually to be understood in the literal, most exact sense when one applies it to the treatment by the French of the German prisoners of war in the Cameroons and in Togo. The thumbscrew, known from the medieval sections of cultural-historical museums, played a role here that one would not believe could again be assigned to this ingenious instrument. The name of Adjutant Venère, who personally took over the torture of the prisoners with horsewhip and lash, deserves to be well remembered. The deeds fit the words. It was a French general—he signs his name Lévy, moreover—who stated that after he had touched a Boche he would consider it purification to put his hands into a pot of manure. What wild rhetoric! What—one must say it—uncivilized exaggeration of national antipathy! I only know of this from the newspapers. But a German officer, who was sent to Reims as a bearer of a flag of truce, told me personally that he was taken prisoner there as a spy, insanely condemned to death, and only saved by British intervention: as he was being taken away after sentencing, the judge called out to him: *"Beaucoup de plaisir!"* Again, what astounding ferocity! Is it then really pharisaism when one attempts to imagine things like this in Germany—and when one cannot succeed in doing so? And what should one think of the relationships between political freedom, people's sovereignty, democracy—and humanity, and human culture, and decency of the heart, when one hears how *the people*, the "people who are by nature just and good," or let us say more carefully: the mob, the diverse local rabble, conducted and conducts itself in France against German civilian and military prisoners? One honors his demands, one reports promptly the arrival of transports to the sovereign in the mother country and in North Africa as well, and truly, he is there to conduct himself like a swine. The violent emotion of the war has caused moral damage everywhere, no one denies that; but who would want to deny that the French spirit has shown the least ability to resist, the most lamentable confusion and derangement? In the Parisian *Temps*, a book was recently praised unreservedly whose author, a respected scholar, Bérillon, a professor of psychiatry, offers the proof that the Germans are not human beings at all, that they belong rather to some kind of inferior species, a fact that can unmistakably be seen from the form of their sense organs, of their abdomens, their smell, as well as the quality of their animal excretions. No, it is *not* pharisaism to conclude that such ghastly idiocy of hatred, such tragicomic capers of patriotic concern, would be impossible in the German sphere—they are also impossible for Slavs, Anglo-Saxons, and Mongols.

Humanity as a political philosophy and as a democratic principle has feet of clay. But why do certain attempts to save it, instead of touching us, seem even more disgusting than the sight of its downfall? When, for example, the Englishmen conclude a trade treaty with a neutral state in which the state is forbidden every further export of goods to Germany *except clothes for women and children*, then I perceive the additional clause, that these products may neither contain wool nor cotton, as a stomach tonic that has long been needed. The present war is the most radical one that has ever been waged; and while Germany was at first completely confused about its character, while she entered it with the naiveté of a fraternity student and thought she could conduct it in the spirit of old-fashioned fair play in a purely soldierly manner, England accurately understood its monstrous nature from the beginning—no wonder, for it was England, of course, that really pressed the stamp on it. From the first day on she conducted the war in the most radical manner by using her seapower not only for her own safety, but also to cut off all imports to Germany, in the attempt, that is, in the most serious and objective sense, to starve her. By the simple and brutal means of cutting the cable, she brought about that morally asphyxiating isolation of Germany that one will always remember here in this country as one remembers a nightmare. With unfurrowed brow she has ignored the concept of private property, and in this her allies cheerfully followed her. She is not waging the war against hostile governments and armies, but against peoples, against the German people, mercilessly, and she was superior to us in her insight into the merciless, limitless, and unfeeling seriousness of the struggle. But what feminine inconsistency, what a hypocritical tribute to "humanity" it is, then, to have such disgusting concern for the importation of "clothes for women and children" to Germany—and to raise a humanitarian cry over the sinking of a luxury liner that had taken on ammunition!

It is true, I hate such attempts at whitewashing, such deceitful efforts to preserve the humanitarian image; but the antipathy they excite in me does not match the one I feel at the sight of the literary spirit that thinks of "humanity" today as a program of opposition against historical events, against the war. Here it is no longer a matter of slyly-sensitive attempts of foreigners to cover up the radical nature of their war of annihilation against Germany, but of something more intellectual and intimate: we are among ourselves, we stand face to face again with the hero of these pages, civilization's literary man—the intellectual politician and champion of political humanity *intra muros*, who, as such, wishes and makes civil war, but as an antinational, international pacifist disavows and outlaws war completely; but particularly the present one;

for it is quite truly Germany's war; Germany bears the "guilt" for it. History will call it the German war, for, if the spirit of civilization's literary man does not gain the domestic victory, the war will complete the historical rise of Germany since the middle of the eighteenth century.

In a recent essay, the German Social Democrat, Paul Lensch, wrote with the greatest impressiveness of this rise as the cause of the World War, which he calls a world revolution. He showed how the great war of the seventeenth century was the result of the German collapse that had been preceded by a century and a half of gradual political decline. For war, he said, has "the general tendency not so much to introduce new developments as to help what already exists to break through, and to complete more quickly what has begun slowly. All the nations hurried to turn Germany into a desert and pressed greedily into the space that Germany's collapse had left empty. French and British world positions could only be maintained so long as Germany was politically impotent and economically weak—both powers were in no doubt about this. England's world dominance in particular required Germany's world-servitude as a prerequisite; as soon as the latter stopped, the former had to collapse. "The present war," Lensch says,

> does not have, as the Thirty Years' War did, a century and a half of decline as its cause but just as long a rise. And it, too, will only complete more quickly what was begun slowly: the rise of central Europe. This time not only almost all the nations of Europe, but almost all the nations on earth, have hurried to transform Germany into a desert. But not one of them has been able to set foot on German soil. Whether we want to or not, we must shatter the existing "balance of power" to bits, which is, of course, only a superiority of Western power, and create a new foundation that corresponds to the true power relationships. A truly revolutionary task!

He says that the war itself has shown that the position the German *Reich* accepted up to the war no longer corresponded to its expanded economic and military capacity. On the other hand, the position of many other nations was also no longer appropriate to their changed, not expanded, but decreased capacities. The war "is putting an end to false appearances, it is helping the present to its right over the past, it is stating what is. That is the world revolution, it is the collapse of the political division of power in Europe and of the world that has gradually developed since the sixteenth century."

Is it foolish to introduce the concept of pacifistic humanity into this purely fateful process that is truly taking place beyond good and evil, in order to dishonor it—or is it not silly? The fact is that it is happening, and indeed, through civilization's literary man. Of course, I am as sure as I am that I am alive that his humanitarian protest would have erupted much less strongly, or that it would not have occurred at all, if it had not been a matter of the "rise" of Germany, but of any other nation. For this depth of his enmity to Germany is immeasurable. I have seen people shake their heads in bitter criticism of the Battle of Tannenberg, who, if not 150,000 Russians but just as many Germans had lost their lives there, would not have denied their moral approval of this result. For have we not been lacking in democracy? Since these people themselves, even though they are literary men and psychologists, do not see this clearly, then we others cannot see clearly enough that it is much less their humanitarian disposition as their disposition of hostility to Germany that determines their position in this war, *on* this war. Nevertheless, we do not want to completely give up a discussion of the relationship of war and humanity.

What is humanitarian is not always and everywhere the same as what is humane—we ran across this truth early, and it continues to pop up again and again. Can one imagine an idea of humanity, a philosophical responsibility for the fate of the human race, or, to express the idea somewhat more concretely, of the European race, that would be antihumanitarian enough to approve of war in principle, and to declare war indispensable? Nietzsche—and again specifically not the late, extremely grotesque Nietzsche, but the enlightened author of *Human, All too Human*—provides the proof of this possibility. "It is vain daydreaming and beautiful-soul idealism," he says, "to expect much more from mankind (or even: much at all), if it has forgotten how to wage war." And at the end of the aphorism that begins in this way, he says with the same certainty and composure: "One will see ever more clearly that a highly cultivated and therefore necessarily weak race such as that of today's Europe not only needs wars, but the greatest and most terrible of wars—temporary lapses into barbarism, in other words—so that it will not forfeit its culture and its very existence to the means of culture."

There we have the example of a nonhumanitarian idea of humanity, of a pedagogical hardness and a thinker's insensivity that, let us admit, is not becoming to everyone. No, we do not presume to adopt the sovereign position of the cultural philosopher, we do not feel dutybound to be indifferent to individual suffering—at least I, for my part, do not do so. But first of all, one can be highly susceptible to pity for the individual and at the same time grant complete justice to the higher point of view of the thinker—that is, one can refuse to follow the principle of pacifism. And most important, if we are to talk about opinions and decisions in principle: if there are opinions that only befit greatness, it is definitely not the opinions that make the greatness. Opinions do not confer rank; this is the point that is important to me— neither the pacifistic nor the war-approving opinion says anything at all in itself about the worth and dignity of the person who advocates it. Opinions are not noble. The most noble and the basest people can have the same opinion, as we see daily before our eyes. If a significant present-day German writer were to pay homage to internationally-democratic pacifism, then he might well be able with his brilliant talent to ennoble this doctrine he shared with both honorable men and the most disgusting of literati; but God knows it is not the doctrine that would ennoble him. It would do so really just as little as the opposite decision and position could be able to dishonor and degrade a person— this is not unnecessary to emphasize since quite obviously, among literary men, at least, the prevailing view is that whoever thinks anything of himself and wants to be a somebody must go overboard in cursing the "criminal insanity" of this war, as well as of war in general, and that whoever does not do this eliminates himself from the community of intellectuals. It is exactly the same as with the hostile disposition to Germany that, as things stand (for Germany is, of course, if one may say so, the leading actor in this war), goes hand in hand with the pacifistic one. That several great Germans, that Hölderlin and Nietzsche, have behaved in a manner hostile to Germany, should not make one believe that one might increase one's own height even by an inch by imitating them today in this point. And that Messrs. Roesemeier, Grumbach, Stillgebauer, Fernau, Michels, and my other honorable compatriots, whatever their names, who are carrying out literary work in Switzerland against Germany, will attain a very high position in the hierarchy of intellectuals, a higher one, for example, than I, to whom their behavior is admittedly extremely disgusting—of this no one will convince me.

Humanity is obvious. If I were in the field, if I saw the horror of destruction with my eyes, if I had to see the insane ripping up of human bodies, to hear the choked voices of the peach-fuzzed young men who had begged for permission to volunteer, and who, childishly breaking down under the intense bombardment, cried, "Mother! Mother!"—does one believe I would remain hard, remain "patriotic," remain "enthusiastic" and would be capable of the grossness of delivering a journalistically suitable report to "my newspaper"? And yet, if the war as reality worked directly on my nerves—would I not remain somewhat distrustful of the disruption that the infinite pity and my own fear of death were inflicting on my heart? Would I not remind myself that the ten thousandth multiple of death is an illusion, that death in reality does not leave individual limits, that the individual still only dies his death, not those of the others as well? Death does not become more terrible when we see it multiplied ten thousand times before our eyes. "Humanity" does not prevent us all from being condemned to bitter death; and there are deaths in bed that are as horrible as any death in the field. Also, each heart is only capable of a limited measure of terror—beyond which something else begins: dullness, ecstasy, or something else again that the inexperienced cannot imagine, namely *freedom*, a religious freedom and serenity, a detachment from life, something beyond fear and hope that undoubtedly signifies the opposite of psychological humiliation, that even signifies the overcoming of death itself. I open again the letter of a young reserve lieutenant from the Flanders front, a student otherwise, and a poet, and I read again what moved me so much at first examination. "In the face of this immeasurable superiority of death," he writes,

> in this complete helplessness of night-and-day bombardment, usually in the rain, in open trenches, in the frightful desolation, in the hellish noise of the defense zone, the individual easily becomes cheerful, *not* despondent; one is so completely free of all cares, so detached from the earth, hopeless, but unburdened! Whoever has survived a week here in the forward position can much more easily survive months—if he lives. I live! At first, I was completely despondent, until in the second night I decided to reconnoiter for myself the battle line that was still three-fourths unknown. For five hours I walked, in spite of mud and fire, by moonlight, past all the battalion trench lines, continually buzzed by English night pilots and strafed from a height of twenty meters with machine gun fire. They fired into all the trenches. The farther forward, the less fire; but those at the very front also have a hard job among stinking bodies, shot-up cannon from earlier battles, etc., *too* hard. This path through death was to me an immensely blessed pain, a liberation. I am as happy as our people, who, with 101 degrees of fever, and with bad lung infections, have still *not* yet reported themselves sick. It is strange, in the face of these *immeasurable* demands for suffering and hardship, one would like to *laugh*, so free is one from all care, all responsibility, so completely in the hands of God.

Does this letter not teach that the human soul cannot be destroyed, cannot be degraded, that its true strength and nobility is only proved in suffering? Every change in and extension of human limits causes dread in him who has not participated in it and causes him to speak of inhumanity. Undoubtedly those trench dwellers, who, with 101 degrees of fever, reject the humanitarian possibility of reporting themselves sick and prefer their monstrous situation to life in the field hospital, are in a state of intoxication, in an intensification of a vital emotion that exceeds all the experience of civilized life. But who would be so philistine as to call the intoxication subhuman? And who would not envy the author of the cited letter his experience of freedom?

The eccentric humanity of war offends and repels the humanitarian sense, as the sight of an enraptured and ecstatic person offends and repels the sober and reasonable one. War's terrifying masculinity, by the way, does not exclude the feminine-charitable principle, and whoever, in order not to have to be a pessimist, justifies suffering teleologically, should not overlook the fact that war offers room, indeed, the widest room, for the organization of love. The expression that explains everything, *c'est la guerre*, is not German. The inadequacy of the French medical service, about which complaints do not die down even in France itself, proves once again that humanity as loftiness does not mean humanity as effectiveness. Furthermore, though war may push the individual's physical and spiritual way of life even far below the ordinary level of civilization—it would obviously still be quite wrong to speak of its brutalizing effect. Generally speaking, according to the reports of reliable observers, war does not brutalize the individual at all. According to them, the *danger* lies much more in the *refinement* of the individual man from such a long war experience, a refinement that may alienate him forever from everyday life. One does not even have to take into account the external expansion of horizon that the farmer or the worker experienced when the times took him to places and among people he would never have allowed himself to dream of meeting in reality: in his deepest inner being he will return home another man, and it will be difficult for him to find his way again in the petty narrowness of everyday life. One does not need the imagination of a poet to measure intuitively what psychological-intellectual, religious elevation, deepening, and ennoblement the year-long daily closeness to death produces in the human being—what nervous changes it must, or at least can, produce. The pitiful wife of the warrior returning from that world will welcome back another man than the one who left; only at first sight will she recognize him again as the one he was, perhaps soon feel a shyness before him, find him strange—and he *would* be a strange one if so many had not shared his fate. Will he still be attracted to her? Will she still be enough for his nerves? The war has made him accustomed to freedom and absence of material concern—which form the soil in which higher humanity and sensitive culture thrive. He has led an extraordinary life—often ghastly, often numbingly heavy, but also highly tense, strange, shocking and educating in a thousand ways. He has developed voluptuous emotions, high-minded comradeship, heartfelt piousness, and *other* things we do not know about. How will he like his home, which has remained narrow, humble, and full of petty cares, and in which he is now supposed to live again without danger and luxury, with the ideal of being a good burgher? What I am hinting at here, together with several other implications, is certainly disquieting enough; but it has nothing at all to do with brutalization, it would signify much more an elevation, intensification and ennoblement of human life by the war.

I put down my pen to open a field letter dated from a military hospital in Lorraine that speaks to the point in the most remarkable manner. In it, a young officer tells, obviously in a gratefully elevated mood, how the war facilitated his acquaintance with good literature that "life" had previously given him no time to think about. Only now, confined to bed and to his room for considerable time by a "not insignificant" wound, does he have the "opportunity" to occupy himself with our recent German poets and writers. "It is a strange corollary of the times," he says, "that I owe such special thanks to the war in general and to the French artillery in particular . . . Not until the war did I find true joy in reading; and, as is well known, a countless host of soldiers has had the same experience as I." War has taught a countless host of young people to read, which is the conscious occupation with the human soul. Is this a fact that belongs in the chapter on war and humanity— or not? I should think so indeed! And is it not precisely democracy that is counting on this fact: on the intellectual education and enhancement of many thousands by the war—as it indeed, in its way, identifies and confuses intellect with politics? "Life," my correspondent declares, had not left him time for occupation with literature; this war had created the necessary leisure for him for the first time. Then the war was more humane and favorable to culture than "life," the life of peace and career, that is. And was it only leisure that it bestowed? Is it certain that just any boring civilian illness would also have led the young man to the discovery of literature? Did not perhaps the exotic experience of the war, of his wound, and of the quiet of the hospital room have to come first to prepare his soul for this discovery?

It is still possible today to think of war as an immortal institution, as an indispensable revolutionary means of helping truth to prevail on earth, although the progress of the technology of war does seem to have carried this argument *ad absurdum.* The judgment that "nothing comes of it anymore" is not valid; for when one stands against all, and nothing comes of it, then this nothing is of such a positive nature that one can well say that something *did* come of it. The human race, Germany included, is pacifist today because the war has already lasted so long and imposed very great sacrifice. To believe it has, in its deepest inner nature, finally and unconditionally renounced war, would be an error; to claim it has *morally* gone beyond war—pure flattery. The Social Democrat, Scheidemann, spoke grossly but honestly when he said the general *exhaustion* would greatly further pacifist democracy. That is certain. But it is not very glorious for democracy that it only seems to thrive on the soil of exhaustion—and on that of failure. A child can observe that the democratic slogan, "No annexations, no reparations," regularly becomes audible in the party that at the moment sees itself losing, and that one immediately puts democracy out of one's mind when a victorious offensive is under way.

The amicable-peaceful society of nations is a chimera. Eternal peace would only be possible with the complete mixture and melting of races and nations—which, whether one says unfortunately or praise God, will take a long time. But whoever considered war to be eternal would not denigrate the human race in doing so—he would do rather the opposite. It is only a superficial truth when one declares that the nations "wanted to live in peace," and that they were led like lambs to the slaughter. In a mythical sense, one may speak of "guilt." The deeper truth is that everyone wanted the war and demanded it, could not do without it anymore. Otherwise it would not have come. And would it not rather honor than shame the human race if, in the long run, it could no longer stand the civic state of security and umbrellas? All in all, the human being is obviously *not* the noble dullard and literary saint that civilization's literary man either now already sees in him or that he wants to make of him as soon as possible. The human being does not perceive civilization, progress, and security as absolute ideals; beyond doubt there lives immortally in him a primitive-heroic element, a deep desire for the fearful, for which all the desired and sought-after exertions and adventures of individuals in peacetime: mountain climbing, polar expeditions, wild animal hunts, and daredevil flying stunts, are only expedients. "Intellect" presses for humanity; but what would a humanity be that had lost its *masculine* component? It, too, still stands equally honored in all nations. After all, there is no antithesis between civilization and masculinity, civilization and *courage*. To be sure, the Italians ran away from the Moors in Aduwa; but the rule is that civilized armies prove more courageous than the primitive ones, and Bismarck remarked in a speech: "Courage is, of course, the same in all civilized nations." In any case, whoever honors, loves, and affirms human nature must above all wish for it to remain *complete*. He will not want it, in its variety of forms, to miss that of the warrior, he will not want human beings to divide up into merchants and literati—which, admittedly, would be democracy.

By the way, however, human life contains so much that is "unworthy of a human being," and "inhumane," that the literary cleric will really never get past protest and disgust even in times of peace. Maupassant, who did not have a weak stomach, once called the act of procreation "filthy and laughable"—"*ordurier et ridicule*." One must certainly be very much in love to contradict this. I have seen people die and people born, and I know that the latter process can far exceed the former in mystical horror. If the horrors of war are hair-raising—well, my hair once stood on end for thirty-six hours while a human being was being born. That was not human, it was *hellish*, and as long as this exists, there can be war, too, as far as I am concerned. Everyone feels and knows that there is a mystic element in war: it is the same element that belongs to all the primordial forces of life, to birth and death, religion and love. But the humanitarian literary man's attitude toward elementary things and toward passion is disconnected and inconsistent. He celebrates passion as rhythm and generous gesture; he lays a claim to it, but still his goal in general is, as in the case of national passion and therefore of war, the thinning of the blood, the "ennoblement," "purification," *sanctification* of the human race—for undoubtably his "progress of the human heart" is headed toward sanctification by the literary spirit—whereby he completely forgets to ask how passion and sanctity are to get along with one another. It is self-evident that he also disapproves of religion. And there is only *one* elementary manifestation that he affirms and in which he strangely enough sees no hindrance to literary sanctification: it is sex. Here his reverence, his liberality and tolerance are completely limitless, one must acknowledge this. For him, sexual love and political humanitarianism, democracy, that is, go closely together; for him the one is only the sublimation of the other; and in strict antithesis to the Christian church and to Schopenhauer, who see in "woman" an *instrumentum diaboli*, he adores in her the inspiring leader on the path of political progress, to wit: virtue. An amazing idea that we will make note of without further comment.

How easy it is today, how easy it *would be*, to please the literary man! Let one just say something like: "Nothing against France! For she has produced this and that great artist"—and one is secure in his good graces. Well, if anyone at all in Germany has ever denied the artistic genius of the French race—I do not believe it has happened—he is a simpleton. I do not covet the applause that is certain to come to everyone today who, in a highly free-thinking manner, champions the war-transcending truth that Stendhal, Delacroix and Flaubert were great artists; for that they were so does not at all hinder the perception that France, in historical decline, is conducting herself in a shockingly bad way; so miserable through hatred and womanishly addicted to insult that no hysterical heroism can reconcile one with the wretchedness of her conduct. But whoever would produce some scorn of "the great times," "the *so-called* great times," would immediately have proved himself to be a member of the society of intellectuals. Why, really? For after all, seen clearly, the times are of course in the end *really* great. Civilization's literary man, precisely he, would have every reason to find them so! To be sure, there is no great man living, but your democratic ideology has of course broken with great men, it found they prevented the great nation. Be proud that nations make history today without a great man! Or rather: that history today is not made at all, but makes itself; that the times give birth to the new without Caesarean assistance. Don't the new times suit you? No one knows yet exactly what they consist of, and every will feels itself revitalized. But that you, precisely you, derive a powerful advantage from them, that your character suddenly stands in the brightest light, your influence and esteem have grown mightily; that the war has brought about your moment of glory, and what you have championed intellectually, namely democracy, is about to be realized politically: do you not see this? Again, you first of all would have reason to call the times great, for they are revolutionary, and you are, of course, revolutionaries. Do you only want to recognize epochs of brilliant culture as great? But I thought you were politicians and not—esthetes? Time and development admittedly continue on their way while the pointer on the clockface of the history of mankind stands still and does not advance. But when it so visibly plunges "forward," as just now, is it not human then to speak of great times? And would it be humane to take away from mothers and widows the consolation that those they gave up died for something great?

Goethe could not love the French Revolution. The experience disturbed him deeply, and he himself said that it paralyzed his productive powers for years. Nevertheless, he has the judge in *Hermann und Dorothea* say:

> Truly, our time is comparable to the strangest of times
> That history, the sacred and the profane, has perceived.
> For whoever has lived yesterday and today in this time
> Has already lived for years: so compact are the events.
> If I think back a little, a gray age seems to me
> To lie on my head, and yet my strength is still alive.
> Oh, we others may well compare ourselves with those
> To whom there appeared in a grave hour in the fiery bush
> The Lord God: He also appeared to us in clouds and fire.*

Great times! Is there, then, one sentence in this speech that does not fit our experience as clothes the body? Goethe loved neither politics nor history. But the old man said to Eckermann:

> I have the great advantage that I was born at a time when the greatest world events were daily routine and continued throughout my long life so that I was a living witness to the Seven Year's War, afterward to the secession of America from England, further to the French Revolution, and finally to the whole era of Napoleon until the hero's fall and the events that followed. Because of this, I have come to quite different conclusions and insights than will be possible for all those who are now being born and who must absorb these great events through books that they do not understand . . .

Can one speak more respectfully of history, or show oneself more willing to call times of powerful political upheaval *great*, and more

---

* Wahrlich, unsere Zeit vergleicht sich den seltensten Zeiten,
  Die die Geschichte bemerkt, die heilige wie die gemeine.
  Denn wer gestern und heut' in diesen Tagen gelebt hat,
  Hat schon Jahre gelebt: so drängen sich alle Geschichten.
  Denk' ich ein wenig zurück, so scheint mir ein graues Alter
  Auf dem Haupte zu liegen, und doch ist die Kraft noch lebendig.
  O, wir anderen dürfen uns wohl mit jenen vergleichen,
  Denen in ernster Stund' erschien im feurigen Busche
  Gott der Herr: auch uns erschien er in Wolken und Feuer.

grateful that one was privileged to experience them? I hear literary men groaning in the newspapers: "Oh, if we had only never seen the 'great times,' we could completely forget their horror!" It seems that Goethe did not think in this way. He called the history of his own days "thoroughly grand and significant. The *battles* of Leipzig and Waterloo," he said, "stand out so powerfully that those of Marathon and others of the like positively are eclipsed." I would like to see the literary man who would not bite off his tongue before he would speak in this tone of the battles in Flanders or at Tannenberg!

A stirring time of feverishly heightened life that intensifies everything tenfold, the noble and the base, and causes changes that are otherwise only the work of many decades; a time of consuming privations and convulsions that force the human being to thought, perception, and profession of faith as no other previous one; that allow him no vegetative existence, but spur him on to take his place with conviction whether it seems honorable or not; a time that works like death: ordering in spite of all confusion, clarifying, defining; that teaches us what we were and are, and that grants us steadfastness and modesty in suffering: why should we not have the right to call such a time great!

Of course it is one thing to be grateful for the experience of great upheavals and world events, and another to believe in an attainable, final goal of happiness for all political history. The latter is rather the affair of the political humanitarian, who, in fact, hates history and scorns "great times," but believes high-mindedly in a perfect and "completely serene" condition of the human race at the end of all the upheavals, and calls everyone who does not share this political belief "ruthless." As far as we are concerned, we find that what Goethe added to those sentences about the advantage of great historical experience is applicable word for word to today:

> It is quite impossible to predict what the coming years will bring us; but I fear we will not come to rest so soon. It is not given to the world to be satisfied; the powerful ones will not consent to a limitation of the use of force, and the masses will not be satisfied with moderate conditions in the expectation of gradual improvements. If the human race could be perfected, then a perfect condition would also be imaginable; but as things stand, everything will fluctuate back and forth, the one group will suffer while the other is comfortable, egotism and envy will always play their roles as evil demons, and there will be no end to the struggle of the factions.

I know very well: love! The decline of brotherhood! Before the war, that is, we were brothers. Oh my God! But where we were not so, for example, there the weapons were "intellectual"—they were indeed. And it is the inhumanity of the weapons that civilization's literary man abhors. Inhumanity begins for him there where blood flows: he cannot stand it. Psychological murder seems to him to be more compatible with progress than struggle with bayonets and hand grenades—and here he is right! I cannot find the place where Karl Moor speaks of the humanitarians who laugh up their sleeves when their neighbor "leaves the stock market bankrupt." But I see how the war has caused tears over mankind to stream from the eyes of fellows whom it would not cost anything in "peacetime" to tear their neighbor's heart out of his breast and cast it before his feet—in an only slightly figurative sense. To confuse culture and humanity: an error worthy of civilization's literary man. To believe that when there is no war then there is peace: a childishness that is not only peculiar to pacifism, but is what it consists of. Do not roll your eyes so! Did the world really look better before the war? Was perhaps this peaceful world, whose collapse we did not experience without awe, more human, milder, kinder, more loving, than the one of today? The war is outlived and rotten, I know: but when it was young, when it broke out and swept away the "peace"—was not Germany on the contrary, *in those days*, for a sacred moment, *beautiful*?

Life is harsh, cruel, and evil at all times and in every place, but it was harshest, most inexorable and unidyllic of all in Germany. Who would not have experienced the feeling on leaving the borders of the *Reich* as if he were suddenly surrounded by a milder, laxer, more "human" atmosphere, as if his nerves, his intellect, his muscles, could *relax*? Truly, this had little or nothing to do with "militarism" and lack of "democracy"; the severity of German life had deeper reasons. A foreigner recently spoke about these reasons: the Dane, Johannes V. Jensen, in a penetrating essay, "Europe Before and After the War." Germany's high development and accomplishment, he says, were more closely connected to the same cultural force that had created northern European culture in general, namely resistance, than was true for any other European state. One of the consequences of Germany's imperiled central geographical position was the inner *social tension* that was not only of an economic but especially of a psychological nature. Jensen calls to mind the significance of the Jews for the total development of the *Reich*—of these hardened children of misfortune whose character clashed with the German spirit that had been disciplined in another type of misfortune. But it was precisely this clash that so honed the German national character that it was momentarily the sharpest, most complete moral apparatus the world had ever seen. "The psychological struggle for life," Jensen says,

> flushed the innermost capacities in both peoples out of their unconscious twilight, spurred all noble and ignoble passions, called up every reserve, with the total result of work and more work. An education such as Germany experienced by the absorption of Jewish elements into her national body is without any counterpart, on both sides the psychological tension emerged in such hair-thin, cutting nuances *that in the last ten years it has really almost hurt to become acquainted with German intellectual works.*

Let us just try it; perhaps we can sympathize with the impression of the foreign observer. One should have the right to quotations, and certainly I am not lacking one in this case: I could speak from strong personal experience about everything the Dane said about "German tension"—perhaps I *have* already done so. Was not the humoristic fictional character of Doctor Überbein, this *malheur* by birth, "committed to accomplishment," the attempt at an expression of precisely this? His humanity was not the best (he had a contemptuous word for it, he spoke of the "laziness of happiness"), and he perished miserably because his unnatural zeal spoiled things with all those who took a more human attitude, a more jovial one, that is, toward "accomplishment," with all friends of a weekend. Who would want to deny that Germany's humanity had suffered because of the tension she stood under? However, against the annoyance that the friends of a weekend found in this, there remains to be said that it was not at all of idealistic origin.

However that may be, we did not live gently, not peacefully, before the war; life was not humane. And when Jensen adds to his analysis: "The war will certainly be perceived in this respect as a *liberation*, the cutting edge is now turned outward—" then we admit: Yes, this is the way it was, the feeling of liberation that the war brought us was partially of this origin—but my God, for what a fleeting moment was it so! The cutting edge has long since been turned against ourselves again, and the handle will be bloodier than ever after the war. We have not complained, we have only expressed our opinions; and we stake our honor on maintaining good form and conduct in the process. This has been our humanity and our luxury—for luxury, even that of "beauty," is immoral voluptuousness if it is not the expression of honor and courage. But whoever acts as if there had been "peace" before the war, and as if there will be "peace" again after the war, we can laugh in his face.

I saw two invalids walking along the street, a blind man and a one-armed one. The blind man stared with artificial eyes, a doll-like look; he allowed himself to be led in his night by his cripple-colleague, on whose robust right arm he went, while on the other side the left field-gray sleeve hung down unoccupied, unwarmed. I, too, am a human being, and I shuddered. They really fixed you, I thought! No, it is monstrous, insane, criminal, and shameful. It must not and will not happen again.

I came closer to them, I stayed with them; one should, without curiosity, with discreet respect, become absorbed in life whenever it appears to one. One should approach it and stay with it with sympathy, love of truth, and without pompousness. From afar, life seems solemn and calls forth wild words such as "monstrous," "insane," "criminal," and "shameful." Closer up, it is simpler, more modest, more unrhetorical, scarcely ever without a touch of humor, in short, it is immediately more human.

The mutilated ones had walked along in silence, and this had undoubtedly reinforced the tragic dignity of their appearance. People almost always seem dignified, beautiful, and esthetically disturbing only as long as they are silent. If they open their mouths, respect for them is usually gone. The dignity and beauty of animals is very much tied to the fact that they cannot speak. Just then they began to speak, the two. They spoke to one another with their nasal, sentimental, upper-Bavarian voices, in their muffled, rumbling dialect full of Middle High German dipthongs such as "oa" and "üa." Something had occurred to one of them that he could just as well express as keep to himself, and so he said it, especially since they had been silent for so long. It was the one-armed one. The doll-eyed one heard him in his night, since he was only blind, not deaf, and without reflecting much, he answered something that made the one-armed one laugh. I had to be careful with him because he did, after all, have living eyes and could see me, something I tended to forget. He did not laugh for the people around, something that would probably not have seemed proper to him with a blind man on his arm, he laughed somewhat hiddenly to himself, and said something again in the process, while at the same time, the blind one added something to complete his answer, and on his face, too, which was still shy from unaccustomed blindness, there appeared a wooden and dark laughter—it was beautiful fall weather.

I hardly understood what they said. Naturally, it was something rather ordinary and not lofty, something connected with life in the field hospital, instruction for blind and one-armed men, or with lunch and digestion. The one-armed one sometimes looked at the people, the blind one could not see them. He stared artificially straight ahead; but of course he knew what most of them looked like, so he had not lost very much there. The weather was beautiful, as I said. They walked and breathed the pleasantly sharp air that smelled like withered leaves, and the sun shone on their noses.

For the moment, they obviously had no worries, and they had had no pain for a long time, either. They had probably had some, probably very bad. But this had almost already been forgotten, and then, of course, pain is experienced quite unequally by different nervous systems; it shocks the human soul in different degrees. The misfortune in the battle, a head wound for the one, the glowing piece of iron that crushed the other's arm, had come with crashing rapidity, at a moment when one was perhaps not afraid at all—suddenly it had happened. Afterwards one had probably lain helpless for a while, under the merciless sky, and one had felt abandoned by God and man. But then, one had learned that human beings still really remain human beings, and to a certain extent set store by their human character, even if they act horribly for the sake of their passions, for power, riches, and honor. One was found, refreshed, bandaged, borne on a stretcher, brought to a bed. After one had done, or rather suffered one's part, one could entrust oneself to the shoulders and arms of fellow human beings who carried the wounded hero that one now was. One had felt caring human hands on one's wounds. One had been operated on while one slept. Doctors who were sometimes gruff but sometimes also made jokes had treated one as well as they had learned how to, and one had to say that they had learned it well and were equipped with all the modern resources. If the pain was bad, one received a little prick with the needle, and then the deep pleasure and gratefulness of relief came, and the divine happiness of painlessness that no one knows of who has not suffered great pain before. And so one had gotten well, one-armed and blind, but one was well, and one did not have to go to war anymore. One went walking in the sun and had perhaps a flattering little idea that one, especially as a pair, made a shocking sight. One was no longer shocked oneself, if one ever had been.

I must add that the sight of the blind man filled me most of all directly with horror. The one-armed one, well, he had, after all, another arm, and the right one, at that. In all possible fields, in agriculture, industry, and as a workman, he could still hold his own, and then, what perfection the progress in the technique of making artificial limbs had reached! But blind. From childhood on, this had seemed for me the most frightening fate. In the course of my life I had seen many blind men who had become so quite without a war, or who had been so from birth, blind men with or without glass eyes, blind men with rectangular, blue glasses in front of their eye sockets, with closed, seemingly grown-together lids, or with open pupils that were dead; I had looked at them and scarcely understood how these people bore their fate, how they were able to live. Later, to be sure, I heard my limitless pity called exaggerated, yes, inadmissible. Blind people, I heard, were generally mild, calm, cheerful people; deafness was a much more embittering handicap and twisted the character, while blindness did rather the opposite. I made the acquaintance of a charming gentleman who has been completely blind since childhood. Moving his cane lightly and gracefully in front of him, he walks unaccompanied and alone in the streets of Berlin, pursuing his business—through the subway tunnel and over Potsdamer Platz. He avoids puddles; how he does it, no one knows. He occupies himself with social welfare, with literature, and also with business speculation—a constantly animated, talkative man. Besides this, he owns a repeating watch with pleasant-sounding chimes that I have always envied him. My acquaintance with him moderated my ideas about the terrors of life in eternal night.

But the strongest impression was made upon me by the statements of a man who lost his sight in his middle years—statements made directly to me about his feelings. After a short period of grief, the man explained, his mood improved greatly, not only toward the time immediately following the loss of sight, but toward the earlier period, as well, toward the time *before*. Darkness is good for the nerves, he feels. He says he has gained in peace of soul, in harmony. All people are good, friendly to him, all show themselves ready to help, show him their best sides, and his relationship to the world and to people has become more cordial, sympathetic, and happy. If he were to be frank, he would have to say: If it were up to him and he were given the choice, he would first answer evasively and say that his misfortune also had very bright sides, if he might express himself in this way. If one pressed him further and demanded a definite answer, then he would have to say: No, it did not tempt him, and frankly, *he had no desire to be able to see again.*

This is, as I have said, the actual statement of a blind man. Now, in the war, I have heard that those in the field hospitals who have been blinded in battle are the most cheerful of all patients. They romp, *they throw their glass eyes at one another.* And this is not out of any hellish despair, but from ordinary high spirits. One cannot understand it, but one must accept it.

The frivolity of the human being, even in the so-called deepest misery, is limitless. His ability to adapt himself, even to circumstances that seem to mock this ability, is just as limitless as long as he stays alive. Furthermore, there is the hope that "*toute trompeuse, qu'elle soit, sert au moins à nous mener à la fin de la vie par un chemin agréable*," as La Rochefoucauld says.

The picturesque and bloodily obvious misery is not the deepest and truly most dreadful one on earth; there are sufferings and pains, degradations of the soul in which the human being loses the desire to throw glass eyes; wounds that are attended to by no human hand and that no public charity worries about, inner mutilations, without honor, iron cross and heroic character that are not paraded out in the fall sun to the edifying shock of one's fellow man, and that the world will be full of even when we are enjoying the blessings of the eternal democratic peace of nations. The world was full of "misery unworthy of human beings" before the war came. The life of the carusi in the Sicilian sulphur mines, the life of the east-end children who succumb in loathsome misery and are crippled by mistreatment; this was before 1914. Shameless injustices, whose perpetrators go unpunished while the victim receives no compensation; bodily pains such as those connected with a broken pelvis or with burns; sickness, debauchery, passion, grief, old age and bitter death, this existed before. Take suffering teleologically, consider that only need creates culture, that without suffering there would be no pity, that only injustice awakens the feeling of justice and without pain, morality would remain undeveloped, human life would remain a vegetation that one would scarcely call happy, since pain is the foil of desire. Or console yourselves in a Christian way with the hope of a life after death. Or be pessimistic and accuse life, life itself, which is sinful and causes guilt and would be better not to exist—this life in which the human being is a wolf to the human being and one only rises by trampling on the other. Be critics of life, strike and punish it with the destructive word! Make of art a torch that may shine mercifully into all terrible depths, into all the shameful and sorrowful abysses of existence; make a fire of intellect and ignite the world everywhere with it so that it flames up and dissolves together with all its shame and torment in redeeming pity! But do not take pleasure in a political-humanitarian lament of opposition to the war! Do not act as if *it* had desecrated the face of the earth—and previously the tiger and the lamb had grazed together. I know nothing more foolish and deceitful than the declamation of the literary man, whom this war made into a humanitarian and who proclaims that whoever does not perceive war as a subhuman outrage and a disgrace is an anti-intellectual, a criminal, and an enemy of the human race.

Love! Humanity! I know it, this theoretical love and this doctrinaire humanity that is hissed out through one's teeth to show one's disgust for one's own nation. I know it, the literary howl of today, know also the works of art in which it is shouted out, works whose humanity is intellectual demand, literary doctrine, something shallow, affected, pontificated—works in which there is no humanity at all, however, and which only prolong their lives by the fact that the public and the critics confuse humanity with the rhetorical-political *demand* for humanity. This demonstrative and programmatic humanity of the literary man who wants to attack and shame with it, who is wonderfully proud of it and seems constantly to be crying, "See how human I am, and you, what are you, ruthless esthetes, that's what you are!" Oh, thanks just the same for this propaganda type of humanity.

War is atrocious, yes! But when, in the midst of this war, the political literary man rises up and declares that the loving breath of the universe is flowing through his breast, then this is the most horrible of all horrors, and to be ignored. "Truly," say servile, foolish people, "that is not only a great artist, that is, above all, a magnificent human being!" Is he not ashamed? For he is, of course, no magnificent human being, and he knows it. Miserable doggedness, together with sentimental verve, doctrinaire callousness, arrogance, rigidly cold impatience, the phariasical sacrificial fervor of "May you perish, *I live in the light*"—all this produces no magnificent human character, and a thousand times worse than "being right for the world," which may come from sympathy, from love—a thousand times worse is *self-righteousness*: it is the sin that is not forgiven. Turgenev once said about the Rousseauean Leo Tolstoy that his ultimate and most frightening secret was that he could love no one but himself. This is the secret of all descendents of Rousseau, who always, in one way or another, put their children into orphanages and write educational novels. To lay stress on their public accomplishments is an evil-success cult. For once again: the only way to see things *humanly* is to see them individually. No literary man has had a greater effect on the world than J. J. Rousseau, and the politician genuflects before him for this reason. Nevertheless, to the human scrutiny of the artist, who can disregard effects, he remains a suspicious fellow. The effect on the public of someone who knows how to say very beautifully, "I love God!" can be significant; but when he, at the same time, "hates his brother," then, according to the Gospel of John, his love of God is nothing other than belles lettres and sacrificial smoke that does not rise.

Apropos of "virtue," I said that it was a matter of taste and mood whether one tended to find the human being more beautiful in an emancipated or in a reverential attitude. Truly, it seems to me that when we are speaking of humanity, the esthetic point of view deserves some consideration. And furthermore, it seems to me that at the very least it bears witness to one-sidedness and limitation when the political humanitarian places all human beauty and dignity in the promethean-emancipatory gesture. I need only look up from my table to delight my eyes with the vision of a moist glade, through whose half-darkness the bright architecture of a temple glistens. From the sacrificial stone the flame blazes up whose smoke disappears in the branches. Flagstones embedded in the swampy-flowered earth lead to its smooth steps, and there sacerdotally covered figures kneel, solemnly humbling their humanity before the savior, while others, upright, in ceremonial bearing, stride from the direction of the temple to the service. Whoever would see an insult to human dignity in this picture by the Swiss artist that I have always valued and held dear, could certainly be called a philistine. Nevertheless, the political humanitarian is undoubtedly duty-bound to see such things in it—and let this much be admitted, it offers an only too excellent example of the undependability of art as a means of progress, of its treacherous tendency toward the antireason that creates beauty. Obviously, however, the humanity of emancipatory progress is either not the true, or not the complete humanity; for how can a work be called inhuman when it offers one's gaze, which has been harassed by impudence, baseness, and mob-greed, a vision and a dream-refuge of dignified-humble human decency?

That there are still places in the midst of a sufficiently liberated world that impose a good measure of such propriety on their visitors, places in which the most disrespectful lout feels obliged to take off his headgear, lower his voice, and assume a serious, almost thoughtful look that is at any rate respectful, not just outwardly for the sake of propriety and order, but also truly inwardly as well; that there are *holy* places, even today, peaceful refuges of the soul, where the human being, who has fled from the evil tumult of some metropolitan street, suddenly stands surrounded by resounding silence and colorful twilight, with the faint smell of centuries in the air, with the eternal, the essential, in short, with the *human* element—this has something fantastic, incredible in it and is a great, magnificent comfort. The political humanitarian may have sufficient tolerance to dignify medieval churches with the antiquarian-esthetic attention of a traveller. But as strongholds of superstition and as hiding places of such a physically expressive soul-bondage as is found there even today, of wretchedness, shame, and misery, in the second decade of the twentieth century, of the *kneeling human being*, they must be an abomination and a despair to his resolute love of humanity. As far as I am concerned, I have always loved time spent in churches, specifically because of an estheticism that had nothing at all to do with the study of culture and with handbook education, but that is rather directed toward what is human. Two steps aside from the amusing highway of progress, and you are surrounded by an asylum where seriousness, quiet, and the thought of death have their proper places, and where the cross is raised for adoration. What a blessing! What *satisfaction*! Here one speaks neither of politics nor of business. The human being is a human being here, he has a heart, and makes no secret of it. Here pure, liberated, nonbourgeois-solemn humanity rules. Here, before one's fellow man, one would be ashamed of rude words, of impudent conduct, but so strong is the right of the human being here, so complete the impotence of civil custom, that no one is ashamed before his fellow man of the expression and display of deep emotion, devotion, surrender and repentance, not even of a bodily posture that would provoke, in all civic situations, displeasure and laughter as theatrical, fantastic, eccentric, and romantic. *The kneeling human being*! No, my humanity feels no displeasure in this picture. On the contrary, it suits it as does no other, specifically because of its anticivil, anachronistic, daringly-human stamp. This posture appears nowhere else anymore, it contradicts in its relaxed humanity all the reserve, skepticism, and hostility to gesture in civilization. Does the lover still kneel before his beloved when he woos her? How nakedly and terribly life in our times would have to break through the uniformity of civilized manners for one to see the human being, who, on his knees, would hide his face in his hands or raise his folded hands in front of him! How *extraordinary* is human nature—which is still the true and essential thing! Religion, however, the place of worship, this sphere of the extraordinary, frees human nature and makes it beautiful. The great individual may be beautiful in an attitude of fiercely defiant emancipation. The great majority of human beings needs the restriction of awe to offer a bearable and even a beautiful sight; and that it grants the human being a posture that is at the same time restricted and human-liberated, is to me a high, esthetic-human merit of the church.

But even if the humanitarian accepts religious humbling, the service to God, that is, as not unworthy of the human being: *service to human beings* must certainly seem to him to be a shocking insult to humanity, to human dignity. Well, I consider it to be prejudicious to set service to human beings against human dignity as incompatible with one another. For as soon, for example, as love comes into play, dignity suffers no harm from service. Pride, honor, and pleasure in obedience seem today to be peculiarly German, and an international incomprehensibility; at any rate, here is a psychological fact that proves that "lack of freedom" is quite compatible with masculine dignity. Whoever, for example, observes a German cadet standing obediently and rigidly at attention before a comrade of officer rank who is scarcely older than he, will notice that this happens with a certain enthusiasm and at the same time a certain humor, in short: there is romantic play in it: the expression of knightly-masculine obedience is obviously bound up with an elevated zest for life, and, particularly as far as the feeling of honor is concerned, it is probably more strongly felt in the one who salutes than in the one who receives the salute. Honor as a life stimulus exists only where there is aristocratic order, the cult of distance, hierarchy; democratic human dignity is in comparison to it the dullest and most lackluster thing in the world. Whoever is something honors himself by stepping back expressively before someone who is something more; the honor of one's own position and rank is always perceived and emphasized as well in the process. Only he who is nothing at all has an interest in emphasizing human equality—an erroneous interest, by the way; for instead of an abstract and doubtful "dignity," he could share in a concrete and personal honor by dedicating himself to voluntary and proud subordination.

In Bismarck's grave inscription, which he wrote himself, "A True German Servant of His Master," there may be a good bit of Germanic-sentimental hypocrisy, for his servant nature was just so-so constituted, even if his master nature made itself felt fully in Germanic-servant and not in Latin-imperial forms. Fontane called him "our civilian Wallenstein," and added that he had more similarity to Schiller's Wallenstein than to the real one, and here again the sentimental part of his character is emphasized. At any rate, that inscription signifies homage to an ideal, and it expresses: "He could after all have become even more if he had wanted to; but this more would, according to German concepts, have been a less, and it was national for him to find his honor in not wanting to be more than the true servant of his master." It was really national to a high degree, and Bismarck was right when he remarked to Latin guests, "Your Caesars would be alien and incomprehensible among us Germans." Just now we are seeing how a powerfully national German servant of his master is trying to prevent possible stirrings of mistrust and jealousy in his master's breast by tirelessly manifesting his loyalty and submissiveness—stirrings in the breast of his master whom he loves *because* he is his master, and whom it would go against his honor not to love. Voltaire's sentence, "*Le premier qui fut roi, fut un soldat heureux*," is a highly un-German thought. The model of the "happy soldier," of the soldierly adventurer, Boulanger, does not exist in Germany, and this is also connected to the fact that a genuine rule of the saber has never existed here.

Proud obedience, I said, seems today to be something specifically German. Originally, however, in predemocratic times, pleasure in service was something generally human, at least generally European. Goethe says, "There is also in the human being a desire to serve; therefore the *chevalerie* of the French is a *servage*." Well, political humanitarianism, with its concept of human dignity, has everywhere thoroughly damaged the instinct of noble servitude, of knightly servitude (the English "knight" and the German "*Knecht*" are actually the same word). Perhaps this humanitarianism has left the picturesque remains of noble servitude in Germany, and now is about to destroy them, too. While the servant class once had its honor, dignity, and beauty, as well as the ruling one, service is increasingly being thought of throughout the world as humanly demeaning, even when it is not a matter of service to people, but is, or ought to be, service to a *cause*, the cause of art, for example, that is after all important for the human race. Even then, I say, the social idea, the idea of right and freedom, greatly predominates, and the cause can go to the devil if only no hair on the head of democratic human dignity is harmed. Let what Felix Mottl experienced in New York at a rehearsal of *Tristan* serve as an example. At exactly twelve o'clock, the concertmaster put on his hat and the orchestra ended the rehearsal, although it was not at all finished; for the gentlemen's contract specified only until twelve o'clock, and if one was not finished by then, so much the worse for the conductor, who stood with his interest in the *cause* alone. No pleading and no outbursts of anger helped; Mottl finally even had to apologize for the latter, for otherwise the performance would have foundered on the human dignity of the musicians. As far as the spirit of service is concerned, there is at least still a human relationship between master and servants on farms; in the cities the last remnants of patriarchal humanity have long been completely destroyed by the inciting, stultifying power of the idea of justice and dignity that makes everything ugly. Loyalty, attachment to house and family, do not appear anymore; the latter are thought of as objects of exploitation, and when it comes to a court clash, the system of justice, which is afraid of socialism, supports this judgment. The solution to the question of domestic service is completely uncertain; all that is clear is that the situation has become untenable.

In spite of all this, the "desire to serve" is certainly something eternal in the human being, and it would have remained clearer as a fact if the modern world had given it more opportunity to prove itself. There are no more servants because there are no more masters—that is, none that can be served with a good aristocratic conscience. Where the order of rank is something completely arbitrary, momentary, and unfounded, the instinct to serve is no longer satisfied; and of course this is indeed the way things stand today with the order of rank. That the servant in a modern hotel serving tea to the swell who is lolling about indecorously in the leather armchair is not, for his part, sitting in the armchair and being himself served by the swell is nothing but pure chance; no one would notice anything if they changed places within a quarter of an hour. But the people—I have already expressed this experience— perceive aristocratically; they have preserved the most natural and the finest feeling of distance, they know how to distinguish with completely undemocratic certainty between a gentleman and a fellow who has luckily gotten rich, and their perception cannot be bribed. Where there is still a possibility of serving with conviction, they like to serve, without in the least feeling that their human dignity has been impaired. That they serve the wife of Mr. Mayer, the wealthy businessman, without conviction, and therefore badly, unfaithfully, with manifestations of recalcitrance, and only for profit, is not to be surprised at.

The idea of human dignity is a product of custom. In the eastern part of Germany the servants still bow down to kiss the hem of the master's gown—a gesture that is carried out with ease, naturalness and dignity, as part of correct behavior, and *accepted* without embarrassment. I emphasize the latter because it seems to me personally to be the more difficult. For just as it is easier (because more comfortable) to obey than to command, it is in general easier to serve than to *be* served, and there is a sensitiveness that makes it impossible. I once told the story of a sensitive prince who had great difficulties in passing by footmen who were standing rigidly at attention, although he knew that they felt quite happy in their posture and satisfied with themselves, and that they would also, with the same self-satisfaction, have thrown themselves on their stomachs if this had been the custom of the country. By this I meant that democracy comes from above, not from below, or at least it should be this way. It should not be pretension, arrogance, insulting demand, but resignation, modesty, renunciation, humanity. Democracy should once again be what it was before the invasion of politics into God's world: brotherhood *above* all differences and with the formal preservation of all differences. Democracy—but I always say the same thing—should be morality, not politics; it should be goodness from person to person, goodness from both sides! For the master needs the goodness of the servant just as much as the servant needs the goodness of the master.

When the war had lasted a few months, one read that Nice and Monte Carlo were at the point of bankruptcy. I do not know whether the report turned out to be true, but I do know that it filled me with the same heartfelt satisfaction as the one that preceded it: namely that *le prince* had telegraphed something humanitarian and anti-German to Wilson, something about civilization and humanity. One wishes disreputable allies for a cause one hates—to this extent, one is a politician. Indeed, one feels oneself reinforced in one's distaste for a world view that is that of a brothelkeeper.

To be sure, nowhere is it more "human" than in this Klingsor magic garden. When one puts oneself into this *etablissement*, one sees quite clearly for the first time what civilization and humanity really mean in the *entente* world. Is it not supposed to have happened that this or that American citizen has hanged himself in the casino park? What of the president's note? But these sacrifices did not fall to "militarism," but to its cheerful opposite. How very offensive to all humanity, at this place of pilgrimage of international civilization, at this amusement coast with palms and showy blue sea, with Parisian women, Russian grand dukes and Rumanian confidence men, with champagne, *Parsifal* performances and warm showers to ward off gamblers' sweat—how inhuman, I say, in this sphere of the "*vie facile*," and of cosmopolitan civilization, the terrible struggle for life and justice of a serious nation must seem!

Bankrupt? And because of this war? What a symbol! But still just a symbol. For the idea that that cosmopolitan civilization, which just before the war had mainly taken on the form of a general dance mania, of a maniacal cult of exotic sexual dances, had been brought to a standstill, to a paling and ghostly disappearance, by the war—this idea was, of course, error and deception. International civilization continues to live, yes, it still lives today and every day just as it lived before the outbreak of the great affliction. At its sporting pleasures in St. Moritz it displays the same foolish costumes of the last time of peace. The ladies' parrot-colored sweaters, the young men's silken tasseled caps. Whoever knows how to get a passport may convince himself and take part in the revelry. The latest of these dance entertainments to which one abandons oneself even during meals, between two courses, is the fox-trot; this I have been told, and I make note of it here; nothing more. As far as I know, the fox-trot was unknown before the war. Not until wartime did it come into favor and flower in Saint Moritz and at other refuges of international civilization; At the time of the battle of the Somme, I believe, it was introduced.

It was in an earlier section of these reflections, dedicated particularly to civilization's literary man, that I tried to describe that Europe we would have had to enjoy in case there had been a rapid and brilliant victory of the *entente* for civilization and humanity. I remember this as I speak of Monte Carlo and Saint Moritz. But I will not neglect to imagine the other possibility, either: the Europe of an overpowering and complete *German* victory—and do not intend to lament that we do not have it, nor will have it. No doubt it would have offered a more decent sight—serious, respectful of the state, social, official, organizational, masculine-soldierly; but also hard, inhospitable, rather gloomy, rather brutal, "militaristic" to the point of pitilessness—and while to be sure I do not believe that "human nature" would ever come off badly on earth under any conditions, no matter how harsh: shall I admit that the idea of humanity in this German Europe would perhaps really have come off badly? Probably there is no Frenchman or Englishman who has not wished for, and does not still wish for, the positive and unconditional triumph of his country in this war. As far as I am concerned, I am completely content that Germany has remained *un*-beaten and commandingly upright, for this was a spiritual necessity and indeed, something so much more positive than the unbeaten condition of France and England that it calls this unbeaten condition in question.

One may believe me or not: I could well imagine that the hatred and enmity among the nations of Europe is finally an illusion, an error—that the sides flaying one another are not basically factions, but working together under God's will, in brotherly pain, for the renewal of the world and the soul. Yes, one may dream of a placated and reconciled Europe—even if goodness and higher harmony will only owe their existence to exhaustion and to that sensitivity and refinement that is created by great suffering. For the refinement from suffering is higher and more human than that from happiness and the life of luxury; I believe in this, and in a hopeful sense I also believe in that future Europe, a Europe that, dedicated to a religious humanity and to tolerant intellectuality, will remember only with shame and scorn today's bitter ideological quarrel: May this Europe be undoctrinaire, undogmatic, and without belief in slogans and antitheses, free, cheerful, and gentle, and only shrug off "aristocracy" and "democracy." Goethe remarked about an ephemeral play that the whole idea was concerned only with aristocracy and democracy, and that this had no general human interest. Thus spoke an antipolitical artist; and will it not be antipolitical and artistic, this postwar Europe? Will it not, in defiance of those who cry for the complete dominance of politics, for "political atmosphere," have humanity and culture as guiding stars? But it should certainly show respect for the *one* aristocractic principle: its own. May it learn to *set great store* in matters of culture and taste, as it did not know how to do before, may it renounce lascivious estheticism and exoticism, the self-betraying tendency to barbarism it pandered to in an unbridled way, taboo crazes in clothes styles and foolish infantilisms in its art, and adopt an attitude of noble rejection of anthropophagic sculpture and South American harbor-saloon dances. By the way, will it not be *poor* for a while, our Europe, will not the sacrifices it has made have taught it to find the simple and the natural precious, and to enjoy gratefully a meal of eggs, ham, and milk rather than some kind of vomitorium-gluttony of the past? Yes, let us imagine it to be filled with disgust for its former negrolike craving for pleasure and the ostentatiousness of civilization, let us think of it as simple and graceful in manners and dedicated to an art that would be the pure expression of its condition: tender, unadorned, kind, intellectual, of the highest humane noblesse, full of form, restrained and powerful through the intensity of its humanity.

Dreams, dreamt on a late summer morning, 1917, while the English-French offensive rages in Flanders. Will they seem inappropriate, implausible, in a writing that admittedly bears the stamp of its warlike origin on its forehead, and that dialectically champions the need and the partisanship of its heart, but that basically struggles against politics and for what is human? I found myself more national than I had known I was, but I was never a politician, never a nationalist. I was not strong or presumptuous enough to be "indifferent" to the war; shaken, stirred up, sharply challenged, I threw myself into the fray and defended by argument what was mine. But God knows I will feel better when my soul will again be permitted to view life and humanity purified of politics; my nature will be able to stand the test better than it has in this book when the nations live alongside one another behind peaceful borders in dignity and honor, and exchange their finest goods: the beautiful Englishman, the polished Frenchman, the human Russian, and the knowing German.

CHAPTER 10

On Belief

For a long time I have tried hard to find a precise, exhaustive, and final definition of the literary man—this book bears witness to this. Now I have finally grasped it, and, far from jealously guarding it, I hurry from a social drive to share it, surprised and amused, as the reader will be, by its simplicity.

A literary man is a being who always knows exactly: "One must now—" and who immediately also *can*. The rest is just commentary. The literary man, you see, *is* not, he only judges—a happy, enviable lot, as I often perceived. For how easy it is for the purely judging person always to jump into the right boat, never to miss the connection, always to be found arm in arm with the latest group of young people. But one can be "backward" and still be even *more*, or, to add a word and put emphasis on it, more *worthy* than many a judging marcher at the *tête*—simply because one is after all something and is therefore heavier, slower, less nimble in running along and running ahead than such a frivolous nothing of literary orientation. Great people, people who *were* much, who were hindered by obligations, solid weights of their being, from unrestrainedly and joyfully plunging into a new opinion of the times without inhibition, have found it *difficult* to come to terms with such new things and to make their peace with them: I refer to Goethe again and to the disturbance and paralysis that he experienced at the intrusion of the Revolution and of politics. Another example is Pascal, whose greatness and power of fascination actually rest on his problematic position between epochs, between middle ages and modernity, Christianity and enlightenment. He belonged to both periods with parts of his being, a critic and a religious man. Such a predicament creates spirit, creates depth, freedom and irony; creates personality. Personality, the only interesting thing on earth, is always a product of mixture and of conflict: epochs, contrasts and contradictions rebound off one another and become intellect, life, form. Personality is being, not opining, and if it tries its hand at giving opinions, then it becomes aware that it consists of opposites and is badly suited to propagate the nothing-but-new, the intellectually strictly up-to-date. Epochs of primarily individualistic and social thought, for example, alternate in history. But only literary weathercocks proclaim and demand one or the other unconditionally, according to the way the wind is blowing, and damn the sinner against the spirit of the times to the bottomless pit. The artist and poet at any rate, in accordance with his deepest nature, will always have an inalienable right to individual ethos; he is the necessary and born protester, the individual with his god. He can and must not be deprived of his loneliness, his "evangelical freedom," even in times of strictest social constraint.

The literary man, then, who as such is nothing, and consequently only has to opine and to judge in a light-hearted way—this adaptable spirit is always up-to-date about what one "must now do" to be up with the times—and then he can do it, too. What must one do now, anyway? One must *believe*. And in what? In belief—would be the correct answer. For here it is, in fact, a matter of a sort of *l'art pour l'art*, of belief as gesture and estheticism, although it is precisely its shabby opposite, doubt, that is perceived as concerned with esthetics, as the source of all *burgherly* estheticism, relativism, impressionism, of all ethical, which here means: *political* irresponsibility and ruthlessness. But as we again say this word, "political," the dominant word of the times, we also express at the same time the content and object of the belief that is new, or renewed, freshened up to be new: It is the belief in politics, that is: in progress, in the human race and its becoming perfect; in a goal, specifically in a goal of happiness in its development; in that "very beautiful and completely serene" condition that its path is brilliantly leading up to; in a kingdom of God that, antimetaphysical and antireligious, has been transferred from the heaven of deceitful clerics to the earthly future, to the human realm; in short, it is the belief in morality, that *democratic* morality of which Nietzsche's contempt said it was striving with all its power for the common green-pasture happiness on earth, to wit, security, safety, comfort, and ease of living, and to cap it all, "if everything goes well, hopes to divest itself of all types of shepherds and bellwethers." "Equality of rights" and "compassion for all suffering" are its two most commonly preached doctrines, and suffering itself is taken as something one simply must abolish. "That such ideas," Nietzsche adds, "can still be modern, speaks badly of this modernity . . ." What was that, still modern? They are so *again*! A philosophy that did not believe in equality of rights and that did not wish the abolishment of suffering had routed these "ideas" twenty years ago; today they again hold the field—and with what a dictatorial expression of triumph! How much inclined to terroristic exclusiveness! Not only do they characterize themselves as *the* morality and *the* truth, but also as *the* intellect itself; intellect that struggles against them and that does not want to share the obligatory belief in politics and democracy is false intellect, is depraved, is ruthless pessimism. Ruthless? We became acquainted with this evil word in *another* connection when we were young. And later we read in a significant letter from Overbeck to Treitschke: "Optimism and pessimism are as old as the world of human beings, and their conflict is not younger—in this I, for my part, already see an argument for pessimism—*both are capable of the same ruthlessness*, both have always proven to be productive, and I, at least, stand up for my conviction of the greater productivity of pessimism."

Truly, this is also a belief, the belief in pessimism and its productivity, and it cannot be denied that the history of intellect and of art gives it nourishment! But the belief in the productivity of a principle should not immediately cause one to believe in the principle itself. This would be adoration of utility. "As if pleasantness were allowed to determine belief!" Pascal cries out—and one believes one is listening to Nietzsche. "As if the pleasure in belief were allowed to dispose one *to* belief!"—we take the liberty of adding, suggesting that we not only mistrust a belief that gives a great deal of pleasure, but also devoutness itself, *because* it gives a great deal of pleasure; that we mistrust the voluptuous gesture of beauty of certain believers of today. "Let," writes Johannes Scherr, a leader of the democratic party of southern Germany, in 1873,

> Let the dreamers whirl around their fixed idea of the maturity of the masses just as whirling dervishes swing around the tips of their own noses. Let them play childishly with their empty, fraudulent bubble called the *self-determination of nations*. We know, of course, how things were, are, and will be with this maturity and self-determination. The masses mature? A boyish dream! Nations determining themselves? A laughable self-deceit! Why don't you finally rub the Rousseauean chimeras from your eyes and look at things the way they are? Where, then, have nations shown that they understood how to be free? Yes, even that they wanted to be free? Nowhere! Even the seemingly liberal, most liberal epochs show themselves everywhere, upon closer examination and impartial investigation, to be

illusions . . . Just take the penal code and the police out of our highly-praised modern civilization for a while, and you will experience humanities whose bestiality will show you what this eternal, self-satisfied sing-song of progress really is.

The creed of an intellect sympathetic to literature and to politics! But should the creed not have the advantage of decency over the progress sing-song of the self-satisfied? The political belief in mankind, the belief in the "very beautiful and completely serene" condition, is an *in*decency today, and nothing else. The human race was comparatively young in 1790, at that time it could hope to realize "happiness," it could believe in politics. This belief is impossible today. Politics has been tried out in all its forms, and it is compromised to the bones. The belief in it is self-delusion. The belief in democracy is an intellectual shelter at any cost, is *obscurantism*; if it is not, as the Swabian thought, self-satisfaction: and indeed, not only in the impersonal sense, in the sense of mankind, but also, above all, personal self-satisfaction—a reason to imagine oneself more virtuous and better than others.

But what does this mean, anyway: to believe in something? Does it mean to believe in its realization? Or does it mean to believe in the desirability of its realization? There is, it seems to me, a difference, and I doubt that the first possibility will satisfy the new imperative of belief. As far as democracy in Germany is concerned, for example, I believe completely in its realization: *this is precisely what makes me pessimistic.* For it is democracy, and not its realization, that I do not believe in.

But let us for the moment set aside all the contents of belief; let us speak of belief itself and in itself, or rather: let us speak above all of its opposite, doubt. Apparently, you see, doubt has changed its intellectual political role in the course of time. Once, at the onset of "modern times," at the time of Petrarca, it was the progressive principle that undermined belief, called authority in question, emancipated the individual, and destroyed the foundations of the unified, medieval-European culture. The way things are today, doubt has become the common denominator of all those outdated intellectual conditions that are hostile and harmful to the will, to resolution, to the intellectual-political *action* in the service of mankind's progress—again I give its critical-scholarly name that by this time has become quite generally understandable: it is called estheticism, relativism, psychologism, impressionism, and all of them, as I have said, which basically mean the same thing, namely doubt, are opposed to belief, are quietistic inhibitions of the will, of resolution, of the political action, which one has, or should, quite truly become used to thinking of as the natural function of the *intellect*, while earlier one wanted and was allowed to distinguish between intellect and action, *knowledge* and action, as quite different and poorly compatible things. The younger Nietzsche still speaks clearly in this sense. "Moderation" is the title he gives to the aphorism that runs: "Complete decisiveness in thought and inquiry, *free thinking* that has become a character trait, that is, causes moderation in action: for it weakens covetousness, draws much of the available energy to itself *in the furtherance of intellectual purposes*, and shows the semi-uselessness, or the uselessness and danger of *all sudden changes*." This is intellect in its antirevolutionary form. Today, intellect declares not only its solidarity, but also its identity with the revolution and scourges as burgherly and pitiful the skeptical suggestion of the semi-useful and dangerous nature of sudden changes.

In the course of these reflections, we have repeatedly given to the word doubt that infamous adjective with which it is today, in the literary-critical sphere, organically bound: the adjective, "burgherly." And truly, the connection between doubt and burgherly nature is, of course, a fact of intellectual history. Doubt stands at the end of the culturally unbroken and secure, authoritarian Christian Middle Ages; it stands at the beginning of the new times, of the period of the enlightenment that conceived a human ideal, the human being who is antifanatical and tolerant, but also no longer intellectually sheltered and bound, but detached and individually isolated. This lax, tolerant, skeptical and isolated human being is the burgher. Has one never heard of "art becoming burgherly"? But all the journals are talking about it! Art becoming burgherly, which means the individualization and detachment of art from a union secure in its culture and belief, was completed at the time of the Renaissance; yes, even if it was the Revolution that helped the burgher to power in an economic sense—he reached artistic and intellectual dominance right at the beginning of the new times, of modernity, of the Renaissance, of the enlightenment of the seventeenth century. This was the time when art and intellect became burgherly, and specifically through criticism, skepticism, and doubt, this progressive principle of the past. The past! For that is now over: now, right now, everything has changed, and the half-thousand year epoch of burgherly detachment has come to an end: the newspapers say so—the newspapers have, like old Goethe, become used "to living in millennia." Do you know who has arrived? Gothic man! Have you not heard of Gothic man? Then you really are not up to date. Gothic man is the man of the new intolerance, of the new antihumanity of the intellect, of the new uniformity and resolution, of belief in belief; he is the no longer burgherly, the *fanatic* human being. One realizes that this is something for the newspapers. What a sensation that the Lamprechtian sensibility, which quite recently was considered so elegant, is suddenly the most despicable, shabby, and burgherly thing on earth; that one may and must contend in damning it in its foundations as soullessness, estheticism, lack of ethics, criminal lack of belief—while it is precisely this sensibility that welcomes the "Gothic man," just as Fiorenza welcomed the roaring monk, with feminine delight!

I fear that Gothic man is no Savonarola, but some kind of literary youth and newspaper contributor with horn-rimmed glasses and a bad complexion. But I am less concerned with his personality than with where he comes from and where he "got it"—for doubtlessly from himself he has nothing at all and the courage to nothing at all. He had to be encouraged to cry out Gothic and fanatic ideas again; this had to be "made possible" again for him, otherwise he would certainly have been afraid of being laughed at; and I think I see who made it possible for him. "Crises in value judgments of the highest order have reduced the realm of tolerance to simple cowardice and weakness of character. To be a Christian—to name just one consequence—becomes from now on *indecent*." This sharp sentence is found in a letter from Nietzsche to Deussen from the year 1888—and I beg pardon for seeing Nietzsche everywhere, and only him; for still finding traces of him everywhere, even today, although his intellectual-political defeat is pasted at every streetcorner today. Now those "value judgments of the highest rank" that Nietzsche spoke of, and whose triumph over the realm of tolerance he announced, were admittedly far from favoring progress, democratic humanity, and social eudaemonism. But it is the gesture, what is esthetic, that finds followers, not what is moral, the opinion—and this should give the fanatics of opinion something to think about. The gesture of fanaticism, which doubtlessly forms a connection between the late Nietzsche and the age of the crusades, was taken over, and by the eccentric drama of his later life, Nietzsche revived a formal—therefore an esthetic—possibility: precisely that of the fanatic attitude—a form that has become full in our times. With what? But let us not yet speak of the content of the belief.

Nietzsche, to spend a little more time with him, was not always the man of the fanatic gesture of the grotesque. Even as Zarathustra, he still demanded from his friends (whom he did not call disciples) not so much belief as *mistrust*. There was even a time—it was the one following the separation from Wagner and Schopenhauer, his real time of free thinking, the time of *Human, All Too Human*—where he loved *one* virtue with his whole soul: *justice*, this moral adversary of fanaticism that he perceived at that time to be a form of genius. At the time, he said, he could not bring himself to consider this form of genius lower than any kind of philosophical, political, or artistic genius. "The nature of justice is to avoid with hearty dislike everything that confuses and blinds the judgment of things; it is therefore an *opponent of convictions*, for justice wants to give everything, whether live or dead, real or imagined, its due—and for this, justice must perceive everything clearly; it therefore puts everything in the best light and surveys it with a careful eye. Finally, it will even give its opponent—blind or short-sighted 'conviction' (as men call it—women call it 'belief') its due—and this is conviction for the sake of truth."

Nietzsche practiced this virtue, he showed the truth of this quality of genius; in the wonderful aphorism, for example, "Reaction as Progress," in which he *did justice to* the great teacher of his youth, Schopenhauer. He says that one of the greatest and quite immeasurable advantages we have derived from Schopenhauer is certainly that he temporarily forces our perception back into older, more powerful ways of looking at the world and at human beings, to which otherwise no path would easily lead us.

> The gain for history and *justice* is very great: I believe that no one now would so easily succeed, without Schopenhauer's help, in doing justice to Christianity and its Asiatic relatives: something that is particularly impossible on the basis of the still-existing Christianity. Only after this great *success of justice*, only after we have corrected in such an essential point the historical method of observation that the Age of Reason brought with it, may we again bear the flag of the Enlightenment—the flag with the three names: Petrarca, Erasmus, Voltaire. Out of reaction we have made progress.

Petrarca, Erasmus, Voltaire—the world of humanism opens up, the realm of fanaticism closes at the sound of these names. Petrarca was a melancholiac, an artist, a lover of contrasts. The German humanist, whose noble burgherly picture by Holbein I love so much, took the same position on the Reformation as Goethe did on the Revolution: that quiet culture is being pushed back by Lutheranism, this was the criticism he made of it, as Goethe did of the French character. And I cannot believe that Voltaire, the Voltaire to whom Nietzsche dedicated his book, only directed his *Ecrasez l'infâme* against Christianity and not against *every* type of fanaticism and intolerance of the stake. Voltaire was not the man of the Revolution; Rousseau was.

There is a magnificent, enchanting series of chapters toward the end of the first volume of *Human, All Too Human*, filled with the spirit of true enlightenment, humanity, and freedom, in which Nietzsche celebrates justice: "that virtue of careful abstinence, that wise moderation that is better known in the area of practical life than in the area of theoretical life, and that, for example, Goethe portrayed in Antonio." He is still enough of a disciple of Schopenhauer to disapprove of the will as an all-too-audible prompter of the intellect, and he says so with words that, as with everything with him, have all the liveliness of experience: he says that everyone who remains ensnared in the net of the first belief that catches him is, under all circumstances, precisely because of this unchangeableness, a representative of backward cultures. Such a person, because of this lack of education (assuming he is educable), is hard, unintelligible, uncorrectable, *without gentility, an eternally suspicious*, unscrupulous person who resorts to all means of making his opinion prevail because he cannot grasp at all that there must also be other opinions; he is, in this respect perhaps, a source of strength, and in cultures that have become all too lax and free, even beneficial, but only because he greatly stimulates opposition to himself. Such minds—Nietzsche called them "unscientific"—are satisfied to find any sort of hypothesis on a matter; they fire up for it and consider the matter closed. To have an opinion already means for them: to be fanatic about it and henceforth to take it to heart as a conviction. "In a matter that is unclear," he says, "they warm up to the first idea that comes into their heads that looks as if it might be an answer: and this, *especially in the field of politics*, always has the direst of consequences." But whoever today, in the style of the Reformation man, still uses insinuations and outbursts of rage to fight against and to put down opinions, clearly shows that he would have burned his opponent if he had lived in other times, and that he would have resorted to all the means of the Inquisition if he had lived as an opponent of the Reformation.

This, as has been said, is how Nietzsche once thought about fanatic convictions, how he spoke of justice and of its deadly enemy, "Gothic man." Truly, at that time, at least, he had more of the *Goethean* man than of the Gothic; for what he said fondly of justice: that it gives to every real or imagined thing its due, and tries to perceive it purely; that it puts everything in the best light and surveys it with a careful eye—is this not just another expression of the Goethean principle that one should, in the observation of a thing, let it stand for itself, and that one should beware of all distortions? The opposite of the Gothic fanatic belief has yet another name that does not come from the moral world as the word, "justice," does, but from the Goethean, artistic one. Nietzsche also uses it repeatedly, and his allegory of the careful treatment of things is particularly close to it: for with it, we are reminded of the plasticity, the three-dimensionality of things. This name is *esthetic education*, and the antifanatic, antimedieval, the renaissance and humanisitc ideal it represents is closely connected to the intellectual rise of the burgher—and this is a new, or repeated, indication of the relationship between burgherly nature and *art*. For "esthetic education" implies something not only passive, but also active; an esthetically educated human being is not just a human being whom his world experience found esthetically educable and who was educated and made passive by it, he is at the same time a person of plastic perception, and if sensuous imagination joins intellectual culture, then he is an artist. If one wanted to define art as "visible justice," the definition might not be accurate in every case in the field of art, but I think it would be accurate in most cases, and it would be a beautiful and pure definition of art, by which one would greatly honor it.

To be sure, a belief is also necessary to serve art in the sense of this definition—belief in art, that is; something like fanaticism is necessary, expressing itself in that sacrificial mania that Turgenev showed in the character of the absurd Westerner: Turgenev, the Goethe-disciple and the humanistic artist, who has said such strong and convincing things about freedom and esthetic education. The greatest pain of his life was Tolstoy's defection from art—a pain, naive as his belief in the divinity of freely creative force, at a loss in his devout naiveté before the fact that the great creator and shaper "had given up literary activity *pour écrire de pareilles billevesées*." He meant Tolstoy's theological writings. And despairing, Turgenev provoked Countess A. A. Tolstoy, Leo's aunt, who records it in her memoirs, to remark that "even Turgenev's style is now like an unfathomable swamp."

The countess was a positively orthodox woman, and took deep offense at her famous nephew's anticlerical religious research. Nevertheless, she saw that he was searching, suffering, and torturing himself, while the author of *Fathers and Sons* persisted almost to the point of complacency in his "negative"—she could also have said: nihilistic—point of view.

She said to him: "It is strange. We have not seen each other for many years, and here I find you again at the same point—*avec ce fond de sable mouvant qui m'a toujours frappé dans vos oeuvres, quelque charmantes qu'elles soient.* I had hoped that the times would have put you on more solid ground ..." *Sable mouvant? On his deathbed,* Turgenev wrote his great, alienated friend, the social-religious prophet, Leo Tolstoy, a letter, a final imploring word, gripping and deeply comical once again in its unshakeable naiveté and belief. "My friend!" he wrote. "Great writer of the Russian country! Listen to the request of a dying man! Return to literature!" Was that "*sable mouvant*"? A belief that persisted in the face of looming death and eternity—much more!—that used its last intellectual and physical powers in the attempt to save apostates: can one deny it the name of belief, or *religiosity*? Estheticism as religion! That is a paradox. But Turgenev's last letter proves its truth and vital power.

In all this there is only one thing that is surprising, yes, that even seems like a psychological deficiency: Turgenev's disconcertedness at Tolstoy's later development, which was definitely organically necessary, and was clearly foreshadowed to the discerning person in his early works. Nekhlyudov in *Resurrection* is Levin in *Anna Karenina*, and again Pierre Besukhov in *War and Peace*, and the true name of this character unity is Leo Tolstoy. Had Turgenev forgotten that even the atmosphere of *Anna Karenina* had smelled to him like Muscovite incense? That he had already written about *War and Peace* (in the epilogue to *Fathers and Sons*): "The saddest example of this lack of true freedom resulting from lack of true esthetic education is seen in Count Leo Tolstoy's latest work, which nevertheless, by virtue of its creative, poetic significance, is probably the best that our literature has produced since the year 1840"? In these weeks I have read the gigantic work again—blessed and shaken by its creative power and full of aversion to everything it contains of idea, of philosophy of history: to this Christian-democratic hard-headedness, this radical and muzhiklike negation of the hero, of the great human being. Here is the gap and unfamiliarity between the German and the national Russian spirit; here begins the resistance of one who breathes in the homeland of Goethe and Nietzsche. But what does not escape me, while it seems to have escaped a Turgenev, is the *unity of force* that holds sway in *War and Peace* as in all of Tolstoy's epic masterworks: it is this, that the "creative poetic significance" of the gigantic epic work that Turgenev admired almost against his will, has the *same* origin as its intellectual rusticity and narrowness; that this narrow-minded Christianity is the same original moral force that effortlessly supports artistic burdens that would have broken Turgenev's culture—that formative power of suffering, that moralistic power of art that makes Tolstoy into a brother of Michelangelo and Richard Wagner. It is truly the opposite of all estheticism—but especially of that final socially made-up and humanitarianly disguised estheticism that hopes to make contact with life and love by plunging into freedom, equality, brotherhood, and the happiness of mankind. The sum total of Pierre Bezukhov's life, the life of a God-seeker—I intend to extract it and to enter it here as a consolation and a tonic:

> He had realized that there was just as rarely a situation in the world in which the human being was happy and completely free as a situation in which he was unhappy and in bondage. He had realized that there was a limit to suffering and a limit to freedom, and that this limit was very near; that the person who suffers because a little leaf has blown onto his rose-colored bed suffers just as much as he was now suffering when he fell asleep on the bare, wet earth and one side of his body became cold and the other warm; that he had suffered just as much earlier when he put on his tight dress shoes as he was now suffering when he went barefoot and his feet were covered with scabs. He realized that he had not been freer at the time when he believed he had married his wife of his own free will than now, when he was locked overnight in the stall . . . What had tortured him earlier, what he had constantly searched for, *the purpose of life*, no longer existed for him. This supposed purpose of life was not just now by chance only momentarily nonexistent for him; he felt rather that there was none and could be none, and this lack of purpose gave him the full, joyful consciousness of freedom that now made up his happiness. He could have no purpose, for he now had the *belief*—not the belief in any kind of principles, words, or ideas, but the belief in a living, constantly perceived God. Previously, he had sought Him in the goals he had set himself; this striving for goals was only a search for God.

No, true belief is no doctrine and no stubborn, rhetorical obstinacy. It is not the belief in some kinds of principles, words and ideas such as freedom, equality, democracy, civilization and progress. It is the belief in God. But what is God? Is He not the universal, the forming principle, omniscient justice, encompassing love? The belief in God is the belief in love, in life, and in art.

When Turgenev criticized Tolstoy's powerful work and accused its creator of "lack of true esthetic education," he was not competing with his great countryman, but speaking as the disciple of a greater man who was even greater than the author of *War and Peace*, as a disciple of

Goethe, and as a representative of the Goethean cultural world in which he breathed and in which he believed. For Turgenev, the friend of French writers—and as an artiste a Frenchifying Slav—was, in his intellectual education, a German. "Esthetic education" is a specifically German concept; it comes from Goethe, from him it has its plastic-artistic character, the sense of freedom, culture, and reverence for life with which Turgenev used the word, through him this concept has been raised in Germany to an educational principle as in no other nation.

Now esthetic education as plastic sense is certainly something different from skepticism—which as such only signifies a manifestation of intellectualism, and indeed, the dullest one. Undoubtedly, however, the idea of esthetic education has in it and brings to maturity a certain depreciating and hostile attitude toward all insipid expression of opinion and speaking, a dissatisfaction and displeasure with all one-sidedness, which is perceived with a certain torment as constrained, impious, inadequate, and hostile to life. There is only one way to stop this inhibition: to desire one-sidedness of speaking and opinion to hold sway for the moment, and consciously, yes, defiantly, to cultivate it, and in this way even the apodictic accent and the gesture of fanaticism can be reached, while at bottom it still always lacks the seriousness of actual stultification, the taste of that grain of salt on one's tongue does not disappear, and everything stays just two steps away from an artistic game. Goethe is talking about this decision, this voluntary renunciation of plastic freedom, when he says, "At the moment of speaking, a person must be one-sided," and of course it remains highly doubtful here whether this is said in favor of one-sidedness or in favor of speaking. At any rate, it has to do here with speaking that perceives *contradiction* as superfluous, tactless, and killjoy, and forbids it, as is expressed in the famous lines:

> You must not confuse me with contradiction;
> As soon as one speaks, one begins to err.*

I believe that such statements by Goethe, statements of a great creator who was devoted to nature, have penetrated deeply into the consciousness of his nation, and have established themselves there: of a nation that already tended toward a musical contrapuntal experience of the world, and that was "esthetically educated" by Goethe, that is: was educated to see things plastically and therefore to be skeptical of simply

---

* Ihr müßt mich nicht durch Widerspruch verwirren;
  Sobald man spricht, beginnt man schon zu irren.

expressing opinions. I believe that in this nation that has been educated in this way there is basically an infinitely higher regard for art, which is what, according to the proverb, brings "*favor*," than the regard for talking and expressing opinions; yes, I believe that here all talk and expression of opinion takes place under the pressure of such over-powering disdain and ingratitude that one is really victimized if one gets involved in it. I think, therefore, that all political palaver disgusts this nation in the deepest reaches of its soul, and I believe precisely for this reason that the civilizing undertaking to create in this nation a democratic, that is, a literary-political atmosphere, is doomed to failure. For there can also be no doubt that esthetic education, "quiet" esthetic education, as Goethe contrasted it with French character, that is: politics, disposes one to be *quietistic*, and that the deeply nonpolitical, antiradical, and antirevolutionary character of the Germans is connected to the supremacy of the idea of esthetic education that has been established with them.

But still a further idea must not be avoided. Some time ago I said to myself that the problematic sphere was actually the sphere of art and of the artist, and perhaps I was thinking then of Goethe's remarkably stern and badtempered demand: "If I am to listen to another's opinion" (just listen to it, not, by chance, to accept it!) "then it must be expressed positively; *I have enough problems in myself.*" It seems to me that this impatient and almost tormented demand, together with this declaration, is a highly German statement, and that it throws light on the interrelationship between esthetic education and what is problematic. Are the Germans really the problematic nation because they are the esthetically educated one? One can also ask the question the other way around. And one can, in this war, be on Germany's side body and soul, one can yearn for a German victory because one feels one's own life, one's own honor inseparably bound to the life and honor of Germany--and still, in one's quietest hour, tend toward the opinion that the esthetically educated, the knowing, and the problematic nation is destined to be the European ferment, and *not* to rule.

We have not stopped speaking of belief, of belief in belief, of belief in itself that, since morality has again "become possible," has been proclaimed on the moral trumpet by that freshly trained virtuoso, the intellectual politician and antiesthete, as what is necessary, what is the prerequisite of all greatness and creative power. With morality, therefore, the "falsification as a matter of principle of great heman beings, great creators, and great times"—for which Nietzsche's ethos of truth reproached morality—has again become possible. "One wants," Nietzsche said, "belief to be the distinguishing mark of great people: but the unscrupulousness, the skepticism, the 'immorality,' and the license to divest oneself of a belief belong to greatness (Caesar, Frederick the Great, Napoleon: but also Homer, Aristophanes, Leonardo, *Goethe*)." And in this connection he names Goethe a second time as he lists:

> Händel, Leibniz, Goethe, and Bismarck—as characteristic *of the strong German type*. Unhesitatingly living between antitheses, full of that versatile strength that avoids convictions and doctrines by playing one against the other and maintaining freedom for itself . . . The great human being is necessarily a skeptic (but this does not say that he has to appear so) . . . Freedom from every type of conviction is part of the strength of his will . . . The need for belief, for any sort of absolute yes and no, is a proof of weakness; all weakness is weakness of the will. The man of belief, the believer, is necessarily a small type of person. Thus "freedom of the intellect," unbelief as instinct, in other words, is the precondition of greatness.

Thus spoke thirty years ago the will to *hard* truth, a stern and masculine pessimism, whose honor it was to practice no swindle with great words and virtues. The reaction is powerful—that *obscurantist* reaction that we have met as the "rehabilitation of virtue." Virtue and belief are not only the prerequisites for active and historical greatness: talent and art must also wither where virtue and belief are lacking, that is: where will, effective loyal behavior, in a word, politics, is wanting. This is what resolute love of mankind claims. *Art*, when it speaks from a pure and majestical-naive mouth, judges otherwise. Ninety years ago in a conversation, Eckermann expressed surprise that in recent times the great events of war really had not stimulated a great deal of imagination. Goethe answered: "They have aroused *more will* than imagination, and more political imagination than artistic, and all *ingenuousness and sensuousness, on the other hand, have been completely lost.*" Thus Goethe. But although it may seem that his words might have a certain timely force in 1917—not Goethe, the esthete is master, hero, and leader of the times. Was Goethe perhaps a fighter? Did he not also express the basest opinions about freedom, equality, progress, and radicalism? Is he not guilty of all the horrors that the ruthless separation of literature and politics has created in Germany? Let another be hero, master, and leader for us, a fighter, a friend of mankind, a man of belief and virtue, a teacher of democracy—let it be Emile Zola, the literary hero of the Dreyfus case, the prophet of the *Quatre Évangiles*.

He is certainly a lost soul who thinks that Zola's appearance, and it best of all, proves one of two things: either that art will descend to feeble boredom and dullness *through* the virtue of belief—or that the virtue of belief is only a form of expression and accompaniment of artistic marasmus. Is it not said that singers whose voices are failing try to save the effect by exaggerated character acting? Is there possibly a connection here with the democratic preaching of Zola's late period? *Fécondité, travail, vérité, justice*—but certainly! Except that social-ethical gesticulation is a poor substitute for a badly tired voice; except that one, to be honest, cannot read the stuff. It is true, Zola never belonged, not even before he threw himself into politics, to the truly great narrators. To compare him with Tolstoy is cruelty, even if instructive cruelty. The difference between epic natural force and ambitiously pumped-up exaggeration jumps up before one's eyes; and while the Emma of the esthete, Flaubert, and the Muscovite Anna are immortal female figures, Nana remains a panting lump of flesh that has been raised to the political-symbolic sphere. Nevertheless, when one speaks of Nana, one speaks of Zola's strong days, of days when he was so much an artist that he neither wanted, could, nor dared be anything else, unless he could be so precisely *as* an artist. At that time, for example, he was democratic as an artist in the same way the "boche," Richard Wagner, and yes, even Beethoven, too, and basically all nineteenth century art was. But the misfortune occurred when he "raised" his artistical-democratic massiveness to political self-consciousness, and began to interpret it in a virtuous-agitative way. We saw what an artist's gain is when being becomes opining and teaching. *Fécondité, travail, vérité, justice* result from this. But one cannot read it.

There are cases that are almost the opposite; cases in which the path leads from belief to unbelief, to pessimism or to irony—and in which, contrary to all morality, this *by no means* implies a decline. As a disciple of Feuerbach, Richard Wagner had been faithful to a humanistic religion, had even taken part in political revolution and believed in "the human being." Then, under Schopenhauer, his Christianity was transformed into a pessimistic Buddhism. When did he create his greatest works? And why is Ibsen's completely skeptical, completely unbelieving, yes, cynical *Wild Duck* (with "life's lie" as a leitmotif)—why is it a masterwork, while the virtuous *Pillars of Society*, with its truly democratic conclusion, is mediocre French theater with a grating technique?

It is not right. It cannot be right. Art does not keep step with virtue— one should not lie. One should not confuse desire with imagination,

political with artistic imagination, just to flatter the spirit of the times—
that spirit of the times that announces in the revues that the esthetic
epoch is at an end and that belief is the order of the day. That talent
and belief belong together is not proven—I do not say that the opposite
has been proven. I do not say that unbelief makes the artist. But when
one says to me that belief makes him, then I reject this as *ideological
impudence.*

"Gothic man," the neofanatic and archenemy of all dissolute-burgh-
erly cultural tolerance—but what does he believe, really? Granted the
sweeping liberal beauty of his gestures—what ideal forms the *content* of
his antihuman, crusading sternness of belief? It is the ideal of humanity!
Who would have imagined it? It is the Renaissance ideal of liberating,
antiauthoritarian doubt, of emancipation, of *freedom*, of the progressing
liberation of the human race from all irrational bonds, the religious, for
example, the national. The revolt of reason is for him the only condition
worthy of a human being; absolute freedom as an orgiastic-nihilistic
goal.

A pretty confusion! Gothic man as civilization's literary man. The
belief in belief as belief in unbelief, in "freedom." The meaning of
European history, according to this belief, is liberation. Renaissance,
Reformation, and Revolution are the names of the previous great acts
of liberation, and only what lies in this direction is good, is European,
is human. Strange! To us, the Reformation seems to stand a little
differently, in a more problematical and *more German* way between the
Renaissance and the Revolution, than the high-minded simplifying
instinct of the liberation enthusiast is ready to admit. We are inclined
to believe that it is not at all a matter of a straight line, and in no way
does Luther's work seem to us to be a pure work of liberation in the
sense of civilization and of enlightenment. To take the Reformation as
a continuation, result, or manifestation of the Renaissance seems to us
to be only very conditionally permissable: To see a disturbance and an
interruption, a relapse into the Middle Ages, a conservative, yes, a
reactionary movement in it is at least acceptable to the same degree;
and the *European* point of view that, for example, Nietzsche took, is
probably actually that a renaissance, disturbed neither by the Reformation nor by the Counter-Reformation, would have brought to the
continent a "more harmonious intellectual liberation." As far as the
Revolution is concerned, on the other hand, it may after all be true that
it would not have been possible without the Reformation: but this is, of
course, only incidentally and approximately true compared to the other

insight that the Revolution would not have been *necessary*, that it may possibly never have occurred, if the Reformation had preceded it everywhere; that it actually has not taken place where the Reformation took place and that obviously the experience of the Reformation *immunizes* against revolution—and in this, beyond doubt, there is an antagonism between the two. It was Thomas Carlyle who said that the Revolution was not at all a consequence and continuation of the Reformation, but only a poor, unfortunate, eternally disquieting substitute for it in those nations that did not accept the Reformation. At any rate, Carlyle is the one who championed it most energetically. The Reformation, he says in his *History of Frederick the Great*, was proffered everywhere, and it is marvelous to see what became of the nations that did not want to listen. He gives examples. Spain, for example, "poor Spain, going about, at this time, making its '*pronuncimientos*'; all the factious attorneys in its little towns assembling to *pronounce* virtually this, 'The Old *is* a lie, then;—good Heavens, after we so long tried hard, harder than any nation, to hold it a truth!—and if it be not Rights of Man, Red Republic and Progress of the Species, we know not what now to believe or to do; and are as a people stumbling on steep places, in the darkness of midnight!'" Or Italy, who also had her Protestants, but killed them and caused Protestantism to be throttled in order to dedicate herself instead to dilettantism and to the fine arts, and to sink from *virtus* into *virtù*. But most emphatically, Carlyle gave the example of France:

> France, with its keen intellect, saw the truth and saw the falsity, in those Protestant times; and, with its ardour of generous impulse, was prone enough to adopt the former. France was within a hairsbreadth of becoming actually Protestant. But France saw good to massacre Protestantism, and end it the night of St. Bartholomew 1572. The celestial Apparitor of Heaven's Chancery, so we may speak, the Genius of Fact and Veracity, had left his Writ of Summons; Writ was read;—and replied to in this manner. The Genius of Fact and Veracity accordingly withdrew;—was staved-off, got kept away, for two hundred years. But the Writ of Summons had been served; Heaven's Messenger could not stay away for ever. No; he returned duly; with accounts run up, on compound interest, to the actual hour, in 1792;—and then, at last, there had to be a "Protestantism"; and we know what kind that was!

Carlyle's interpretation agrees, as one sees, with Hegel's prophecy in a remarkable way: France will, because she missed the Reformation, never come to rest. If, however, missing the Reformation has eternal restlessness in the political sphere as a consequence—could one not say that surrender to it creates political quietism? That the experience of metaphysical freedom makes one somewhat indifferent to political freedom and makes one badly disposed toward enthusiasm for human rights, red republic and progress, in a word, toward political enthusiasm? Luther was really, no matter how considerable his political accomplishments may have been, for his part, definitely a nonpolitical man. It is certain that he had neither political talent nor political interest nor political intentions and goals. He was not concerned with things of this world, he was concerned with the salvation of his soul—yes, not even directly with the salvation of those of others, but with his own. Nietzsche wrote quite incidentally (in the *Antichrist*) the critically brilliant sentence: "*A religious person thinks only of himself.*" That is the truth: It was what moved that political professor to say of Dostoyevsky that his work lacked every indication of social ideals. It is not by chance that the country that brought forth the Reformation is also the country of that much-talked-about political "immobility," about which much is said in Europe. The Reformation in relation to the Renaissance is a disturbance, in relation to the Revolution, it is a hindrance and a *sedative*: I call to mind the possibility of this interpretation in order to ward off a convenient simplification, yes a fatuous interpretation of history by civilization's literary man, and to characterize as very inexact and frivolous his interpretation of Luther's work as a work of liberation and of progress in *his* sense.

In truth, one has in the Reformation an event of genuine German majesty to admire, an event and fact of the soul—actually not capable of interpretation or criticism, like life. The critical work of interpretation pales before it and sinks into helplessness. One can call this event revolutionary or reactionary, rebellious or preserving, democratic or aristocratic: it is all this at once, it is deep, defiant, fateful, antiprogrammatic, personal, and great. For it is, in a good German way, completely the work of a great man, of a personality that was, to be sure, powerfully national but just as powerfully and richly individual—born from his most personal struggles and needs, marked with their stamp forever. Was the Reformation "good fortune"? No, not at all. The consequences for Germany were what one calls the "sobering" of our north, furthermore the division of the nation, furthermore the Thirty Years' War. We have already mentioned Goethe's opinion of Luther, of the misfortune of the repression of "quiet culture" by the pressure of belief. And now even Nietzsche—one remembers his rage and despair over the incident of "Luther in Rome," about this vulgar man and monk who "rose up *against the Renaissance*," and restored the church, who restored *Christianity* after it had been conquered at its very seat. "Ah, these Germans!" he cried in French. "What they have already cost us!" And in a strongly schoolmasterlike way he accuses them of always "having something else in mind" than what was important in decisive moments: at the time of the Renaissance, the Reformation, at the time of Napoleon, the wars of liberation, and now, while *he* was philosophizing, they had the "*Reich*" on their minds. I draw attention to all of this because I am angered at the frivolousness with which civilization's literary man claims the Reformation for his doctrine as if it were obviously simply an act of liberation and progress between the Renaissance and the Revolution. If he were to see in it an act of German obstinacy, I would like it better; for it would be more logical in the spirit of his Germanophobia.

But wait a minute! Would *liberation*, more and more liberation, be the word and sense of the hour—and not rather something quite different, namely commitment? Is not our intellectual politician's need for "simplification" and resolution, is not the proclamation of "Gothic man" the most convincing proof that this latter is the case?

Freedom—of course this negative does not contain its dignity in itself (for negation in itself is without dignity), but receives it only from its complement, from what is negated by it. In Dostoyevsky's *Bobock*, the corpses that converse at night in the graveyard reach the splendid resolution *never to be ashamed of themselves anymore*. Well, this, too, is freedom, a freedom, to be sure, for conversing corpses. But one does not have to be a decided misanthrope to find the suspicion not completely unjustified that the majority of human beings secretly mean freedom from shame and from the requirement of being decent when they cry for freedom. The negative character of the idea of freedom is completely limitless, it is a nihilistic idea and therefore only salutary in the smallest doses, it is a medicinal poison. Again, is this means indicated at a moment when the innermost desire of the world, of the whole world, is not at all for further anarchization by the idea of freedom, but for new commitments, and when the belief in belief, as we have seen, is reaching the point of psychological obscurantism?

"*Et certe*," Claudel has his leprous Violaine say, "*le malheur de ce temps est grand. Ils n'ont point de père. Ils regardent et ne savent plus òu est le Roi et le Pape. C'est pourquoi voici mon corps en travail à la place de la chrétienté qui se dissout.*" Is this not the voice of the times? It is a Gothic voice—

France still understands Gothic style best of all. Just listen to the sentences that Auguste Rodin published at the beginning of the war, and in, of all magazines, an American one. He said that before the ordeal France had been taking rapid and irreversible steps toward decay, all of France, and especially her art. Why? Because of freedom. French artistic genius had reached its greatest height in Gothic creations; after this, it gradually became weaker, even though the following centuries still produced new, original forms of expression. Rodin sees in *empire* style the last genuinely French art—from there on the decline begins. "The nineteenth century gave artists freedom and—ruined them in doing so. *As if freedom could inspire art! It has killed art!* With freedom, the magnificent styles of the older times have disappeared, and we have only been able to make poor imitations of them. *With the Revolution,* art became a shopkeeper, and of this change it died."

All truths are temporal truths. Intellect is the courtier of the will, and the requirements, the pressing needs of a time, appear to it as "insights," as "truths." Freedom as the ruin of art: this is such a temporal insight, a truth that testifies to the will of the times—and not only among Frenchmen. "Things are bad today," Nietzsche said, "with the higher artists: are they not almost all being destroyed by inner lack of discipline? No longer are they tyrannized from the outside by the *absolute table of values* of a church or of a court: nor do they learn any longer to rear their own, inner tyrant, their *will*." The longing, striving, seeking of the times, which definitely is *not* for freedom, but which is longing for an "inner tyrant," for an "absolute system of values," for constraint, for the moral return to certainty—it is a striving for *culture,* for dignity, for bearing, for form—and I may speak of this, for I knew about it before many others did, I harkened to it and tried to present it: not as a prophet, not as a propagandist, but novelistically, that is: experimentally and without final commitment. I experimented in a story with the renunciation of the psychologism and relativism of the dying epoch; I had an artist say good-bye to "knowledge for its own sake," renounce sympathy for the "abyss," and turn to the will, to value judgment, to intolerance, to "resolution." I gave all this a catastrophic, that is: a skeptical-pessimistic ending. I cast doubt on the possibility of an artist's gaining *dignity,* I had my hero, who tried it, discover and admit that it was not possible. I know well that the "new will" that I had frustrated would never have become a problem for me at all, an object of my artistic instinct, if I had not had a part in it, for in the realm of art there is no objective knowledge, there is only an intuitive and lyrical one. But to frustrate it, this "new will," to give the experiment a skeptical-pessimistic ending: precisely this seemed *moral* to me—as it seemed artistic to me. For my nature is such that doubt, yes, despair, seems to me more moral, decent, and artistic than any kind of leader-optimism, let alone that politicizing optimism that would like to be saved at any cost by belief—by belief in what? In democracy!

The fact is paradoxical and remarkable enough that the European war has greatly strengthened the belief in "the human being," in a goal of happiness for the development of the human race, in progress toward the ideal, in an earthly kingdom of God and of love, a kingdom of freedom, equality, brotherhood—in short, that it has greatly strengthened the revolutionary optimism *à la française* and brought it to a veritable hothouse blossoming. Is it not most highly probable that reactionary psychic manifestations will have to return, as the Europe of the Restoration produced them? Dostoyevsky has described in the most concise and clear way the psychology of the so-called romantic discontent of "*Byronism*." "Byronism," he says,

> arose at a time of general disappointment, not to say despair. One had accepted with exuberant enthusiasm the ideals of the *new belief* that had been proclaimed by France toward the end of the eighteenth century—when suddenly the course of events in the leading nation of Europe took a turn that corresponded so little to the great expectations, and disappointed the people so deeply in their hopeful belief, that precisely that time was for searching intellects the saddest in the history of Western Europe. And the idols that for a moment had been raised did not only collapse for external reasons, but just as much as a result of their *inner bankruptcy*, something all leading intellects and strong hearts immediately recognized.

Whoever would suggest the possibility, yes, the certainty, that we are going toward a new Byronism, a "general disappointment, if not even despair," that will necessarily have to follow on the heels of the "exuberant enthusiasm" for the "new belief," *and whoever in the process lets even a bit of satisfaction with this certain probability slip out*: he would have to be prepared to be accused of malicious and basely wicked enmity to mankind—and to console himself with the inner knowledge that this accusation did not apply to him. For when it is once again a matter of "humanity," I not only believe that *doubt* makes one more human and kinder than belief, fanaticism, the arrogance of the possession of truth and "resolute love of mankind," I even believe that *despair* is a better, more human, more moral—I mean: more religious condition than the rhetorical faith of revolutionary optimism, and that the human race will be closer to salvation in a state of despair than in one of belief—in democracy! All disbelief in political revolutionary ideology, all belief in its necessary "inner bankruptcy," all despair of it, is of religious nature and rests on the contrast between religiosity and political activism—just as Dostoyevsky clearly and with unmistakable sympathy considered the European movement that he christened with the name of Byron to be a *religious* movement in contrast to the political movement that came from France: Dostoyevsky was one of the deepest and most powerful religious men of all times, and beside this moralist's work the anarchistic social-utopia of the aged Tolstoy seems like a youngster's first stumbling philosophical effort.

"Christ does not trouble himself over politics," Luther said. Dostoyevsky did not trouble himself over it, either; the religious genius is essentially nonpolitical. That Dostoyevsky *dealt* with politics, that he wrote essays about it, is no objection: he wrote them *against* politics, his political writings are the reflections of a nonpolitical man—one could also say: of a conservative man. For all conservatism is antipolitical, it does not believe in politics, only the partisan of progress does this. There is only *one* genuine political type, the Western revolutionary; and since Dostoyevsky was an antirevolutionary, he was antipolitical. In his introduction to the *Literary Writings*, Strakhov says the following about Dostoyevsky's burial:

> Among the thousands who accompanied the dead man on his last journey, there were naturally probably representatives of the most varied opinions, but the great majority buried in Dostoyevsky their educator, their teacher, the one who said to them: *"Humble yourself, proud human being! Work (on yourself), idle human being!"* All who sought a moral support saw in him a leader who showed them the paths on which one can and must seek salvation. One respected and loved in him not only the patriot and conservative; for many, he was also a consolation and a hope, and this not only because he scourged and combatted the revolutionary intrigues, but because he understood the highest, purely spiritual interests of the Russian character; not only because in his words religious mood, honest love of the nation, was revealed, but above all because our national power, *our national unity, and our political mission,* for which we have long sacrificed so much and are still at all times ready to sacrifice, were very dear to him . . .

"His death," Strakhov even added, "was not the death of a meritorious artist who had lived his days to an end in peace, but the death of a political fighter." And nevertheless, even though the national power and the political mission of Russia were in his heart; even though he scourged revolutionary intrigues, progress, and Western liberalism, which he called nihilism, and even though one may in this sense call him a "political fighter"—still I am right when I say that Dostoyevsky was of a nonpolitical nature, that he was antipolitical and did not believe in politics.

Whoever is not convinced of this by his teaching and command: "*Humble* yourself, proud human being! Work, idle human being! (namely on yourself!)" let him, in order to have the proof in hand, read in the volume, *Literary Writings*, the magnificent essay entitled: "On the occasion offered, A Few Lectures on Diverse Subjects on the Basis of an Argument that Mr. A. Gradovsky Made Against Me." This Mr. A. Gradovsky was the same sly old fox and Western liberal professor *à la* Milykov who polemicized against Dostoyevsky's demand: "Humble yourself and work on yourself!"—and declared to him that with these words he had expressed what made up both the strength and the weakness of the author of *The Brothers Karamazov*: These words, he said, contained a great *religious* ideal, a powerful sermon on *personal* ethics, but every trace of *social* ideals was lacking. "Mr. Dostoyevsky," he wrote, "calls us to work, to work on ourselves. Personal perfection in the spirit of Christian love is naturally the first prerequisite of every activity, no matter whether it is great or small! But from this it still does not follow that people who are individually perfect in the Christian sense neces- sarily form a perfect state." He went on to say that there had always been good people, even in times of slavery, but that the latter had still been a disgrace before God, and the Tsar-emancipator fulfilled not only the demands of *personal*, but also of *social* morality, about which one had no correct ideas in olden times. Personal and social morality were not one and the same, he continued, and from this it followed that social perfection could not be reached solely by the improvement of the personal qualities of human beings: not solely by work on one's own person and by personal humility. "Working on oneself and educating oneself to humility can also be done in the desert or on an uninhabited island. But as a member of society, of a state, human beings develop and improve themselves only by working alongside one another, with one another, and for one another. This is also the reason why the social perfection of human beings depends to such a great extent upon the perfection of *social institutions* that teach people values that are, if not Christian, at least civic."

Now then, *that* is the voice of the politician, raised in a doctrinaire manner against him who is *not* one, against the moralist. The reply, refutation, beating that the great moral poet gives the political social-moralist is done in a characteristically dramatic tone and style, it is loquacious-passionate, careless, cheerful, conversational, and all the time glowing with anger and contempt, light and radical, humorous and overpowering. To read it today affords one indescribable happiness, indescribable satisfaction. I admit that only the war and its distress have brought me this stormy gratefulness of reading—my pencil moves enraptured along whole pages, exclamation points of intimate agreement fall heavily in the margins. Never before did one read like this. One has often done so with passion, previously as well, but it was more abstract. All things were more abstract, more intellectual, more distant, they were only "interesting," not such burning issues, there was basically no timeliness before this time. Today it not only exists, it is comprehensive, and all things are caught in its urgency. It is possible while reading to writhe with hatred and opposition. It is possible for one's eyes to look up from the book, moist with gratefulness for consolation received, for confirmation, reinforcement, liberation, justification, for a word of salvation.

With ultimate irony, Dostoyevsky speaks of the humanitarian politicians of the first half of his century who so heartily hated and combatted slavery—hated and combatted it "in a European way," namely by running to Paris to the barricades, while never even thinking, for example, that they might first simply free their own peasants and distribute part of their own land among them, in order at least to relieve their own consciences of responsibility. "The milieu," they said, prevented them in this, and so they went to "their dear little Paris" where they fought at the barricades. With the rent money the peasants sent them they helped publish French radical journals and reviews, and by the by learned the little song:

> *Ma commère, quand je danse,*
> *Comment va mon cotillon?*

Oh, their civic lament was loud, and their concern for the peasant in bondage was acute. And still, it was less a concern about the slavery of the Russian peasant than the *very abstract* concern about the serfdom of the human race in general: "It should definitely not exist anymore, it is backward, it does not agree with the enlightenment! *Liberté, égalité et fraternité!*"—they thought only of this. But Dostoyevsky finds that *one can live quite well, yes, even extremely well*, with such concern, especially when in the process one can nourish oneself spiritually *with the thought of one's own moral beauty* and sublimity that one had developed in the flight of one's civic ideas, and bodily—well, bodily still from the rent money of these same peasants. As far as the peasant and the Russian people themselves were concerned, however, the Russians in Paris were not only deeply convinced of the hopeless vulgarity of the peasants, this conviction had already turned into feeling: "A *physical perception of disgust* already betrayed itself there—oh, naturally only an involuntary, almost unconscious feeling that they themselves perhaps did not notice at all . . ."

Does not all this seem somehow well known and familiar to us? Do we not know them from home, these lovers of the human race who gravitate to Paris—abstract, but "resolute" lovers and prophets of *liberté, égalité et fraternité*, with their civic lamentations and their great concern? Do they not also live quite well, yes, even extremely well in the process, glorious and spoiled, as they nourish themselves spiritually with the thought of their own civic-moral beauty, but bodily, perhaps, with the help of a smart impresario from the capitalistic world system that they curse as they receive the greatest benefit from it? But above all: do we not know that deep conviction of the vulgarity of the German people, combined with the most stupid adoration of foreign things, especially of "our dear little Paris"—a conviction that has already become feeling, so that already a physical perception of disgust for everything German is betrayed, a literal not-being-able-to-stand-them that made it so easy for us, so very easy and obvious, to take sides in this war against Germany and for "justice"?

But let us continue! With humorous passion Dostoyevsky combats the scholar's view that "personal perfection in the spirit of Christian love" is not much use in national affairs, and that the social perfection of the individual depends upon the perfection of *social institutions*. He talks about serfdom. Wherever, he says, true and perfect Christianity would rule on an estate, serfdom would certainly cease to exist, therefore there would be nothing to worry about any more, even if all the official documents and bills of sale were ignored. "What would it matter *then* to 'Korobochka,' the *true* Christian woman, whether her peasants were slaves or not? She would be 'mother' to them, a real mother, and the 'mother' in her would have simply eliminated the previous 'mistress,' and this would have happened quite automatically. The previous relationship—that of mistress to slave—would in this case have disappeared *like mist before the sun*, and the old people would have been supplanted by others who stood in a completely new relationship to one another that would have been unthinkable before . . . I assure you, Mr. Gradovsky, that Korobochka's peasants would then voluntarily have stayed with her, indeed, for the simple reason that everyone sees where he is best off. Or do you think that *the peasants would be better off with your institutions* than with the female landowner who loves them and cares for them like their real mother . . . In Christianity, in true Christianity, there will be masters and servants, but a slave is unimaginable. I am speaking of the true, perfect Christianity. Servants are not slaves. The disciple Timothy served the Apostle Paul when they traveled together, but just read the letters of Paul to Timothy: is he writing to a slave, or even to a servant at all? Certainly not! These are clearly letters to his 'son, Timothy'—to his 'beloved son'!" And Dostoyevsky's voice rises up to the passage, to the immortal and universally valid axiom: "You must realize, my dear professor, that purely social ideals that have no organic connection with ethical ideals, that stand rather by themselves, ideals that are therefore separated from the whole as you imagine you can separate things with your learned little knife, social ideals, furthermore, *that could be taken over from outside and transplanted to any desired place* and that could blossom there as 'institutions,' as you call them—that such ideals, I say, do not exist at all, have never existed and also never can exist! And after all, what is a social ideal, anyway, how is one to understand this phrase at all?"

Dostoyevsky teaches the religious origin of national ideas and the resultant national dependence of the social ideal. For ages, he says, people have sought to find a formula for their social organization, a formula that would be as perfect as possible, one that would do justice to all; people have sought this formula for thousands of years, since the beginning of their historical development, and have not been able to find it. "The ant knows the formula of its hill, the bee of its hive, but the human being does not know his formula." But then how did the ideal of a social organization come into human society? It is purely and simply the product of the moral perfection of individual human beings: it begins with this and it has always been this way and will always remain so. The moral idea has always and everywhere preceded the appearance of a nation, *for it is precisely what forms the special national character*; it first creates the nation. But the moral idea has emerged from transcendental convictions that have always and everywhere become religious confession, and then always, scarcely after the new religion has come into being, a new nation has been formed.

> *To preserve the spiritual treasure that has been received*, people immediately begin to join together, and only then do they begin in eager cooperation to look for ways to organize themselves so that nothing of the received treasure will be lost; then they look for a social formula of communal life, for *a governmental form best suited for them*. They seek to develop the moral treasure they have acquired *over the whole world if possible, to its fullest splendor and to raise it to its greatest glory*.

Here, in the clearest, simplest, and most heartfelt words, we have not only the moral perfection of the individual, the personal ethos as the primary one that precedes the social idea, we also have here the origin of nationality from the religious element, the national idea *as* religion; we understand national war, in which self-assertion and expansion merge and cannot be differentiated, as *religious war*.

"And mark my words," Dostoyevsky continues,

> As soon as *the spiritual ideal* in a nation *has begun to decay* in the course of time and years, the nation has also begun to decay at the same time, and with it, too, its whole governmental structure, and the social ideal, which was formed in it in the meantime has also died . . . When in the nation the need for general individual perfection, *in the spirit that has evoked this need, is extinguished*, then all "civic institutions" gradually also disappear, because *then there is nothing left to preserve*.

Therefore one cannot possibly agree with the professor's doctrine that the social perfection of the human being is dependent upon the perfection of social institutions that imbue in people "if not Christian, then at least civic values." "A nation," George's voice resounds—

> A nation is dead when its gods are dead.

But the Russian continues:

> When the moral-religious idea in the nation has had its day, there has always begun a panicky, anxious need for union in order "to save one's neck" if something should happen—civic unity then knows no other goals . . . And what could then the institution, as such, taken for itself alone, still save, anyway? If there were brothers, there would also be brotherhood. But if there are no brothers, brotherhood cannot be achieved through any "institution" at all. What sense is there in creating an "institution,"

and in providing it with the inscription, *"liberté, égalité, fraternité"*? *You will definitely not achieve anything with such an institution*, and one would therefore probably—or rather inevitably—have to add something else to the three words as a fourth element, namely: *"ou la mort."* *"Fraternité ou la mort"*—and the brothers will cut their brothers' heads off in order to establish brotherhood through a "civic institution". . .

You, Mr. Gradovsky, are seeking salvation in externals. You think: Even if here in Russia there are mainly only idiots and rascals among us—one only has to transplant some kind of European "institution" from Europe to Russia, and everything would be saved. The mechanical taking over of European forms (forms that may well collapse there tomorrow) that are alien to our nation and not attuned to its nature, is as is generally known, the main idea of the Russian Westerner. "For the present," they say, "we cannot even find our way in those questions and contradictions that Europe has long ago answered and overcome." What, Europe? And already overcome? Who could have hoodwinked you so?

And here Dostoyevsky becomes the prophet, the herald of the judgment he feels to be so close and about whose appearance he is mistaken in detail, but in the essential part proves himself to be a true seer.

"This Europe," he cries (1880!),

has definitely already reached the eve of its fall, of a fall that will be general and terrible without exception. This anthill, with its moral principle that has been shaken to the core, that has forfeited everything in common and everything absolute, is, I claim, already as good as destroyed. The Fourth Estate has begun to rise, already it is knocking at the door and demanding entry, and if entry is not granted, it will break the door to bits. It does not want the former ideals, it casts every law aside that has been in effect up to now. It no longer agrees to compromises and concessions. *Acquiescence in small things only inflames*, and the Fourth Estate wants to have everything. Something will begin that no one has considered possible up to now. All these parliamentary governmental systems, all presently dominant social theories, all accumulated fortunes, all the banks, sciences, and Jews, all these things will disappear in a trice—except the Jews, naturally, who even then will not lose their heads and will rise to the top again so that the uproar even becomes profitable for them. All this "is standing right at the door." Do you wish to laugh? Blessed are those who laugh! May God grant them long life so they may see everything with their own eyes . . . The symptoms are terrible. The eternally old, unnatural political situation of the European states could suffice in itself to form a beginning . . . This unnaturalness, and these "insoluble" political problems (which are, by the way, known to all) must inevitably lead to the great, final, account-settling political war into which everyone will be drawn, and which will break out in this century yet, perhaps even in this decade. What do you think: *Can the society there still withstand a long political war?* The factory owner is fearful and easy to frighten, and the Jew, too. As soon as the war becomes protracted, or even threatens to become protracted, they will immediately close all their factories and banks, and the millions of hungry, discharged proletarians will be put out in the street. Or do you perhaps put your hope in the wisdom of the statesmen, that they will not allow a war to come? But when has one ever been able to trust in this wisdom? Or do you perhaps place hope in the *parliaments?*— that they will not grant the means for the war because they might perhaps foresee the consequences? Yes, but when have parliaments ever foreseen any kind of consequences and refused the means to a statesman who was only a little energetic, or at least persistent? And thus the war puts the proletarian in the street. What do you think, will he still wait patiently now and starve as he used to?—Now, after the victories of political socialism, after the "Internationale," the congresses of the socialists, and the Parisian Commune? No, now it will be different: The proletarian will throw himself upon Europe and destroy all the old things forever. Only on our Russian shore will the waves shatter, for then it will be revealed for the first time clearly to all how much our national organism is different from those of Europe . . . And these people, you say, had long ago solved their problems at home? With twenty constitutions in less than a century, and after almost ten revolutions?. . .

The European catastrophe, the great, account-settling political war into which everyone was drawn, came just about two decades later than Dostoyevsky predicted. The statesmen have not hindered it, and the parliaments have granted the means. The factory owners and the Jews in the meantime have not failed, and the war has not yet put the proletarian in the street, but has given him twenty to fifty marks a day in wages. In a different way from what Dostoyevsky thought, it has been shown that the national organism of Russia is different from those of Europe, for the revolution has broken out in Russia, and not yet in the West. Professor Gradovsky and his "institutions" came to power in the person of Mr. Milykov. The burgher president was followed by an ingenious dictator who politicized against a peasant-and-soldier council that, for its part, knows more of Tolstoy than of Dostoyevsky. "Dostoyevsky is forgotten in Russia." But his question of whether European society could withstand a long political war has found only an unclear answer up to now.

We stop at the end of October, 1917. Görz has been retaken, Austrian-German divisions have broken open the Alpine passes and descended into the Venetian plain. What happened in Russia and in Rumania can be repeated in Italy. It will be repeated—is there anyone at all who did *not* know that this country is not seriously equal to this war? What a joy the news of these days is! What liberation, salvation, and refreshment the "power," the clear and majestic act of war, brings, after the rotten-choking gloom and confusion of domestic affairs, of Germany's psychological anarchy, of her self-treacherous flirting with submission to "democracy," her "political" attempts to conform, to "reach an understanding" by stooping in her diplomatic notes to the language of Wilson! Once again one can breathe joyfully. Italy's defeat would be the defeat of Mazzini and of d'Annunzio, of the democratic-republican incendiary orator and of the esthetic-political clown, both of whom I hate from the bottom of my heart.

But still, I no longer believe, if I ever did, that the problems, Europe's insoluble political problems, can be solved by the force of arms. Germany has been victorious too often to still believe in victories. The war is incalculable, "peace" farther away than ever. It becomes daily more improbable that the present "democratic" and "absolutist" governments will end it; the representatives of the revolutionary nations will do it when the time is ripe. The proletarian will scarcely find it necessary "to throw himself upon Europe" in order to seize power for himself; it will fall to him of itself. The socialist tyranny that began before the war and gained strength in the war will be limitless and crushing after the war; all opposing spirit, all satirical fury, will have to arm itself against it and against nothing else. In any case, the radical revolutionary ideology will see good days. The wave of blissful political hopefulness that has, as we said, been stirred up by this war will swell up immeasurably, the exuberant enthusiasm of the end of the eighteenth century will even be exceeded in ardor by the "new belief." "Toward the Beginning" is the title that a poet of strong literary mannerisms, Walter Hasenclever, gives to a lyrical-dramatic fragment he has just published in a pamphlet for young people. Here are a few verses from it:

> Palaces are trembling. *Power is at an end.*
> Whoever was great, plunges into the abyss,
> The gates crash shut.
> He who had everything, has lost everything;
> The slave by dint of his work
> Is richer than he.
> Follow me! I shall lead you.

The wind is rising from the ruins,
The new world is dawning.*

The people of the peace conference will "believe." They will believe they have found, or are close to finding, the formula for the social organization of the human race, the formula of the human anthill, of the human beehive, the faultless formula that does justice to all, that they have been seeking for millennia. *Liberté, égalité, fraternité ou la mort*— and the brothers will cut off their brothers' heads to establish brotherhood through "civic institutions." The kingdom of God will appear on earth, justice, eternal peace and happiness in the form of the *république démocratique, sociale et universelle.* Thereupon the course of things will take a turn that will scarcely come up to the great expectations; and not just for external reasons will the momentarily raised idols fall, but especially because of their inner bankruptcy they always bore within themselves. Deeply disappointed in their hopeful belief, people will throw themselves into the arms of *Weltschmerz*, of a new "Byronism." Scorn, bitterness, and despair will be the dominant moods on earth— and once more: would someone who is not a malicious devil, not a sneering enemy of mankind, someone who can say of himself that he is still open to enthusiasm for adventure, for beauty born of loneliness, someone who almost sees life itself in admiration, belief, and dedication, and who does not have to pursue love and sympathy for all creatures either in an esthetic or in a political way—would such a person have to hide it if he looked forward to this probable and unavoidable turn of events with anticipatory satisfaction? I must confess that I am such a person. For I hate politics and the belief in politics because it makes one arrogant, doctrinaire, stubborn and inhuman. I do not believe in the formula for the human anthill, the human beehive, do not believe in the *république démocratique, sociale et universelle*, do not believe that the human race is destined for "happiness," or even that it *wants* happiness— do not believe in "belief," but rather more in despair, because it is

---

* Paläste wanken. *Die Macht ist zu Ende.*
  Wer groß war, stürzt in den Abgrund,
  Die Tore donnern zu.
  Wer alles besaß, hat alles verloren;
  Der Knecht im Schweiß seiner Hände
  Ist reicher als er.
  Folgt mir! Ich will euch führen.
  Der Wind steigt aus den Trümmern,
  Die neue Welt bricht an.

despair that frees the path to salvation; I believe in humility and in work—work on oneself, which, in its highest and most moral, its strictest and most cheerful form, seems to me to be art. And this I also believe, that a politically resolute lover of the human race who wants art to be political, and who, as a man of the hour, calls me a ruthless person and a parasite because I do not want this—that such a person commits a crime against a human soul, a crime that invalidates, gives the lie to, and forever destroys all his chatter about love.

I heard that Dostoyevsky was forgotten in Russia. Apparently so. As far as Germany is concerned, one can see that even today young writers cling to the great prophet of the soul as they scarcely do to any other, but that everyone who embodies literature, radicalism, and politics swears much more by Tolstoy—not by Tolstoy the artist: he seems quite outmoded to them, and Dostoyevsky's apocalyptic, grotesque psychology stands decidedly nearer to their "expressionism" than Tolstoy's plastic art; but they get along well with the old Tolstoy who is no longer an artist, with the social prophet and Christian-anarchic utopian, the pacifist, antimilitarist and enemy of the state: and quite rightly so. For in contrast to Dostoyevsky, who was *not* one, this Tolstoy is indeed a politician—I insist upon this because it is very important to me to bring out quite clearly the idea of the politician and his opposite.

I say: Dostoyevsky, even though the power and the political mission of Russia were dear to him, and even though—or rather: *because* he scourged revolutionary intrigues, was no politician. Tolstoy, who did not at all hold dear the power and political mission of Russia, who was an antinationalist and pacifist and would have read, or did read Dostoyevsky's essay in favor of war with the greatest disgust—he, for his part, was one. Why? Because in him Christianity is completely socialized; because in him social life is raised to a religion. "Tolstoy's religion," Emil Hammacher says, "falls mainly in the social sphere." This means: it serves the promotion of social welfare; its ideal result is "happiness." But here Tolstoy is a democrat, he is a politician. Tolstoy is *enlightenment*, that is: a moralist of happiness, a philosopher of welfare. Tolstoy is—pardon the word, there is today none more characteristic— he is *entente*, he is, even without exactly being a "Westerner," the representative of Russian democracy, the West-East alliance of today is spiritually justified in him—it is *not* justified in Dostoyevsky.

Five days before his last, Dostoyevsky received a few letters from Tolstoy to read in which the latter had developed his ideas in the often

confused, touching, and struggling way that we know. Dostoyevsky held
his head and cried out in despair: "Not that! Above all, not that!" He
sympathized, it is said, with none of Tolstoy's thoughts. Nevertheless,
he picked up everything that lay on the table, originals and copies of
the letters, and took them along. He intended to combat Tolstoy's ideas;
but he died, and Russia buried a patriot and a conservative—a "political
fighter," but only as far as he scourged "revolutionary intrigues," only
as far as one becomes a politician by fighting politics.

At the same time, Tolstoy was corresponding with an *American pastor*
who addressed him as "My dear brother." In my opinion, this was not
more and not less than a world historical scandal; and it was Tolstoy's
fault that things could go so far, the fault of his degeneration from the
great Slavic novelist to the prophet of a democratic, worldwide welfare
state. His success in the Anglo-Saxon world was extraordinary—and
this says something of his level. Who in America would understand
anything of Dostoyevsky? It was left to a cosmopolitan Dane, Johannes
V. Jensen, to create a sensational synthesis of Dostoyevsky and America.
But the fate of being addressed by a reverend with "My dear brother,"
was spared the author of the "Karamazovs."

Dostoyevsky wrote to a mother: "Teach your child to believe in God,
and indeed, strictly according to tradition. Otherwise you cannot make
your child into a good person, but at best only into a *sufferer*, and at
worst—into an indifferent, *fat* one, and this is much worse." I cannot
say that I believe in God—it would take a long time, I think, before I
would say so, even if I did. Doubt has not made me *fat*; I even tend to
think that it is belief (and not doubt) that makes one fat, and it may be
more courageous, more moral, and more truthful to live in a resigned
and in a dignified way in a godless world than to escape the deep and
empty look of the sphinx with a blind faith such as that in democracy.
I called such an attempt at escape the betrayal of the cross—may it
make him who commits it fat and blessed! Meanwhile, I know two
things. First, I know that it would be comparatively easier for me to
believe in God than in "mankind"; and second I know that mankind
needs belief in God more than in democracy. For putting aside the
question of whether the individual person can be good without God, it
is absolutely certain that the masses of people will never find the
slightest reason to be good without the belief in God, without religion.

Religion! I have heard civilization's literary man talk about religion!
A poet had died, a son of man who was, with all the scintillating cunning
of his intellect, still infinitely naive and demoniacally tortured, and it

was said that his last hours were filled with religious efforts (which had, by the way, always been a part of his life), that he had struggled with God, struggled up to the last to reach God, and had—perhaps—died believing in Him. How did civilization's literary man go about excusing him? How did he extricate himself from the situation? "*The commitment to the spirit,*" he said at the grave, "that we call religion,"—was obviously something the deceased was most clearly aware of! But one knows, of course, what civilization's literary man understands by "spirit." He understands literature by it, he understands politics by it, together with that thing called: democracy. And this he calls religion! When I had heard this, when I had heard this "liberal religious" Sunday preacher's unctuous, counterfeit reasoning, when I had had to witness this attempt to reclaim for politics a soul that was seeking its salvation in its final hour of need, I put on my top hat and went home.

No, religion is not the commitment to the spirit of civilization's literary man. Belief in God is different from belief in progress. One knows the objective result of this "liberal religious" belief; at best it is "happiness," the positivistic happiness in the figure of Fourier's Phalanstère. But one also knows its *personal* result—at least I know it. It is the preacherly arrogance of being something better through belief, the self-righteous bigotry of the missionary and the pharisee, combined with constant aggressiveness against the rotten ones who do not "believe." By "humanity" it understands a rational principle, rigidly moral and morally rigid. It is basically never social, not friendly out of individual human friendliness that charms forth goodness, and that makes everyone show his best and most noble side. It knows nothing of tolerance, but is hard, divisive, doctrinaire all the way to the guillotine, humorless, in truth without love in spite of all its screaming about love, without music, without tenderness, fanatically rhetorical—abominable.

Whether he now says "belief" or "freedom"—the politician is abominable. But when I say: not politics, but religion, I do not boast of having religion. Far from it. No, I have none. If, however, one may understand by *religiosity* the freedom that is a path, not a goal; that means openness, tenderness, openness for life, humility; a searching, probing, doubting and erring; a path, as I have said, to God, or, as far as I am concerned, to the Devil as well—but for heaven's sake not the hardened certainty and philistinism of the possession of belief—well, then perhaps I may call some of this freedom and religiosity my own.

I want to end this chapter with two German aphorisms that speak of religiosity and freedom. "This life," Luther says, "is not piousness, but becoming pious, not health, but becoming healthy, not being, but becoming." And Lessing says: "Not the possession of truth, but the search for it, expands the powers of the human being; in it alone lies his continually growing perfection."

CHAPTER 11

The Politics of Estheticism

Strange! I walk around midst the small collection of books that has accrued to me through the years. I leaf through them, come upon places here and there that I have, according to good custom, marked with a pencil while I was reading—and find that they are all *moralistic* passages, passages, that is, that have nothing at all to do with "beauty," but with moral-psychological things. The year is indicated in which I first made a book my own; many an emphasis dates far back. I was young, I read; I amused myself, admired, loved and learned. But the esthetic element, no matter how much I loved it and tried to learn from it, seems to have been obvious to me; my pencil did not begin to move in those places where it revealed itself most exquisitely. What I sought, what was important to me, what I emphasized, was ethics, was morality; and it was art that had a moral emphasis, that was bound up with morality, that I looked up to, that I perceived as *my* sphere, as what was proper for me, as what had always been familiar to me.

When my novel-chronicle about the decline of a family appeared, a year passed before it was noticed. Then I gleaned much praise and honor from it. Among the reviews, however, there was one that satisfied me most of all, not because it praised, but because it characterized, and especially because it treated the book together with an Italian one, a novel by d'Annunzio that had just been translated, and juxtaposed the pessimistic moralism of my story to the voluptuous estheticism of the Latin one. *This* clipping I carried in my breast pocket, and I liked to show it. This was it. This was the way I was and wanted to be. I also wanted to be *seen* in this way; and there was opposition in this will— opposition to a world view and to a type of art that was alien and hostile to me, that seemed to me to be without conscience, or to use the more colorful word instead, *ruthless*. "You have kindled orgies in honor of the shining surface of the world and called it art." This was such an expression of this opposition, an expression stylized into monkish ferocity and exaggerated, but meant personally.

Strange! The direction of my opposition seems to have changed. It seems that in these pages I have been opposing morality; clearly I have been holding art up against it; and "ruthless": this terrible word is hurled out—not against me, it would certainly be presumptuous to apply it to me; but still, against an opinion and negation that I agree with and that I assert. Seriously, have the roles been reversed? At most the names! And not of my wanting, but from a simple whim of my adversary and opposite type. The point of this chapter is that in truth things are as they were before; that we have essentially remained true to ourselves, I, and especially also my opponent; that the direction of my opposition has *not* changed, only that its target has taken on a different name today, that it is now calling itself "morality," that is, "politics," and me a ruthless, parasitic esthete.

"Ruthless": Schopenhauer first gave the word life for us, and specifically in a thoroughly negative way as the strongest moral condemnation, as a scathing attribute of every optimism that the herald of the reversal of the will understood as counterredemptive insensitivity to the monstrous suffering of the world. We encountered the word again in Nietzsche, but how changed in its sense and sound! "Ruthless," or also "unscrupulous," *"scrupulously unscrupulous"*: this was no longer a moral judgment, by this time the word was "free of moral hypocrisy" and highly positive, highly affirmative, yes, it was meant as downright glorification: "ruthless"—a dionysian word, an almost feminine-enraptured praise and tribute to life, the strong, sublime, powerful, innocent, victorious, violent, and particularly *beautiful* life, the Cesare-Borgia-life as the weak person, eternally separated from this life, would dream of in his hectic-sentimental yearning. Yes, "life" was perceived here above all as *beautiful*, as beauty itself in its amoral and exuberant masculine brutality, celebrated, flattered and wooed; it was an esthetically interpreted, an esthetically viewed beauty, and "ruthless" became the private pet word of all estheticism originating from Nietzsche.

Now is the time for me to acknowledge publicly that I have never, neither at twenty nor at forty, had anything at all to do with this estheticism that undoubtably goes back to Nietzsche's "life" romanticism that was in full bloom when I began writing—which does not mean that it did not trouble and excite me. At that time, one was devoted to the senses with conviction and with sufficient ruthlessness, one dreamed of thickly gilded renaissance plafonds and fat women, there was a continual dinning in my ears about the "strong and beautiful life" in sentences that ran something like: "Only people with strong, brutal instincts can create great works!"—while I definitely knew that works such as the "Last Supper," which I had seen in Rome, and the novel, *Anna Karenina*, which strengthened me while I was writing *Buddenbrooks*, had been produced by people of the highest moral, Christianly scrupulous character who were willing to suffer. "You are staying too long with the criticism of reality," I heard very close at hand. "But in good time you will get to art, too." To art? But criticism of reality, plastic moralism, this was precisely what I perceived to be art, and I despised the programmatically ruthless gesture of beauty to which today's virtue wanted to encourage me at that time.

Yes, in years in which there was otherwise little to despise, I could despise the esthetic, renaissance-Nietzscheanism that was all around me and that seemed to me to be a boyishly mistaken imitation of Nietzsche. The representatives of this school took Nietzsche at his word, took him literally. It was not Nietzsche whom they had viewed and experienced, but the ideal image of his self-negation, and they cultivated this mechanically. They innocently believed him to be the "immoralist" he called himself; they did not see that this descendent of Protestant ministers had been the most sensitive moralist who ever lived, a morally possessed man, Pascal's brother. But then, what did they see, really? They did not miss a single misunderstanding that his demeanor ever offered them opportunity for. The element of romantic *irony* in his eros—they had no sense for this at all. And his philosophizing inspired them to create quite prosaic celebrations of beauty, novels full of aphrodisiacal, high-school boy's fantasy, catalogues of vices in which absolutely nothing was omitted.

No matter how false it would be to present Nietzsche as in any way the father of European estheticism, it is still true that among the intellectual currents that emanate from him there is one that is nothing but esthetic, that one can indeed be educated by Nietzsche into an esthete. It was that estheticism that, since for all its eagerness to achieve "plasticity," it was not at all naive, but highly analytical, could give itself the most accurate abusive name: It called itself the "hysterical renaissance." This readiness for self-criticism was conciliatory. The element that is hostile to life and that recognizes itself may live and develop as colorfully as it can; it will do no harm; the self-recognition basically prevents it from being aggressive. It would be something else if it took itself seriously and became impudent, if it claimed to be truth, life, art itself, and finally even virtue, too, and tried to defame the opposition! The "hysterical renaissance" did not do that. It knew and did not forget that it was basically lifeless and loveless, that it was a gesticulative, highly talented impotence, even in life and love, and its intellectual dignity consisted precisely in the pain over this condition: it was a tragic dignity that had to disappear as soon as any kind of seeming "development" and new nomenclature caused the self-knowledge and self-doubt to disappear.

I repeat that I have never had anything intrinsically to do with the renaissance-estheticism of certain "Nietzscheans." But what held me away may have been—I had this feeling early—my German character. "Beauty," as those dionysians interpreted and glorified it with sharp gestures, always seemed to me something for Latins and Latinists, a "bit of the south" of rather suspicious, contemptible character; and even though I boundlessly admired Nietzsche as a prose writer and psychologist in all stages of his life: the Nietzsche who really mattered to me and who, in accordance with my nature, had to affect me pedagogically most deeply, was the one who was still very close to Wagner and Schopenhauer, or who always remained close to them, the one who singled out from all plastic art *one* picture with lasting love—Dürer's "Knight, Death, and Devil"; the one who had told Rohde of his natural pleasure in all art and philosophy in which "ethical air, Faustian smell, cross, death and grave" could be detected: a phrase I immediately seized upon as a symbol for a whole world, *my world*, a northern-moral-Protestant, *id est, German* one that is strictly in opposition to that world of ruthless estheticism.

We have recently received a beautiful book: *The Work of Conrad Ferdinand Meyer* by Franz Ferdinand Baumgarten. In it the author characterizes Meyer with a quotation; he calls him "a burgher gone astray and an artist with a bad conscience." "The prejudices that are in the burgher's blood," he adds by way of explanation, "spoiled the freedom of the artist for him, and the temptations of the artist's blood gave the burgher a bad conscience." Meyer knew he belonged to those who wore the crown of sorrows, as did his "Saint"; he rejected *passion, brutality, unscrupulousness*, as did Pescara and Angela Borgia. That is very good. Never has the characteristic charm that flows from the work of this Swiss writer been perceived and defined more subtly: this charm rests on a special and personal mixture of burgherly and artistic nature, on the permeation of a world of beautiful ruthlessness by the

Protestant spirit. Conrad Ferdinand was hardly like the Nietzsche-influenced renaissance esthete of 1900 who mechanically accepted Nietzsche's theoretical anti-Christianity; he could never commit the "betrayal of the cross," "*Car malgré tous mes efforts d'échapper au christianisme,*" he says in a letter, "*au moins à ses dernières conséquences, je m'y sens ramené par plus fort que moi chaque année davantage . . .*" He was a Christian in that he did not confuse himself with what he longed to portray: the ruthless-beautiful life; he remained true to suffering and to conscience, Christianity, burgherly nature, German character, these are, in spite of all Latinizing tendencies in artistic matters, if not the components, then at least the basic qualities of his artistic genius, and the characteristic of all three is conscientiousness, this opposite of passion. "A matter of conscience." "It really has to do with a matter of conscience." He liked to use such turns of phrase when he talked about his work by letter. People such as he do not flame up at all for "rights"; the "right of passion" is the first thing they despise. Tonio Kröger found a humorous-modest expression for this mood and antipathy when he said to his girl friend: "Lord, you can have Italy, Lisaweta! I am indifferent to Italy to the point of contempt! It has been a long time since I imagined I belonged there. Art, right? Velvet blue sky, hot wine, and sweet sensuality . . . In short, I don't like that. I renounce it. All the *bellezza* makes me nervous. Nor can I stand all those frightfully lively people down there with their black animal looks. These Latins have no conscience in their eyes . . ." No, that was no esthete, this youthful writer with the mixed name and character.

He was, of course, also the one who wrote to Lisaweta: "I admire the proud and cold ones who seek adventure in the paths of great, demonic beauty and who despise the 'human being'—but I do not envy them. For if anything at all is capable of making a literary man into a creative writer, it is this, my burgherly love for what is human, alive, and ordinary. All warmth, all goodness, all humor, come from it, and it almost seems to me as if it is that same love about which is written that with it one can speak with the tongues of men and of angels, and without it one is only as sounding brass or a tinkling cymbal." Here, to be sure, an attitude toward "life" was expressed that was considerably different from the dionysian cult of life of those adventurers on the paths of ruthless beauty. "*Proud and cold,*" I called them; for I knew—knew as I know today, that in my "burgherly" pessimism, my life denial that had "not yet gotten to art," there was more love of life and its children than in their theoretical glorification of life. Irony as love—

not one fiber of their being knew anything of such an experience. Self-renunciation—he who did not know this was the egotist. He believes he has found it today; in what? Most gracious Lord, *in politics* he thinks he has found it! And "ruthless"—the triumphant, amoral sense of this word has not changed for him into something moral, but into a clumsy righteousness: ruthless, this is what he calls today the separation of art and politics!

In these pages, I seem to have accepted and adopted as my own the antithesis of political or politicized art, and the art of estheticism. But that was a game; for seriously, I know better what the nature of this antithesis is, I know that it rests on a desired, nobly desired, self-deception that has gradually become all too successful for the one who decrees it, that it is wrong, that it does not exist, that one need not be an esthete when one does not believe in politics, but that one can, as a "serving" social-moralist and herald of resolute love of mankind, remain an arch-esthete. Has remained: it is quite obvious, and the only person who can miss it is one who wants to miss it because he wants "to find others worse than he." We had the hysterical renaissance—now we have the hysterical democracy. Only that the latter no longer has the cheerful honesty and artistic impudence to call itself hysterical. Only that it takes itself seriously, utterly seriously, rigidly morally, takes itself as virtue itself and had "repressed" what long ago was written about it:

> I have given virtue a new charm—it has the effect of something forbidden. It has our most subtle honesty against it, it is seasoned with the "*cum grano salis*" of the scientific pangs of conscience; it is old-fashioned in odor and has an antique effect, so that now it is finally alluring the smart people and making them curious—in short, it works like vice . . .
>
> (Nietzsche)

But what is this state of allurement and this curiosity, what, in a word, is this *fornication with virtue*, other than estheticism?

When I acted as if that fabricated antithesis really existed, I tried to define estheticism in different ways, as culture, as justice, as freedom, as belief in art. In truth, there is only one definition for it, and I have already given it, too. Estheticism, whether it expresses itself as a frenetic cult of ruthless-beautiful life, or as rhetorically resolute "love of mankind," is the gesture-rich, highly talented impotence in life and love. Nothing else. One should know less about the essence of this exalted "universal love of mankind." It is peripheral eroticism. Wherever it is proclaimed, wherever one boasts of it, there tends to be something wrong in the middle. It is the motto and the battle cry of an antiestheticism that betrays itself by its propagandalike moral combat posture as what it is: as also-and-still-estheticism. I do not know whether the antipolitician is also a politician. But I have the clearest certainty that the antiesthete, the intellectual politician and belles-lettres-democrat, is *also* an esthete, that his political ideology is only a new and sensational form of *bellezza*.

Above all, his radicalism is *bellezza*. Estheticism that politicizes itself will always be radical, precisely because of *bellezza*. It is quite common to confuse radicalism with depth. Nothing is more incorrect. Radicalism is beautiful shallowness—a liberal cult of gestures that leads directly into choreography, as a word of the intellectual politician proves. "Freedom," he said one day, "Freedom is the bacchanalian dance of reason!" Now, if that is not *bellezza*, I do not know where to look for it. It is a poetic paraphrase of the nihilistic-orgiastic idea of freedom, dancer-politics, demonized Dalcroze. In the *Italian Journey* one finds an expression of disdainful calm—I mean: calm disdain about this political esthete-orgy. "Freedom and equality," it says there, "can only be enjoyed in the ecstasy of madness."

What political estheticism and the *bellezza*-and-belles-lettres-politician lack in a generous way may be a sense of responsibility, may be conscience. But where should this come from, anyway, since no one, not even he himself, presumes his responsibility, nor evaluates his statements in this spirit? On the contrary, everyone, including him, evaluates them first and last from the point of view of beauty, and whatever opinion there is in them is justified because it shows itself capable of beauty. Heavens above, he is, after all, an artist—and what do opinions matter in the realm of art? He *knows* basically that they do not matter at all. Who would want to judge a great artist by his opinions—or a work of art, even one whose medium is the word, by its possible *consequences*? He *knows* that one asks these questions—and he secretly asks them of himself. It is not the consequences that count, but the effect: The political artist is the one who is *most hungry for effect*, but he covers up this hunger for effect with the doctrine that art must have consequences, and specifically, political ones.

No matter how elevated his moralistic talk about the "responsible" and "irresponsible" writer may become, it is talk in which he himself, in unruffled calm, does not believe. Art is not objective, its charm is that it "consumes the material through form." Art is irresponsible: it is concerned with gesture, beauty, and passion, and an artist is an artist and wants to be appreciated as an artist not only when he creates, but also when he speaks: Everyone knows this, and he himself knows it secretly best of all. Artistic nature is something *one can retreat behind* when the objective world becomes a bit confused—behind which one is happily sheltered and still derives honor from the confusion. The *bellezza* politician says the most flagrantly unprincipled things because he knows perfectly well: it cannot hurt him at all. For in what would one not make allowance for the artist's "temperament"? At worst, he has creatively missed the point. And even if he acts as if he were demanding to be taken seriously—he himself is only to a certain extent serious in all that. He speaks for the sake of "passion," of *beautiful* "passion," and if one finds him frivolous to the point of foolishness, of repulsiveness, then he retreats into his artistic nature that has remained untouched by this, that is even made pleasing by it. It is possible that the opinions he tossed out yesterday are no longer his today, just as little as the Flaubert-estheticism that they replaced is still credo, either. To be sure, he expressed them with the highest claim for validity, the most extreme apodicticity and dogmatism, with them he has insulted, wounded, tyrannized, and possibly defamed and killed—what of it! He is an artist, he has the "right of passion," and so the whole world, and he himself, turns a blind eye to what he does.

But what if this right of passion did not exist here at all, because, that is, true artistic nature, which itself never makes such vulgar misuse of the right to passion and of passion, does not exist here at all? If it were only a matter of a false, half-baked, intellectual, would-be, artificial artistic nature, and of a passion that was no passion, but only a twisted, self-satisfied hot-headedness and lack of conscience, a poor surrogate? In a word: if it were a matter of estheticism? I make no secret of my insight that this is what it is, since every reason not to be quite frank about it has been taken from me. As an artist and as a politician as well one is an esthete when one to be sure proclaims oratorically that art must be political and have consequences, but when one is, at the same time, ready at any moment to retreat with one's politics behind art—personally and objectively. The politicized artist has taste, he does not want to be thought of as a simple moralizer, he would have to be afraid that this would injure his reputation as an artist. Therefore he is intent on veiling and camouflaging the morality in an artistic-psychological way: he takes virtue a bit pathologically—oh, not too much so, just so far that one can still take its blarney seriously, but so that it also seems all right not to take it seriously. He is even capable of concealing the democratic-political message in such a way that he treats its representative with grotesque humor—not from Turgenevian motives, but to save face and to avoid the reproach of moralizing. Besides that, in the description of vice, for example, the fact that flagrant estheticism stands right next to virtue also helps to "dim" virtue and to reconcile it artistically; and if all this should lead one or another naive reader to a complete misunderstanding of the whole thing—well, only assuming there is any effect at all present, any really strong effect, then the insensitivity of the artist-politician to such misunderstanding is as good as complete. To cap it all off, he is always an artist who, the devil take it, wants his success; and if the undertaking is a success, it does no harm at all that one has noticed nothing and the product has in no way had a political but only an artistic-sensational effect.

All this is estheticism; but a half-baked, cowardly one that retreats behind virtue. It is also virtuousness, but a half-baked and cowardly one that uses art as a breastplate. Greatness is consistent. Old Tolstoy damned art altogether and put *Uncle Tom's Cabin* high above Beethoven and Shakespeare. This is strange, but it has character. On the other hand, there is something completely respectable in pure and insolent estheticism. Baudelaire wrote in his diary, "1848 was *only* amusing because everyone was then building castles in the air—1848 was *only* charming because of the excess of ridiculousness—Robespierre is *only* estimable because he has created *a few literarily beautiful sentences.*" I like that. Pure estheticism is capable of the most intensive effects. Oscar Wilde's *Salome*, for example, is a work of immortal precision and force; the hard artistry of this sincere and upright estheticism has the truth of the wicked and beautiful life. But the politicized and moralizing estheticism with "ardent ethos," the estheticism mixed with tearful revolutionary humanitarianism—is a mixture that has, to be sure, democracy and democratic effect in its favor, but that has good taste strongly against it.

The cultural point of view cannot be completely neglected. Morality always has a tendency to iconoclasm. Rule of opinion easily leads to hostility to culture and art. One knows virtue's aversion to beauty, form, polish, and elegance—these things seem frivolous to it, esthetic; and indeed its mistrust is all the more intense, it feels it must act even more harshly, when it itself comes from estheticism, when it is an esthetic renegade. Out of fear of artistry, one begins to write with a broom, puritanically-ascetically, in chopped-up sentences—to symbolize virtue. The style is considered saved if only the syntax is French. But if excellence in this leads the way—the little ones follow only too willingly, and the floodgates are open to every bungling expression of conviction. Again it turns out that revolutionary times such as these bring to light "more will than imagination, and more political imagination than artistic." But where the political spirit, that is, conviction, is trumps, very little talent is asked for, and the bunglers enjoy good times. The danger, for example, that "patriotic" loyalty of conviction could be confused with talent is insignificant compared to the new and different one: the conviction of literary love of mankind, the charm of a pacifistically opposing attitude, has an effect on a public considering itself exacting that is much more fascinating than "patriotism"—here one forgets that convictions lie on the street and that everyone can pick them up and make them his own: the advocate of such a conviction is immediately "one of our most subtle minds." Cultural guardians still think they must rail against bad war novels and Iron Hindenburgs; but they should not keep such a close eye on the patriotic bunglers, who are harmless and fool no one, as on the gentlemen who think they can replace talent with an inverse loyalty of conviction. After quite a few years, it seemed as if German prose could again show itself alongside other European prose, something that had not been the case for a few decades. Under the stamp of conviction, what has been reached seems likely to be lost again, and again "French character" (politics, that is) is pushing back "quiet culture."

The politics of esthetes—the components of this phrase teach us right away—is not a German growth, but a Latin one. It is clear that its transplantation to Germany is part of the "democratization" of Germany. D'Annunzio and Barrès are excellent examples of politicized estheticism; particularly the latter, a one-time decadent and esthete who "developed" himself into a politician, nationalist, *patriotard*, and crier of revenge. For him the revenge idea is *"un excitant"*—just as politics doubtless is for our belles-lettres-politicians; only that here it nourishes radicalistic contents instead of nationalistic ones. This is a difference, but it is also the whole difference; there is no other. The national differentiation, the German character of our belles-lettres-politicians, exhausts itself in this—in its antinationalism. I do not say: in its cosmopolitanism—for German cosmopolitanism may after all be quite another thing. One can hardly establish oneself as a German cosmopolite in this war simply by speaking just like the French parliamentary president about "saber" and "justice." This is, quite frankly, not the level of German cosmopolitanism. A simple-Germanophobic, rhetorical-revolutionary French way of thinking—appealing to the humanist, Goethe, and to the European, Nietzsche, as precedents because they, too, were antinationalists—makes many demands on our readiness for approval and tolerance, a readiness that is simply not up to these demands today. Not for three years now. The game was possible "in the semidarkness of the esthetic epoch." Today, one has had enough of it. One has had enough of putting up with sentences such as, for example, "What is written in the German language is German." "Every artistic and intellectual movement that blossoms on German soil is German, whether we like it or not." This is not true. We are no longer hoodwinked, and we, we see no reason to make a secret of our thoughts, out of pure good-naturedness to call something white when it is quite obviously black. Why the game with the word, "German," anyway? Why claim a title for oneself, or even tolerate it, when one despises it? Let one be consistent! Let one reject it! "German character is not in the blood, but in the mind," Lagarde says. Let one refer to this judgment! Let one declare: No, then, I am not German, I am, although of German blood, in my basic intellectual nature, my whole culture, French, and I act accordingly. This would be honest. It would be a statement of a fact that could be evaluated as an advantage, or as something else. Possibly not everyone would unreservedly regard it as an advantage; there might be people who see in the fact that a man who is in spite of everything German by birth and surroundings and who in all ways thinks, feels, speaks and writes just like a Frenchman rather an oddity, a freak of nature, and they might react to it as one reacts to freaks of nature: fascinated, even if also somewhat repelled. That, as I said, could be. But it is completely out of the question that such a declaration, made among Germans, could prove to be in any way dangerous or harmful for the one who makes it.

I want this to go on record: it would be neither dangerous nor harmful. Why the sleight of hand: "By being anti-German, am I German?" That is quite unnecessary. In Germany, no one is hurt by insulting Germany: on the contrary! And our belles-lettres-politician *knows this very well*. Really, I deny all boldness here. The likes of it would be bold in France—much less of it would be bold there. But among ourselves? One *finds* it bold: with this it stops being bold. "Byzantinism" before the nation—as if that brought honor in Germany! As if the opposite, the most unjust "justice," did not bring honor in Germany! One speaks of "speculation in nationalism." If anything like that exists, it is not important. What is important is the speculation in antination-alism: it is not the less in bloom because it is blossoming in a "more intellectual" sphere, and *courage*—no, courage is not necessary at all for it. Only quite crude outward appearances, the naive imprudence of "power," which creates highly welcome martyrdoms, can confuse one about this. "Practical life," "reality," with its silencing of the "intellect" by power (whatever is silenced by power must naturally have "intellect")—this reality informs only insufficiently about the true state of things, yes, it even leads one astray. Courage is necessary today for one to declare oneself a German, a burgherly German—to commit oneself with at least a part of one's being, probably the best part, to the national element. The opposite requires only as much courage today as every literary rascal can muster.

I repeat: Why the sleight of hand, for civilization's literary man clearly *knows very well* that hostility to Germany hurts no one in Germany, that it is completely safe, yes, that its display even brings honor? Unnecessarily he cried: "I—antinational? Long after me, traits of mine will be called national that would never have become so without me. Your national character will become closer to its true nature than it is today because of me; I am giving you an example of what you are to become!" What intellectual bluff! What a twisted refutation of modest reason! Not in this way, not as civilization's literary man believes, or convinces himself he believes, is a national character ever strengthened and enriched. It is strengthened and enriched, it becomes aware of itself, looking at its most genuine, strongest, most characteristic, most paradigmatically perfect representatives, its great men. But this strengthening recognition is always only a recognizing again of what has been deeply familiar from the beginning. No trait of the Luthers, Goethes, and Bismarcks became German through them—while it has been Celto-Latin before. Was not the image of Bismarck's character poetically-prophetically anticipated in Kleist's Armin? In his country, Mazzini was genuine and not foreign—the political Freemason with the "dogma of equality" and the "revolutionary symbol." His spirit is foreign in Germany; but not, to repeat, in his homeland. He was of genuine birth, a familiar expression of the race. He might arouse hatred, suffer persecution: not for a moment could he seem truly strange, confusing, twisted, or monstrous; he could never seem for a moment like a ghostly oddity and two-headed calf—nor should we quite forget that in Mazzini's case (and even in Zola's case, as well) "unity of thought and deed" did not remain a literary phrase, but that Mazzini's political manifestoes and proclamations are only the literary reflection of the genuine life of a fighter and martyr whose effort was the human being himself and that therefore had to find not only national understanding, but also human respect, even with his opponents. But what does our belles-lettres-activist hold up to us as an example? Does he seriously believe that the wildly gesticulating, revolutionary world of letters he holds up to us will ever be called German?

He cried further: "I—an apostate? Whether I love the fatherland or not: I am it myself!" But that is simply the obvious, bluffing, and twisted untruth. He is not the fatherland; not only is he not so, he has carried his intellectual, political cult of what is alien so far that he has no thought, no idea, no feeling in common with his own national character anymore. And it became easy for him to attain this type of identity with the fatherland. Never has German music touched his heart, enriched his spirit—he does not understand a tone and does not want to, either. Never has he enjoyed the high ecstasy of German metaphysics—it does not promote progress and is therefore inopportune. His relationship to the great German character is embarrassed rejection, deep hostility. We have long known how he stands toward Goethe, the antipolitician, quietist, and esthete. As far as Bismarck is concerned, there even exists, by the hand of the literary man, a portrait of him. "Bismarck" is not written under it; "passion" does not make one lose all caution; but there can be no doubt. Here is the image: "This is the man of power, the master par excellence, and quite useless when he cannot be master. The purposeless weight of the massive shoulders!—in a man of power who has been overthrown and who is waiting for his return, and only waiting, *without intellectual interests, without any activity besides power*, ready for anything so that he may exercise it again, ready to deny his entire past, yes, if necessary, to risk the life of his prince—for the prince was always only the pretext for the power instinct of his most loyal servant . . ." In every barracks there is a grammar school teacher serving a one-year hitch who complains that "intellectual interests" are neglected in the military. No matter. Here we have the founder of worldly Germany—*vu à travers un temperament*. The great Germans are divided into esthetes and power louts. At any rate, they are vermin. But whether civilization's literary man loves them or not: he himself is a great German.

A manifestation of the political esthetic character is that *exoticism* that consists of a real physical disgust for close, native reality, and an ardent, romantic, enthusiastically embellished belief in the superiority, the nobility, and the beauty of what is distant and foreign. Whoever completely perceives the life of his own people, the human reality as it surrounds him, as basically hateful and common, as what is only artistically suited for the most ferocious satire, and whoever on the other hand seeks what is beautiful, true, and nobly human beyond the national borders, and finds it, or imagines that he finds it there—is without doubt an esthete. This is a statement; and only half-way is it a criticism. Revulsion at reality, the inability to react to it except in a furious, satirical way, the transfer of beauty into the unreal or suprareal world, is quite appropriate for the critical intellect, for the sensitive, artistic human being—and in a certain sense, of course, what is distant, what is not present, is unreal. But when lovingly transfigured unreality, when what has been idealistically dreamed of, is now treated as reality, as something that exists somewhere, in short, as life, in order to chastise life *at hand*, to tyrannize, to debase, and to insult the life of one's own people with it, then it becomes absurd, childish, and shockingly unjust.

This is the exoticism that our political esthete becomes guilty of when he speaks of France. We have already recognized several times that France is his country, the homeland of his soul. Why should he not love her, and place her above all fatherlands on earth? The rule of politics! The rule of women! The rule of literature! The rule of reason! And when one reads in Rolland: "Christophe was completely shattered at the conversations he had with some of these crazy protagonists of reason. They completely reversed his ideas about France. He had shared the common opinion of France as a well-balanced, sociable, tolerant, *freedom-loving* nation. And he found fanatics of abstraction, taken ill with logic, who were always ready to sacrifice others as well as themselves to one of their syllogisms. They constantly spoke of freedom, and no one was less prepared to understand and to tolerate it. Nowhere were there characters *whom intellectual or dogmatic passion had made into colder and crueler despots . . .*" I say that when one reads this, every word forms a recognition, and one understands with finality: yes, our intellectual politician is a Frenchman, his love for France is the most natural patriotic love.

But patriotic love should be bridled and disciplined somewhat by understanding, by a little skepticism and criticism, by a sense of reality and justice, otherwise it degenerates into blind, malicious-enthusiastic chauvinism. Good Lord, what is civilization's literary man making of France, republican France, whose reality lies so open to the undeluded gaze, both in literature and in life! The realm of truth, of freedom, of light, of absolute magnanimity, the realm of democracy and of the intellect opens up if one gives oneself only for a moment to the heroic prose that he develops in honor of his exotic homeland: the country of the "least pressure" is what his republican France is to him, of the *vie facile*, under the protection of the spirit. When one listens to him, one could forget that in the judgment of real French writers, "dear little Paris" is, of all cities, the one that treats the poor in the harshest, cruelest way. One could also forget that although democratic progress in France has, to be sure, reached the stage of separation of church and state, it nevertheless laid down its arms (or even turned them against the people) before the hard interests of the bourgeoisie capitalist, when it was necessary to fulfill the simplest demands of social decorum. The whole despairing and anarchic misery of this political life, the disintegration of the party system, the dirty competition of the cliques, the decay of political morality, the thick, foul air of corruption and scandal that surrounds the Third Republic—our enthusiast is not disturbed by these things. I have said that it seems to me that the misuse of that criticism that a foreign nation directs toward itself through its writers is the true international disloyalty. Still, it may be permissible to use it, to refer to it to fellow countrymen who see beauty abroad but only hatefulness and meanness at home. We have recently received in German the volume of Rolland's great novel containing Jean-Christophe's Parisian experiences—less described than analyzed. I will not again forget, as I tend to do, that the book is available to the whole world—to our radical literary man as well, who will, however, avoid it. I promise not to lose myself in quotations, not to cite page after page from it to describe republican France and to give evidence in a childlike way that this France is a reality like any other, and in many ways more miserable and hopeless than many others.

The scathing portrait—scathing because of passionate love, deep involvement, deep concern, not because of alienation and hatred—the portrait is magnificent and comprehensive. Here is art: "the religion of numbers—the size of the audience and of the receipts—dominated the artistic sense of this shopkeeper republic." Here is criticism—that subjects itself to the "divinity of the moment," to general suffrage. Here, in intellectual life, is anarchistic dilettantism, the "mechanical pleasure in dissolution, dissolution in the extreme," together with "the sensuality of a literary prostitute"—and on the other hand, fanaticism, political zealotry, the daily challenge to civil war, usually only rhetorical, "but there was no lack of naive souls who transferred into deed a moral that others had written." Then there are splendid spectacles: "Administrative districts that planned to secede from France, deserting regiments, burned-down governors' buildings, tax collectors on horseback leading companies of gendarmes, farmers armed with scythes holding kettles of boiling water ready to defend the churches from being stormed by freethinkers in the name of freedom, national liberators who climbed up trees to speak to the vintners of the south who have risen up against the northern alcohol provinces . . . *The Republic flattered the people—and then cut them down with the saber.* For their part, the people crushed the heads of some of the nation's children—officers and soldiers. Thus one proved to the other the goodness of his cause . . ." Here are the politicians, socialistic and radical-socialistic ministers, these apostles of the miserable and the hungry, and they pose as connoisseurs of refined pleasures. Skeptics, sensualists, nihilists, and anarchists in their private entertainments, they become fanatics as soon as the action begins.

> The greatest dilettantes among them had scarcely achieved *power* before they acted like little oriental despots. Their intellect was skeptical and their temperament tyrannical. At their disposal they had the power, the magnificent mechanism of the central administration that the greatest of all despots had created, and the temptation to misuse it was too great. From this, a sort of republican empire developed . . .

More, it gets better. It turns into what would also happen in Germany if wishes came true.

> Politics was regarded as a lucrative, if not much higher, branch of business and industry. The intellectual workers despised the politicians, and vice versa. Recently, however, an overture was made, and shortly thereafter an *alliance between the politicians and the worst class of intellectuals took place.* A new power had arisen that claimed absolute dominion over thought: the freethinkers. They had made advances to the other power that saw in them a perfect mechanism for *political despotism* . . . It was an unbelievable joke that these thousands of poor, ignorant animals had to band together into herds in order to think "liberally." To be sure, their freedom of thought consisted in denying others freedom of thought in the name of reason: for they believed in reason as the Catholics in the holy virgin . . .

Oh, yes, this is quite a lot of fun, but we are not comtemplating the portrait for the sake of enjoying others' suffering, not with national self-righteousness, certainly not; but just with a certain satisfaction for our pessimism and our sense of justice, for our dislike of the German gallomaniac's exotic addiction to glorification. Espionage and informing are in bloom; the clerics compete with the Freemasons, but the republican state secretly promotes the latter, the reign of terror of these mendicant monks and Jesuits of reason over the army, the university, over all government bodies. A retired major, an old African, swallows his grief at the misery in the army: at "the encouragement to denunciation and the distrust that has resulted among the officers; at the humiliation of *having to carry out the shameless orders of irresponsible and malicious politicians*"; his grief at the army "being misused for low police work, for taking church inventories, for suppressing worker strikes, for serving private interests and for the vengeful lust of the leading party of the moment—of those radical and anticlerical philistines who stood against the rest of the country . . ." They "began the purification of art. They purged the classical writers of the seventeenth century quite thoroughly and would not permit the name of God to besmirch La Fontaine's fables. Nor would they allow it to remain in music, and radicalism was enraged because one dared to sing Beethoven's spiritual songs at a people's concert. It demanded that other words be substituted." "What?" Christophe asked, beside himself. "The Republic?"

But this Republic is the anarchy in which the leaders set the example; "where one followed an inconsistent policy of chasing ten rabbits at the same time and of letting them all get away one after another in the process, where a hostile diplomacy existed alongside a peace-loving Ministry of War, where ministers of war destroyed the army to ennoble it, where naval ministers incited the arsenal workers to revolt, military instructors preached about the horrors of war, where there were dilettante officers, dilettante judges, dilettante revolutionaries, and dilettante patriots . . . And, as a disastrous echo of the above example, there came the destructive work from below: teachers who taught contempt for authority and rebellion against one's native land; postal officials who burned letters and telegrams; factory workers who threw sand or emery into the gears of the machines; arsenal workers who destroyed the arsenals, the burning of ships, a monstrous devaluation of work by the workers themselves—the destruction not only of the rich, but of the riches of the world. And to crown the work, an intellectual elite saw fit to justify such national suicide with reason and justice by proclaiming *the sacred right of the human being to happiness*. A pathological enthusiasm for humanitarianism undermined the ability to distinguish between good and evil and bewailed with senile senti-mentality the 'irresponsible and sanctified person' of the criminal:— one laid down one's weapons before crime and handed society over to it."

I promised too much, I have not been able to resist. These scathing pages are all too full of reminiscences of the basic motifs of this book, with references to its opposition. Freedom, equality, brotherhood! How do they look, according to Rolland, in the blessed country of their birth? "Courtly customs ruled in this republic without republicans; there were socialistic newspapers, socialistic representatives, who lay on their stomachs before passing kings, servile souls who stood at attention before titles, braid, and medals; to keep them on the leash, one only had to throw them a few bones to chew on, or the Legion of Honor. If the kings had ennobled all the citizens of France, all the citizens of France would have remained loyal to the kings . . ." Oh, yes, democracy! Here we have the national festival with its bustle of people, its amusement "that is so painful to the ones who are not mirthful and who have need of quiet."

> Shots resounded, steam-driven merry-go-rounds snorted, and barrel organs whined from noon to midnight. The silly noise lasted a week. Then the President of the Republic, in order to maintain his popularity, allowed the revelers an additional half week. It cost him nothing; he did not hear the noise . . .

Delightful. M. Romain Rolland scolded me severely, but this is delightful. It is also charming the way he speaks of the republican transportation system, of seating arrangements in second-class trains "where one could not even lean back to sleep; for this belongs to the privileges that the French railroad companies, which are, of course, extremely democratic, try as much as possible to deny the poorer passengers in order to leave the rich ones the pleasant consciousness of being the only ones to enjoy sleeping." And then brotherhood. What the foreigner particularly notices in the French landscape

> is the extreme division of real estate into lots. Every person had his garden; and every garden, every speck of earth, was separated from the others by walls, by fences of all kinds. At the most one found here and there a few common fields and forests, or one saw that the occupants of a river bank of necessity found themselves closer to one another than to the occupants of the other bank. Each person locked himself in his house; and it seemed as if these jealous solitary ways, instead of becoming weaker after so many centuries of closeness, were now stronger than ever. Christophe thought: "How lonely they are!"

In the capital they are the same as in the country: cold, lonely, sullen, isolated from one another. Brotherhood? Warm-hearted togetherness?

> This would require a mutual tolerance and a force of affection that only can be born of inner happiness, of the happiness of a healthy, normal, harmonious life . . . This would require a nation to be content, it would require one's native land to be in an epoch of greatness, or, what is even better, to be on the way to greatness. And besides this, there would also have to be—both belong together—*a power* that could set all the driving forces of the nation in motion, a wise and strong power that stood above the factions. But there cannot be any other power over the factions than one *that draws its strength from itself* and not from the great mass, one that does not try to lean on the anarchical majority, as is the case today when it lays itself at the feet of the average people, but one that forces itself on all through services rendered: a victorious general, a welfare dictatorship, a supremacy of intelligence . . . How do I know? . . .

How does he know, Rolland's little Olivier, who says this? He only knows that France is a reality that is not content, not more so than other realities, probably less so; and that one should not scorn her by tendentiously glorifying her as the country of the "lightest pressure" and of blessed humanity.

But this is what the German belles-lettres-politician is doing. *He is careful* not to take notice of French reality, either through literature or even personal observation, through personal compassion, which is really the path of love. For him, France is not a reality, but an idea. Very good! But he measures this idea by German reality! This is absurd. Everything would be all right if he would measure German reality by the German ideal—and then be shocked. But to measure one's native reality by a foreign ideal, this is insane. This is exotic estheticism.

In Germany there lives a man, a writer, whose behavior in this war has been exposed to quite contradictory evaluation. Born in England, raised in France, Houston Stewart Chamberlain was from an early age a passionate student and promulgator of German culture. He did not come to us by chance, like Chamisso, but by convinced choice; he settled down and became totally German; he celebrated Kant, Goethe, and Wagner in great works; yes, his German character had, perhaps because he was an Englishman, a strong political coloring, he seemed like a German nationalist, a pan-German, and in the war he took an intellectual and passionate part in the struggle of his chosen fatherland—against the country of his fathers. One has criticized this. One found that at this time a painful silence would have stood him in better stead. As far as I am concerned, I admit that to me his behavior seems *comparatively* excusable, yes, justified. I see the similarity of this remarkable case of estrangement to the ease of our literary-political Frenchman by choice—the similarity and the *difference* between them. Chamberlain has really become a German to the same extent that our radical literary man has become a Frenchman. The difference is: he lives in Germany, personally, bodily. The difference is: he thinks himself capable, and indeed he is, of maintaining his belief and his love in spite of the highly imperfect reality that he sees before his eyes and that he is co-enduring. Civilization's literary man, on the other hand, *shuns* Paris. Yes, just as Heinrich Heine went there to be able to love Germany in a romantic way—from a distance—our hero does *not* go there, ever, not for a week, for he wants to save his abstract, exotic love for France. For he knows deep down that French reality would sober him up within forty-eight hours. What is this? If it deserves a milder name than that of cowardice, then it is: estheticism.

One more thing!—and that will be enough. The assertion that politicized art is the exact opposite of estheticized art must accordingly be considered by us as finally refuted.

We know the political moralist, the man of domestic policy and of national self-criticism, as a satirist. Satire, "scourging" satire, is obviously the most important instrument of his political-social-critical pedagogy. But satire, since it is art, is always to a certain extent an end in itself: it gives pleasure, it pleases the one who exercises it as well as the one who receives it—regardless of its pedagogical value. From a crassly artistic point of view, one could say that the former Russian "conditions" were *justified* by two or three works of brilliant satire they gave rise to, and that these works would necessarily have been weaker if the "conditions" had been less strong.

To a certain extent, then, the satirist *likes* the object of satire, the "conditions," for they are what make his effects possible. But our political satirist does not really like the German "conditions"—one must understand this. Not only does he not like them from a moral point of view, he does not really like them from the artistic point of view of political satire, either. Let us admit that the socio-political conditions in Germany do not, by far, have the direct literary adaptiveness, the satirical charm, of those of the "genuinely political nations." Therefore the satirist feels the need to stylize them, to perfect them according to his taste, that is: to Westernize them, to democratize them: The perfect and artistically desirable object of satire is first the thoroughly politicized, democratized society—and the satirist anticipates it for Germany. Therefore he does not satirize a real Germany, but an ideal, amusing one, one that is as he wishes it already were, a Germany with "political atmosphere." He anticipates democracy, and to this extent, he is creative; his satire "gives you an example of what you are to become."

An example—harmless and unpretentious. I still remember a modern comedy scene in which a politician, legislator, or let us say more correctly: a deputy, makes a rhetorical-patriotic campaign speech before some citizens, his constituents, naturally, or the ones who are supposed to send him to the chamber, I mean to the senate or the house. "Industry!" he cries, and every word is a pompous-patriotic pledge. "Business! Agriculture! The army!" This is all I remember. Now it would be wrong to believe that our satirist had no ear for the completely un-German, the thoroughly alien accent of this scene. He has an ear for it—*but this ear is delighted by it.* But a satire that, bored with the national reality, "whips" a foreign theme until it becomes national— such a satire may well be called esthetic.

This is the cheerful side of the matter. But it has a serious one—and now it is necessary to say a word about *social-critical expressionism.* Expressionism, to put it quite generally and very briefly, is that artistic direction that, in strong contrast to the passivity, to the humble manner of reception and presentation of impressionism, most deeply despises the imitation of reality, that resolutely dismisses all obligation to reality and replaces it with the sovereign, explosive, ruthlessly creative decree of the intellect. Oh, excellent—even if naturally not completely new. Art was never an imitation of reality; copies of nature have never been considered art. Nor has art ever been simple passivity; passive art is not conceivable, it has always been active, it has been the desire for spirit, for beauty, its inner essence has always been style, form and selection, reinforcement, elevation, a rising above the material, and every artist's life work, whether small or large, has been a cosmos, resting in itself, stamped with the mark of its creator. Impression and expression have always been necessary elements of art, one without the other has been helpless. Even if their proportions changed, if in one case delight, faithfulness and power of natural perception, in the other the instinct for the grotesque, predominate and form the psychological law of artistic creation. The antithesis of impressionistic and expressionistic art is that of realism and grotesqueness. Tolstoy and Dostoyevsky: the realistic, plastic writer, and the visionary artist of the grotesque, stand there opposite one another in all their grandeur in one nation and epoch. It would be idle to ask who was the greater. It would be impudent to claim that the will in the expressionist, Dostoyevsky, was stronger.

Nothing exceeds the ethical will, the moral strength, that speaks from Tolstoy's serious, gigantic work. But if we accept the principle that the expressionistic artistic tendency contains more of an intellectual impetus to do violence to life, then one will definitely have to set certain limits to the "artistic freedom" under discussion here—art will have to set them for itself. The grotesque is the supratrue and the exceedingly real, not the arbitrary, false, antireal, and absurd. And an artist who would deny all obligation to life, who would carry disgust for the impression so far that he practically divests himself of all obligation to real forms of life, and who only allows the dictatorial emanations of some kind of absolute art demon to hold sway: such an artist may well be called the greatest of all radical fools.

Here lie the dangers of *satire*. It seems to me that satire's inner conflict is that it is of necessity grotesque art, that is: expressionism, and that therefore its receptivity to love and suffering is more weakly developed, its bonds to nature exposed to loosening—while at the same time there is no type of art that must remain more responsible and intimately bound to life and to reality than satire, since it clearly wants to accuse, judge, and castigate life and reality. This conflict and this danger—the danger, that is, of degeneration into *mischief* (for a distorted picture without basis in reality that is nothing other than an "emanation" is neither distortion nor image, but mischief)—this danger, then, appears strangely enough less often and is probably to a lesser extent present so long as it is a matter of satire on a grand scale, satire of the world and of mankind. It becomes a burning issue, however, when the satire descends to political and to social criticism, with the appearance, in short, of the expressionistic-satirical social novel. At this point it becomes a political, an international danger. For a social-critical expressionism without impression, responsibility, and conscience, that described entrepreneurs who do not exist, workers who do not exist, "social conditions" that may have existed perhaps in England around 1850, and that brewed its inflammatory stories of love and murder from such ingredients—such a social satire would be mischief, and if it deserved a more noble name, more noble than that of international defamation and national slander, then it is: ruthless estheticism.

What I have said here—as with everything I say—is the expression of my anger against the shamelessness with which the intellectual politician decrees the identity of politics and morality; against the arrogance with which he denies and slanders every morality that seeks to answer the question of human nature in another, more psychological way than that of politics—that uncultivated, I mean: un-Germanly cultivated arrogance that reviles everything that is not politics as estheticism, and that presumes to schoolmaster the German way of life with a hostile, foreign spirit. I have given three or four examples of what his antiestheticism, his "responsibility," his high moral combination of literature and politics, are like: his unscrupulous "passion," his fornication with virtue, his *bellezza* radicalism, the artist's irresponsibility behind which he retreats as soon as it seems necessary, his expressionism, that is, his inability to love the close and the real, his childish cult of what is foreign and at the same time the caution with which he avoids the experience of foreign reality, and finally, the alien, playful, and irresponsibly false element in his satire—all this is estheticism of the first water, and with his boastingly proclaimed, optimistic-revolutionary belief in "mankind," "progress," and "happiness," "the cross is betrayed" and denied in the same way as it was with some kind of beautiful ruthlessness of the past. But his false apostasy has the intolerance of the genuine one, for his hostility to life has forgotten shame, self-doubt, and irony, it takes itself completely seriously now, it is aggressive to the point of insanity, and its self-righteousness cries aloud to heaven. Truly, the "hysterical renaissance" was morally better than the hysterical democracy.

CHAPTER 12

Irony and Radicalism

This is an antithesis and an either-or. The intellectual human being has the choice (*as far as* he has the choice) of being either an ironist or a radical; a third choice is not decently possible. What he proves to be is a question of final argumentation. It is decided by which argument is for him the final, decisive, and absolute one: life or intellect (intellect as truth or as justice or as purity). For the radical, life is no argument. *Fiat justitia* or *veritas* or *libertas, fiat spiritus—pereat mundus et vita!* Thus speaks all radicalism. "But is truth an argument—when life is at stake?" This question is the formula of irony.

Radicalism is nihilism. The ironist is conservative. Nevertheless, a conservatism is only ironical if it does not imply the voice of life, which wants itself, but the voice of intellect, which does not want itself, but life.

Here eros comes into play. One has defined it as "the affirmation of a human being apart from his *worth*." Now this is not a very intellectual, not a very moral affirmation, and neither is the affirmation of life by intellect. It is ironical. Eros was always an ironist. And irony is eroticism.

The relationship of life and intellect is an extremely delicate, difficult, exciting, and painful one, charged with irony and eroticism, and it cannot be disposed of by the thesis I once read in an activist writing: The goal is to form the world by intellect in such a way "that it no longer needs intellect." I knew this turn of phrase. There was already talk in contemporary literature of those who "did not need intellect"— and indeed, with that sly longing that perhaps forms the real philosophical and poetic relationship of intellect to life, perhaps is intellect itself. Life so formed that it "no longer needs" intellect (or art, either, perhaps?)! Is this another utopia? But then, it is a nihilistic utopia, one born of hatred and of tyrannical negation, of the fanaticism of purity.

It is the sterile utopia of the absolute intellect, of "intellect for intellect's sake," which is stiffer and colder than any *l'art pour l'art*, and which should not be surprised if life puts no trust in it. Longing, you see, goes back and forth between intellect and life. Life also wants intellect. Two worlds whose relationship is erotic without a clear sexual polarity, without the one representing the masculine, and the other the feminine principle: this is life and intellect. Therefore there is no union between them, but only the short, intoxicating illusion of union and understanding, eternal tension without resolution. *It is the problem of beauty* that intellect perceives life, and life perceives intellect, as "beauty." Intellect that loves is not fanatic, it is ingenious, it is political, it woos, and its wooing is erotic irony. One has a political term for this: it is "conservatism." What is conservatism? The erotic irony of the intellect.

It is time to speak of art. One finds today it must have a goal, must be concerned with the perfection of the world, must have moral consequences. Well, the artist's way of *perfecting* life and the world was, at least originally, quite different from that of political melioration: it was that of transfiguration and glorification. Original, natural, "naive" art was an acclamation and a celebration of life, of beauty, of the hero, of the great deed; it offered life a mirror in which it saw its image in blissfully embellished and purified truth: from this sight it received a new delight in itself. Art was a stimulus, a seduction to life, and it will always be so in good part. What has made it problematic, what has so complicated its character, is its connection with *intellect*, pure intellect, the critical, negative, and destructive principle—a connection of magical paradoxy, inasmuch as it combined the most ardent, the sensually most talented, creative affirmation of life with the finally nihilistic emotional appeal of radical criticism. Art, creative writing, stopped being naive. It became, to use the older expression, "sentimental," or, as one says today, "intellectual"; art, creative writing, was and is now no longer simply life, but also *criticism* of life, and indeed, a criticism far more terrible and shocking than that of pure intellect, as its methods are richer, more emotional, more varied—and more amusing.

Art, therefore, became moral—and there was no lack of taunts from a skeptical psychology that claimed it had become so because of ambition to heighten and to deepen its effects; for, it said, art's main purpose was effect; one should not take its morality all too morally; it gained dignity through it, or thought it did; talent was by nature something low, yes, apelike, but it aimed for solemnity, and for this purpose, intellect was just the thing. But what psychology can cope with art, this enigmatic being with the deeply cunning eyes that is serious in play and in all seriousness plays a game of form that by deception, brilliant imitation, and earnest illusion, deeply shakes people with ineffable sobbing and ineffable laughter, both at the same time! Art has, of course, through its connection with morality, with radical intellect, that is, in no way lost its nature as a stimulus to life: it could not avoid it even if it wanted to do otherwise, and at times it believes it wants, or seems to want, to do otherwise—enthusiastically giving life new pleasure and excitement in itself by bringing it to sensual-suprasensual self-observation, to a most intensive self-consciousness and self-esteem, even in cases where its critical nature seems to be radically hostile to life, nihilistic.

We know of such cases: Tolstoy's *Kreutzer Sonata* is such a one, and art "betrays" itself in a double sense here, betrays its character because in order to turn against life, it must turn against itself. A talented prophet preaches against art and for purity. One objects: In this way life dries up. The artist prophet answers: Let it! Thus speaks intellect. "After all, is life an argument?" Here we have its question, and admittedly it brings silence. But how very strange, what a childlike contradiction, to offer such a message and question to people in the form of an artistic story, in the form of entertainment, that is!

And still it is precisely this that makes art so lovable and worthy of practice; it is this wonderful contradiction that it is, or at least can be, by its delightful imitation and critical-moral destruction of life, at the same time life's comfort and judgment, praise and glory, that it can have the effect of giving pleasure and awakening *conscience* to the same degree. To put it diplomatically, its mission lies in maintaining equally good relations with life and with pure intellect, in being at the same time conservative and radical; it lies in its central and mediating position between intellect and life. Here is the source of irony. But here is also, if anywhere, the relationship, the similarity, of art to politics: for politics, too, in its way, takes a mediating position between pure intellect and life, and it is not worthy of its name if it is nothing but conservative *or* radically destructive! But it would be a misunderstanding to want to make the artist into a politician because of this situational similarity; for the artist's task of awakening the *conscience* of life, and of keeping it awake, is not at all a political task, but much more a religious one. A great neurologist once defined conscience as "social fear." With all respect, this is an unpleasantly "modern" definition—a typical example of how today all morality and religiosity are absorbed into the social sphere. I would like to know what, for example, Luther's lonely troubles and struggles of conscience in a monastery, before he unexpectedly became a reformer and therefore social, could have had to do with the social idea. But if someone declared it to be a task of art to awaken the *fear of God* by bringing life before the judging countenance of pure intellect, then I would not want to contradict.

One will not want to say that a world experience in the sense of the radical intellect would be quite proper for art. The personal result would be constant rage against everything that human political and social life offers to one's view, for example, on a trip. "Intellect" sees churches, factories, proletarians, military, police, prostitutes, the power of technology and industry, bank buildings, poverty, riches, a thousand forms of life that human beings have developed. All this is stupid, crude, mean, and opposed to intellect; to chaste nirvana, that is. "The intellectual" never gets over his anger, his quiet fury and inner contradiction, his hatred and protest. What this attitude toward life, this way of seeing, this continual rebellion in the name of decent nothingness, is supposed to have to do with art, you must ask those who confuse the artist with the intellectual; I do not know. I do not believe that an artist who always maintained this political-critical view, who had forever lost the childlike, naive and believing attitude toward things in the world, and who was no longer capable of seeing a thing as something that is happy in its God-willed state, looks happily at the world, and may demand to be looked back at just this way: I do not believe that such an artist would be particularly suited to the fulfillment of his special task.

But since art cannot be radical, would it therefore be ironical? It is certain that art's central and mediating position between intellect and life makes the ironical sphere quite native to it, and if I do not say that art must always be ironic, I still call irony, in contrast to radicalism, an artistic element; for intellect becomes conservative and erotic in irony, while in radicalism it remains nihilistic and selfish.

But irony is always irony toward both sides; it directs itself against life as well as against intellect, and this takes the grand gesture away from it, this makes it melancholy and modest. To the extent that it is ironic, art is also melancholy and modest—or let us say more correctly: the artist is so. For the area of morality is the personal one. The artist, then, to the extent that he is an ironist, is melancholy and modest; "passion," the grand gesture, the great word, are denied to him, yes, intellectually he cannot even attain dignity. The ambivalence of his central position, his hybrid nature of intellect and sensuality, the "two souls in his breast," prevent it. An artist's life is no dignified life, the path of beauty no dignified path. Beauty, you see, is indeed intellectual, but also sensual ("divine and visible at the same time," Plato said), and therefore it is the artist's path to intellect. But whether anyone who tries to reach intellect through the senses can gain wisdom and a man's true dignity I once questioned in a story in which I had an artist who had "become dignified" realize that people like him must necessarily remain immoral and adventurers of feeling; that the magistral posture of his style had been lies and foolishness, his noble attitude a trick, the confidence the masses had in him quite ridiculous, and educating the nation and youth through art a risky undertaking to be forbidden.

Having him realize this in a melancholy, ironic way, I remained true to myself—which is the point I am interested in. At a very young age I sent a magazine that had requested it an autobiographical sketch in which I said:

> Those who have leafed through my writings will remember that I have always regarded the artist's, the creative writer's way of life with extreme mistrust. Indeed, my astonishment at the honors society grants this species will never end. I know what a creative writer is, for verifiably I am one, myself. Briefly, a creative writer is a fellow who is completely useless in all fields of serious endeavor, only bent on making merry, not only not useful to the state, but even rebellious to it, who does not even have to possess special gifts of intelligence, but may be of as slow and dull an intellect as I have always been—for the rest, a childish charlatan inside, with a tendency to debauchery and in every way disreputable, who should have nothing else to expect from society—and basically expects nothing else—than quiet contempt. But the fact is that society grants this type of person the possibility of attaining the highest honors in its midst.

This was the irony of a youthful artistic nature and I know well that irony, although it is definitely something passably "intellectual," even if not precisely in the virtuous sense, has in the meantime become very much *vieux jeu*, a sign of burgherly nature and of shabby quietism. The activist has arrived—*pulcher et fortissimus*.* And still I wonder, in a quiet

---

* In Section I, paragraph 8 of *Beyond Good and Evil*, Nietzsche says:

> In every philosophy there is a point where the "conviction" of the philosopher steps out on stage: or, to say it in the language of an old, mysterious ritual:
>
> *adventavit asimus*
> *pulcher et fortissimus.*

These are the opening lines of the text of the medieval "Prose of the Ass." Thomas Mann could be sure that his brother, Heinrich, had read the Nietzschean passage.

state of being behind the times, whether ironic modesty will not always remain the really *decent* relationship of the artist—no, not to art, but to artistic nature.

It is strange that the desire of an artistic nature to *judge* life and human nature from the point of view of pure intellect implies less lack of irony, melancholy, and modesty than the will to *improve* it politically according to one's conviction. But that this latter purpose exists at all usually will turn out to be a mistaken conclusion of the observer. Why not give another example from my own practice? It is the most convenient at hand. The criticism of the new German intermediate school toward the end of *Buddenbrooks*—is it directed in more than a quite vague and indirect way toward school reform? It is certainly an indictment, but a quite loosely stipulated indictment: stipulated and qualified by the nature of the one who experiences that institution, through whose experience it appears, with whose eyes it is seen. Something is breaking down there—but what is breaking down is not so much the new German intermediate school, which, to be sure, comes off badly, as rather the little prince of decline and of too much music, Hanno Buddenbrook, and he is failing in life in general, which is symbolized and provisionally outlined in the school. Art—is it not always a criticism of life made by a little Hanno? The others, this is clear, are quite happy with life as it is, and in their element—like Hanno's classmates at school. He—through whose experience the school appears, and indeed as ludicrous, tormenting, stupid, and disgusting—is actually quite far from thinking of his experience and judgment as generally valid and authoritative; for he recognizes himself as a nervous exception. That is his pride and his modesty, and it is, it seems to me, the pride and the modesty of the artist before life. It is basically disloyal to use art's criticism of life for ameliorative propaganda purposes; neither the school nor life in general can be arranged so that the highest moral and esthetic sensitivity, that sensitivity and intellect, can feel at home in them. Nevertheless, such a critique may cause ameliorative effects in the real world—political effects, that is—because the sensitive exception, even though he cannot be politically authoritative, still expresses the conscience of the human race. He is, in a higher, more tender, esthetically moral sense, even against, and precisely against, his will, *its suffering leader*—so that in fact, artistic criticism of life has improving, ennobling, moralizing, beneficial effects. But this is something else, a separate situation, and must in no way mislead us to define art—because it can have political consequences—as a political instrument, or to want to make the artist into a politician. An artist who misunderstood his special and ironic type of leadership in such a way that he understood it to be directly political and began to act accordingly would fall victim to self-righteousness and moral security, to an insufferable pose of virtue—the result would be the emergence of a philistinism of respectability and a schoolmasterly attitude toward the people that would doubtlessly be followed directly by artistic ruin—and not necessarily followed.

Irony as modesty, as skepticism turned backward, is a form of morality, is personal ethics, is "domestic policy." But all politics, in the civic sense as well as in the sense of the intellectual man of action, of the activist, is foreign policy. Let us skip over everything that can make an artist into a nonpolitician, into an impossible politician. There is the consideration that no definite governmental form is a life-necessity and a sine qua non for art, but that it has blossomed under the most varied of earthly conditions. There is, precisely in the artist, an innate horror of shoddy work, the reluctance to tamper in a dilettante way with obviously difficult and complicated situations. There is the fact that the artist's work, the highest, most subtle, most responsible and consuming work there is, will scarcely leave him the exuberance to play the political complainer. All these inhibitions are not as strong as the one I called modesty, the modesty of skepticism turned backward. An artist who is so at peace with his conscience, so lacking in all irony, so much at harmony with his humanity, so virilely satisfied with his work, all in all so civically solid that he would find the gait with which the ordinary citizen, sure of his cause, strides to the ballot box to exercise his right to vote, perhaps the new Prussian right—such an artist is hard to imagine.

But where can I find words to show the degree of incomprehension, amazement, disgust, and *scorn* I feel in the face of a Latin poet-politician and warmonger such as Gabriele d'Annunzio? Is such a rhetorical demagogue ever alone at all? Is he always "on stage"? Does he know no loneliness, no self-doubt, no worry and anguish about his soul and his work, no irony toward fame, no shame at being "adored"? And in his country they took the vain, delirious artistic fool *seriously*, at least for a while! No one stood up and said: "If he knows the times, I know his moods—away with the belled fool!" Was that perhaps only possible in a country that has remained childlike, in a country in which all political-democratic critical philosophy still does not prevent criticism and skepticism in that grander style from being lacking, in a country, therefore, that has had no experience of a critique of reason and of morality, but least of all a critique of artistic nature?

D'Annunzio, the aper of Wagner, the ambitious word-reveler whose talent "rings all the bells," and to whom Latin character and nationalism form just a means of effect and enthusiasm, the irresponsible adventurer who wanted his ecstasy and his great hour, his "historical moment," his marriage with the people, and nothing more—one took him seriously, one took the artist seriously as a politician, in a fateful hour for the country! The artist as a panegyrist of war. "And you?" And I! Where is the German artist who incites to war, who has cried out for war— whose conscience and morality would have even thought it possible at the last moment, and even beyond the last moment? And I! It seems to me that it is one thing, after the war has become fate, to stand by one's nation with one's modest word and intellect, and still to doubt one's right to "patriotism"—and quite another thing to misuse one's talent, one's soul, one's ability to become orgiastic, one's fame, to incite millions of human beings into a bloody hell, and then, "from the heaven of his fatherland" (what a rhetorical outrage!), to cast his brocadelike prose down upon them. There you have it, then, your activism! There you have him, the politicized esthete, the poetic seducer of the people, the blasphemer of the people, the libertine of rhetorical enthusiasm, the belles-lettres-politician, the dago of the intellect, the *miles gloriosus* of democratic "humanity"! And *that* should come up in our country? That should become master here? Never will that happen. And I, at least, am grateful for belonging to a country that will never grant "intellect" the power to commit such miserable mischief.

I showed a situational similarity between politics and art. I said they both took a middle, mediating position between life and intellect, and I derived a tendency to irony from this that one will perhaps concede to me at least as far as art is concerned. But "ironic" politics? The word combination seems all too strange and especially all too frivolous for one ever to find it valid, much less to admit that politics is altogether and always of ironical character. Let us at least be convinced that it can never be the opposite, that it can never be radical, that this contradicts its nature, that it would have the logic of wooden iron to speak of "radicalistic politics"! Politics is necessarily the will to mediation and to a positive result, it is cleverness, flexibility, politeness, diplomacy, and in all this it does not in any way have to lack the power of always remaining the opposite of its opposite: of the destructive absolute, of radicalism.

As a boy, I heard that Prince Bismarck had said that the Russian nihilists had much more in common with our liberals than with social democracy. This surprised me; for on the parliamentary-political scale, one had of course thought of the socialists as being between the more right-leaning liberals and the nihilists who formed the far left, and it was hard for me to think that those bomb-throwers should stand intellectually closer to the members of a burgherly-liberal progress than to revolutionary social democracy. Later I learned that bomb-throwing was not at all a necessary part of Russian nihilism, that it was rather quite simply Western European liberalism, the political enlightenment, that in Russia—and specifically through literature—had received the name of nihilism: Bismarck and Dostoyevsky agreed in this that Western European enlightenment, the rational, progressive politics of liberalism, had a nihilistic character, and it was probably true that the terrorists of the East simply *did* what the nihilists of the West thought and taught.

"Intellect" that *acts*, active "intellect," reveals and proves the total radicalism of its character, for from a decent and clean point of view, the act of pure intellect can never be anything but the most radical act. The intellectual who becomes convinced he must act is immediately at the point of political *murder*—or, if not this, then the morality of his action is always such that political murder would be the consequence of his way of acting. The slogan, "The intellectual must act!", as far as it is meant in the sense of pure intellect, is a rather questionable slogan, for all experience definitely teaches that the intellectual who is carried by his passion into reality enters an element that is wrong for him, in which he behaves badly, dilettantishly, and wretchedly, suffers human damage and must immediately cover himself in the melancholy martyrdom of moral self-sacrifice in order to stand up at all before himself and the world.

"The man of action," Goethe said, "is always without conscience. Only the observer has a conscience." But the opposite is also true: in his relationship to reality, the observer has much less need for conscience, or at least he needs a different type of conscience than the man of action; he can allow himself the fine luxury of radicalism. The man who is called to action in reality cannot do this. He will rapidly rid himself of absolute values as boyish immaturity, for he knows that his business is the *political* mediation of thought and reality, and that he must therefore have the ability to compromise—an ability that the "observer" completely lacks, because, you see, the unnatural effort it costs him to overcome his inborn shyness and timidity in the face of reality does not leave him the strength for compromise, for moderation, and for good sense. The activity of one born to observation will always be an unnatural, monstrous, distorted, and self-destructive activity; the *action directe*, the action of the intellect, will always be only an abortion of action.

It is pure luck that this slogan: "The intellectual must act!" remains a highly literary slogan, a fashionable doctrine and sensation of the newspapers. The artist-activist does not think of action at all—and indeed, characteristically, he thinks even less of it the greater the talent he enjoys. Tell me about the regard the highly talented person has for himself, for his personal preciousness, the smiling vanity with which he receives the admiration accorded to the vibrating high-mindedness, the hard brilliance of his periods! Is this man capable of a self-destructive act, a personal sacrifice? Never his whole life long has he been able to pass the smallest test of this. One wants fame, money, love, applause, applause. One stands with one's neck nestled against fur, surrounded by the lenses of the movie cameramen, and lyricizes about "spirit." At least in his person one realizes democracy by doing business with virtue—he leaves the assassination of ministers, and even speaking at strikes, to the less select people, ones who have nothing to lose, poor, talentless fanatics, desperate Jew boys. In a word, his relationship to action (and to the man of action) is thoroughly urbane-aristocratic. But if this is so, if the seriously compromising act is the business of the less gifted, of subordinates: how about the rank and dignity of the act itself, of action altogether? The comedy scene must be written in which the young idealist comes to the master of revolu-tionary rhetoric and says to him the time has come, the moment has arrived, when one must step up and act. The master will fail. The expectant, burning eyes of the young disciple will see, instead of a fanatic, a man of the world, an—artist. Perhaps, in front of this pair of black, burning, demanding eyes, the man of the world will blush a little: but then he will speak with a smile: "Oh, no, young man, you are asking the wrong thing of me. I think I have some reason to value my personal safety. My health, which in spite of everything seems to be dear to the younger generation, would not, I fear, stand up under a long period of investigatory arrest. I wrote *Robespierre*, at the premiere of which you and your friends applauded so, although I had not neglected to put my hero under the suspicion of a syphilitic brain disease. Although? Precisely for this reason! You would have applauded less if I had not left you the option of this suspicion. But a constitution from which works of such melancholy depth arise, precious manifestations of *vertu sans y croire*—such a constitution is not made to expose itself politically. Just imagine that the authorities should lay a hand on me. No, no, dear friend, good-bye! You interrupted me in an animated passage on freedom and happiness that I would like to finish before I travel to the spa. Go, go and do your duty! *Votre devoir, jeunes hommes de vingt ans, sera le bonheur!*"

Irony. It is possible that I see it where other people do not see it; but it just seems to me that one cannot grasp this concept comprehensively enough, that it should never be taken too ethically and too politically. When Kant, after a terrible and only too successful epistemological campaign, reintroduced everything again under the name of "Postulates of *Practical* Reason," and made possible again what he had just critically crushed, because, you see, as Heine says, "Old Lampe must have a god"—then I see political irony in this. When Nietzsche and Ibsen, the one through philosophy and the other through comedy, question the value of truth for *life*, I see in this the same ironic ethos. When the Christian Middle Ages, with its dogma of original sin, the doctrine, that is, of an essential sinfulness of the world that is insuperable for the masses, always winked at the ideal, lived in a constant compromise of the ideal with the all-too-human, clearly distinguished the higher spiritual culture from its natural *basis* and ascribed the latter in very large part to sin in order to show it wrong in principle and still to allow for it in practice—this again, in my eyes, is nothing other than ironic politics. Another example is found in Adam Müller, this thinker who is in bad repute with all the advocates of progress, but who has said the wisest and most ingenious things in the world about politics. He does not confuse politics with *justice*, but defines justice positively and beyond all doubt as something naturally and historically given, as legitimate, in short as the visible power, while he defines politics, or statecraft, in contrast to justice, as the principle that teaches us "to be somewhat indulgent" in the administration of positive-historical and absolute justice, to reconcile it with conscience, common sense, the present and the future, and with utility. He calls politics the principle of mediation, tolerance, persuasion, and bargaining, which scientifically must be completely separated from jurisprudence and still go hand in hand with it in a practical sense—and here again we have politics in that specifically ironical and conservative sense that is its characteristic sense and spirit. But the most beautiful, magnificently resigned expression of conservative irony seems to me to be a political letter from the old Friedrich von Gentz to a young female friend, in which he says:

> The history of the world is a constant passage from the old to the new. In the continual cycle of things, everything destroys itself, and the fruit that has ripened separates itself from the plant that has produced it. But if this cycle is not to bring about the rapid decline of all existing things, therefore also everything that is just and good, then besides the large, and *finally always overwhelming* number of those working for the new, there must also be a smaller number who defend the old with moderation and purpose and who try to keep the stream of the times, even if they cannot and do not want to stop it, within a regulated bed . . . I was always aware that in spite of all the majesty and the strength of my principals, and in spite of all the individual victories that they achieved, the spirit of the times would finally be more powerful than we, that the press, no matter how much I despised it in its excesses, would not lose its terrible superiority over all our wisdom, and that art is just as little able to put a spoke in the wheel of the world as is force. *But this was no reason* for me not to follow faithfully and patiently the task that had befallen me; only a bad soldier deserts his flag when fortune seems to be becoming unfavorable; and I also have enough pride to say to myself in darker moments: *victrix causa Diis placuit, sed victa Catoni.*

"Intellect" is the spirit of the times, the spirit of the new, the spirit of democracy, for which the "finally always overwhelming" majority is working. But a document such as the one above teaches that the most intellectually gifted ones are those whose task it is to control "intellect"— perhaps because they "need intellect most of all."

Irony and conservatism are closely related moods. One could say that irony is the intellect of conservatism—as far, that is, as conservatism has intellect, something that obviously is just as little the rule as in the case of progress and radicalism. Conservatism can be a simple and strong emotional tendency, without wit and melancholy, as robust as dashing, happy-go-lucky progressiveness; then it feels good, and it strikes to defend against dissolution. It only becomes witty and melancholy when international intellectual emphasis joins national emotional emphasis; when a bit of democracy, of literature, complicates its essence. Irony is a form of intellectualism, and ironic conservatism is intellectual conservatism. In it, being and effect contradict one another to a certain extent, and it is possible that it may promote democracy and progress in the way it fights them.

The more unintellectually dashing and happy-go-lucky progress is itself, the more dearly it cherishes the belief that conservatism is necessarily based on coarseness and malicious stupidity. It is hardly worthwhile to dispute this belief. The burgher, Jacob Burckhardt, was neither stupid nor bad, but his politically conservative disposition, his aristocratic aversion to the penetration of a noisy liberalism into the city hall and church of old Basel, his unshakable steadfastness in support of the resistance offered by a quiet and proud conservative minority, is well known. And also his love for the people—a quality of so many conservative politicians of antiquity and of modern times. Goethe and Nietzsche were conservative—all German intellect has been conservative from the beginning, and it will remain so, as long, that is, as it itself lasts, and is not democratized, done away with, that is.

Strakhov, in his often-mentioned introduction to Dostoyevsky's political writings, says of the novelist's joining the Slavophile party:

> Slavophilism is definitely not a theory severed from life; it is a completely natural phenomenon, both in its positive side—as conservatism—and in its negative one—as reaction, that is, as the wish to throw off the intellectual and moral yoke of the West. Therefore it is understandable *that Fyodor Mikhailovitch developed a whole series of viewpoints and many sympathies that were completely Slavophile,* and that he came forward with them without at first noticing his agreement with the party that had already existed for a long time, and only later did he confess his agreement with it directly and openly.

But the positive reason why Dostoyevsky, as a politician, hesitated for a long time before joining the conservative-Slavophile party, was his writing, his love of literature. "For he loved literature," Strakhov said, "and this love was the most important reason why he did not immediately join the Slavophiles. *He perceived quite vividly the hostility* that they, in accordance with their principles, had always had for contemporary literature."

Undoubtedly there is a certain antithesis between conservatism and writing, and literature. Just as in the combination, "radicalistic politics," "conservative writing" contains a certain contradiction in the adjective. For literature is analysis, intellect, skepticism, psychology; it is democracy, the "West," and where it joins the conservative-national disposition, that schism of which I spoke appears, the one between being and effect. Conservative? Naturally I am not; for if I wanted to be so in opinion, I would still not be so according to my nature, which, finally, is what has effect. In cases such as mine, destructive and conserving tendencies meet, and as far as one can speak of effect, it is just this double effect that takes place.

Today I know pretty well what my "cultural political" position is: As a matter of fact, it was even statistics that gave me clues about it. They show that in 1876 (a year after my own birth) the "highest number of live births" per thousand persons was reached in Germany. It amounted to 40.9. There followed, up to the turn of the century, a *slow* decline in births, which was, in the meantime, well compensated by the decline in the number of deaths. Suddenly, starting just after 1900, over thirteen years, there has been a fall in the birthrate from 37 to 27—a fall, statistics assures us, that *no civilized nation has experienced in such a short time.* There is no possibility here of an actual weakening of the race. Venereal diseases and alcoholism have declined, hygiene has progressed. The causes are purely moral, or, to say it in a more indifferent-scientific way, cultural-political; they lie in the "civilization," in the progressive development of Germany in the Western sense. In these years, to put it briefly, and also to emphasize it, German prose has improved; at the same time, advocacy of and information on birth control methods have penetrated every village.

In 1876, when the nation stood at the peak of its fertility, Bismarck, Moltke, Helmholtz, Nietzsche, Wagner, and Fontane were living in Germany. They were not radical literary men, but they were markedly intellectual just the same. What do we have today? The average. Democracy. Why, we have it already! The "refinement," "humanization," literarization, democratization of Germany has, of course, been moving at the most rapid pace for almost twenty years! Why does one still scream and agitate so much? Would not a little conservatism be appropriate to the times?

I know very well why it was precisely in 1900 when I, for my part, had become twenty-five years old, that the sudden fertility decline began that had been unheard of in a civilized nation. At this time, precisely in the year that *Buddenbrooks* appeared, the story of the refinement, sublimation, and decay of a German burgher family, this undoubtedly very German book that is, however, also undoubtedly a sign of a decline in national health, and that in fifteen years has reached seventy editions: at this time, with me and with those like me, there began the moral-political-biological process behind which civilization's literary man is standing with his agitating whip. I know exactly how much I am a part of it, how much my activity is also an expression and a promotion of this process. But in contrast to the radical literary man, I have also always cherished conservative countertendencies in myself, and, without understanding myself politically, expressed them quite early. This came from the concept of life that I had from Nietzsche, and from my relationship to this concept, a relationship that may have been ironic, but that was not more ironic than my relationship to "intellect." This concept of life takes on national timeliness around the year 1900, when the fall in fertility begins. It is a *conservative* idea, and scarcely has the novel of decay been finished than conservative opposition in the form of irony appears, as the words "life" and "conserving" begin to play a role in my production. I wrote:

> The realm of art is increasing, and that of health and innocence is declining on earth. One should most carefully *conserve* what is left of it, and one should not want to seduce people to poetry who much prefer to read photographically illustrated horse books! It is ridiculous to love *life* and still to strive with all one's talents to win it over to one's side, to win it for the subtleties and melancholies, for the whole sick nobility of literature.
>
> (*Tonio Kröger*)

One sees that I used these ideas for things that were only moral-intellectual, but undoubtedly in the process there was political will alive in me that I was unaware of, and here again we see that one does not have to play the political activist and demonstrant, that one can be an "esthete" and still have deep feeling for the political element.

I close these reflections on the day on which the beginning of the armistice negotiations between Germany and Russia is being announced. If all is not deception, the long-cherished wish I have had in my heart almost from the beginning of the war will be fulfilled: Peace with Russia! Peace with her first of all! And the war, if it continues, will continue against the West alone, against the "*trois pays libres*," against "civilization," "literature," politics, the rhetorical bourgeois. The war continues; for this is no war. This is an historical period that may continue like the one from 1789 to 1815, or from 1618 to 1648. "And not before," we read in the poem from *Fraternal Strife in Hapsburg:*

> And not before the grave has taken those now men,
> And those now children have become then men,
> Will the ferment stop that is now in the blood.*

The war goes on; and this book, too, in which it is reflected in

---

* Und eh nicht, die nun Männer, faßt das Grab,
  Und die nun Kinder, Männer sind geworden,
  Legt sich die Gärung nicht, die jetzt im Blut.

miniature, repeated personally, could go on with it—even if it lasted thirty years. I am happy that I can do what the nations punishing each other so terribly cannot do for a long time—that I can finish. Some of these pages are beautiful; these are the ones where love was allowed to speak. There where strife and bitter separation rule, I will never look again. But it is true that unjust insult was repulsed there, and this, too, was only a reflection of the great insult that a nation received from a whole articulate world.

What is this world? It is the world of politics, of democracy; and that I had to take a position against it, that I had to stand with Germany in this war, and not, like civilization's literary man, with the enemy—this necessity stands out clearly to every discerning person in everything I wrote and put together in fifteen years of peace. But the impression that I stand alone today among German intellectuals with my belief that the human question is never, never to be solved politically, but only spiritually-morally, can be simply nothing more than an impression, it must be based on a delusion. The legitimacy of such ways of viewing and feeling has been reinforced by too many statements of noble spirits who have remained German by being exceedingly German. *Wieland* was national in the highest and most intellectual sense when he said that the eternal refrain of all his political dreams was that if the human race was ever to improve, the reform had to begin not with forms of government and constitutions, but with *the individual human being.* He was also national when he burst out with the question: "What German in whose breast only a spark of national feeling glows can bear the thought that a foreign people would presume to *force* upon us at gun point a political *delusion* that is destructive of all our domestic and burgherly relations, and that they, just at the moment when they have nothing but human rights, freedom, equality, world citizenship, and universal brotherhood on their lips, should give us the disgusting choice of either becoming traitors to the laws of our fatherland, to our lawful rulers, and to ourselves and our children, or of letting ourselves be treated like the most depraved slaves?" And he knew that he was not alone, and that he was committing no betrayal of intellect when he completed his series of essays on the French Revolution with the words: "True to my principles and convictions that I have set forth for more than thirty-five years, I will continue as long as I live to work as a writer to further everything I hold to be for the general good of the human race; and precisely for this reason I will, as long as it is necessary, work with all my might against all false, confused, and deceptive concepts of freedom